Color-Coded Accounting Equation

This color-coded accounting equation is a tool you will use throughout your first accounting course. This tool is so important that we have to put it here for quick reference. You may find this helpful when preparing your homework assignments. Each financial statement is identified by a unique color. You will see these colors throughout the chapters when we present a financial statement.

1 The **income statement**, enclosed in the red box, provides the details of revenues earned and expenses incurred.

2 The revenue and expense transactions are then condensed into one number—in this case net income—that becomes part of the **statement of owner's equity**, which appears in the yellow box.

3 The ending balance of owner's equity flows into the **balance sheet**, shown in the blue box.

4 The **statement of cash flows**, as indicated by the green box, provides details of how a company got its cash and how it spent cash during the accounting period.

Relationships Between Financial Statements for Kay Torres Travel Agency

KAY TORRES TRAVEL AGENCY
Statement of Cash Flows*
Month Ended June 30, 2008

Cash flows from operating activities:		
Receipts:		
Collections from customers		$ 2,300
Payments:		
To suppliers ($ 600 + $ 900 + $ 300)	$(1,800)	
To employees	(1,100)	
Total payments		(2,900)
Net cash used for operating activities		(600)
Cash flows from investing activities:		
Acquisition of equipment	$(9,000)	
Net cash used for investing activities		(9,000)
Cash flows from financing activities:		
Investment by owner	$20,000	
Withdrawal by owner	(1,000)	
Loan from bank	15,000	
Net cash provided by financing activities		34,000
Net increase in cash		$24,400
Cash balance, June 1, 2008		0
Cash balance, June 30, 2008		$24,400

*Chapter 13 shows how to prepare this statement.

KAY TORRES TRAVEL AGENCY
Income Statement
Month Ended June 30, 2008

Revenue:		
Service revenue		$7,500
Expenses:		
Building rent expense	$ 900	
Salary expense	1,100	
Utilities expense	300	
Total expenses		2,300
Net income		$5,200

KAY TORRES TRAVEL AGENCY
Statement of Owner's Equity
Month Ended June 30, 2008

Kay Torres, capital, June 30, 2008	$ 0
Add: Investment by owner	20,000
Net income for the month	5,200
Subtotal	25,200
Less: Withdrawals by owner	(1,000)
Kay Torres, capital, June 30, 2008	$24,200

KAY TORRES TRAVEL AGENCY
Balance Sheet
June 30, 2008

Assets		Liabilities	
Cash	$24,400	Accounts payable	$600
Accounts receivable	5,200	Notes payable	15,000
Supplies	1,200	Total liabilities	15,600
Equipment	9,000		
		Owner's Equity	
		Kay Torres, capital	24,200
Total assets	$39,800	Total liabilities and owner's equity	$39,800

PRINCIPLES OF ACCOUNTING

Chapters 1–10 & 14

Custom Edition for
Washtenaw Community College

Taken from:

Principles of Accounting: Chapters 1-12
by Meg Pollard, Sherry K. Mills and Walter T. Harrison Jr.

Principles of Accounting: Chapters 11-21
by Meg Pollard, Sherry K. Mills and Walter T. Harrison Jr.

Taken from:

Principles of Accounting: Chapters 1-12
by Meg Pollard, Sherry K. Mills and Walter T. Harrison Jr.
Copyright © 2007 by Pearson Education
Published by Prentice Hall
Upper Saddle River, New Jersey 07458

Principles of Accounting: Chapters 11-21
by Meg Pollard, Sherry K. Mills and Walter T. Harrison Jr.
Copyright © 2007 by Pearson Education
Published by Prentice Hall

This special edition published in cooperation with Pearson Custom Publishing.

Printed in the United States of America

10 9 8 7 6 5 4 3 2 1

ISBN 0-536-48231-4

2007160572

LH

Please visit our web site at *www.pearsoncustom.com*

PEARSON CUSTOM PUBLISHING
501 Boylston Street, Suite 900, Boston, MA 02116
A Pearson Education Company

Brief Contents

Contents

Taken from: *Principles of Accounting: Chapters 1-12*
by Meg Pollard, Sherry K. Mills, and Walter T. Harrison Jr.

Contents

Taken from: *Principles of Accounting: Chapters 11-21*
by Meg Pollard, Sherry K. Mills, and Walter T. Harrison Jr.

14 Financial Statement Analysis   746

The *Principles of Accounting* Demo Doc System: For professors whose greatest joy is hearing students say "I get it!"

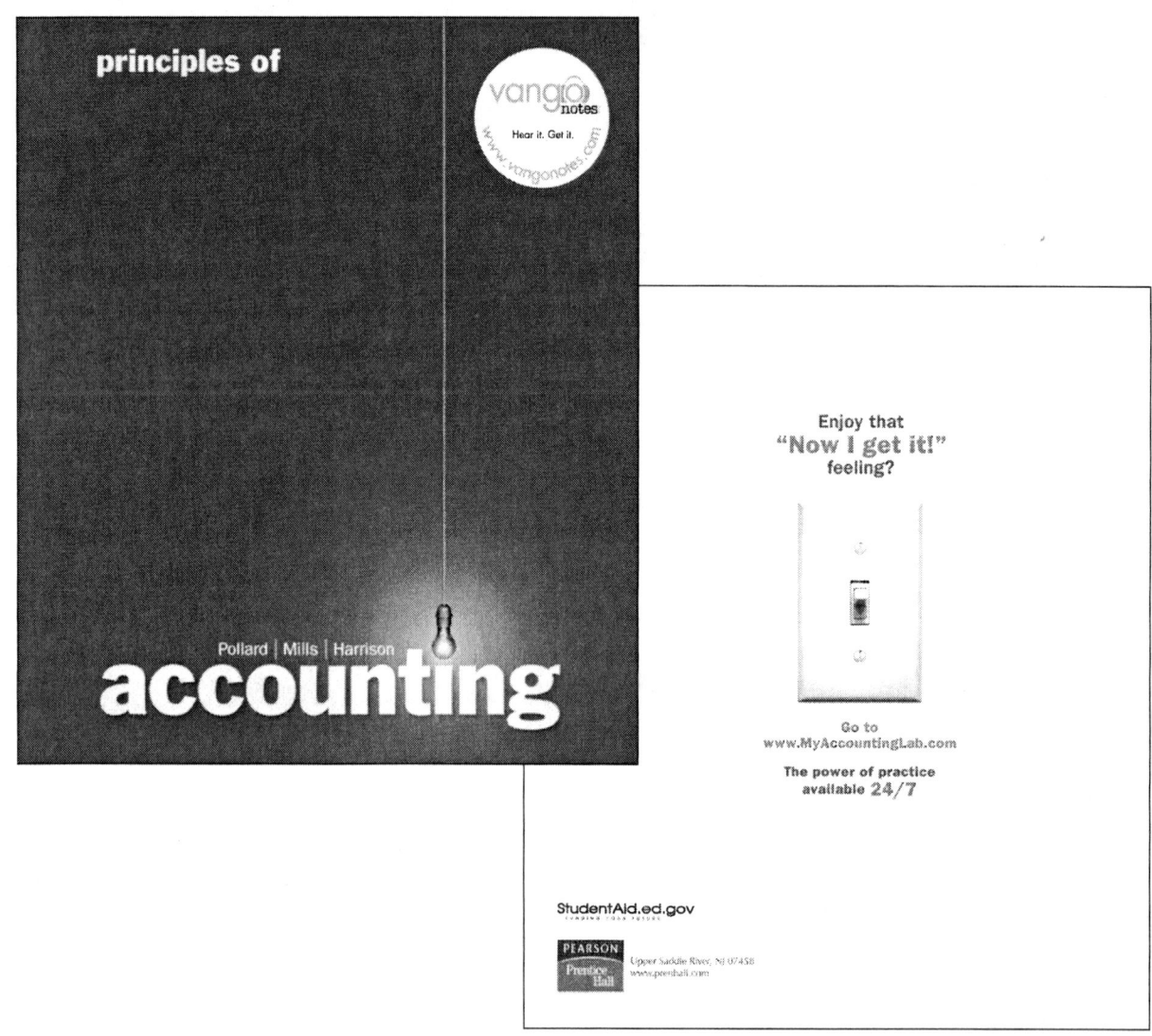

Help your students achieve "I get it!" moments when you're with them AND when you're NOT.

When you're there showing how to solve a problem in class, students "get it." When you're not there, they get stuck—it's only natural.

Our system is designed to help you deliver the best "I get it!" moments. (Instructor's Edition, Instructor Demo Docs)

But it's the really tricky situations that no one else has zeroed in on— the 2 A.M. outside-of-class moments, when you're not there—that present the greatest challenge.

That's where we come in: at these critical "they have the book, but they don't have you" moments. *Principles of Accounting's* Demo Doc System will help in those critical times. The ability of the Horngren System to help in those times is what makes this package different from all other textbooks.

The *Principles of Accounting* Demo Doc System

Duplicate the classroom experience anytime, anywhere. When is your "I get it!" moment?

THE FIRST EDITION

1. A system of instruction that duplicates the classroom experience anytime, anywhere.

2. Demo Docs: entire problems worked through step-by-step from start to finish with the kind of comments around it that YOU would say in class. Available in Flash and in print.

3. A "no clutter" layout, so critical content is clear.

4. Consistency of voice and visual exhibits across all mediums.

5. MyAccountingLab Online Homework and Assessment tool: Marry the "I get it!" moment with the Power of Practice.

6. Your "I get it!" moment on your time.

Details

1. **CHAPTERS 1–4** We know it's critical that students nail the fundamentals and language before they can move to practice. We're spending extra time developing the accounting cycle chapters (Chs 1-4) to make sure they will help students succeed. We're including extra visuals, comprehensive problems, and a Demo Doc for every chapter to give students enough to go on.

2. **THE ULTIMATE SYSTEM: FUELED BY DEMO DOCS**–This is the System of Learning (Text + Study Guide with Demo Docs + MyAccountingLab).

▶ *NEW* **DEMO DOCS** – Introductory accounting students consistently tell us, "When doing homework, I get stuck trying to solve problems the way they were demonstrated in class." Instructors consistently tell us, "I have so much to cover in so little time; I can't afford to go backward and review homework in class." Those challenges inspired us to develop Demo Docs. Demo Docs are comprehensive worked-through problems available for every chapter of our introductory accounting text to help students when they are trying to solve exercises and problems on their own.

The idea is—help students duplicate the classroom experience outside of class.

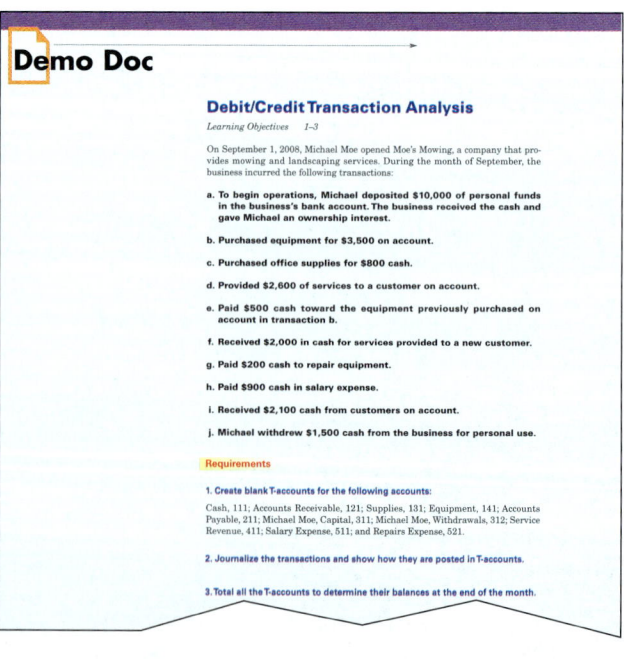

Demo Doc

Debit/Credit Transaction Analysis

Learning Objectives   1–3

On September 1, 2008, Michael Moe opened Moe's Mowing, a company that provides mowing and landscaping services. During the month of September, the business incurred the following transactions:

a. To begin operations, Michael deposited $10,000 of personal funds in the business's bank account. The business received the cash and gave Michael an ownership interest.

b. Purchased equipment for $3,500 on account.

c. Purchased office supplies for $800 cash.

d. Provided $2,600 of services to a customer on account.

e. Paid $500 cash toward the equipment previously purchased on account in transaction b.

f. Received $2,000 in cash for services provided to a new customer.

g. Paid $200 cash to repair equipment.

h. Paid $900 cash in salary expense.

i. Received $2,100 cash from customers on account.

j. Michael withdrew $1,500 cash from the business for personal use.

Requirements

1. Create blank T-accounts for the following accounts:

Cash, 111; Accounts Receivable, 121; Supplies, 131; Equipment, 141; Accounts Payable, 211; Michael Moe, Capital, 311; Michael Moe, Withdrawals, 312; Service Revenue, 411; Salary Expense, 511; and Repairs Expense, 521.

2. Journalize the transactions and show how they are posted in T-accounts.

3. Total all the T-accounts to determine their balances at the end of the month.

Entire problems that mirror the end-of-chapter material are shown solved and annotated with explanations written in a conversational style, essentially imitating what an instructor might say if standing over a student's shoulder. All Demo Docs will be available online in Flash and in print so students can easily refer to them when they need them.

3. **CONSISTENCY** – The small, incremental stuff matters. Consistency in form, function, and language. From medium to medium. So when students ask "Where do the numbers come from?" they can go to our text **OR** go online and know what to do. If it's worded one way here, it's worded the same way there. In the case where alternate terms *could* be used, we reference them in the definition at the end of the chapter for students so they "get it." It looks one way here, it looks the same way there.

4. **CLUTTER-FREE** – We're getting rid of clutter. Less is more. Extraneous boxes and features, non-essential bells and whistles…gone. Too much excess crowds out what really matters—the concepts, the problems, the learning objectives. Instructors asked for fewer "features" in favor of more exercises with better cross referencing. So, that's what we've done. Based on feedback, important items such as ethics and business cases are now located as part of the end of chapter materials so that the student can follow the sequence of learning accounting *uninterrupted*.

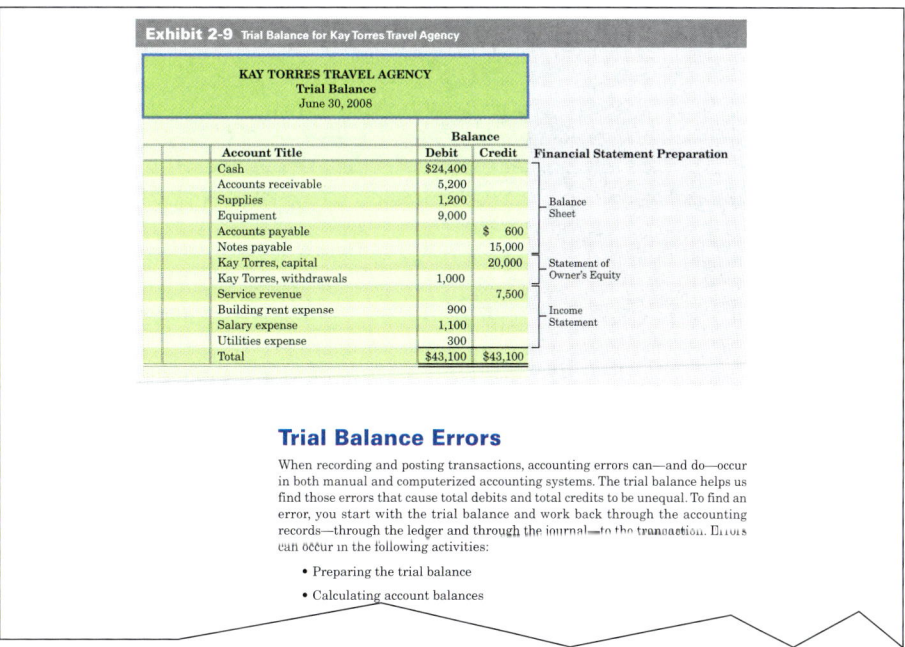

Exhibit 2-9 Trial Balance for Kay Torres Travel Agency

KAY TORRES TRAVEL AGENCY
Trial Balance
June 30, 2008

Account Title	Balance Debit	Balance Credit	Financial Statement Preparation
Cash	$24,400		
Accounts receivable	5,200		
Supplies	1,200		Balance Sheet
Equipment	9,000		
Accounts payable		$ 600	
Notes payable		15,000	
Kay Torres, capital		20,000	Statement of Owner's Equity
Kay Torres, withdrawals	1,000		
Service revenue		7,500	
Building rent expense	900		Income Statement
Salary expense	1,100		
Utilities expense	300		
Total	$43,100	$43,100	

Trial Balance Errors

When recording and posting transactions, accounting errors can—and do—occur in both manual and computerized accounting systems. The trial balance helps us find those errors that cause total debits and total credits to be unequal. To find an error, you start with the trial balance and work back through the accounting records—through the ledger and through the journal—to the transaction. Errors can occur in the following activities:

- Preparing the trial balance
- Calculating account balances

5. **MyAccountingLab** – This online homework and assessment tool represents when the "I get it!" moment meets the power of practice. The power of repetition, when you get it, means that learning happens. MyAccountingLab is about helping students at their teachable moment, whether that is 1 P.M. or 1 A.M., but whenever you are not there. MyAccountingLab is packed with algorithmic problems because practice makes perfect. It's also packed with the exact same end-of-chapter material that you're used to assigning for homework. It includes a Demo Doc for each of the end-of-chapter exercises and problems that students can refer to as they work through the question. It helps students when it's 1 A.M., and they're trying to solve a problem the way it was demonstrated in class.

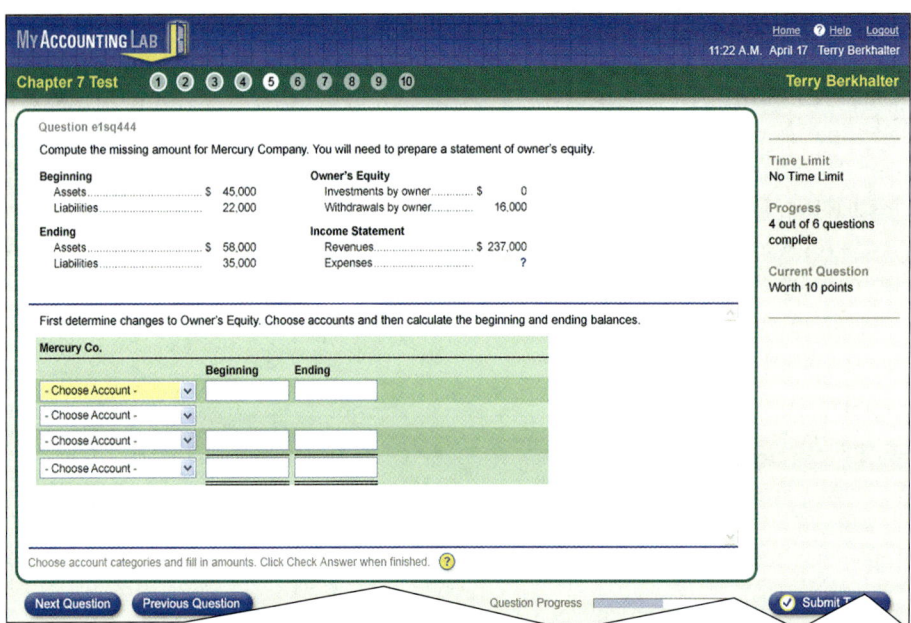

6. **Your "I get it!" moment on your time.**

INSTRUCTOR SUPPLEMENTS

Instructor's Edition featuring Instructor Demo Docs

▶ **The New Look Instructor's Edition**

We've asked a lot of instructors how we can help them successfully implement new course-delivery methods (e.g. online) while maintaining their regular campus schedule of classes and academic responsibilities. In response, we developed a system of instruction for those of you who are long on commitment and expertise—but short on time and assistance.

The primary goal of the **Instructor's Edition** is **ease of implementation, using any delivery method**—traditional, self-paced, or online. That is, the Instructor's Edition quickly answers for you, the professor, the question "What must the student do?" Likewise, the Instructor's Edition quickly answers for the student, "What must I do?", and offers time saving tips with "best of" categories for in class discussion and strong examples to illustrate difficult concepts to a wide variety of students. The Instructor's Edition also offers a quick one-shot cross reference at the exact point of importance with key additional teaching resources, so everything is in one place. The **Instructor's Edition** includes summaries and teaching tips, pitfalls for new students, and "best of" practices from instructors from across the world.

▶ **The Instructor's Edition also includes *Instructor Demo Docs***

In **Instructor Demo Docs,** we walk the students through how to solve a problem, as if it were the first time they've seen it. There are no lengthy passages of text. Instead, bits of expository text are woven into the steps needed to solve the problem, in the exact sequence—for you to provide at the teachable *"I get it!"* moment. This is the point at which the student has a context within which he or she can understand the concept. We provide conversational text around each of the steps so the student stays engaged in solving the problem. We provide notes to the instructor for key teaching points around the Demo Docs, and "best of" practice tid-bits before each *Instructor Demo Doc.*

The *Instructor Demo Docs* are written with all of your everyday classroom realities in mind—and trying to save your time in prepping new examples each time your book changes. Additionally, algorithmic versions of these Demo Docs are provided to students in their student guide. We keep the terminology consistent with the text, so there are no surprises for students as they try and work through a problem the first time.

Solutions Transparencies

These transparency masters are the **Solutions Manual** in an easy-to-use format for class lectures.

Instructor's Resource Center CD or www.prenhall.com

The password protected site and resource CD includes the following:

- **The Instructor's Edition with *Instructor Demo Docs***
- **Problem Set C**

- **Solutions Manual with Interactive Excel Solutions**

  The Solutions Manual contains solutions to all end-of-chapter questions, multiple-choice questions, short exercises, exercise sets, problems sets, and Internet exercises. The Solutions Manual is available in Microsoft Excel, Microsoft Word, and in print. You can access the solutions in MS Excel and MS Word formats by visiting the Instructor's Resource Center on the Prentice Hall catalog site at www.prenhall.com or on the Instructor's CD. You will need a Pearson Educator username and password to retrieve materials from the Web site.

  Solutions to select end-of-chapter exercises and problems are available in *interactive MS Excel format* so that instructors can present material in dynamic, step-by-step sequences in class. The interactive solutions were prepared by Kathleen O'Donnell of the State University of New York, Onondaga Community College.

- **Test Bank** The test item file includes more than 2,000 questions:
  - Multiple Choice
  - Matching
  - True/False
  - Computational Problems
  - Essay

- **Test Bank** is formatted for use with WebCT, Blackboard, and Course Compass.

- **PowerPoints (instructor and student)** summarize and reinforce key text materials. They capture classroom attention with original problems and solved step-by-step exercises. These walk-throughs are designed to help faciliate classroom discussion and demonstrate where the numbers come from and what they mean to the concept at hand. There are approximately 35 slides per chapter. PowerPoints are available on the Instructor's CD and can be downloaded from www.prenhall.com.

MyAccountingLab Online Homework and Assessment Manager

The "I get it" moment meets *power of practice.* The power of repetition when you "get it" means learning happens. **MyAccountingLab** is about helping students at their teachable moments, whether it's 1 P.M. or 1 A.M.

MyAccountingLab is an online homework and assessment tool, packed with algorithmic versions of every text problem since practice makes perfect. It's also packed with the exact same end of chapter that you're used to assigning for homework. Additionally, **MyAccountingLab** includes:

1. A **Demo Doc** for each of the end-of-chapter exercises and problems that students can refer to as they work through the question.

2. A **Guided Solution** to the exact problem they are working on. It helps students when they're trying to solve a problem the way it was demonstrated in class.

3. A full **e-book** so the students can reference the book at the point of practice.

4. New **topic specific videos** that walk students through difficult concepts.

Companion Web Site

The book's Web site at www.prenhall.com/pollard—contains the following:

- Self-study quizzes—interactive study guide for each chapter
- MS Excel templates that students can use to complete homework assignments for each chapter (e-working papers)
- Samples of the Flash Demo Docs for students to work through the accounting cycle

Online Courses with WebCT/BlackBoard

Prentice Hall offers a link to MyAccountingLab through the Bb and WebCT Course Management Systems.

Classroom Response Systems (CRS)

CRS is an exciting new wireless polling technology that makes large and small classrooms even more interactive, because it enables instructors to pose questions to their students, record results, and display those results instantly. Students can easily answer questions using compact remote control–type transmitters. Prentice Hall has partnerships with leading classroom response-systems providers and can show you everything you need to know about setting up and using a CRS system. Prentice Hall will provide the classroom hardware, text-specific PowerPoint slides, software, and support.

Visit **www.prenhall.com/crs** to learn more.

STUDENT SUPPLEMENTS

Runners Corporation PT Lab Manual

Containing numerous simulated real-world examples, the **Runners Corporation** practice set is available complete with data files for Peachtree, QuickBooks, and PH General Ledger. Each practice set also includes business stationery for manual entry work.

A-1 Photography-Manual PT Lab Manual

Containing numerous simulated real-world examples, the **A-1 Photography** practice set is available complete with data files for Peachtree, QuickBooks, and PH General Ledger. Each set includes business stationery for manual entry work.

Study Guide including DEMO DOCS and e-Working Papers

Introductory accounting students consistently tell us, "When doing homework, I get stuck trying to solve problems the way they were demonstrated in class." Instructors consistently tell us, "I have so much to cover in so little time; I can't afford to go backwards and review homework in class." Those challenges inspired us to develop **Demo Docs. Demo Docs** are comprehensive worked-through problems available for nearly every chapter of our introductory accounting text to help students when they are trying to solve exercises and problems on their own. The idea is to help students duplicate the classroom experience outside of class. Entire problems that mirror end-of-chapter material are shown solved and annotated with explanations written in a conversational style, essentially imitating what an instructor might say if standing over a student's shoulder. All **Demo Docs** will be available in the Study Guide—in print and on CD in Flash, so students can easily refer to them when they need them. The Study Guide also includes a summary overview of key topics and multiple-choice and short-answer questions for students to test their knowledge. Free electronic working papers are included on the accompanying CD.

MyAccountingLab Online Homework and Assessment Manager

The "I get it!" moment meets *power of practice*. The power of repetition when you get it; means that learning happens. **MyAccountingLab** is about helping students at their teachable moment, whether that is 1 P.M. or 1 A.M.

MyAccountingLab is an online homework and assessment tool, packed with algorithmic versions of every text problem because practice makes perfect. It's also packed with the exact same end-of-chapter that you're used to assigning for homework. Additionally, **MyAccountingLab** includes:

1. A **Demo Doc** for each of the end-of-chapter exercises and problems that students can refer to as they work through the question.
2. A **Guided Solution** to the exact problem they are working on. It helps students when they're trying to solve a problem the way it was demonstrated in class.
3. A full **e-book** so the students can reference the book at the point of practice.
4. New **topic specific videos** that walk students through difficult concepts.

PowerPoints

For student use as a study aide or note-taking guide, these PowerPoint slides may be downloaded at the Companion Web site at www.prenhall.com/pollard.

Companion Web Site – www.prenhall.com/pollard

The book's Web site at www.prenhall.com/pollard—contains the following:

- Self-study quizzes—interactive study guide for each chapter
- MS Excel templates that students can use to complete homework assignments for each chapter (e-working papers)
- Samples of the Flash Demo Docs for students to work through the accounting cycle.

Classroom Response Systems (CRS)

CRS is an exciting new wireless polling technology that makes large and small classrooms even more interactive because it enables instructors to pose questions to their students, record results, and display those results instantly. Students can easily answer questions using compact remote-control–type transmitters. Prentice Hall has partnerships with leading classroom response-systems providers and can show you everything you need to know about setting up and using a CRS system. Prentice Hall will provide the classroom hardware, text-specific PowerPoint slides, software, and support.

Visit **www.prenhall.com/crs** to learn more.

- **VangoNotes in MP3 Format**

  Students can study on the go with VangoNotes, chapter reviews in downloadable MP3 format that offer brief audio segments for each chapter:

  - Big Ideas: the vital ideas in each chapter
  - Practice Test: lets students know if they need to keep studying
  - Key Terms: audio "flashcards" that review key concepts and terms
  - Rapid Review: a quick drill session—helpful right before tests

  Students can learn more at **www.vangonotes.com**

Hear it. Get It.

partnership with **Audible** Education

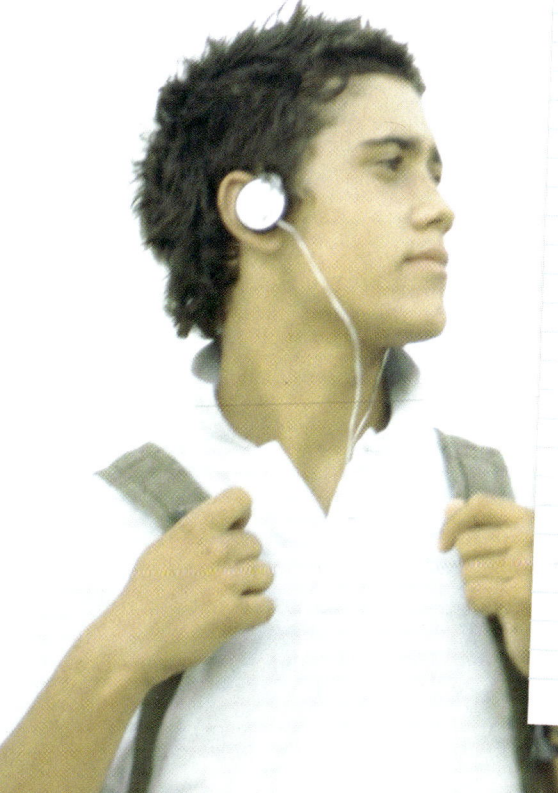

Study on the go with VangoNotes.

Just download chapter reviews from your text and listen to them on any mp3 player. Now wherever you are-- whatever you're doing--you can study by listening to the following for each chapter of your textbook:

Big Ideas: Your "need to know" for each chapter

Practice Test: A gut check for the Big Ideas--tells you if you need to keep studying

Key Terms: Audio "flashcards" to help you review key concepts and terms

Rapid Review: A quick drill session--use it right before your test

VangoNotes.com

Acknowledgments

We'd like to thank the following contributors:

Florence McGovern *Bergen Community College*
Helen Brubeck *San Jose State University*

Suzanne Oliver *Okaloosa Walton College*
Bill Smith *New Mexico State University*

We'd like to extend a special thank-you to the following members of our advisory panel:

Laurel Berry *Bryant and Stratton College*
Jerry Millier *Chaparral College*
Kathy Hepner *Central Pennsylvania College*
Trisha King *Colorado Technical University*
Karen Wisniewski *County College of Morris*
Michael Stamos *Devry University*

Patty Holmes *DMACC*
Georgia Buckles *Manchester Community College*
Bill Smith *New Mexico State University*
Jane Konditi *Northwood University*
Barbara Pughsley *South University*
Jay Siegel Union *County College*

We'd also like to thank the following reviewers:

Shi-Mu (Simon)Yang *Adelphi University*
Thomas Stolberg *Alfred State University*
Thomas Branton *Alvin Community College*
Maria Lehoczky *American Intercontinental University*
Suzanne Bradford *Angelina College*
Judy Lewis *Angelo State University*
Roy Carson Anne *Arundel Community College*
Paulette Ratliff-Miller *Arkansas State University*
Joseph Foley *Assumption College*
Jennifer Niece *Assumption College*
Bill Whitley *Athens State University*
Shelly Gardner *Augustana College*

Becky Jones *Baylor University*
Betsy Willis *Baylor University*
Michael Robinson *Baylor University*
Kay Walker-Hauser *Beaufort County Community College, Washington*
Joe Aubert *Bemidji State University*
Florence McGovern *Bergen Community College*
Calvin Fink *Bethune Cookman College*
Michael Blue *Bloomsburg University*
Scott Wallace *Blue Mountain College*
Lloyd Carroll *Borough Manhattan Community College*
Ken Duffe *Brookdale Community College*
Chuck Heuser *Brookdale Community College*
Shafi Ullah *Broward Community College South*
Lois Slutsky *Broward Community College South*
Ken Koerber *Bucks County Community College*

Julie Browning *California Baptist University*
Richard Savich *California State University – San Bernardino*
David Bland *Cape Fear Community College*
Robert Porter *Cape Fear Community College*
Vickie Campbell *Cape Fear Community College*
Cynthia Thompson *Carl Sandburg College – Carthage*
Liz Ott *Casper College*

Joseph Adamo *Cazenovia College*
Julie Dailey *Central Virginia Community College*
Jeannie Folk *College of DuPage*
Lawrence Steiner *College of Marin*
Dennis Kovach *Community College Allegheny County - Allegheny*
Norma Montague *Central Carolina Community College*
Debbie Schmidt *Cerritos College*
Janet Grange *Chicago State University*
Bruce Leung *City College of San Francisco*
Pamela Legner *College of DuPage*
Bruce McMurrey *Community College of Denver*
Martin Sabo *Community College of Denver*
Jeffrey Jones *Community College of Southern Nevada*
Tom Nohl *Community College of Southern Nevada*
Christopher Kelly *Community College of Southern Nevada*
Patrick Rogan *Cosumnes River College*
Kimberly Smith *County College of Morris*

Jerold Braun *Daytona Beach Community College*
Greg Carlton *Davidson County Community College*
Irene Bembenista *Davenport University*
Thomas Szczurek *Delaware County Community College*
Charles Betts *Delaware Technical and Community College*
Patty Holmes *Des Moines Area Community College – Ankeny*
Tim Murphy *Diablo Valley College*

Phillipe Sammour *Eastern Michigan University*
Saturnino (Nino) Gonzales *El Paso Community College*
Lee Cannell *El Paso Community College*
John Eagan *Erie Community College*

Ron O'Brien *Fayetteville Technical Community College*
Patrick McNabb *Ferris State University*
John Stancil *Florida Southern College*
Lynn Clements *Florida Southern College*

Alice Sineath *Forsyth Technical Community College*
James Makofske *Fresno City College*
Marc Haskell *Fresno City College*
James Kelly *Ft. Lauderdale City College*

Christine Jonick *Gainesville State College*
Bruce Lindsey *Genesee Community College*
Constance Hylton *George Mason University*
Cody King *Georgia Southwestern State University*
Lolita Keck *Globe College*
Kay Carnes *Gonzaga University, Spokane*
Carol Pace *Grayson County College*
Rebecca Floor *Greenville Technical College*
Geoffrey Heriot *Greenville Technical College*
Jeffrey Patterson *Grove City College*
Lanny Nelms *Gwinnet Technical College*
Chris Cusatis *Gwynedd Mercy College*

Tim Griffin *Hillsborough Community College*
Clair Helms *Hinds Community College*
Michelle Powell *Holmes Community College*
Greg Bischoff *Houston Community College*
Donald Bond *Houston Community College*
Marina Grau *Houston Community College*
Carolyn Fitzmorris *Hutchinson Community College*

Susan Koepke *Illinois Valley Community College*
William Alexander *Indian Hills Community College – Ottumwa*
Dale Bolduc *Intercoast College*
Thomas Carr *International College of Naples*
Lecia Berven *Iowa Lakes Community College*
Nancy Schendel *Iowa Lakes Community College*
Michelle Cannon *Ivy Tech*
Vicki White *Ivy Tech*
Chuck Smith *Iowa Western Community College*

Stephen Christian *Jackson Community College*
DeeDee Daughtry *Johnston Community College*
Richard Bedwell *Jones County Junior College*

Ken Mark *Kansas City Kansas Community College*
Ken Snow *Kaplan Education Centers*
Charles Evans *Keiser College*
Bunney Schmidt *Keiser College*
Amy Haas *Kingsborough Community College*

Jim Racic *Lakeland Community College*
Doug Clouse *Lakeland Community College*
Patrick Haggerty *Lansing Community College*
Patricia Walczak *Lansing Community College*
Humberto M. Herrera *Laredo Community College*
Christie Comunale *Long Island University*
Ariel Markelevich *Long Island University*
Randy Kidd *Longview Community College*
Kathy Heltzel *Luzerne County Community College*

Lori Major *Luzerne County Community College*

Fred Jex *Macomb Community College*
Glenn Owen *Marymount College*
Behnaz Quigley *Marymount College*
Penny Hanes *Mercyhurst College, Erie*
John Miller *Metropolitan Community College*
Denise Leggett *Middle Tennessee State University*
William Huffman *Missouri Southern State College*
Ted Crosby *Montgomery County Community College*
Beth Engle *Montgomery County Community College*
David Candelaria *Mount San Jacinto College*
Linda Bolduc *Mount Wachusett Community College*

Barbara Gregorio *Nassau Community College*
James Hurat *National College of Business and Technology*
Denver Riffe *National College of Business and Technology*
Asokan Anandarajan *New Jersey Institute of Technology*
Robert Schoener *New Mexico State University*
Stanley Carroll *New York City Technical College of CUNY*
Audrey Agnello *Niagara County Community College*
Catherine Chiang *North Carolina Central University*
Karen Russom *North Harris College*
Dan Bayak *Northampton Community College*
Elizabeth Lynn Locke *Northern Virginia Community College*
Debra Prendergast *Northwestern Business College*
Nat Briscoe *Northwestern State University*
Tony Scott *Norwalk Community College*

Deborah Niemer *Oakland Community College*
Suzanne Oliver *Okaloosa Walton Junior College*
John Boyd *Oklahoma City Community College*
Kathleen O'Donnell *Onondaga Community College*
J.T. Ryan *Onondaga Community College*

Toni Clegg *Palm Beach Atlantic College*
David Forsyth *Palomar College*
John Graves *PCDI*
Carla Rich *Pensacola Junior College*
Judy Grotrian *Peru State College*
Judy Daulton *Piedmont Technical College*
John Stone *Potomac State College*
Betty Habershon *Prince George's Community College*

Kathi Villani *Queensborough Community College*

William Black *Raritan Valley Community College*
Verne Ingram *Red Rocks Community College*
Paul Juriga *Richland Community College*
Patty Worsham *Riverside Community College*
Margaret Berezewski *Robert Morris College*
Phil Harder *Robert Morris College*
Shifei Chung *Rowan University of New Jersey*

Charles Fazzi *Saint Vincent College*
Lynnette Yerbuy *Salt Lake Community College*
Susan Blizzard *San Antonio College*
Hector Martinez *San Antonio College*
Audrey Voyles *San Diego Miramar College*
Margaret Black *San Jacinto College*
Merrily Hoffman *San Jacinto College*
Randall Whitmore *San Jacinto College*
Carroll Buck *San Jose State University*
Helen Brubeck *San Jose State University*
Cynthia Coleman *Sandhills Community College*
Barbara Crouteau *Santa Rosa Junior College*
Pat Novak *Southeast Community College*
Susan Pallas *Southeast Community College*
Al Case *Southern Oregon University*
Gloria Worthy *Southwest Tennessee Community College*
Melody Ashenfelter *Southwestern Oklahoma State
  University*
Douglas Ward *Southwestern Community College*
Brandi Shay *Southwestern Community College*
John May *Southwestern Oklahoma State University*
Jeffrey Waybright *Spokane Community College*
Renee Goffinet *Spokane Community College*
Susan Anders *St. Bonaventure University*
John Olsavsky *SUNY at Fredonia*
Peter Van Brunt *SUNY College of Technology at Delhi*

David L. Davis *Tallahassee Community College*
Kathy Crusto-Way *Tarrant County Community College*
Sally Cook *Texas Lutheran University*
Bea Chiang *The College of New Jersey*
Matt Hightower *Three Rivers Community College*

Susan Pope *University of Akron*
Joe Woods *University of Arkansas*
Allen Blay *University of California, Riverside*
Barry Mishra *University of California, Riverside*
Laura Young *University of Central Arkansas*

Jane Calvert *University of Central Oklahoma*
Bambi Hora *University of Central Oklahoma*
Joan Stone *University of Central Oklahoma*
Kathy Terrell *University of Central Oklahoma*
Harlan Etheridge *University of Louisiana*
Pam Meyer *University of Louisiana*
Sandra Scheuermann *University of Louisiana*
Tom Wilson *University of Louisiana*
Lawrence Leaman *University of Michigan*
Larry Huus *University of Minnesota*
Brian Carpenter *University of Scranton*
Ashraf Khallaf *University of Southern Indiana*
Tony Zordan *University of St. Francis*
Gene Elrod *University of Texas, Arlington*
Cheryl Prachyl *University of Texas, El Paso*
Karl Putnam *University of Texas, El Paso*
Stephen Rockwell *University of Tulsa*
Chula King *University of West Florida*
Charles Baird *University of Wisconsin – Stout*

Mary Hollars *Vincennes University*
Lisa Nash *Vincennes University*
Elaine Dessouki *Virginia Wesleyan College*

Sueann Hely *West Kentucky Community and
  Technical College*
Darlene Pulliam *West Texas A&M University, Canyon*
Judy Beebe *Western Oregon University*
Michelle Maggio *Westfield State College*
Kathy Pellegrino *Westfield State College*
Nora McCarthy *Wharton County Junior College*
Sally Stokes *Wilmington College*
Maggie Houston *Wright State University*

Gerald Caton *Yavapai College*
Chris Crosby *York Technical College*
Harold Gellis *York College of CUNY*

About the Authors

Meg Pollard is Professor of Accounting at American River College in Sacramento, California. She received her B.A. in Economics-Business from UCLA and her M.B.A. in Business Administration from California State University, Sacramento, graduating as the Outstanding Graduate Student of the Year with memberships in Phi Kappa Phi Honor Society and Beta Gamma Sigma Honor Society.

Professor Pollard began her career in accounting in the audit department of the Los Angeles office of Touche Ross & Co. and was employed as a financial analyst in the corporate headquarters of the *Fortune* 500 firm, Lear Siegler, Inc. Her industry experience also has included service as director of finance for a non-profit organization.

Pollard is a Certified Public Accountant with an active license in California and is a member of the California Society of Certified Public Accountants, CalCPA. She is listed in both *Who's Who Among Executive and Professional Women Educators* and *Who's Who Among America's Teachers*.

Professor Pollard has taught Fundamentals of College Accounting, Financial Accounting, Managerial Accounting, Intermediate Accounting, Payroll Accounting, Auditing, Computer Spreadsheet Applications for Accounting, Careers in Accounting, Concepts in Personal Finance, and Business Mathematics. She is co-founder and co-instructor of the Volunteer Income Tax Assistance (VITA) program at American River College, an Internal Revenue Service program in which student volunteers electronically prepare and file income tax returns for low-income individuals free of charge.

Sherry Mills is Associate Professor of Accounting at New Mexico State University. She received her M.A. and Ph.D. in Accounting from Texas Tech University.

Professor Mills also has taught at the University of Texas, San Antonio, and Texas Tech University. She is the recipient of numerous teaching awards including NMSU's Westhafer Award for Teaching Excellence, the New Mexico Professor of the Year Award, New Mexico Society of CPA's Accounting Educator of the Year, and the Award for Innovation in Accounting Education by the American Accounting Association. As a member of the American Accounting Association and the American Institute of Certified Public Accountants, Professor Mills has served on numerous committees representing innovation in accounting education.

Walter T. Harrison, Jr. is Professor Emeritus of Accounting at the Hankamer School of Business, Baylor University. He received his B.B.A. degree from Baylor University, his M.S. from Oklahoma State University, and his Ph.D. from Michigan State University.

Professor Harrison, recipient of numerous teaching awards from student groups as well as from university administrators, has also taught at Cleveland State Community College, Michigan State University, the University of Texas, and Stanford University.

A member of the American Accounting Association and the American Institute of Certified Public Accountants, Professor Harrison has served as Chairman of the Financial Accounting Standards Committee of the American Accounting Association, on the Teaching/Curriculum Development Award Committee, on the Program Advisory Committee for Accounting Education and Teaching, and on the Notable Contributions to Accounting Literature Committee.

Professor Harrison has lectured in several foreign countries and published articles in numerous journals, including *The Accounting Review*, *Journal of Accounting Research*, *Journal of Accountancy*, *Journal of Accounting and Public Policy*, *Economic Consequences of Financial Accounting Standards*, *Accounting Horizons*, *Issues in Accounting Education*, and *Journal of Law and Commerce*.

He is co-author of *Financial Accounting*, Sixth Edition, 2006 (with Charles T. Horngren), published by Prentice Hall. Professor Harrison has received scholarships, fellowships, and research grants or awards from PriceWaterhouse Coopers, Deloitte & Touche, the Ernst & Young Foundation, and the KPMG Foundation.

principles of
accounting

LEARNING OBJECTIVES

1 Describe the nature and types of business organizations.

2 Explain the role of accounting in business organizations.

3 Define Generally Accepted Accounting Principles and describe the basic accounting concepts.

4 Use the accounting equation to analyze business transactions.

5 Prepare financial statements and explain the relationships between them.

6 Explain the role of ethics in accounting and business.

Accounting and the Business Environment

o you have a hobby or enjoyable activity? Have you ever thought about how you can transform a favorite pastime into your life's work? Let's say your dream is to be involved in car racing. You could make a career of racing cars. Or, you could build racing tracks, design the race cars, manufacture and supply the specialty tires, manage pit crews, track the money made and spent on each racing event, broadcast the race, or own the racetrack. You could take any one of these activities and make it into a business. Many of the businesses that operate in the United States began as someone's dream. •

Look Back

While you have probably not yet studied accounting, you may have noticed that different kinds of businesses exist. Also, chances are good that you have already seen the need for accounting in keeping track of your bank account balance and the amount you owe on your credit card or student loan.

Look Ahead

You will discover and examine different business types. You will learn how to account for business transactions and, following accounting rules, report their results.

In this chapter you will learn about different types of businesses and about accounting as the language of business. You will see that accounting rules, which we call principles, are necessary to guide accountants and managers in tracking the results of a business's activities. You will also see the basic financial reports that communicate these results.

Business Organizations

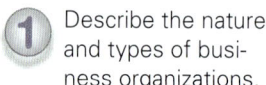 **1** Describe the nature and types of business organizations.

To start a business you need the following:

- An idea that will become a product or service, and
- A market of customers who want the product or service you offer

A **business** is an organization that sells products or services to customers. One major goal of a business is to generate a **profit**, which is the difference between the sales price of the goods or services sold by the business and the cost of the resources used to provide these goods or services. The other major goal of a business is to stay **liquid**. Being liquid means being able to generate enough cash from selling goods or services to pay bills on time.

Types of Business Organizations

A business organization can be classified by what it provides to its customers.

- **Service companies** perform services for customers. Some service companies provide legal, accounting, medical, or banking services that require lots of expertise, and others help with personal services such as lawn mowing, oil changing, hair styling, painting, plumbing, or cleaning. Examples include H&R Block, Bank of America, Jiffy Lube, and Merry Maids.
- **Merchandise companies**, also known as **retail companies**, sell products that are made by another company. Examples of merchandise companies include Wal-Mart, Sears, Amazon.com, and Ace Hardware. Many of these companies keep large volumes of goods on hand for sale, such as Toys "R" Us.
- **Manufacturing companies** make their own products that are sold directly to the final customer or to other companies who distribute the products to customers. Toyota, Intel, and Apple are all examples of manufacturing companies.

Some companies are actually combinations of these three types. For example, Wal-Mart and Sears are primarily merchandising companies because they sell goods such as clothing, televisions, washers and dryers, and laundry detergent to their customers. However, both companies are also service businesses because they contain auto shops that will change the oil in a customer's car or rotate the car's tires.

Forms of Business Organizations

A business organization can also be classified based on how it is organized, and a business can be organized in one of three basic forms, as a **proprietorship**, a **partnership**, or a **corporation**.

- A proprietorship
  - Has a single owner, called the proprietor, who is often the manager.
  - Tends to be a small merchandising store or the professional business of a physician, attorney, or accountant.

From the accounting viewpoint, each proprietorship is separate from its owner. The accounting records of the proprietorship do not include the owner's personal financial records. However, from a legal perspective, the business *is* the proprietor. If the organization stops operating, the owner is personally responsible for all debts that the business owed to creditors. In this book, we begin discussing the accounting process by looking at a proprietorship.

- A partnership
  - Joins two or more individuals as co-owners. Each owner is a partner.
  - Is a business such as a retail store or professional organization of physicians, attorneys, or accountants.
  - Is small or medium-sized, but may be gigantic, exceeding 2,000 partners.

Accounting treats the partnership as a separate organization, distinct from the personal, financial affairs of each partner. But again, from a legal perspective, a partnership *is* the partners. If the organization stops operating, the partners are personally responsible for all debts that the organization owes to creditors.

- A corporation
  - Is owned by **stockholders**, or **shareholders**. Stockholders purchase an ownership interest in a corporation by buying shares of its stock.
  - Can be small, with as few as one stockholder, but are usually quite large because they get funds from many owners or stockholders.
  - Begins when the state approves its articles of incorporation.
  - Is a legal entity separate from its owners that conducts business in its own name.

Like a proprietorship or partnership, the accounting records of a corporation are separate from the records of its owners. However, unlike the proprietorship and the partnership, the owners of a corporation do not lose personal assets if the corporation goes bankrupt and is unable to pay its bills. So, the amount that the stockholders risk when buying stock is the amount that they paid for the stock. This **limited liability** of stockholders for corporate debts explains why corporations are so popular.

Accounting and Accountability

Business organizations are part of a larger community because businesses provide goods and services to the community, as well as employment for some community members. As an owner or manager of a business organization, you are accountable, or responsible, for the actions of that business.

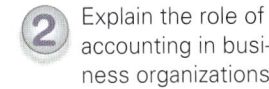 **2** Explain the role of accounting in business organizations.

Organization Accountability

Accountability is responsibility for one's actions. **Organization accountability** is the organization's **fiduciary** responsibility to manage its resources carefully. Many different individuals and groups of people, called stakeholders, have an interest in organizations. Stakeholders include investors, creditors, suppliers, employees, customers, government agencies, and investees.

Stakeholders have an interest in the activities of a business, especially in those activities that most directly affect them. A business's activities can be grouped into three categories.

- **Financing activities.** Organizations and their management attract investors and creditors who provide cash or other assets to the organization. In exchange, organizations and their management use these resources responsibly to operate the business profitably, and repay amounts owed when due while maintaining a positive cash balance.

- **Investing activities.** Organizations and their management obtain items needed to operate the business. Some of these are physical, long-term things such as building space, equipment, and furniture. Others include stock in or loans to other companies as a way of using extra cash profitably. In exchange, organizations and their management pay suppliers and investees for these items in a timely manner.

- **Operating activities.** Organizations and their management generate a profit from the sale of goods or services.

  - Organizations use resources to sell goods or services. In exchange for the resources used, management pays suppliers and employees on time and provides a safe work environment.

  - Customers buy goods or services. In exchange, management provides quality goods or services in a timely manner.

  - Organizations and their management meet various regulatory obligations to the Securities and Exchange Commission, the Internal Revenue Service, the Federal Trade Commission, and other federal and local government agencies by reporting financial information, paying taxes, and obeying laws.

Financial Accounting and Management Accounting

To satisfy the needs of stakeholders, managers are required to provide information that communicates the decisions made and the results obtained from those decisions. Because organizations are accountable to others for actions taken, managers communicate using **accounting** as the language of business. As the language of business, accounting is the information system that measures business activity, processes results of activities into reports, and communicates the results to decision makers. Thus, organization accountability requires two forms of accounting based on who is being communicated with:

- **Financial accounting** for external reporting

- **Management accounting** for internal planning, control, and decision making

Financial accounting produces reports called **financial statements** that show financial information about a business. These historical, objective reports communicate financial information about a business in monetary terms to its external stakeholders and must follow **Generally Accepted Accounting Principles**

(GAAP). GAAP are the rules that govern financial accounting, the "law" of financial accounting, and must be followed when preparing financial statements.

- Financial statements allow investors and creditors to make investment decisions.
- Financial statements allow suppliers and customers to determine the financial condition of a business.
- Financial statements report to regulatory agencies such as the Securities and Exchange Commission, the Internal Revenue Service, and the Federal Trade Commission.

Management accounting provides financial and nonfinancial information inside the organization. This forward-looking information helps managers plan, control, and make decisions consistent with the fiduciary role managers have in operating a business. Management accounting information must be useful, and the benefits of this information must be greater than the costs of obtaining it. However, because it is used internally, it does not need to follow GAAP.

If you plan to turn your hobby into your own business, accounting will help you. You are accountable to many, just as they are accountable to you. In this course, you will learn how financial accounting can help you demonstrate that you have acted responsibly in your business dealings. Management accounting can help you develop plans, make decisions, and control your operations so that you can be profitable and pay your bills. Exhibit 1-1 illustrates the differences between financial accounting and management accounting.

Exhibit 1-1 Management Accounting Versus Financial Accounting

	Management Accounting	Financial Accounting
1. Primary users	Internal: the company's managers	External: investors, creditors, suppliers, customers, and government agencies
2. Purpose of information	Help managers plan and control business operations	Help investors, creditors, and others make investment, credit, and other decisions
3. Timing	Information about future performance	Information about past performance
4. Type of report	Internal reports not regulated by GAAP (determined by cost-benefit analysis)	Financial statements regulated by GAAP

Accounting Concepts and Principles

Financial statements are used to communicate with those outside the business and must follow GAAP. GAAP are the established rules, principles, and concepts established by the accounting profession. Existing and potential investors and creditors can compare different companies if the companies have prepared financial statements using these rules.

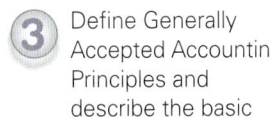

3 Define Generally Accepted Accounting Principles and describe the basic accounting concepts.

GAAP rests primarily on a conceptual framework written by the **Financial Accounting Standards Board (FASB)**, the seven-person group that is the "designated organization in the private sector for establishing standards of financial accounting and reporting." The framework specifies that: *The primary objective of financial reporting is to provide information useful for making investment and lending decisions.* To be useful, information must be relevant, reliable, and comparable. We begin our discussion of GAAP by introducing basic accounting concepts and principles.

The Entity Concept

The most basic concept in accounting is that of the **entity**. An accounting entity is an organization or a section of an organization that stands apart as a separate economic unit. The entity concept specifies that boundaries must be drawn around each entity so as not to confuse its financial affairs with those of other entities.

Let's assume you want to start your own business designing and building roller coasters for amusement parks. To measure the financial position of your company you must keep sales to customers, money borrowed from banks, and assets purchased for future use separated from your personal activities.

Even large companies can use the entity concept to separate the company into several divisions. Toyota, for example, creates divisions by car line, so that Toyota's management can evaluate the divisions' profitability. If sales in the Lexus division drop, Toyota can focus on the operating activities for that division only. Thus, the entity concept applies to any economic unit that needs to be evaluated separately.

The Reliability (Objectivity) Principle

Accounting information is based on the most reliable data available so that investors and creditors can use this information to make decisions. This guideline is the **reliability**, or **objectivity, principle**. Reliable data is verifiable, which means that it may be confirmed by any independent observer. For example, a bank loan is supported by a promissory note, which is objective evidence of the loan. Without the reliability principle, accounting data might be based on whims and opinions.

Suppose you want to buy a building for your electronics store. You choose a small building that you believe is worth $150,000. To confirm its value to the business, you hire a real estate appraiser, who values the building at $140,000. The appraisal of $140,000 is the more reliable value because it is supported by an independent observation.

The Cost Principle

The cost principle states that acquired assets and services should be recorded at their actual cost, also called **historical cost**. Suppose your electronics store purchases TV equipment from a supplier who is going out of business. Assume that you get a good deal and pay only $2,000 for equipment that would have cost you $3,000 elsewhere. The cost principle requires you to record the equipment at its actual cost of $2,000, not the $3,000 that you believe the equipment is worth.

The cost principle also holds that the accounting records should keep the historical cost of an asset throughout its useful life because this cost is a reliable measure. Even though the value of the TV equipment may change before you sell it, you still show the $2,000 as its cost.

The Going-Concern Concept

Another reason for measuring assets at historical cost is the **going-concern** concept. This concept assumes that the entity will stay in business for the foreseeable future, long enough to use existing resources for their intended purpose. Also, creditors who loan money to a business or investors who provide money or assets in a business do so assuming the business will remain in operation indefinitely. To reassure stakeholders that the business is a going concern, the business may have its financial statements audited by a CPA firm. If the CPA firm believes the business is in jeopardy of going out of business, the firm will report this opinion to the stakeholders.

In summary, GAAP allows external stakeholders to see reliable financial statements reported showing the historical costs of assets that reflect the entity's ability to continue as a business.

The Accounting Equation

The basic tool of accounting is the **accounting equation**. It measures the economic resources of a business and the claims to those resources.

4 Use the accounting equation to analyze business transactions.

Assets, Liabilities, and Owner's Equity

Assets are the economic resources of a business that are expected to provide benefits to the business in the future. Assets are what the business owns. Cash, merchandise inventory, furniture, and land are examples of assets.

Claims to those assets come from two sources:

- **Liabilities** are *outsider* claims to the assets of a business—liabilities are debts owed to outsiders. These outside parties, called creditors, include organizations that loan money or provide supplies, merchandise, furniture, or buildings. These creditors have a claim, or legal right, to part of the company's assets until the company pays them.

- **Owner's equity**, or **capital**, represents the *insider* claims to the assets of a business. Equity means ownership, so owner's equity is the owner's claim to the company's assets that comes from investing in the business.

The accounting equation shows how assets, liabilities, and owner's equity are related. Since it shows what the business owns and the claims against those items, it also shows the **financial position** of the business. Assets appear on the left side of the equation, and the liabilities and owner's equity appear on the right side. Exhibit 1-2 shows that the two sides must always be equal.

(Economic Resources)   (Claims to Economic Resources)
ASSETS   = LIABILITIES + OWNER'S EQUITY

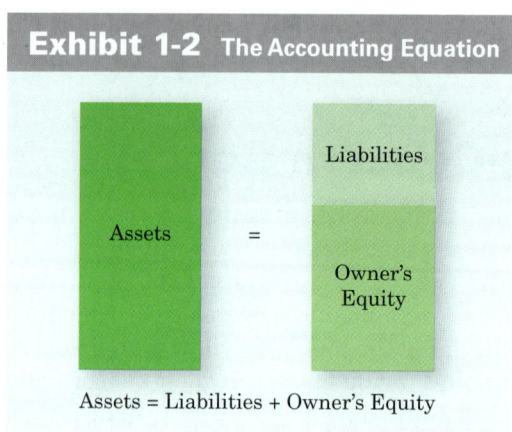

Exhibit 1-2 The Accounting Equation

Liabilities

Assets = Owner's Equity

Assets = Liabilities + Owner's Equity

Components of Owner's Equity

By rearranging the accounting equation, we see that owner's equity is the amount of an entity's assets left after its liabilities are subtracted. Let's assume a company's assets are $10,000, liabilities are $4,000, and owner's equity is $6,000:

$$\text{ASSETS} - \text{LIABILITIES} = \text{OWNER'S EQUITY}$$
$$\$10,000 - \$4,000 = \$6,000$$

A major goal of business is to increase owner's equity through financing, investing, and operating activities. The owner's equity, or capital, of a business can increase in two ways:

- **Owner investments** increase equity when the owner invests cash and other assets in the business. For example, Kay Torres invested $20,000 to start a travel agency called Kay Torres Travel Agency. Owner's equity of the business increased by $20,000.

- **Revenues** increase owner's equity when the business sells goods or services to customers. For example, Kay Torres Travel Agency earned revenue by planning vacations and other trips for customers. Kay arranged travel for a family reunion in Hawaii and the business earned $2,300 for this work. Owner's equity of the business increased by $2,300. Types of revenue include sales revenue when goods are sold, service revenue for services rendered, and interest revenue for interest earned on savings accounts and cash loans to others.

The owner's equity of a business can decrease in two ways:

- **Owner withdrawals** decrease owner's equity when the owner takes assets out of the business for personal use. For example, Kay Torres withdrew $1,000 from her travel agency's checking account for personal use. This owner withdrawal decreased the owner's equity of the business by $1,000.

- **Expenses** decrease owner's equity when the business uses up resources to deliver goods or provide services to customers. For example, Kay Torres Travel Agency paid $900 for one month of building rent. Owner's equity decreased by $900. To operate, businesses use a variety of resources that become expenses, such as employee salary expense, advertising expense, insurance expense, supplies expense, and utilities expense.

Revenues represent the increase to owner's equity from selling goods and services. Expenses show the decreases from using resources to earn this revenue. By matching expenses against the revenues they produced, the profitability of the business can be measured:

Revenues – Expenses = Net Income or Net Loss

When revenues are greater than expenses, the business earns **net income**, or profit. When expenses are greater than revenues, the business has a **net loss**. Exhibit 1-3 shows the following formula to calculate the owner's equity balance:

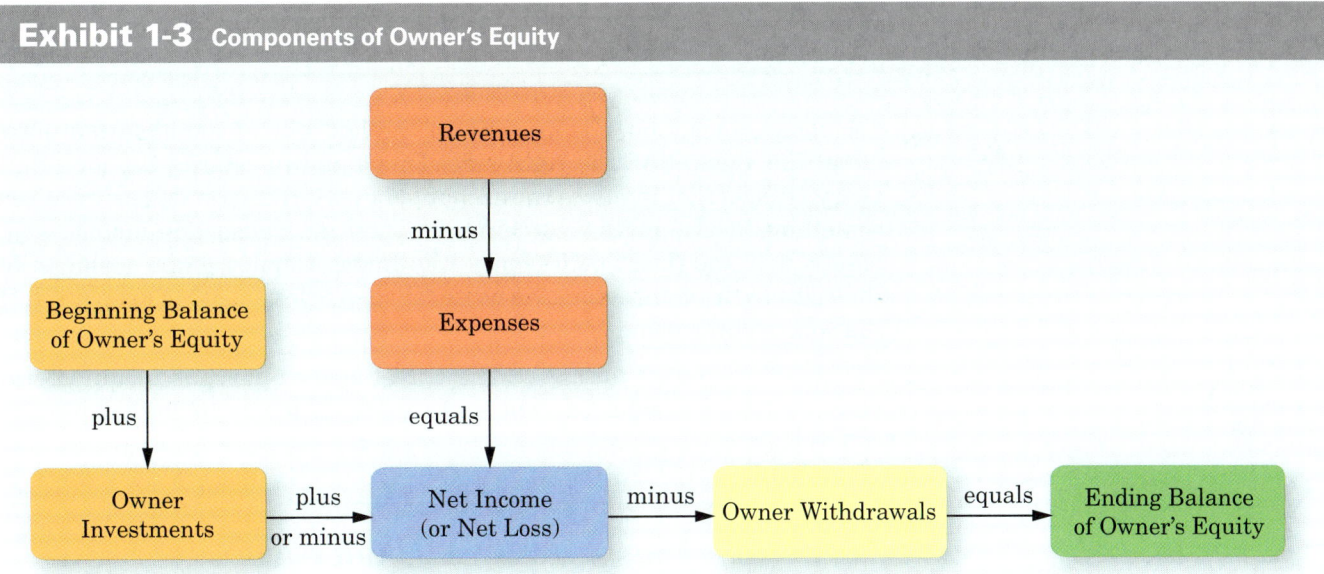

Exhibit 1-3 Components of Owner's Equity

Accounting for Business Transactions

Because a business is an organization that is accountable to its stakeholders, the business must account for all actual transactions. A **transaction** is any event that affects the financial position of the business *and* can be measured reliably. A transaction involves an exchange. In any transaction, something is received by the business, and something is given.

You are involved in transactions every day. In the past month you may have purchased food, gas, clothing, use of an apartment and utilities, parking space, and entertainment. In return you may have given cash or, if you used a credit card, your promise to pay cash later. If you work, you received cash in exchange for your time and expertise. These transactions affect your financial position.

To see how transactions affect the financial position of a company, we will use the accounting equation to account for some common transactions. Let's look at Kay Torres Travel Agency that began on June 1, 2008.

Kay Torres uses a Web site she developed to plan and pay for customer trips. The Web site is linked to airlines, hotels, and cruise lines, so clients can obtain the latest information 24 hours a day, 7 days a week. Torres's Web site allows the agency to transact more business than it could through the phone, fax, or e-mail. As a result, Torres can operate with few employees, which reduces expenses. She can pass along the savings to clients by charging them lower fees, which attracts more customers and helps her business grow.

Now let's analyze some of the transactions of Kay Torres Travel Agency.

1. *Investment by owner.* Kay Torres invests $20,000 of her own money to start the business. She deposits $20,000 in a bank account titled Kay Torres Travel Agency. In trade for the cash that the business receives, the owner receives an equity interest in the business. The effect of this transaction on the accounting equation of the Kay Torres Travel Agency business entity is

	ASSETS	=	LIABILITIES	+	OWNER'S EQUITY	TYPE OF OWNER'S EQUITY TRANSACTION
	Cash	=			Kay Torres, Capital	
(1)	+$20,000	=		+	$20,000	*Owner investment*
Bal.	$20,000	=			$20,000	

For each transaction, the amount on the left side of the equation must equal the amount on the right side. This equality reflects the idea that every transaction involves an exchange: every time a business receives something, it also gives something up. The first transaction increases an asset, Cash, and the owner's equity, Kay Torres, Capital, of the business. To the right of the transaction, we write "Owner investment" to keep track of the source of the owner's equity.

2. *Purchase equipment for cash.* The travel agency purchases equipment, paying cash of $9,000. The effect of this transaction on the accounting equation is

	ASSETS			=	LIABILITIES	+	OWNER'S EQUITY
	Cash	+	Equipment	=		+	Kay Torres, Capital
Bal.	$20,000			=			$20,000
(2)	− 9,000		+$ 9,000	=			
Bal.	$11,000		+$ 9,000	=			$20,000
			$20,000	=			$20,000

The cash purchase of equipment increases one asset, Equipment, and decreases another asset, Cash, by the same amount. After the transaction is completed, Torres's business has cash of $11,000, equipment of $9,000, and owner's equity of $20,000. Note that the total balances, abbreviated as "Bal.," on both sides of the equation are always equal.

3. *Borrow cash from the bank.* The travel agency borrows $15,000 cash from the bank and signs a 2-year note payable to the bank. The effect of this transaction on the accounting equation is

	ASSETS			=	LIABILITIES	+	OWNER'S EQUITY
					Notes Payable		Kay Torres, Capital
	Cash	+	Equipment	=		+	
Bal.	$11,000	+	$ 9,000	=			$20,000
(3)	+ 15,000			=	+ $15,000		
Bal.	$26,000	+	$ 9,000	=	$15,000	+	$20,000
			$35,000	=	$35,000		

A **note payable** is a written promise of future payment. Often businesses will borrow money from the bank in order to purchase assets or to make sure enough cash is available to pay suppliers. Borrowing cash from the bank increases the asset Cash and increases the liability Notes Payable by $15,000. Now the total assets of $35,000 equal the total liabilities and owner's equity of $35,000.

4. *Purchase supplies on credit.* The travel agency purchases office supplies for the agency, agreeing to pay $1,200 within 30 days. Its effect on the accounting equation increases the asset Supplies and increases the liability Accounts Payable by $1,200.

		ASSETS			=	LIABILITIES				OWNER'S EQUITY
	Cash	+	Supplies	+	Equipment	=	Accounts Payable	+ Notes Payable +		Kay Torres, Capital
Bal.	$26,000	+			$ 9,000	=		$15,000	+	$20,000
(4)			+ $1,200			=	+ $ 1,200			
Bal.	$26,000	+	$1,200	+	$ 9,000	=	$ 1,200	+ $15,000	+	$20,000
					$36,200	=	$36,200			

The Supplies account is an asset, not an expense, because the supplies purchased haven't been used yet. Supplies are an example of a **prepaid expense**. Like other prepaid expenses, the cost of the supplies will remain an asset until they are used in the business operations. The agreement to pay for them later creates an **accounts payable**, which is the amount of unpaid credit purchases from suppliers. Accounts payable is backed only by the reputation and the credit standing of the company.

5. *Provide services for cash.* The Travel Agency earns service revenue by providing travel services for clients. Kay makes $2,300 of travel arrangements and collects this amount in cash. The effect on the accounting equation is

		ASSETS			=	LIABILITIES			OWNER'S EQUITY	TYPE OF OWNER'S EQUITY TRANSACTION
	Cash	+	Supplies	+ Equipment	=	Accounts Payable +	Notes Payable +		Kay Torres, Capital	
Bal.	$26,000	+	$1,200	+ $ 9,000	=	$ 1,200	+ $15,000	+	$20,000	
(5)	+ 2,300				=				+ 2,300	*Service revenue*
Bal.	$28,300	+	$1,200	+ $ 9,000	=	$ 1,200	+ $15,000	+	$22,300	
				$38,500	=	$38,500				

Providing services increases both Cash and Kay Torres, Capital, by $2,300. A revenue transaction grows the business, as shown by the increases in assets and owner's equity.

6. *Provide services on credit.* Businesses can also earn service revenue even if it hasn't yet been paid for these services. Torres performs $5,200 of

services and, in return, Kay Torres Travel Agency receives clients' promises to pay this $5,200 within one month. In accounting, we say that Torres performed this service **on account**. A client's promise to pay is called an **account receivable** and is an asset because the travel agency owns the right to collect the cash in the future.

The act of performing the service, not collecting the cash, earns the revenue. This $5,200 of service revenue increases the wealth of Torres's business just like the $2,300 of revenue that she collected immediately in transaction (5). The effect on the accounting equation is an increase in the asset Accounts Receivable and an increase in Kay Torres, Capital, as follows:

		ASSETS			=	LIABILITIES			+	OWNER'S EQUITY	TYPE OF OWNER'S EQUITY TRANSACTION
	Cash	+ Accounts Receivable	+ Supplies	+ Equipment	=	Accounts Payable	+ Notes Payable	+		Kay Torres, Capital	
Bal.	$28,300 +		+ $1,200	+ $ 9,000	=	$ 1,200	+ $15,000	+		$22,300	
(6)		+ $5,200			=					+ 5,200	*Service revenue*
Bal.	$28,300 +	$5,200	+ $1,200	+ $ 9,000	=	$ 1,200	+ $15,000	+		$27,500	
				$43,700	=	$43,700					

7. *Partial payment of accounts payable.* The travel agency pays $600 to the store where it purchased $1,200 worth of supplies in transaction (4). In accounting, we say that it pays $600 on account. The effect on the accounting equation is a decrease in the asset Cash and a decrease in the liability Accounts Payable, as shown next.

		ASSETS			=	LIABILITIES			+	OWNER'S EQUITY
	Cash	+ Accounts Receivable	+ Supplies	+ Equipment	=	Accounts Payable	+ Notes Payable	+		Kay Torres, Capital
Bal.	$28,300 +	$5,200	+ $1,200	+ $ 9,000	=	$ 1,200	+ $15,000	+		$27,500
(7)	− 600				=	− 600				
Bal.	$27,700 +	$5,200	+ $1,200	+ $ 9,000	=	$ 600	+ $15,000	+		$27,500
				$43,100	=	$43,100				

The payment of cash on account has no effect on Supplies because the payment does not affect the amount of supplies owned by the business. Likewise, the payment on account does not affect expenses because the business is paying off an amount owed, not using those supplies.

8. (8), (9), and (10) *Payment of expenses.* During the month, the travel agency pays $900 in cash for building rent, $1,100 for salaries, and $300 for utilities. The effects on the accounting equation are

	ASSETS				=	LIABILITIES			+	OWNER'S EQUITY	TYPE OF OWNER'S EQUITY TRANSACTION
	Cash	+ Accounts Receivable	+ Supplies	+ Equipment	=	Accounts Payable	+ Notes Payable	+		Kay Torres, Capital	
Bal.	$27,700 +	$5,200	+ $1,200	+ $ 9,000	=	$ 600	$15,000	+		$27,500	
(8)	– 900				=					– 900	*Building rent expense*
Bal.	$26,800 +	$5,200	+ $1,200	+ $ 9,000	=	$ 600	+ $15,000	+		$26,600	
(9)	– 1,100				=					–1,100	*Salary expense*
Bal.	$25,700 +	$5,200	+ $1,200	+ $ 9,000	=	$ 600	+ $15,000	+		$25,500	
(10)	– 300				=					– 300	*Utilities expense*
Bal.	$25,400 +	$5,200	+ $1,200	+ $ 9,000	=	$ 600	+ $15,000	+		$25,200	
				$40,800	=	$40,800					

For each of these transactions, Cash decreases and so does Kay Torres, Capital. Each expense is recorded separately, because they are different kinds of expenses. After every transaction, total assets must still equal total liabilities and owner's equity so that the accounting equation continues to balance.

Expenses are a necessary part of business. Resources have to be used to earn revenue. So, to increase owner's equity for revenue earned, a business must decrease owner's equity by using its resources. The goal is to earn more revenue than the expenses used to earn that revenue.

11. *Cash withdrawal by owner.* Torres withdraws $1,000 cash from the business for her personal use. The effect on the accounting equation is

	ASSETS				=	LIABILITIES			+	OWNER'S EQUITY	TYPE OF OWNER'S EQUITY TRANSACTION
	Cash	+ Accounts Receivable	+ Supplies	+ Equipment	=	Accounts Payable	+ Notes Payable	+		Kay Torres, Capital	
Bal.	$25,400 +	$5,200	+ $1,200	+ $ 9,000	=	$ 600	+ $15,000	+		$25,200	
(11)	– 1,000				=					– 1,000	*Owner withdrawal*
Bal.	$24,400 +	$5,200	+ $1,200	+ $ 9,000	=	$ 600	+ $15,000	+		$24,200	
				$39,800	=	$39,800					

Torres's withdrawal of $1,000 cash decreases the asset Cash and the equity account of Kay Torres, Capital. The withdrawal is not an expense because the cash is used for the owner's personal affairs. The cash withdrawal was not used to earn revenue. We record this decrease in owner's equity as Withdrawals or as Drawings.

12. *Remodel of Torres's home.* Torres remodels her home at a cost of $40,000, paying cash from personal funds. This event is *not* a transaction of Kay Torres Travel Agency and therefore is not recorded by the business. It is a transaction of Kay Torres, not Kay Torres Travel Agency. This transaction illustrates the entity concept, the idea that Kay Torres Travel Agency is an entity separate from Kay Torres.

Evaluating Business Transactions

Exhibit 1-4 summarizes Kay Torres Travel Agency's transactions. Panel A lists the descriptions of the transactions, and Panel B shows the analysis. As you study the exhibit, note that every transaction keeps the equation in balance.

Financial Statements

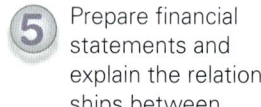 **5** Prepare financial statements and explain the relationships between them.

To present the results of the transactions we analyzed, we need to prepare financial statements. These reports show the entity's financial information to interested stakeholders including the owner, Kay Torres, and her banker. Let's examine the business's financial statements at the end of the period in the order in which they are prepared. These financial statements are presented in different colors to help you see the relationship between the transaction analysis we prepared and the financial statements.

Financial statements include the following:

- **Income statement**
- **Statement of owner's equity**
- **Balance sheet**
- **Statement of cash flows**

The Income Statement

The accountant prepares the income statement to answer the question, "Are we making a profit?" Just as a scoreboard shows how many points a team earned for a specific period of time, a business prepares an income statement to show, for a specific time period, the revenue earned and the expenses incurred to produce that revenue. Further, like the scoreboard that shows whether the team is winning or losing, the income statement holds one of the most important pieces of information about a business—whether it earned

- Net income (total revenues are greater than total expenses) or
- Net loss (total revenues are less than total expenses)

To prepare the income statement, we set up a format that includes the heading and the body of the statement. The heading includes the name of the business, the "Who", the name of the financial statement, the "What", and the time period it

Exhibit 1-4 Descriptions and Analysis of Transactions, Kay Torres Travel Agency, June 2008

PANEL A—Descriptions of Transactions

1. As the owner, Torres invested $20,000 cash in the business, Kay Torres Travel Agency.
2. The travel agency purchased $9,000 of equipment for cash.
3. The travel agency borrowed $15,000 cash from the bank.
4. The travel agency purchased $1,200 of supplies on credit.
5. The travel agency provided $2,300 of services for cash.
6. The travel agency provided $5,200 of services on credit.
7. The travel agency made a partial payment of $600 on the account payable in transaction 4.
8. The travel agency paid $900 of building rent expense.
9. The travel agency paid $1,100 of salary expense.
10. The travel agency paid $300 of utilities expense.
11. Torres, the owner, withdrew $1,000 cash for personal use.
12. Torres remodeled her home with $40,000 of personal funds. This transaction does not involve the business and is not included in the following analysis of transactions.

PANEL B—Analysis of Transactions

			ASSETS			=	LIABILITIES			+	OWNER'S EQUITY	TYPE OF OWNER'S EQUITY TRANSACTION
	Cash	+	Accounts Receivable +	Supplies +	Equipment	=	Accounts Payable	+	Notes Payable	+	Kay Torres, Capital	
(1)	+$20,000										+$20,000	Owner investment
Bal.	20,000					=					20,000	
(2)	−9,000				+$9,000							
Bal.	11,000	+			9,000	=					20,000	
(3)	+15,000								+$15,000			
Bal.	26,000	+			9,000	=			15,000	+	20,000	
(4)				+$1,200			+$1,200					
Bal.	26,000	+		1,200 +	9,000	=	1,200	+	15,000	+	20,000	
(5)	+2,300										+2,300	Service revenue
Bal.	28,300	+		1,200 +	9,000	=	1,200	+	15,000	+	22,300	
(6)			+$5,200								+5,200	Service revenue
Bal.	28,300	+	5,200 +	1,200 +	9,000	=	1,200	+	15,000	+	27,500	
(7)	−600						−600					
Bal.	27,700	+	5,200 +	1,200 +	9,000	=	600	+	15,000	+	27,500	
(8)	−900										−900	Building rent expense
Bal.	26,800	+	5,200 +	1,200 +	9,000	=	600	+	15,000	+	26,600	
(9)	−1,100										−1,100	Salary expense
Bal.	25,700	+	5,200 +	1,200 +	9,000	=	600	+	15,000	+	25,500	
(10)	−300										−300	Utilities expense
Bal.	25,400	+	5,200 +	1,200 +	9,000	=	600	+	15,000	+	25,200	
(11)	−1,000										−1,000	Owner withdrawal
Bal.	$24,400	+	$5,200 +	$1,200 +	$9,000	=	$ 600	+	$15,000	+	$24,200	
					$39,800	=	$39,800					

covers, the "When". The body of the income statement lists the revenues, then the expenses, and finally the net income or net loss.

Where do we find this information? In this chapter, we introduced you to the accounting equation as a way of accounting for a business's transactions. Panel B of Exhibit 1-4 shows how the accounting equation was used to analyze and keep track of transactions for Kay Torres Travel Agency for June 2008. Let's get the information to prepare the income statement by looking at it. In the equity column of the accounting equation, you will see the revenue and expense activity for June. These transactions represent the operating activity of the business, the activities necessary to generate a profit and to grow the business.

Now, let's look at Exhibit 1-5 to see how we prepare the income statement using the information from the equity column. In the first month of operations, Kay Torres Travel Agency earned $7,500 in revenue and expended $2,300 in resources to serve her customers. The difference is net income of $5,200. This amount can remain part of her equity in the business and can be used to "grow" or expand her business. Or, because Kay owns the business, she may choose to withdraw all or part of the business's net income to be used for other reasons.

Exhibit 1-5   Preparation of Income Statement and Statement of Owner's Equity for Kay Torres Travel Agency

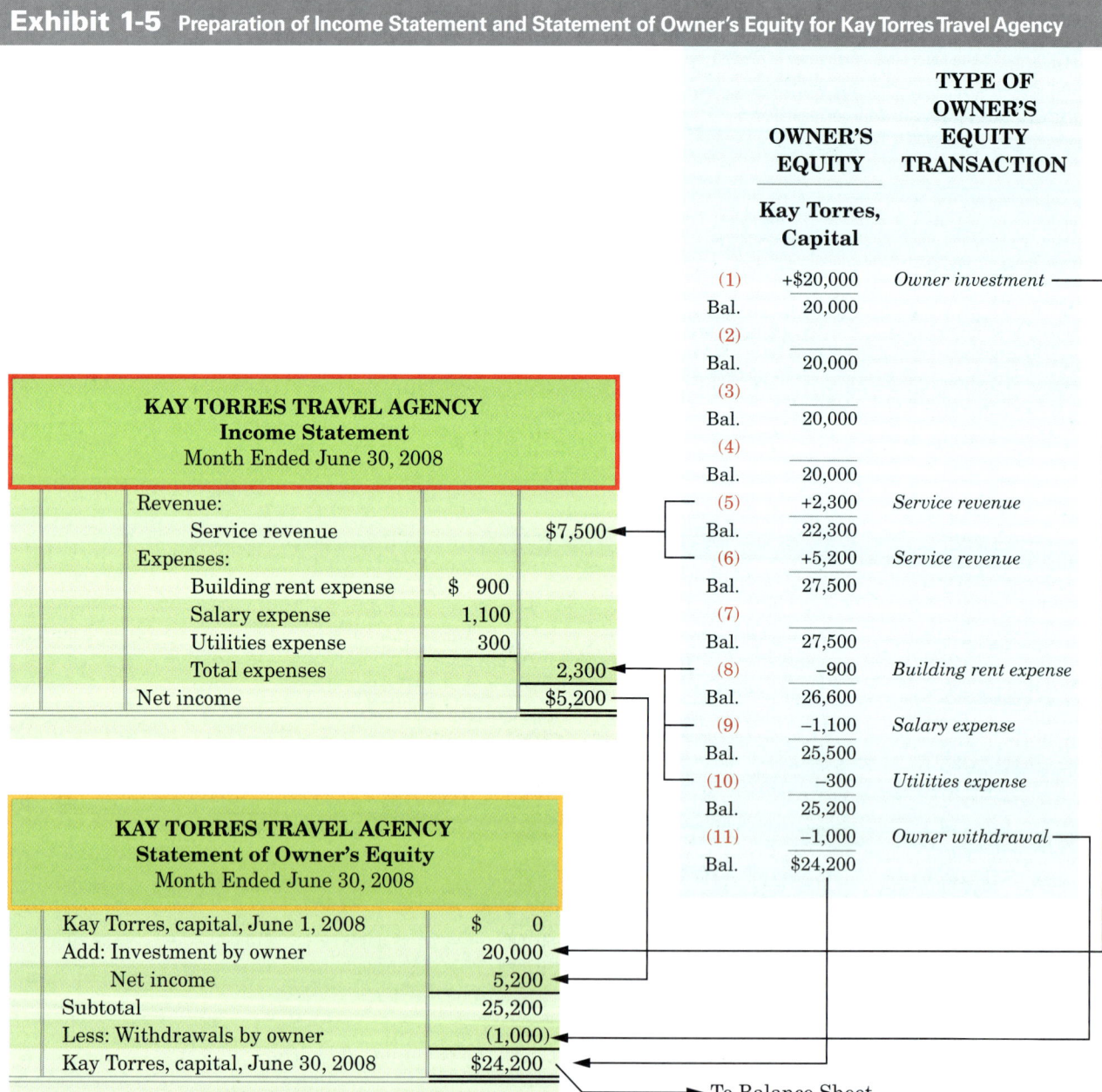

KAY TORRES TRAVEL AGENCY
Income Statement
Month Ended June 30, 2008

Revenue:		
Service revenue		$7,500
Expenses:		
Building rent expense	$ 900	
Salary expense	1,100	
Utilities expense	300	
Total expenses		2,300
Net income		$5,200

KAY TORRES TRAVEL AGENCY
Statement of Owner's Equity
Month Ended June 30, 2008

Kay Torres, capital, June 1, 2008	$ 0
Add: Investment by owner	20,000
Net income	5,200
Subtotal	25,200
Less: Withdrawals by owner	(1,000)
Kay Torres, capital, June 30, 2008	$24,200

		OWNER'S EQUITY	TYPE OF OWNER'S EQUITY TRANSACTION
		Kay Torres, Capital	
(1)	+$20,000		Owner investment
Bal.	20,000		
(2)			
Bal.	20,000		
(3)			
Bal.	20,000		
(4)			
Bal.	20,000		
(5)	+2,300		Service revenue
Bal.	22,300		
(6)	+5,200		Service revenue
Bal.	27,500		
(7)			
Bal.	27,500		
(8)	–900		Building rent expense
Bal.	26,600		
(9)	–1,100		Salary expense
Bal.	25,500		
(10)	–300		Utilities expense
Bal.	25,200		
(11)	–1,000		Owner withdrawal
Bal.	$24,200		

To Balance Sheet

The Statement of Owner's Equity

"How much equity do I have in the business?" The statement of owner's equity answers this question by presenting the amount of the owner's claim to assets and the changes to that claim during a specific time period, such as a month or a year, as follows:

Remember that increases in owner's equity come from

- Owner investments

- Net income (Revenues – Expenses, when revenues are greater than expenses)

Decreases in owner's equity result from

- Owner withdrawals

- Net loss (Revenues – Expenses, when expenses are greater than revenues)

To prepare the statement of owner's equity, we set up a format that, like the income statement, includes a heading and body. The heading includes the name of the business, the name of the financial statement, and the time period it covers. The body of the statement lists the beginning owner's equity balance, any additional owner investments, net income or net loss, any owner withdrawals, and the ending balance of owner's equity.

Where do we find the information? Again, let's look again at Panel B of Exhibit 1-4. In the equity column of the accounting equation, you will see the investment and withdrawal activity for June. Combining these amounts with the net income or net loss, we can calculate the ending balance of owner's equity on June 30.

Now, let's look at Exhibit 1-5 to see how we prepare the statement of owner's equity using the information from the equity column. Because the business just opened, the beginning owner's equity balance was $0. In the first month of operations, Kay Torres Travel Agency received an owner investment of $20,000 and had an owner withdrawal of $1,000. Combined with the $5,200 net income of June, Kay Torres's ending equity balance at June 30 is $24,200. Because Torres's initial investment was $20,000, and the ending owner's equity balance is $24,200, the increase in her equity is $4,200, and this amount stays in the business to help her expand it.

The Balance Sheet

"What is the financial position of my business at this point in time? Owners and creditors periodically need to see the resources of the business and the claims to those resources. The balance sheet lists all the entity's assets, liabilities, and owner's equity as of a specific date, usually the end of a month or a year. *The balance sheet gets its name from the fact that it shows how the accounting equation for a business balances*, that the assets of the business still equal the liabilities and owner's equity of a business, even after transactions have occurred. For this reason, the balance sheet is like a picture of the entity, and is also known as the **statement of financial position**.

To prepare the balance sheet, we set up a format that includes the heading and the body of the statement. The heading includes the business name, the name of the financial statement, and the point in time at which it was prepared. The body of the statement presents the amounts of the assets, liabilities, and owner's equity at that point in time.

Where do we find the information? Let's look again at Panel B of Exhibit 1-4. This time we focus on the last row of the exhibit, which shows the balances for each asset, liability, and owner's equity at the end of the period, June 30, 2008.

Now, let's look at Exhibit 1-6 to see how we prepare the balance sheet using the information from that last row. Each amount in this row represents the balance for the assets, liabilities, or owner's equity at a point in time, so we include

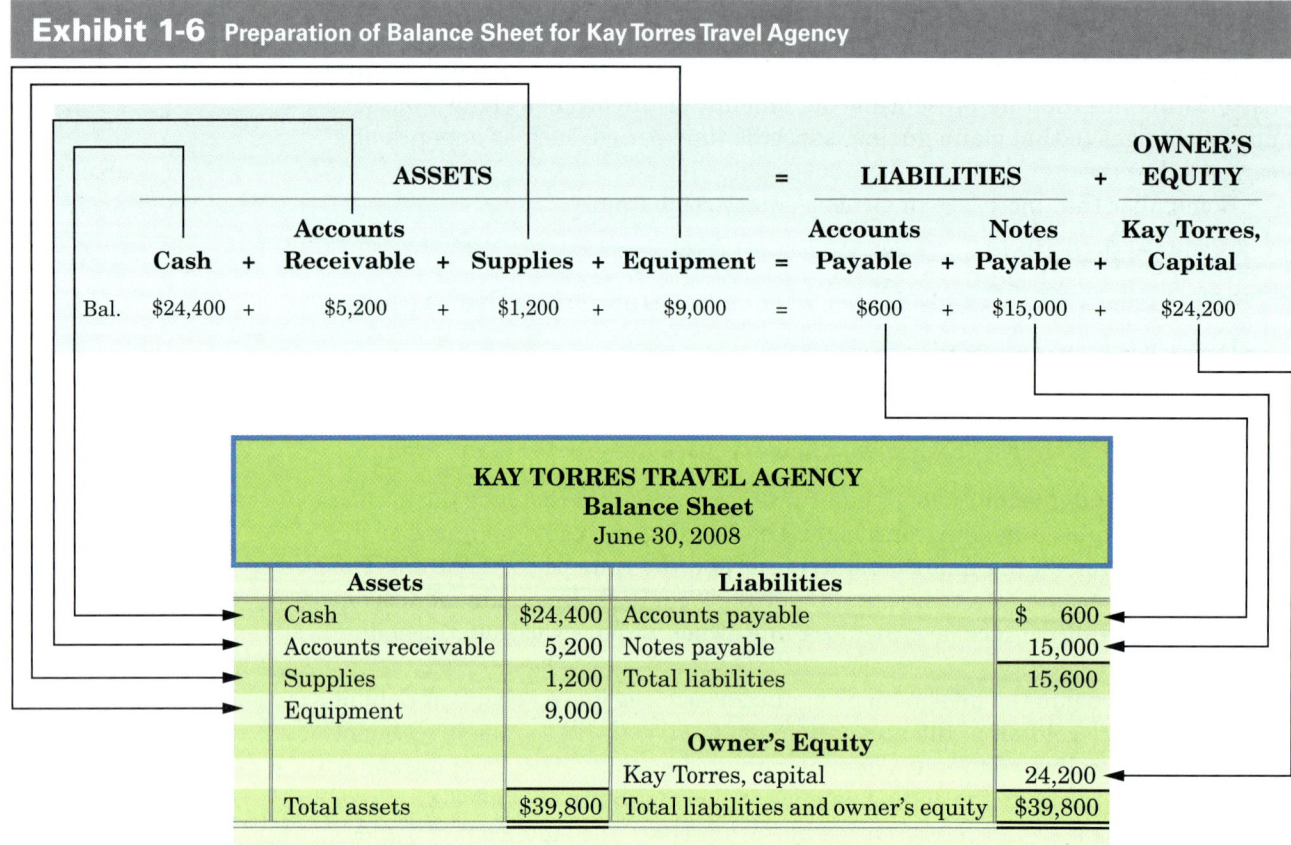

Exhibit 1-6 Preparation of Balance Sheet for Kay Torres Travel Agency

these amounts on the balance sheet. Notice that total assets equal total liabilities and owner's equity.

The Statement of Cash Flows

"Did we generate more cash than we used?" Owners and creditors want to see how liquid the business is, how well it can pay its bills, and they want to see the source of that liquidity. A business's liquidity is the result of its financing, investing, and operating activities, and this financial statement demonstrates how those activities either produced or used cash. The statement of cash flows reports the amount of cash coming in and cash going out during a period. It also shows the resulting cash balance at the end of that period, which matches the amount of cash shown in the balance sheet. The statement of cash flows shown in Exhibit 1-7 illustrates that cash for Kay Torres Travel Agency increased by $24,200 during June, and it shows the sources of that increase. We will learn how to prepare the statement of cash flows in Chapter 13.

Relationships Between the Financial Statements

Exhibit 1-8 illustrates all four financial statements. The statements were prepared using data in the transaction analysis in Exhibit 1-4, which covers the month of June 2008 and is shown in the center of Exhibit 1-8.

1. First, we prepared the income statement for the month ended June 30, 2008. This amount appears on the statement of owner's equity as an increase to owner's equity.

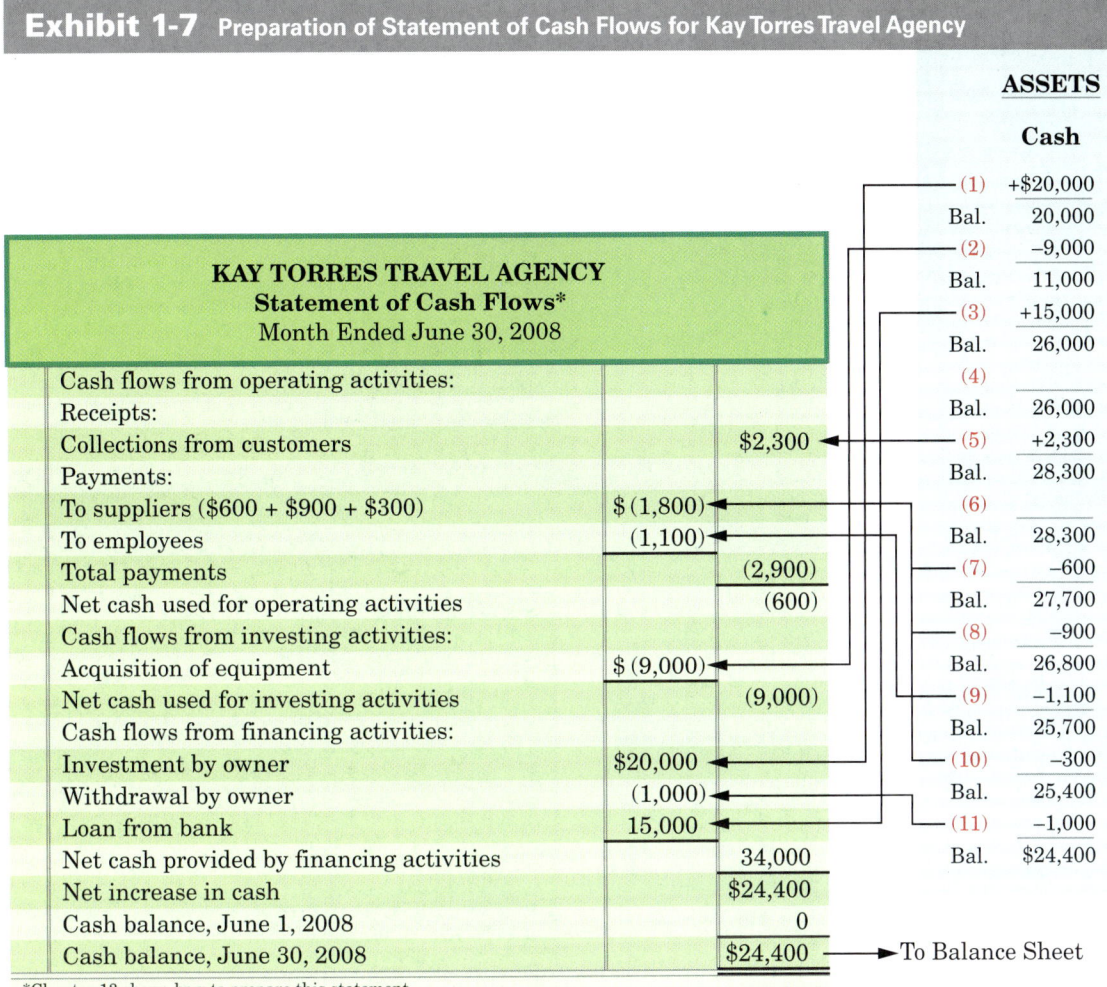

Exhibit 1-7 Preparation of Statement of Cash Flows for Kay Torres Travel Agency

	ASSETS
	Cash
(1)	+$20,000
Bal.	20,000
(2)	−9,000
Bal.	11,000
(3)	+15,000
Bal.	26,000
(4)	
Bal.	26,000
(5)	+2,300
Bal.	28,300
(6)	
Bal.	28,300
(7)	−600
Bal.	27,700
(8)	−900
Bal.	26,800
(9)	−1,100
Bal.	25,700
(10)	−300
Bal.	25,400
(11)	−1,000
Bal.	$24,400

KAY TORRES TRAVEL AGENCY
Statement of Cash Flows*
Month Ended June 30, 2008

Cash flows from operating activities:		
Receipts:		
Collections from customers		$2,300
Payments:		
To suppliers ($600 + $900 + $300)	$(1,800)	
To employees	(1,100)	
Total payments		(2,900)
Net cash used for operating activities		(600)
Cash flows from investing activities:		
Acquisition of equipment	$(9,000)	
Net cash used for investing activities		(9,000)
Cash flows from financing activities:		
Investment by owner	$20,000	
Withdrawal by owner	(1,000)	
Loan from bank	15,000	
Net cash provided by financing activities		34,000
Net increase in cash		$24,400
Cash balance, June 1, 2008		0
Cash balance, June 30, 2008		$24,400

→ To Balance Sheet

*Chapter 13 shows how to prepare this statement.

2. Second, we prepared the statement of owner's equity for the month ended June 30, 2008. The owner's equity balance at the end of June appears on the balance sheet.

3. Third, we prepared the balance sheet at June 30, 2008. The balance sheet reports all assets, all liabilities, and owner's equity as of that date. Notice that total assets equal total liabilities and total owner's equity.

4. Fourth, we examined the statement of cash flows for the month ended June 30, 2008. The ending cash balance is the same cash amount that appears on the balance sheet.

Ethical Decision Making

Ethics in Accounting and Business

To be truly accountable to stakeholders, all members of an organization should behave ethically. **Ethics** are the principles of right behavior that guide decision making. These principles are based on values of responsibility, fairness, trustworthiness, respect, caring, and citizenship; the general rule of ethics is to bring no

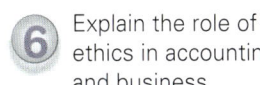

6 Explain the role of ethics in accounting and business.

Exhibit 1-8 Relationships Between Financial Statements for Kay Torres Travel Agency

KAY TORRES TRAVEL AGENCY — Transaction Analysis

	Cash	+ Accounts Receivable	+ Supplies	+ Equipment	=	Accounts Payable	+ Notes Payable	+ Kay Torres, Capital	TYPE OF OWNER'S EQUITY TRANSACTION
(1)	+$20,000				=			+$20,000	Owner investment
Bal.	20,000				=			20,000	
(2)	−9,000			+$9,000	=				
Bal.	11,000 +			9,000	=			20,000	
(3)	+15,000				=		+$15,000		
Bal.	26,000 +			9,000	=		15,000 +	20,000	
(4)			+$1,200		=	+$1,200			
Bal.	26,000 +		1,200 +	9,000	=	1,200 +	15,000 +	20,000	
(5)	+2,300				=			+2,300	Service revenue
Bal.	28,300 +		1,200 +	9,000	=	1,200 +	15,000 +	22,300	
(6)		+$5,200			=			+5,200	Service revenue
Bal.	28,300 +	5,200 +	1,200 +	9,000	=	1,200 +	15,000 +	27,500	
(7)	−600				=	−600			
Bal.	27,700 +	5,200 +	1,200 +	9,000	=	600 +	15,000 +	27,500	
(8)	−900				=			−900	Building rent expense
Bal.	26,800 +	5,200 +	1,200 +	9,000	=	600 +	15,000 +	26,600	
(9)	−1,100				=			−1,100	Salary expense
Bal.	25,700 +	5,200 +	1,200 +	9,000	=	600 +	15,000 +	25,500	
(10)	−300				=			−300	Utilities expense
Bal.	25,400 +	5,200 +	1,200 +	9,000	=	600 +	15,000 +	25,200	
(11)	−1,000				=			−1,000	Owner withdrawal
Bal.	$24,400 +	$5,200 +	$1,200 +	$9,000	=	$ 600 +	$15,000 +	$24,200	

KAY TORRES TRAVEL AGENCY
Statement of Cash Flows*
Month Ended June 30, 2008

Cash flows from operating activities:		
Receipts:		
Collections from customers		$ 2,300
Payments:		
To suppliers ($600 + $900 + $300)	$ (1,800)	
To employees	(1,100)	
Total payments		(2,900)
Net cash used for operating activities		(600)
Cash flows from investing activities:		
Acquisition of equipment	$ (9,000)	
Net cash used for investing activities		(9,000)
Cash flows from financing activities:		
Investment by owner	$20,000	
Withdrawal by owner	(1,000)	
Loan from bank	15,000	
Net cash provided by financing activities		34,000
Net increase in cash		$24,400
Cash balance, June 1, 2008		0
Cash balance, June 30, 2008		$24,400

*Chapter 13 shows how to prepare this statement.

KAY TORRES TRAVEL AGENCY
Income Statement
Month Ended June 30, 2008

Revenue:		
Service revenue		$7,500
Expenses:		
Building rent expense	$ 900	
Salary expense	1,100	
Utilities expense	300	
Total expenses		2,300
Net income		$5,200

KAY TORRES TRAVEL AGENCY
Statement of Owner's Equity
Month Ended June 30, 2008

Kay Torres, capital, June 1, 2008		$ 0
Add: Investment by owner	20,000	
Net income	5,200	25,200
Subtotal		25,200
Less: Withdrawals by owner		(1,000)
Kay Torres, capital, June 30, 2008		$24,200

KAY TORRES TRAVEL AGENCY
Balance Sheet
June 30, 2008

Assets		Liabilities	
Cash	$24,400	Accounts payable	$ 600
Accounts receivable	5,200	Notes payable	15,000
Supplies	1,200	Total liabilities	15,600
Equipment	9,000	**Owner's Equity**	
		Kay Torres, capital	24,200
Total assets	$39,800	Total liabilities and owner's equity	$39,800

Note: Remember…
1. The income statement, enclosed in the red box, provides the details of revenues earned and expenses incurred.
2. The revenue and expense transactions are then condensed into one number—in this case, net income—which becomes part of the statement of owner's equity as indicated by the yellow box.
3. The ending balance of owner's equity flows into the balance sheet, as indicated by the blue box.
4. The statement of cash flows, as indicated by the green box, provides details of how a company got its cash and how it spent cash during the accounting period.

physical or emotional harm to others. Organizations create a culture with standards representing the expected behavior of its members, sometimes in the form of a code of ethics. As individuals, we also have beliefs about what is right or wrong. Ethical dilemmas can arise when personal beliefs or organizational culture differ from ethical principles.

Stakeholders need relevant, reliable, and comparable information about a company. Companies naturally want to look as good as possible. The potential for conflict here is significant. To provide reliable information for the public, the Securities and Exchange Commission requires companies that sell stocks and bonds publicly to have their financial statements audited by independent accountants. An **audit** is an examination of a company's financial statements by a **Certified Public Accountant (CPA)** in order to determine whether those statements give a fair presentation of the company's situation.

The vast majority of accountants do their jobs quietly, professionally, and ethically. We never hear about them. Unfortunately, only those who bend the rules make the headlines. In recent years we've seen more accounting scandals than at any time since the 1920s.

Enron Corp., for example, was the seventh-largest company in the United States before the company admitted reporting fewer debts on its financial statements than it really owed. WorldCom, a major long-distance telephone provider, admitted accounting for expenses as though they were assets. Xerox Corp. was accused of manipulating reported profits. These and other scandals rocked the business community and hurt investor confidence. Innocent people lost their jobs, and the stock market suffered when stock prices dropped. The courts are still sorting out who was responsible for the flawed information and its consequences.

Standards of Professional Conduct

The American Institute of Certified Public Accountants (the AICPA), has a Code of Professional Conduct that provides guidance to CPAs in their work. The preamble to the Code states: "[A] certified public accountant assumes an obligation of self-discipline above and beyond the requirements of laws and regulations . . . [and] an unswerving commitment to honorable behavior. . . ."

Similarly, **Certified Management Accountants (CMAs)** have standards. The opening paragraph of the Standards of Ethical Conduct of the Institute of Management Accountants (IMA) states: "Management accountants have an obligation to the organizations they serve, their profession, the public, and themselves to maintain the highest standards of ethical conduct."

As mentioned previously, companies can also set standards of ethical conduct for employees. For example, The Boeing Company, a leading manufacturer of aircraft, has a highly developed set of business conduct guidelines. The chairperson of the board states: "We owe our success as much to our reputation for integrity as we do to the quality and dependability of our products and services. This reputation is fragile and can easily be lost."

As one chief executive stated, "Ethical practice is simply good business." Truth is always better than dishonesty—in accounting, in business, and in life.

Have you ever thought of having your own business? The Accounting in Action feature shows how to make some of the decisions that you will face if you start a business. Accounting in Action appears in each chapter.

Demo Doc

Transaction Analysis Using the Accounting Equation/Financial Statement Preparation

Learning Objectives   4, 5

On March 1, 2008, David Richardson opened a painting business near a historical housing district and named it DR Painting. David is the sole owner of the proprietorship. During March 2008, David engaged in the following transactions:

a. **David invested $40,000 of personal cash to start the business.**

b. **The business paid $20,000 cash to acquire a truck.**

c. **The business purchased supplies costing $1,800 on account.**

d. **The business painted a house for a client and received $3,000 cash.**

e. **The business painted a house for a client for $4,000. The client agreed to pay next week.**

f. **The business paid $800 cash toward the supplies purchased in transaction c.**

g. **The business paid employee salaries of $1,000 in cash.**

h. **David withdrew $1,500 cash from the business for personal use.**

i. **The business collected $2,600 from the client in transaction e.**

j. **David paid $100 cash for personal groceries.**

Requirements

1. Analyze these transactions in terms of their effects on the accounting equation of DR Painting. Use Exhibit 1-4 (p. 17) as a guide.

2. Prepare the income statement, statement of owner's equity, and balance sheet of the business after recording the transactions. Use Exhibit 1-8 (p. 22) as a guide.

Demo Doc Solutions

Analyze these transactions in terms of their effects on the accounting equation of DR Painting. Use Exhibit 1-4 (p. 17) as a guide.

 Use the accounting equation to analyze business trans-actions.

Part 1	Part 2	Part 3	Part 4	Demo Doc Complete

a. David invested $40,000 of personal cash to start the business.

David is using his own money, but he is giving it *to the business*. Because the business is involved, it is a recordable transaction.

From the business's perspective, this transaction will increase Cash (an asset) by $40,000 and increase David Richardson, Capital (owner's equity) by $40,000.

The effect of this transaction on the accounting equation is:

	ASSETS	=	LIABILITIES	+	OWNER'S EQUITY	TYPE OF OWNER'S EQUITY TRANSACTION
	Cash	=			David Richardson, Capital	
(a)	+$40,000	=			+$40,000	*Owner investment*
Bal.	$40,000	=			$40,000	

To record this transaction in the equation, we add $40,000 under Assets: Cash and add $40,000 under Owner's Equity. To the right of the transaction, we write "Owner investment" to help us keep track of changes in the equity account. This note will also be helpful when we prepare the financial statements. Before we move on, we should double-check to see that the left side of the equation equals the right side. It is important to remember that the equation must balance after each transaction is recorded.

b. The business paid $20,000 cash to acquire a truck.

Truck (an asset) is increased by $20,000, while Cash (an asset) is decreased by $20,000.

The effect of this transaction on the accounting equation is:

	ASSETS			=	LIABILITIES	+	OWNER'S EQUITY
	Cash	+	Truck	=			David Richardson, Capital
Bal.	$40,000			=			$40,000
(b)	−20,000	+	$20,000	=			
Bal.	$20,000	+	$20,000	=			$40,000
		$40,000		=	$40,000		

Notice that transactions do not have to affect both sides of the equation. However, the accounting equation *always* holds, so *both sides must always balance*. It helps to check that this is true after every transaction.

c. The business purchased supplies costing $1,800 on account.

Supplies is an asset that is increased by $1,800. However, the supplies were not paid for in cash, but instead *on account*. This transaction involves accounts *pay*able (because it will have to be *paid* later). Because we now have *more* money that has to be paid later, it is an increase in Accounts Payable (a liability) of $1,800.

The effect of this transaction on the accounting equation is:

	ASSETS			=	LIABILITIES	+	OWNER'S EQUITY
	Cash	+ Supplies +	Truck	=	Accounts Payable	+	David Richardson, Capital
Bal.	$20,000		+ $20,000	=			$40,000
(c)		+ $1,800		=	+ $ 1,800		
Bal.	$20,000 +	$1,800 +	$20,000	=	$ 1,800	+	$40,000
			$41,800	=	$41,800		

Remember that the supplies will be recorded as an asset until the time that they are used by the business (this adjustment will be addressed in a later chapter). The obligation to pay the $1,800 will remain in Accounts Payable until it is paid.

d. The business painted a house for a client and received $3,000 cash.

When the business paints houses, it means that it is doing work for clients. Doing work for clients (or performing services) is the way that the business makes money. By performing these services, the business is earning service revenues.

Painting this house provides services for a customer. This means that Service Revenues increases (which increases owner's equity) of $3,000. Because the customer paid in cash, this transaction also results in an increase in Cash (an asset) of $3,000.

Remember: Revenues *increase* net income, which increases owner's equity.

The effect of this transaction on the accounting equation is:

	ASSETS			=	LIABILITIES	+	OWNER'S EQUITY	TYPE OF OWNER'S EQUITY TRANSACTION
	Cash	+ Supplies +	Truck	=	Accounts Payable	+	David Richardson, Capital	
Bal.	$20,000 +	$1,800 +	$20,000	=	$ 1,800	+	$40,000	
(d)	+ 3,000			=			+ 3,000	*Service revenue*
Bal.	$23,000 +	$1,800 +	$20,000	=	$ 1,800	+	$43,000	
			$44,800	=	$44,800			

Notice that we write "Service revenue" to the right of the owner's equity column.

e. The business painted a house for a client for $4,000. The client agreed to pay next week.

Again, the business is performing services for clients, which means that it is earning service revenues. This transaction results in an increase in Service Revenues (owner's equity) of $4,000.

This transaction is similar to transaction **d**, except that the business is not receiving the cash immediately. Should we wait to record the revenue until the cash is received? No, DR Painting should recognize the revenue when the service is performed, regardless of whether or not it has received the cash.

However, this time the client did not pay in cash but instead agreed to pay later, which is the same as charging the services *on account*. The business will *receive* this money in the future (when the customers eventually pay), so it is called accounts *receiv*able. Accounts Receivable (an asset) is increased by $4,000. Accounts Receivable represents amounts owed to the business and decreases when a customer pays.

The effect of this transaction on the accounting equation is:

		ASSETS			=	LIABILITIES	+	OWNER'S EQUITY	TYPE OF OWNER'S EQUITY TRANSACTION
	Cash	+ Accounts Receivable +	Supplies +	Truck	=	Accounts Payable	+	David Richardson, Capital	
Bal.	$23,000 +		$1,800 +	$20,000	=	$ 1,800	+	$43,000	
(e)		+ $4,000			=		+	+ 4,000	*Service revenue*
Bal.	$23,000 +	$4,000 +	$1,800 +	$20,000	=	$ 1,800	+	$47,000	
				$48,800	=	$48,800			

f. The business paid $800 cash toward the supplies purchased in trans-action c.

Think of Accounts Payable (a liability) as a list of companies to which the business owes money. In other words, it is a list of companies to which the business will *pay* money. In this particular problem, the business owes money to the company from which it purchased supplies on account in transaction **c**. When the business *pays* the money in full, it can cross this company off of the list. Right now, the business is paying only *part* of the money owed.

This transaction results in a decrease to Accounts Payable (a liability) of $800 and a decrease to Cash (an asset) of $800. Because the business is only paying part of the money it owes to the supply store, the balance to Accounts Payable is still:

$$\$1,800 - \$800 = \$1,000$$

You should note that this transaction does not affect Supplies because we are not buying more supplies. We are simply paying off a liability, not acquiring more assets or incurring a new expense.

The effect of this transaction on the accounting equation is:

	Cash	+	Accounts Receivable	+	Supplies	+	Truck	=	Accounts Payable	+	David Richardson, Capital
			ASSETS					=	**LIABILITIES**	+	**OWNER'S EQUITY**
Bal.	$23,000	+	$4,000	+	$1,800	+	$20,000	=	$ 1,800	+	$47,000
(f)	−800							=	−800		
Bal.	$22,200	+	$4,000	+	$1,800	+	$20,000	=	$ 1,000	+	$47,000
							$48,000	=	$48,000		

g. The business paid employee salaries of $1,000 in cash.

The work the employees have given to the business has *already been used*. By the end of March, DR Painting's employees have worked and painted for customers for the entire month. Therefore, the *benefit* of the employees' work has *already been received*, which means that it is a salary *expense*. Salary Expense increases by $1,000, which is a decrease to owner's equity.

Remember: Expenses *decrease* net income, which decreases owner's equity.

The salaries were paid in cash, so Cash (an asset) also decreases by $1,000.

The effect of this transaction on the accounting equation is:

		ASSETS			=	LIABILITIES	+	OWNER'S EQUITY	TYPE OF OWNER'S EQUITY TRANSACTION
	Cash +	Accounts Receivable +	Supplies +	Truck =		Accounts Payable	+	David Richardson, Capital	
Bal.	$22,200 +	$4,000 +	$1,800 +	$20,000 =		$ 1,000	+	$47,000	
(g)	−1,000			=				−1,000	Salary expense
Bal.	$21,200 +	$4,000 +	$1,800 +	$20,000 =		$ 1,000	+	$46,000	
				$47,000 =		$47,000			

h. David withdrew $1,500 cash from the business for personal use.

Although David is taking the money, the cash is coming from the *business*, so this is a recordable transaction for the business. A decrease of $1,500 to Cash (an asset) is recorded. Because David is the owner, this transaction results in an increase of $1,500 to Owner Withdrawals, which is a decrease to owner's equity.

You should note that *the withdrawal is not an expense* because the cash is not used by the business. The cash withdrawn is for the owner's personal use rather than to earn revenue for the business.

The effect of this transaction on the accounting equation is:

		ASSETS			=	LIABILITIES	+	OWNER'S EQUITY	TYPE OF OWNER'S EQUITY TRANSACTION
	Cash +	Accounts Receivable +	Supplies +	Truck =		Accounts Payable	+	David Richardson, Capital	
Bal.	$21,200 +	$4,000 +	$1,800 +	$20,000 =		$ 1,000	+	$46,000	
(h)	−1,500			=				−1,500	Owner withdrawal
Bal.	$19,700 +	$4,000 +	$1,800 +	$20,000 =		$ 1,000	+	$44,500	
				$45,500 =		$45,500			

i. The business collected $2,600 from the client in transaction e.

Think of Accounts Receivable (an asset) as a list of people/companies from which the business will *receive* money at some point in the future. Later, when the business collects (receives) the cash in full from any particular customer, it can cross that customer off the list.

In transaction **e**, DR Painting performed services for a client who did not pay at that time. Now DR is receiving *part* of the money owed ($2,600). This collection decreases Accounts Receivable (an asset) by $2,600.

Because the cash is received, this is an increase to Cash (an asset) of $2,600. The effect of this transaction on the accounting equation is:

		ASSETS				=	LIABILITIES	+	OWNER'S EQUITY
	Cash	+ Accounts Receivable	+ Supplies	+ Truck	=		Accounts Payable	+	David Richardson, Capital
Bal.	$19,700 +	$4,000	+ $1,800	+ $20,000	=		$ 1,000	+	$44,500
(i)	+ 2,600	− 2,600			=				
Bal.	$22,300 +	$1,400	+ $1,800	+ $20,000	=		$ 1,000	+	$44,500
				$45,500	=		$45,500		

j. David paid $100 cash for personal groceries.

These groceries were purchased with David's *personal* money for David's *personal* use. Therefore, this transaction does *not* relate to the business and is *not* a recordable transaction for DR Painting. This transaction has no effect on the business's accounting equation. Had David used the business's cash to purchase groceries, then the business would record the transaction.

		ASSETS			=	LIABILITIES	+	OWNER'S EQUITY	TYPE OF OWNER'S EQUITY TRANSACTION
	Cash	+ Accounts Receivable	+ Supplies	+ Truck	=	Accounts Payable	+	David Richardson Capital	
(a)	+$40,000				=			+ $40,000	*Owner investment*
(b)	− 20,000			+ $20,000	=				
(c)			+ $1,800		=	+ $1,800			
(d)	+ 3,000				=			+ 3,000	*Service revenue*
(e)		+ $4,000			=			+ 4,000	*Service revenue*
(f)	− 800				=	− 800			
(g)	− 1,000				=			− 1,000	*Salary expense*
(h)	− 1,500				=			− 1,500	*Owner withdrawal*
(i)	+ 2,600	− 2,600			=				
(j)	Not a transaction of the business.								
	$22,300 +	$1,400	+ $1,800	+ $20,000	=	$1,000	+	$44,500	
		$45,500			=		$45,500		

Prepare the income statement, statement of owner's equity, and balance sheet of the business after recording the transactions. Use Exhibit 1-8 (p. 22) as a guide.

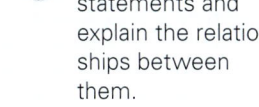 Prepare financial statements and explain the relationships between them.

Part 1	**Part 2**	Part 3	Part 4	Demo Doc Complete

Income Statement

The income statement is the first statement that should be prepared because the other financial statements rely upon the net income number calculated on the income statement.

The income statement reports the profitability of the business. To prepare an income statement, begin with the proper heading. A proper heading includes the name of the company (DR Painting), the name of the statement (Income Statement), and the time period covered (Month Ended March 31, 2008). Notice that we are reporting income for a period of time, rather than a single date.

The income statement lists all revenues and expenses. It uses the following formula to calculate net income:

$$\text{Revenues} - \text{Expenses} = \text{Net income or Net Loss}$$

First, you should list revenues. Secondly, list the expenses. Having trouble finding the revenues and expenses? Look in the equity column of the accounting equation. After you have listed and totaled the revenues and expenses, you subtract the total expenses from total revenues to determine net income or net loss. If you have a positive number, then you report net income. A negative number indicates that expenses exceeded revenues, and you will report a net loss.

In the case of DR Painting, transactions **d** and **e** increased service revenue (by $3,000 and $4,000, respectively). These transactions mean that total service revenue for the month was:

$$\$3,000 + \$4,000 = \$7,000$$

The only expenses incurred were in transaction **g**, which resulted in a salary expense of $1,000. On the income statement, these transactions would be recorded as follows:

DR PAINTING Income Statement Month Ended March 31, 2008		
Revenue:		
Service revenue		$7,000
Expenses:		
Salary expense		1,000
Net income		$6,000

Note the result is a net income of $6,000:

$$\text{Revenues} - \text{Expenses} = \text{Net income}$$
$$\$7,000 \ - \ \$1,000 \ = \ \$6,000$$

You will use this amount on the statement of owner's equity.

Part 1	Part 2	**Part 3**	Part 4	Demo Doc Complete

Statement of Owner's Equity

The statement of owner's equity shows the changes in owner's equity for a period of time. To prepare a statement of owner's equity, begin with the proper heading. A proper heading includes the name of the company (DR Painting), the name of the statement (Statement of Owner's Equity), and the time period covered (Month Ended March 31, 2008). As with the income statement, we are reporting equity for a period of time, rather than a single date.

Net income is used on the statement of owner's equity to calculate the new balance in the Capital account. This calculation uses the following formula:

Beginning Owner's Equity

+ Owner Investments

+ Net Income or – Net Loss

– Owner Withdrawals

= Ending Owner's Equity

You will begin the body of the statement by reporting the owner's capital at the beginning of the period (March 1). List the owner's name, Capital, and beginning date to the left, and enter the dollar amount of capital to the right. Then you will list additions to equity, such as additional investment by the owner or net income. You should notice that the amount of net income comes directly from the income statement. Following additions, you will report deductions from equity, such as withdrawals made by the owner or a net loss. After reporting the additions and deductions, you should compute the owner's ending capital for the period.

In this case, because the company is new, the beginning capital is zero. Additions to capital include the initial investment by the owner ($40,000 from transaction **a**), plus the net income as reported on the income statement ($6,000), for a subtotal of $46,000. A deduction from equity occurred in transaction **h**, when David withdrew $1,500 from the business for personal use. On the statement of owner's equity, these transactions would be shown as follows:

DR PAINTING
Statement of Owner's Equity
Month Ended March 31, 2008

David Richardson, capital, March 1, 2008	$ 0
Add: Investment by owner	40,000
Net income for the month	6,000
Subtotal	46,000
Less: Withdrawals by owner	(1,500)
David Richardson, capital, March 31, 2008	$44,500

Note the result is an ending capital amount of $44,500 ($46,000 − $1,500 = $44,500). You will use this amount on the balance sheet.

| Part 1 | Part 2 | Part 3 | **Part 4** | Demo Doc Complete |

Balance Sheet

The balance sheet reports the financial position of the business. To prepare a balance sheet, begin with the proper heading. A proper heading includes the name of the company (DR Painting), the name of the statement (Balance Sheet), and the date (March 31, 2008). Unlike the income statement and statement of owner's equity, we are reporting the financial position of the company for a *specific date*, rather than a period of time.

The balance sheet is just a listing of all assets, liabilities, and equity, with the equality of the accounting equation verified at the bottom.

To prepare the body of the statement, begin by listing assets. Next, list liabilities and owner's equity. Notice that the balance sheet is organized in the same order as the accounting equation. You should also note that the amount of owner's equity comes directly from the ending capital on your statement of owner's equity. You should then total both sides to make sure that they are equal. If they are not equal, you need to look for an error.

In this case, assets include the total cash balance of $22,300, accounts receivable of $1,400, supplies worth $1,800, and the truck's value of $20,000, for a total of $45,500 in assets. Liabilities total $1,000: the balance on the Accounts Payable account. The figures for assets and liabilities come directly from the accounting equation worksheet. From the statement of owner's equity, we have an ending capital amount of $44,500. This gives us a total for liabilities and owner's equity of $1,000 + $44,500 = $45,500, confirming the accounting equation:

Assets = Liabilities + Owner's Equity

DR PAINTING Balance Sheet March 31, 2008			
Assets		**Liabilities**	
Cash	$22,300	Accounts payable	$ 1,000
Accounts receivable	1,400		
Supplies	1,800		
Truck	20,000	**Owner's Equity**	
		David Richardson, capital	44,500
Total assets	$45,500	Total liabilities and owner's equity	$45,500

| Part 1 | Part 2 | Part 3 | Part 4 | Demo Doc Complete |

Accounting in Action

ACCOUNTING AND THE BUSINESS ENVIRONMENT

Suppose you open a business. Here are some factors you must consider if you expect to be profitable:

Decision	Guidelines
• How to organize the business?	If a single owner—a *proprietorship*. If two or more owners, but not incorporated—a *partnership*. If stock issued to stockholders—a *corporation*.
• What to account for?	*Transactions* that affect the business and can be measured reliably, separate from those of its owners, according to the *entity* concept.
• How much to record for assets and services?	Actual, *historical cost* according to the cost principle.
• How to analyze a transaction?	*Accounting equation:* Assets = Liabilities + Owner's Equity
• How to measure profits and losses?	*Income statement:* Revenues – Expenses = Net Income or Net Loss
• Did owner's equity increase or decrease?	*Statement of owner's equity*: Beginning Owner's Equity + Owner Investments + Net Income or – Net Loss – Owner Withdrawals = Ending Owner's Equity
• Where does the business stand financially?	*Balance sheet (accounting equation):* *Assets = Liabilities + Owner's Equity*

Review

Accounting and the Business Environment
Word Power

Accounts payable A liability backed by the general reputation and credit standing of the debtor.

Accounts receivable An asset representing amounts due from customers to whom the business has sold goods or for whom the business has performed services.

Accounting The information system that measures business activity, processes the results of activities into reports, and communicates the results to decision makers.

Accounting equation The basic tool of accounting that measures the resources of the business and the claims to those resources: Assets = Liabilities + Owner's Equity.

Assets Economic resources that are expected to be of benefit in the future.

Audit An examination of a company's financial statements by a Certified Public Accountant to determine their fairness.

Balance sheet An entity's assets, liabilities, and owner's equity as of a specific date. Also called the *statement of financial position*.

Business An organization that sells products or services to customers.

Capital The insider claims to the assets of a business by the owner; the owner's interest in the business. Also called *owner's equity*.

Certified Management Accountant (CMA) A licensed accountant who works for a single company.

Certified Public Accountant (CPA) A licensed accountant who serves the general public rather than one particular company.

Corporation A business owned by stockholders that is an entity legally separate from its owners.

Entity An organization or a section of an organization that, for accounting purposes, stands apart as a separate economic unit.

Ethics Principles of right behavior.

Expenses Decreases to owner's equity from using resources to deliver goods or provide services to customers.

Fiduciary Fiscally responsible; legally and financially trustworthy.

Financial accounting Accounting that provides information for people outside the business.

Financial Accounting Standards Board (FASB) The primary organization that determines how accounting is practiced in the United States.

Financial statements Historical, objective reports, prepared according to GAAP, that communicate financial information about a business to those outside the business.

Financing activities The activities of a business that involve transactions with long-term creditors and stockholders.

Financial position The resources of a business and the claims against those resources.

Generally Accepted Accounting Principles (GAAP) Accounting rules, created by the Financial Accounting Standards Board, that govern how accountants measure, process, and communicate financial information.

Going concern The assumption that a business will continue indefinitely.

Historical cost Actual cost of assets and services acquired.

Income statement Summary of a business's revenues, expenses, and net income or net loss for a specific period.

Investing activities The activities of a business that involve buying or disposing of long-term assets.

Liabilities Outsider claims to the assets of a business; the debts owed to outsiders.

Limited liability Owners of a corporation are not legally responsible for its debts; the amount that stockholders put at risk is limited to the amount they paid for the stock.

Liquid Able to generate enough cash from selling goods or services to pay bills on time.

Management accounting Accounting that provides information for managers inside a business.

Manufacturing companies Businesses that make their own products that are sold to the final customer or to other companies.

Merchandise companies Businesses that sell products made by another company. Also called *retail companies*.

Net income The excess of total revenues over total expenses. Also called *profit*.

Net loss The excess of total expenses over total revenues.

Note payable A written promise of future payment made by the business.

Objectivity Verifiable, confirmable by any independent observer. Also called *reliability*.

On account Buying or selling on credit.

Operating activities The activities of a business that determine net income or net loss.

Organization accountability The organization's fiduciary responsibility to manage its resources carefully.

Owner's equity The insider claims to the assets of a business by the owner; the owner's interest in the business. Also called *capital*.

Owner investments Amounts added to a business by the owner.

Owner's withdrawals Amounts removed from the business by the owner.

Partnership A business with two or more owners.

Prepaid expenses Amounts that are assets of a business because they represent items to be used later but are already paid for.

Profit The difference between the revenues, the sales price of the goods or services sold by the business, and expenses, the cost of the resources used to provide these goods and services. Also called *net income*.

Proprietorship A business with a single owner.

Reliability Verifiable, confirmable by any independent observer. Also called *objectivity*.

Retail companies Businesses that sell products made by another company. Also called *merchandise companies*.

Revenues Increases to owner's equity earned by delivering goods or providing services to customers.

Service companies Businesses that provide services to customers.

Shareholder A person who owns stock in a corporation. Also called *stockholder*.

Statement of cash flows Summary of the changes in a business's cash balance for a specific period.

Statement of financial position A business's assets, liabilities, and owner's equity as of a specific date. Also called the *balance sheet*.

Statement of owner's equity Summary of the changes in a business's owner's equity during a specific period.

Stockholder A person who owns stock in a corporation. Also called *shareholder*.

Transaction An event that affects the financial position of a particular entity and can be measured reliably.

Quick Check

1. Generally Accepted Accounting Principles (GAAP) are created by the:

   a. Securities and Exchange Commission (SEC).
   b. Financial Accounting Standards Board (FASB).
   c. Institute of Management Accountants (IMA).
   d. American Institute of Certified Public Accountants (AICPA).

2. Which type of business organization is owned by its stockholders?

   a. Proprietorship
   b. Partnership
   c. Corporation
   d. All the above are owned by stockholders

3. Which accounting concept or principle specifically states that we should record transactions at amounts that can be verified?

   a. Entity concept
   b. Reliability principle
   c. Cost principle
   d. Going-concern concept

4. Fossil is famous for fashion wristwatches and leather goods. At the end of a recent year, Fossil's total assets added up to $381 million, and owners' equity was $264 million. How much did Fossil owe creditors?

   a. Cannot determine from the data given
   b. $381 million
   c. $264 million
   d. $117 million

5. Assume that Fossil sold watches for $50,000 to a department store on account. How would this transaction affect Fossil's accounting equation?

   a. Increase both assets and owners' equity by $50,000
   b. Increase both assets and liabilities by $50,000
   c. Increase both liabilities and owners' equity by $50,000
   d. No effect on the accounting equation because the effects cancel out

6. Refer to Fossil's sale of watches on account in the preceding question. Which parts of the accounting equation does a sale on account affect?

   a. Accounts Receivable and Accounts Payable
   b. Accounts Payable and Cash
   c. Accounts Payable and Owner, Capital
   d. Accounts Receivable and Owner, Capital

7. Assume that Fossil paid expenses totaling $35,000. How does this transaction affect Fossil's accounting equation?

    a. Increases assets and decreases liabilities
    b. Increases both assets and owners' equity
    c. Decreases both assets and owners' equity
    d. Decreases assets and increases liabilities

8. Consider the overall effects of transactions in questions 5 and 7 on Fossil. What is Fossil's net income or net loss?

    a. Net income of $50,000
    b. Net loss of $35,000
    c. Net income of $15,000
    d. Cannot determine from the data given

9. The balance sheet reports:

    a. Financial position on a specific date.
    b. Results of operation on a specific date.
    c. Financial position for a specific period.
    d. Results of operations for a specific period.

10. The income statement reports:

    a. Financial position on a specific date.
    b. Results of operations on a specific date.
    c. Financial position for a specific period.
    d. Results of operations for a specific period.

Answers are given after Apply Your Knowledge (p. 55).

Accounting Practice

Short Exercises

S1-1. Place the corresponding letter of the definition next to the term.

③ Generally Accepted Accounting Principles.

a. An organization that stands as a separate economic unit must not have its financial affairs confused with that of other entities.

b. Data must be verifiable.

c. The entity will remain in operation for the foreseeable future.

d. Acquired assets and services should be recorded at their actual cost.

_____ 1. Cost principle

_____ 2. Entity concept

_____ 3. Going-concern concept

_____ 4. Reliability principle

S1-2. Mac Cummings owns and operates Mac's Floral Designs. He proposes to account for the shop's assets at their current market value in order to have current amounts on the balance sheet. Which accounting concept or principle does Cummings's view violate?

③ Generally Accepted Accounting Principles.

a. Cost principle

b. Entity concept

c. Going-concern concept

d. Reliability principle

S1-3. Determine the missing amounts in the following accounting equations.

	ASSETS	=	LIABILITIES	+	OWNER'S EQUITY
a.	$90,000	=	$45,000	+	?
b.	?	=	$35,000	+	$45,000
c.	$85,000	=	?	+	$70,000

S1-4. Place the corresponding letter of the definition next to the term.

④ Using the accounting equation.

a. Debts that are owed to creditors

b. Economic resources that are expected to be of benefit in the future

c. Claims of the owner of the business

_____ 1. Assets

_____ 2. Liabilities

_____ 3. Owner's equity

Using the account-
ing equation.

S1-5. Ashley Briggs owns Curtain Call Casting Service near the campus of Beverly Hills Community College. The business has cash of $5,000 and furniture that cost $12,000. Debts of the business include accounts payable of $8,000 and a $6,000 note payable. Determine the amount of owner's equity Briggs has in the business. Using Briggs's figures, write the accounting equation of the casting service. Refer to Exhibit 1-4 for assistance.

④ Using the account-
ing equation.

S1-6. Westside Counseling, Inc., has cash of $3,000, supplies costing $1,300, and owner's equity of $2,000. Determine the liabilities of the business. Using Westside's figures, write the accounting equation of the counseling service.

④ Using the account-
ing equation.

S1-7. Uptown Dental Professionals started a business when Dr. Higuera invested $10,000 of his own money in the business. Before starting operations, Uptown borrowed $8,000 cash by signing a note payable to Community State Bank. Account for these two transactions in the accounting equation.

④ Using the account-
ing equation.

S1-8. Roadway Towing Service earns service revenue by towing vehicles for AAA. Roadway's main expenses are the salaries paid to its employees. Account for the following transactions in the accounting equation:

a. Roadway earned $10,000 of service revenue on account.

b. Roadway paid $6,000 in salaries expense.

④ Using the account-
ing equation.

S1-9. Match each of the following items with its location in the accounting equation:

a. Assets

b. Liabilities

c. Owner's Equity

d. Revenues

e. Expenses

___e___ 1. Utilities Expense

___a___ 2. Accounts Receivable

___c___ 3. Gay Gillen, Capital

___t___ 4. Office Supplies

___e___ 5. Lease Expense, Computer

___e___ 6. Salary Expense

___a___ 7. Cash

___e___ 8. Rent Expense, Office

___d___ 9. Service Revenue

___b___ 10. Accounts Payable

_____ 11. Land

S1-10. Label each of the items listed with the abbreviation of the financial statement on which it appears.

5 Preparing financial statements.

Income Statement (IS)

Balance Sheet (BS)

Statement of Owner's Equity (OE).

_____ 1. Accounts Receivable

_____ 2. Notes Payable

_____ 3. Advertising Expense

_____ 4. Service Revenue

_____ 5. J. P., Capital, June 1

_____ 6. Office Supplies

Exercises

E1-11. Place the corresponding letter of the definition next to the term.

1 Nature and types of businesses.

_____ 1. Liabilities

4 Using the accounting equation.

_____ 2. Assets

_____ 3. Audit

5 Preparing financial statements.

_____ 4. Corporation

_____ 5. Owner's Withdrawal

_____ 6. Proprietorship

_____ 7. Partnership

_____ 8. Transaction

a. Any event that affects financial position.

b. Organization form with a single owner

c. Organization form with two or more owners

d. Organization form that can have an indefinite life

e. Examination of the financial statements

f. Debt owed to outsiders

g. Economic resource of the business

h. Removal of the assets of the business by the owner for personal use

E1-12. As a manager of a sporting goods store, you must deal with a variety of business transactions. Place the letter of each of the following transactions next to the effect it has on the accounting equation.

a. Owner withdrew cash from the business for personal use.

b. Purchased land for building site.

c. Paid cash on an account payable.

d. Received a cash investment from the owner.

e. Received cash from the bank in exchange for a note payable.

_____ 1. Increase an asset and increase owner's equity.

_____ 2. Increase an asset and increase a liability.

_____ 3. Increase one asset and decrease another asset.

_____ 4. Decrease an asset and decrease owner's equity.

_____ 5. Decrease an asset and decrease a liability.

E1-13. Chips Galore, a proprietorship, supplies snack foods. The business experienced the following events. State whether each event (a) increased, (b) decreased, or (c) had no effect on the total assets of the business, and identify the asset(s) involved in each transaction.

1. Chips Galore received a cash investment from the owner.

2. Purchased land as a building site for cash.

3. Paid cash on accounts payable.

4. Purchased machinery and equipment for a manufacturing plant; signed a promissory note in payment.

5. Performed service for a customer on account.

6. The owner withdrew cash from the business for personal use.

7. Received cash from a customer on accounts receivable.

8. The owner used personal funds to purchase a swimming pool for his home.

9. Sold land for a price equal to the cost of the land; received cash.

10. Borrowed money from the bank.

E1-14. Determine the missing amounts in the following accounting equations.

	ASSETS	=	LIABILITIES	+	OWNER'S EQUITY
Gemstone	?	=	$61,800	+	$21,000
Sampson Hardware	$ 72,000	=	?	+	$34,000
Lundy Plumbing	$102,700	=	$79,800	+	?

E1-15. Gullion Web Design started business in 2009 with total assets of $25,000 and total liabilities of $11,000. At the end of 2009, Gullion's total assets stood at $31,000, and total liabilities were $14,000.

4 Using the accounting equation.

After analyzing the data, answer the following questions:

1. What was the amount of the increase or decrease in owner's equity?

2. Identify two possible reasons for the change in owner's equity during the year.

E1-16. Bear Veterinarian Services balance sheet data at May 31, 2009, and June 30, 2009, follow:

5 Preparing financial statements.

	May 31, 2009	**June 30, 2009**
Total assets	$150,000	$195,000
Total liabilities	109,000	131,000
Total owner's equity	?	?

Requirements

The following are three *independent* assumptions about investments and withdrawals by the owner of the business during June. For each assumption, compute the amount of net income or net loss during June 2009. Find the solution by preparing the statement of owner's equity. First, use the amounts of total assets and total liabilities given above and the accounting equation to determine the beginning and ending owner's equity amounts. Then plug those and the other amounts given in each assumption into the statement to determine the net income or net loss.

1. The owner invested $10,000 in the business and made no withdrawals.

2. The owner made no additional investments in the business but withdrew $5,000 for personal use.

3. The owner invested $30,000 in the business and withdrew $6,000 for personal use.

4 Using the accounting equation.

E1-17. Presented here are nine transactions and the analysis used to account for them. Evaluate each of the suggested accounting treatments and indicate whether it is true or false.

1. Received cash of $25,000 from the owner, who was investing in the business.

   Answer: Increase asset, increase owner's equity. ○ True ○ False

2. Paid $700 cash to purchase supplies.

   Answer: Increase asset, increase owner's equity. ○ True ○ False

3. Earned rental revenue on account, $500.

   Answer: Increase asset, increase owner's equity ○ True ○ False

4. Purchased on account office furniture at a cost of $600.

   Answer: Increase asset, increase liability. ○ True ○ False

5. Received cash on account, $900.

   Answer: Increase asset, decrease asset. ○ True ○ False

continued.....

6. Paid cash on account, $250.

Answer: Increase asset, increase liability. ○ True ○ False

7. Sold land for $12,000, which was the cost of the land.

Answer: Increase asset, decrease asset. ○ True ○ False

8. Rented automobiles and received cash of $680.

Answer: Increase asset, increase owner's equity. ○ True ○ False

9. Paid monthly office rent of $800.

Answer: Decrease asset, increase owner's equity. ○ True ○ False

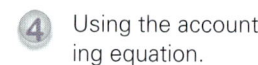

Using the accounting equation.

E1-18. Ken Hobt opened a dental practice. During the first month of operation, July, the business titled Ken Hobt, D.D.S., experienced the following events:

July 6	Hobt invested $60,000 in the business by opening a bank account in the name of K. Hobt, D.D.S.
9	The business paid $55,000 cash for land. Ken plans to build an office building on the land.
12	The business purchased dental supplies for $2,000 on account.
15	The business officially opened for business.
15	The business treated patients and earned service revenue of $7,000, receiving cash.
17	The business paid office rent, $1,000.
28	The business sold supplies to another dentist for the cost of those supplies, $500.
31	The business paid $1,500 on account related to the July 12 purchase.

Requirements

Using the accounting equation.

Analyze the effects of these events on the accounting equation of the dental practice of K. Hobt, D.D.S. Use a format similar to Exhibit 1-4, with headings for Cash; Dental Supplies; Land; Accounts Payable; and K. Hobt, Capital.

Preparing financial statements.

E1-19. The analysis of Maximum Refund Tax Service's first seven transactions follows. The owner of the business made only one investment to start the business and no withdrawals.

		ASSETS		=	LIABILITY +		OWNER'S EQUITY	
	Cash	+ Accounts Receivable	+ Equipment =		Accounts Payable	+ Note Payable	+ Owner Capital
1.	+$50,000			=			+$50,000
2.	−750		+$750	=			
3.			+100,000	=		+$100,000	
4.		+$800		=			+800
5.	−2,000			=			−2,000
6.	+2,200			=			+2,200
7.	+150	− 150		=			

continued.....

Requirements

1. Label each of the transactions in the preceding analysis with the corresponding letter of the description that best fits it:

a. Earned revenue for tax services, but customer will pay later.

b. Customers paid cash for services completed earlier in the month.

c. Received cash for revenue earned by providing tax services.

d. Paid cash for expenses incurred to operate the business.

e. Paid cash to purchase equipment.

f. Invested cash to start the tax service business.

g. Borrowed money from the bank to purchase equipment.

2. If these transactions fully describe the operations of Maximum Refund Tax Service during the month, what was the amount of its net income or net loss?

E1-20. The following are the balances of the assets, liabilities, and owner's equity of Hawkins Graphic Design at November 30, 2009:

① Nature and types of businesses.

⑤ Preparing financial statements.

Cash	$ 2,000	Office Equipment	$15,500
Accounts Receivable	6,900	Supplies	600
Accounts Payable	2,500	Note Payable	8,000
J.D. Hawkins, Capital	14,500		

Requirements

1. What type of business organization is Hawkins Graphic Design?

2. Prepare the balance sheet of the business at November 30, 2009.

3. What does the balance sheet report?

E1-21. The assets, liabilities, owner's equity, revenues, and expenses of Sullivan, Architect, a drafting business, at December 31, 2009, have the following balances at the end of its first year. During the year, T. Sullivan, the owner, invested $15,000 in the business.

④ Using the accounting equation.

⑤ Preparing financial statements.

Office Furniture	$ 56,000	Note Payable	$41,000
Utilities Expense	6,800	Rent Expense	24,000
Accounts Payable	3,300	Cash	3,600
T. Sullivan, Capital	27,100	Office Supplies	4,800
Service Revenue	161,200	Salary Expense	60,000
Accounts Receivable	9,000	Salaries Payable	2,000
Supplies Expense	4,000	Property Tax Expense	1,200

continued.....

1. Identify each as an asset, liability, owner's equity, revenue, or expense.

2. Prepare the income statement of Sullivan, Architect, for the year ended December 31, 2009. What is the result of operations for 2009?

3. What was the amount of the owner's withdrawals during the year? Answer by preparing a statement of owner's equity to solve for the withdrawals. Recall that the business has just completed its first year and has no beginning balance for T. Sullivan, Capital.

5 Preparing financial statements.

E1-22. Presented here is information for Pod Company for the year ended December 31, 2009.

Pod Company	
Beginning:	
Assets	$ 50,000
Liabilities	20,000
Ending:	
Assets	$ 70,000
Liabilities	35,000
Owner's Equity:	
Investments by owner	$ 0
Withdrawals by owner	40,000
Income Statement:	
Revenues	$230,000
Expenses	185,000

Requirements

Answer the following questions.

1. What is the beginning owner's equity of Pod Company?

2. What is the ending owner's equity of Pod Company?

3. What is the net income or net loss for the year?

4 Using the accounting equation.

5 Preparing financial statements.

Problems (Group A)

P1-23A. Morgan Madison practiced law with a partnership for 10 years. Recently she opened her own law office, which she operates as a proprietorship. The name of the new entity is Morgan Madison, Attorney.

continued.....

Madison experienced the following events during the first month of operations. Some of the events were personal and did not affect the law practice. Others were business transactions and should be accounted for by the business.

July 1	Sold 1,000 shares of Wal-Mart stock, which she had owned for several years, for $68,000 cash that she deposited in her personal bank account.
5	Deposited $100,000 cash in a new business bank account titled Morgan Madison, Attorney.
6	A representative of a large company telephoned Madison and told her of the company's intention to hire Morgan Madison as its attorney.
7	Paid $500 cash for letterhead stationery supplies for the new law office.
9	Purchased office furniture for the law office, agreeing to pay the account, $9,500, within 3 months.
23	Finished court hearings on behalf of a client and submitted a bill for legal services, $3,000.
30	Paid office rent, $1,860.
31	Withdrew $10,000 cash from the business for personal use.

Requirements

1. Using a format similar to Exhibit 1-4, account for each transaction, calculating new balances after each transaction, for the proprietorship of Morgan Madison, Attorney.

2. Determine the following items:

   a. Total assets

   b. Total liabilities

   c. Total owner's equity

   d. Net income or net loss for the month

P1-24A. Daniel Laird owns and operates an architectural firm called Laird Design. The following amounts summarize the financial position of his business on April 30, 2009:

④ Using the accounting equation.

⑤ Preparing financial statements.

ASSETS				=	LIABILITIES	+	OWNER'S EQUITY
Cash	+ Accounts Receivable	+ Supplies	+ Land	=	Accounts Payable	+	Daniel Laird, Capital
Bal. $1,720 +	$3,240 +		$24,100 =		$5,400	+	$23,660

continued.....

During May 2009, the following events occurred:

a. Laird received $12,000 as a gift and deposited the cash in the business bank account.

b. Paid off the beginning balance of Accounts Payable.

c. Performed services for a client and received cash of $1,100.

d. Collected cash from a customer on account, $750.

e. Purchased supplies on account, $720.

f. Consulted on the interior design of a major office building and billed the client for services performed, $5,000.

g. Invested personal cash of $1,700 in the business.

h. Paid office rent, $1,860.

i. Sold supplies at cost to another interior designer for $80 cash.

j. Withdrew cash of $4,000 for personal use.

Requirements

1. Using a format similar to Exhibit 1-4, account for each transaction, calculating new balances after each transaction, for the proprietorship of Laird Design.

2. Prepare the income statement of Laird Design for the month ended May 31, 2009.

3. Prepare the statement of owner's equity of Laird Design for the month ended May 31, 2009.

4. Prepare the balance sheet of Laird Design at May 31, 2009.

⑤ Preparing financial statements.

P1-25A. Moore Photographic Studio provides pictures for high school yearbooks. The capital balance of L. Moore, owner of the company, was $50,000 at December 31, 2008. During 2009 he withdrew $16,000 for personal use but made no additional investments. At December 31, 2009, the business's accounting records show these balances:

Accounts Receivable	$ 8,000	Rent Expense	$ 7,000
Note Payable	12,000	Cash	16,000
L. Moore, Capital	?	Accounts Payable	6,000
Salary Expense	22,000	Advertising Expense	4,000
Equipment	65,000	Service Revenue	70,000

Prepare the following financial statements for Moore Photographic Studio:

a. Income statement for the year ended December 31, 2009

b. Statement of owner's equity for the year ended December 31, 2009

c. Balance sheet at December 31, 2009

P1-26A. Presented here are the amounts of assets, liabilities, revenues, and expenses of Speedy Delivery Service at December 31, 2009. The items are listed in alphabetical order.

④ Using the accounting equation.

⑤ Preparing financial statements.

Accounts Payable	$12,000	Note Payable	$31,000
Accounts Receivable	3,000	Property Tax Expense	2,000
Building	56,000	Rent Expense	14,000
Cash	7,000	Salary Expense	38,000
Equipment	21,000	Service Revenue	108,000
Interest Expense	4,000	Supplies	7,000
Interest Payable	1,000	Utilities Expense	3,000
Land	8,000		

The capital balance of Kurt Davis, the owner, was $43,000 at December 31, 2008. During 2009, Kurt withdrew $32,000 for personal use but made no additional investments.

Requirements

1. Identify each amount shown as an asset, liability, owner's equity, revenue, or expense.

2. Prepare the income statement of Speedy Delivery Service for the year ended December 31, 2009.

3. Prepare the company's statement of owner's equity for the year ended December 31, 2009.

4. Prepare the company's balance sheet at December 31, 2009.

5. Answer the following questions about the company:

   a. What was the profit or loss for the year?

   b. What was the increase or decrease of capital for the year?

   c. What is the amount of economic resources on December 31, 2009?

   d. What is the amount owed on December 31, 2009?

P1-27A. The systems manager of Geeks-R-Us Computer Service prepared the balance sheet of the company while the accountant was ill. The balance sheet contains numerous errors. In particular, the systems manager knew that the balance sheet should balance, so she plugged in the owner's equity amount to achieve this balance. The owner's equity amount, however, is not correct. All other amounts are accurate, but some are out of place.

④ Using the accounting equation.

⑤ Preparing financial statements.

Requirements

1. Identify each amount shown as an asset, liability, owner's equity, revenue, or expense.

2. Prepare a new, corrected balance sheet and date it correctly. Compute total assets, total liabilities, and owner's equity.

continued.....

GEEKS-R-US COMPUTER SERVICE
Balance Sheet
Month Ended October 31, 2009

Assets		Liabilities	
Cash	$ 2,400	Notes receivable	$ 3,000
Insurance expense	300	Interest expense	2,000
Land	31,500	Office supplies	800
Salary expense	3,300	Accounts receivable	2,600
Office furniture	6,700	Notes payable	19,000
Accounts payable	3,000	**Owner's Equity**	
Utilities expense	2,100	Owner's equity	22,900
Total assets	$49,300	Total liabilities	$52,300

Problems (Group B)

④ Using the accounting equation.

⑤ Preparing financial statements.

P1-28B. Matthew Bond practiced law with a partnership for 5 years. Recently he opened his own law office, which he operates as a proprietorship. The name of the new entity is Matthew Bond, Attorney. Bond experienced the following events during his first month of operations. Some of the events were personal and did not affect his law practice. Others were business transactions and should be accounted for by the business.

Feb. 4	Received $100,000 cash from former law partners.
5	Deposited $80,000 cash in a new business bank account titled Matthew Bond, Attorney.
6	Paid $300 cash for letterhead stationery supplies for the new law office.
7	Purchased office furniture for the law office. Bond agreed to pay the account payable, $7,000, within 3 months.
10	Sold 500 shares of Disney stock, which he had owned for several years, receiving $75,000 cash. Deposited the cash from the sale of stock in his personal bank account.
12	A representative of a large company telephoned Bond and told him of the company's intention to hire Matthew Bond as its attorney.
18	Finished court hearings on behalf of a client and submitted a bill for legal services, $5,000. Bond expected to collect from this client within 2 weeks.
25	Paid office rent, $1,000.
28	Withdrew $10,000 cash from the business for personal use.

Requirements

1. Using a format similar to Exhibit 1-4, account for each transaction, calculating new balances after each transaction, for the proprietorship of Matthew Bond, Attorney.

continued.....

2. Determine the following items:

    a. Total assets

    b. Total liabilities

    c. Total owner's equity

    d. Net income or net loss for February

P1-29B. Sara Carlson owns and operates a photography studio for pets called Lasting Friends. The following amounts summarize the financial position of her business on August 31, 2009:

④ Using the accounting equation.

⑤ Preparing financial statements.

	ASSETS			= LIABILITIES	+	OWNER'S EQUITY
Cash +	Accounts Receivable	+ Supplies + Land =		Accounts Payable	+	Sara Carlson, Capital
Bal. $2,250 +	$1,500	+	$12,000 =	$8,000	+	$7,750

During September 2009, the following events occurred:

a. Carlson inherited $20,000 and deposited the cash in the business bank account.

b. Performed services for a client and received cash of $700.

c. Paid off the beginning balance of Accounts Payable.

d. Purchased supplies on account, $1,000.

e. Collected cash from a customer on account, $1,000.

f. Invested personal cash of $1,000 in the business.

g. Consulted on the magazine layout of pets and billed the client for services rendered, $2,400.

h. Paid office rent, $1,000.

i. Sold supplies at cost to another business for $150 cash.

j. Withdrew cash of $2,000 for personal use.

Requirements

1. Using a format similar to Exhibit 1-4, account for each transaction, calculating new balances after each transaction, for the proprietorship of Sara Carlson.

2. Prepare the income statement of Lasting Friends for the month ended September 30, 2009.

3. Prepare the statement of owner's equity for the month ended September 30, 2009.

4. Prepare the balance sheet at September 30, 2009.

P1-30B. Quality Wood Furniture Store restores antique furniture. The capital balance of J. Wood, the owner of the company, was $56,000 at December 31, 2008. During 2009 he withdrew $50,000 for personal use but made no additional investments. At December 31, 2009, the business's accounting records show these balances:

Accounts Receivable............	$ 3,000	Insurance Expense...............	$ 4,000
Note Payable......................	35,000	Cash	5,000
J. Wood, Capital	?	Accounts Payable.................	1,000
Salary Expense...................	14,000	Advertising Expense	2,000
Automobiles	80,000	Service Revenue	66,000

Prepare the following financial statements for Quality Wood Furniture Store:

a. Income statement for the year ended December 31, 2009

b. Statement of owner's equity for the year ended December 31, 2009

c. Balance sheet at December 31, 2009

P1-31B. Presented here are the amounts of assets, liabilities, revenues, and expenses of Sky King Flying Training at December 31, 2009. The items are listed in alphabetical order.

Accounts Payable	$ 19,000	Land.....................................	$ 60,000
Accounts Receivable	12,000	Note Payable........................	85,000
Advertising Expense.........	13,000	Property Tax Expense.........	4,000
Building.............................	170,000	Rent Expense.......................	23,000
Cash....................................	14,000	Salary Expense....................	63,000
Equipment..........................	20,000	Salary Payable.....................	1,000
Insurance Expense	2,000	Service Revenue	178,000
Interest Expense...............	9,000	Supplies	3,000

The capital balance of Brian King, the owner, was $150,000 at December 31, 2008. During 2009, Brian withdrew $40,000 for personal use but made no additional investments.

Requirements

1. Identify each amount shown as an asset, liability, owner's equity, revenue, or expense.

2. Prepare the company's income statement and statement of owner's equity for the year ended December 31, 2009.

3. Prepare the company's balance sheet at December 31, 2009.

4. Answer these questions about the company:

continued.....

a. What was the profit or loss for the year?

b. What was the increase or decrease of capital for the year?

c. What is the amount of economic resources on December 31, 2009?

d. What is the amount owed on December 31, 2009?

P1-32B. The son of the owner of Bring-on-the-Show Entertainment prepared the company's balance sheet while the accountant was ill. The balance sheet contains numerous errors. In particular, the son of the owner knew that the balance sheet should balance, so he plugged in the owner's equity amount needed to achieve this balance. The owner's equity amount, however, is not correct. All other amounts are accurate, but some are out of place.

④ Using the accounting equation.

⑤ Preparing financial statements.

BRING-ON-THE-SHOW ENTERTAINMENT
Balance Sheet
Month Ended July 31, 2009

Assets		Liabilities	
Cash	$ 12,000	Accounts receivable	$ 23,000
Office supplies	1,000	Service revenue	68,000
Land	44,000	Property tax expense	800
Salary expense	2,500	Accounts payable	9,000
Office furniture	8,000		
Notes payable	36,000	**Owner's Equity**	
Rent expense	4,000	Owner's equity	6,700
Total assets	$107,500	Total liabilities	$107,500

Requirements

1. Identify each amount shown as an asset, liability, owner's equity, revenue, or expense.

2. Prepare a new, correct balance sheet and date it correctly. Compute total assets, total liabilities, and owner's equity.

for 24/7 practice, visit www.MyAccountingLab.com

Apply Your Knowledge

BE ON GUARD

Case 1. Mary Kay and her husband Bob were the owners of B&M Enterprises. They applied for a small business loan, and the bank requested the most recent business financial statements. When Mary compiled the balance sheet, she noticed that the business assets and related owner's equity were small. Accordingly, she told Bob that they should contribute some of their personal assets to the business so that the assets and equity would appear much larger and thus the bank would more likely agree to the business loan. Bob agreed that the balance sheet would appear stronger with more assets and equity but his concern was with the income statement. The sales for the latest period were low, which resulted in a slight net loss because expenses were slightly higher than revenues. Bob reasoned that contributing assets would show a stronger balance sheet but felt something had to be done to also improve the income statement. He then told Mary that their business could "sell" back some of the assets they had contributed and report higher sales on the income statement, which would result in net income rather than the actual net loss. Mary did not feel comfortable buying back assets from their business just to increase reported sales.

Discuss any ethical concerns you may have with Mary's proposal. Discuss any ethical concerns you may have with Bob's proposal. Do you think it is ethical for businesses to "dress up" their financial statements when applying for a loan?

Case 2. Bright Desert Developers was in the final phase of completing a land development project it started earlier in the year. Bright Dessert had acquired 50 acres of raw land for $200,000 and then spent an additional $1,450,000 in land development costs to create a new subdivision with 220 residential lots. With a total cost of $1,650,000 and 220 lots, each lot had a cost of $7,500; however, the lots were listed for sale at $35,000 per lot. Bright Desert was applying for a business loan and needed to provide current financial statements to the bank. John Dolan, the company president, wanted to include the total current value of the lots of $7,700,000, 220 lots x $35,000 per lot, rather than the total cost currently listed on the balance sheet at $1,650,000. Dan Jones, the company accountant, told John that the lots were inventory and the cost principle required that they be included on the balance sheet at the $1,650,000 rather than the fair market value. Furthermore, even though the lots were listed for sale at $35,000 each, there was no guarantee that they would actually all sell at this value, and according to the objectivity principle, the more reliable cost figure should be used for this reason, too.

Should the Bright Desert balance sheet list the lots at the total cost of $1,650,000 or the total selling price of $7,700,000? Could Bright Desert provide one balance sheet using historical cost and another balance sheet using market value?

KNOW YOUR BUSINESS

This case is designed to familiarize you with the financial reporting of a real company to further your understanding of the chapter material you are learning. Each chapter will have a financial statement case that will focus on material contained in that chapter. You will be asked questions and you will then refer to Appendix A at the end of the book where you will find the annual report for Target Corporation. Use the annual report to answer these questions; additional information necessary to answer some questions is available at http://investors.target.com. As you progress through each chapter, you will gain a real understanding of actual corporate financial reporting in addition to the basic accounting concepts you are learning within each textbook chapter. This added learning experience will further reinforce your understanding of accounting.

Refer to the Target Corporation financial statements in Appendix A at the end of the book and to the Target web site when necessary.

Requirements

1. Look at all the financial statements starting on page A-1 of the appendix and see whether you can identify the balance sheet, income statement, and statement of cash flows. (Note that the term *Consolidated* simply means combined.)

2. Did you see that Target titled its balance sheet as "Statement of Financial Position"? Were you able to identify it? (Note that some companies use this title.)

3. What was the total amount of assets Target reported as of January 2005? (Keep in mind that the numbers are in the millions.) Did the total assets increase or decrease from January 2004?

4. Did you see that Target titled its income statement as "Results of Operations"? Were you able to identify it? (Note that some companies use this title.)

5. What was the total amount of sales Target reported for 2004? (Keep in mind that the numbers are in the millions.) Did the sales increase or decrease from the previous years presented?

For Internet Exercises, Excel in Practice, and additional online activities, go to the Web site www.prenhall.com/pollard.

Quick Check Answers

1. *b* 2. *c* 3. *b* 4. *d* 5. *a* 6. *d* 7. *c* 8. *c* 9. *a* 10. *d*

LEARNING OBJECTIVES

1 Describe the role of accounts in summarizing business transactions.

2 Explain double-entry accounting.

3 Record and summarize business transactions.

4 Prepare and use a trial balance to create financial statements.

Recording Business Transactions

You have been shopping for the car of your dreams. You found it! But you don't have enough cash to pay for it. Before you close the deal, you go to the bank to get a car loan.

The loan officer wants some information about your financial condition before she will loan you the money. You have to answer lots of questions. What do you own? What is its value? Do you owe money to anyone? How much? What is your salary? What expenses do you have?

You should have this important financial information available for banks and other creditors. Businesses need to keep this information available, too. Suppose FedEx wants to buy a new fleet of delivery trucks this year. Imagine how complicated gathering all this data would be! How do individuals and businesses keep track of this information? The answer is accounting. •

Look Back

You have examined the various forms of businesses, and learned to account for transactions and summarize their results in financial statements.

Look Ahead

You will see how to use the formal, double-entry system of accounting to record transactions in a journal, post them to accounts in the ledger, and prepare a trial balance and financial statements.

Remember from Chapter 1 that accounting is the information system that measures business activity, processes results of activities into reports, and communicates the results to decision makers. In this chapter, you will learn about the use of accounts, double-entry accounting, and the accounting process that helps businesses accomplish these tasks.

The Role of Accounts in Summarizing Business Transactions

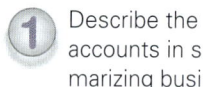 Describe the role of accounts in summarizing business transactions.

Transactions

As customers, most of us engage in transactions every day. You receive something, and you give something in return. For example, to get a haircut, you pay cash. For a good meal at a restaurant, you may pay cash by using a debit card. To score tickets for a ballgame, you may use a credit card.

Companies also transact business every day. A business receives cash, goods, services, or promises of future payment from others. In trade, a business gives cash, goods, services, or its promise to pay amounts owed later.

All business transactions, like personal transactions, involve an exchange. So, **transactions** are the economic events—the exchanges—that have a measurable impact on the financial position of the business.

Accounts

The key summary device of accounting is the **account**. This is the detailed record of all the changes that have occurred in a particular asset, liability, or owner's equity as a result of transactions.

As we saw in Chapter 1, the accounting equation is the basic tool—the framework—of accounting because it shows how assets, liabilities, and owner's equity are related. It measures the assets of the business and the claims to those assets. Following the accounting equation, there are three broad types of accounts:

Assets = Liabilities + Owner's Equity

Assets

Remember from Chapter 1 that assets are the economic resources of a business expected to provide benefits to the business in the future. Most businesses use the following asset accounts:

- *Cash.* The Cash account is a record of cash transactions. Cash includes money, such as the business's bank account balance, paper currency, coins, and checks.

- *Accounts Receivable.* A business may sell goods or services in exchange for an oral or implied promise of future cash receipt. Such sales are made on credit, on account. The Accounts Receivable account holds the amounts that customers owe the business for goods or services that have already been provided, how much the company can expect to *receive* from customers in the future.

- *Notes Receivable.* A business may sell goods or services or loan money and receive a **promissory note**. A **note receivable** is a written pledge that the customer or borrower will pay a fixed amount of money by a certain date. Notes Receivable is a record of the promissory notes that the business expects to collect in cash.

- *Prepaid Expenses.* A business often pays certain expenses, such as rent and insurance, in advance. A prepaid expense is an asset because the prepayment provides a future benefit for the business. A separate asset account is used for each prepaid expense. Prepaid Rent and Prepaid Insurance are examples of prepaid expense accounts.

- *Land.* The Land account is a record of the cost of land a business owns and uses in its operations.

- *Buildings.* The cost of a business's buildings, its offices, warehouses, and stores, for example, appear in the Buildings account.

- *Equipment, Furniture, and Fixtures.* A business has a separate asset account for each type of equipment. Examples include Computer Equipment, Office Equipment, and Store Equipment. The Furniture and Fixtures account likewise shows the cost of these assets.

Liabilities

As defined in Chapter 1, liabilities are debts owed to outsiders. A business generally has fewer liability accounts than asset accounts because a business's liabilities can be summarized in a few categories:

- *Accounts Payable.* A business may purchase goods or services in exchange for an oral or implied promise of future payment. Such purchases are made on credit, on account. The Accounts Payable account shows how much cash the business must *pay* suppliers for goods or services that have already been received.

- *Notes Payable.* Notes Payable represents amounts the business must pay because it signed promissory notes to borrow money or to purchase goods or services.

- *Accrued Liabilities.* An accrued liability is a liability for an expense that has been incurred but has not yet been paid. Taxes Payable, Interest Payable, and Salary Payable are accrued liability accounts.

Owner's Equity

As we saw in Chapter 1, the owner's claim to the assets of the business is called owner's equity, or capital. In a proprietorship or a partnership, owner's equity is split into separate accounts:

- *Capital.* The Capital account *summarizes* the owner's claim to the assets of the business. Capital can be computed by subtracting its total liabilities from its total assets. The Capital balance equals the owner's investments in the business plus net income and minus any net loss and owner withdrawals.

- *Withdrawals.* When a business owner withdraws cash or other assets from the business for personal use, the business's assets and owner's equity decrease. The amounts taken out appear in a separate account titled Withdrawals or Drawing. The Withdrawals account decreases owner's equity. If withdrawals were recorded directly in the Capital account, the amount of owner withdrawals might be lost among the other Capital account changes.

- **Revenues.** The increases in owner's equity created by selling goods or services to customers are called revenues. This account represents amounts *earned* by the company even if the company has not yet been paid for the goods and services provided. A business will have as many revenue accounts as needed, depending on how many ways it earns its revenue.

- **Expenses.** Expenses are the decreases in owner's equity from using resources to deliver goods or provide services to customers. A business needs a separate account for each type of expense, such as Salary Expense, Rent Expense, Advertising Expense, and Utilities Expense. Businesses strive to minimize their expenses in order to maximize net income.

Chart of Accounts

Organizations use a **chart of accounts** to list all their accounts along with the numbers they assign to them. Accounting is consistent; accounts are listed in the chart of accounts in the balance sheet order of assets, liabilities, capital, withdrawals, revenues, and expenses. Account numbers usually have two or more digits. The first digit indicates the type of account. Usually, if an account starts with:

- 1, it is an asset account.
- 2, it is a liability account.
- 3, it is a capital or withdrawals account.
- 4, it is a revenue account.
- 5, it is an expense account.

The second and third digits in an account number indicate where the account fits within the category. For example, Cash may be account number 101, the first asset account. Accounts Receivable may be account number 111, the second asset. Accounts Payable may be number 201, the first liability. All accounts used by a business are numbered by this system. The chart of accounts usually varies from business to business because every business has accounts based on its own needs.

The chart of accounts for Kay Torres Travel Agency, the business we discussed in Chapter 1, appears in Exhibit 2-1. Notice the gap in account numbers between 111 and 141. Gaps allow accounts to be added later. Torres may need to add another category of receivables—for example, Notes Receivable, which she might number 122. Or the business may start selling some type of inventory, account number 132.

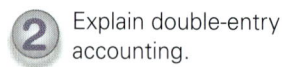

Double-Entry Accounting

2 Explain double-entry accounting.

As we used the accounting equation in the last chapter to track the transactions of a business, you saw that each transaction affected at least two accounts. Transactions demonstrate that an exchange occurred between the business and an entity outside of the business. The accounts provide a summary of all the exchanges, or trans-

Exhibit 2-1   Chart of Accounts for Kay Torres Travel Agency

KAY TORRES TRAVEL AGENCY
Balance Sheet Accounts

Assets		Liabilities	
111 Cash		211 Accounts payable	
121 Accounts receivable		221 Notes payable	
131 Supplies			
141 Equipment		**Owner's Equity**	
		311 Kay Torres, capital	
		312 Kay Torres, withdrawals	

KAY TORRES TRAVEL AGENCY
Income Statement Accounts

Revenue		Expenses	
411 Service revenue		511 Building rent expense	
		512 Salary expense	
		513 Utilities expense	

actions, that affect the accounts for the accounting period. Certain rules apply to help us summarize business transactions in accounts. The rule that reflects the fact that every transaction involves at least two accounts is called **double-entry accounting**.

Rules of Debits and Credits

To understand double-entry accounting, you need to know the rules of **debits** and **credits**. The left side of *any* account is called the debit side, sometimes abbreviated as *Dr.* The right side of *any* account is called the credit side, sometimes shown as *Cr.* You may be confused by the words *debit* and *credit*, especially if you use a debit or credit card. Just remember that, in accounting, to debit an account simply means putting a transaction on its left side. Conversely, to credit an account just means putting an entry on its right side. *To reflect the fact that every transaction involves an exchange—to show that every transaction affects at least two accounts—every business transaction will include at least one debit and at least one credit, so that equal amounts of debits and credits represent every transaction.*

T-Account

A **T-account** is an informal account form used to summarize transactions. It isn't really used in accounting for business transactions, but it does provide a handy way of getting used to debits and credits. The T-account gets its name from the fact that it is shaped like the letter "T". Check out the following T-account. The vertical line in the letter T divides the account into its two sides: left and right. The account title appears at the top of the T.

Account Title

Debit = left side	Credit = right side
Dr.	Cr.

The type of account determines where we record increases and decreases in the T-account. In other words, whether increases are shown as debits or credits depends on what type of account is involved and where that account appears in the accounting equation. Here's how the rules apply to the different account types:

- **Assets.** Because assets are on the left side of the equation, increases are placed on the left, or debit, side of the account and decreases are placed on the right, or credit, side. For example, if you receive cash, you record the increase in cash as a debit in the Cash account. If you pay cash, you record the decrease in cash as a credit in the Cash account.

- **Liabilities.** Liabilities are located on the right of the accounting equation. Show increases on the right, or credit, side of the account and decreases on the left, or debit, side of the account. For example, when you borrow money from the bank and sign a note, you record the increase in Notes Payable as a credit. As you make monthly payments, you decrease the amount due to the bank with a debit in the Notes Payable account.

- **Capital and Withdrawals.** Like liabilities, owner's equity is on the right side of the equation. Record increases on the right, or credit, side of the account and decreases on the left, or debit, side of the account. When an owner invests in the business, you record the increase in the Capital account as a credit. A withdrawal by the owner decreases owner's equity so transactions affecting the Withdrawals account are exceptions to the location rule. Increases are shown opposite of how they are shown in the Capital account, so increases are presented on the left, or debit, side. When the owner takes money out of the business for personal use, you record the increase in withdrawals as a debit in the Withdrawals account.

- **Revenues.** As you know, revenues are increases to owner's equity. So, record increases in revenues on the right, or credit, side. When you perform a service as part of your business operations, you record the increase in owner's equity as a credit in the Revenue account.

- **Expenses.** Like withdrawals, expenses decrease owner's equity, so they too are exceptions to the rule. Increases are shown opposite of how they are shown in the Capital account. Show increases in expenses on the left, or debit, side. When you incur expenses in operating your business, record the increase in expenses as a debit in the Expense account.

The rules of debits and credits are summarized in Exhibit 2-2.

Exhibit 2-2 Rules of Debits and Credits with Normal Account Balances

Assets		=	Liabilities		+		Owner's Equity			

Assets		Liabilities		Capital		Withdrawals	
Debit	Credit	Debit	Credit	Debit	Credit	Debit	Credit
+	−	−	+	−	+	+	−
Bal.		Bal.		Bal.		Bal.	

Revenues		Expenses	
Debit	Credit	Debit	Credit
−	+	+	−
	Bal.	Bal.	

Exhibit 2-3 Normal Account Balances and Changes to Account Balances

	Normal Balance		Increase		Decrease	
Balance sheet accounts						
Assets	Debit		Debit			Credit
Liabilities		Credit		Credit	Debit	
Capital		Credit		Credit	Debit	
Withdrawals	Debit		Debit			Credit
Income statement accounts						
Revenues		Credit		Credit	Debit	
Expenses	Debit		Debit			Credit

Normal Balance

An account's **normal balance** falls on the side of the account where increases are recorded.

- Assets increase on the debit side, so the normal balance of an asset is on its debit side.

- Liabilities increase on the credit side, so the normal balance of a liability is on its credit side.

- Owner's capital increases on the credit side, so the normal balance of the Capital account is on the credit side.

- Owner's withdrawals increase on the debit side, so the normal balance of the Withdrawals account is on the debit side.

- Revenues increase on the credit side, so the normal balance of a revenue is on its credit side.

- Expenses increase on the debit side, so the normal balance of an expense is on its debit side.

Exhibit 2-2 shows the normal balance of accounts in T-account format. Exhibit 2-3 illustrates the normal balance of all the assets, liabilities, and owner's equity accounts, including revenues, which increase an owner's equity in the business, and expenses, which decrease an owner's equity in the business.

Recording and Summarizing Business Transactions

Remember using the accounting equation as a way of tracing the transactions of a business? Although that approach worked for us in Chapter 1, imagine how hard it would be to use the equation to account for all of the transactions of large businesses such as Wal-Mart, FedEx, or Bank of America.

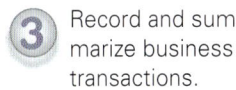
Record and summarize business transactions.

In real life, the accounting process actually begins when business transactions are entered in a **journal**. The journal is the chronological, or date order, record of the transactions of a business. The accounting system tracks each exchange by creating a record in the journal showing the transaction, the date it occurred, and how it affected the business's accounts. Because of the double-entry system of accounting—where each exchange involves at least two accounts—every journal entry includes an equal amount of debits and credits.

To enter a transaction in a journal means to **record** or **journalize** the transaction. Take the following steps to record a journal entry:

1. Record the date.

2. Record the debit entry by entering the account title and then entering the amount in the debit column.

3. Record the credit entry on the next line by indenting the account title and then entering the amount in the credit column.

4. Write an explanation describing the entry.

Although the journal tells you about events that had a financial impact on your business for a particular day, the journal does not provide enough information to make decisions. You need a summary of your business activities to tell you how much cash you have in your checking account, how much you owe your suppliers, or what your equity is in the business on any given day. The **ledger** is a grouping of all the accounts and their balances in balance sheet order to show the amount of assets, liabilities, and owner's equity on a given date. Instead of using an actual ledger, we will first use the T-account form of accounts to understand how accounting summarizes transactions in accounts.

A necessary step in the process of summarizing transactions is to post the transactions in the journal to the ledger. **Posting** in accounting just means copying the amounts from the journal to the ledger. Debits in the journal are posted as debits in the ledger, and credits in the journal are credits in the ledger. Debits never become credits, and credits never become debits.

Check out Exhibit 2-4, which shows us how transactions are entered in the accounting records of a business. Preparation of the trial balance and financial statements will be discussed later in the chapter.

Exhibit 2-4 How Transactions Are Entered into Accounting Records

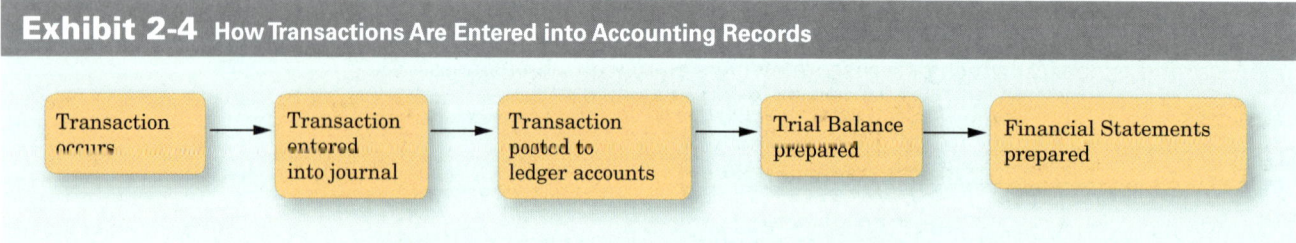

Remember Kay Torres Travel Agency from Chapter 1? The investment that Kay Torres made to open the business is posted to the ledger in Exhibit 2-5 as an example of the posting process. Notice that the journal has a column labeled "Post Ref." It stands for **posting reference**, a notation that links the two records, the journal and the ledger, together. When posting the amount from the journal to the ledger, place the account numbers of the accounts to which the entry was posted in the Post Ref. column of the journal. Remember that the chart of accounts shows the numbers of each account.

Exhibit 2-5 Posting a Journal Entry to the Accounts

PANEL A—Journal Entry:

Date	Accounts	Post Ref.	Dr.	Cr.
	Cash	111	20,000	
	Kay Torres, Capital	311		20,000
	Received investment from owner.			

PANEL B—Posting to the Accounts:

Cash 111	Kay Torres, Capital 311
20,000	20,000

The Transaction Analysis

To properly record, or journalize, transactions in the journal and summarize them in the T-accounts, you will complete a five-step transaction analysis. Steps 1 through 4 analyze the transaction for the journal entry. Step 5 reflects the posting of the transaction from the journal into the accounts. For now we will omit explanations of journal entries so that we can focus on the recording process.

For each transaction, ask the following questions:

STEP 1
What accounts are affected? *Example*: Cash, Accounts Payable, or Salary Expense.

STEP 2
For each account affected, what type of account is it? Is it an asset, liability, capital, withdrawal, revenue, or expense? *Example*: Cash is an asset.

STEP 3
Does the account balance increase or decrease? *Example*: If you receive cash, then that account increases.

STEP 4
Do you debit or credit the account in the journal entry? See Exhibit 2-2 or Exhibit 2-3 for a summary of the rules of debits and credits. *Example*: Cash is an asset and it increases; increases in assets are recorded as debits.

STEP 5
What does the T-account look like? See Exhibit 2-3 for a summary of normal balances and changes to account balances.

The five-step analysis looks like the following in chart form:

Step 1 Accounts Affected	Step 2 Type	Step 3 ↑↓	Step 4 Dr. or Cr.

Once you complete steps 1–4, then you are ready to make the entry in the journal:

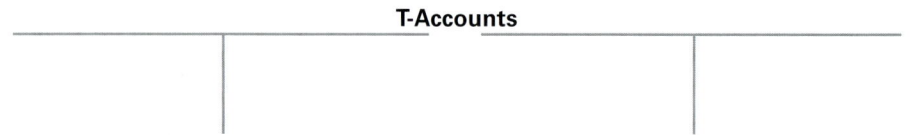

Journal Entry:

Date	Accounts	Post Ref.	Dr.	Cr.

After you have recorded the transaction in the journal, you are ready to post it to the accounts:

T-Accounts

Be sure to work through the first three steps before trying to debit or credit an account!

In the next section, we will practice the five-step process. Our goal is to successfully analyze transactions, record the transactions using journal entries, and post the transactions to accounts.

Applying Transaction Analysis

Check out how the transactions for the first month of business of Kay Torres Travel Agency are analyzed and recorded.

1. ***Investment by owner.*** Kay Torres invested $20,000 cash in the business.

Analysis of Transaction (1)

STEP 1
What accounts are affected? The travel agency received cash from its owner. In exchange, the owner received an equity interest in the business. The accounts involved are Cash and Kay Torres, Capital. These account titles come from the chart of accounts.

STEP 2
What type of account is it? Cash is an asset. Kay Torres, Capital, is capital.

STEP 3
Does the account balance increase or decrease? Because cash was received, Cash is increased. Kay's ownership interest, Kay Torres, Capital, is also increased because she invested money in the business.

STEP 4
Do you debit or credit the account in the journal entry? According to the rules of debits and credits, an increase in an asset is recorded with a debit. An increase in capital is a credit.

STEP 5

What does the T-account look like? The amount of the transaction affecting Cash is entered on the debit side. The amount for Kay Torres, Capital, is entered on the credit side.

1 Accounts Affected	2 Type	3 ↑↓	4 Dr. or Cr.
Cash	Asset	↑	Dr.
Kay Torres, Capital	Capital	↑	Cr.

Journal Entry:

Date	Accounts	Post Ref.	Dr.	Cr.
1.	Cash	111	20,000	
	Kay Torres, Capital	311		20,000

	Cash	111		Kay Torres, Capital	311
(1)	20,000			(1)	20,000

Notice that the name of the account being credited is indented in the journal. This is a standard way to differentiate between the account being debited and the account being credited.

Also note again that every transaction affects at least two T-accounts and that the total amount added to the debit side equals the total amount added to the credit side. This form of analysis is a double-entry analysis of transactions; it reflects the exchange nature of every transaction and keeps the accounting equation in balance.

We will continue with more brief explanations for each transaction.

2. ***Purchase equipment for cash.*** The travel agency purchased $9,000 of equipment for cash.

Analysis of Transaction (2)

STEP 1

The travel agency received equipment in exchange for cash paid to the equipment manufacturing company. The accounts involved in the transaction are Equipment and Cash.

STEP 2

Equipment and Cash are assets.

STEP 3

The asset Equipment is increased. The asset Cash is decreased because Kay wrote a check to pay for the equipment.

STEP 4

An increase in the asset Equipment is a debit; a decrease in the asset Cash is a credit.

STEP 5

The amount for Equipment is entered on the debit side. The amount for Cash is entered on the credit side.

1 Accounts Affected	2 Type	3 ↑↓	4 Dr. or Cr.
Equipment	Asset	↑	Dr.
Cash	Asset	↓	Cr.

Journal Entry:

Date	Accounts			Post Ref.	Dr.	Cr.
2.	Equipment			141	9,000	
	Cash			111		9,000

	Cash		111		Equipment		141
(1)	20,000	(2)	9,000	(2)	9,000		

3. ***Borrow cash from the bank.*** The travel agency borrowed $15,000 cash from the bank and signed a 2-year note payable to the bank.

Analysis of Transaction (3)

STEP 1

The travel agency received cash from the bank in exchange for a signed note agreeing to pay the cash back in 2 years. The accounts involved in the transaction are Cash and Notes Payable.

STEP 2

Cash is an asset; Notes Payable is a liability.

STEP 3

The asset Cash is increased. The liability Notes Payable is also increased because it represents an obligation owed to the bank.

STEP 4

An increase in the asset Cash is a debit; an increase in the liability Notes Payable is a credit.

STEP 5

The amount for Cash is entered on the debit side. The amount for Notes Payable is entered on the credit side.

1 Accounts Affected	2 Type	3 ↑↓	4 Dr. or Cr.
Cash	Asset	↑	Dr.
Notes Payable	Liability	↑	Cr.

Journal Entry:

Date	Accounts	Post Ref.	Dr.	Cr.
3.	Cash	111	15,000	
	Notes Payable	221		15,000

	Cash	111			Notes Payable	221
(1)	20,000	(2) 9,000			(3)	15,000
(3)	15,000					

4. **Purchase supplies on credit.** The travel agency purchased $1,200 of supplies on account.

Analysis of Transaction (4)

STEP 1

The travel agency received supplies in exchange for a promise to pay cash to the supplier next month. The accounts involved in the transaction are Supplies and Accounts Payable.

STEP 2

Supplies is an asset; Accounts Payable is a liability.

STEP 3

The asset Supplies is increased. The liability Accounts Payable is increased because it represents an obligation to pay the supplier.

STEP 4

An increase in the asset Supplies is a debit; an increase in the liability Accounts Payable is a credit.

STEP 5

The amount for Supplies is entered on the debit side. The amount for Accounts Payable is entered on the credit side.

1 Accounts Affected	2 Type	3 ↑↓	4 Dr. or Cr.
Supplies	Asset	↑	Dr.
Accounts Payable	Liability	↑	Cr.

Journal Entry:

Date	Accounts	Post Ref.	Dr.	Cr.
4.	Supplies	131	1,200	
	Accounts Payable	211		1,200

Supplies	131		Accounts Payable	211
(4) 1,200			(4) 1,200	

5. ***Provide services for cash.*** The travel agency received $2,300 cash at the time travel services were provided to customers.

Analysis of Transaction (5)

STEP 1

The travel agency received cash in exchange for services rendered to help clients plan vacations. The agency *earned* this money. The accounts involved in the transaction are Cash and Service Revenue.

STEP 2

Cash is an asset; Service Revenue is a revenue.

STEP 3

The asset Cash is increased. The revenue Service Revenue is increased, too.

STEP 4

An increase in the asset Cash is a debit; an increase in the revenue Service Revenue is a credit.

STEP 5

The amount for Cash is entered on the debit side. The amount for Service Revenue is entered on the credit side.

1 Accounts Affected	2 Type	3 ↑↓	4 Dr. or Cr.
Cash	Asset	↑	Dr.
Service Revenue	Revenue	↑	Cr.

Journal Entry:

Date	Accounts	Post Ref.	Dr.	Cr.
5.	Cash	111	2,300	
	Service Revenue	411		2,300

		Cash		111		Service Revenue		411
(1)	20,000	(2)	9,000				(5)	2,300
(3)	15,000							
(5)	2,300							

6. ***Provide services on credit.*** The travel agency provided $5,200 of services on credit.

Analysis of Transaction (6)

STEP 1
The travel agency received promises from customers to send cash next month in exchange for services rendered to help clients plan vacations. Again, the business *earned* this money, although it has not received it yet. We keep track of the amounts owed by each customer by creating an accounts receivable account for each customer. The accounts involved in the transaction are Accounts Receivable and Service Revenue.

STEP 2
Accounts Receivable is an asset; Service Revenue is a revenue.

STEP 3
The asset Accounts Receivable is increased. The revenue Service Revenue is increased, too.

STEP 4
An increase in the asset Accounts Receivable is a debit; an increase in the revenue Service Revenue is a credit.

STEP 5
The amount for Accounts Receivable is entered on the debit side. The amount for Service Revenue is entered on the credit side.

1 **Accounts Affected**	2 **Type**	3 ↑↓	4 **Dr. or Cr.**
Accounts Receivable	Asset	↑	Dr.
Service Revenue	Revenue	↑	Cr.

Journal Entry:

Date	Accounts	Post Ref.	Dr.	Cr.
6.	Accounts Receivable	121	5,200	
	Service Revenue	411		5,200

	Accounts Receivable	121		Service Revenue		411
(6)	5,200			(5)	2,300	
				(6)	5,200	

7. ***Partial payment of accounts payable.*** The travel agency paid $600 of the $1,200 owed to a supplier.

Analysis of Transaction (7)

STEP 1
The travel agency owed a supplier $1,200, but only paid $600. The travel agency received a reduction in the amount owed to the supplier in exchange for making a cash payment. The accounts involved in the transaction are Accounts Payable and Cash.

STEP 2
Accounts Payable is a liability; Cash is an asset.

STEP 3
The liability Accounts Payable is decreased. The asset Cash is also decreased.

STEP 4
A decrease in the liability Accounts Payable is a debit; a decrease in the asset Cash is a credit.

STEP 5
The amount for Accounts Payable is entered on the debit side. The amount for Cash is entered on the credit side.

1 Accounts Affected	2 Type	3 ↑↓	4 Dr. or Cr.
Accounts Payable	Liability	↓	Dr.
Cash	Asset	↓	Cr.

Journal Entry:

Date	Accounts	Post Ref.	Dr.	Cr.
7.	Accounts Payable	211	600	
	Cash	111		600

	Cash	111			Accounts Payable	211
(1)	20,000	(2)	9,000	(7)	600	(4) 1,200
(3)	15,000	(7)	600			
(5)	2,300					

8. ***Payment of building rent expense for cash.*** The travel agency paid $900 for rent on the building it occupied.

Analysis of Transaction (8)

STEP 1
The travel agency paid $900 in exchange for the *use* of the building as part of operating the business. The accounts involved in the transaction are Building Rent Expense and Cash.

STEP 2
Building Rent Expense is an expense; Cash is an asset.

STEP 3
The expense Building Rent Expense is increased. The asset Cash is decreased.

STEP 4
An increase in an expense Building Rent Expense is a debit; a decrease in the asset Cash is a credit.

STEP 5
The amount for Building Rent Expense is entered on the debit side. The amount for Cash is entered on the credit side.

1 Accounts Affected	2 Type	3 ↑↓	4 Dr. or Cr.
Building Rent Expense	Expense	↑	Dr.
Cash	Asset	↓	Cr.

Journal Entry:

Date	Accounts	Post Ref.	Dr.	Cr.
8.	Building Rent Expense	511	900	
	Cash	111		900

	Cash		111		Building Rent Expense	511
(1)	20,000	(2)	9,000	(8)	900	
(3)	15,000	(7)	600			
(5)	2,300	(8)	900			

9. ***Payment of salary expense for cash.*** At the end of the month, the travel agency paid an employee a salary of $1,100.

Analysis of Transaction (9)

STEP 1
The travel agency received the *use* of the employee's time and expertise in exchange for $1,100 cash. The accounts involved in the transaction are Salary Expense and Cash.

STEP 2
Salary Expense is an expense; Cash is an asset.

STEP 3
The expense Salary Expense is increased. The asset Cash is decreased.

STEP 4
An increase in the expense Salary Expense is a debit; a decrease in the asset Cash is a credit.

STEP 5

The amount for Salary Expense is entered on the debit side. The amount for Cash is entered on the credit side.

1 Accounts Affected	2 Type	3 ↑↓	4 Dr. or Cr.
Salary Expense	Expense	↑	Dr.
Cash	Asset	↓	Cr.

Journal Entry:

Date	Accounts	Post Ref.	Dr.	Cr.
9.	Salary Expense	512	1,100	
	Cash	111		1,100

	Cash		111		Salary Expense	512
(1)	20,000	(2)	9,000	(9)	1,100	
(3)	15,000	(7)	600			
(5)	2,300	(8)	900			
		(9)	1,100			

10. ***Payment of utilities expense for cash.*** The travel agency received an electric bill and paid cash of $300.

Analysis of Transaction (10)

STEP 1

The travel agency received an electric bill and paid cash for the *use* of electricity. The accounts involved in the transaction are Utilities Expense and Cash.

STEP 2

Utilities Expense is an expense; Cash is an asset.

STEP 3

The expense Utilities Expense is increased. The asset Cash is decreased.

STEP 4

An increase in the expense Utilities Expense is a debit; a decrease in the asset Cash is a credit.

STEP 5

The amount for Utilities Expense is entered on the debit side. The amount for Cash is entered on the credit side.

1 Accounts Affected	2 Type	3 ↑↓	4 Dr. or Cr.
Utilities Expense	Expense	↑	Dr.
Cash	Asset	↓	Cr.

Journal Entry:

Date	Accounts	Post Ref.	Dr.	Cr.
10.	Utilities Expense	513	300	
	Cash	111		300

Cash			111		Utilities Expense		513
(1)	20,000	(2)	9,000	(10)	300		
(3)	15,000	(7)	600				
(5)	2,300	(8)	900				
		(9)	1,100				
		(10)	300				

11. ***Cash withdrawal by owner.*** Kay Torres withdrew $1,000 from the travel agency's checking account for personal use.

Analysis of Transaction (11)

STEP 1
The owner withdrew cash for personal use. The agency received a reduction in equity interest in exchange for cash paid to the owner. The accounts involved in the transaction are Kay Torres, Withdrawals, and Cash.

STEP 2
Kay Torres, Withdrawals, is a withdrawal account; Cash is an asset.

STEP 3
The withdrawal account Kay Torres, Withdrawals, is increased because the amount of money withdrawn from the business has increased. The asset Cash is decreased.

STEP 4
An increase in the withdrawal account Kay Torres, Withdrawals, is a debit; a decrease in the asset Cash is a credit.

STEP 5
The amount for Kay Torres, Withdrawals, is entered on the debit side. The amount for Cash is entered on the credit side.

1 Accounts Affected	2 Type	3 ↑↓	4 Dr. or Cr.
Kay Torres, Withdrawals	Withdrawal	↑	Dr.
Cash	Asset	↓	Cr.

Journal Entry:

Date	Accounts	Post Ref.	Dr.	Cr.
11.	Kay Torres, Withdrawals	312	1,000	
	Cash	111		1,000

	Cash		111		Kay Torres, Withdrawals 312
(1)	20,000	(2)	9,000	(11) 1,000	
(3)	15,000	(7)	600		
(5)	2,300	(8)	900		
		(9)	1,100		
		(10)	300		
		(11)	1,000		

Balancing the Accounts

After transactions are recorded and posted to accounts, you will calculate each account's balance. A **balance** is the difference between the account's total debits and its total credits. Every account has a balance, shown as "Bal." in the following T-account:

	Accounts Payable		211
		(1) Bal.	0
		(2)	5,000
(3)	2,000		
		(4) Bal.	3,000

1. The beginning balance for the current accounting period is the ending balance brought forward from the previous period. In this example, the business is new, so its beginning balance is $0.

2. If, for example, the business purchases $5,000 of supplies on credit during the first accounting period, this transaction will show up as a credit to the Accounts Payable account.

3. If the company then pays $2,000 of its debt for these supplies, the amount will be entered on the debit side of the account.

4. The Accounts Payable account normally has a credit balance because credits increase this account. Because the company just started, this account had a beginning credit balance of $0. Add increases of $5,000 that appear on the credit side, and subtract decreases of $2,000 that appear on the debit side. The resulting ending balance of Accounts Payable is $3,000.

   A horizontal line separates the transaction amounts from the account balance at the end of an accounting period. The "Bal. 3,000" under the horizontal line shows that the balance in Accounts Payable at the end of the accounting period was $3,000. In the next accounting period, this balance will be the new beginning balance and will change as the business makes more credit purchases and more payments against amounts charged on account.
   If an account's total debits are more than its total credits, then that account has a debit balance. If an account's total credits are more than its total debits, then that account has a credit balance. For example, the Accounts Payable credit balance of $3,000 is the difference between its total credits, including the beginning balance, of $5,000 and its total debits of $2,000.
   This formula, shown here for Accounts Payable, works for calculating the ending balance of any account.

Ending Balance = Beginning Balance + Increases − Decreases
$3,000   = $0   + $5,000 − $2,000

Accounts After Posting to the Ledger

Exhibit 2-6 shows the accounts after all transactions have been posted. The accounts have been grouped under assets, liabilities, and owners' equity as shown using Kay Torres Travel Agency's chart of accounts in Exhibit 2-1.

Exhibit 2-6 Kay Torres Travel Agency's T-Accounts (Ledger) After Posting

Assets

Cash			111
(1)	20,000	(2)	9,000
(3)	15,000	(7)	600
(5)	2,300	(8)	900
		(9)	1,100
		(10)	300
		(11)	1,000
Bal.	24,400		

Accounts Receivable		121
(6)	5,200	
Bal.	5,200	

Supplies		131
(4)	1,200	
Bal.	1,200	

Equipment		141
(2)	9,000	
Bal.	9,000	

Liabilities

Accounts Payable			211
(7)	600	(4)	1,200
		Bal.	600

Notes Payable			221
		(3)	15,000
		Bal.	15,000

Owner's Equity

Kay Torres, Capital			311
		(1)	20,000
		Bal.	20,000

Kay Torres, Withdrawals		312
(11)	1,000	
Bal.	1,000	

Service Revenue			411
		(5)	2,300
		(6)	5,200
		Bal.	7,500

Building Rent Expense		511
(8)	900	
Bal.	900	

Salary Expense		512
(9)	1,100	
Bal.	1,100	

Utilities Expense		513
(10)	300	
Bal.	300	

Details of Journals and Ledgers

In practice, the journal and the ledger provide information that creates a "trail" that can be used to follow transactions through the accounting records of a business. For example, a supplier may bill us twice for an item that we purchased. To prove we paid the first bill, we would search the records to find our payment. To see how this process really works when a ledger is used to hold account summaries instead of T-accounts, let's take a closer look at the journal and the ledger.

DETAILS IN THE JOURNAL

Exhibit 2-7, Panel A, describes a transaction, and Panel B shows this transaction in the journal. The page number of the journal appears in its upper right corner. The journal displays the following information about the transaction.

- The *date* when the transaction occurred.

- The *accounts* debited and credited, the *amounts* of the debit and credit, and an *explanation* of the transaction.

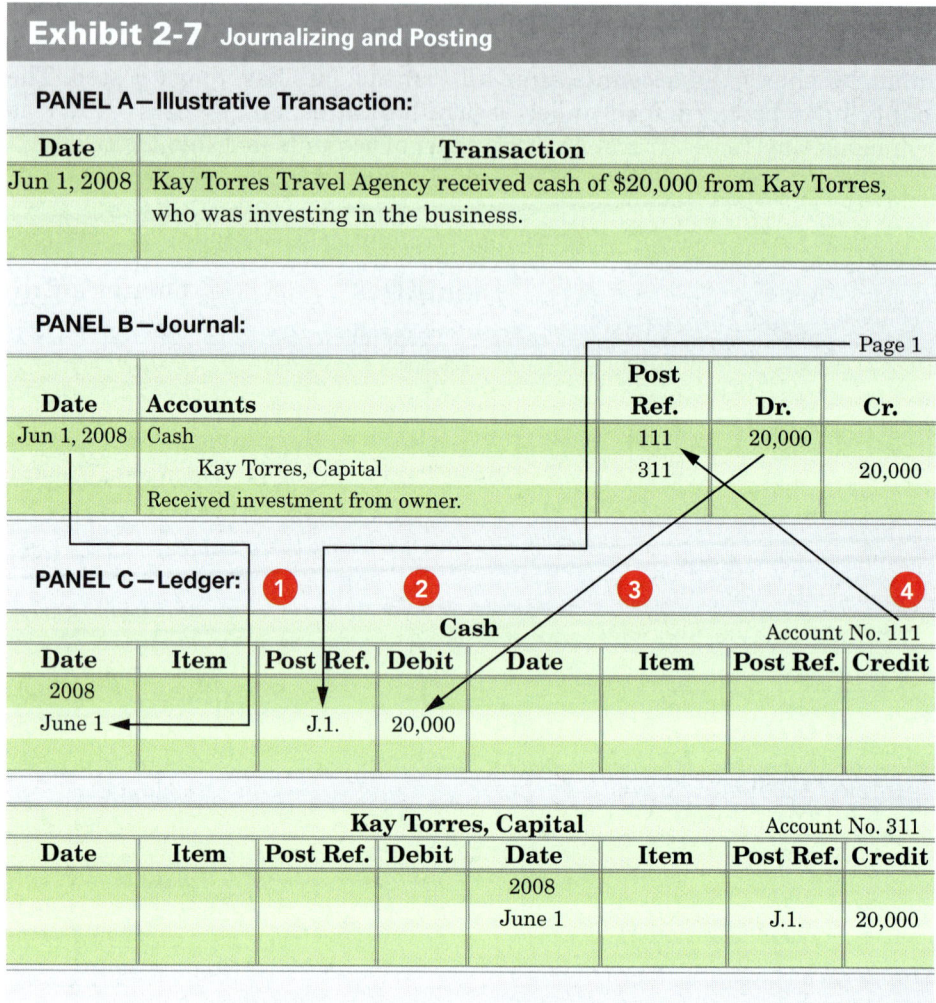

Exhibit 2-7 Journalizing and Posting

PANEL A—Illustrative Transaction:

Date	Transaction
Jun 1, 2008	Kay Torres Travel Agency received cash of $20,000 from Kay Torres, who was investing in the business.

PANEL B—Journal:

Page 1

Date	Accounts	Post Ref.	Dr.	Cr.
Jun 1, 2008	Cash	111	20,000	
	Kay Torres, Capital	311		20,000
	Received investment from owner.			

PANEL C—Ledger: ① ② ③ ④

Cash   Account No. 111

Date	Item	Post Ref.	Debit	Date	Item	Post Ref.	Credit
2008							
June 1		J.1.	20,000				

Kay Torres, Capital   Account No. 311

Date	Item	Post Ref.	Debit	Date	Item	Post Ref.	Credit
				2008			
				June 1		J.1.	20,000

- The *posting reference*, abbreviated as "Post Ref."—a notation that links the two records, the journal and the ledger, together. The posting reference shows the account numbers of the accounts to which the entry was posted and links the journal to the ledger to form a trail.

DETAILS IN THE LEDGER

Exhibit 2-7, Panel C, shows the accounts affected by the first transaction: Cash and Kay Torres, Capital. The account number appears at the upper right corner of each account. Each account has a separate column for:

- The *date*.

- The *item*, which can be used for any special notation.

- The *posting reference*, abbreviated as "Post Ref." This column is used to show the page number of the journal where the transaction was recorded. In this way, it shows where this information came from, and links the two records, the journal and ledger.

- The *debit* column with the amount of any debits.

- The *credit* column with the amount of any credits.

Posting

As we discussed earlier, posting means copying information from the journal to the ledger. But how do we handle the details? Exhibit 2-7 illustrates the steps. Panel A describes the first transaction of the business entity, Kay Torres Travel Agency; Panel B presents the journal; Panel C shows the ledger.

The posting process includes four steps. After recording the transaction in the journal:

ARROW ❶

Copy the transaction date from the journal to the Cash account in the ledger.

ARROW ❷

Copy the journal page number from the journal to the Cash account in the ledger. "J.1" refers to Journal page 1.

ARROW ❸

Copy the dollar amount of the debit, $20,000, from the journal as a debit into the Cash account in the ledger.

ARROW ❹

Copy the account number, 111, from the Cash account in the ledger back to the journal. This step demonstrates that the $20,000 debit to Cash was posted to Cash. The journal entry is posted to Cash first because this is the first account listed in the entry. Once posting to Cash is complete, repeat the process to post the entry to Kay Torres, Capital.

Four-Column Account

The ledger accounts illustrated in Exhibit 2-7 use a format similar to that of a T-account because they present the debit amount on the left of the account and the credit amount on the right. Another account format, the more formal form, is more commonly used and has four amount columns, as illustrated in Exhibit 2-8.

The first pair of debit and credit columns holds the individual transaction amounts posted from journal entries, such as the $20,000 debit. The second pair of debit and credit columns keeps the account balance. The four-column format keeps a running, or ongoing, balance in the account. For this reason, it is used in actual practice instead of the T-account format. In Exhibit 2-8, Cash has a debit balance of $20,000 after the first transaction and a debit balance of $11,000 after the second transaction.

Exhibit 2-8 Account in Four-Column Format

Cash — Account No. 111

Date	Item	Post Ref.	Debit	Credit	Balance Debit	Balance Credit
2008						
June 1		J.1	20,000		20,000	
3		J.1		9,000	11,000	

Trial Balance

4 Prepare and use a trial balance to create financial statements.

Now that the transactions have been recorded in the journal and posted to accounts in the ledger, a trial balance can be prepared. The **trial balance** lists all the accounts of a business and their balances in balance sheet order. A trial balance can be constructed at any time, but is most commonly put together at the end of the accounting period. Because the total of the debit balances should equal the total of the credit balances, the purpose of the trial balance is to summarize all account balances to be certain that total debits equal total credits before the financial statements are prepared. Exhibit 2-9 is the trial balance for Kay Torres Travel Agency after all transactions have been journalized and posted for June 2008.

Exhibit 2-9 Trial Balance for Kay Torres Travel Agency

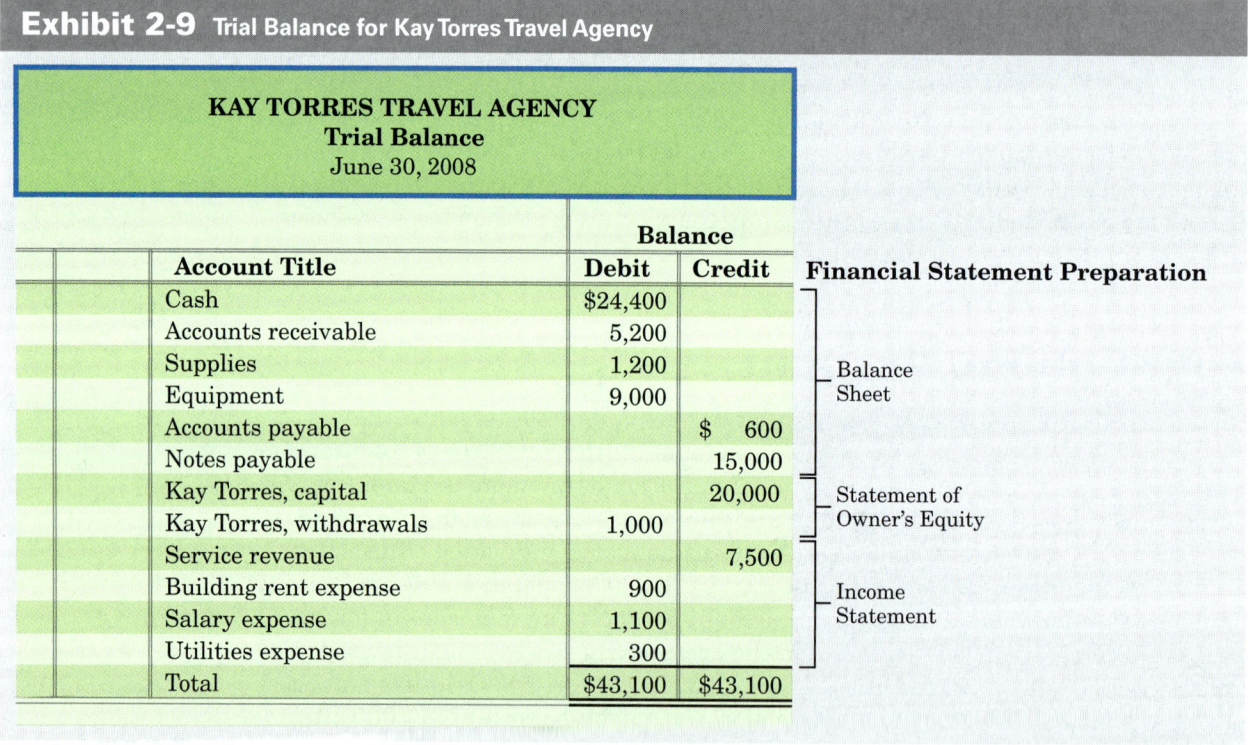

KAY TORRES TRAVEL AGENCY
Trial Balance
June 30, 2008

Account Title	Balance Debit	Credit	Financial Statement Preparation
Cash	$24,400		
Accounts receivable	5,200		
Supplies	1,200		Balance
Equipment	9,000		Sheet
Accounts payable		$ 600	
Notes payable		15,000	
Kay Torres, capital		20,000	Statement of
Kay Torres, withdrawals	1,000		Owner's Equity
Service revenue		7,500	
Building rent expense	900		Income
Salary expense	1,100		Statement
Utilities expense	300		
Total	$43,100	$43,100	

Trial Balance Errors

When recording and posting transactions, accounting errors can—and do—occur in both manual and computerized accounting systems. The trial balance helps us find those errors that cause total debits and total credits to be unequal. To find an error, you start with the trial balance and work back through the accounting records—through the ledger and through the journal—to the transaction. Errors can occur in the following activities:

- Preparing the trial balance
- Calculating account balances

- Posting amounts into the accounts

- Recording journal entries

Exhibit 2-10 shows nine common trial balance errors that can occur and cause the trial balance to be out of balance.

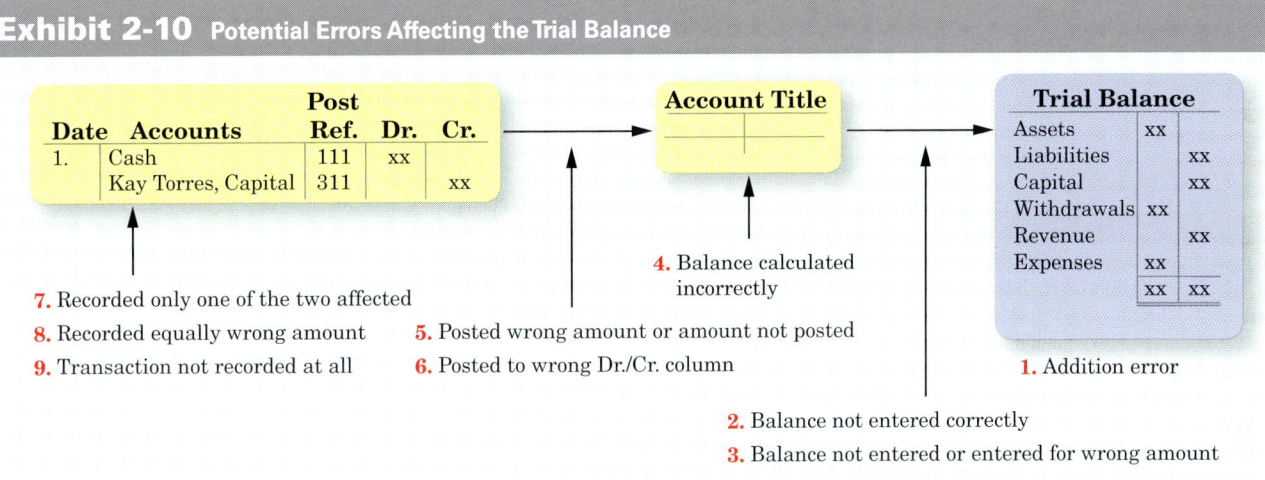

Exhibit 2-10 **Potential Errors Affecting the Trial Balance**

The following steps can be taken if the trial balance does not balance:

1. Begin by recalculating the totals on the trial balance.

2. If the trial balance is still out of balance, then calculate the difference between the total debits and total credits. Divide this difference by 2. Are any of the account balances equal to this amount? If so, then a debit balance was entered as a credit balance or a credit balance as a debit balance. You can also divide the difference by 9 to find a transposition error where the order of two digits has accidentally been reversed. For example, a balance of $2,100 in an account may have been shown as $1,200 in the trial balance. The difference is $900, which is a multiple of 9. Occasionally, an error occurs by dropping or adding zero(s) to an amount such as entering $21 as $210. This mistake is called a slide and will also cause a difference in the totals that is evenly divisible by 9.

3. If the trial balance columns are still unequal, then trace accounts and their balances back to the accounts in the ledger. An account(s) may have been excluded from your list, or its balance was incorrectly listed.

4. If you find that the accounts are all listed and the balances are correct, then you need to examine each account. Recalculate account balances to find any errors in addition or subtraction.

5. If the account balances are correctly calculated, then trace all postings back to the journal where the transactions were recorded. You might find that one of the amounts was posted for the wrong amount or not posted to the account.

6. You also might find that one of the amounts was posted into the wrong column of the account.

7. If the posting has occurred correctly, check the journal. Maybe a journal entry was made for only one of the two accounts affected.

KAY TORRES TRAVEL AGENCY
Trial Balance
June 30, 2008

Account Title	Balance	
	Debit	Credit
Cash	$24,400	
Accounts receivable	5,200	
Supplies	1,200	
Equipment	9,000	
Accounts payable		$ 600
Notes payable		15,000
Kay Torres, capital		20,000
Kay Torres, withdrawals	1,000	
Service revenue		7,500
Building rent expense	900	
Salary expense	1,100	
Utilities expense	300	
Total	$43,100	$43,100

At this point, the errors should be corrected and the total debits and total credits will be equal in the trial balance.

Keep in mind that errors may still occur in the trial balance, even though total debits and credits are the same and the trial balance "balances." Perhaps a transaction was recorded for the wrong amount in a journal entry, or perhaps an entire entry was recorded twice, or not recorded at all. These errors correspond to items 8 and 9 in Exhibit 2-10. You may also check your entries by looking at the documents that support each transaction. Exhibit 2-11 shows the steps that can be taken to correct each type of error.

Exhibit 2-11 Steps to Correct Errors in the Trial Balance

Error	Steps to Correct the Trial Balance
1. Addition error in the trial balance	Correct the totals in the trial balance.
2. Balance not entered correctly	Enter balance correctly to fix transposition, slide, or balance entered in wrong column.
3. Balance not entered into trial balance or entered for wrong amount	Add account and balance, or correct balance in the trial balance.
4. Balance incorrectly calculated in account	Recalculate the account balance. Correct the amount in the account. Insert the correct balance into the trial balance.
5. Posted the wrong amount from the journal to the account or amount was not posted at all	Correct the amount in the account. Recalculate the account balance. Insert the correct balance into the trial balance.
6. Posted journal entry into the wrong column of the account	Post journal entry amount into the correct column. Recalculate the account balance. Insert the correct balance into the trial balance.
7. Recorded in the journal only one of the two accounts affected	Record the missing portion of the journal entry and post it into its account. Recalculate the account balance. Insert the correct balance into the trial balance.
8. Recorded wrong amount in the journal	Prepare a new, correcting journal entry and post it to the accounts. Recalculate the account balances. Insert the correct balances into the trial balance.
9. Transaction not recorded in the journal	Prepare the journal entry and post to the accounts. Recalculate the account balances. Insert the correct balances into the trial balance.

Using the Trial Balance to Prepare Financial Statements

After completing the trial balance, you can prepare the financial statements. Set up the financial statements as we did in Chapter 1. Get the account balances from the trial balance. Insert account names and their balances into the financial statements, starting with the income statement, then the statement of owner's equity, and finishing with the balance sheet. Make sure the balance sheet is in balance!

The preceding page shows the income statement, statement of owner's equity, and balance sheet for Kay Torres Travel Agency at June 30, 2008. Notice again the flow of information from one financial statement to the other.

Demo Doc

Debit/Credit Transaction Analysis

Learning Objectives   1–3

On September 1, 2008, Michael Moe opened Moe's Mowing, a company that provides mowing and landscaping services. During the month of September, the business incurred the following transactions:

a. To begin operations, Michael deposited $10,000 of personal funds in the business's bank account. The business received the cash and gave Michael an ownership interest.

b. Purchased equipment for $3,500 on account.

c. Purchased office supplies for $800 cash.

d. Provided $2,600 of services to a customer on account.

e. Paid $500 cash toward the equipment previously purchased on account in transaction b.

f. Received $2,000 in cash for services provided to a new customer.

g. Paid $200 cash to repair equipment.

h. Paid $900 cash in salary expense.

i. Received $2,100 cash from customers on account.

j. Michael withdrew $1,500 cash from the business for personal use.

Requirements

1. Create blank T-accounts for the following accounts:

Cash, 111; Accounts Receivable, 121; Supplies, 131; Equipment, 141; Accounts Payable, 211; Michael Moe, Capital, 311; Michael Moe, Withdrawals, 312; Service Revenue, 411; Salary Expense, 511; and Repairs Expense, 521.

2. Journalize the transactions and show how they are posted in T-accounts.

3. Total all the T-accounts to determine their balances at the end of the month.

Demo Doc Solutions

Requirement 1

Create blank T-accounts for the following accounts:

Cash, 111; Accounts Receivable, 121; Supplies, 131; Equipment, 141; Accounts Payable, 211; Michael Moe, Capital, 311; Michael Moe, Withdrawals, 312; Service Revenue, 411; Salary Expense, 511; and Repairs Expense, 521.

1 Describe the role of accounts in summarizing business transactions.

2 Explain double-entry accounting.

Part 1	Part 2	Part 3	Demo Doc Complete

Opening a T-account simply means drawing a blank account (the T) and putting the account title (and the account number, if used) on top. To help find the accounts later, they are usually organized into assets, liabilities, owner's equity, revenue, and expenses (in that order). Note that the account numbers also follow this order.

Draw empty T-accounts for every account listed in the question.

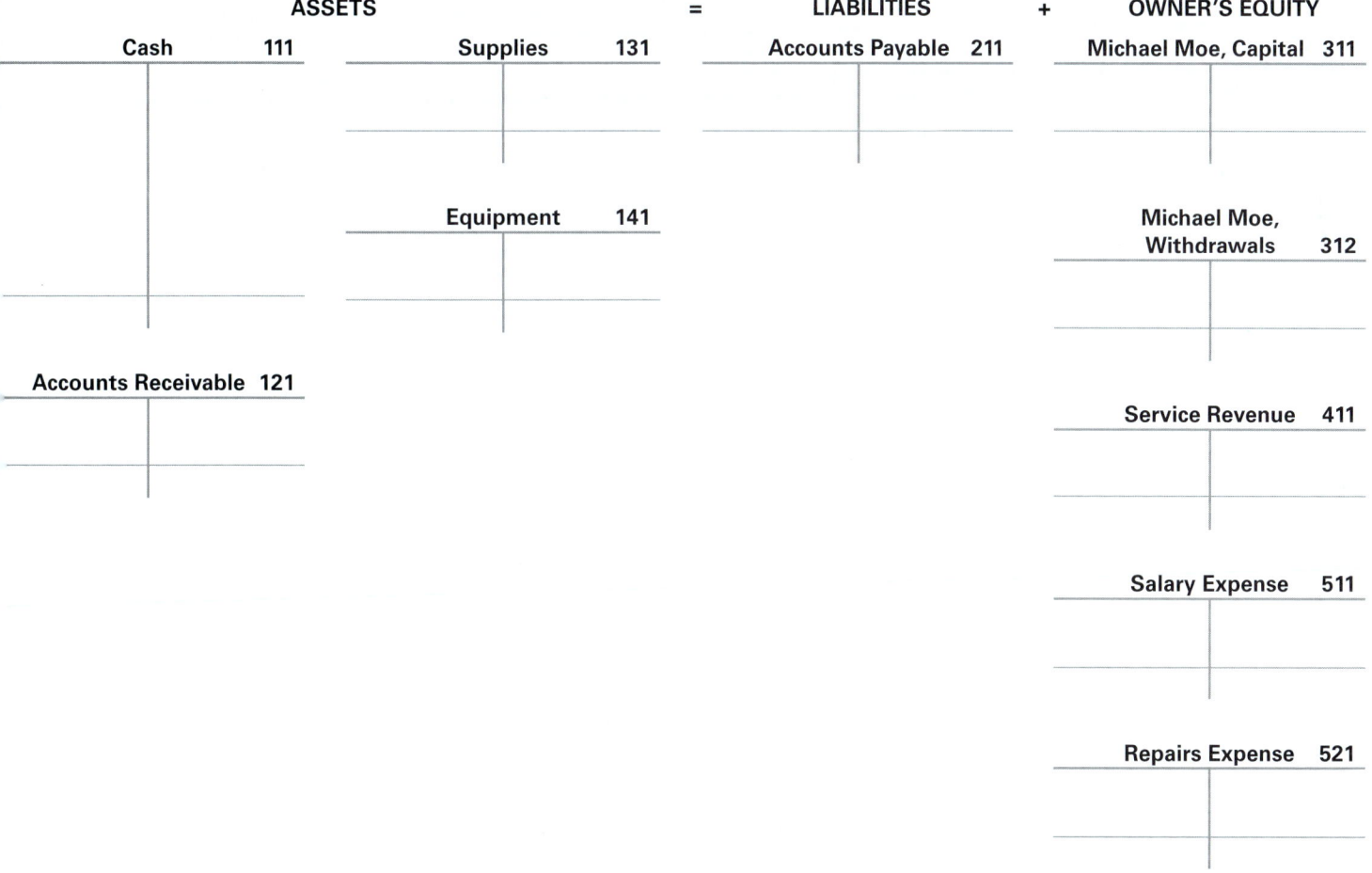

1. Describe the role of accounts in summarizing business transactions.

2. Explain double-entry accounting.

3. Record and summarize business transactions.

Journalize the transactions and show how they are posted in T-accounts.

Part 1	Part 2	Part 3	Demo Doc Complete

a. **To begin operations, Michael deposited $10,000 of personal funds in the business's bank account. The business received the cash and gave Michael an ownership interest.**

Remember the transaction analysis steps (listed on p. 65). First, we must determine which accounts are affected.

The business received $10,000 cash from its owner (Michael Moe). In exchange, Michael received an equity interest in the business. So, the accounts involved are Cash and Michael Moe, Capital.

The next step is to determine what type of accounts they are. Cash is an asset, while capital accounts are capital, part of owner's equity.

You can also determine account types by looking at the account numbers. Asset account numbers begin with a 1, liabilities with a 2, owner's equity with a 3, revenues with a 4, and expenses with a 5 (see Exhibit 2-1, p. 61).

The next step is to determine whether these accounts increased or decreased. From *the business's* point of view, Cash (an asset) increased. Michael Moe, Capital (equity), also increased.

Now we must determine whether these accounts should be debited or credited. Look at Exhibit 2-2 (p. 62). According to the rules of debits and credits, an increase in assets is a debit, while an increase in capital (equity) is a credit.

So, Cash (an asset) increases, which is a debit. Michael Moe, Capital (equity), also increases, which is a credit.

1 Accounts Affected	2 Type	3 $\uparrow \downarrow$	4 Dr. or Cr.
Cash	Asset	$\uparrow$	Dr.
Michael Moe, Capital	Capital	$\uparrow$	Cr.

The journal entry would be as follows:

Journal Entry:

Date	Accounts	Post Ref.	Dr.	Cr.
a.	Cash (Asset, $\uparrow$; debit)	111	10,000	
	Michael Moe, Capital (Capital, $\uparrow$; credit)	311		10,000
	Received investment from owner.			

Note that the total dollar amounts of debits will equal the total dollar amounts of credits.

Remember to use the transaction letters for references. This will help when we post this entry to the T-accounts.

Posting to the T-accounts is the last step in transaction analysis (see p. 65).

To post the transaction to the T-accounts, simply transfer the amount of each debit to its correct account as a debit (left side) entry, and transfer the amount of each credit to its correct account as a credit (right side) entry.

For this transaction, a debit of $10,000 to Cash means that we enter $10,000 on the left side of the Cash T-account. A credit of $10,000 to Michael Moe, Capital, means that we enter $10,000 on the right side of the Michael Moe, Capital, T-account.

Cash	111		Michael Moe, Capital	311
(a) 10,000			(a) 10,000

b. Purchased equipment for $3,500 on account.

Because it is a new transaction, we perform the transaction analysis steps (p. 65) again.

The business received equipment in exchange for a promise to pay for the cost ($3,500) at a future date. So the accounts involved in the transaction are Equipment and Accounts Payable.

Equipment is an asset, and Accounts Payable is a liability. Equipment (an asset) increased. Accounts Payable (a liability) also increased.

Looking at Exhibit 2-2 (p. 62), we see that an increase in assets is a debit, while an increase in liabilities is a credit.

So, Equipment (an asset) increases, which is a debit. Accounts Payable (a liability) also increases, which is a credit.

1 Accounts Affected	2 Type	3 ↑↓	4 Dr. or Cr.
Equipment	Asset	↑	Dr.
Accounts Payable	Liability	↑	Cr.

The journal entry would be as follows:

Journal Entry:

Date	Accounts	Post Ref.	Dr.	Cr.
b.	Equipment (Asset, ↑ ; debit)	141	3,500	
	Accounts Payable (Liability, ↑ ; credit)	211		3,500
	Purchased equipment on account.			

We enter $3,500 on the debit (left) side of the Equipment T-account and $3,500 on the credit (right) side of the Accounts Payable T-account.

Equipment		141		Accounts Payable		211
(b)	3,500				(b)	3,500

c. Purchased office supplies for $800 cash.

The business purchased supplies in exchange for cash ($800). The accounts involved in the transaction are Supplies and Cash.

Supplies and Cash are both assets. Supplies (an asset) increased. Cash (an asset) decreased.

Looking at Exhibit 2-2 (p. 62), we see that an increase in assets is a debit, while a decrease in assets is a credit.

So Supplies (an asset) increases, which is a debit. Cash (an asset) decreases, which is a credit.

1 Accounts Affected	2 Type	3 ↑↓	4 Dr. or Cr.
Supplies	Asset	↑	Dr.
Cash	Asset	↓	Cr.

The journal entry would be as follows:

Journal Entry:

Date	Accounts	Post Ref.	Dr.	Cr.
c.	Supplies (Asset, ↑; debit)	131	800	
	Cash (Asset, ↓; credit)	111		800
	Purchased supplies for cash.			

We enter $800 on the debit (left) side of the Supplies T-account and $800 on the credit (right) side of the Cash T-account.

Cash		111		Supplies		131
(a)	10,000			(c)	800	
	(c)	800				

Notice the $10,000 already on the debit side of the Cash account from transaction **a**.

d. Provided $2,600 of services to a customer on account.

The business received promises from customers to send cash ($2,600) next month in exchange for services rendered. So the accounts involved in the transaction are Accounts Receivable and Service Revenue.

Accounts Receivable is an asset and Service Revenue is revenue. Accounts Receivable (an asset) increased. Service Revenue (revenue) also increased.

Looking at Exhibit 2-2 (p. 62), we see that an increase in assets is a debit, while an increase in revenue is a credit.

So Accounts Receivable (an asset) increases, which is a debit. Service Revenue (revenue) increases, which is a credit.

1 Accounts Affected	2 Type	3 ↑↓	4 Dr. or Cr.
Accounts Receivable	Asset	↑	Dr.
Service Revenue	Revenue	↑	Cr.

The journal entry is as follows:

Journal Entry:

Date	Accounts	Post Ref.	Dr.	Cr.
d.	Accounts Receivable (Asset, ↑ ; debit)	121	2,600	
	Service Revenue (Revenue, ↑ ; credit)	411		2,600
	Provided services on credit.			

We enter $2,600 on the debit (left) side of the Accounts Receivable T-account and $2,600 on the credit (right) side of the Service Revenue T-account.

Accounts Receivable	121		Service Revenue	411
(d) 2,600			(d)	2,600

e. Paid $500 cash toward the equipment previously purchased on account in transaction b.

The business paid *some* of the money that was owed on the purchase of equipment in transaction **b**. The accounts involved in the transaction are Accounts Payable and Cash.

Accounts Payable is a liability, and Cash is an asset. Accounts Payable (a liability) decreased. Cash (an asset) also decreased.

Remember, the Accounts Payable account is the total amount owed to creditors to which the business will have to make payments in the future (a liability). When the business makes these payments to the creditors, the amount of this account decreases, because the business now owes less (in this case, it reduces from $3,500—in transaction **b**—to $3,000).

Looking at Exhibit 2-2 (p. 62), we see that a decrease in liabilities is a debit, while a decrease in assets is a credit.

So Accounts Payable (a liability) decreases, which is a debit. Cash (an asset) decreases, which is a credit.

1 Accounts Affected	2 Type	3 ↑↓	4 Dr. or Cr.
Accounts Payable	Liability	↓	Dr.
Cash	Asset	↓	Cr.

The journal entry is as follows:

Journal Entry:

Date	Accounts	Post Ref.	Dr.	Cr.
e.	Accounts Payable (Liability, ↓; debit)	211	500	
	Cash (Asset, ↓; credit)	111		500
	Made partial payment on Accounts Payable.			

We enter $500 on the debit (left) side of the Accounts Payable T-account and $500 on the credit (right) side of the Cash T-account.

	Cash		111			Accounts Payable		211
(a)	10,000						(b)	3,500
		(c)	800	(e)	500			
		(e)	500					

f. Received $2,000 in cash for services provided to a new customer.

The business received cash ($2,000) in exchange for mowing and landscaping services rendered to a client. The accounts involved in the transaction are Cash and Service Revenue.

Cash is an asset, and Service Revenue is revenue. Cash (an asset) increased. Service Revenue (revenue) also increased.

Looking at Exhibit 2-2 (p. 62), we see that an increase in assets is a debit, while an increase in revenue is a credit.

So Cash (an asset) increases, which is a debit. Service Revenue (revenue) increases, which is a credit.

1 Accounts Affected	2 Type	3 ↑↓	4 Dr. or Cr.
Cash	Asset	↑	Dr.
Service Revenue	Revenue	↑	Cr.

The journal entry is as follows:

Journal Entry:

Date	Accounts	Post Ref.	Dr.	Cr.
f.	Cash (Asset, ↑; debit)	111	2,000	
	Service Revenue (Revenue, ↑; credit)	411		2,000
	Provided services for cash.			

We enter $2,000 on the debit (left) side of the Cash T-account and $2,000 on the credit (right) side of the Service Revenue T-account.

	Cash	111		Service Revenue	411
(a)	10,000			(d)	2,600
	(c)	800		(f)	2,000
	(e)	500			
(f)	2,000				

Notice how we keep adding onto the T-accounts. The values from previous transactions are already in place.

g. Paid $200 cash to repair equipment.

The business paid $200 cash to repair equipment. Because the benefit of the repairs has already been used, the repairs are recorded as Repairs Expense. Because the repairs were paid in cash, the Cash account is also involved.

Repairs Expense is an expense and Cash is an asset. Repairs Expense (an expense) increased. Cash (an asset) decreased.

Looking at Exhibit 2-2 (p. 62), we see that an increase in expenses is a debit, while a decrease in an asset is a credit.

So Repairs Expense (an expense) increases, which is a debit. Cash (an asset) decreases, which is a credit.

1 Accounts Affected	2 Type	3 ↑↓	4 Dr. or Cr.
Repairs Expense	Expense	↑	Dr.
Cash	Asset	↓	Cr.

The journal entry is as follows:

Journal Entry:

Date	Accounts	Post Ref.	Dr.	Cr.
g.	Repairs Expense (Expense, ↑; debit)	521	200	
	Cash (Asset, ↓; credit)	111		200
	Made payment for repairs.			

We enter $200 on the debit (left) side of the Repairs Expense T-account and $200 on the credit (right) side of the Cash T-account.

	Cash		111			Repairs Expense		521
(a)	10,000				(g)	200		
		(c)	800					
		(e)	500					
(f)	2,000							
		(g)	200					

h. Paid $900 cash in salary expense.

The business paid employees $900 in cash. Because the benefit of the employee's work has already been used, the salary is recorded as Salary Expense. Because the salary was paid in cash, the Cash account is also involved.

Salary Expense is an expense, and Cash is an asset. Salary Expense (an expense) increased. Cash (an asset) decreased.

Looking at Exhibit 2-2 (p. 62), an increase in expenses is a debit, while a decrease in an asset is a credit.

So Salary Expense (an expense) increases, which is a debit. Cash (an asset) decreases, which is a credit.

1 Accounts Affected	2 Type	3 ↑↓	4 Dr. or Cr.
Salary Expense	Expense	↑	Dr.
Cash	Asset	↓	Cr.

The journal entry is as follows:

Journal Entry:

Date	Accounts	Post Ref.	Dr.	Cr.
h.	Salary Expense (Expense, ↑; debit)	511	900	
	Cash (Asset, ↓; credit)	111		900
	Made payment of salary using cash.			

We enter $900 on the debit (left) side of the Salary Expense T-account and $900 on the credit (right) side of the Cash T-account.

	Cash		111			Salary Expense		511
(a)	10,000				(h)	900		
		(c)	800					
		(e)	500					
(f)	2,000							
		(g)	200					
		(h)	900					

i. Received $2,100 cash from customers on account.

The business received payments ($2,100) from customers for services previously provided in transaction **d**. The accounts involved in this transaction are Cash and Accounts Receivable.

Cash and Accounts Receivable are both assets. Cash (an asset) increased. Accounts Receivable (an asset) decreased.

Remember, accounts receivable is the total amount due from customers from which the business will receive money. When the business receives these payments from its customers, the amount of this account decreases, because the business now has less to receive in the future (in this case, it reduces from $2,600—in transaction **d**—to $500).

Looking at Exhibit 2-2 (pg. 62), we see that an increase in assets is a debit, while a decrease in assets is a credit.

So Cash (an asset) increases, which is a debit. Accounts Receivable (an asset) decreases, which is a credit.

1 Accounts Affected	2 Type	3 ↑↓	4 Dr. or Cr.
Cash	Asset	↑	Dr.
Accounts Receivable	Asset	↓	Cr.

The journal entry is as follows:

Journal Entry:

Date	Accounts	Post Ref.	Dr.	Cr.
i.	Cash (Asset, ↑ ; debit)	111	2,100	
	Accounts Receivable (Asset, ↓ ; credit)	121		2,100
	Received payment from customers on account.			

We enter $2,100 on the debit (left) side of the Cash T-account and $2,100 on the credit (right) side of the Accounts Receivable account.

	Cash		111			Accounts Receivable		121
(a)	10,000				(d)	2,600		
		(c)	800				(i)	2,100
		(e)	500					
(f)	2,000							
		(g)	200					
		(h)	900					
(i)	2,100							

j. Michael withdrew $1,500 cash from the business for personal use.

Michael (the owner of the business) withdrew cash from the business. The business paid cash to Michael, whose ownership interest (equity) decreased. The accounts involved in the transaction are Michael Moe, Withdrawals, and Cash.

Michael Moe, Withdrawals, is a withdrawal, and Cash is an asset. Michael Moe, Withdrawals (withdrawal) increased. Cash (an asset) decreased.

Looking at Exhibit 2-2 (p. 62), we see that an increase in withdrawals is a debit, while a decrease in an asset is a credit.

So Michael Moe, Withdrawals (withdrawal) increases, which is a debit. Cash (an asset) decreases, which is a credit.

1 Accounts Affected	2 Type	3 ↑↓	4 Dr. or Cr.
Michael Moe, Withdrawals	Withdrawal	↑	Dr.
Cash	Asset	↓	Cr.

Journal Entry:

Date	Accounts	Post Ref.	Dr.	Cr.
j.	Michael Moe, Withdrawals (Withdrawal, ↑ ; debit)	312	1,500	
	Cash (Asset, ↓ ; credit)	111		1,500
	Cash withdrawal by owner.			

We enter $1,500 on the debit (left) side of the Michael Moe, Withdrawals, T-account and $1,500 on the credit (right) side of the Cash account.

	Cash		111			Michael Moe, Withdrawals	312
(a)	10,000				(j)	1,500	
		(c)	800				
		(e)	500				
(f)	2,000						
		(g)	200				
		(h)	900				
(i)	2,100						
		(j)	1,500				

Now we will summarize the journal entries for the month:

Journal Entry:

Date	Accounts	Post Ref.	Dr.	Cr.
a.	Cash		10,000	
	Michael Moe, Capital			10,000
	Received investment from owner.			

Journal Entry:

Date	Accounts	Post Ref.	Dr.	Cr.
b.	Equipment		3,500	
	Accounts Payable			3,500
	Purchased equipment on account.			
c.	Supplies		800	
	Cash			800
	Purchased supplies for cash.			
d.	Accounts Receivable		2,600	
	Service Revenue			2,600
	Provided services on credit.			
e.	Accounts Payable		500	
	Cash			500
	Made partial payment on Accounts Payable.			
f.	Cash		2,000	
	Service Revenue			2,000
	Provided services for cash.			
g.	Repairs Expense		200	
	Cash			200
	Made payment for repairs.			
h.	Salary Expense		900	
	Cash			900
	Made payment of salary using cash.			
i.	Cash		2,100	
	Accounts Receivable			2,100
	Received payment from customers on account.			
j.	Michael Moe, Withdrawals		1,500	
	Cash			1,500
	Cash withdrawal by owner.			

Requirement 3

Total all the T-accounts to determine their balances at the end of the month.

3 Record and summarize business transactions.

Part 1	Part 2	**Part 3**	Demo Doc Complete

To compute the balance in a T-account (total the T-account), add up the numbers on the debit/left side of the account and (separately) the credit/right side of the account. Subtract the smaller number from the bigger number and put the difference on the side of the bigger number. This procedure gives the balance in the T-account (the net total of both sides combined).

For example, for the Cash account, the numbers on the left side total $10,000 + $2,000 + $2,100 = $14,100. The credit/right side = $800 + $500 + $200 + $900 + $1,500 = $3,900. The difference is $14,100 − $3,900 = $10,200. We put the $10,200 on the debit side because it is the side of the bigger number of $14,100.

Another way to think of adding up (totaling) T-accounts is the following:

$$
\begin{array}{rl}
& \text{Beginning Balance in T-Account} \\
+ & \text{Increases to T-Account} \\
- & \text{Decreases to T-Account} \\
\hline
= & \text{Ending Balance in T-Account (total)}
\end{array}
$$

The T-accounts should look like the following after posting all transactions and totaling each account:

ASSETS   =   **LIABILITIES**   +   **OWNER'S EQUITY**

Cash			111
(a)	10,000		
		(c)	800
		(e)	500
(f)	2,000		
		(g)	200
		(h)	900
(i)	2,100		
		(j)	1,500
Bal.	10,200		

Accounts Receivable			121
(d)	2,600		
		(i)	2,100
Bal.	500		

Supplies			131
(c)	800		
Bal.	800		

Equipment			141
(b)	3,500		
Bal.	3,500		

Accounts Payable			211
		(b)	3,500
(e)	500		
		Bal.	3,000

Michael Moe, Capital			311
		(a)	10,000
		Bal.	10,000

Michael Moe, Withdrawals			312
(j)	1,500		
Bal.	1,500		

Service Revenue			411
		(d)	2,600
		(f)	2,000
		Bal.	4,600

Salary Expense			511
(h)	900		
Bal.	900		

Repairs Expense			521
(g)	200		
Bal.	200		

Part 1	Part 2	Part 3	Demo Doc Complete

Accounting in Action

RECORDING BUSINESS TRANSACTIONS

Here are some decisions that you would make as you record and summarize transactions in your business:

Decision	Guidelines
• Has a transaction occurred?	*Yes,* if the event is an exchange that has a measurable impact on the entity's financial position
	No, if the event is not an exchange or does not affect the entity's financial position
• How do I keep track of transactions?	In the *journal,* the chronological record of transactions
• How do I record each transaction?	By recording *increases and / or decreases* in all the accounts affected by the transaction
• How do I record increases/decreases?	*Rules of debits and credits:*

Account Type	Increase (also Normal Balance)	Decrease
Asset	Debit	Credit
Liability	Credit	Debit
Owner's Capital	Credit	Debit
Owner's Withdrawals	Debit	Credit
Revenue	Credit	Debit
Expense	Debit	Credit

• How do I know the amount of assets, liabilities, or owner's equity in the business at any point in time?	In the *ledger,* the record holding the accounts and their balances after increases and/or decreases have been recorded
• How do I know if my accounts balance?	By preparing the *trial balance*
• Where do I report the results of operations?	In the *income statement:*

       Revenues − Expenses = Net Income or Net Loss

• Where do I report the ownership interest?   In the *statement of owner's equity:*

       Beginning Owner's Equity

       + Owner Investments

       + Net Income or − Net Loss

       − Owner Withdrawals

       = Ending Owner's Equity

• Where do I report the financial position at a point in time?   In the *balance sheet:*

       Assets = Liabilities + Owner's Equity

Review

Recording Business Transactions
Word Power

Account The basic summary device of accounting; the detailed record of all the changes in a particular asset, liability, or owner's equity as a result of transactions.

Balance The difference between an account's total debit and total credit amounts; the ending value of an account.

Chart of accounts A list of all the accounts of a business and the numbers assigned to those accounts.

Credit The right side of any account; an entry made to the right side of an account.

Debit The left side of any account; an entry made to the left side of an account.

Double-entry accounting The rule of accounting that specifies, because transactions are measurable exchanges, every transaction involves at least two accounts and will thus be recorded with equal amounts of debits and credits.

Journal The chronological accounting record of the transactions of a business.

Journalize Enter a transaction in a journal. Also called *record*.

Ledger The accounting record summarizing, in accounts, the transactions of a business and showing the resulting account balances.

Normal balance The balance that appears on the side of an account where increases are recorded; the expected balance of an account.

Note receivable A written promise of future payment received by the business.

Posting Copying amounts from the journal to accounts in the ledger.

Posting reference A notation in the journal and ledger that links these two accounting records together.

Promissory note A written pledge to pay a fixed amount of money at a later date.

Record Enter a transaction in a journal. Also called *journalize*.

T-account An informal account form used to summarize transactions, where the top of the T holds the account title and the base divides the debit and credit sides of the account.

Transactions The economic events, or exchanges, that have a measurable impact on the financial position of a business.

Trial balance A list of all the accounts of a business and their balances in balance sheet order; its purpose is to verify that total debits equal total credits.

Quick Check

1. Which sequence of actions correctly summarizes the accounting process?

   a. Prepare a trial balance, journalize transactions, post to the accounts.
   b. Post to the accounts, journalize transactions, prepare a trial balance.
   c. Journalize transactions, post to the accounts, prepare a trial balance.
   d. Journalize transactions, prepare a trial balance, post to the accounts.

2. The left side of an account is used to record

   a. Debits
   b. Credits
   c. Debits or credits, depending on the type of account
   d. Increases

3. Suppose Toni's T-Shirt Shop has cash of $50,000, receivables of $60,000, and furniture and fixtures totaling $200,000. The shop owes $80,000 on account and has a $100,000 note payable. How much is the shop's owner's equity?

   a. $20,000
   b. $310,000
   c. $180,000
   d. $130,000

4. Toni's T-Shirt Shop purchased supplies of $1,000 on account. The journal entry to record this transaction is:

Journal Entry:

Date	Accounts	Post Ref.	Dr.	Cr.
a.	Inventory		1,000	
	Accounts Payable			1,000
b.	Accounts Payable		1,000	
	Supplies			1,000
c.	Supplies		1,000	
	Accounts Payable			1,000
d.	Supplies		1,000	
	Accounts Receivable			1,000

5. Posting a $1,000 purchase of supplies on account appears as follows:

a.

Supplies	Accounts Receivable
1,000	1,000

c.

Supplies	Accounts Payable
1,000	1,000

b.

Supplies	Accounts Payable
1,000	1,000

d.

Cash	Supplies
1,000	1,000

6. Which journal entry records Toni's obtaining a bank loan of $11,000?

Journal Entry:

Date	Accounts	Post Ref.	Dr.	Cr.
a.	Notes Payable		11,000	
	Accounts Receivable			11,000
b.	Notes Payable		11,000	
	Cash			11,000
c.	Cash		11,000	
	Notes Payable			11,000
d.	Cash		11,000	
	Accounts Payable			11,000

7. Lisa's Tax Service paid $500 for supplies and purchased additional supplies on account for $700. Lisa's Tax Service also paid $300 of the accounts payable. What is the balance in the Supplies account?

a. $500
b. $900
c. $1,200
d. $1,500

8. Quick Copies recorded a cash collection on account by debiting Cash and crediting Accounts Payable. What will the trial balance show for this error?

a. Too much for liabilities
b. Too much for assets
c. The trial balance will not balance
d. Both a and b

9. Ray Gomez, an attorney, had a law business that began the year with total assets of $120,000, total liabilities of $70,000, and owner's equity of $50,000. During the year the business earned revenue of $110,000 and paid expenses of $30,000. Ray also invested an additional $20,000 in the business and withdrew $60,000 for living expenses. How much is the owner's equity in the business at year-end?

a. $90,000
b. $120,000
c. $130,000
d. $160,000

10. How would Ray Gomez record his expenses for the year in the preceding question?

Journal Entry:

Date	Accounts	Post Ref.	Dr.	Cr.
a.	Expenses		30,000	
	Cash			30,000
b.	Expenses		30,000	
	Accounts Payable			30,000
c.	Cash		30,000	
	Expenses			30,000
d.	Accounts Payable		30,000	
	Cash			30,000

Answers are given after Apply Your Knowledge (p. 123).

Accounting Practice

Short Exercises

① The role of accounts.

S2-1. Match the accounting terms at the left with the corresponding definitions at the right.

____ 1. Account a. Any economic event that has a financial impact on the business

____ 2. Assets b. The detailed record of the changes in a particular asset, liability, or owner's equity

____ 3. Owner's equity c. Economic resources that provide a future benefit for a business

____ 4. Expenses d. Debts or obligations of a business

____ 5. Liabilities e. Owner's claim to the assets of a business

____ 6. Revenues f. Increases in owner's equity from selling goods or services to customers

____ 7. Transactions g. Decreases in owner's equity from using resources to sell goods or services

① The role of accounts.

S2-2. For each of the following accounts, place the corresponding letter(s) of its account type in the space provided.

(A) Asset (L) Liability (OE) Owner's Equity (R) Revenue (E) Expense

 OE John Ebbs, Withdrawals

____ 1. Accounts Payable

____ 2. Cash

____ 3. Fee Revenue

____ 4. Prepaid Rent

____ 5. Rent Expense

____ 6. John Ebbs, Capital

③ Recording and summarizing transactions.

S2-3. The following list names the activities involved in the accounting process of recording and summarizing business transactions. Place the activities in the order they occur, starting with 1.

 1 Transaction occurs.

____ Record the transaction in the journal.

____ Prepare the trial balance.

continued.....

_____ Post the transaction from the journal to the accounts.

_____ Prepare the financial statements.

S2-4. For each of the following accounts, indicate the account type by labeling it as an asset (A), liability (L), owner's equity (OE), revenue (R), or expense (E). Also give the digit each account number would begin with in the chart of accounts.

① The role of accounts.

_A,1_ Land

_____ 1. Service Revenue

_____ 2. R. Peters, Withdrawals

_____ 3. Accounts Receivable

_____ 4. Salary Expense

_____ 5. Notes Payable

_____ 6. R. Peters, Capital

_____ 7. Rent Expense

S2-5. Demonstrate your knowledge of accounting terminology by filling in the blanks to review some key definitions.

② Double-entry accounting.

④ Using a trial balance for preparing financial statements.

Lynn Bratton is describing the accounting process for a friend who is a philosophy major. Lynn states, "The basic summary device in accounting is the _____. The left side of an account is called the _____ side, and the right side is called the _____ side. We record transactions first in a _____. Then we post, or copy, the data to the _____. It is helpful to list all the accounts with their balances on a _____ _____."

S2-6. For each of the following accounts, indicate if the account's normal balance is a debit balance (DR) or a credit balance (CR).

② Double-entry accounting.

_DR_ Cash

_____ 1. Rent Expense

_____ 2. Accounts Payable

_____ 3. Service Revenue

_____ 4. Office Furniture

continued.....

_____ 5. J. Byrd, Capital

_____ 6. Land

_____ 7. J. Byrd, Withdrawals

③ Recording and sum-
marizing transactions.

S2-7. Calculate each account balance.

Cash			110		S. Roman, Capital		311
8/9	4,000	9/8	500			4/5	10,000
10/14	8,000					6/10	4,000
						7/5	2,000

② Double-entry
accounting.

③ Recording and summa-
rizing transactions.

S2-8. Complete the following table. For each account listed, identify the type of account, how the account is increased (debit or credit), and how the account is decreased (debit or credit).

Account	Type	↑	↓
Office Equipment	Asset	Dr.	Cr.
G. Day, Withdrawals			
Service Revenue			
Accounts Payable			
Rent Expense			
Cash			

③ Recording and summa-
rizing transactions.

S2-9. Nolan Tarkington opened a medical practice in San Diego. The following transactions took place in September:

Sept. 1	Tarkington invested $30,000 cash in a business bank account to start his medical practice.
2	Purchased medical supplies on account, $10,000.
2	Paid monthly office rent of $4,000.
3	Provided $5,000 of medical services to patients. Received cash of $2,000 for these services and sent bills to patients for the remainder.

Using the steps outlined in the five-step transaction analysis, record the transactions in the journal.

continued.....

Journal Entry:

Date	Accounts	Post Ref.	Dr.	Cr.
Sept. 1	Cash		30,000	
	Nolan Tarkington, Capital			30,000
	Received investment from owner.			

S2-10. After operating for a month, Nolan Tarkington's medical practice completed the following transactions during the latter part of October:

③ Recording and summarizing transactions.

Oct. 15	The business borrowed $50,000 from the bank, signing a note payable.
22	Performed service for patients on account, $3,600.
30	Received cash on account from patients, $2,000.
31	Received a utility bill, $200, which will be paid during November.
31	Paid the monthly salary to its nurse, $3,000.
31	Paid interest expense of $200 on the bank loan.

Using the steps outlined in the five-step transaction analysis, record the transactions in the journal.

Journal Entry:

Date	Accounts	Post Ref.	Dr.	Cr.
Oct. 15	Cash		50,000	
	Notes Payable			50,000
	Borrowed money from the bank and signed			
	a promissory note.			

S2-11. The accounting records for Airborne Services contain the following amounts on December 31, 2009. The accounts appear in no particular order and dollar amounts are in millions.

④ Using a trial balance for preparing financial statements.

Revenues	$29	Other Liabilities	$19
Other Assets	40	Cash	12
Accounts Payable	1	Expenses	22
Capital	25		

Prepare the trial balance for Airborne Services at December 31, 2009. List the accounts in proper order.

4 Using a trial balance for preparing financial statements.

S2-12. To the left of each account listed on the trial balance, indicate the financial statement that will include the account: income statement (IS), statement of owner's equity (OE), or balance sheet (BS).

EARTH CONNECT
Trial Balance
October 31, 2009

			Balance	
	Account Title		Debit	Credit
	Cash		$2,500	
	Accounts receivable		300	
	Supplies		100	
	Office equipment		1,000	
	Accounts payable			$ 90
	Z. Mann, capital			2,810
	Z. Mann, withdrawals		1,200	
	Fee revenue			5,500
	Advertising expense		750	
	Rent expense		800	
	Salary expense		1,500	
	Utilities expense		250	
	Total		$8,400	$8,400

4 Using a trial balance for preparing financial statements.

S2-13. The total debits do not equal the total credits for Luna's Personal Training. Pita Luna realized she made an error by recording her withdrawal as $600 instead of the correct amount of $100. She also made another error but she needs your help to find it.

LUNA'S PERSONAL TRAINING
Trial Balance
April 30, 2009

			Balance	
	Account Title		Debit	Credit
	Assets		$3,000	
	Liabilities			$1,000
	P. Luna, capital			2,100
	P. Luna, withdrawals			600
	Total		$3,000	$3,700

Find the second error and prepare a new, correct trial balance.

S2-14. Accounting has its own vocabulary and basic relationships. Match the accounting terms at the left with the corresponding phrase at the right.

① The role of accounts.

② Double-entry accounting.

_____1. Posting   a. Chronological record of transactions

_____2. Normal balance   b. An asset

_____3. Payable   c. Left side of an account

_____4. Journal   d. Side of an account where increases are recorded

_____5. Receivable   e. Copying data from the journal to the ledger

_____6. Capital   f. Resources used while operating a business

_____7. Debit   g. A liability

_____8. Expense   h. Grouping of accounts

_____9. Ledger   i. Owner's equity in the business

Exercises

E2-15. Review basic accounting definitions by completing the following crossword puzzle.

① The role of accounts.

② Double-entry accounting.

Down:

1. Left side of an account
4. Record holding the grouping of accounts
5. An economic resource
7. Record of transactions

Across:

2. Records an increase in a liability
3. List of accounts with their balances
6. Another word for liability

E2-16. Dirk Woods House Repair began operations on March 1, 2009. The seven transactions recorded during March by Hilda, the accountant, are shown in the following T-accounts.

Cash			111
(1)	15,000	(2)	3,000
		(5)	250
		(6)	2,300
		(7)	1,000
Bal.	8,450		

Accounts Receivable		112
(4)	4,500	
Bal.	4,500	

Supplies		113
(3)	600	
Bal.	600	

Equipment		114
(2)	3,000	
Bal.	3,000	

Accounts Payable			211
(5)	250	(3)	600
		Bal.	350

Dirk Woods, Capital			311
		(1)	15,000
		Bal.	15,000

Dirk Woods, Withdrawals		312
(7)	1,000	
Bal.	1,000	

Service Revenue			411
		(4)	4,500
		Bal.	4,500

Operating Expenses		511–524
(6)	2,300	
Bal.	2,300	

Complete the following table. For each transaction shown, determine the accounts affected, the type of account, whether the account increases or decreases, and whether it would be recorded in the journal on the debit or credit side. Transaction (1) is an example.

Transaction	Accounts Affected	Type	↑↓	Dr. or Cr.
(1)	Cash	Asset	Increase	Dr.
	Dirk Woods, Capital	Capital	Increase	Cr.

E2-17. Using the steps outlined in the five-step transaction analysis, prepare the seven journal entries from the postings made to the T-accounts in E2-16 for Dirk Woods House Repair. Explanations for each transaction are not required.

E2-18. Using the steps outlined in the five-step transaction analysis, record the following transactions in the journal for Elkins Enterprises. Explanations are not required. Follow the pattern given for the December 1 transaction.

Journal Entry:

Date	Accounts	Post Ref.	Dr.	Cr.
Dec. 1	Interest Expense		500	
	Cash			500

continued.....

Dec. 1	Paid interest expense, $500.
5	Purchased office furniture on account, $800.
10	Performed service on account for a customer, $1,600.
12	Borrowed $7,000 cash, signing a note payable.
19	Sold for $29,000 land that had cost the company $29,000.
21	Purchased building for $140,000; signed a note payable.
27	Paid the liability from December 5.

E2-19. The following T-accounts have been opened, or set up, for Elkins Enterprise.

③ Recording and summarizing transactions.

④ Using a trial balance for preparing financial statements.

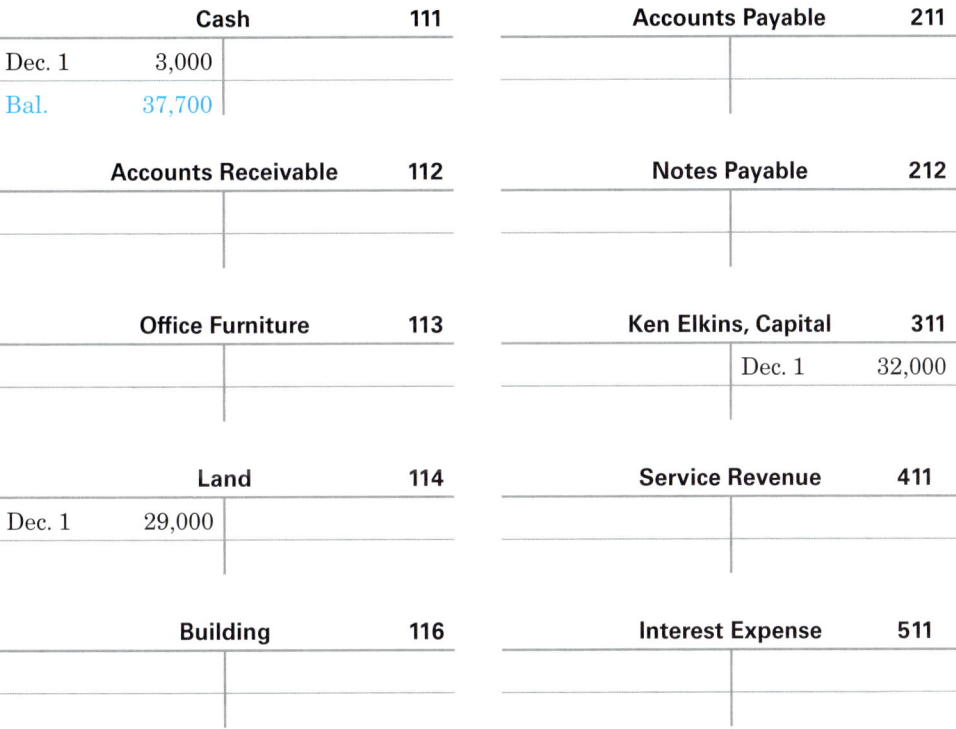

	Cash	111
Dec. 1	3,000	
Bal.	37,700	

Accounts Payable	211

Accounts Receivable	112

Notes Payable	212

Office Furniture	113

Ken Elkins, Capital	311
Dec. 1	32,000

	Land	114
Dec. 1	29,000	

Service Revenue	411

Building	116

Interest Expense	511

Requirements

1. Post the journal entries recorded for Elkins Enterprise in E2-18 to the appropriate T-accounts. Identify all items by date. Formal posting references are not required.

2. Calculate the balance of each account at December 31, 2009. Beginning balances are already in the accounts. Use the formula for calculating the ending balance of an account (page 76), or calculate each account's total debits and total credits and write the difference between the two on the side with the larger total.

3. Prove that the total of all the debit balances equals the total of all of the credit balances by preparing a trial balance.

3 Recording and sum-
marizing transactions.

E2-20. Ponderosa Landscaping completed the following transactions during March 2009, its first month of operations:

Mar. 1	Ray Pines invested $70,000 of cash to start the business.
2	Purchased supplies on account, $200.
4	Paid cash for a building to use for storage, $60,000.
6	Performed service for customers and received cash, $3,000.
9	Paid on accounts payable, $100.
17	Performed service for customers on account, $1,600.
23	Received cash from a customer on account, $1,200.
31	Paid the following expenses: salary, $1,200, and rent, $500.

Using the steps outlined in the five-step transaction analysis, record the transactions of Ponderosa Landscaping. List transactions by date. Use the following accounts: Cash; Accounts Receivable; Supplies; Building; Accounts Payable; Ray Pines, Capital; Service Revenue; Salary Expense; Rent Expense.

3 Recording and summa-
rizing transactions.

E2-21. The March transactions for Ponderosa Landscaping from E2-20 are posted in the following T-accounts.

	Cash		111
Mar. 1	70,000	Mar. 4	60,000
6	3,000	9	100
23	1,200	31	1,700
Bal.			

	Accounts Receivable		112
Mar. 17	1,600	Mar. 23	1,200
Bal.			

	Supplies		113
Mar. 2	200		
Bal.			

	Building		114
Mar. 4	60,000		
Bal.			

	Accounts Payable		211
Mar. 9	100	Mar. 2	200
		Bal.	

	Ray Pines, Capital		311
		Mar. 1	70,000
		Bal.	

	Service Revenue		411
		Mar. 6	3,000
		17	1,600
		Bal.	

	Salary Expense		501
Mar. 31	1,200		
Bal.			

	Rent Expense		502
Mar. 31	500		
Bal.			

Requirements

4 Using a trial balance
for preparing financial
statements.
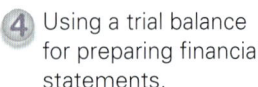

1. Calculate account balances. Use the formula for calculating the ending balance of an account (page 42), or calculate each account's total debits and total credits and write the difference between the two on the side with the larger total.

2. Prepare the trial balance for Ponderosa Landscaping at March 31, 2009.

E2-22. The first five October transactions for Agetro, a styling salon, have been posted to the accounts as follows:

③ Recording and summarizing transactions.

Cash					Supplies			Equipment			Building	
(1)	22,000	(3)	40,000	(2)	400		(5)	6,000		(3)	40,000	
(4)	37,000	(5)	6,000									

Accounts Payable			Notes Payable			Liz Agetro, Capital	
	(2)	400		(4)	37,000	(1)	22,000

Requirements

④ Using a trial balance for preparing financial statements.

1. Prepare the journal entries that served as the sources for the five transactions.

2. Calculate the balance in each account. Use the formula for calculating the ending balance of an account (page 76), or calculate each account's total debits and total credits and write the difference between the two on the side with the larger total.

3. Prepare the trial balance for Agetro at October 31, 2009.

4. Prepare a balance sheet for Agetro as of October 31, 2009.

E2-23. Rita Bebe, Consultant, completed these transactions during the first half of December:

③ Recording and summarizing transactions.

④ Using a trial balance for preparing financial statements.

Dec. 2	Invested $14,000 to start a consulting practice titled Rita Bebe, Consultant.
2	Paid monthly office rent, $500.
3	Paid cash for a Dell computer, $2,000. The computer is expected to remain in service for 5 years.
4	Purchased office furniture on account, $3,600. The furniture should last for 5 years.
5	Purchased supplies on account, $300.
9	Performed consulting service for a client on account, $1,700.
12	Paid utility expenses, $200.
18	Performed service for a client and received cash for the full amount of $800.

Requirements

1. Open, or set up, T-accounts in the ledger: Cash, 111; Accounts Receivable, 112; Supplies, 113; Equipment, 114; Furniture, 115; Accounts Payable, 211; Rita Bebe, Capital, 311; Service Revenue, 411; Rent Expense, 510; Utilities Expense, 520.

continued.....

2. Record transactions in the journal. Explanations are not required.

3. Post them to the T-accounts. Identify all items by date. Formal posting references are not required.

4. Calculate the balance in each account. Use the formula for calculating the ending balance of an account (page 76), or calculate each account's total debits and total credits and write the difference between the two on the side with the larger total.

5. Prepare a trial balance at December 31, 2009. No transactions occurred between December 18 and December 31 because the owner closed the business and took a two-week vacation.

4 Using a trial balance for preparing financial statements.

E2-24. Petras Gorav has trouble keeping his debits and credits equal. During a recent month, Petras made the following errors:

a. In journalizing a receipt of cash for service revenue, Petras debited Cash for $80 instead of the correct amount of $800. Petras also credited Service Revenue for $80, the incorrect amount.

b. Petras recorded a $120 purchase of supplies on account by debiting Supplies and crediting Accounts Payable for $210.

c. In preparing the trial balance, Petras omitted a $50,000 note payable.

d. Petras posted a $700 utility expense as $70. The credit posting to Cash was correct.

e. In recording a $400 payment on account, Petras debited Supplies and credited Accounts Payable.

Requirements

1. For each of these errors, state whether Petras's mistake would cause the total debits and total credits on the trial balance to be unequal.

2. Identify each account with an incorrect balance, and indicate the amount and direction of the error

Use the following format.

Effect on Trial Balance	Account(s) Misstated
a. Total debits = Total credits	Cash
	$720 too low
	Service Revenue
	$720 too low

Problems (Group A)

P2-25A. John Ortiz practices medicine under the business title John Ortiz, M.D. During June, his medical practice engaged in the following transactions:

Recording and sum-marizing transactions.

June 1	Ortiz deposited $55,000 cash in the business bank account. The business gave Ortiz owner's equity in the firm.
5	Paid monthly rent on medical equipment, $700.
9	Paid $22,000 cash to purchase land for an office site.
10	Purchased supplies on account, $1,200.
19	Borrowed $20,000 from the bank. Ortiz signed a note payable to the bank in the name of the business.
22	Paid $1,000 on account.
30	Revenues earned during the month included $6,000 cash and $5,000 on account.
30	Paid employees' salaries, $2,400; office rent, $1,500; and utilities, $400.
30	Withdrew $10,000 from the business for personal use.

Ortiz's business uses the following accounts: Cash; Accounts Receivable; Supplies; Land; Accounts Payable; Notes Payable; John Ortiz, Capital; John Ortiz, Withdrawals; Service Revenue; Salary Expense; Rent Expense; Utilities Expense.

Requirements

Journalize each transaction, as shown for June 1.

Journal Entry:

Date	Accounts	Post Ref.	Dr.	Cr.
June 1	Cash		55,000	
	John Ortiz, Capital			55,000
	Received investment from owner.			

P2-26A. Josh Groben opened a law office on December 2 of the current year. During the first month of operations, the business completed the following transactions:

Recording and sum-marizing transactions.

Using a trial balance for preparing financial statements.

Dec. 2	Groben deposited $30,000 cash in the business bank account, Josh Groben, Attorney.
3	Purchased supplies, $500, and furniture, $2,600, on account.
4	Performed legal service for a client and received cash, $1,500.
7	Paid cash to acquire land for a future office site, $22,000.
11	Prepared legal documents for a client on account, $900.

continued.....

Recording Business Transactions **113**

15	Paid secretary's salary, $570.
16	Paid for the furniture purchased December 3 on account.
18	Received $1,800 cash for helping a client sell real estate.
19	Defended a client in court and billed the client for $800.
29	Received partial collection from client on account, $400.
31	Paid secretary's salary, $570.
31	Paid rent expense, $700.
31	Withdrew $2,200 for personal use.

Requirements

1. Open, or set up, the following T-accounts: Cash; Accounts Receivable; Supplies; Furniture; Land; Accounts Payable; Josh Groben, Capital; Josh Groben, Withdrawals; Service Revenue; Salary Expense; Rent Expense.

2. Journalize transactions. Explanations are not required.

3. Post the transactions to the T-accounts, using transaction dates as posting references.

4. Calculate the balance in each account. Use the formula for calculating the ending balance of an account (page 76), or calculate each account's total debits and total credits and write the difference between the two on the side with the larger total.

5. Prepare the trial balance for Josh Groben, Attorney, at December 31 of the current year.

3 Recording and summarizing transactions.

4 Using a trial balance for preparing financial statements.

P2-27A. The trial balance for Robert Quiroga, Registered Dietician, at November 15, 2009, follows:

ROBERT QUIROGA, REGISTERED DIETICIAN
Trial Balance
November 15, 2009

Acct #	Account Title	Balance Debit	Balance Credit
11	Cash	$ 3,000	
12	Accounts receivable	8,000	
13	Supplies	600	
14	Equipment	15,000	
21	Accounts payable		$ 4,600
31	Robert Quiroga, capital		20,000
32	Robert Quiroga, withdrawals	2,300	
41	Service revenue		7,100
51	Salary expense	1,800	
52	Rent expense	1,000	
	Total	$31,700	$31,700

continued.....

During the remainder of November, Quiroga completed the following transactions:

Nov. 16	Collected $6,000 cash from a client on account.
17	Performed a nutritional analysis for a hospital on account, $1,700.
21	Used personal funds to pay for the renovation of private residence, $55,000.
22	Purchased supplies on account, $800.
23	Withdrew $2,100 for personal use.
23	Paid on account, $2,600.
24	Received $1,900 cash for consulting with Kraft Foods.
30	Paid rent, $700.
30	Paid employees' salaries, $2,100.

Requirements

1. Journalize the transactions that occurred November 16 to November 30 on page 6 of the journal.

2. Open the ledger accounts listed in the trial balance together with their beginning balances at November 15. Use the four-column account format illustrated in the chapter. Enter "Bal." for the previous balance in the Item column. Post the transactions to the ledger, using dates, account numbers, and posting references. Calculate the new account balances.

3. Prepare the trial balance for Robert Quiroga, Registered Dietician, at November 30, 2009.

P2-28A. The accounts of Sautter Graphics follow with their normal balances at December 31, 2009. The accounts are listed in no particular order.

④ Using a trial balance for preparing financial statements.

Account	Balance
P. Sautter, Capital	$ 48,800
Insurance Expense	700
Accounts Payable	4,300
Service Revenue	86,000
Land	29,000
Supplies Expense	300
Cash	5,000
Salary Expense	6,000
Building	125,000
Rent Expense	2,000
P. Sautter, Withdrawals	6,000
Utilities Expense	400

continued.....

Accounts Receivable	9,500
Notes Payable	45,000
Supplies	200

Requirements

1. Prepare the company's trial balance at December 31, 2009, listing accounts in the proper order. For example, Supplies comes before Building and Land. List the largest expense first, the second-largest expense next, and so on.

2. Prepare the financial statements: income statement, statement of owner's equity, and balance sheet. Assume no investments were made by the owner during the year.

4 Using a trial balance for preparing financial statements.

P2-29A. The trial balance for Online Cable Service does not balance. The following errors were detected:

a. The Cash balance is understated by $400.

b. Rent expense of $350 was erroneously posted as a credit rather than a debit.

c. An $8,300 credit to Service Revenue was not posted.

d. A $600 debit to Accounts Receivable was posted as $60.

e. The balance of Utilities Expense is understated by $60.

f. A $100 purchase of supplies on account was neither journalized nor posted.

g. Office Furniture should be listed in the amount of $21,300.

ONLINE CABLE SERVICE
Trial Balance
March 31, 2009

Account Title	Balance Debit	Balance Credit
Cash	$ 6,200	
Accounts receivable	2,000	
Supplies	500	
Office furniture	22,300	
Computers	46,000	
Accounts payable		$ 2,700
Notes payable		18,300
Meredith Ballard, capital		50,800
Meredith Ballard, withdrawals	5,000	
Service revenue		4,900
Salary expense	1,300	
Rent expense	500	
Advertising expense	300	
Utilities expense	200	
Total	$84,300	$76,700

continued.....

Requirements

1. Prepare the correct trial balance at March 31.

2. Prepare Online Cable Service's income statement for the month ended March 31, 2009, to determine whether the business had a net income or a net loss for the month.

Problems (Group B)

P2-30B. Mann Theaters owns movie theaters in the shopping centers of a major metropolitan area. It engaged in the following business transactions during April:

③ Recording and summarizing transactions.

April 1	Mann invested $500,000 personal cash in the business by depositing that amount in a bank account titled Mann Theaters. The business gave Mann owner's equity in the company.
2	Paid $400,000 cash to purchase a theater building.
5	Borrowed $220,000 from the bank. Mann signed a note payable to the bank in the name of Mann Theaters.
10	Purchased theater supplies on account, $1,700.
15	Paid $800 on account.
15	Paid property tax expense on theater building, $1,200.
16	Paid employee salaries, $2,800, and rent on equipment, $1,800.
17	Withdrew $6,000 from the business for personal use.
30	Received $20,000 cash from revenue and deposited that amount in the bank.

Mann Theaters uses the following accounts: Cash; Supplies; Building; Accounts Payable; Notes Payable; M. Mann, Capital; M. Mann, Withdrawals; Sales Revenue; Salary Expense; Rent Expense; Property Tax Expense.

Requirements

Journalize without explanation each transaction of Mann Theaters as shown for April 1.

Journal Entry:

Date	Accounts	Post Ref.	Dr.	Cr.
April 1	Cash		500,000	
	M. Mann, Capital			500,000

③ Recording and summarizing transactions.

④ Using a trial balance for preparing financial statements.

P2-31B. Emily Smith started her practice as a registered dietician on September 3 of the current year. During the first month of operations, the business completed the following transactions:

Sept. 3	Smith transferred $20,000 cash from her personal bank account to a business account titled Emily Smith, Registered Dietician. The business gave Smith owner's equity in the firm.
4	Purchased supplies, $200, and furniture, $1,800, on account.
6	Performed services for a hospital and received $4,000 cash.
7	Paid $15,000 cash to acquire land for a future office site.
10	Performed a nutritional analysis for a hotel and received its promise to pay the $800 within one week.
14	Paid for the furniture purchased September 4 on account.
15	Paid secretary's salary, $600.
17	Received partial collection from client on account, $500.
20	Prepared a nutrition plan for a school on account, $800.
28	Received $1,500 cash for consulting with Procter & Gamble.
30	Paid secretary's salary, $600.
30	Paid rent expense, $500.
30	Withdrew $2,900 for personal use.

Requirements

1. Open, or set up, the following T-accounts: Cash; Accounts Receivable; Supplies; Furniture; Land; Accounts Payable; Emily Smith, Capital; Emily Smith, Withdrawals; Service Revenue; Salary Expense; Rent Expense.

2. Record each transaction in the journal. Explanations are not required.

3. Post the transactions to the T-accounts, using transaction dates as posting references.

4. Calculate the balance in each account. Use the formula for calculating the ending balance of an account (page 76), or calculate each account's total debits and total credits and write the difference between the two on the side with the larger total.

5. Prepare the trial balance for Emily Smith, Registered Dietician, at September 30 of the current year.

P2-32B. The trial balance for Mark Power, CPA, is dated February 14, 2009:

3 Recording and summarizing transactions.

4 Using a trial balance for preparing financial statements.

MARK POWER, CPA
Trial Balance
February 14, 2009

Acct #	Account Title	Balance Debit	Credit
11	Cash	$ 2,000	
12	Accounts receivable	9,500	
13	Supplies	800	
14	Land	18,600	
21	Accounts payable		$ 3,000
31	Mark Power, capital		26,500
32	Mark Power, withdrawals	1,200	
41	Service revenue		7,200
51	Salary expense	3,600	
52	Rent expense	1,000	
	Total	$36,700	$36,700

During the remainder of February, Power completed the following transactions:

Feb. 15	Power collected $3,500 cash from a client on account.
16	Performed tax services for a client on account, $700.
20	Paid on account, $1,000.
21	Purchased supplies on account, $100.
21	Withdrew $1,200 for personal use.
21	Paid for a deck for private residence, using personal funds, $9,000.
22	Received cash of $5,500 for consulting work just completed.
28	Paid rent, $800.
28	Paid employees' salaries, $1,800.

Requirements

1. Record the transactions that occurred from February 15 to February 28 in page 3 of the journal.

2. Open the ledger accounts listed in the trial balance together with their balances at February 14. Use the four-column account format

continued.....

illustrated in the chapter. Enter "Bal." for the previous balance in the Item column. Post the transactions to the ledger, using dates, account numbers, and posting references. Calculate the new account balances.

3. Prepare the trial balance for Mark Power, CPA, at February 28, 2009.

④ Using a trial balance for preparing financial statements.

P2-33B. The accounts of Lenahan Graphics follow with their normal balances at December 31, 2009. The accounts are listed in no particular order.

Account	Balance
P. Lenahan, Capital.....................	$ 60,700
Insurance Expense.......................	600
Accounts Payable	3,300
Service Revenue	86,000
Land..	9,000
Supplies Expense	300
Cash	5,000
Salary Expense	6,000
Building	115,000
Rent Expense	2,000
P. Lenahan, Withdrawals.............	6,000
Utilities Expense..........................	400
Accounts Receivable.....................	9,500
Notes Payable..............................	4,000
Supplies	200

Requirements

1. Prepare the company's trial balance at December 31, 2009, listing accounts in the proper order. For example, Supplies comes before Building and Land. List the largest expense first, the second-largest expense next, and so on.

2. Prepare the financial statements: income statement, statement of owner's equity, and balance sheet. Assume no investments were made by the owner during the year.

④ Using a trial balance for preparing financial statements.

P2-34B. The trial balance for Inner Balance Fitness Center does not balance. The following errors were detected:

a. The cash balance is understated by $700.

b. The cost of the building was $93,000, not $96,000.

c. A $200 purchase of supplies on account was neither journalized nor posted.

continued.....

d. The balance of Utilities Expense is overstated by $70.

e. Rent Expense of $200 was erroneously posted as a credit rather than a debit.

f. A $300 debit to Accounts Receivable was posted as $30.

g. A $4,300 credit to Service Revenue was not posted.

		Balance	
INNER BALANCE FITNESS CENTER **Trial Balance** June 30, 2009			
Account Title		**Debit**	**Credit**
Cash		$ 3,000	
Accounts receivable		10,000	
Supplies		900	
Equipment		85,100	
Building		96,000	
Accounts payable			$ 55,000
Notes payable			72,000
Rico Smith, capital			62,500
Rico Smith, withdrawals		2,900	
Service revenue			6,500
Salary expense		2,100	
Rent expense		1,000	
Advertising expense		600	
Utilities expense		400	
Total		$202,000	$196,000

Requirements

1. Prepare the correct trial balance at June 30.

2. Prepare the company's income statement for the month ended June 30, 2009, in order to determine the business's net income or net loss for the month.

for 24/7 practice, visit
www.MyAccountingLab.com

Apply Your Knowledge

Case 1. Sandra Gomez was recording the daily transactions of her business, Wind Enterprises, into the accounting records so she could prepare financial statements and apply for a bank loan. Some of the business expenses were higher than she had expected, and Sandra was worried about the affect of these expenses on net income. Sandra was recording a $5,000 payment for legal fees incurred by her business by debiting Legal Expense and crediting Cash to properly record the journal entry. She then thought that, rather than debiting the expense account for the $5,000 payment, she could debit the Withdrawals account, which also had a normal debit balance. Sandra knew that debits had to equal credits so debiting the Withdrawals account instead of the Legal Expense account would not affect the trial balance. Further, the net income would be $5,000 higher because now no legal expense would be recorded. She thought that either way the owner's equity would be reduced, and besides, it really didn't matter how the $5,000 payment was shown as long as she showed it somewhere.

Should Sandra debit the Withdrawals account rather than the Legal Expense account? Do you agree with her thought that it really doesn't matter how the $5,000 payment is shown as long as it is shown somewhere? Considering that Wind Enterprises is *her* business, does Sandra have any ethical responsibilities to properly record each business transaction?

Case 2. Steve Jones was recording the transactions of his client, Canton Construction. Numerous payments were listed for wages paid, and therefore he was properly debiting the Wage Expense account and crediting Cash. Steve became concerned that if he kept debiting the Wage Expense account it would end up with a balance much higher than any of the other expense accounts. Accordingly, he began debiting other expense accounts for some of the wage payments and thus "spread the expenses around" to other expense accounts. When he was done posting all the journal entries to the ledger accounts, he printed a trial balance. He saw that the Wage Expense debit balance was $32,000 and the total of all the other expense accounts was $26,000. Had he properly posted all the wage expense transactions, Wage Expense would have totaled $46,000 and the other expense accounts would have totaled $12,000. Steve reasoned that his actions provided for "more balanced" expense account totals and, regardless of his postings, the total expenses were still $58,000 so the overall net income would be the same.

Were Steve's actions justified? Do they cause any ethical concerns? If you were the owner of Canton Construction, would you have a problem with what Steve did?

This case will help you understand the impact of business transactions that accountants record in journal entries and that ultimately affect the financial statements. Although we do not have access to the journals used by Target, we can still understand various business transactions that Target had as seen on the financial statements in their annual report. Refer to the Target Income Statements, "Consolidated Results of Operations," and the Target balance sheet's

"Consolidated Statements of Financial Position" in Appendix A. Assume Target completed the following transactions during 2004:

Dec. 3	Purchased $250,000 of equipment for cash.
7	Recorded cash sales of $12,645,000.
10	Purchased $1,485,000 of inventory on account.
15	Earned $328,000 of sales revenue on account.
29	Paid $1,000,000 on account from the December 10 purchase.

Requirements

1. Prepare journal entries to record the transactions listed. Use the account titles found in the Target financial statements: Cash, Accounts Receivable, Fixtures and Equipment, Accounts Payable, and Sales.

2. Look at the financial statements and locate the accounts that you included in your journal entries. Note that the balances Target reported include millions of dollars in transactions for the year. Imagine how much activity and how many transactions Target has every day!

For Internet Exercises, Excel in Practice, and additional online activities, go to the Web site www.prenhall.com/pollard.

Quick Check Answers

1. *c* 2. *a* 3. *d* 4. *c* 5. *b* 6. *c* 7. *c* 8. *d* 9. *a* 10. *a*

LEARNING OBJECTIVES

1. Describe the accounting principles that help businesses measure income.

2. Describe the four types of adjusting entries.

3. Make adjusting entries.

4. Prepare an adjusted trial balance.

5. Prepare financial statements from an adjusted trial balance.

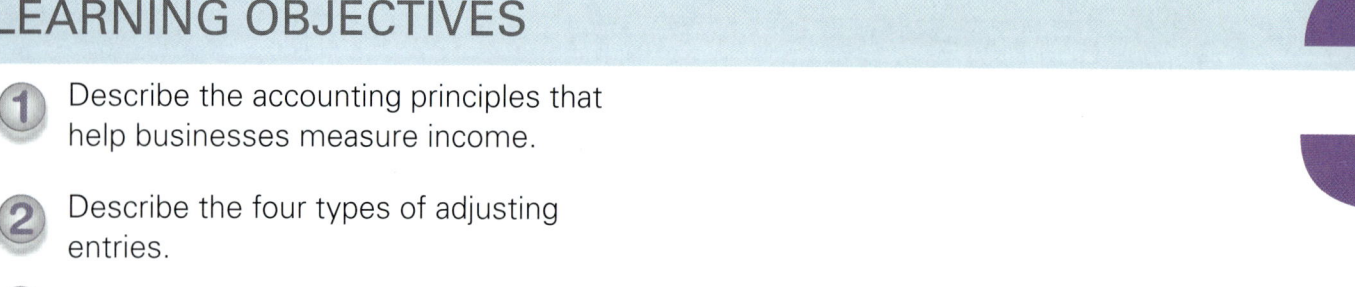

The Adjusting Process

Have you ever paid cash for something before you received it, or received cash for work you haven't performed yet? Perhaps you joined a health club, subscribed to a magazine, or purchased season tickets to see your favorite team, symphony, or theatre company. Maybe you received cash in advance from a neighbor in return for your promise to paint a fence, mow a yard, or walk the dogs later on.

On the other hand, have you ever purchased a good or received a service and promised to pay for it in a while? Have you ever worked but not been paid for your efforts until later? Maybe you used a credit card to buy food, clothing, or gasoline for your car, and paid the bill at the end of the month. Perhaps you worked part-time at a fast-food restaurant or interned one summer at a company in a large city and didn't get paid until the end of the week or even the summer.

These situations occur almost every day in business. We might think that cash is received or paid right away in every transaction, but this isn't always practical. Sometimes goods or services are sold to customers on account, and other times customers pay for goods or services in advance of receiving them. Sometimes supplies, utilities, employees' efforts, and other items are obtained before they are paid for, and sometimes they are paid for before they are received. If businesses only recorded transactions that involved cash, then they would fail to report all the transactions that they engage in where cash is not immediately transferred. In this way, they would mislead stakeholders about their financial position. ●

Look Back

You have learned how to use the double-entry system of accounting to record transactions in a journal, post them to accounts in the ledger, and prepare a trial balance and financial statements.

Look Ahead

You will learn how to adjust revenues and expenses to measure income accurately and prepare an adjusted trial balance and use it to prepare financial statements.

In Chapters 1 and 2 you learned how to use accounts, the accounting equation, and the rules of debits and credits to measure, process, and communicate the results of a business's transactions in reports called financial statements. In this chapter, we will focus on when revenues and expenses happen. We will see how the accounting system adjusts accounts as necessary to reflect these events and then prepare accurate financial statements.

Measuring Business Income Using Accounting Principles

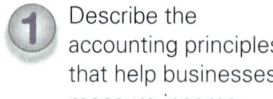 Describe the accounting principles that help businesses measure income.

One of the primary goals in business is to earn a profit. Profit, also called net income, occurs when revenues earned by a business are more than expenses incurred to operate that business. Generally Accepted Accounting Principles (GAAP) guide us in measuring net income accurately, and according to GAAP, we account for transactions on an accrual basis to make this happen. **Accrual basis accounting** dictates that we record revenues when they are earned and expenses when they are incurred in order to produce revenues. In this way, revenues of a period are matched against the expenses of that period. To summarize:

- We record revenues when they are earned by providing goods or services, according to the **revenue recognition principle**.

- We record expenses when incurred by using resources to produce those revenues according to the **matching principle**.

- In this way, we accomplish *accrual basis accounting*, the idea of recording revenues and the related expenses in the same time period so that we can compare them and correctly measure income.

- The **time period concept** says that organizations must prepare financial reports for a specific period of time, and that these time periods should always be the same length so that results presented are comparable.

Thus, to measure income accurately, companies need to update their revenue and expense accounts at the end of each period.

To illustrate these principles, let's assume that Sheila Jones visited Jack Thomas Automotive to select a Mustang GT and found the car of her dreams. The price on the car sticker is $25,000, but Sheila and Jack agreed on a price of $22,000. Before buying it, however, Sheila needs to talk to her parents. She plans to come back next week to sign the loan and get the car.

Revenue will be earned later when Sheila signs the sales agreement and loan papers and drives the car off the lot. At that time, Thomas Automotive will record the sale for $22,000, the amount on the sales agreement. Jack's dealership cannot record the sale until the transaction occurs. Jack will have the Mustang's gas tank filled with gas before Sheila drives it home. Similarly, the business will record the cost of the gas used to fill the tank at the time the sale is recorded because the two events go together; the gas expense relates to the revenue from the sale. To measure income accurately, both must be reported in the same time period.

The basic accounting period is typically one year long, and nearly all businesses prepare annual financial statements. The annual accounting period for most large companies runs the calendar year from January 1 through December 31, although some companies use a **fiscal year** that does not coincide with the calendar year. A fiscal year is any consecutive 12 months that a business chooses. It may begin on January 1 and end December 31, but may also begin at any other point and end 12 months later. Usually, the year-end date is the low point in business activity for the year. **Fiscal year-end (FYE)** refers to the date that the business's fiscal year ends. Although we will focus primarily on an annual time period, know that financial statements can be, and usually are, also prepared monthly, quarterly, or semiannually so that businesses have an idea of how they are doing before the year ends.

Exhibit 3-1 highlights the need for accrual basis accounting and the revenue recognition, matching, and time period principles.

Exhibit 3-1 Accounting Principles for Measuring Income: Accrual Basis Accounting

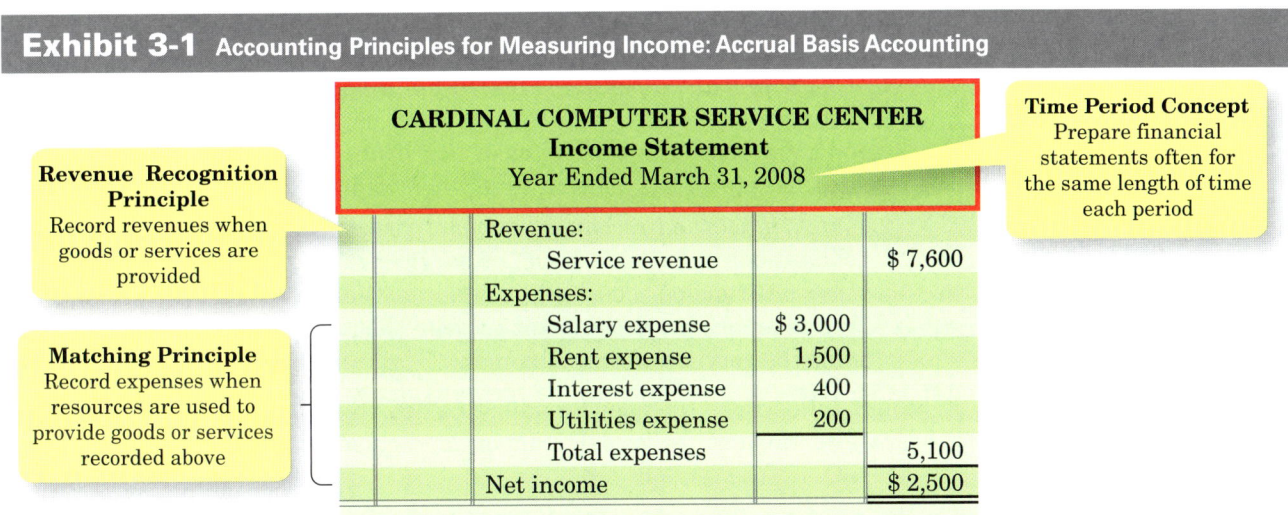

Types of Adjusting Entries

As we saw in Chapter 2, a business records transactions throughout the accounting period as the transactions occur. At the end of that period, the accountant prepares a trial balance and uses it to prepare financial statements. However, before most business can prepare correct financial statements, the accountant will have to prepare **adjusting entries**.

Describe the four types of adjusting entries.

Adjusting entries are journal entries needed to ensure that accrual basis accounting is accomplished so that business income can be measured accurately. Remember discussing the time lag that can occur when goods or services are transferred at a point in time different from when cash for those items is paid or received? Because some transactions cover more than one accounting period, adjusting entries are necessary to assign revenues to the period when they are earned and expenses to the period when they are incurred. So, adjusting entries properly measure:

1. The period's income on the income statement and

2. The assets and the liabilities on the balance sheet

Each adjusting entry affects an income statement account, a revenue or an expense, and a balance sheet account, an asset or a liability. *Cash is never included in an adjusting entry because cash is always recorded accurately at the time it is received or paid.*

Adjusting entries fall into two categories: **deferrals** and **accruals**. Adjustments are made for deferrals because, in the transactions creating the deferrals, the cash is exchanged before a revenue or expense is recorded; adjustment is necessary to record the correct amount of revenue earned or expense incurred since the cash exchange took place. Adjustments are needed for accruals for exactly the opposite reason; in the transactions creating the accruals, the revenues have been earned or the expenses have been incurred before cash has been exchanged.

- Two types of adjustments are made for *deferrals*:

   1. *Divide prepaid expenses, supplies, buildings, equipment, or other assets* between periods. These assets will be used, or expensed, over more than one time period after the cash has been paid. We wait to record the expenses until the point in time when we use the items.

   2. *Divide unearned revenues* between periods. These liabilities represent obligations to provide goods or services and will be earned over more than one time period after the cash has been received. We wait to record the revenues until the point in time that we deliver the goods or provide the services to the customer.

Exhibit 3-2 illustrates the need for adjusting deferred items. We will describe and prepare adjusting entries for deferrals in the next section of this chapter.

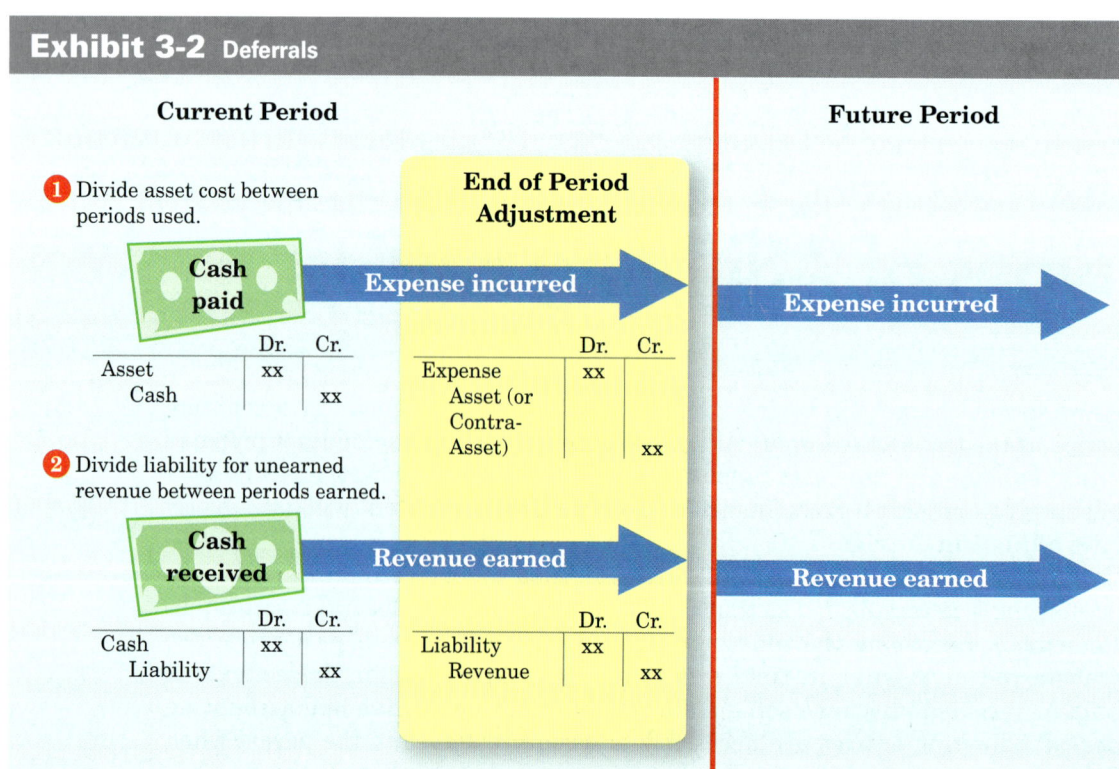

Exhibit 3-2 Deferrals

- Two types of adjustments are made for *accruals*:

  1. *Accrue, or record, unrecorded expenses.* These liabilities represent the company's obligation to pay for unrecorded expenses that have been incurred, or used, in the current period. We record the expenses in the current period even though we have not yet paid for them.

  2. *Accrue, or record, unrecorded revenues.* These assets represent the company's right to receive payments from customers or other parties for unrecorded revenues that have been earned. We record the revenues in the current period, even though we have not yet received cash from the customers.

Exhibit 3-3 illustrates the need for adjusting accrued items. We will describe and prepare adjusting entries for accruals in the next section of this chapter.

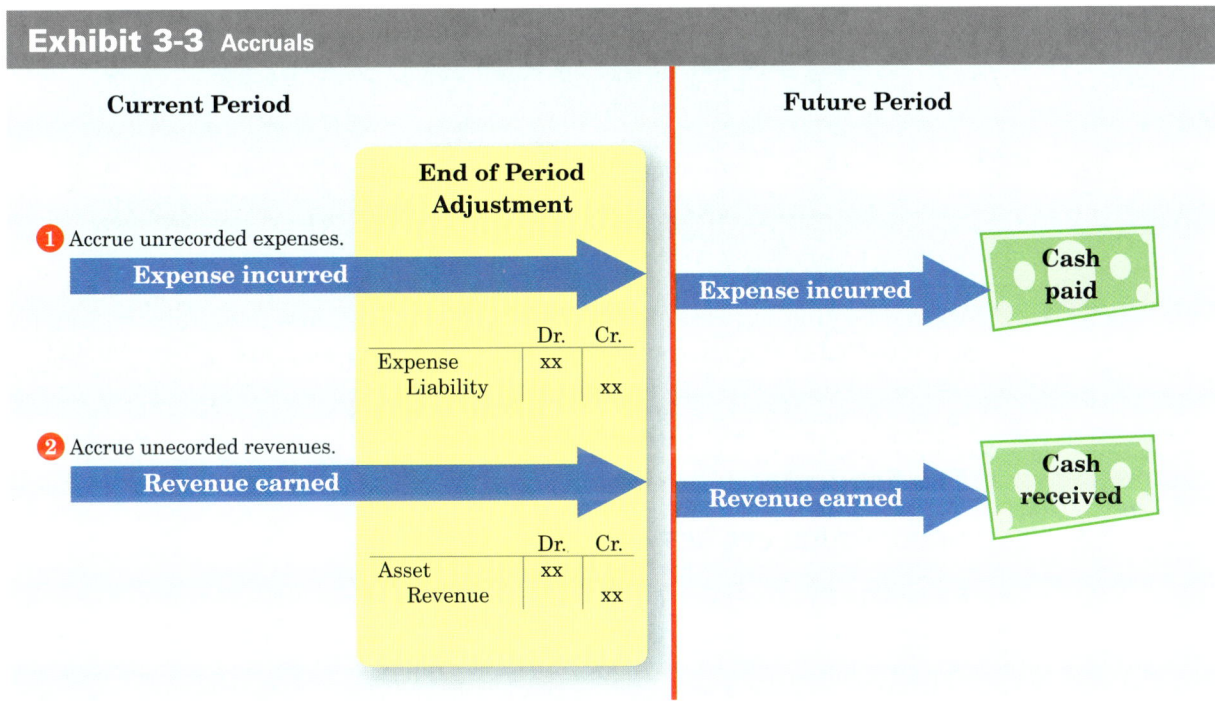

Exhibit 3-3 Accruals

Adjusting the Accounts

At the end of the accounting period, the accountant prepares the financial statements by first preparing a trial balance. Remember Kay Torres and her travel business from Chapter 2? Exhibit 3-4 shows the trial balance of Kay Torres Travel Agency at September 30, 2008, a few months later than we saw the business in Chapter 2. This *unadjusted trial balance* lists most of the revenues and expenses of the travel agency for September, but these amounts are incomplete because they do not reflect certain revenue and expense transactions that affect more than one accounting period. Although this preliminary trial balance is *unadjusted*, we usually refer to it simply as the trial balance, without the label "unadjusted."

Remember from Chapter 2 that the accounting process records transactions in the journal and posts them to accounts in the ledger. This process is still used

3 Make adjusting entries.

Exhibit 3-4 Unadjusted Trial Balance

KAY TORRES TRAVEL AGENCY
(Unadjusted) Trial Balance
September 30, 2008

Account Title	Balance Debit	Balance Credit
Cash	$ 26,300	
Accounts receivable	3,100	
Supplies	900	
Prepaid rent	3,000	
Equipment	12,600	
Accounts payable		$ 13,100
Unearned service revenue		450
Kay Torres, capital		29,500
Kay Torres, withdrawals	3,200	
Service revenue		7,000
Salary expense	550	
Utilities expense	400	
Total	$ 50,050	$ 50,050

when adjusting the accounts. In this chapter we will show how adjusting entries are recorded then copied to accounts. However, instead of using the real, ledger account form, we will post adjustments to T-accounts, because this approach makes it easier to see how these entries affect the accounts.

Deferrals

DIVIDING ASSETS BETWEEN PERIODS

PREPAID RENT Prepaid rent and prepaid insurance are examples of prepaid expenses, items that are paid for before they are used. Often, landlords require tenants to pay rent in advance and this prepayment creates an asset for the renter. Suppose Kay Torres Travel Agency moves to a new office and prepays three months' office rent on September 1, 2008. If the lease specifies a monthly rental of $1,000, then the amount of cash paid is $3,000 ($1,000 $\times$ 3 months). The entry to record the payment is

Journal Entry:

Date	Accounts	Post Ref.	Dr.	Cr.
Sept. 1	Prepaid Rent ($1,000 $\times$ 3 months)		3,000	
	Cash			3,000
	Paid 3 months' rent in advance.			

After posting, Prepaid Rent has a $3,000 debit balance.

ASSETS

Prepaid Rent

Sept. 1	3,000

Throughout September, Prepaid Rent holds this beginning balance. The trial balance at September 30, 2008, in Exhibit 3-4, lists Prepaid Rent with its debit balance of $3,000. However, Prepaid Rent should be decreased for the amount of the asset that has been used during the month. *The cost of the rent used during the month becomes rent expense, because expenses are the value of what is used in business operations to earn revenue.*

The business used the rented space for one month, so the adjusting entry transfers $1,000 ($3,000/3 months) of the Prepaid Rent to Building Rent Expense. The Building Rent Expense account is increased by a debit, which will reduce owner's equity, to reflect a cost of operating the business. The Prepaid Rent account is an asset that decreases by a credit for the same amount. The adjusting entry is

Journal Entry:

Date	Accounts	Post Ref.	Dr.	Cr.
Sept. 30	Building Rent Expense ($3,000/3 months)		1,000	
	Prepaid Rent			1,000
	Record rent expense for September.			

After posting, Prepaid Rent and Building Rent Expense show correct ending balances:

ASSETS				EXPENSES		
Prepaid Rent				**Building Rent Expense**		
Sept. 1	3,000	Sept. 30	1,000	Sept. 30	1,000	
Bal.	2,000			Bal.	1,000	

Correct Asset Amount: $2,000 → Total Accounted for: $3,000 ← Correct Expense Amount: $1,000

If Kay Torres Travel Agency had prepaid insurance, then the same analysis would apply to this asset account, too. The only difference in the adjusting entry would be in the account titles, which would be Prepaid Insurance instead of Prepaid Rent, and Insurance Expense instead of Building Rent Expense, and of course, the amount of the entry.

SUPPLIES Supplies are accounted for in the same way as prepaid expenses. On September 2, Kay Torres paid $900 for office supplies. Two asset accounts were affected, Supplies and Cash. Supplies increased by $900 while Cash decreased by $900, as shown here:

Journal Entry:

Date	Accounts	Post Ref.	Dr.	Cr.
Sept. 2	Supplies		900	
	Cash			900
	Paid cash for office supplies.			

The September 30 trial balance, therefore, lists Supplies with a $900 debit balance, as shown in Exhibit 3-4. But Torres's September 30 balance sheet should *not* report supplies of $900, because during September, Torres used some of these supplies to conduct business. *The cost of the supplies used becomes supplies expense.*

To measure supplies expense, Torres counts the supplies on hand at the end of September. These supplies counted are still available to the business. Assume that the travel agency still owns supplies costing $600 at September 30. The supplies purchased ($900) minus the supplies on hand at the end of September ($600) determines the value of the supplies consumed during the month ($300).

Cost of Asset Available, Beginning Balance + Supplies Purchased:	–	Cost of Asset on Hand at the End of the Period:	=	Cost of Asset Used During the Period:
$900	–	$600	=	$300

The September 30 adjusting entry updates the Supplies account and records Supplies Expense for the month.

Journal Entry:

Date	Accounts	Post Ref.	Dr.	Cr.
Sept. 30	Supplies Expense ($900 – $600)		300	
	Supplies			300
	Record supply expense for September.			

After posting, Supplies and Supplies Expense hold correct ending balances:

	ASSETS				EXPENSES	
	Supplies				**Supplies Expense**	
Sept. 2	900	Sept. 30	300	Sept. 30	300	
Bal.	600			Bal.	300	

Correct Asset Amount:	→	Total Accounted for:	←	Correct Expense Amount:
$600		$900		$300

DEPRECIATION ON LONG-TERM ASSETS A special type of deferral relates to long-term assets. **Long-term assets** are long-lived, tangible assets used in the operation of a business. Long-term assets last for more than a year. Examples include land, buildings, equipment, and furniture. All of these assets, except land, are used up over time. As an asset is used, part of the asset cost becomes an expense, just as supplies consumed become supplies expense. This allocation of the asset's cost to expense over its useful life is called **depreciation**; in other words, depreciation is the process of using up of long-term assets. We record no depreciation for land because it is never really used up.

We use the same idea to account for long-term assets as we did for prepaid expenses and supplies because they are all assets. The major difference is the length of time it takes for the asset to be used up. Prepaid expenses and supplies are typically used within a year, while most long-term assets remain functional for several years.

Consider Kay Torres Travel Agency, which already owns $9,000 of equipment from an earlier purchase made in June. Suppose that on September 3, Torres purchased additional equipment on account for $3,600 and made this journal entry:

Journal Entry:

Date	Accounts	Post Ref.	Dr.	Cr.
Sept. 3	Equipment		3,600	
	Accounts Payable			3,600
	Purchased equipment on account.			

After posting, the Equipment account has a $12,600 balance:

ASSETS

Equipment

Bal.	9,000
Sept. 3	3,600
Bal.	12,600

Because Kay did not know about adjusting entries before September, the travel agency never recorded depreciation on the original equipment purchased and now needs to record the depreciation on both the new and older equipment. Even though actually measuring the value of an asset used up is difficult, several methods are available for estimating the amount of depreciation. One computation uses the **straight-line depreciation** method. Torres believes the equipment will remain useful for 3 years and will be worthless, having no salvage value at the end of its life, so depreciation on this equipment is calculated using the straight-line method as follows:

$$\frac{\text{Depreciation Expense}}{\text{per Year}} = \frac{\text{Cost of Asset} - \text{Salvage Value of Asset}}{\text{Useful Life of Asset}} = \frac{\$12,600}{3} = \$4,200$$

Depreciation for the month of September is $350 ($4,200/12 months).

THE ACCUMULATED DEPRECIATION ACCOUNT Depreciation expense for September is recorded by this entry:

Journal Entry:

Date	Accounts	Post Ref.	Dr.	Cr.
Sept. 30	Depreciation Expense, Equipment		350	
	Accumulated Depreciation, Equipment			350
	Record depreciation on equipment for September.			

After posting the depreciation entry, Kay Torres's accounts appear as follows:

	ASSETS			EXPENSES
ASSET		**CONTRA-ASSET**		
Equipment		**Accumulated Depreciation, Equipment**		**Depreciation Expense, Equipment**
Bal. 9,000			Sept. 30 350	Sept. 30 350
Sept. 3 3,600				
Bal. 12,600			Bal. 350	Bal. 350

Notice that the value of the equipment used during the month was not deducted from the Equipment account. Instead, the used-up value for the month was added to the **Accumulated Depreciation** account, and this account holds all of the depreciation recorded for an asset's life. The Accumulated Depreciation, Equipment, account increases over the life of the asset as the asset expires. By keeping the cost of the equipment separate from its accumulated depreciation, financial statement users can look at the Equipment account to see how much the asset cost and look also at the Accumulated Depreciation, Equipment, account to see how much of that cost has been used.

Accumulated Depreciation, Equipment, is a contra-asset. A **contra-account** has two main characteristics:

- A contra-account follows a companion account.
- A contra-account's normal balance is opposite that of the companion.

Accumulated Depreciation, Equipment, is the contra-account that follows Equipment. Equipment, an asset, has a debit balance, so Accumulated Depreciation, Equipment, a contra-asset, has a credit balance. *All contra-assets have credit balances*. Because it relates to the asset account, Equipment, it will appear on the balance sheet.

The balance sheet reports both Equipment and Accumulated Depreciation, Equipment. Because it's a contra-account, the balance of Accumulated Depreciation, Equipment is subtracted from Equipment. The resulting net amount of a long-term asset is called its **book value**, or **carrying value**, and is calculated as follows:

Book Value of a Long-Term Asset		
Cost	Equipment	$12,600
– Accumulated Depreciation	Less: Accumulated Depreciation, Equipment	(350)
= Book (or Carrying) Value	Book Value	$12,250

A business usually keeps an accumulated depreciation account for each type of depreciable asset. If Kay Torres Travel Agency had both buildings and equipment, it would use two accumulated depreciation accounts, Accumulated Depreciation, Buildings, and Accumulated Depreciation, Equipment.

DIVIDING LIABILITIES BETWEEN PERIODS

UNEARNED REVENUES Some businesses collect cash from customers in advance. Receiving cash from a customer before earning it creates a liability called **unearned revenue**, or **deferred revenue**, because the company *owes* a product or a service to the customer. Don't let the title fool you: Only when the product or service is delivered will the business *earn* the revenue.

Suppose Intel Corporation hires Torres's agency to provide travel services, agreeing to pay her $450 monthly, beginning immediately. Torres collects the first amount from Intel on September 20. Torres records the cash receipt and a liability as follows:

Journal Entry:

Date	Accounts	Post Ref.	Dr.	Cr.
Sept. 20	Cash		450	
	Unearned Service Revenue			450
	Collected revenue in advance.			

Now the liability account Unearned Service Revenue shows that the travel agency owes $450 of services because of its obligation to make travel arrangements for Intel.

LIABILITIES

Unearned Service Revenue

	Sept. 20 450

The September 30 trial balance in Exhibit 3-4 lists Unearned Service Revenue as a liability with a $450 credit balance. However, during the last 10 days of the month, September 21 through September 30, Torres *earned* one-third of the $450, or $150 ($450 × 10/30 days). Therefore, Torres makes the following adjustment to account for earning $150 of the revenue:

Journal Entry:

Date	Accounts	Post Ref.	Dr.	Cr.
Sept. 30	Unearned Service Revenue ($450 × 10/30 days)		150	
	Service Revenue			150
	Record service revenue earned from			
	September 20–30.			

This adjusting entry shifts $150 of the $450 total from liability to revenue. Service Revenue increases by $150, and Unearned Service Revenue decreases by $150. Now both accounts are up to date at September 30:

LIABILITIES				REVENUES		
Unearned Service Revenue				**Service Revenue**		
Sept. 30	150	Sept. 20	450		Bal.	7,000
		Bal.	300		Sept. 30	150
					Bal.	7,150

Correct Liability Amount:		Total Accounted for:		Correct Revenue Amount:
$300	→	$450	←	$150

Accruals

ACCRUING EXPENSES

SALARY PAYABLE Suppose Kay Torres pays her employee a monthly salary of $1,100, half on the 15th of the month and half on the last day of the month. If either payday falls on a weekend, Torres pays the salary the following Monday. During September, Torres paid the first half-month salary of $550 ($1,100 × 1/2 month) on Friday, September 15, and made the following entry:

Journal Entry:

Date	Accounts	Post Ref.	Dr.	Cr.
Sept. 15	Salary Expense ($1,100 × 1/2 month)		550	
	Cash			550
	Paid salary for September 1–15.			

After posting, Salary Expense shows its balance:

EXPENSES

Salary Expense

Sept. 15	550

The trial balance at September 30 in Exhibit 3-4 includes Salary Expense with a debit balance of $550. This salary expense relates to the first half of September only. Because the next payday, September 30, falls on a Saturday, the second half of September's salary will actually be paid in October. This salary is really an expense of September, so Torres must accrue salary of $550. At September 30, Torres makes an adjusting entry as follows:

Journal Entry:

Date	Accounts	Post Ref.	Dr.	Cr.
Sept. 30	Salary Expense ($1,100 × 1/2 month)		550	
	Salary Payable			550
	Accrue salary for September 16–30.			

Accrued expenses, such as the accrual for salary expense, are expenses that the business has incurred but not yet paid. The adjusting entry to accrue the expense always creates a liability, such as Salary Payable, Taxes Payable, Interest Payable. Companies don't make weekly journal entries to accrue expenses. Instead, they make an adjusting entry at the end of the period to bring each expense and the related liability up to date before preparing financial statements.

This is accrual accounting in action; look at the Salary Expense and Salary Payable balances at September 30 after posting:

EXPENSES				LIABILITIES		
Salary Expense				**Salary Payable**		
Sept. 15	550				Sept. 30	550
Sept. 30	550				Bal.	550
Bal.	1,100					

Salary Expense holds a full month's salary as it should, and Salary Payable shows the liability the company owes its employee at September 30.

ACCRUING REVENUES

ACCOUNTS RECEIVABLE As we just discussed, some expenses occur before they are paid, which creates an accrued expense. Likewise, businesses sometimes also earn revenue before they receive the cash. Assets such as Accounts Receivable and Interest Receivable hold this accrued revenue amount until cash is received.

Assume that Kay Torres Travel Agency is hired on September 15 to perform travel services for an engineering firm. Under this agreement, the business will earn \$500 monthly. During September, it will earn half a month's fee, \$250 (\$500 × 1/2 month), for work performed September 15 through September 30. On September 30, Torres makes the following adjusting entry to accrue the revenue earned during this period:

Journal Entry:

Date	Accounts	Post Ref.	Dr.	Cr.
Sept. 30	Accoounts Receivable (\$500 × 1/2 month)		250	
	Service Revenue			250
	Accrue service revenue for September 15–30.			

The unadjusted trial balance in Exhibit 3-4 shows that Accounts Receivable has an unadjusted balance of \$3,100. Service Revenue's unadjusted balance is \$7,000. Posting the adjustment increases both accounts to their correct balances at September 30.

ASSETS			REVENUES		
Accounts Receivable			**Service Revenue**		
Bal.	3,100			Bal.	7,000
				Sept. 30	150
Sept. 30	250			Sept. 30	250
Bal.	3,350			Bal.	7,400

Without the adjustment, the agency's financial statements would be incomplete and misleading: They would understate both Accounts Receivable and Service Revenue.

Exhibit 3-5 summarizes the timing of deferral and accrual adjustments.

Exhibit 3-5 Deferral and Accrual Adjustments

				Adjusting Entries		
Deferrals: Cash transaction comes first.						
	First	**Dr.**	**Cr.**	**Later**	**Dr.**	**Cr.**
Prepaid expenses,	*Pay cash and record an asset:*			*Record an expense and decrease the asset:*		
depreciable assets	Prepaid Rent	XXX		Rent Expense	XXX	
	Cash		XXX	Prepaid Rent		XXX
Unearned Revenues	*Receive cash and record a liability:*			*Record a revenue and decrease the liability:*		
	Cash	XXX		Unearned Service Revenue	XXX	
	Unearned Service Revenue		XXX	Service Revenue		XXX
Accruals: Cash transaction comes later.						
	First	**Dr.**	**Cr.**	**Later**	**Dr.**	**Cr.**
Accrued Expenses	*Accrue an expense and the related liability:*			*Pay cash and decrease the liability:*		
	Salary Expense	XXX		Salary Payable	XXX	
	Salary Payable		XXX	Cash		XXX
Accrued Revenues	*Accrue a revenue and the related asset:*			*Receive cash and decrease the asset:*		
	Accounts Receivable	XXX		Cash	XXX	
	Service Revenue		XXX	Accounts Receivable		XXX

Summary of the Adjusting Process

The adjusting process has two purposes:

1. Measure net income or net loss accurately on the *income statement*. Every adjusting entry affects a *revenue* or an *expense*.

2. Update the *balance sheet*. Every adjusting entry also affects an *asset* or a *liability* related to the revenue or expense account adjusted.

Remember the key differences between deferrals and accruals:

1. A *deferred revenue or expense* is paid first, and recorded as a revenue or expense later as the revenue is earned or the expense is incurred.

2. An *accrued revenue or expense* is recorded as a revenue or expense first as the revenue is earned or the expense is incurred, and paid later.

Exhibit 3-6 summarizes the effects of the various adjusting entries.

Exhibit 3-6 Summary of Adjusting Entries

Category of Adjusting Entry	Debit	Credit
1. Deferred expense................................ Expense		Asset or Contra-Asset
2. Deferred revenue............................... Liability		Revenue
3. Accrued expense................................ Expense		Liability
4. Accrued revenue................................ Asset		Revenue

Source: Adapted from material provided by Beverly Terry.

Exhibit 3-7 summarizes the adjusting entries of Kay Torres Travel Agency at September 30. Panel A gives the information needed to make each adjustment, Panel B shows the adjusting entries, and Panel C gives the accounts after posting. Each adjustment is identified by a letter.

Exhibit 3-7 Journalizing and Posting the Adjusting Entries of Kay Torres Travel Agency

PANEL A—Descriptions of Transactions

a.	Prepaid rent expired, $1,000.
b.	Supplies used, $300.
c.	Depreciation on equipment, $350.
d.	Service revenue collected in advance now earned, $150.
e.	Accrued salary expense, $550.
f.	Accrued service revenue, $250.

PANEL B—Adjusting Entries

Date	Accounts	Post Ref.	Dr.	Cr.
Sept. 30	a. Building Rent Expense ($3,000/3 months)		1,000	
	Prepaid Rent			1,000
	Record rent expense for September.			
30	b. Supplies Expense ($900 – $600)		300	
	Supplies			300
	Record supply expense for September.			
30	c. Depreciation Expense, Equipment		350	
	Accumulated Depreciation, Equipment			350
	Record depreciation on equipment for September.			
30	d. Unearned Service Revenue ($450 × 10/30 days)		150	
	Service Revenue			150
	Record service revenue earned from September 20–30.			
30	e. Salary Expense ($1,100 × 1/2 month)		550	
	Salary Payable			550
	Accrue salary for September 16–30.			
30	f. Accounts Receivable ($500 × 1/2 month)		250	
	Service Revenue			250
	Accrue service revenue for September 16–30.			

continued.....

Exhibit 3-7 (Continued)

PANEL C—Accounts

ASSETS

Cash

Bal.	26,300	

Accounts Receivable

Bal.	3,100	
(f)	250	
Bal.	3,350	

Supplies

Sept. 2	900	(b)	300
Bal.	600		

Prepaid Rent

Sept. 1	3,000	(a)	1,000
Bal.	2,000		

Equipment

Bal.	9,000	
Sept. 3	3,600	
Bal.	12,600	

Accumulated Depreciation, Equipment

		(c)	350
		Bal.	350

LIABILITIES

Accounts Payable

		Bal.	13,100

Salary Payable

		(e)	550
		Bal.	550

Unearned Service Revenue

(d)	150	Sept. 20	450
		Bal.	300

OWNER'S EQUITY

Kay Torres, Capital

		Bal.	29,500

Kay Torres, Withdrawals

Bal.	3,200	

Service Revenue

		Bal.	7,000
		(d)	150
		(f)	250
		Bal.	7,400

Building Rent Expense

(a)	1,000	
Bal.	1,000	

Salary Expense

Sept. 15	550	
(e)	550	
Bal.	1,100	

Supplies Expense

(b)	300	
Bal.	300	

Depreciation Expense, Equipment

(c)	350	
Bal.	350	

Utilities Expense

Bal.	400	

The Adjusted Trial Balance

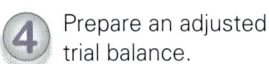

4 Prepare an adjusted trial balance.

This chapter began with a trial balance prepared before any adjustments had been made, the unadjusted trial balance shown in Exhibit 3-4. After adjustment, the accounts appear as presented in Exhibit 3-7, Panel C. A useful step in preparing the financial statements is to list the accounts and their adjusted balances on an **adjusted trial balance** to make sure total debits still equal total credits after adjusting entries have been recorded and posted. Exhibit 3-8 is a **worksheet** that shows how to prepare the adjusted trial balance using the following steps:

STEP 1:
Copy account titles and trial balance amounts directly from the trial balance. Place debit balances in the debit column and credit balances in the credit column of the Trial Balance columns.

STEP 2:
Enter the adjusting journal entries into the correct debit or credit column of the Adjustments section of the worksheet. Label each entry with the letter that identifies it as one of the adjusting entries recorded in Exhibit 3-7.

STEP 3:
Calculate new, adjusted balances for each account. Start with the balance from the Trial Balance columns. Add or subtract the change in the balance as shown in the Adjustments section. Enter the new balance into the correct debit or credit

column of the Adjusted Trial Balance columns. Remember that accounts will be affected differently by adjusting entries:

- Some accounts may be affected by one adjustment, such as Accounts Receivable.
- Some accounts may affected by more than one adjustment, such as Service Revenue.
- Some accounts may not be affected by adjustments at all: Cash, Equipment, Accounts Payable, Capital, Withdrawals, and Utilities Expense. So, their balances will be the same on both the unadjusted and adjusted trial balances.

Exhibit 3-8 Preparation of Adjusted Trial Balance on the Worksheet

KAY TORRES TRAVEL AGENCY
Worksheet
September 30, 2008

Account Title	Trial Balance Dr.	Trial Balance Cr.	Adjustments Dr.	Adjustments Cr.	Adjusted Trial Balance Dr.	Adjusted Trial Balance Cr.	
Cash	26,300				26,300		
Accounts receivable	3,100		f. 250		3,350		
Supplies	900			b. 300	600		
Prepaid rent	3,000			a. 1,000	2,000		
Equipment	12,600				12,600		Balance Sheet *(Exhibit 3-11)*
Accumulated depreciation, equipment				c. 350		350	
Accounts payable		13,100				13,100	
Salary payable				e. 550		550	
Unearned service revenue		450	d. 150			300	
Kay Torres, capital		29,500				29,500	Statement of Owner's Equity *(Exhibit 3-10)*
Kay Torres, withdrawals	3,200				3,200		
Service revenue		7,000		d. 150		7,400	
				f. 250			
Building rent expense			a. 1,000		1,000		
Salary expense	550		e. 550		1,100		Income Statement *(Exhibit 3-9)*
Supplies expense			b. 300		300		
Depreciation expense, equipment			c. 350		350		
Utilities expense	400				400		
Total	50,050	50,050	2,600	2,600	51,200	51,200	

Preparing the Financial Statements

The September financial statements of Kay Torres Travel Agency can be prepared from the adjusted trial balance in Exhibit 3-8. In the right margin, we see how the accounts are distributed to the financial statements. The financial statements should be prepared in this order, the same order that we used in previous chapters:

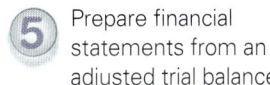

5 Prepare financial statements from an adjusted trial balance.

1. The income statement (Exhibit 3-9) reports the revenues and the expenses to determine net income or net loss for a period of time.

2. The statement of owner's equity (Exhibit 3-10) shows the changes in owner's equity during the period and computes the ending balance of owner's equity. Kay Torres did not make any additional investments in Kay Torres Travel Agency during the month of September, but remember from previous chapters that these additional investments would be shown as increases in her owner's equity.

3. The balance sheet (Exhibit 3-11) reports the assets, liabilities, and owner's equity to see the financial position of the business at a point in time.

Exhibit 3-9 Income Statement

KAY TORRES TRAVEL AGENCY
Income Statement
Month Ended September 30, 2008

Revenue:		
Service revenue		$ 7,400
Expenses:		
Salary expense	$ 1,100	
Building rent expense	1,000	
Utilities expense	400	
Depreciation expense, equipment	350	
Supplies expense	300	
Total expenses		3,150
Net income		$ 4,250

Exhibit 3-10 Statement of Owner's Equity

KAY TORRES TRAVEL AGENCY
Statement of Owner's Equity
Month Ended September 30, 2008

Kay Torres, capital, September 1, 2008	$ 29,500
Add: Net income	4,250
Subtotal	33,750
Less: Withdrawals by owner	(3,200)
Kay Torres, capital, September 30, 2008	$ 30,550

Exhibit 3-11 Balance Sheet

KAY TORRES TRAVEL AGENCY
Balance Sheet
September 30, 2008

Assets			Liabilities	
Cash		$ 26,300	Accounts payable	$ 13,100
Accounts receivable		3,350	Salary payable	550
Supplies		600	Unearned service revenue	300
Prepaid rent		2,000	Total liabilities	13,950
Equipment	$12,600			
Less: Accumulated depreciation,			**Owner's Equity**	
equipment	(350)	12,250	Kay Torres, capital	30,550
Total assets		$ 44,500	Total liabilities and owner's equity	$ 44,500

As we first discussed in Chapter 1, all financial statements include these elements:

- Heading
    - Name of the entity, such as Kay Torres Travel Agency
    - Title of the statement: income statement, statement of owner's equity, or balance sheet
    - Date, or period, covered by the statement: Month ended September 30, 2008, or September 30, 2008
- Body of the statement

The income statement often lists expenses in descending order from largest amount to smallest amount, as shown in Exhibit 3-9. However, know that some companies will list expenses in some other order, such as alphabetical order.

Relationships Between the Financial Statements

The arrows in Exhibits 3-9, 3-10, and 3-11 show how the financial statements relate to each other. In Chapter 1, we discussed the relationships between the financials. As a review of these connections, follow the arrow that takes net income from the income statement to the statement of owner's equity. Then follow the arrow that takes the ending balance of owner's equity to the balance sheet.

1. Net income from the income statement in Exhibit 3-9 increases owner's equity in Exhibit 3-10. A net loss decreases owner's equity.

2. Ending capital from the statement of owner's equity in Exhibit 3-10 is transferred to the balance sheet in Exhibit 3-11. The owner's ending capital is needed to balance the balance sheet.

Demo Doc

Preparation of Adjusting Entries, Adjusted Trial Balance, and Financial Statements

Learning Objectives 3–5

Cloud Break Consulting has the following information at June 30, 2008:

Account Title	Balance Debit	Balance Credit
CLOUD BREAK CONSULTING (Unadjusted) Trial Balance June 30, 2008		
Cash	$131,000	
Accounts receivable	104,000	
Supplies	4,000	
Prepaid rent	27,000	
Land	45,000	
Building	300,000	
Accumulated depreciation, building		$155,000
Accounts payable		159,000
Unearned service revenue		40,000
Susan Cloud, capital		152,000
Susan Cloud, withdrawals	57,000	
Service revenue		450,000
Salary expense	255,000	
Rent expense	25,000	
Miscellaneous expense	8,000	
Total	$956,000	$956,000

Cloud must make adjusting entries related to the following items:

a. Supplies on hand at year-end, $1,000.

b. Nine months of rent ($27,000) was paid in advance on April 1, 2008. No rent expense has been recorded since that date.

c. Depreciation expense has not been recorded on the building for 2008. The building has a useful life of 25 years.

d. Employees work Monday through Friday. The weekly payroll is $5,000 and is paid every Friday. June 30, 2008, is a Thursday.

e. Service revenue of $15,000 must be accrued.

f. A client paid $40,000 in advance for consulting services to be provided evenly from January 1, 2008, through August 31, 2008. None of the revenue from this client has been recorded.

Requirements

1. Open the ledger T-accounts with their unadjusted balances.

2. Journalize Cloud's adjusting entries at June 30, 2008, and post the entries to the T-accounts.

3. Total all the T-accounts in the ledger.

4. Write the trial balance on a worksheet, enter the adjusting entries, and prepare an adjusted trial balance.

5. Prepare the income statement, the statement of owner's equity, and the balance sheet. Draw arrows linking the three financial statements.

Demo Doc Solutions

Open the ledger T-accounts with their unadjusted balances.

Part 1	Part 2	Part 3	Part 4	Part 5	Demo Doc Complete

Remember from Chapter 2 that opening a T-account means drawing a blank account that looks like a capital T and putting the account title across the top. To help find the accounts later, they are usually organized into assets, liabilities, owner's equity, revenue, and expenses (in that order). If the account has a beginning balance, it ***must*** be put in on the correct side.

Remember that debits are always on the left side of the T-account and credits are always on the right side. This rule is true for *every* account.

The correct side to enter each account's beginning balance is the side of *increase* in the account. We expect all accounts to have a *positive* balance, or more increases than decreases.

For assets, an increase is a debit, so we would expect all assets to have a debit balance. For liabilities and owner's equity, an increase is a credit, so we would expect all of these accounts to have a credit balance. By the same reasoning, we expect revenues to have a credit balance and expenses and withdrawals to have a debit balance.

The unadjusted balances to be posted into the T-accounts are simply the amounts from the unadjusted trial balance.

ASSETS

Cash

| Bal. | 131,000 | |

Building

| Bal. | 300,000 | |

OWNER'S EQUITY

Susan Cloud, Capital

| | | Bal. | 152,000 |

Salary Expense

| Bal. | 255,000 | |

Accounts Receivable

| Bal. | 104,000 | |

Accumulated Depreciation, Building

| | | Bal. | 155,000 |

Susan Cloud, Withdrawals

| Bal. | 57,000 | |

Rent Expense

| Bal. | 25,000 | |

Supplies

| Bal. | 4,000 | |

Land

| Bal. | 45,000 | |

Service Revenue

| | | Bal. | 450,000 |

Miscellaneous Expense

| Bal. | 8,000 | |

Prepaid Rent

| Bal. | 27,000 | |

LIABILITIES

Accounts Payable

| | | Bal. | 159,000 |

Unearned Service Revenue

| | | Bal. | 40,000 |

Requirement 2

Journalize Cloud's adjusting entries at June 30, 2008, and post the entries to the T-accounts.

③ Make adjusting entries.

Part 1	**Part 2**	Part 3	Part 4	Part 5	Demo Doc Complete

a. Supplies on hand at year-end, $1,000.

On June 30, 2008, the unadjusted balance in supplies was $4,000. However, a count shows that only $1,000 of supplies actually remains on hand. The supplies that are no longer there have been used. When assets/benefits are used, an expense is created.

Cloud will need to make an adjusting journal entry to reflect the correct amount of supplies on the balance sheet. The "cost of asset on hand at the end of the period" to be shown on the balance sheet is the actual amount of supplies on hand of $1,000. However, right now the Supplies account shows $4,000 (as we can see from the trial balance). This $4,000 is the "cost of asset available."

Cost of Asset Available	–	Cost of Asset on Hand at the End of the Period	=	Cost of Asset Used (Expense) during the Period
$4,000	–	$1,000	=	$3,000

The supplies have decreased because they have been used up. The $3,000 of supplies expense must be recorded to show the value of supplies that were used.

Journal Entry:

Date	Accounts	Post Ref.	Dr.	Cr.
June 30	Supplies Expense ($4,000 – $1,000) (Expense, ↑; debit)		3,000	
	Supplies (Asset, ↓; credit)			3,000
	Record supply expense.			

After posting, Supplies and Supplies Expense hold correct ending balances:

	ASSETS Supplies			EXPENSES Supplies Expense	
Bal	4,000	(a) 3,000	(a)	3,000	
Bal.	1,000		Bal.	3,000	

b. Nine months of rent ($27,000) was paid in advance on April 1, 2008. No rent expense has been recorded since that date.

When something is prepaid, it is a *future* benefit (an asset) because the business is now entitled to receive goods or services for the terms of the prepayment. Once those goods or services are received (in this case, once Cloud has occupied the building being rented), they become a *past* benefit, and therefore an expense.

Cloud prepaid $27,000 for nine months of rent on April 1, which means that Cloud pays $27,000/9 = $3,000 a month for rent. At June 30, prepaid rent is adjusted for the amount of the asset that has been used up. Because Cloud occupied the building being rented for three months, we know that three months of the prepayment have been used. The amount of rent used is:

$$3 \times \$3,000 = \$9,000$$

The "correct asset amount" is the amount of prepaid rent that will appear on the balance sheet. In this case, six months' worth of prepaid rent has not been used. $6 \times \$3,000 = \$18,000$. However, right now the Prepaid Rent account shows $27,000 (as we can see from the trial balance). This $27,000 is the "total asset accounted for."

Correct Asset Amount: → Total Accounted for: ← Correct Expense Amount:
$18,000 $27,000 $9,000

Because the $9,000 of prepaid rent is a *past* benefit, an expense is recorded. Rent Expense must be increased (a debit) and Prepaid Rent (an asset) must be decreased (a credit).

Journal Entry:

Date	Accounts	Post Ref.	Dr.	Cr.
June 30	Rent Expense (Expense, ↑; debit)		9,000	
	Prepaid Rent (Asset, ↓; credit)			9,000
	Record rent expense.			

	ASSETS				**EXPENSES**		
	Prepaid Rent				**Rent Expense**		
Bal.	27,000			Bal.	25,000	
		(b)	9,000	(b)	9,000	
Bal.	18,000			Bal.	34,000	

c. Depreciation expense has not been recorded on the building for 2008. The building has a useful life of 25 years.

Depreciation expense per year is calculated as:

$$\text{Depreciation Expense per Year} = \frac{\text{Cost of Asset} - \text{Salvage Value of Asset}}{\text{Useful Life of Asset}}$$

The cost principle compels us to keep the original cost of a plant asset in that asset account. Because the Building account has a balance of $300,000, we know that this is the original cost of the building. No salvage value is mentioned in the question, so we assume it is $0. We are told in the question that the building's useful life is 25 years.

$$\text{Depreciation Expense per Year} = \frac{(\$300{,}000 - \$0)}{25 \text{ years}}$$

$$= \$12{,}000 \text{ per year.}$$

We will record depreciation of $12,000 in the adjusting journal entry.

The journal entry to record depreciation expense is *always* the same. It is only the *number* (dollar amount) in the entry that changes. It always involves an increase to Depreciation Expense (a debit) and an increase to the contra-asset account of Accumulated Depreciation (a credit).

Journal Entry:

Date	Accounts	Post Ref.	Dr.	Cr.
June 30	Depreciation Expense, Building (Expense, ↑; debit)		12,000	
	Accumulated Depreciation, Building (Asset, ↓; credit)			12,000
	Record depreciation on building.			

ASSETS

ASSET

Building

Bal. 300,000	
Bal. 300,000	

CONTRA-ASSET

Accumulated Depreciation, Building

	Bal. 155,000
	(c) 12,000
	Bal. 167,000

EXPENSES

Depreciation Expense, Building

(c) 12,000	
Bal. 12,000	

The book value of the building is its original cost (the amount in the Building T-account) minus the accumulated depreciation on the building:

Book value of plant assets	
Building	$300,000
Less: Accumulated Depreciation, Building	(167,000)
Book Value of the Building	$133,000

d. Employees work Monday through Friday. The weekly payroll is $5,000 and is paid every Friday. June 30, 2008, is a Thursday.

Salary is an accrued expense. That is, it is a liability that incurs from an *expense* that hasn't been paid yet. Most employers pay their employees *after* the work has been done, which means that the work is a *past* benefit. This is Salary Expense, and it grows each pay period until payday.

Cloud's employees are paid $5,000 for five days of work (Monday through Friday), which means they earn $5,000/5 = $1,000 per day. By the end of the day on Thursday, June 30, the employees have worked for four days and have not been paid. Therefore, Cloud owes employees $1,000 × 4 = $4,000 of salary at June 30.

If the salaries have not been paid, then they are pay*able* (or in other words, they are *owed*). They must be recorded as some kind of payable account. We might be tempted to use Accounts Payable, but this account is usually reserved for *bills* received. Employees do not typically send their employers a bill. They simply expect to be paid and Cloud knows that the salaries are owed. For this reason, we put this amount into another payable account. In this case, Salary Payable is most appropriate.

Because salary is not owed until work is performed, we know that Cloud's employees have already worked. For a *past* benefit, we need to record an expense (in this case, Salary Expense).

We record an increase to Salary Expense (a debit) and an increase to the liability Salary Payable (a credit) of $4,000.

Journal Entry:

Date	Accounts	Post Ref.	Dr.	Cr.
June 30	Salary Expense (Expense, ↑; debit)		4,000	
	Salary Payable (Liability, ↑; credit)			4,000
	Accrue salary expense.			

	EXPENSES					LIABILITIES	
	Salary Expense					Salary Payable	
Bal.	255,000					(d)	4,000
(d)	4,000					Bal.	4,000
Bal.	259,000						

e. Service revenue of $15,000 must be accrued.

Accrued revenue is another way of saying "receivable" (or receipt in the future). If *accrued* revenue is recorded, it means that a receivable is also recorded. Customers have received goods or services from the business, but the business has not yet received the cash. The business is entitled to these receivables because the revenue has been earned.

Service Revenue must be increased by $15,000 (a credit) and the Accounts Receivable asset must be increased by $15,000 (a debit).

Journal Entry:

Date	Accounts	Post Ref.	Dr.	Cr.
June 30	Accounts Receivable (Asset, ↑; debit)		15,000	
	Service Revenue (Revenue, ↑; credit)			15,000
	Accrue service revenue.			

ASSETS

Accounts Receivable

Bal.	104,000		
(e)	15,000		
Bal.	119,000		

REVENUES

Service Revenue

		Bal.	450,000
		(e)	15,000
		Bal.	465,000

f. A client paid $40,000 in advance for consulting services to be provided evenly from January 1, 2008, through August 31, 2008. None of the revenue from this client has been recorded.

Cloud received cash in advance for work not yet performed for the client. By accepting the cash, Cloud also accepted the obligation to perform that work (or provide a refund if they did not). In accounting, an obligation is a liability. We call this liability "unearned revenue" because it *will* be revenue (after the work is performed) but it is not revenue *yet*.

The $40,000 paid in advance is still in the Unearned Revenue account. However, some of the revenue has been earned as of June 30. Six months of the earnings period have passed (January 1 through June 30), so six months' worth of the revenue has been earned.

The entire revenue earnings period is eight months (January 1 through August 31), so the revenue earned per month is $40,000/8 = $5,000. The six months of revenue earned total:

$$6 \times \$5,000 = \$30,000$$

The "correct liability amount" is the amount of unearned revenue that will appear on the balance sheet. In this case, two months of unearned revenue remain: $2 \times \$5,000 = \$10,000$. However, right now the Unearned Revenue account shows a balance of $40,000 (as we can see from the trial balance). This $40,000 is the "total accounted for."

Correct Liability Amount: → Total Accounted for: ← Correct Revenue Amount:

$10,000 $40,000 $30,000

So Unearned Revenue, a liability, must be decreased by $30,000 (a debit). Because the revenue is now earned, it can be recorded as normal service revenue. Therefore, Service Revenue also increases by $30,000 (a credit).

Journal Entry:

Date	Accounts	Post Ref.	Dr.	Cr.
June 30	Unearned Service Revenue (Liability, ↓; debit)		30,000	
	Service Revenue (Revenue, ↑; credit)			30,000
	Record service revenue that was collected in			
	advance and has now been earned.			

Essentially, the $30,000 has been shifted from "unearned" to "earned" revenue.

	LIABILITIES				REVENUES	
	Unearned Service Revenue				**Service Revenue**	
(f)	30,000	Bal.	40,000		Bal.	450,000
		Bal.	10,000		(e)	15,000
					(f)	30,000
					Bal.	495,000

Now we will summarize all of the adjusting journal entries:

Journal Entry:

Date	Accounts	Dr.	Cr.
June 30	a. Supplies Expense	3,000	
	Supplies		3,000
	Record supply expense.		
30	b. Rent Expense	9,000	
	Prepaid Rent		9,000
	Record rent expense.		
30	c. Depreciation Expense, Building	12,000	
	Accumulated Depreciation, Building		12,000
	Record depreciaton on building.		
30	d. Salary Expense	4,000	
	Salary Payable		4,000
	Accrue salary expense.		
30	e. Accounts Receivable	15,000	
	Service Revenue		15,000
	Accrue service revenue.		
30	f. Unearned Service Revenue	30,000	
	Service Revenue		30,000
	Record service revenue that was collected in advance		
	and has now been earned.		

Requirement 3

Total all the T-accounts in the ledger.

3 Make adjusting entries.

| Part 1 | Part 2 | **Part 3** | Part 4 | Part 5 | Demo Doc Complete |

After posting all of these entries and totaling all of the T-accounts, we have:

ASSETS

Cash

| Bal. | 131,000 | | |

Accounts Receivable

Bal.	104,000		
(e)	15,000		
Bal.	119,000		

Supplies

| Bal. | 4,000 | (a) | 3,000 |
| Bal. | 1,000 | | |

Prepaid Rent

Bal.	27,000		
		(b)	9,000
Bal.	18,000		

Land

| Bal. | 45,000 | | |

Building

| Bal. | 300,000 | | |

Accumulated Depreciation, Building

		Bal.	155,000
		(c)	12,000
		Bal.	167,000

LIABILITIES

Accounts Payable

| | | Bal. | 159,000 |

Salary Payable

| | | (d) | 4,000 |
| | | Bal. | 4,000 |

Unearned Service Revenue

		Bal.	40,000
(f)	30,000		
		Bal.	10,000

OWNER'S EQUITY

Susan Cloud, Capital

| | | Bal. | 152,000 |

Susan Cloud, Withdrawals

| Bal. | 57,000 | | |

Service Revenue

		Bal.	450,000
		(e)	15,000
		(f)	30,000
		Bal.	495,000

Salary Expense

Bal.	255,000		
(d)	4,000		
Bal.	259,000		

Supplies Expense

| (a) | 3,000 | | |
| Bal. | 3,000 | | |

Rent Expense

Bal.	25,000		
(b)	9,000		
Bal.	34,000		

Depreciation Expense, Building

| (c) | 12,000 | | |
| Bal. | 12,000 | | |

Miscellaneous Expense

| Bal. | 8,000 | | |

Make adjusting entries.

Prepare an adjusted trial balance.

Write the trial balance on a worksheet, enter the adjusting entries, and prepare an adjusted trial balance.

| Part 1 | Part 2 | Part 3 | **Part 4** | Part 5 | Demo Doc Complete |

First, we copy the account titles and trial balance amounts directly from the trial balance (shown at the beginning of the question) into the Trial Balance section (columns). Place the amounts in the correct debit or credit column.

Next we record the adjusting journal entries into the correct debit or credit columns of the Adjustments section (columns) of the worksheet. Each entry should include a letter identifying the adjusting entry recorded.

Now calculate the new balances for each account by adding the debits and credits across. These balances should be the same as the balances you calculated for the T-accounts in Requirement 3. Place these amounts into the Adjusted Trial Balance columns and give the adjusted account balances.

CLOUD BREAK CONSULTING
Worksheet
June 30, 2008

Account Title	Trial Balance Dr.	Trial Balance Cr.	Adjustments Dr.	Adjustments Cr.	Adjusted Trial Balance Dr.	Adjusted Trial Balance Cr.
Cash	131,000				131,000	
Accounts receivable	104,000		e. 15,000		119,000	
Supplies	4,000			a. 3,000	1,000	
Prepaid rent	27,000			b. 9,000	18,000	
Land	45,000				45,000	
Building	300,000				300,000	
Accumulated depreciation, building		155,000		c. 12,000		167,000
Accounts payable		159,000				159,000
Salary payable				d. 4,000		4,000
Unearned service revenue		40,000	f. 30,000			10,000
Susan Cloud, capital		152,000				152,000
Susan Cloud, withdrawals	57,000				57,000	
Service revenue		450,000		e. 15,000		495,000
				f. 30,000		
Salary expense	255,000		d. 4,000		259,000	
Supplies expense			a. 3,000		3,000	
Rent expense	25,000		b. 9,000		34,000	
Depreciation expense, building			c. 12,000		12,000	
Miscellaneous expense	8,000				8,000	
Total	956,000	956,000	73,000	73,000	987,000	987,000

You should be sure that the debit and credit columns equal before moving on to the next section.

Requirement 5

Prepare the income statement, the statement of owner's equity, and the balance sheet. Draw arrows linking the three financial statements.

⑤ Prepare financial statements from an adjusted trial balance.

| Part 1 | Part 2 | Part 3 | Part 4 | **Part 5** | Demo Doc Complete |

CLOUD BREAK CONSULTING
Income Statement
Year Ended June 30, 2008

Revenue:		
Service revenue		$495,000
Expenses:		
Salary expense	$259,000	
Rent expense	34,000	
Depreciation expense, building	12,000	
Supplies expense	3,000	
Miscellaneous expense	8,000	
Total expenses		316,000
Net income		$179,000

CLOUD BREAK CONSULTING
Statement of Owner's Equity
Year Ended June 30, 2008

Susan Cloud, capital, July 1, 2007	$152,000
Add: Net income	179,000
Subtotal	331,000
Less: Withdrawals by owner	(57,000)
Susan Cloud, capital, June 30, 2008	$274,000

CLOUD BREAK CONSULTING
Balance Sheet
June 30, 2008

Assets			Liabilities	
Cash		$131,000	Accounts payable	$159,000
Accounts receivable		119,000	Salary payable	4,000
Supplies		1,000	Unearned service revenue	10,000
Prepaid rent		18,000	Total liabilities	173,000
Land		45,000		
Building	$300,000		**Owner's Equity**	
Less: Accumulated depreciation	(167,000)	133,000	Susan Cloud, capital	274,000
Total assets		$447,000	Total liabilities and owner's equity	$447,000

| Part 1 | Part 2 | Part 3 | Part 4 | Part 5 | Demo Doc Complete |

Accounting in Action

THE ADJUSTING PROCESS

Here are some decisions you would make as you use accrual basis accounting in your business:

Decision	Guidelines
• How to measure business income accurately?	*Accrual basis accounting*, because it provides more complete reports of operating performance and financial position
• How to measure revenues?	*Revenue recognition principle*—Record revenues only when they're earned
• How to measure expenses?	*Matching principle*—Subtract expenses from the revenues they relate to in order to measure net income
• What period to measure income?	*Time period concept*—measure income for fiscal years of equal length
• Where to start measuring income at the end of the period?	Unadjusted trial balance, usually referred to simply as the *trial balance*
• How to update the accounts before preparing the financial statements?	*Make adjusting entries* at the end of the period

Decision

• What are the categories of adjusting entries?

• How do the adjusting entries differ from other journal entries?

• Where are the accounts with their adjusted balances summarized?

Guidelines

Deferred expenses   Accrued revenues
Deferred (unearned) revenues   Accrued expenses

1. Made only at the end of the period
2. Never affect cash
3. Debit or credit
   • At least one *income statement* account
   • At least one *balance sheet* account

Adjusted trial balance, which aids in preparation of the financial statements

Review

The Adjusting Process
Word Power

Accrual basis accounting Accounting that records revenues when earned and expenses when incurred to produce those revenues; recognizes the impact of transactions as they occur regardless of whether they involve a transfer of cash.

Accruals Revenues earned or expenses incurred before cash has been exchanged.

Accumulated depreciation A contra-asset account that holds the cumulative sum of all depreciation recorded for an asset.

Adjusted trial balance A list of all the accounts of a business with their adjusted balances.

Adjusting entry Entry made at the end of the accounting period to measure the period's income accurately and bring the related asset and liability accounts to correct balances before the financial statements are prepared.

Book value The asset's cost minus its accumulated depreciation. Also called *carrying value*.

Carrying value The asset's cost minus its accumulated depreciation. Also called *book value*.

Contra-account An account that always has a companion account and whose normal balance is opposite that of the companion account.

Deferrals Cash received or paid before revenues have been earned or expenses have been incurred.

Deferred revenue A liability created when a business collects cash from customers in advance of providing goods or services. Also called *unearned revenue*.

Depreciation Allocation of the cost of a long-term asset to expense over its useful life.

Fiscal year Any consecutive, 12-month period that a business adopts as its accounting year.

Fiscal year-end (FYE) The ending date of a business's fiscal year.

Long-term assets Long-lived, tangible assets such as land, buildings, equipment, and furniture, used in the operation of a business lasting for more than a year.

Matching principle Recording expenses in the time period they were incurred to produce revenues, thus matching them against the revenues earned during that same period.

Straight-line depreciation A method of estimating depreciation: (Cost of the Asset – Salvage Value)/Useful Life of the Asset.

Revenue recognition principle Recording revenues when they are earned by providing goods or services to customers.

Time period concept Accounting periods must be of equal length so that income measurement is comparable from one period to another; ensures that information is reported at regular intervals.

Unearned revenue A liability created when a business collects cash from customers in advance of providing goods or services. Also called *deferred revenue*.

Worksheet A document holding the trial balance, adjustments, and adjusted trial balance of a business and is used to prepare financial statements.

Quick Check

1. What are the features of accrual accounting?

   a. Accrual accounting records all transactions.
   b. Revenues are only recorded for cash receipts.
   c. Expenses are only recorded for cash payments.
   d. All the above are true.

2. The revenue recognition principle says:

   a. Record revenue only after you have earned it.
   b. Record revenue only when you receive cash.
   c. Match revenues and expenses in order to compute net income.
   d. Divide time into equal periods to measure net income or net loss properly.

3. Adjusting the accounts is the process of:

   a. Recording transactions as they occur during the period.
   b. Updating the accounts at the end of the period.
   c. Zeroing out account balances to prepare for the next period.
   d. Subtracting expenses from revenues to measure net income.

4. Which terms describe the types of adjusting entries?

   a. Deferrals and depreciation
   b. Expenses and revenues
   c. Deferrals and accruals
   d. Prepaid expenses and prepaid revenues

5. Assume that the weekly payroll of It's Just Lunch is $5,000. December 31, the end of the year, falls on Monday, but the company won't pay employees for the full week until its usual payday, Friday. What adjusting entry will It's Just Lunch make on Monday, December 31?

Journal Entry:

Date	Accounts	Post Ref.	Dr.	Cr.
	a. Salary Expense		a. 1,000	
	Salary Payable			1,000
	b. Salary Expense		b. 1,000	
	Cash			1,000
	c. Salary Payable		c. 1,000	
	Salary Expense			1,000
	d. Salary Expense		d. 1,000	
	Accumulated Salary			1,000

6. Assume It's Just Lunch gains a client who prepays $600 for a package of six dates. It's Just Lunch collects the $600 in advance and will provide the date arrangements later. After setting up two dates for the client, what should It's Just Lunch report on its income statement for this transaction?

   a. Cash of $600
   b. Service Revenue of $600
   c. Service Revenue of $200
   d. Unearned Service Revenue of $400

7. After setting up two dates for the client, what should It's Just Lunch report on its balance sheet for this transaction?

   a. Accrued expense
   b. Prepaid expense
   c. Accrued revenue
   d. Unearned revenue

8. Unearned Revenue is always:

   a. A liability.
   b. Revenue.
   c. An asset.
   d. Owner's equity.

9. The adjusted trial balance shows:

   a. Amounts that may be out of balance.
   b. Revenues and expenses only.
   c. Assets, liabilities, and owner's equity only.
   d. Amounts that are ready for the financial statements.

10. Which correctly represents the flow of information from one financial statement to another?

    a. Income statement to the statement of owner's equity.
    b. Statement of owner's equity to the balance sheet.
    c. Both a and b are correct.
    d. None of the above is correct.

Answers are given after Apply Your Knowledge (p. 227).

Accounting Practice

Short Exercises

① Accounting principles that help measure income.

S3-1. Match the accounting term with the corresponding definition.

   ___ **1.** Accrual basis accounting

   ___ **2.** Matching principle

   ___ **3.** Revenue recognition principle

   ___ **4.** Time period concept

   a. Ensures that information is reported at regular intervals

   b. Records the impact of a business event as it occurs regardless of whether the transaction affected cash.

   c. Records expenses when incurred to sell goods or provide services.

   d. Records revenue when it is earned.

② The four types of adjusting entries.

S3-2. The trial balance of Moore Engineering includes the following balance sheet accounts. For each account, identify the type of adjusting entry that typically is made for the account (deferred expense, deferred revenue, accrued expense, or accrued revenue), and give the related income statement account used in that adjustment.

   a. Interest Payable

   b. Unearned Service Revenue

   c. Accounts Receivable

   d. Supplies

   e. Accumulated Depreciation

   Example: Prepaid Insurance: deferred expense; Insurance Expense

③ Making adjusting entries.

S3-3. Tory's Camera Shop's Prepaid Rent balance is $3,000 on September 1. This prepaid rent represents 5 months' rent. Journalize and post the adjusting entry on September 30 to record one month's rent. Compute the balances of the two accounts involved.

③ Making adjusting entries.

S3-4. Tory's Camera Shop's Advertising Supplies balance on September 1 is $2,000 and the balance in Advertising Supplies Expense is $0. On September 30, there are $1,300 of supplies on hand. Journalize and post the adjusting entry on September 30 for the supplies used. Compute the balances of the two accounts involved.

③ Making adjusting entries.

S3-5. Jones & Jones uses computers for data searches. Suppose that on April 1 the company paid cash of $30,000 for Hewlett-Packard computers that

continued.....

are expected to remain useful for two years. At the end of two years, the value of the computers is expected to be zero.

Requirements

1. Journalize entries to record the following:

    a. The purchase of the computers on April 1
    b. The depreciation on the computers on April 30

    Include dates and use the following accounts: Computer Equipment; Accumulated Depreciation, Computer Equipment; and Depreciation Expense, Computer Equipment.

2. Post the entries to the accounts listed in requirement 1, and show their balances at April 30.

3. What is the equipment's book value at April 30?

S3-6. In order to purchase computers and other supplies, Jones & Jones borrowed $50,000 on April 1 by signing a note payable to Community Bank. Interest expense for Jones & Jones is $250 per month. Journalize an adjusting entry to accrue interest expense at December 31, assuming no other adjusting entries have been made for the year. Post to the two accounts affected by the adjustment.

    ③ Making adjusting entries.

S3-7. Wheatfield Nature Magazine collected $2,400 on October 1 for one-year subscriptions from subscribers in advance. Journalize and post the adjusting entry on December 31 that Wheatfield Nature Magazine has earned, assuming no other adjusting entries have been made for the year.

    ③ Making adjusting entries.

S3-8. The accountant for Becker Supply asks you to journalize the following adjusting entries at December 31:

    ③ Making adjusting entries.

1. Services provided but not recorded, $1,000.

2. Salaries earned by employees but not recorded, $1,200.

3. Accrued interest on a note payable, $200.

S3-9. The adjusted trial balance of Forever Fresh Decorations at December 31, 2009 includes the following accounts: Depreciation Expense, $500; Supplies Expense, $50; Interest Expense, $80; Utilities Expense, $25; Service Revenue, $1,200; J. Kanse, Capital, $5,200; and J. Kanse, Withdrawals, $800. Prepare an income statement for the year. List the expenses from the largest amount to the smallest.

    ⑤ Preparing financial statements.

S3-10. Use the data from S3-9 to prepare a statement of owner's equity. No additional investments were made by the owner.

    ⑤ Preparing financial statements.

S3-11. Suppose you work summers doing photo shots for senior pictures. Most of your customers pay you immediately after their photo session, but a

    ③ Making adjusting entries.

continued.....

few customers ask you to bill them at the end of the month. It is now September 30 and you have collected $900 from cash-paying customers. Your remaining customers owe you $300. How much service revenue would you record according to accrual basis accounting?

3 Making adjusting entries.

S3-12. Stone Photos uses databases from the school to create mailings to send to potential clients. In order to manage the data, Stone Photos purchases a PowerBook for $3,000 cash. How would Stone Photos account for the $3,000 expenditure under the accrual basis of accounting?

Exercises

2 The four types of adjusting entries.

3 Making adjusting entries.

4 Preparing an adjusted trial balance.

E3-13. Match the accounting term with the corresponding definition.

_____ **1.** Accumulated depreciation

_____ **2.** Adjusted trial balance

_____ **3.** Adjusting entry

_____ **4.** Book value

_____ **5.** Contra-account

_____ **6.** Depreciation

_____ **7.** Long-term asset

a. An account whose normal balance is opposite that of its companion account.

b. Entry made to assign revenues to the period in which they are earned and expenses to the period incurred.

c. A list of accounts with their adjusted balances.

d. The cumulative sum of all depreciation recorded for an asset.

e. The allocation of a long-term asset's cost to expense over its useful life.

f. The asset's cost less its accumulated depreciation.

g. Long-lived asset used to operate the business.

1 Accounting principles that help measure income.

E3-14. Identify the accounting concept or principle (more than one may apply) that gives the most direction on how to account for each of the following situations:

a. Unpaid expenses of $1,200 must be accrued at the end of the period to measure income properly.

b. You sign a contract and receive $3,200 to provide services for a customer next month.

continued.....

c. The owner of a business desires monthly financial statements to measure the progress of the entity on an ongoing basis.

d. Total salaries for the period were $5,700. The salaries were paid to employees who washed cars at your car wash.

E3-15. Suppose you started up your own photography business to videotape events for high school seniors. The senior class paid you $300 in advance to film the prom. You videotaped the senior class awards ceremony but the high school hasn't paid you the $200 fee yet. Five parents each pay you $50 cash for filming their children at graduation. Answer the following questions about the correct way to account for your revenue under accrual basis accounting:

     1. Name the accounts used to record these events.

     2. Prepare the journal entries to record the three transactions.

③ Making adjusting entries.

E3-16. Calculate the missing amounts for each of the following Prepaid Advertising situations. For situation A, journalize the adjusting entry. Consider each situation separately.

③ Making adjusting entries.

	Situation			
	A	**B**	**C**	**D**
Beginning Prepaid Advertising	$400	$500	$900	$600
Payments for Prepaid Advertising during the year	1,400	?	1,100	?
Total amount to account for	?	?	2,000	1,500
Ending Prepaid Advertising	300	400	?	700
Advertising Expense	$?	$900	$1,200	$800

E3-17. Journalize the adjusting entries for the following adjustments at January 31, the end of the accounting period, omitting explanations.

③ Making adjusting entries.

     a. Employee salaries owed for Monday through Thursday of a five-day workweek, $10,000.

     b. Unearned service revenue now earned, $500.

     c. Depreciation, $3,000.

     d. Prepaid rent expired, $300.

     e. Interest revenue accrued, $3,800.

E3-18. If the entries in E3-17 were omitted at year-end, compute the amount of overstatement or understatement of each transaction on the income

⑤ Preparing financial statements.

continued.....

statement. What is the total understatement or overstated caused by not recording the adjustments? Use the following format to help analyze the transactions.

Transaction	Overstatement/Understatement	Amount
Sample		
a.	Overstatement	$10,000

E3-19. Journalize the adjusting entry needed at December 31, the fiscal year-end, for each of the following independent situations. No other adjusting entries have been made for the year.

a. On October 1, we collected $6,000 rent in advance. We debited Cash and credited Unearned Rent Revenue. The tenant was paying one year's rent in advance.

b. Interest revenue of $800 has been earned but not yet received. The business holds a $20,000 note receivable.

c. Salary expense is $1,500 per day, Monday through Friday, and the business pays employees each Friday. This year, December 31 falls on a Wednesday.

d. The unadjusted balance of the Supplies account is $3,100. Supplies on hand total $1,200.

e. Equipment was purchased last year at a cost of $10,000. The equipment's useful life is four years.

f. On September 1, when we prepaid $1,200 for a two-year insurance policy, we debited Prepaid Insurance and credited Cash.

E3-20. The accounting records of Carson Graphic Designers include the following unadjusted balances at March 31: Accounts Receivable, $1,000; Supplies, $600; Salary Payable, $0; Unearned Service Revenue, $400; Service Revenue, $4,700; Salary Expense, $1,200; and Supplies Expense, $0. Carson's accountant gathered the following data for the March 31 adjusting entries:

a. Service revenue accrued, $2,000.

b. Unearned service revenue that has been earned, $200.

c. Supplies on hand, $100.

d. Salary owed to employee, $400.

Record the adjustments, then post them to T-accounts, labeling each adjustment by letter. Calculate each account's adjusted balance.

E3-21. The adjusted trial balance of Shawn Peterson, Web Designer, is incomplete. Enter the adjustment amounts directly in the adjustment columns.

continued.....

SHAWN PETERSON, WEB DESIGNER Worksheet May 31, 2008							
	Trial Balance		Adjustments		Adjusted Trial Balance	
Account Title	Dr.	Cr.	Dr.	Cr.	Dr.	Cr.
Cash	4,000				4,000	
Accounts receivable	4,500				7,600	
Supplies	1,000				800	
Equipment	22,300				22,300	
Accumulated depreciation, equipment		15,000				15,400
Salary payable						900
S. Peterson, capital		16,400				16,400
S. Peterson, withdrawals	5,100				5,100	
Service revenue		9,600				12,700
Salary expense	2,700				3,600	
Rent expense	1,400				1,400	
Depreciation expense, equipment					400	
Supplies expense					200	
Total	41,000	41,000			45,400	45,400

E3-22. Make the journal entry for each adjustment needed to complete the adjusted trial balance in E3-21. Date the entries.

③ Making adjusting entries.

E3-23. Using the adjusted trial balance in E3-21, prepare the Shawn Peterson, Web Designer, income statement and statement of owner's equity for the month ended May 31, 2008; also prepare its balance sheet on that date.

⑤ Preparing financial statements.

E3-24. The accountant for Brian Lynn Studio posted adjusting entries (a) through (e) to the accounts at December 31, 2008. Selected balance sheet accounts and all the revenues and expenses of the entity follow in T-account form.

⑤ Preparing financial statements.

Accounts Receivable		Supplies		Accumulated Depreciation, Equipment		Accumulated Depreciation, Building	
23,000		3,000	(a) 1,000		5,000		33,000
(e) 1,000					(b) 1,000		(c) 5,000

Salary Payable						Service Revenue	
	(d) 1,500						105,000
							(e) 1,000

Salary Expense		Supplies Expense		Depreciation Expense, Equipment		Depreciation Expense, Building	
10,000		(a) 1,000		(b) 1,000		(c) 5,000	
(d) 1,500							

continued.....

1. Calculate balances in the accounts and use the appropriate accounts to prepare the income statement of Brian Lynn Studio for the year-ended December 31, 2008. List expenses in order from largest to smallest.

2. Were the 2008 operations successful? Give the reason for your answer.

E3-25. Weave Roofing began the year with capital of $30,000. On July 12, Slade Weave invested $12,000 cash in the business. On September 10, he invested land in the business valued at $50,000 by transferring his personal asset to the company. The income statement for the year-ended December 31, 2008, reported a net loss of $28,000. During this fiscal year, Weave withdrew $1,500 each month for personal use.

⑤ Preparing financial statements.

Requirements

1. Prepare Weave Roofing's statement of owner's equity for the year-ended December 31, 2008.

2. Did the owner's equity of the business increase or decrease during the year? What caused this change?

③ Making adjusting entries.

E3-26. The adjusted trial balances of Bonds Electronic Shop at December 31, 2009, and December 31, 2008, include these amounts:

⑤ Preparing financial statements.

	2009	2008
Supplies	$ 2,100	$2,000
Salary Payable	3,800	3,700
Unearned Service Revenue	18,000	16,300

Analysis of the accounts at December 31, 2009, reveals these transactions for 2009:

Purchases of supplies	$ 8,400
Cash payments for salaries	45,600
Cash receipts in advance for service revenue	95,200

Compute the amount of supplies expense, salary expense, and service revenue to report on the Bonds Electronics income statement for 2009. Solve by making T-accounts and posting the information to solve for the unknown amounts.

E3-27. Country Inn completed the following selected transactions and prepared the following adjusting entries during July:

③ Making adjusting entries.

July 1	Prepaid advertising for three months, $2,100.
5	Paid electricity expenses, $500.
9	Received cash for the day's room rentals, $600.
14	Paid cash for six cable hookups, $600.
23	Served a banquet, receiving a note receivable, $1,600.
31	Made the adjusting entry for advertising related to the July 1 transaction.
31	Accrued salaries, $900.

State whether each transaction would increase revenues, decrease revenues, increase expenses, decrease expenses, or have no effect on revenues or expenses. If revenues or expenses are affected, give the amount of the impact on revenues or expenses for July. Use the following illustration of the July 1 entry as the format for your answers.

Revenues and Expenses for July		
Date	Impact on Revenues or Expenses	$ Effect on Revenues or Expenses
July 1	No effect	0

Problems (Group A)

P3-28A. Journalize the adjusting entry needed on December 31, the end of the current accounting year, for each of the following independent cases affecting Wisconsin Alps. No other adjusting entries have been made for the year.

③ Making adjusting entries.

a. Prior to making the adjusting entry on December 31, the balance in Prepaid Insurance is $3,600. Wisconsin Alps pays liability insurance each year on March 31.

b. Wisconsin Alps pays employees each Friday. The amount of the weekly payroll is $5,000 for a five-day workweek. December 31, the fiscal year-end, is a Monday.

c. Wisconsin Alps borrowed money, signing a note payable. For the current year, accrued interest amounts to $600 and will be paid next year.

d. The beginning balance of Supplies was $1,600. During the year, it purchased supplies for $4,900, and at December 31 the supplies on hand total $2,100.

continued.....

e. Wisconsin Alps contracts with corporations who reward their employees with skiing vacations. The corporations paid $16,000 in advance. This receipt was journalized and posted as a debit to Cash and credit to Unearned Service Revenue. The owner determines that Wisconsin Alps earned one-fourth of the total fee received during the current year.

f. Depreciation for the current year includes Ski Lifts, $3,850, and Lighting Equipment, $1,300.

(3) Making adjusting entries.

P3-29A. Assume the unadjusted and adjusted trial balances for YOYO Games at September 30, 2009, show the following data:

YOYO GAMES
Adjusted Trial Balance
September 30, 2009

Account Title	Adjusted Trial Balance Dr.	Adjusted Trial Balance Cr.	Trial Balance Dr.	Trial Balance Cr.
Cash	$ 5,200		$ 5,200	
Accounts receivable	5,000		5,700	
Interest receivable			300	
Notes receivable	6,100		6,100	
Supplies	1,000		300	
Prepaid rent	2,400		1,600	
Equipment	46,400		46,400	
Accumulated depreciation, equipment		$16,000		$17,200
Accounts payable		6,900		6,900
Wages payable				300
Bailey Cole, capital		39,500		39,500
Bailey Cole, withdrawals	3,600		3,600	
Rental revenue		9,500		10,200
Interest revenue				300
Wage expense	1,600		1,900	
Rent expense			800	
Depreciation expense, equipment			1,200	
Insurance expense	400		400	
Supplies expense			700	
Utilities expense	200		200	
Total	$71,900	$71,900	$74,400	$74,400

Requirements

(3) Making adjusting entries.

Journalize the adjusting entries that account for the differences between the two trial balances.

(4) Preparing an adjusted trial balance.

(5) Preparing financial statements.

P3-30A. The trial balance of Padre Paradise at December 31, 2008, and the data needed for the month-end adjustments follow:

a. Insurance coverage still remaining at December 31, $300.

b. Supplies used during the month, $200.

continued.....

c. Depreciation for the month, $900.

d. Accrued advertising expense at December 31, $300. (Use Accounts Payable as the liability account needed.)

e. Accrued salaries at December 31, $100.

f. Service revenue still unearned at December 31, $1,000.

	PADRE PARADISE Trial Balance December 31, 2008		
		Balance	
	Account Title	**Debit**	**Credit**
	Cash	$ 22,200	
	Accounts receivable	44,100	
	Prepaid insurance	3,100	
	Supplies	800	
	Building	412,700	
	Accumulated depreciation, building		$321,600
	Accounts payable		1,900
	Salary payable		
	Unearned service revenue		2,300
	Jane Carlsen, capital		155,000
	Jane Carlsen, withdrawals	2,900	
	Service revenue		7,900
	Salary expense	2,100	
	Insurance expense		
	Depreciation expense, building		
	Advertising expense	800	
	Supplies expense		
	Total	$488,700	$488,700

Requirements

1. Open T-accounts for the accounts listed in the trial balance and insert their December 31 unadjusted balances.

2. Journalize the adjusting entries and post them to the T-accounts. Reference the posted amounts by letters, (a) through (f).

3. Prepare the adjusted trial balance.

4. How will the company use the adjusted trial balance?

P3-31A. The adjusted trial balance of American Central at December 31, 2008, follows:

 Preparing financial statements.

continued.....

AMERICAN CENTRAL Adjusted Trial Balance December 31, 2008		
	Balance	
Account Title	**Debit**	**Credit**
Cash	$ 2,100	
Accounts receivable	3,000	
Supplies	2,300	
Prepaid rent	1,600	
Office furniture	37,700	
Accumulated depreciation, office furniture		$ 5,600
Accounts payable		2,600
Unearned service revenue		600
Dakota Sloan, capital		26,000
Dakota Sloan, withdrawals	29,000	
Service revenue		106,000
Depreciation expense, office furniture	2,300	
Salary expense	39,900	
Rent expense	17,400	
Utilities expense	2,600	
Supplies expense	2,900	
Total	$140,800	$140,800

Requirements

1. Prepare American Central's 2008 income statement, statement of owner's equity, and year-end balance sheet. List expenses in decreasing order on the income statement.

2. a. Which financial statement reports American Central's results of operations? Were operations successful during 2008? Cite specifics from the financial statements to support your evaluation.

b. Which statement reports the company's financial position? Does American Central's financial position look strong or weak? Give the reason for your evaluation.

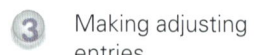

Making adjusting entries.

P3-32A. Edward Russell, an attorney, has a law practice that completed these transactions and recorded these adjusting journal entries during October:

Oct. 2	Prepaid insurance for October through December, $600.
4	Paid water bill, $450.
5	Performed services on account, $3,000.
9	Withdrew cash for personal use, $1,400.
12	Received cash for services performed, $8,400.
14	Purchased office equipment on account, $300.

continued.....

28   Collected $500 on account from the October 5 transaction.

29   Paid salary expense, $1,100.

30   Paid the account payable from October 14.

31   Recorded an adjusting entry for October insurance expense related to the October 2 transaction.

31   Recorded an adjusting entry for unearned revenue now earned, $700.

Requirements

1. State whether the transaction would increase revenues, decrease revenues, increase expenses, decrease expenses, or have no effect on revenues or expenses. If revenues or expenses are affected, give the amount of the impact on revenues or expenses for October. Use the following format for your answer.

Revenues and Expenses for October		
Date	Impact on Revenues or Expenses	$ Effect on Revenues or Expenses

2. Using the results from Requirement 1, compute October net income or net loss under the accrual basis of accounting.

3. Why does the accrual basis of accounting result in an accurate measurement of income?

Problems (Group B)

P3-33B. Journalize the adjusting entry needed on December 31, the end of the current accounting period, for each of the following independent cases affecting Burke's Restoration. No other adjusting entries have been made for the year.

 Making adjusting entries.

a. Each Friday, Burke pays employees for the current week's work. The amount of the payroll is $10,000 for a five-day workweek. December 31, the fiscal year-end, is a Thursday.

b. Burke pays $1,500 for insurance coverage each year on September 30.

c. Burke received notes receivable from some clients for professional services rendered. During the current year, Burke earned interest of $600, which will be collected next year.

d. The beginning balance of Supplies was $3,800. During the year, Burke purchased supplies costing $5,500, and at December 31, the supplies on hand total $2,700.

e. Burke managed an antique show, and the client paid Burke $16,000 at the start of the project. Burke recorded this amount as Unearned Service Revenue. The campaign will run for several

continued.....

months. Burke estimates that the company has earned three-fourths of the total fee during the current year.

f. Depreciation for the current year includes: Office Furniture, $4,500, and Office Equipment, $1,700.

③ Making adjusting entries.

P3-34B. Jordan Brokers' unadjusted and adjusted trial balances at December 31, 2008, follow.

	JORDAN BROKERS Adjusted Trial Balance December 31, 2008				
		Trial Balance		Adjusted Trial Balance	
	Account Title	Dr.	Cr.	Dr.	Cr.
	Cash	$ 2,200		$ 2,200	
	Accounts receivable	5,200		13,200	
	Supplies	800		300	
	Prepaid insurance	2,900		2,300	
	Office furniture	16,400		16,400	
	Accumulated depreciation, office furniture		$ 6,200		$ 7,800
	Accounts payable		6,400		6,400
	Salary payable				1,000
	Interest payable				400
	Notes payable		8,600		8,600
	Megan Jordan, capital		13,500		13,500
	Megan Jordan, withdrawals	9,400		9,400	
	Commission revenue		46,900		54,900
	Depreciation expense, office furniture			1,600	
	Supplies expense			500	
	Utilities expense	5,000		5,000	
	Salary expense	26,600		27,600	
	Rent Expense	12,200		12,200	
	Interest expense	900		1,300	
	Insurance expense			600	
	Total	$81,600	$81,600	$92,600	$92,600

Requirements

③ Making adjusting entries.

Journalize the adjusting entries that account for the differences between the two trial balances.

④ Preparing an adjusted trial balance.

P3-35B. The trial balance of Pod Electronics at August 31, 2008, and the data needed for the month-end adjustments follow:

⑤ Preparing financial statements.

continued.....

		POD ELECTRONICS Trial Balance August 31, 2008		

		Balance	
Account Title		**Debit**	**Credit**
Cash		$ 4,100	
Accounts receivable		15,800	
Prepaid rent		2,400	
Supplies		1,200	
Furniture		19,700	
Accumulated depreciation, furniture			$ 3,600
Accounts payable			3,300
Salary payable			
Unearned service revenue			2,800
William Pod, capital			31,500
William Pod, withdrawals		5,300	
Service revenue			12,600
Salary expense		3,800	
Rent expense			
Depreciation expense, furniture			
Advertising expense		1,500	
Supplies expense			
Total		$ 53,800	$ 53,800

a. Unearned service revenue still unearned at August 31, $800.

b. Rent still prepaid at August 31, $600.

c. Supplies used during the month, $500.

d. Depreciation for the month, $450.

e. Accrued advertising expense at August 31, $600. (Use Accounts Payable as the liability account needed.)

f. Accrued salaries at August 31, $500.

Requirements

1. Open T-accounts for the accounts listed in the trial balance and insert their August 31 unadjusted balances.

2. Journalize the adjusting entries and post them to the T-accounts. Reference the posted amounts by letters (a) through (f).

3. Prepare the adjusted trial balance.

4. How will Pod Electronics use the adjusted trial balance?

P3-36B. The adjusted trial balance of Jason's Art & Coffee Experience at December 31, 2008, follows.

 Preparing financial statements.

continued.....

JASON'S ART AND COFFEE EXPERIENCE		
Adjusted Trial Balance		
December 31, 2008		

	Balance	
Account Title	**Debit**	**Credit**
Cash	$ 5,300	
Accounts receivable	12,100	
Prepaid rent	1,350	
Supplies	970	
Equipment	54,000	
Accumulated depreciation, equipment		$ 22,240
Accounts payable		13,600
Unearned service revenue		4,520
Interest payable		1,570
Salary payable		930
Notes payable		15,000
J. Moore, capital		22,380
J. Moore, withdrawals	48,000	
Service revenue		115,000
Depreciation expense, equipment	13,710	
Salary expense	35,000	
Rent expense	12,000	
Interest expense	4,200	
Utilities expense	3,770	
Insurance expense	3,150	
Supplies expense	1,690	
Total	$195,240	$195,240

Requirements

1. Prepare Jason's 2008 income statement and statement of owner's equity and year-end balance sheet. List expenses in decreasing order on the income statement.

2. **a.** Which financial statement reports Jason's results of operations? Were 2008 operations successful? Cite specifics from the financial statements to support your evaluation.

   b. Which statement reports the company's financial position? Does Jason's financial position look strong or weak? Give the reason for your evaluation.

 Making adjusting entries.

P3-37B. Hertz Management completed the following selected transactions and prepared these adjusting entries during January:

Jan. 1	Prepaid insurance for January through March, $600.
4	Performed management service on account, $2,200.
5	Purchased office furniture on account, $150.
8	Paid property tax expense, $450.

continued.....

11	Purchased office equipment for cash, $800.
19	Performed management services and received cash, $7,700.
24	Collected $400 on account.
26	Paid the account payable from the January 5 transaction.
29	Paid salary expense, $2,000.
31	Recorded an adjusting entry for January insurance expense related to the January 1 transaction.
31	Recorded an adjusting entry for unearned revenue now earned, $600.

Requirements

1. State whether the transaction would increase revenues, decrease revenues, increase expenses, decrease expenses, or have no effect on revenues or expenses. If revenues or expenses are affected, give the amount of the impact on revenues or expenses for October. Use the following format for your answer.

Revenues and Expenses for January		
Date	Impact on Revenues or Expenses	$ Effect on Revenues or Expenses

2. Compute January net income or net loss under the accrual basis of accounting.

3. State why the accrual basis of accounting results in an accurate measurement of income.

for 24/7 practice, visit www.MyAccountingLab.com

Apply Your Knowledge

BE ON GUARD

Case 1. Lisa Sweet was preparing the adjusting journal entries for Sweet Enterprises, a business that uses the accrual basis of accounting, in order to prepare the adjusted trial balance and financial statements. She knew that $1,300 of salaries related to the current accounting period had accrued but wouldn't be paid until the next period. Lisa thought that simply not including the adjustment for these salaries would mean no additional salary expense for the current period, and reported net income would be higher than it would have been if she had made the adjustment. Further, she knew that the Salary Payable account would be zero, so the liabilities reported on the balance sheet would be less, and her business would look even better. Besides, she reasoned that these salaries would be reported eventually, so it was merely a matter of showing them in one period instead of another. Dismissing the reporting as just a timing issue, she ignored the adjustment for the additional salary expense.

Is Lisa acting unethically by failing to record the adjustment for accrued salaries? Does it matter that, shortly into the new accounting period, the wages will ultimately be paid? Is it really simply a matter of timing? What are the potential problems of failing to include all the adjusting journal entries?

Case 2. On December 30, Michael Smith was posting the year-end adjustments for his business, Excel Limited. The income statement he was completing for a bank loan was not as strong as Michael thought it would be, with low sales revenue for the year. He was talking the situation over with his sister when he had an idea. Michael asked his sister if she would buy some products from Excel Limited so that the December Sales Revenue would be higher. His sister told him that she did not need any of the products Excel Limited sold. Michael then told her to simply buy the products now, and return them in January for a refund. His sister said that she did not have any money and couldn't buy them, even if she was eventually going to return them. Michael then said that she could buy the goods on account, then in January her account would be credited in full when she returned them. Michael realized that he would not only be able to increase Sales Revenue for the month, but he would also show an increase in assets because of a greater Accounts Receivable balance. His sister asked Michael if what they were contemplating was an acceptable business practice. Michael explained that any customer could return merchandise purchased within 30 days, so what they were doing was a perfectly acceptable business transaction.

Is Michael's plan to sell products in the current year only to have them returned in the next accounting period unethical? Does the fact that all customers have a 30-day return privilege affect your answer? What are the implications of Michael's plan?

KNOW YOUR BUSINESS

This case will help you to better understand the effect of adjusting journal entries on the financial statements. You know that adjusting journal entries are entered in the journal and then posted to the ledger accounts. We do not have access to the journals and ledgers used by Target but we can see some of the adjusted accounts on their financial statements. Refer to the Target Income Statements,

"Consolidated Results of Operations," and the Target Balance Sheets, "Consolidated Statements of Financial Position" in Appendix A. Also find the footnote titled "Accrued Liabilities," which is one of the many footnotes included after the financial statements.

Requirements

1. Open T-accounts for the following accounts and their balances as of January 2004. (Note that amounts from the Target financial statements are in millions.)

Accumulated Depreciation	$4,727
Accrued Liabilities	$1,288

2. Using the information below for Target's 2004 operations, make the appropriate journal entries. Use the Accrued Liabilities account for all accrued liabilities.
   a. Depreciation expense, $685.
   b. Full payment of the January 2004 Accrued Liabilities balance, $1,288.
   c. Accrued wages and benefits expense, $412.
   d. Accrued taxes payable, $287.
   e. Accrued gift card liability, $214.
   f. Other accrued expenses, $720.

3. Post the journal entries to the two T-accounts you set up. Check the updated ending balances in each account against the balances reported on the Target balance sheet as of January 2005, "Consolidated Statements of Financial Position."

For Internet Exercises, Excel in Practice, and additional online activities, go to the Web site www.prenhall.com/pollard.

Quick Check Answers

1. *a* 2. *a* 3. *b* 4. *c* 5. *a* 6. *c* 7. *d* 8. *a* 9. *d* 10. *c*

LEARNING OBJECTIVES

1. Explain the steps in the accounting cycle.

2. Prepare a worksheet.

3. Prepare financial statements using the worksheet.

4. Close the revenue, expense, and withdrawals accounts.

5. Classify assets and liabilities as current or long-term.

4

Completing the Accounting Cycle

Most games, such as golf, baseball, soccer, and chess, involve competition between two or more people with specific goals to achieve and rules to follow. Some games have time constraints; the individual or team that wins the most points within a certain time period wins the game. In these games, the scoreboard is wiped clean when the game ends so that a new game can begin.

Like those games mentioned, businesses have goals to achieve and rules to follow. Remember from Chapter 1 that the two primary goals of business include making a profit and being liquid, generating enough cash from selling goods or services to pay bills on time. Rules and regulations, such as GAAP, protect those who interact with the business. Further, just as the scoreboard is reset before a new game begins, businesses keep track of their operating activities for a period of time; at the end of that time, the accounting process sets the scoreboard back to zero so that the business may account for a new game in a new accounting period. •

Look Back

You have learned how to record and post transactions, prepare a trial balance, adjust accounts, and prepare an adjusted trial balance and financial statements.

Look Ahead

You will learn how to prepare closing entries and complete the accounting cycle. You will also find out how to classify assets and liabilities as either current or long-term.

In Chapters 2 and 3, we learned how to account for transactions, prepare a trial balance, adjust accounts as necessary to measure income accurately, and prepare an adjusted trial balance and financial statements. These steps are part of a process known as the **accounting cycle**. The practice of resetting the scoreboard in business is called closing the books, and it is covered in the last steps of the cycle. In this chapter, we learn how to prepare closing entries and finish the accounting process.

The Accounting Cycle

1 Explain the steps in the accounting cycle.

In the first chapter, we talked about the need for accountability in business. Owners and managers make decisions about the financing, investing, and operating activities of a business. These individuals have a fiduciary responsibility to stakeholders of the business, including investors, suppliers, creditors, customers, employees, and government agencies.

Accountants use financial accounting to prepare financial statements that communicate the decisions made and the results obtained from those decisions. The financial statements "tell the story" of the business's past activities. The accounting cycle is the process of gathering financial information and preparing these financial statements. Exhibit 4-1 shows the eight steps in the accounting cycle.

STEP 1
The accountant identifies business transactions by examining source documents, contracts, and internal business reports.

- Source documents are documents that represent a business transaction. For example, sales invoices reflect customer sales, while remittance advices with customer checks reflect cash collections from customers. Purchase orders reflect purchases of supplies or services, while cancelled checks reflect payments to suppliers.

- Business contracts include bank loans, mortgage loans, lease agreements, and other arrangements. Contracts obligate the business to repay the loan or mortgage, pay for the use of assets owned by someone else, or fulfill some other requirement agreed to in the document.

- Internal business reports include lists of assets used to calculate depreciation as well as payroll registers that show payments to employees.

STEP 2
The accountant records these transactions in the journal.

STEP 3
The accountant posts the journal entries into accounts in the ledger.

Steps 1 through 3 happen throughout the accounting period as the business engages in transactions.

Exhibit 4-1 The Accounting Cycle

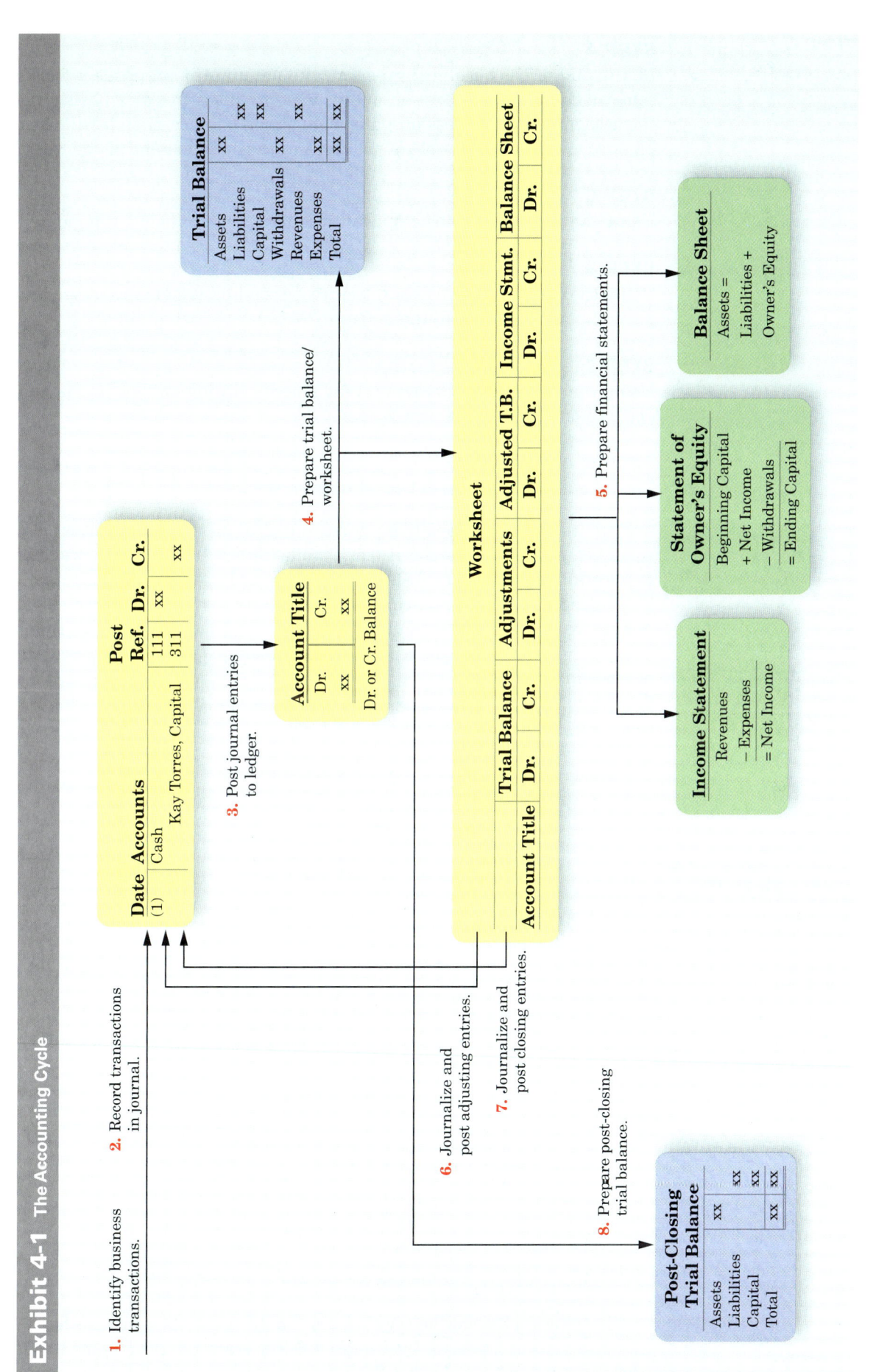

1. Identify business transactions.

2. Record transactions in journal.

3. Post journal entries to ledger.

4. Prepare trial balance/worksheet.

5. Prepare financial statements.

6. Journalize and post adjusting entries.

7. Journalize and post closing entries.

8. Prepare post-closing trial balance.

STEP 4

At the end of the accounting period, the accountant prepares a worksheet, or sometimes simply prepares a trial balance, and uses this as a basis for adjusting the accounts. If a business prepares only a trial balance, then it will use this trial balance to complete the rest of the steps in the cycle instead of the worksheet.

STEP 5

Using the worksheet, the accountant prepares the financial statements.

STEP 6

Using the worksheet, the accountant records adjusting entries in the journal and posts them to accounts in the ledger.

STEP 7

Using the worksheet, the accountant records closing entries in the journal and posts them to accounts in the ledger.

STEP 8

The accountant prepares a post-closing trial balance.

In Chapter 1, we used the accounting equation to track transactions and saw that each exchange affected at least two accounts. In Chapter 2, we learned how to account for transactions formally by completing steps 1 through 3 of the accounting cycle, and preparing a trial balance, part of step 4. We also practiced producing financial statements using unadjusted account balances from the trial balance. We witnessed the need to adjust accounts and prepare an adjusted trial balance in Chapter 3, continuing our coverage of step 4. Once again, we prepared financial statements by using adjusted account balances. In this chapter, we will complete the accounting cycle by studying steps 4 through 8, demonstrating the worksheet as a useful tool for accomplishing steps 5, 6, and 7.

The Worksheet

 Prepare a worksheet.

Accountants often use a worksheet, a document that holds the trial balance, adjustments, and adjusted trial balance, to summarize data for the financial statements. The worksheet is not part of the ledger or the journal, and it is not a financial statement. It is merely a tool that accountants use to gather information before financial statements are prepared. Listing all the accounts and their unadjusted balances helps identify the accounts that need adjustment. Once completed, the worksheet is useful when journalizing adjusting and closing entries and when preparing financial statements.

The heading at the top of the worksheet includes the following:

- The name of the business

- The title of the document

- The period covered by the worksheet

In this chapter, we once again examine the accounting process for Kay Torres Travel Agency. Exhibits 4-2 through 4-6 illustrate the development of a typical worksheet using Torres's agency as an example A step-by-step description of the worksheet follows in these exhibits. Simply turn the acetate pages to follow from one exhibit to another. To prepare the worksheet:

1. *Prepare the trial balance by entering account titles and their unadjusted balances in the Trial Balance columns of the worksheet and totaling the columns.* Exhibit 4-2 shows the September 30 trial balance for Torres's business. Remember from previous chapters that this information comes directly from the ledger accounts. Accounts are listed in balance sheet order, and total debits must equal total credits.

    An account may have a zero balance, such as Supplies Expense. A zero balance indicates that an account may need adjustment.

2. *Enter the adjusting entries in the Adjustments columns, and total the columns.* Exhibit 4-3 includes the September adjusting entries for Kay Torres Travel Agency. Recall that we made these same adjustments in Chapter 3.

    We can identify adjustments needed by examining the accounts on the trial balance and considering what we know about the business's transactions. Looking at the first account listed, we see that Cash needs no adjustment because we know all cash transactions are recorded as they occur during the period. Consequently, Cash's balance is up-to-date.

    Accounts Receivable is listed next. At September 30, Torres has earned $250 that she has not yet recorded. For service revenue earned but not yet collected, Torres debits Accounts Receivable and credits Service Revenue on the worksheet. A letter links the debit and the credit of each adjusting entry together.

    This process may seem a bit mysterious, but know that the accountant for a business is usually quite familiar with the transactions of a business, largely because they hear about those transactions and see the source documents and contracts of an entity. Further, they are often the ones who assemble the internal reports of the business. So, it is likely that the person who accounts for the travel agency, in this case, Kay Torres, knows about the $250 of revenue earned but not yet collected. Seeing Accounts Receivable on the trial balance reminds her that an adjustment for the $250 is needed.

    By moving down the trial balance, Torres identifies the remaining accounts that need adjustment. In this way, the other adjustments are entered on the worksheet as we did in Chapter 3. After the adjustments are entered, the amount columns are totaled. Again, total debits equal total credits.

3. *Compute each account's adjusted balance by combining the trial balance and adjustment figures. Prepare the adjusted trial balance by entering each account's adjusted amount in the Adjusted Trial Balance columns and totaling the columns.* Exhibit 4-4 shows the worksheet with the adjusted trial balance completed. Cash, for example, is up-to-date, so it receives no adjustment, and its balance is the same as it was on the trial balance. Accounts Receivable's adjusted balance of $3,350 is computed by adding the unadjusted debit amount of $3,100 to the $250 debit adjustment. We compute the $600 adjusted balance for Supplies by subtracting the $300 credit adjustment from the unadjusted debit balance of $900. Remember that an account may receive more than one adjustment, as Service Revenue does. On the adjusted trial balance, total debits still equal total credits.

Exhibit 4-2 Trial Balance

KAY TORRES TRAVEL AGENCY
Worksheet
September 30, 2008

Account Title	Trial Balance Dr.	Trial Balance Cr.	Adjustments Dr.	Adjustments Cr.	Adjusted Trial Balance Dr.	Adjusted Trial Balance Cr.	Income Statement Dr.	Income Statement Cr.	Balance Sheet Dr.	Balance Sheet Cr.
Cash	26,300									
Accounts receivable	3,100									
Supplies	900									
Prepaid rent	3,000									
Equipment	12,600									
Accumulated depreciation, equipment		13,100								
Accounts payable										
Salary payable		450								
Unearned service revenue		29,500								
Kay Torres, capital	3,200									
Kay Torres, withdrawals		7,000								
Service revenue										
Building rent expense										
Salary expense	550									
Supplies expense										
Depreciation expense, equipment										
Utilities expense	400									
	50,050	**50,050**								
Net income										

Write the account titles and their unadjusted balances in the Trial Balance columns of the worksheet. Total the columns.

4. *Extend, or copy, the asset, liability, and owner's equity amounts from the adjusted trial balance to the Balance Sheet columns. Copy the revenue and expense amounts to the Income Statement columns. Total both sets of statement columns.* Every account is either a balance sheet account or an income statement account. Each account's balance should appear in only one column, as shown in Exhibit 4-5. Total the income statement columns first, then total the balance sheet columns.

5. *Compute net income or net loss by subtracting total expenses from total revenues. Enter this net income or loss as the balancing amount in the Income Statement columns and as the balancing amount in the Balance Sheet columns by writing it below the smallest total for each pair of columns. Then compute the new column totals.* Exhibit 4-6 presents the completed accounting worksheet, which shows net income of $4,250, computed as follows:

| | | Income Statement | | Balance Sheet | |
		Dr.	Cr.	Dr.	Cr.
Revenues – Expenses = Net Income					
$7,400 – $3,150 = $4,250		(Expenses) 3,150	(Revenues) 7,400	48,050	43,800
	Net income	4,250			4,250
		7,400	7,400	48,050	48,050

Net income of $4,250 is entered in the debit column of the Income Statement columns; the debit column had the smallest total because expenses are less than revenues. This entry brings total debits equal to total credits in the Income Statement columns. *The net income amount is then extended to the credit column of the Balance Sheet columns* because the credit column had the smallest total. Net income brings the balance sheet amounts into balance.

If expenses exceed revenues, the result is a net loss. In that event, the net loss is entered on the worksheet. *The loss amount should be entered in the credit column of the Income Statement columns to balance them and also in the debit column of the Balance Sheet columns to balance these columns as well.* After completion, total debits equal total credits in both the Income Statement columns and in the Balance Sheet columns.

Completing the Accounting Cycle

The worksheet helps accountants prepare the financial statements, record the adjusting entries, and close the accounts. Let's see how this happens.

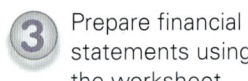

Prepare financial statements using the worksheet.

Preparing the Financial Statements

We can prepare financial statements for Kay Torres Travel Agency immediately after completing the worksheet. Exhibits 4-7 and 4-8 repeat the September financial statements seen in Chapter 3 so we can understand how they are assembled based on information gathered from the worksheet completed in Exhibit 4-6.

Recording the Adjusting Entries

Adjusting the accounts requires recording adjusting entries in the journal and posting them to accounts in the ledger. Panel A of Exhibit 4-9 repeats the September adjusting entries of Kay Torres Travel Agency that we saw in Chapter 3 and on the worksheet in Exhibit 4-3. The adjusting entries should be journalized after they are entered on the worksheet. Panel B shows the revenue and the expense accounts after all adjustments have been posted. "Adj." identifies an amount posted from an adjusting entry. Only the revenue and expense accounts are presented in the exhibit so that we can turn our attention to the closing process.

Accountants can use the worksheet to prepare monthly or quarterly statements without actually entering the adjusting entries into the formal accounting records. By adjusting the accounts on the worksheet, the accountant can assemble accurate balances to prepare the financial statements. Because the balances in many of the accounts needing adjustment will need adjustment again at the end of the next month or quarter, some businesses think there is no point in the process of journalizing and posting these adjusting entries. Many companies journalize and post the adjusting entries only once annually, at the end of the year.

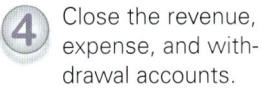

Close the revenue, expense, and withdrawal accounts.

Closing the Accounts

One of the primary goals of a business is to earn a profit, or net income. The business performs a number of operating activities to generate net income during the year. The business creates revenue and expense accounts to store amounts related to these operating activities.

Revenues and expenses hold the results of the operating activities of a business much like the scoreboard holds the results of a game. In this sense, the income statement used to report revenues and expenses is like a scoreboard. It tells whether the business is winning—earning net income, or losing—producing a net loss. Like the scoreboard, the amounts on the income statement must be set back to zero in order to account for a new game, or new period's activities.

By separating the net income generated during each accounting period, the owner can compare the business's net income over time, as well as measure the profitability of the business against the profitability of other, similar businesses. As with the cumulative, win/loss records for most teams, a cumulative record of the net income or loss for the business is kept—not on the scoreboard—but in owner's equity. As you prepared the statement of owner's equity in previous chapters, you saw that net income increases owner's equity, and you know that net loss decreases it. Because the owner owns the business, the owner also owns the income or loss from the business. Closing entries are how the accounting system keeps score, adding income or subtracting loss from the owner's investment in the business.

Closing entries are the end-of-period journal entries that get these temporary, scoreboard accounts ready for the next period. In accounting, the period, or "game," is a year long, so closing entries are made at the end of the fiscal year. To close an account means to makes its balance equal to zero, just as closing a bank

Exhibit 4-7 Using the Worksheet to Prepare the Income Statement

KAY TORRES TRAVEL AGENCY
Worksheet
September 30, 2008

| | Income Statement | |
Account Title	Dr.	Cr.
Service revenue		7,400
Building rent expense	1,000	
Salary expense	1,100	
Supplies expense	300	
Depreciation expense, equipment	350	
Utilities expense	400	
	3,150	7,400
Net income	4,250	
	7,400	**7,400**

KAY TORRES TRAVEL AGENCY
Income Statement
Month Ended September 30, 2008

Revenue:		
Service revenue		$7,400
Expenses:		
Salary expense	$ 1,100	
Building rent expense	1,000	
Utilities expense	400	
Depreciation expense, equipment	350	
Supplies expense	300	
Total expenses		3,150
Net income		$4,250

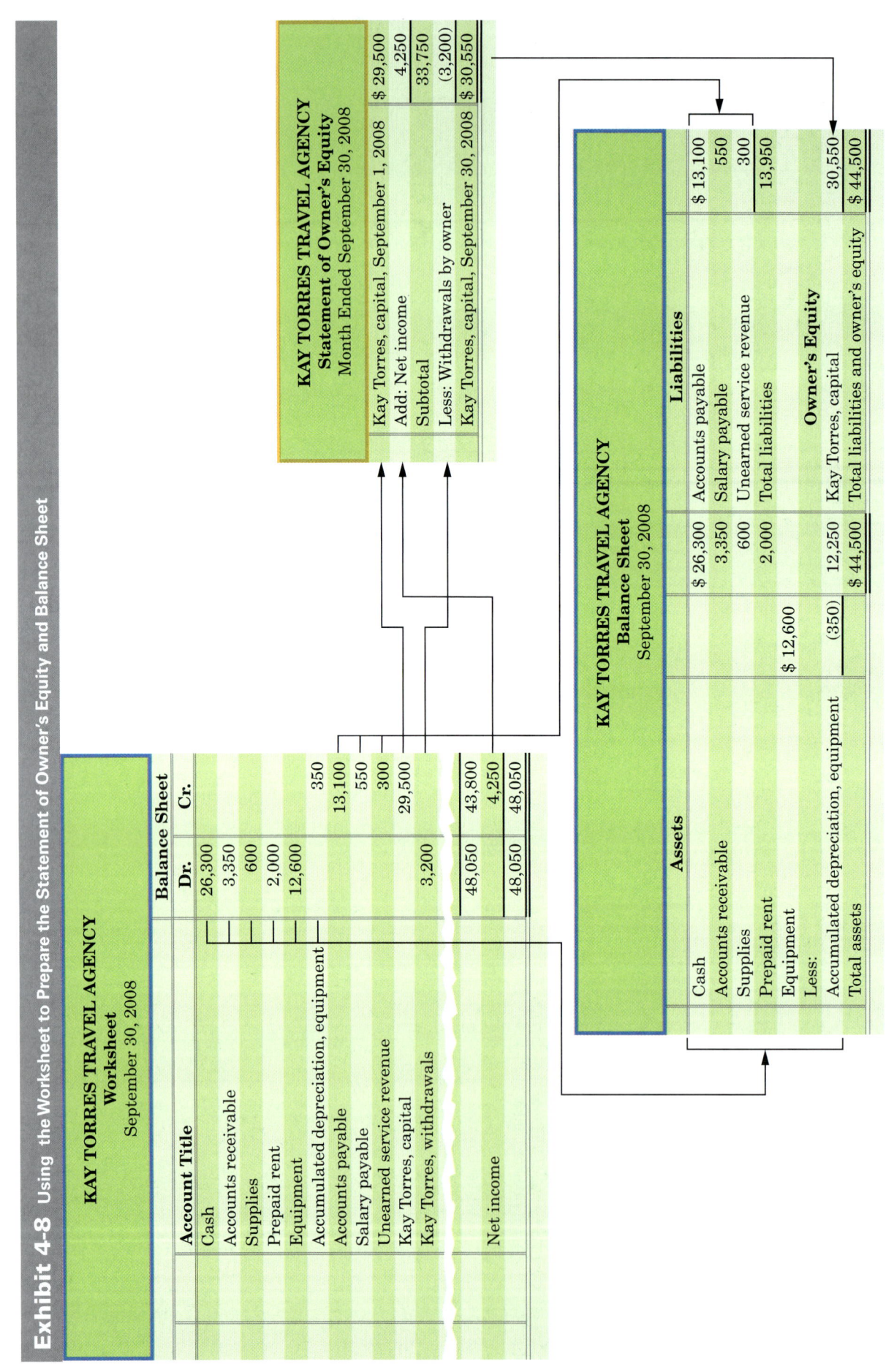

Exhibit 4-9 Journalizing and Posting the Adjusting Entries

PANEL A—Journalizing the Adjusting Entries

Date	Accounts	Post Ref.	Dr.	Cr.
Sept. 30	Building Rent Expense ($3,000/3 months)		1,000	
	Prepaid Rent			1,000
	Record rent expense for September.			
30	Supplies Expense ($900 − $600)		300	
	Supplies			300
	Record supply expense for September.			
30	Depreciation Expense, Equipment		350	
	Accumulated Depreciation, Equipment			350
	Record depreciation on equipment for September.			
30	Unearned Service Revenue ($450 × 10/30 days)		150	
	Service Revenue			150
	Record service revenue earned from September 20–30.			
30	Salary Expense ($1,100 × 1/2 month)		550	
	Salary Payable			550
	Accrue salary for September 16–30.			
30	Accounts Receivable ($500 × 1/2 month)		250	
	Service Revenue			250
	Accrue service revenue for September 15–30.			

PANEL B—Posting the Adjusting Entries to the Revenue and Expense Accounts

REVENUE

Service Revenue

	Bal.	7,000
	Adj.	150
	Adj.	250
	Bal.	7,400

EXPENSES

Building Rent Expense

Adj.	1,000	
Bal.	1,000	

Salary Expense

Sept. 15	550	
Adj.	550	
Bal.	1,100	

Supplies Expense

Adj.	300	
Bal.	300	

Depreciation Expense, Equipment

Adj.	350	
Bal.	350	

Utilities Expense

Bal.	400	

Adj. = Amount posted from an adjusting entry; Bal. = Balance.

account means to withdraw all of the funds in that account. Closing entries then do several things:

- First, they reset the scoreboard accounts, the revenues and expenses, back to zero balances so that accounting for a new period can begin. The owner's withdrawals account is also closed because it measures the owner's withdrawals for only one period.

- Next, they transfer the result of the game, the net income or net loss, to its permanent home, owner's equity. Withdrawal amounts for the period are also transferred to owner's equity because they decrease the owner's investment in the business.

- After closing, the Capital account will hold its correct balance.

Temporary accounts are the revenue and expense accounts used to hold financial information temporarily during the accounting period. The Withdrawals account is also a temporary account.

Before closing the accounts, the accounting equation for a sole proprietorship would be:

$$\text{Assets} = \text{Liabilities} + \text{Owner's Equity (Capital} - \text{Withdrawals} + \text{Revenues} - \text{Expenses)}$$

After closing the accounts, the accounting equation for a sole proprietorship would be:

$$\text{Assets} = \text{Liabilities} + \text{Owner's Equity (Capital)}$$

The accounts that remain in the accounting equation are called **permanent accounts**. The asset, liability, and capital accounts are *not* closed at the end of the period because their balances are not used to measure income. Consider Cash, Accounts Receivable, Accounts Payable, and Kay Torres, Capital. These accounts do not represent business activity for a single period, so they are not closed at the end of the period. Their balances carry over to the next period. For example, the Cash balance at December 31, 2007, becomes the beginning balance for 2008.

The Four Closing Entries

At the end of the accounting period, the results of the business's operating activities and owner withdrawal activity move from the temporary accounts to the owner's equity permanent account. To journalize closing entries, complete the following steps:

STEP 1
Close the revenue accounts and move their balances into the **Income Summary** account. Income Summary is a temporary, holding account that collects revenue and expense amounts during the closing process. The Income Summary account is only used during this process.

STEP 2
Close the expense accounts and move their balances into the Income Summary account.

STEP 3
At this point, Income Summary now holds revenues and expenses, which means it now holds net income or net loss. Close the Income Summary account by moving its balance, the net income or net loss, into the owner's capital account.

STEP 4

Close the owner's withdrawals account and move the total amount withdrawn into the owner's capital account.

Exhibit 4-10 illustrates these four steps. The process for making closing entries is the same as it is for making any entry; record these entries in the journal and post them to accounts in the ledger. The worksheet provides a useful tool in completing these four closing entries because it lists the current balances of the accounts needing closure.

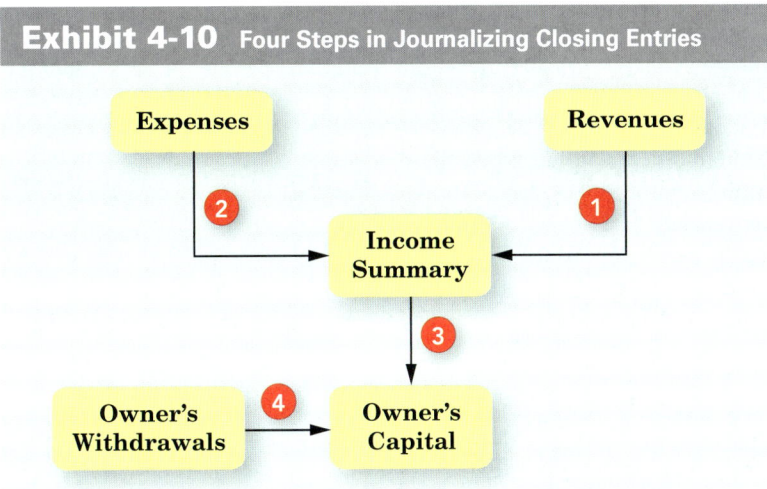

Exhibit 4-10 Four Steps in Journalizing Closing Entries

Now, let's apply this process to the Kay Torres Travel Agency. Although the travel agency has not yet concluded its first year of business, we will illustrate closing entries for this business because we are already familiar with it.

STEP 1

Close the revenue accounts and move their balances into the Income Summary account. Revenues show credit balances to reflect the increase in owner's equity. To close revenues, debit each revenue account for the amount of its credit balance. Credit the Income Summary account for the total of the revenues. This closing entry transfers total revenues to the *credit* side of Income Summary.

At September 30, Kay Torres Travel Agency has $7,400 in Service Revenue. This amount is found in the Income Statement Cr. column of the abbreviated worksheet in Exhibit 4-11. Exhibit 4-12 shows the closing entry in Panel A and the posting of the entry in Panel B. Notice that the balance for Service Revenue is zero after posting the closing entry.

STEP 2

Close the expense accounts and move their balances into the Income Summary account. Expenses show debit balances to reflect the decrease in owner's equity. To close expenses, credit each expense account for the amount of its debit balance. Debit the Income Summary account for the total of the expenses. This closing entry transfers total expenses to the *debit* side of Income Summary.

At September 30, Kay Torres Travel Agency has a total of $3,150 in expenses including Building Rent Expense, $1,000; Salary Expense, $1,100; Supplies Expense, $300, Depreciation Expense, Equipment, $350; and Utilities Expense, $400. These amounts are found in the Income Statement Dr. column of the abbreviated worksheet in Exhibit 4-11. Exhibit 4-12 shows the closing entry in Panel A and the posting of the entry in Panel B. Notice that the balance for each of the expense accounts is zero after posting the closing entry.

Exhibit 4-11 Using the Worksheet to Prepare Closing Entries

KAY TORRES TRAVEL AGENCY
Worksheet
September 30, 2008

Account Title	Income Statement Dr.	Cr.	Balance Sheet Dr.	Cr.
Cash			26,300	
Accounts receivable			3,350	
Supplies			600	
Prepaid rent			2,000	
Equipment			12,600	
Accumulated depreciation, equipment				350
Accounts payable				13,100
Salary payable				550
Unearned service revenue				300
Kay Torres, capital				29,500
Kay Torres, withdrawals			3,200	
Service revenue		7,400		
Building rent expense	1,000			
Salary expense	1,100			
Supplies expense	300			
Depreciation expense, equipment	350			
Utilities expense	400			
	3,150	7,400	48,050	43,800
Net income	4,250			4,250
	7,400	7,400	48,050	48,050

STEP 3

Close the Income Summary account by moving its balance, the net income or net loss, into the owner's capital account. Because revenues and expenses have been transferred to the Income Summary account, the account now holds the net income or net loss of the period, but only for a moment. To close Income Summary, we debit it for the amount of its credit balance, and credit the owner's capital account. This closing entry transfers net income to the owner's capital account. If a net loss had occurred, then the Income Summary account would have a debit balance. To close it, we would credit it for this balance and debit the capital account.

At September 30, Kay Torres Travel Agency has a credit balance of $4,250 in the Income Summary account. This amount is found in the Income Statement Dr. column of the abbreviated worksheet in Exhibit 4-11. Notice that the Income Summary account is not on the worksheet because it only exists to shift revenues and expenses to the capital account. Exhibit 4-12 shows the closing entry in Panel A and the posting of the entry in Panel B. After the posting, you will see that the Income Summary account has a zero balance.

STEP 4

Close the owner's withdrawals account and move the total amount withdrawn into the owner's capital account. To close the withdrawals account, credit it for the amount of its debit balance and debit the owner's capital account. This entry transfers the owner's withdrawals to the *debit* side of the capital account. At September 30, Kay Torres Travel Agency has a debit balance of $3,200 in the Withdrawals account. This amount is found in the Balance Sheet Dr. column of the abbreviated worksheet in Exhibit 4-11. Exhibit 4-12 shows the closing entry

Exhibit 4-12 Journalizing and Posting Closing Entries

PANEL A—Journalizing the Closing Entries

Date	Accounts	Post Ref.	Dr.	Cr.
Sept. 30	Service Revenue		7,400	
	Income Summary			7,400
30	Income Summary		3,150	
	Building Rent Expense			1,000
	Salary Expense			1,100
	Supplies Expense			300
	Depreciation Expense, Equipment			350
	Utilities Expense			400
30	Income Summary ($7,400 – $3,150)		4,250	
	Kay Torres, Capital			4,250
30	Kay Torres, Capital		3,200	
	Kay Torres, Withdrawals			3,200

PANEL B—Posting the Closing Entries

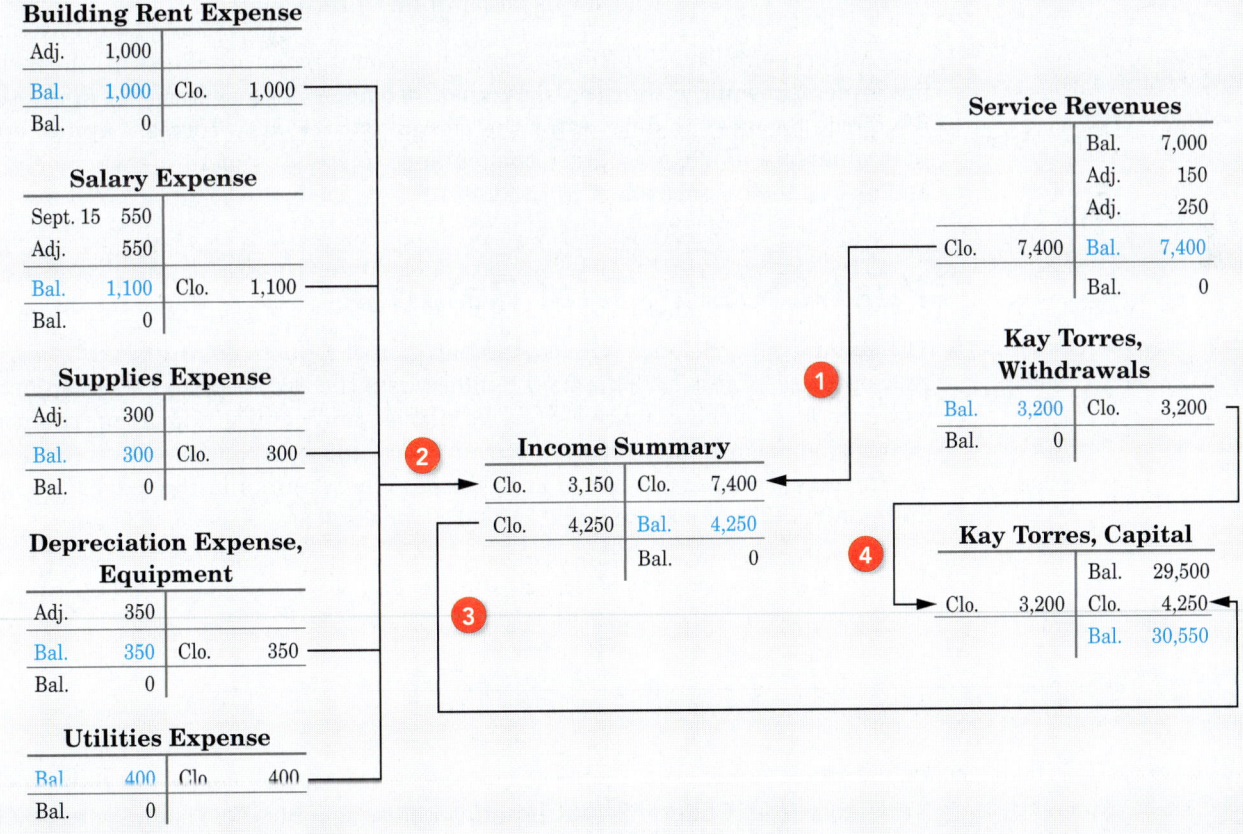

Adj. = Amount posted from an adjusting entry; Clo. = Amount posted from a closing entry; Bal. = Balance.

Exhibit 4-13 Post-Closing Trial Balance

KAY TORRES TRAVEL AGENCY
Post-Closing Trial Balance
September 30, 2008

Account Title	Balance	
	Debit	Credit
Cash	$ 26,300	
Accounts receivable	3,350	
Supplies	600	
Prepaid rent	2,000	
Equipment	12,600	
Accumulated depreciation, equipment		$ 350
Accounts payable		13,100
Salary payable		550
Unearned service revenue		300
Kay Torres, capital		30,550
Total	$ 44,850	$ 44,850

in Panel A and the posting of the entry in Panel B. After the posting, you will see that the Kay Torres, Withdrawals, account has a zero balance.

At this point, the Kay Torres, Capital, account balance reflects all the owner investments, owner withdrawals, and net income or net loss incurred during the life of the business to date. After the closing entries, Kay Torres, Capital, ends with a balance of $30,550. Trace this balance to the statement of owner's equity and also to the balance sheet in Exhibit 4-8.

Post-Closing Trial Balance

The accounting cycle ends with the preparation of a **post-closing trial balance**, as seen in Exhibit 4-13. This trial balance lists the accounts and their adjusted balances after closing. Only assets, liabilities, and capital appear on the post-closing trial balance. No temporary accounts—revenues, expenses, or withdrawals—are included because they have been closed. The accounts in the ledger are now up-to-date and ready for the next period's transactions.

Classifying Assets and Liabilities

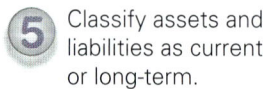

5 Classify assets and liabilities as current or long-term.

Remember from Chapter 1 that liquidity refers to a business's ability to pay its bills. Since bill-paying ability relies on cash, liquidity depends on how quickly a company can convert assets into cash. Managers are interested in liquidity because business difficulties arise from a shortage of cash. A **classified balance sheet** lists assets and liabilities in classes in the order of their liquidity, so that the financial statement users can analyze the business's ability to pay its bills on time.

Accordingly, Cash is listed as the first asset because it is the most liquid. Accounts receivable is a relatively liquid asset because the receivables are expected to be collected in the near future. Supplies are less liquid than receivables, and furniture and buildings are even less liquid because of their long lives. Similarly, liabilities are listed in order of liquidity, based on when they will be paid or fulfilled, with accounts payable generally being shown first.

Assets

CURRENT ASSETS

Current assets are assets that will be converted to cash, sold, or used up during the next 12 months or within the business's normal operating cycle if the cycle is longer than a year. The **operating cycle** is the length of time a business needs to obtain resources, use the resources to sell goods and services to customers, and collect cash from theses customers.

For most businesses, the operating cycle is a few months. Cash, Accounts Receivable, Notes Receivable due within a year, and Prepaid Expenses are current assets. Merchandising companies such as Intel, Sears, and Dell have another current asset, Inventory. Inventory shows the cost of the goods available for sale to customers.

LONG-TERM ASSETS

Long-term assets are generally long-lived, tangible assets, although this category usually includes all assets other than current assets. One category of long-term assets is called **plant assets** or **fixed assets** and can be seen on the balance sheet as **property**, **plant**, **and equipment**. Land, buildings, furniture, fixtures, and equipment are examples of these assets.

Liabilities

CURRENT LIABILITIES

Current liabilities are the debts or obligations of the business that must be paid with cash or fulfilled with goods and services within one year or the entity's operating cycle if the cycle is longer than a year. Accounts Payable, Notes Payable due within one year, Salary Payable, Interest Payable, and Unearned Revenue are current liabilities.

LONG-TERM LIABILITIES

Long-term liabilities are obligations that extend beyond one year. Often, a business owner signs a contract to repay a note or mortgage over several years. The portion of the note or mortgage payable within one year will be a current liability. The remaining balance will be a long-term liability.

A Classified Balance Sheet

Thus far we have presented the *unclassified* balance sheet of Kay Torres Travel. Now let's look at its classified balance sheet, presented in Exhibit 4-14.

By classifying each asset and liability as current or long-term, the classified balance sheet in Exhibit 4-14 reports more information, totals for current assets and current liabilities, than does the unclassified version. Exhibit 4-14 presents the balance sheet in **account form** because the balance sheet lists the assets at the left and the liabilities and owner's equity at the right, just as these accounts

Exhibit 4-14 Classified Balance Sheet of Kay Torres Travel Agency

KAY TORRES TRAVEL AGENCY
Balance Sheet
September 30, 2008

Assets			Liabilities	
Current Assets:			Current Liabilities:	
Cash		$26,300	Accounts payable	$13,100
Accounts receivable		3,350	Salary payable	550
Supplies		600	Unearned service revenue	300
Prepaid rent		2,000	Total current liabilities	13,950
Total current assets		32,250	Long-Term Liabilities (None)	
Fixed Assets:			Total liabilities	13,950
Equipment	$12,600			
Less: Accumulated			**Owner's Equity**	
depreciation, equipment	(350)	12,250	Kay Torres, capital	30,550
Total assets		**$44,500**	Total liabilities and owner's equity	**$44,500**

appear in the accounting equation. Another way to complete the balance sheet is to use a **report form** that lists the assets at the top and the liabilities and owner's equity below.

Demo Doc

Preparing Closing Entries

Learning Objective   4

This question continues on from the Cloud Break Consulting question in the Chapter 3: Demo Doc (pp. 144–155).

Use the data from the adjusted trial balance of Cloud Break Consulting at June 30, 2008:

	CLOUD BREAK CONSULTING Adjusted Trial Balance June 30, 2008		
		Adjusted Trial Balance	
	Account Title	Debit	Credit
	Cash	$131,000	
	Accounts receivable	119,000	
	Supplies	1,000	
	Prepaid rent	18,000	
	Land	45,000	
	Building	300,000	
	Accumulated depreciation, building		$167,000
	Accounts payable		159,000
	Salary payable		4,000
	Unearned service revenue		10,000
	Susan Cloud, capital		152,000
	Susan Cloud, withdrawals	57,000	
	Service revenue		495,000
	Salary expense	259,000	
	Supplies expense	3,000	
	Rent expense	34,000	
	Depreciation expense, building	12,000	
	Miscellaneous expense	8,000	
	Total	$987,000	$987,000

Requirement

1. Journalize and post Cloud's closing entries.

Demo Doc Solution

4 Close the revenue, expense, and withdrawal accounts.

Journalize and post Cloud's closing entries.

We prepare closing entries for two reasons. First, we need to clear out the temporary accounts (the revenue, expense, and withdrawals accounts) to a zero balance. They need to begin the next year empty so that next year's income statement can begin fresh. Second, we need to update the Capital account.

These goals can be met by closing the accounts. If you look at Exhibit 4-10 (p. 191), you can see the process through which closing the accounts is done.

Part 1	Part 2	Part 3	Part 4	Demo Doc Complete

By preparing closing entries, we "close" the revenue accounts to Income Summary. We move the revenues out of their T-accounts and into the Income Summary T-account.

The Income Summary is a new account that is created *only* for the closing entries. Its purpose is to summarize net income; that is, to calculate net income. The Income Summary account is like an income statement collapsed into a T-account. Because the first component of net income is revenues, it is also the first component of Income Summary.

Let's look at the Service Revenue T-account:

Service Revenue

	Bal. 495,000

Remember the first reason to prepare closing entries: We need to clear out the income statement accounts so that they are empty to begin the next year. What do we need to do to bring the Service Revenue account to zero? It has a *credit* balance of $495,000, so to bring that to zero, we need to *debit* $495,000.

We know the first part of our first closing entry:

Journal Entry:

Date	Accounts	Post Ref.	Dr.	Cr.
1.	Service Revenue		495,000	
	???			495,000

What is the credit side of this entry? The reason we look first at Service Revenue is to help calculate net income using the Income Summary. So the other side of the entry must go to the Income Summary:

Journal Entry:

Date	Accounts	Post Ref.	Dr.	Cr.
1.	Service Revenue		495,000	
	Income Summary			495,000

With this entry, we close the Service Revenue account to zero:

Service Revenue

		Bal.	495,000
Clo.	495,000		
		Bal.	0

Part 1	**Part 2**	Part 3	Part 4	Demo Doc Complete

Next, the closing entries "close" expenses to the Income Summary. We move expenses from their T-accounts into the Income Summary T-account. In this question, we need to close the five different expense accounts:

Salary Expense

Bal.	259,000

Supplies Expense

Bal.	3,000

Rent Expense

Bal.	34,000

Depreciation Expense, Building

Bal.	12,000

Miscellaneous Expense

Bal.	8,000

Each of these expenses shows a *debit* balance. In order to bring these accounts to zero, we must *credit* them. The balancing debit will go to the Income Summary account:

Journal Entry:

Date	Accounts	Post Ref.	Dr.	Cr.
2.	Income Summary		316,000	
	Salary Expense			259,000
	Supplies Expense			3,000
	Rent Expense			34,000
	Depreciation Expense, Building			12,000
	Miscellaneous Expense			8,000

	Salary Expense					Supplies Expense		
Bal.	259,000				Bal.	3,000		
		Clo.	259,000				Clo.	3,000
Bal.	0				Bal.	0		

	Rent Expense					Depreciation Expense, Building		
Bal.	34,000				Bal.	12,000		
		Clo.	34,000				Clo.	12,000
Bal.	0				Bal.	0		

	Miscellaneous Expense		
Bal.	8,000		
		Clo.	8,000
Bal.	0		

Now let's look at the Income Summary account:

	Income Summary		
		Clo.	495,000
Clo.	316,000		
		Bal.	179,000

Remember that the credit of $495,000 is from the first closing entry prepared earlier.

The purpose of creating this account was to combine all of the revenues and expenses to summarize and calculate net income. Notice that this balance is the same net income number that appears on the income statement and in the accounting worksheet in Chapter 3: Demo Doc.

The Income Summary account is *only* for closing entries, however. It does *not* appear on the financial statements. It "disappears" (goes to a zero balance) before the financial statements are prepared, which brings us to step 3.

Part 1	Part 2	**Part 3**	Part 4	Demo Doc Complete

We next "close" the Income Summary account to the Capital account. In other words, we move the amount in the Income Summary account to the Capital account.

How do we remove the balance from Income Summary? The Income Summary T-account shows a *credit* balance of $179,000; to remove this number, we *debit* Income Summary for $179,000:

Journal Entry:

Date	Accounts	Post Ref.	Dr.	Cr.
3.	Income Summary		179,000	
	???			179,000

What is the credit side of this entry? The purpose of step 3 is to move the Income Summary data to the Capital account, so the credit side of the entry goes to Susan Cloud, Capital:

Journal Entry:

Date	Accounts	Post Ref.	Dr.	Cr.
3.	Income Summary		179,000	
	Susan Cloud, Capital			179,000

This entry adds the net income to the Capital account. Notice that it also brings the Income Summary account to a zero balance.

Income Summary

		Clo.	495,000
Clo.	316,000		
		Bal.	179,000
Clo.	179,000		
		Bal.	0

Part 1	Part 2	Part 3	**Part 4**	Demo Doc Complete

"Closing" the Withdrawals account to the Capital account moves the amount from the Withdrawals account to the Capital account.

Susan Cloud, Withdrawals

Bal.	57,000

What do we need to do to bring the Withdrawals account to zero? It shows a *debit* balance of $57,000, so to bring that to zero, we *credit* $57,000. The balancing debit goes to the Susan Cloud, Capital, account:

Journal Entry:

Date	Accounts	Post Ref.	Dr.	Cr.
4.	Susan Cloud, Capital		57,000	
	Susan Cloud, Withdrawals			57,000

This journal entry moves the withdrawals to the Capital account.

Susan Cloud, Withdrawals

Bal.	57,000		
		Clo.	57,000
Bal.	0		

The Capital account now has the following transactions:

Susan Cloud, Capital

			Bal.	152,000	Beginning capital amount
			Clo.	179,000	Net income
Withdrawals	Clo.	57,000			
			Bal.	274,000	Ending capital amount

Notice that all temporary accounts (that is the revenue, the expense, the withdrawals, and the income summary account) now return to a zero balance and are ready to begin the next year.

Part 1	Part 2	Part 3	Part 4	Demo Doc Complete

Accounting in Action

COMPLETING THE ACCOUNTING CYCLE

In completing the accounting cycle for your business, you might encounter the following decisions:

Decision	Guidelines
Where to summarize the effects of all the entity's transactions and adjustments during the period?	Accountant's *worksheet* with columns for: • Trial balance • Adjustments • Adjusted trial balance • Income statement • Balance sheet
What is the last major step in the accounting cycle?	Prepare *closing entries* for the *temporary accounts:* • Revenues • Expenses • Owner's withdrawals
Why close out the revenues, expenses, and owner's withdrawals?	These *temporary accounts* have balances that relate only to one accounting period and need to be reset to $0 before accounting for the next period can begin
Which accounts do *not* get closed out?	*Permanent, balance sheet accounts* that do carry their balances into the next period: • Assets • Liabilities • Owner's capital
How do businesses classify their assets and liabilities on the balance sheet?	*Current*, if within one year or the entity's operating cycle if longer than a year *Long-term*, if not current

Review

Completing the Accounting Cycle
Word Power

Account form Balance sheet format that lists assets on the left of the report and liabilities and owner's equity on the right, just as those accounts appear in the accounting equation.

Accounting cycle The process of accounting for the transactions of a business for a period of time so that results of these transactions can be reported in financial statements.

Classified balance sheet A balance sheet that separates its assets and liabilities into groups or classes, based on the relative liquidity of those items.

Closing entries Journal entries that complete the accounting cycle at the end of the accounting period; close the revenue, expense, and withdrawals accounts to set their balances to zero so that accounting can begin for the next period.

Current assets Assets that are expected to be converted to cash, sold, or consumed within one year or the business's operating cycle if the cycle is longer than a year.

Current liabilities Debts due to be paid with cash or fulfilled with goods and services within one year or the entity's operating cycle if the cycle is longer than a year.

Fixed assets The tangible, long-lived assets of a business including land, buildings, furniture, fixtures, and equipment. Also called plant assets and are commonly shown on the balance sheet as property, plant, and equipment.

Income summary A temporary account used to hold revenues and expenses during the closing process until their balances are transferred to capital.

Long-term liabilities Liabilities other than those that are current.

Operating cycle The time span during which the business obtains resources, uses them to sell goods and services to customers, and collects cash from these customers.

Permanent accounts Accounts that are not closed at the end of the period—the asset, liability, and capital accounts.

Plant assets The tangible, long-lived assets of a business including land, buildings, furniture, fixtures, and equipment. Also called fixed assets and are commonly shown on the balance sheet as property, plant, and equipment.

Post-closing trial balance A list of the accounts and their balances at the end of the accounting period after closing entries have been journalized and posted.

Property, plant, and equipment A heading often seen on the balance sheet used to describe fixed, or plant, assets.

Report form Balance sheet form that reports assets at the top of the report, followed by liabilities, and ending with owner's equity at the end of the report.

Temporary accounts Accounts that are closed at the end of the period—revenues, expenses, and withdrawals—that relate to a particular accounting period.

Quick Check

1. Consider the steps in the accounting cycle in Exhibit 4-1. Which part of the accounting cycle provides information to help a bank decide whether to lend money to a company?

   a. Financial statements
   b. Adjusting entries
   c. Closing entries
   d. Post-closing trial balance

2. Which columns of the worksheet show unadjusted amounts?

   a. Trial Balance
   b. Adjustments
   c. Income Statement
   d. Balance Sheet

3. Which columns of the worksheet show net income?

   a. Adjusted Trial Balance
   b. Income Statement
   c. Balance Sheet
   d. Both b and c

4. Which situation involving the Income Statement columns of the worksheet indicates a net loss?

   a. Total debits equal total credits
   b. Total debits exceed total credits
   c. Total credits exceed total debits
   d. None of the above

5. Assume that Supplies has a $6,000 unadjusted balance on the trial balance of Dell's accounting worksheet. At year-end Dell counts supplies on hand of $2,000. What adjustment will appear on Dell's worksheet?

Date	Accounts	Post Ref.	Dr.	Cr.
a.	Supplies		4,000	
	Supplies Expense			4,000
b.	Supplies Expense		4,000	
	Supplies			4,000
c.	Supplies		2,000	
	Supplies Expense			2,000
d.	No adjustment is needed because the Supplies account already has a correct balance.			

6. Which of the following accounts is not closed?

    a. Salary Expense
    b. Service Revenue
    c. Accumulated Depreciation, Equipment
    d. Owner, Withdrawals

7. What do closing entries accomplish?

    a. Transfer revenues, expenses, and owner withdrawals to capital
    b. Zero out the revenues, expenses, and owner withdrawals to prepare these accounts for the next period
    c. Bring the capital account to its correct ending balance
    d. All of the above

8. Which of the following is not a closing entry?

Date	Accounts	Post Ref.	Dr.	Cr.
a.	Income Summary		XXX	
	Building Rent Expense			XXX
b.	Salary Payable		XXX	
	Income Summary			XXX
c.	Service Revenue		XXX	
	Income Summary			XXX
d.	Owner, Capital		XXX	
	Owner, Withdrawals			XXX

9. Assets and liabilities are listed on the balance sheet in order of their:

    a. Purchase date
    b. Liquidity
    c. Market value
    d. Adjustments

10. Examine Kay Torres Travel Agency's classified balance sheet in Exhibit 4-14. Torres's current assets at September 30, 2008, are:

    a. $13,950
    b. $32,250
    c. $12,250
    d. $30,550

Answers are given after Apply Your Knowledge (p. 227).

Accounting Practice

Short Exercises

S4-1. Organize the following activities to indicate the normal sequence of steps in the accounting cycle. Label the steps as 1 through 8.

① Steps in the accounting cycle.

   a. Close the accounts.

   b. Identify business transactions.

   c. Prepare the financial statements.

   d. Post the journal entries to the ledger.

   e. Journalize and post the adjusting entries.

   f. Record the transactions in the journal.

   g. Prepare the post-closing trial balance.

   h. Prepare the worksheet.

S4-2. The following steps in preparing a worksheet are shown in random order. Indicate the correct order in which the steps would be performed. Label them 1 through 9.

② Preparing a worksheet.

   a. Add the debit and credit columns of the Adjusted Trial Balance.

   b. Enter the adjusting entries in the worksheet.

   c. Add the debit and credit columns of the Balance Sheet and Income Statement.

   d. Enter the amount of net income or net loss for the period.

   e. Extend the adjusted trial balance amounts to the Income Statement and Balance Sheet columns.

   f. Enter the unadjusted account names and balances from the ledger to the worksheet.

   g. Add the debit and credit columns of the Adjustments.

   h. Add or deduct adjustments and extend to the Adjusted Trial Balance.

   i. After entering the net income or net loss, verify that the Balance Sheet debit and credit columns and the Income Statement debit and credit columns equal.

S4-3. The following accounts appear in the adjusted trial balance. Identify each as an (a) asset, (b) liability, (c) revenue, or (d) expense.

② Preparing a worksheet.

   _____ 1. Accounts Payable

   _____ 2. Lease Expense

continued.....

_____ 3. Computer

_____ 4. Prepaid Insurance

_____ 5. Service Revenue

_____ 6. Notes Payable

② Preparing a worksheet.

S4-4. The adjusted trial balance on the worksheet contains the following accounts. Identify the set of worksheet columns to which each account is extended. Use IS for Income Statement columns and BS for Balance Sheet columns.

_____ 1. Accounts Receivable

_____ 2. Supplies

_____ 3. Service Revenue

_____ 4. Furniture

_____ 5. J.D., Withdrawals

_____ 6. Building Rent Expense

_____ 7. Accumulated Depreciation, Furniture

_____ 8. Salaries Payable

④ Closing the revenue, expense, and withdrawal accounts.

S4-5. From the following list of accounts from the adjusted trial balance, identify each as an asset, liability, owner's equity, revenue, or expense. Also state whether each account is a permanent or temporary account, and if it is an account that gets closed at the end of the accounting period. Following the accounts is a sample of the format to use.

1. Depreciation Expense

2. Sales Revenue

3. Building

4. Cash

5. Unearned Service Revenue

6. Prepaid Rent

7. Peterson, Withdrawals

8. Peterson, Capital

Account	Type of Account	Permanent/Temporary	Closed
Supplies	Asset	Permanent	No

S4-6. The following accounts and balances appear on TJ Services' adjusted trial balance on December 31, 2009:

③ Preparing financial statements.

④ Closing the revenue, expense, and withdrawal accounts.

Service Revenue	$1,000
Building Rent Expense	200
Salary Expense	300
T. Roy, Withdrawals	700
T. Roy, Capital	7,000

Requirements

1. Journalize the closing entries required.

2. What is the net income or net loss?

3. What is the change in capital?

S4-7. For the following series of journal entries, indicate whether each is an adjusting entry (ADJ) or a closing entry (CL).

② Preparing a worksheet.

④ Closing the revenue, expense, and withdrawal accounts.

Date	Accounts	Post Ref.	Dr.	Cr.
a.	Salary Expense		500	
	Salary Payable			500
b.	Service Revenue		800	
	Income Summary			800
c.	JD, Capital		300	
	JD, Withdrawals			300
d.	Unearned Revenue		600	
	Service Revenue			600

S4-8. After closing its accounts at May 31, 2009, Hall's Boarding had the following account balances:

④ Closing the revenue, expense, and withdrawal accounts.

Notes Payable	$2,000	Building	$1,800
Prepaid Rent	825	Cash	1,786
Accounts Receivable	2,479	Service Revenue	0
Prepaid Insurance	1,182	Hall, Capital	5,788
Accounts Payable	284	Salary Expense	0

continued.....

Prepare Hall's post-closing trial balance at May 31, 2009. List accounts in proper order, as shown in Exhibit 4-11.

(5) Classifying assets and liabilities.

S4-9. Story County Ethanol Plant had sales revenue of $1,320 million during the fiscal year ended January 31, 2009, and total assets of $456 million at January 31, 2009, the end of the company's fiscal year. The financial statements of Story County reported the following amounts (in millions):

Sales Revenue.....................	$1,320	Land and Buildings......................	$ 103
Prepaid Insurance.............	162	Accounts Payable.........................	75
Receivables	18	Total Expenses............................	1,073
Interest Expense	2	Accumulated Depreciation,	
Equipment	176	Equipment	117
Prepaid Expenses..............	22	Accrued Liabilities (such as Salary Payable)............................	44

Identify the assets, including contra-assets, and liabilities. Classify each asset and each liability as current or long-term.

(5) Classifying assets and liabilities.

S4-10. From the following list of categories found on the balance sheet and list of balance sheet accounts, match each account with the category in which it would appear.

a. Current assets

b. Long-term assets

c. Current liabilities

d. Long-term liabilities

_____ 1. Mortgage Payable

_____ 2. Equipment

_____ 3. Prepaid Insurance

_____ 4. Notes Payable, due in two years

_____ 5. Accumulated Depreciation, Building

Exercises

(1) Steps in the accounting cycle.

E4-11. Match the terms listed on the left with the corresponding accounting definitions listed on the right.

_____ 1. Accounting cycle   a. Liabilities that are not due for two years.

continued.....

_____ 2. Closing entries

   b. Entries that transfer the balances of revenues, expenses, and withdrawals to capital.

(2) Preparing a worksheet.

_____ 3. Current assets

   c. Debts due to be paid within one year or the operating cycle.

(4) Closing the revenue, expense, and withdrawals accounts.

_____ 4. Fixed assets

   d. Multicolumn document designed to organize information before preparing the financial statements.

(5) Classifying assets and liabilities.

_____ 5. Current liabilities

   e. List of the accounts and their balances after closing entries have been prepared.

_____ 6. Long-term liabilities

   f. Assets expected to be converted to cash or used up within a year.

_____ 7. Post-closing trial balance

   g. Assets not used up within a year.

_____ 8. Worksheet

   h. Process by which companies produce their financial statements for a specific period.

E4-12. The following is a list of accounts and balances for Green Horizon in random order. The information is for the month ended March 31, 2009.

(2) Preparing a worksheet.

Accounts Payable	$ 4
Accounts Receivable	7
Accumulated Depreciation, Office Equipment	1
Cash	4
Office Equipment	8
Prepaid Insurance	2
Service Revenue	23
Supplies	4
Toni Green, Capital	12
Toni Green, Withdrawals	6
Unearned Revenue	3
Utilities Expense	2
Wage Expense	10
Supplies Expense	0
Depreciation Expense, Office Equipment	0
Wages Payable	0
Insurance Expense	0

continued.....

Prepare a worksheet, entering accounts in the trial balance in the proper order, listing the expenses in decreasing amounts. All accounts have normal balances. Complete the worksheet using the following information:

a. Expired insurance, $1.

b. Unearned revenue now earned, $2.

c. Estimated depreciation on office equipment, $1.

d. Accrued wages, $1.

e. Supplies on hand, $1.

 Preparing a worksheet.

E4-13. The following is the trial balance of Christine's Piano Service:

		Balance	
Account Title		**Debit**	**Credit**

CHRISTINE'S PIANO SERVICE
Trial Balance
September 30, 2009

Account Title	Debit	Credit
Cash	$ 3,500	
Accounts receivable	3,400	
Prepaid rent	1,200	
Supplies	3,300	
Equipment	32,600	
Accumulated depreciation, equipment		$ 1,800
Accounts payable		3,600
Salary payable		
C. Smith, capital		35,300
C. Smith, withdrawals	2,000	
Service revenue		7,000
Depreciation expense, equipment		
Salary expense	1,800	
Building rent expense		
Supplies expense		
Total	$ 47,800	$ 47,800

Additional information at September 30, 2009:

a. Accrued service revenue, $600.

b. Depreciation on equipment, $100.

c. Accrued salary expense, $500.

d. Prepaid rent expired, $800.

e. Supplies used, $1,600.

continued.....

Complete the worksheet for the month ended September 30, 2009. How much was net income for September?

③ Preparing financial statements.

E4-14. Using the information from the completed E4-13, journalize Christine's adjusting and closing entries.

④ Closing the revenue, expense, and withdrawals accounts.

E4-15. Using the following selected accounts of Karl's Auto Shop at September 30, 2009, prepare the entity's closing entries:

④ Closing the revenue, expense, and withdrawals accounts.

K. Karl, Capital	$ 21,600	Interest Expense	$ 2,200
Service Revenue	110,000	Accounts Receivable	14,000
Unearned Revenues	1,300	Salary Payable	800
Salary Expense	12,500	Depreciation Expense	10,200
Accumulated Depreciation	35,000	Building Rent Expense	5,900
Supplies Expense	1,700	K. Karl, Withdrawals	40,000
Interest Revenue	700	Supplies	1,400

What is Karl's ending capital balance at September 30, 2009?

E4-16. The accountant for Sandvold_Investments.com has posted adjusting entries (a) through (e) to the following accounts at December 31, 2009:

④ Closing the revenue, expense, and withdrawals accounts.

Accounts Receivable	
126,000	
(a) 9,500	

Supplies	
4,000	(b) 2,000

Accumulated Depreciation, Furniture	
	5,000
	(c) 1,100

Accumulated Depreciation, Building	
	33,000
(d)	6,000

Salary Payable	
	(e) 700

Marcia Sandvold, Capital	
	52,400

Marcia Sandvold, Withdrawals	
61,400	

Service Revenue	
	108,000
	(a) 9,500

Salary Expense	
26,000	
(e) 700	

Supplies Expense	
(b) 2,000	

Depreciation Expense, Furniture	
(c) 1,100	

Depreciation Expense, Building	
(d) 6,000	

continued.....

1. Journalize Sandvold_Investments.com's closing entries at December 31, 2009.

2. Determine Marcia Sandvold's ending capital balance at December 31, 2009.

③ Preparing financial statements.

E4-17. From the following accounts of Hernandez Realty, prepare the business's statement of owner's equity for the year ended December 31, 2009:

Paul Hernandez, Capital				Paul Hernandez, Withdrawals				Income Summary			
Clo.	72,000	Jan. 1	163,000	Mar. 31	19,000			Clo.	85,000	Clo.	228,000
		Clo.	143,000	Jun. 30	17,000			Clo.	143,000	Bal.	143,000
		Bal.	234,000	Sep. 30	19,000						
				Dec. 31	17,000						
				Bal.	72,000	Clo.	72,000				

③ Preparing financial statements.

④ Closing the revenue, expense, and withdrawals accounts.

E4-18. The trial balance and adjusted income statement amounts from the April worksheet of The Major Sports Company follow:

		THE MAJOR SPORTS COMPANY Worksheet				

		Trial Balance		Income Statement	
Account Title		**Dr.**	**Cr.**	**Dr.**	**Cr.**
Cash		15,200			
Supplies		1,400			
Prepaid rent		1,100			
Equipment		51,100			
Accumulated depreciation, equipment			4,200		
Accounts payable			6,600		
Salary payable					
Unearned service revenue			4,400		
Notes payable, long-term			10,000		
Chad Majors, capital			34,800		
Chad Majors, withdrawals		1,000			
Service revenue			14,800		16,000
Salary expense		3,000		3,800	
Building rent expense		1,200		1,400	
Depreciation expense, equipment				300	
Supplies expense				400	
Utilities expense		800		800	
		74,800	74,800	6,700	16,000
Net income or net loss				?	

continued.....

Requirements

1. Journalize Major's adjusting and closing entries at April 30.

2. How much net income or net loss did Major earn for April? How can you tell?

E4-19. Use the data from E4-18 to prepare a classified balance sheet in report form.

⑤ Classifying assets and liabilities.

E4-20. The accountant prepared the following post-closing trial balance. Prepare a corrected post-closing trial balance. Assume all accounts have normal balances and the amounts are correct.

④ Closing the revenue, expense, and withdrawals accounts.

MICHAEL'S FRAMING SERVICE
Post-Closing Trial Balance
September 30, 2009

Account Title	Balance Debit	Credit
Cash	$ 9,225	
Accounts receivable	33,300	
Supplies		$ 1,980
Equipment		63,000
Accumulated depreciation, equipment	19,980	
Accounts payable	11,250	
Salary payable		2,700
Unearned rent	5,400	
Michael Good, capital	68,175	
Total	$147,330	$ 67,680

E4-21. The following is the adjusted trial balance of Olivia Wilson for December 31, 2009.

OLIVIA WILSON, CONSULTANT
Adjusted Trial Balance
December 31, 2009

Account Title	Balance Debit	Balance Credit
Cash	$ 8,700	
Accounts receivable	1,500	
Supplies	100	
Equipment	2,000	
Accumulated depreciation, equipment		50
Furniture	6,600	
Accumulated depreciation, furniture		60
Accounts payable		4,600
Salary payable		500
Unearned service revenue		600
Olivia Wilson, capital		13,000
Olivia Wilson, withdrawals	1,600	
Service revenue		3,200
Building rent expense	500	
Utilities expense	200	
Salary expense	500	
Depreciation expense, equipment	50	
Depreciation expense, furniture	60	
Supplies expense	200	
Total	$ 22,010	$ 22,010

Requirements

1. Journalize and post the closing entries at December 31. Denote each closing amount as Clo. and account balance as Bal.

2. Prepare a classified balance sheet at December 31 in account form.

E4-22. The following is the adjusted trial balance for Peterson's Catering Service at December 31, 2009. Prepare a classified balance sheet in account form. Assume the Mortgage Payable is a current liability.

continued.....

PETERSON'S CATERING SERVICE Adjusted Trial Balance December 31, 2009		
	Balance	
Account Title	**Debit**	**Credit**
Cash	$ 48,040	
Accounts receivable	24,520	
Prepaid rent	4,680	
Supplies	3,300	
Equipment	62,400	
Accumulated depreciation, equipment		$ 18,720
Accounts payable		12,300
Mortgage payable		54,780
G. Peterson, capital		54,540
G. Peterson, withdrawals	2,000	
Service revenue		8,700
Depreciation expense, equipment	500	
Salary expense	1,800	
Rent expense	900	
Utilities expense	700	
Supplies expense	200	
Total	$149,040	$149,040

Problems (Group A)

P4-23A. The trial balance of Cole's Interiors at May 31, 2009, follows:

 Preparing a worksheet.

Additional data at May 31, 2009:

a. Depreciation: furniture, $500; building, $400.

b. Accrued salary expense, $600.

c. Supplies on hand, $400.

d. Prepaid insurance expired, $300.

e. Accrued interest expense, $200.

f. Unearned service revenue earned during May, $4,400.

g. Accrued advertising expense, $100 (credit Accounts Payable).

h. Accrued interest revenue, $200.

Requirement

Complete Cole's Interior's worksheet for May. Label adjusting entries by letter.

continued.....

	COLE'S INTERIORS **Trial Balance** **May 31, 2009**		
			Balance
	Account Title	**Debit**	**Credit**
	Cash	$ 4,300	
	Notes receivable	10,300	
	Interest receivable		
	Supplies	500	
	Prepaid insurance	1,700	
	Furniture	27,400	
	Accumulated depreciation, furniture		$ 1,400
	Building	53,900	
	Accumulated depreciation, building		34,500
	Land	18,700	
	Accounts payable		14,700
	Interest payable		
	Salary payable		
	Unearned service revenue		8,800
	Notes payable, long-term		18,700
	K. Cole, capital		29,900
	K. Cole, withdrawals	3,800	
	Service revenue		16,800
	Interest revenue		
	Depreciation expense, furniture		
	Depreciation expense, building		
	Salary expense	2,100	
	Insurance expense		
	Interest expense		
	Utilities expense	1,100	
	Advertising expense	1,000	
	Supplies expense		
	Total	$124,800	$124,800

P4-24A. The unadjusted T-accounts of Josh Murray, J.D., at December 31, 2009, appear on the next page and the related year-end adjustment data is as follows:

Preparing a worksheet.

Preparing financial statements.

Adjustment data at December 31, 2009:

a. Depreciation for the year, $5,000.

b. Supplies on hand, $2,000.

c. Accrued service revenue, $4,000.

d. Unearned service revenue earned during the year, $2,000.

e. Accrued salary expense, $4,000.

continued.....

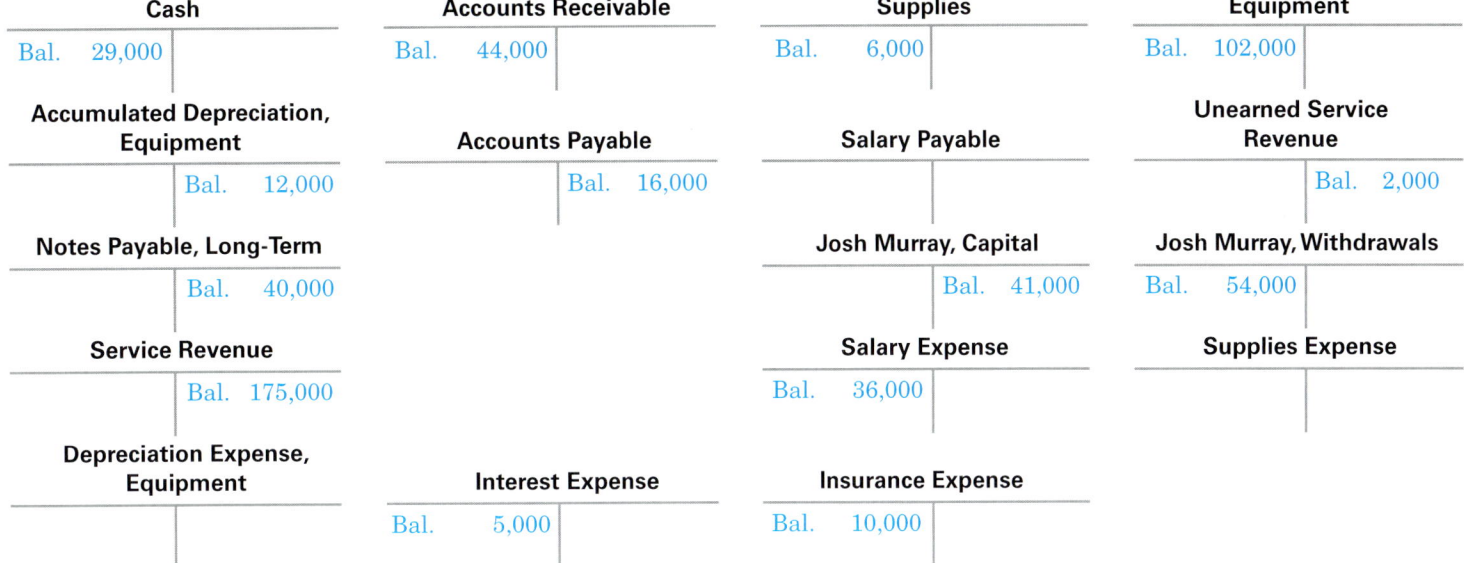

Requirements

1. Enter the account balances in the Trial Balance columns of a worksheet and complete the worksheet. Label each adjusting entry by letter. List all the accounts, including those with zero balances. Leave a blank line under Service Revenue.

2. Prepare the income statement, the statement of owner's equity, and the classified balance sheet in account form.

3. What was the amount of income and what was the amount of the increase in capital for the year?

P4-25A. The adjusted trial balance of Truman Doors Service at April 30, 2009, follows. Adjusting data at April 30, 2009, consists of:

a. Accrued service revenue, $2,200.

b. Depreciation for the year: equipment, $6,900; building, $3,700.

c. Accrued wage expense, $800.

d. Unearned service revenue earned during the year, $4,100.

e. Supplies used, $500.

f. Prepaid insurance expired, $700

g. Accrued interest expense, $1,200.

③ Preparing financial statements.

④ Closing the revenue, expense, and with-drawals accounts.

continued.....

TRUMAN DOORS SERVICE		
Adjusted Trial Balance		
April 30, 2009		

	Balance	
Account Title	**Debit**	**Credit**
Cash	$ 14,500	
Accounts receivable	43,700	
Supplies	3,600	
Prepaid insurance	2,200	
Equipment	63,900	
Accumulated depreciation, equipment		$ 28,400
Building	74,300	
Accumulated depreciation, building		18,200
Land	30,600	
Accounts payable		40,700
Interest payable		1,200
Wages payable		800
Unearned service revenue		3,600
Notes payable, long-term		69,900
Jeff Truman, capital		51,700
Jeff Truman, withdrawals	27,500	
Service revenue		98,500
Depreciation expense, equipment	6,900	
Depreciation expense, building	3,700	
Wage expense	32,800	
Insurance expense	700	
Interest expense	8,100	
Supplies expense	500	
Totals	$313,000	$313,000

Requirements

1. Journalize the adjusting entries.

2. Journalize the closing entries.

③ Preparing financial statements.

P4-26A. The adjusted trial balance of Jane's Tutoring Success Company October 31, 2009, is shown on the following page.

Requirement

Prepare the income statement, statement of owner's equity, and classified balance sheet in account form for the month of October, 2009.

continued.....

JANE'S TUTORING SUCCESS COMPANY
Adjusted Trial Balance
October 31, 2009

Acct. #	Account Title	Debit	Credit
11	Cash	$ 4,900	
12	Accounts receivable	15,310	
13	Prepaid rent	2,200	
14	Supplies	840	
15	Equipment	26,830	
16	Accumulated depreciation, equipment		$ 3,400
21	Accounts payable		7,290
23	Unearned service revenue		5,300
31	Jane Carlsen, capital		29,390
32	Jane Carlsen, withdrawals	3,900	
41	Service revenue		12,560
51	Salary expense	2,860	
52	Rent expense	100	
54	Depreciation expense, equipment	800	
56	Supplies expense	200	
	Total	$ 57,940	$ 57,940

P4-27A. Following are selected accounts randomly listed for Myra Laird, M.D., on December 31, 2009.

③ Preparing financial statements.

Accounts Payable	$34,700	Insurance Expense	$ 600
Accounts Receivable	41,500	Notes Payable, Long-Term	3,200
Accumulated Depreciation,		Other Assets (long-term)	2,300
Building	47,300	Other Current Liabilities	1,100
Accumulated Depreciation,		Prepaid Insurance	600
Equipment	7,700	Prepaid Rent	4,700
Building	55,900	Salary Expense	17,800
Cash	3,400	Salary Payable	2,400
Depreciation Expense	1,900	Service Revenue	71,100
Myra Laird, Capital	38,300	Supplies	3,800
Equipment	24,200	Unearned Service Revenue	1,700

Requirement

Prepare Laird's classified balance sheet dated December 31, 2009, in account form.

Problems (Group B)

 Preparing a worksheet.

P4-28B. The trial balance of Jordan's Personal Training at September 30, 2009, follows.

	JORDAN'S PERSONAL TRAINING Trial Balance September 30, 2009		
		Balance	
Account Title		**Debit**	**Credit**
Cash		$ 21,200	
Accounts receivable		37,800	
Supplies		17,600	
Prepaid insurance		2,300	
Equipment		32,600	
Accumulated depreciation, equipment			$ 26,200
Building		42,800	
Accumulated depreciation, building			10,500
Land		28,300	
Accounts payable			22,600
Interest payable			
Wages payable			
Unearned service revenue			10,500
Notes payable, long-term			22,400
Dan Jordan, capital			79,100
Dan Jordan, withdrawals		4,200	
Service revenue			20,100
Depreciation expense, equipment			
Depreciation expense, building			
Wage expense		3,200	
Insurance expense			
Interest expense			
Utilities expense		1,100	
Advertising expense		300	
Supplies expense			
Total		$191,400	$191,400

Additional data at September 30, 2009:

a. Depreciation: equipment, $600; building, $300.

b. Accrued wage expense, $200.

c. Supplies on hand, $14,300.

d. Prepaid insurance expired during September, $500.

e. Accrued interest expense, $100.

f. Unearned service revenue now earned during September, $4,900.

g. Accrued advertising expense, $100 (credit Accounts Payable).

h. Accrued service revenue, $1,100.

continued.....

Requirement

Complete Jordan's Personal Training worksheet for September. Label adjusting entries by letter. Leave a blank line under Service Revenue.

P4-29B. The unadjusted T-accounts of Zimmerman's Studio, at December 31, 2009, and the related year-end adjustment data follow.

 Preparing a worksheet.

3 Preparing financial statements.

Cash	
Bal. 15,000	

Accounts Receivable	
Bal. 36,000	

Supplies	
Bal. 9,000	

Equipment	
Bal. 99,000	

Accumulated Depreciation, Equipment	
	Bal. 13,000

Accounts Payable	
	Bal. 6,000

Salary Payable	

Unearned Service Revenue	
	Bal. 5,000

Notes Payable, Long-Term	
	Bal. 60,000

B. Zimmerman, Capital	
	Bal. 36,000

B. Zimmerman, Withdrawals	
Bal. 62,000	

Service Revenue	
	Bal. 182,000

Salary Expense	
Bal. 53,000	

Supplies Expense	

Depreciation Expense, Equipment	

Interest Expense	
Bal. 6,000	

Building Rent Expense	
Bal. 15,000	

Insurance Expense	
Bal. 7,000	

a. Unearned service revenue now earned during the year, $5,000.

b. Supplies on hand, $1,000.

c. Depreciation for the year, $9,000.

d. Accrued salary expense, $1,000.

e. Accrued service revenue, $2,000.

Requirements

1. Enter the account balances in the Trial Balance columns of a worksheet, and complete the worksheet. Label each adjusting entry by letter. List all the accounts, including those with zero balances. Leave a blank line under Service Revenue.

2. Prepare the income statement, the statement of owner's equity, and the classified balance sheet in account format.

3. Discuss the success of the company during the year.

3 Preparing financial
statements.

4 Closing the revenue,
expense, and with-
drawals accounts.

P4-30B. The adjusted trial balance of Emeroff Framing at September 30, 2009, and the adjusting data for September 30, 2009, follow:

EMEROFF FRAMING Adjusted Trial Balance September 30, 2009		
	Balance	
Account Title	**Debit**	**Credit**
Cash	$ 12,300	
Accounts receivable	26,400	
Supplies	31,200	
Prepaid insurance	3,200	
Equipment	135,800	
Accumulated depreciation, equipment		$ 16,400
Building	34,900	
Accumulated depreciation, building		16,800
Land	30,000	
Accounts payable		39,100
Interest payable		1,400
Wages payable		
Notes payable, long-term		104,000
Dakota Emeroff, capital		49,400
Dakota Emeroff, withdrawals	45,300	
Service revenue		139,800
Depreciation expense, equipment	7,300	
Depreciation expense, building	3,900	
Wage expense	21,400	
Insurance expense	2,200	
Interest expense	8,500	
Utilities expense	4,300	
Supplies expense	200	
Total	$366,900	$366,900

a. Prepaid insurance expired, $2,200.

b. Accrued interest expense, $500.

c. Accrued service revenue, $900.

d. Accrued wage expense, $700.

e. Depreciation for the year: equipment, $7,300; building, $3,900.

f. Supplies used, $200.

Requirements

1. Journalize the adjusting entries.
2. Journalize the closing entries.

P4-31B. The adjusted trial balance of Myers Food Consultants at August 31, 2009, follows:

continued.....

		Balance	
Acct. #	Account Title	Debit	Credit
	MEYERS FOOD CONSULTANTS Adjusted Trial Balance August 31, 2009		
11	Cash	$ 3,800	
12	Accounts receivable	15,560	
13	Prepaid rent	1,290	
14	Supplies	20,900	
15	Equipment	15,350	
16	Accumulated depreciation, equipment		$ 12,800
17	Building	89,900	
18	Accumulated depreciation, building		28,600
21	Accounts payable		4,240
23	Unearned service revenue		8,900
31	Cory Meyers, capital		71,920
32	Cory Meyers, withdrawals	4,800	
41	Service revenue		34,300
51	Salary expense	2,160	
52	Rent expense	5,000	
54	Depreciation expense, equipment	1,000	
55	Depreciation expense, building	1,000	
	Total	$160,760	$160,760

Requirement

Prepare the income statement, the statement of owner's equity, and the classified balance sheet in account form for the month of August, 2009.

P4-32B. Selected accounts of Cornerstone Services at December 31, 2009, follow:

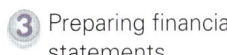 Preparing financial statements.

Accounts Payable	$ 15,100	Sandra Stone, Capital	$67,100
Accounts Receivable	6,600	Notes Payable, Long-Term	27,800
Accumulated Depreciation,		Other Assets (Long-Term)	3,600
Equipment	37,800	Other Current Liabilities	4,700
Accumulated Depreciation,		Prepaid Insurance	1,100
Computers	11,600	Prepaid Rent	6,600
Equipment	114,400	Salary Expense	24,600
Cash	16,500	Salary Payable	3,900
Service Revenue	93,500	Supplies	2,500
Computers	22,700	Unearned Service Revenue	5,400
Interest Payable	600		

Requirement

Prepare Cornerstone's classified balance sheet in account form at December 31, 2009.

for 24/7 practice, visit
www.MyAccountingLab.com

Apply Your Knowledge

Case 1. Larry Foster and his banker were reviewing the monthly income statements for his antique business, Foster's Collectibles. The banker was impressed with the growth of sales revenue and net income for January as compared to January of last year. Larry knew it had been a good month, but didn't think it had been spectacular. Suddenly, Larry realized that he failed to close out the revenue and expense accounts for the prior year, which ended in December. Because those temporary accounts were not closed out, their balances were included in the January amounts for the current year. Larry then realized that the banker had the financial statements but not the general ledger or any trial balances. Thus, the banker would not be able to see that the accounting cycle was not properly closed and that this failure was creating a misstated income statement for January of the current year. The banker then commented that the business appeared to be off to such a strong start that he would approve a line of credit for the business. Larry decided to not say anything because he did not want to lose the line of credit. Besides, he thought, it really did not matter that the income statement was misstated because his business would be sure to repay any amounts borrowed.

Should Larry have informed the banker of the mistake made and redone the current year's January income statement? Was Larry's failure to close the prior year's revenue and expense accounts unethical? Does the fact that the business will repay the loan matter?

Case 2. Sally Jones, the owner of Travel Unlimited, was meeting with her accountant to review the financial statements. The accountant expressed some concerns over the business's lack of liquidity. Even though the total assets were $1,240,000, only $60,000 were current. Of the $420,000 in total liabilities, $200,000 were current. Sally did not care because she knew she had plenty of equity. Further, she believed that the bank would see a strong balance sheet because the total assets were greater than the total liabilities. Her accountant argued, saying that the bank would become concerned with Travel Unlimited's ability to pay its current liabilities as they become due and payable. After all, the business only had $60,000 of current assets available to cover current liabilities of $200,000. Sally then told the accountant to simply reclassify some of the long-term assets as current and thereby "fix" the liquidity issue of Travel Unlimited. Sally argued that it really did not matter because the business had lots of assets and could sell some of them for cash if it had to meet any current liabilities that became due.

Should the accountant reclassify some long-term assets as current? Is the argument that the business has lots of assets and could sell some for cash if it had needed to meet any current liabilities a valid argument? What should Sally do?

This case will help you to better understand and become more familiar with the format and content of a balance sheet. Refer to the Target Balance Sheets, "Consolidated Statements of Financial Position," in Appendix A. Use the information from the balance sheets to answer the following questions:

Requirements

1. Which balance sheet format does Target use?

2. What is the largest current asset and current liability reported by Target as of January 2005?

3. Under what category does Target include its buildings and improvements?

4. Does Target have more long-term debt than total current liabilities in each year presented? Has the total long-term debt increased or decreased?

For Internet Exercises, Excel in Practice, and additional online activities, go to the Web site www.prenhall.com/pollard.

Quick Check Answers

1. *a* 2. *a* 3. *d* 4. *b* 5. *b* 6. *c* 7. *d* 8. *b* 9. *b* 10. *b*

LEARNING OBJECTIVES

1. Describe the supply chain that links suppliers, retailers, and customers.

2. Journalize transactions between the supplier and retailer.

3. Journalize transactions between the retailer and customer.

4. Journalize shipment transactions and identify other selling expenses in a retail business.

5. Prepare a retailer's financial statements.

6. Compute the gross profit percentage and inventory turnover rate.

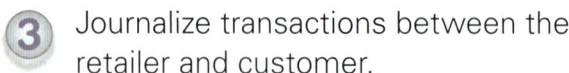

Accounting for a Retail Business

Your friend is looking for a present for her sister's birthday. Her sister enjoys the beach so you suggest that she buy her sister a swimsuit cover-up. Your friend could shop for one at a department store, a specialty beachwear store, in a mail-order catalogue, or online. Department and specialty stores would allow her to touch the fabric and check out clothing sizes. Mail order and online sellers provide colorful pictures and information about colors, patterns, and sizes. Your friend decides to buy a swimsuit cover-up at a specialty store and mails it to her sister just in time for her sister's birthday.

The department, specialty, mail-order, and online stores are all retail businesses. Remember from Chapter 1 that retail, or merchandise, companies buy goods in order to resell them to their customers. Businesses such as Sears, Target, and Wal-Mart are major retailers that buy and sell thousands of products to customers like you and your friend. ●

Look Back

You have now mastered the accounting cycle for a service business by recording and posting transactions, preparing a worksheet and financial statements, and closing temporary accounts. You have also learned to assemble a classified balance sheet.

Look Ahead

Understanding the relationships between suppliers, retailers, and customers, you will account for a business that buys and sells merchandise and report the results of these activities in financial statements.

In previous chapters, we completed the accounting cycle for a service business using Kay Torres Travel Agency as an example. We recorded and posted its transactions in accounts, adjusted those accounts on a worksheet, prepared financial statements, and closed the temporary accounts used to track a single year's activity. In this chapter, we turn our attention to the accounting cycle of a merchandising business, one that sells goods to its customers. By examining Baja Beachwear, we will see how retail merchandisers record purchases and sales transactions between it, suppliers, and customers. We will also prepare financial statements for a retail business.

The Supply Chain

1 Describe the supply chain that links suppliers, retailers, and customers.

A **supply chain** is the chain of transactions between businesses that supply goods and the customers that ultimately use these goods; it begins when a manufacturer purchases raw materials and uses them to produce products. Merchandisers, **wholesalers** and retailers, buy these manufactured goods and deliver them to the ultimate user, the customer. Wholesalers typically buy large lots of products from manufacturers and resell them to retailers. Retailers buy goods from manufacturers or wholesalers, then sell smaller quantities to the public, the final consumers. Thus, this sequence of events involves the flow of materials, completed goods, and related information between manufacturers, wholesale and/or retail merchandisers, and customers.

Exhibit 5-1, Panel A shows the flow of goods in a supply chain and the retailer's relationship with its suppliers, manufacturers and wholesalers, and its customers.

We are all familiar with merchandisers like the retail store, Target, and the e-retailer, Amazon.com. In the remainder of this chapter, we will focus on retailers to illustrate merchandising operations. We look at the retailer's relationship with its suppliers and its customers and examine the journal entries needed to record transactions between these links in the supply chain.

The Supplier/Retailer Relationship

Exhibit 5-1, Panel B, illustrates activities between suppliers and retailers. Retailers:

- Identify suppliers, either manufacturers or wholesalers.
- Purchase goods from these suppliers, often on credit.
- Pay cash to suppliers for goods purchased.
- Return goods purchased from suppliers as necessary.

Amy Toms grew up in California, working for several different retail beachwear companies. After graduation from college, she started her own business, Baja Beachwear. Baja Beachwear sells bathing suits, beach towels, sunglasses, shirts, sandals, and other similar items. Her stores will attract and keep customers if she provides a wide selection of goods in convenient store locations at reasonable prices. Amy works hard to find suppliers that can provide merchandise that her customers want.

Exhibit 5-1 The Supply Chain and Supplier/Retailer and Retailer/Customer Relationships

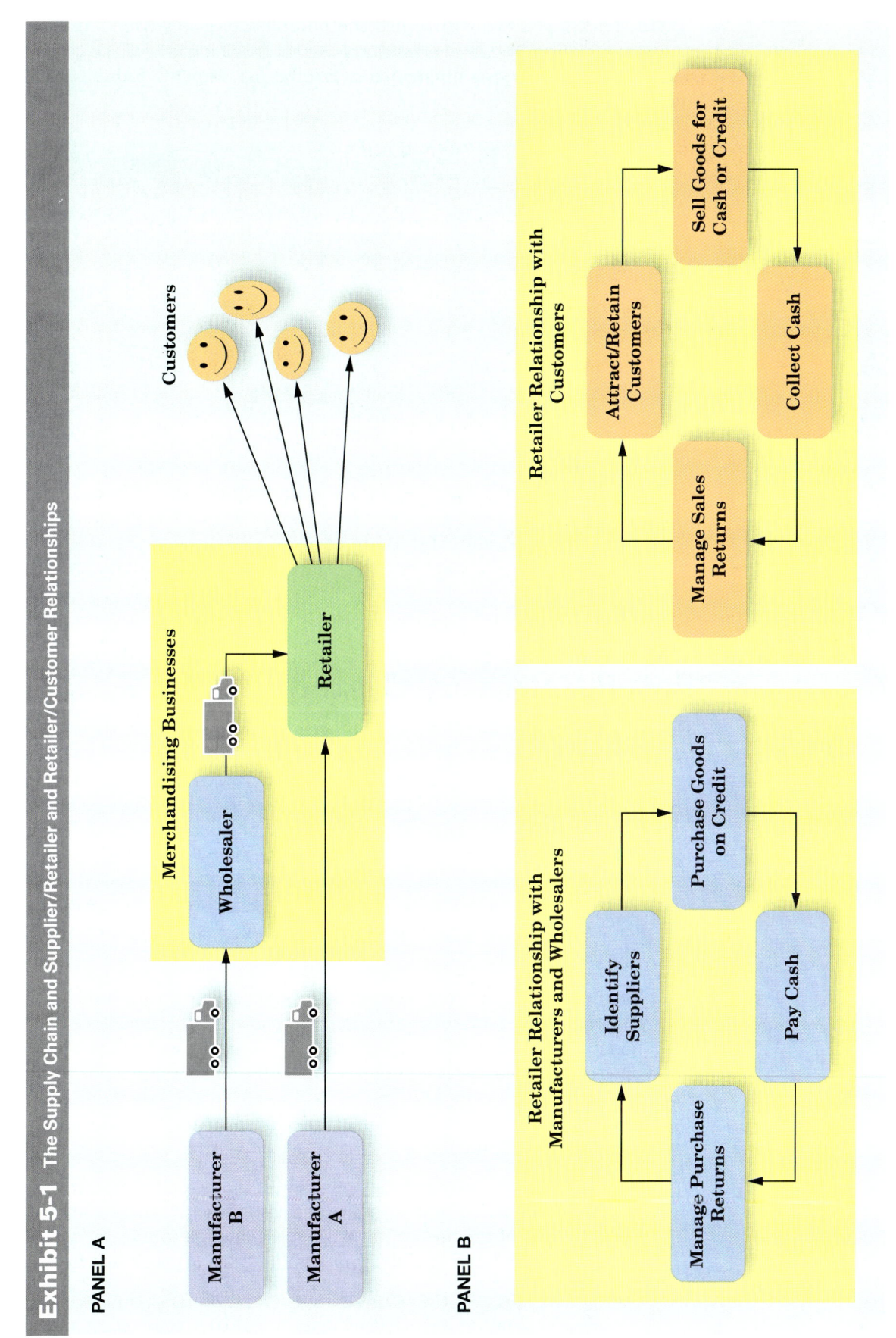

PANEL A

PANEL B

In this chapter we will record the purchase of goods from suppliers, payments to suppliers for these goods, and the return of some of these goods to suppliers when necessary, as illustrated in Exhibit 5-1, Panel B. Exhibit 5-2 shows a supply chain for Baja Beachwear.

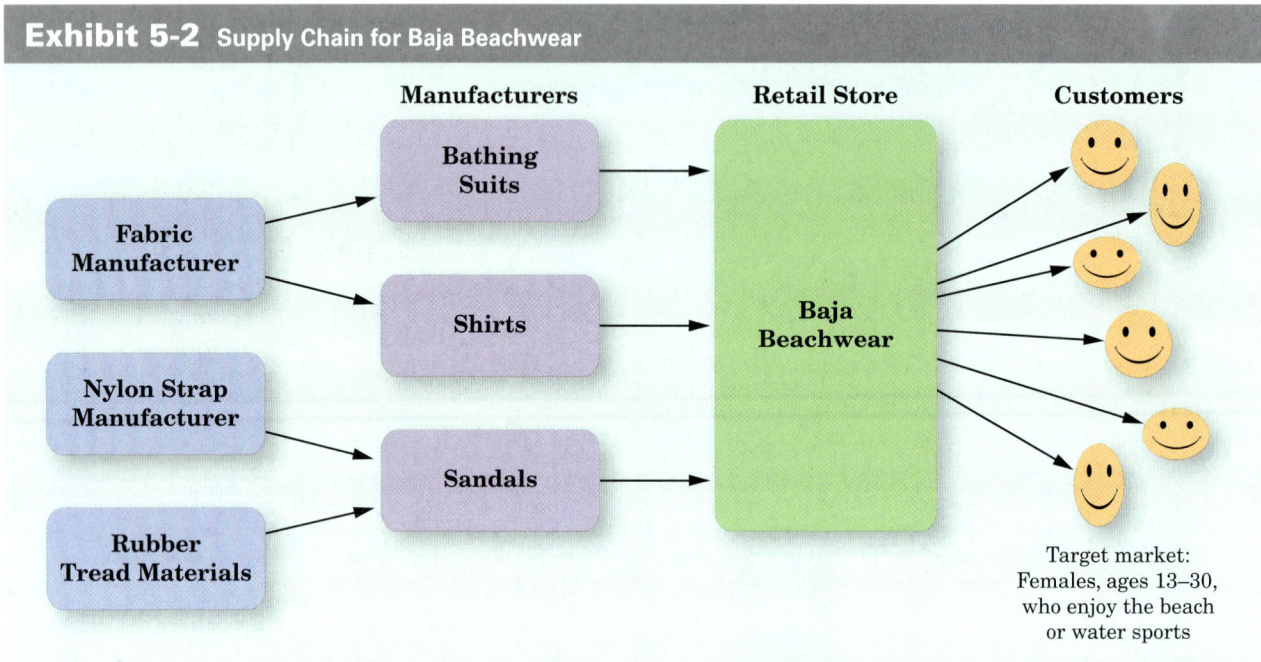

Exhibit 5-2 Supply Chain for Baja Beachwear

Retail Inventory Systems

The products that manufacturing and wholesale businesses supply retailers become **inventory** of the retailer. Inventory refers to the goods that the retailer owns and has available to sell to its customers; it is the products that the business holds for sale as part of its normal operations. Retail businesses buy and sell products, also called **merchandise inventory**, instead of services. Throughout the remainder of the book we refer to merchandise inventory simply as inventory. It is typically a retailer's most important asset because it is probably the business's largest current asset, as well as the center of merchandising transactions.

Businesses that have inventory use one of two systems to keep track of the cost of goods:

- The **periodic inventory system** is a system of accounting for inventory that does *not* keep a continuous, running record of all goods owned. Instead, it only updates the inventory account *periodically*. Under this method, the business physically counts the goods in inventory at the end of the accounting period. It then multiplies the number of each item owned by the cost of the item to get a total value for the product. Finally, it then adds the total value of each product type together to calculate a new balance for the inventory account.

  Similarly, a business calculates the value of the inventory that it has sold at the end of the period. It determines the cost of the products sold by comparing the value of the goods that were available for sale to the value of the goods left in inventory; the difference is the value of goods sold to customers.

  Businesses may use the periodic inventory system if they sell relatively inexpensive goods and lots of them, making it time consuming and costly to keep track of each sale as it occurs. Also, businesses will typically utilize this system if they do not have optical-scanning cash registers and technology to track items sold automatically.

- The **perpetual inventory system** is a system of accounting for inventory that keeps a running record of inventory owned and the cost of the inventory sold. Every time the business engages in a transaction involving inventory, it immediately adjusts the balance in the inventory account. In this way, the inventory balance is *perpetually* up-to-date. However, the business still counts inventory at least once a year to see whether any goods have been stolen, lost, or damaged; just because accounting records indicate that a certain amount of inventory is owned, doesn't necessarily mean that this amount is actually present and in good condition. The physical count establishes the correct amount of ending inventory and also serves as a check on the perpetual records. In this way, this inventory system achieves better control over the inventory than does the periodic system.

  Technology makes it easier for businesses to use the perpetual system. Usually, the cash register in a perpetual system is a computer terminal that records a sale and simultaneously updates inventory records. It does so by employing a laser that scans bar codes on products. The bar coding identifies inventory items and their cost and are thus used to track each item sold. Because it is more commonly used, we will use the perpetual inventory system to illustrate the transactions for a retail business.

The Retailer/Customer Relationship

Exhibit 5-1, Panel B, also shows activities between the retailer and the customer. Retailers:

- Attract and retain customers.
- Sell goods for cash or credit to customers.
- Collect cash from customers.
- Accept returns of goods sold to customers as necessary.

  Retail business, like Baja Beachwear, must identify the types of customers they want to attract into their stores. Market research helps them focus, or target, their advertising and sales efforts on a portion of the total market. Amy chose to target her sales efforts on females, ages 13–30, who enjoy the beach or water sports. With this market in mind, Amy directs her advertising and sales activities to attract and retain these customers.

  In this chapter, we will record the sale of goods to customers, cash collection from these customers, and the return of goods from customers, as shown in Exhibit 5-1, Panel B.

Accounting for the Supplier/Retailer Relationship

Throughout the year, the retailer engages in a number of inventory transactions with suppliers:

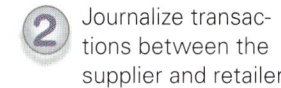
2 Journalize transactions between the supplier and retailer.

- Cash purchases: Purchase goods for cash paid immediately.
- Credit purchases: Purchase goods on account and promise to pay cash later.

- Purchase discounts: Receive deduction from the amount due by paying cash earlier than the due date.

- Purchase returns and allowances: Return damaged goods to supplier for a refund or accept an allowance on those goods.

Cash and Credit Purchases

Amy Toms wants to sell bathing suits in her Baja Beachwear business. She locates an appropriate supplier, Janz Swimwear, and purchases 300 bathing suits from Janz on account at a cost of $25 each. Thus, the total value of Baja's purchase is $7,500 (300 bathing suits × $25). Baja Beachwear receives the goods on February 1 and records this purchase as follows:

Journal Entry:

Date	Accounts	Post Ref.	Dr.	Cr.
Feb. 1	Inventory		7,500	
	Accounts Payable—Janz Swimwear			7,500
	Record purchase of inventory on account.			

The purchase of inventory on account increases both Baja Beachwear's assets and liabilities. The Inventory account accumulates the cost of goods purchased for resale, and its balance increases every time inventory is purchased. Purchases of other resources used in the business, such as office supplies, equipment, sales vehicles, furniture, and warehouses are recorded in their own accounts because, unlike inventory, they are not going to be resold to customers. Inventory is an asset until it is sold because, as we first discussed in Chapter 1, assets are items owned by the business.

Notice that the name of the supplier is listed in the journal entry following Accounts Payable. This is because a record of the amount owed to each supplier is kept in a **subsidiary ledger** so that the retailer knows the amount of the accounts payable to each one. A subsidiary ledger is an accounting record that keeps track of details, in this case, the amount owed to each individual vendor.

Some manufacturers and wholesalers may require cash to be paid at the time of shipment. If Janz required cash payment for the 300 bathing suits at the time of sale, then Baja Beachwear would record the cash purchase as follows:

Journal Entry:

Date	Accounts	Post Ref.	Dr.	Cr.
Feb. 1	Inventory		7,500	
	Cash			7,500
	Record purchase of inventory for cash.			

Purchase Discounts

Exhibit 5-3 illustrates Janz's invoice for Baja's $7,500 purchase of inventory. A **sales invoice** is a bill that documents the sale of goods to a business customer. The invoice includes **credit terms**, or the payment terms, for customers who buy

Exhibit 5-3 Invoice

Janz

Janz Swimwear
P.O. Box 1492
Miami, Florida

Invoice	
Date	Number
2/1/08	644

Shipped to: Baja Beachwear
18 Shoreline Drive
Laguna Beach, CA

Terms: 3/15, n30

Quantity	Item	Unit Price	Total
300 each	Bathing suits	$ 25	$ 7,500

Subtotal	$ 7,500
Shipping Charge	–
Tax	–
Total	$ 7,500

on account. A customer may pay cash when it receives the goods or it may pay within a period of time following the receipt of those goods. Merchandisers, usually wholesalers, use credit terms on sales to retail businesses to communicate when payment is due. Often, merchandisers will use the term **n/30**, which means that the sales price for the goods must be paid within 30 days after the date of the invoice. If the amount is due at the end of the month, the invoice will include the phrase **n/eom** or **eom**.

All businesses want to have enough cash to pay their bills on time. Retailers are frequently offered **purchase discounts** for early payment by suppliers in order to improve the cash inflow of the supplier. By getting the retailer to pay amounts before the due date, these companies get cash sooner. The time period in which the retailer may pay and receive the discount is called the **discount period**. If the retailer takes advantage of this offer and pays early, then these discounts represent a reduction in the cost of the merchandise purchased.

Check out Janz's invoice in Exhibit 5-3; Janz's credit terms of "3/15, n/30" mean that Baja Beachwear may deduct 3% of the total amount due to Janz if it pays Janz within 15 days of the invoice date. Otherwise, the full amount is due in 30 days. In this case, the discount period covers 15 days. However, if Janz listed terms of "n/30" instead of "3/15, n/30," it would mean that it was not offering a discount at all, and payment is due 30 days after the invoice date.

If Baja Beachwear chooses to pay within the discount period, it will pay $7,275, or 97% of the purchase invoice amount of $7,500, calculated as follows:

Invoice Total	$ 7,500	(100% of invoice amount)
− Purchase Discount	(225)	(3% of invoice amount, or .03 × $7,500)
= Cash Paid	$ 7,275	(97% of invoice amount, or .97 × $7,500)

Baja records its payment on February 13, which is within the discount period, as shown:

Journal Entry:

Date	Accounts	Post Ref.	Dr.	Cr.
Feb. 13	Accounts Payable—Janz Swimwear		7,500	
	Cash			7,275
	Inventory			225
	Record payment of inventory purchases within the discount period.			

Note that the discount is credited to the Inventory account, because the discount decreases the cost of the bathing suits that Baja Beachwear bought from Janz.

However, if Baja Beachwear paid this invoice after the discount period, Baja Beachwear would have paid the full amount of $7,500. In that case, it would have recorded the payment this way:

Journal Entry:

Date	Accounts	Post Ref.	Dr.	Cr.
Feb. 24	Accounts Payable—Janz Swimwear		7,500	
	Cash			7,500
	Record payment of inventory purchases after the discount period.			

Purchase Returns and Allowances

Occasionally, retailers buy goods that they are not fully satisfied with. In these cases, manufacturers and wholesalers usually allow retailers to return goods that are defective, damaged, or otherwise unsuitable. Or, they may allow the retailer to keep the unsuitable merchandise and receive a deduction, or an allowance, from the amount they owe for that merchandise. **Purchase returns and allowances** both decrease the retailer's cost of the inventory.

Suppose Baja Beachwear buys 20 pair of Tiva sandals for $20 per pair, and these sandals become damaged in shipment. If Baja returns the merchandise to Tiva Sandals, the manufacturer, it will issue a **debit memorandum**, a document that supports the return of goods to the supplier and makes an adjustment to the balance owed to the supplier, as illustrated in Exhibit 5-4. A debit memorandum is named based on the effect that the memo has on the Accounts Payable account of the issuer; upon issuing the debit memorandum, Baja will *debit*, or reduce, its Accounts Payable balance for the value of the merchandise returned. It records the purchase return as follows:

Journal Entry:

Date	Accounts	Post Ref.	Dr.	Cr.
Apr. 5	Accounts Payable—Tiva Sandals		400	
	Inventory			400
	Record inventory returned to manufacturer.			

A purchase return decreases both Baja Beachwear's assets and its liabilities.

Exhibit 5-4 Debit Memorandum

Baja Beachwear
18 Shoreline Drive
Laguna Beach, California

DEBIT MEMORANDUM #69

To: Tiva Sandals   Date: April 5, 2008
9 Rio Rancho Drive
San Antonio, TX

We debit your account balance for the following:

20 pairs of T180 Sandals @ $20 per pair   **$400**

Accounting for the Retailer/Customer Relationship

The retailer engages in several different types of business transactions with its customers:

 3 Journalize transactions between the retailer and customer.

- Cash sales: Sell goods for cash received immediately.

- Credit sales: Sell goods on account and receive customer's promise to pay cash later.

- Sales discounts: Grant reduction in the amount receivable from customer as an incentive for customer's payment within the discount period.

- Sales returns and allowances: Accept damaged goods from customer for a refund or grant customer an allowance for them.

Cash Sales

Retailers, such as Baja Beachwear, often receive cash at the time of the sale of merchandise. On June 9, Baja Beachwear sells goods of $3,000 to customers for cash. The journal entry to record the sale increases the asset, Cash, and also increases the revenue account, **Sales Revenue**. Sales Revenue is the account used by retailers to track the value of merchandise sold to customers at the prices that the retailer charges those customers.

Remember that Baja Beachwear, like most retailers, uses the perpetual inventory system to account for its inventory. Under this system, at the time of the sale, Baja must also reduce the Inventory balance for the value of the merchandise sold so that the Inventory account always, or perpetually, holds the current balance. The value of the merchandise sold is accounted for in the **Cost of Goods Sold** account. This income statement account holds the cost of merchandise sold so its value can be deducted from Sales Revenue as a step in determining the amount of net income or loss for the business.

Assume that the goods that Baja sold its customers for $3,000 cost Baja $1,900. The entity transfers the $1,900 cost of the goods from the Inventory account to Cost of Goods Sold by decreasing Inventory and increasing Cost of Goods Sold, at the same time that it records the increase to Cash and Sales Revenue, as follows:

Journal Entry:

Date	Accounts	Post Ref.	Dr.	Cr.
June 9	Cash		3,000	
	Sales Revenue			3,000
	Cost of Goods Sold		1,900	
	Inventory			1,900
	Record sale of inventory for cash.			

Remember that when a product is sold, a retail business recognizes:

1. Sales revenue for the selling price of the product to the customer.

2. Cost of goods sold for the retailer's cost of the product.

This type of journal entry involving more than two accounts is called a **compound journal entry**. A compound entry is a journal entry including more than one debit amount and/or more than one credit amount. It is used when a transaction affects more than two accounts.

In some computerized systems, the computer routinely records the cost of goods sold entry when the cashier uses an optical scanner to scan the item's bar code into the accounting system. Scanning the item indicates that the item is being sold, and both Inventory and Cost of Goods Sold are automatically adjusted accordingly. In this case, the retailer would only record the first part of the journal entry:

Journal Entry:

Date	Accounts	Post Ref.	Dr.	Cr.
June 9	Cash		3,000	
	Sales Revenue			3,000
	Record sale of inventory for cash.			

Some retailers allow customers to use credit cards and debit cards rather than currency. These transactions are still essentially cash sales because the company issuing the cards bears the responsibility of collecting the amount due from the customer. The retailer, however, usually has to pay a service charge to the credit/debit card company in exchange for their processing of the transactions.

- Retailers record the amount of the sale at the time of sale.

- Retailers also record service charges for credit and debit cards related to the sale.

While transaction details vary, if Baja Beachwear accepted debit or credit cards for its June sales, it could record its $25 credit/debit card service charge as follows:

Journal Entry:

Date	Accounts	Post Ref.	Dr.	Cr.
June 9	Credit/Debit Card Expense		25	
	Cash			25
	Record payments for service charges on credit/debt card sales.			

Credit Sales

Many retail businesses will establish charge accounts for their customers. Baja Beachwear sold bathing suits, sandals, and towels to Julie Sneed on June 11 for $500. These goods cost the retailer $290. It records this sale on account and the cost of goods sold as follows:

Journal Entry:

Date	Accounts	Post Ref.	Dr.	Cr.
June 11	Accounts Receivable—Julie Sneed		500	
	Sales Revenue			500
	Cost of Goods Sold		290	
	Inventory			290
	Record sale of inventory on account, invoice no. 322.			

When Julie sends Baja her payment for this merchandise, the retailer records the cash receipt on account as follows:

Journal Entry:

Date	Accounts	Post Ref.	Dr.	Cr.
June 19	Cash		500	
	Accounts Receivable—Julie Sneed			500
	Record payment received on invoice no. 322.			

Notice that the name of the customer is listed in the journal entry following Accounts Receivable because a charge account is established for each customer to whom the retailer allows sales on account. Each charge account has its own number and is kept in a subsidiary ledger for accounts receivable so that the retailer can keep track of the amount of accounts receivable owed by each individual customer.

Sales Discounts to Other Businesses— The Supplier's Perspective

Remember the discount that Janz offered Baja Beachwear for early payment? It is not common practice for a retailer to offer discounts to its customers for early payment; however, wholesalers and manufacturers such as Janz do, so we will illustrate sales discounts by looking at them from the perspective of Janz, the seller. The credit terms of the sale between Janz and Baja are 3/15, n/30. Baja chose to pay the invoice within the 15-day discount period, and it got a 3% or $225 discount on its $7,500 purchase ($7,500 × .03). Janz was paid $7,275, or 97% of the invoice amount of $7,500. As we discussed previously, this discount reduces the cost of the merchandise purchased by Baja. As the seller, this discount represents a reduction in the value of sales to Baja.

Businesses like Janz want to keep track of these amounts so they can measure the impact of discounts on the business's sales revenue. So, the accounting system accumulates these amounts in a separate, contra-account, called **Sales Discounts**. Remember from Chapter 3 that a contra-account is an account with a balance opposite of its related companion account. Because it is related to Sales Revenue, the Sales Discounts is a contra-account to Sales Revenue and typically holds a debit balance. This account marks the decreases in sales revenue incurred by granting discounts to the customer.

Janz received this payment of $7,275 from Baja on February 13. The journal entry that Janz made to record the receipt of cash and the sales discount is:

Journal Entry:

Date	Accounts	Post Ref.	Dr.	Cr.
Feb. 13	Cash		7,275	
	Sales Discounts		225	
	Accounts Receivable—Baja Beachwear			7,500
	Record payment received within the discount period.			

If Baja failed to pay within the 15-day discount period, it would have had to pay the full invoice price of $7,500 and Janz would have recorded the payment as follows:

Journal Entry:

Date	Accounts	Post Ref.	Dr.	Cr.
Feb. 24	Cash		7,500	
	Accounts Receivable—Baja Beachwear			7,500
	Record payment received after the discount period.			

Sales Returns and Allowances

In the course of business, retailers may allow customers to return merchandise or they may let customers keep the damaged goods and request an allowance for the damage. Businesses want to keep track of these activities so they can analyze and manage the situations causing the damage and measure the costs of damage to the business. So, the accounting system accumulates these amounts in a separate, contra-account, called **Sales Returns and Allowances**. Because Sales

Returns and Allowances is related to Sales Revenue, it is a contra-account to Sales Revenue. Sales Revenue normally has a credit balance, which means that Sales Returns and Allowances typically holds a debit balance. Its balance tracks the decreases to sales arising from a customer's return of merchandise or from the retailer's giving an allowance to the customer.

SALES RETURNS

Occasionally, a retail business makes an error sending goods to a customer. Reasons why the items sent to a customer may not agree with the customer's order include, but are not limited to, the following situations:

- Wrong item description (e.g., customer wanted a two-piece swimsuit, but Baja sent a one-piece swimsuit)

- Wrong size (e.g., customer wanted sandals in a size 8, but Baja sent a size 10)

- Too many items sent (e.g., customer wanted three shirts, but Baja sent and billed customer for five shirts)

Exhibit 5-5 illustrates a **credit memorandum**, a document that supports the return of goods from the customer and the adjustment to the customer's account balance. The credit memo gets its name from the effect that it has on the balance of the customer's account. Because the credit memo decreases the amount due from the customer, the retailer will *credit* the accounts receivable balance for that customer. The retailer will send a credit memorandum to the customer as notification that an adjustment has been made to the amount the customer owes the retailer.

Exhibit 5-5 Credit Memorandum

Baja Beachwear
18 Shoreline Drive
Laguna Beach, California

CREDIT MEMORANDUM #14

To: Harrison Brooks   Date: August 15, 2008
     297 Lees Drive
     San Diego, CA

We credit your account balance for the following:

3 Blue Hawaiian shirts @ $25 per shirt	**$75**

When the customer returns the goods, the retailer will:

- Decrease sales revenue by increasing Sales Returns and Allowances, and decrease the customer's Accounts Receivable account balance for the sales price of those goods.

- Decrease Cost of Goods Sold and increase Inventory for the cost of the goods, if the goods are in good condition and can be resold.

Now let's see how Baja records the return of three shirts for $75 from Harrison Brooks, a customer. The shirts that Harrison Brooks returned cost Baja $30. Baja Beachwear records the sales return as follows:

Journal Entry:

Date	Accounts	Post Ref.	Dr.	Cr.
Aug. 15	Sales Returns and Allowances		75	
	Accounts Receivables—Harrison Brooks			75
	Inventory		30	
	Costs of Goods Sold			30
	Record receipt of returned goods, credit memo no. 14.			

Accounts Receivable decreases because Baja will never collect cash for the returned goods. Instead, Baja receives the returned merchandise and updates its inventory records because its perpetual inventory system needs to reflect the increase to Inventory from the return. Baja Beachwear must also decrease Cost of Goods Sold because the goods are no longer sold.

SALES ALLOWANCES

Rather than return goods to the retailer, some customers may be willing to keep goods that were damaged in shipment and accept an allowance for the damage. Baja Beachwear grants Logan Randall a $100 sales allowance for damaged goods. It records the sales allowance as follows:

Journal Entry:

Date	Accounts	Post Ref.	Dr.	Cr.
Aug. 29	Sales Returns and Allowances		100	
	Accounts Receivables—Logan Randall			100
	Record sales allowance for damaged goods, credit memo no. 15.			

Notice that the journal entry for a sales allowance does not affect Inventory or Cost of Goods Sold because the customer returned no goods to the retailer.

Accounting for Delivery and Other Selling Expenses

 4 Journalize shipment transactions and identify other selling expenses in a retail business.

In addition to purchases and sales transactions, a retailer must also manage shipping costs and other selling expenses. Retailers often pay the following costs:

- To receive goods from suppliers
- To deliver goods to customers
- To advertise and sell goods

Costs to Receive Goods from Suppliers

Have you ever purchased something from a catalog or online and had to pay shipping and handling charges in addition to the cost of the item you bought? Shipping and handling increases the cost of what you purchased. The same thing happens when retail businesses buy merchandise from suppliers. When retailers order items, they often have to pay the cost of getting those items shipped to their place of business in addition to paying the purchase price of the items themselves. For a business, these shipping costs are often referred to as **freight** charges.

Buyers and sellers specify who will pay shipping costs by setting shipping terms. Shipping terms specify the point at which ownership of the goods transfers from seller to buyer and also fix responsibility for paying shipping costs.

- Under **free on board (FOB) shipping point**, ownership, or **title**, transfers from the seller to the buyer at the point where the goods are *shipped*. Because the seller no longer owns the merchandise at this point, this term also means that the buyer must pay shipping charges to get the merchandise sent to its place of business. The retailer, as the buyer, will add the shipping costs to inventory by debiting Inventory because these amounts increase the cost of the goods purchased.

- **Free on board (FOB) destination** denotes the opposite arrangement; ownership transfers from the seller to the buyer when the goods reach their *destination*, so the seller must pay to ship goods to that point. The supplier, as the seller, records them with a debit to Delivery Expense.

Exhibit 5-6 summarizes FOB terms.

Exhibit 5-6 FOB Terms Determine Who Pays Freight

FOB Shipping Point — Seller → Buyer — Title passes to buyer. Buyer pays shipping costs.

FOB Destination — Seller → Buyer — Seller pays shipping costs. Title passes to buyer.

Let's see how Baja Beachwear records shipping costs when it purchases goods. When it buys products under FOB shipping point, Baja can either pay the shipping company directly or reimburse the seller for the transportation cost that the seller prepays. When Baja buys products under FOB destination, the supplier pays these costs.

FOB SHIPPING POINT, PAY THE SHIPPING COMPANY

Suppose Baja Beachwear incurs shipping costs for the purchase of swimsuits from Janz, FOB shipping point. Baja pays $60 to the carrier for the February 1 shipment. Baja Beachwear's entry to record payment of the shipping charge is as follows:

Journal Entry:

Date	Accounts	Post Ref.	Dr.	Cr.
Feb. 1	Inventory		60	
	Cash			60
	Record payment of shipping bill for the February 1 purchase.			

Baja debits Inventory to increase the cost of the swimsuits bought and credits Cash for the shipping costs. Although shipping costs increase the cost of goods, they are not included in the calculation of any purchase discount. We compute purchase discounts only on the amount due to the supplier for the goods themselves.

FOB SHIPPING POINT, REPAY THE SELLER FOR PREPAID SHIPPING COSTS

Under FOB shipping point, the seller sometimes prepays the shipping costs as a convenience and lists these costs on the invoice for the merchandise. If the buyer pays the invoice within the discount period, the discount will be computed only on the merchandise cost, not on the shipping costs.

Let's see how Baja records the following purchase transactions. On July 15 it buys $1,000 of goods on account, under FOB shipping point, with $80 of shipping costs added. The invoice total is $1,080. Invoice credit terms are 2/10, n/30. Baja then returns $100 of these goods for credit on July 20. It makes payment in full for the purchase on July 25.

First, Baja records the purchase of goods:

Journal Entry:

Date	Accounts	Post Ref.	Dr.	Cr.
July 15	Inventory		1,080	
	Accounts Payable—Golden Beachwear			1,080
	Record purchase of inventory on account.			

Next, Baja records the return of inventory, as follows:

Journal Entry:

Date	Accounts	Post Ref.	Dr.	Cr.
July 20	Accounts Payable—Golden Beachwear		100	
	Inventory			100
	Record inventory returned to the manufacturer.			

Finally, it records the payment for the purchase by calculating the purchase discount and the balance due. Baja pays on July 25, which is within the 10-day discount period, so it receives a discount of $18: 2% of the $1,000 original purchase amount minus $100 of returned goods, or .02 × $900. The cash paid is $962, as shown:

Purchase Amount	$1,000
+ Shipping Costs	80
− Purchase Return	(100)
− Purchase Discount ($1,000 − $100 = $900; $900 × .02 = $18)	(18)
= Cash Paid	$ 962

The journal entry to record the cash payment is shown here:

Journal Entry:

Date	Accounts	Post Ref.	Dr.	Cr.
July 25	Accounts Payable—Golden Beachwear ($1,000 + $80 − $100)		980	
	Inventory [($1,000 − $100) × 0.02]			18
	Cash ($1,000 + $80 − $100 − $18)			962
	Record payment of inventory puchases within the discount period.			

FOB DESTINATION

Under FOB destination, the seller pays to have the goods shipped to their destination. As the buyer in an agreement covered by these terms, Baja Beachwear has no shipping costs to record because its supplier pays the freight.

Costs to Deliver Goods to Customers

The cost of shipping goods to customers is usually recorded in a Delivery Expense account. Delivery Expense is an expense on the income statement and, as an expense account, normally holds a debit balance. This cost occurs when the seller agrees to ship goods to the final destination, shipping terms FOB destination. Let's see how the sale of goods and payment of shipping costs affect Baja Beachwear in different situations.

Jorge Klooney, a frequent customer at Baja Beachwear, has an account with the store. Jorge wants to buy a swimming suit cover-up as a Christmas gift for his sister living in Miami. Baja purchased the cover-up for $45 and sells it to Jorge for $100. Shipping costs to Miami total $15.

FOB DESTINATION

Let's first assume that, to stimulate sales before Christmas, Baja advertises that shipping costs are free if the customer purchases merchandise before December 1. Assume Jorge buys the cover-up on November 30 and charges it to his account. He also asks Baja to ship it to Miami. Baja would record the sale and payment of shipping costs as follows:

Journal Entry:

Date	Accounts	Post Ref.	Dr.	Cr.
Nov. 30	Accounts Receivable—J. Klooney		100	
	Sales Revenue			100
	Cost of Good Sold		45	
	Inventory			45
	Record sale of inventory on account.			

Journal Entry:

Date	Accounts	Post Ref.	Dr.	Cr.
Nov. 30	Delivery Expense		15	
	Cash			15
	Record shipping on sale.			

In this case, income from the sale would be $40 ($100 − $45 − $15).

FOB SHIPPING POINT

Now let's assume Jorge buys the cover-up on December 3 and gets it home to wrap and send with another gift. Because Jorge makes the purchase after the offer of free shipping expired on December 1, he would have to pay for shipping the item to Miami anyway. Baja would record the sale as follows:

Journal Entry:

Date	Accounts	Post Ref.	Dr.	Cr.
Dec. 3	Accounts Receivable—J. Klooney		100	
	Sales Revenue			100
	Cost of Goods Sold		45	
	Inventory			45
	Record sale of inventory on account.			

In this situation, income from sale would be $55 ($100 − $45).

FOB SHIPPING POINT, SELLER AGREES TO PREPAY SHIPMENT COSTS

Now assume that Jorge buys the cover-up on December 2 and asks Baja to ship the cover-up for him. Again, Baja's free shipping offer expired on December 1, but Baja would record the sale, including the payment of shipping costs as follows:

Journal Entry:

Date	Accounts	Post Ref.	Dr.	Cr.
Dec. 2	Accounts Receivable—J. Klooney		100	
	Sales Revenue			100
	Cost of Goods Sold		45	
	Inventory			45
	Record sale of inventory on account.			

Journal Entry:

Date	Accounts	Post Ref.	Dr.	Cr.
Dec. 2	Accounts Receivable—J. Klooney		15	
	Cash			15
	Record prepayment of shipping costs.			

Income from the sale is again $55 ($100 − $45 + $15 − $15). When you compare the three scenarios, you will see that the income from the sale under FOB shipping point will be the same whether or not Baja prepays for shipment:

	FOB Destination	FOB Shipping Point	FOB Shipping Point, Seller Prepays
Sales Revenue	$100	$100	$100
− Cost of Goods Sold	(45)	(45)	(45)
− Delivery Expense	(15)	—	—
= Income from Sale	$ 40	$ 55	$ 55

Other Selling Costs

Retail businesses use resources to support their relationships with customers. The costs of advertising and selling merchandise are expenses of operating a business that sells goods. Examples of **selling expenses** usually found on a retailer's income statement include:

- Sales salaries, wages, and commissions

- Advertising and promotion

- Depreciation for the use of stores, parking lots, counters, displays, shelves, vehicles of salespeople, and storage space such as warehouses and refrigerators

- Delivery of merchandise to customers

Preparing a Retailer's Financial Statements

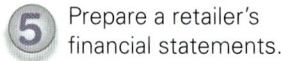

Prepare a retailer's financial statements.

In the previous chapter, we studied the completion of the accounting cycle. Recall that the cycle includes the following steps:

- Identify business transactions, record them in the journal, and post them to the ledger.
- Prepare a trial balance or worksheet, adjusting the accounts as necessary.
- Prepare financial statements.
- Journalize and post adjusting and closing entries.
- Prepare a post-closing trial balance.

The appendix to Chapter 5 explains how to prepare adjusting and closing entries for a retailer using a worksheet. Exhibit 5-7 shows Baja Beachwear's financial statements for 2008 based on the worksheet completed in the appendix.

Income Statement

INCOME STATEMENT FORMATS: MULTISTEP AND SINGLE-STEP

Remember the account form of the balance sheet from a previous chapter? We used it to show the balance sheet of Kay Torres Travel Agency, but in this chapter we used the report form to present Baja Beachwear's balance sheet. Just as this statement can take two different forms, the income statement also comes in two formats. After you check out Baja Beachwear's multistep income statement in Exhibit 5-7, look at its single-step version in Exhibit 5-8. Notice that, in both formats, net income is exactly the same. The format of the income statement does not change the net income or net loss of a business; it simply changes how the calculation of net income or net loss is presented.

THE MULTISTEP INCOME STATEMENT

The **multistep income statement** calculates net income or net loss in steps by computing important subtotals. Investors like this format because it provides step-by-step information about the profitability of the business and is thus useful for making investment decisions. Baja Beachwear's multistep income statement for the year ended December 31, 2008, appears in Exhibit 5-7. The multistep format is by far the more popular of the two choices.

Much like the income statement for a service business, the income statement of a retailer begins with revenue and can include the items listed below. *Know that, because businesses vary, not all of the items shown will appear on every multi-step income statement.*

- **Net Sales Revenue** is presented first, and is calculated by subtracting both Sales Discounts and Sales Returns and Allowances from Sales Revenue. Keep in mind, though, that as a retailer, Baja granted no sales discounts so no amount will appear on its income statement for this item.
- The cost of the merchandise that was sold appears next as Cost of Goods Sold.
- **Gross Profit**, also called **Gross Margin**, is a subtotal computed next as Net Sales Revenue minus Cost of Goods Sold.

Exhibit 5-7 Financial Statements of Baja Beachwear

BAJA BEACHWEAR
Income Statement
Year Ended December 31, 2008

Sales revenue		$171,300	
Less: Sales returns and allowances		(3,400)	
Net sales revenue			$167,900
Cost of goods sold			(90,300)
Gross profit			77,600
Operating expenses:			
Selling expenses:			
Advertising	$ 1,000		
Delivery expense	200	$ 1,200	
General and administrative expenses:			
Wage expense	10,200		
Rent expense	8,400		
Insurance expense	1,000		
Depreciation expense, office equipment	600		
Supplies expense	550	20,750	(21,950)
Net income			$ 55,650

BAJA BEACHWEAR
Statement of Owner's Equity
Year Ended December 31, 2008

Amy Toms, capital, December 31, 2007	$32,900
Add: Net income	55,650
Subtotal	88,550
Less: Withdrawals by owner	(52,900)
Amy Toms, capital, December 31, 2008	$35,650

BAJA BEACHWEAR
Balance Sheet
December 31, 2008

Assets		
Current assets:		
Cash		$ 3,150
Accounts receivable		4,600
Supplies		100
Inventory		39,700
Prepaid insurance		200
Total current sssets		47,750
Long-term assets:		
Office equipment	$32,000	
Less: Accumulated depreciation, office equipment	(3,000)	29,000
Total assets		$76,750
Liabilities		
Current liabilities:		
Accounts payable		$40,000
Wages payable		400
Unearned sales revenue		700
Total current liabilities		41,100
Owner's Equity		
Amy Toms, capital		35,650
Total liabilities and owner's equity		$76,750

Exhibit 5-8 Single-Step Income Statement

BAJA BEACHWEAR
Income Statement
Year Ended December 31, 2008

Revenues:		
Net sales revenue		$167,900
Expenses:		
Cost of goods sold	$90,300	
Selling expenses	1,200	
General and administrative expenses	20,750	
Total expenses		112,250
Net income		**$55,650**

- **Operating Expenses**, expenses of operating the business other than cost of goods sold, are shown after Gross Profit. Many companies report operating expenses in two categories:

  - Selling Expenses include the costs of advertising and selling merchandise such as sales salaries, commissions, advertising, promotion, depreciation for items used in sales, and delivery costs to customers, as we mentioned earlier.

  - **General and Administrative Expenses** include office expenses, such as the salaries of the company president and office employees, depreciation of items used in administration, rent, utilities, and property taxes on the office building.

- On the statement, Gross Profit minus Operating Expenses equals **Operating Income**, or **Income from Operations**. Operating income measures the results of the entity's primary, ongoing activities.

- The last section of an income statement is **Other Revenues and Expenses**. This category reports revenues and expenses that fall outside of a business's main operations. Examples include interest revenue, interest expense, dividends revenue, and gains and losses on the sale of long-term assets. Because not all businesses have revenues and expenses from other sources, not all income statements will include this section.

- The last line of the income statement is Net Income or Net Loss, which is calculated by adding Other Revenues and subtracting Other Expenses from Operating Income. We often hear the term *bottom line*, and the bottom line of the income statement is net income or net loss; it is the final result of operations.

THE SINGLE-STEP INCOME STATEMENT

The **single-step income statement** groups all revenues together and all expenses together, and then subtracts total expenses from total revenues in a single step, without calculating any subtotals. The advantage of the single-step format is that it clearly distinguishes revenues from expenses, as Exhibit 5-8 shows. This format works well for service entities because they have no gross profit to report.

Statement of Owner's Equity

A retailer's statement of owner's equity looks exactly like that of a service business.

Balance Sheet

If the business is a retailer, then the major difference between its balance sheet and that of a service business is that it shows inventory as a major current asset. Service businesses usually have no inventory. Exhibit 5-7 shows the report form of the balance sheet so we can trace owner's equity from the statement of owner's equity to the balance sheet.

Two Key Ratios for Decision Making

Inventory is the most important asset for a retail business because it is often the largest current asset and the focus of retail operations. Statement readers use several ratios to evaluate operations involving inventory, including the **gross profit percentage** and the rate of **inventory turnover**.

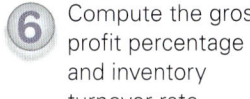
6 Compute the gross profit percentage and inventory turnover rate.

The Gross Profit Percentage

Gross profit, also called gross margin, is a key tool in evaluating retail operations; remember that gross profit is net sales revenue minus the cost of goods sold. Thus, gross profit is the amount left over from sales after deducting the cost of the merchandise sold. Retailers strive to maximize gross profit, and the gross profit percentage shows how well they are meeting this goal. Gross profit percentage, also called the **gross margin percentage**, measures the relationship between gross profit and sales. It is computed by dividing gross profit by net sales revenue. Based on information provided from the income statement in Exhibit 5-7, the gross profit percentage for Baja Beachwear is 46.2%, calculated as follows:

$$\text{Gross Profit Percentage} \; = \; \frac{\text{Gross Profit}}{\textit{Net } \text{Sales Revenue}} = \frac{\$77,600}{\$167,900} = 0.462 = 46.2\%$$

A 46.2% gross margin percentage means that each dollar of net sales generates 46.2 cents of gross profit. Every time Baja Beachwear sells $1 of merchandise, it produces 46 cents of gross profit that can be used to cover operating expenses and perhaps create net income.

The gross profit percentage is one of the most carefully watched measures of profitability. This information can be used to compare changes in gross profit from year to year for the business, or it can be used to compare the company to other businesses in the same industry. For most businesses, the gross profit percentage changes little from year to year. A significant change in the gross profit margin indicates a significant change in the business's operations and warrants investigation.

The Rate of Inventory Turnover

Owners and managers strive to sell inventory quickly because inventory generates no profit until it is sold. The faster a business produces sales, the higher the sales revenue available to create income will be. Inventory turnover, the ratio of cost of goods sold to average inventory, measures the number of times a company sells, or *turns over*, its average level of inventory during a period. It is computed as follows for Baja Beachwear using the financial statements in Exhibit 5-7:

$$\text{Inventory Turnover} = \frac{\text{Cost of Good Sold}}{\text{Average Inventory}} = \frac{\text{Cost of Goods Sold}}{(\text{Beginning Inventory} + \text{Ending Inventory}) / 2}$$

$$= \frac{\$90,300}{(40,000^* + \$39,700) / 2} = 2.27 \text{ Times Per Year}$$

Baja's inventory turnover rate shows that it is selling its merchandise inventory a little more than two times a year.

Inventory turnover is usually computed for an annual period, so the cost of goods sold figure is the amount for the entire year. Average inventory is computed by adding the beginning inventory balance to the ending inventory balance, and dividing the total by 2. Remember that balance sheet accounts, such as inventory, carry their balances from one period to the next, so the ending inventory for one year becomes the beginning inventory for the next year. A high turnover rate is desirable because it indicates that the inventory is turning over, or being sold, fast; an increase in the turnover rate usually means increasing profits will result from increasing sales.

Exhibit 5-9 compares Baja Beachwear to a national retailer. Notice that the national retailer moves its merchandise about six times as fast as Baja Beachwear. Regardless of the turnover rate, retailers need to keep sufficient levels of inventory to meet sales demand; however, retailers also need to avoid purchasing too much inventory, because high levels of inventory require more money to buy the inventory and store it until the goods are sold. These actions will increase interest expense if the funds needed are borrowed, and warehouse rent expense, if warehouse storage space is rented.

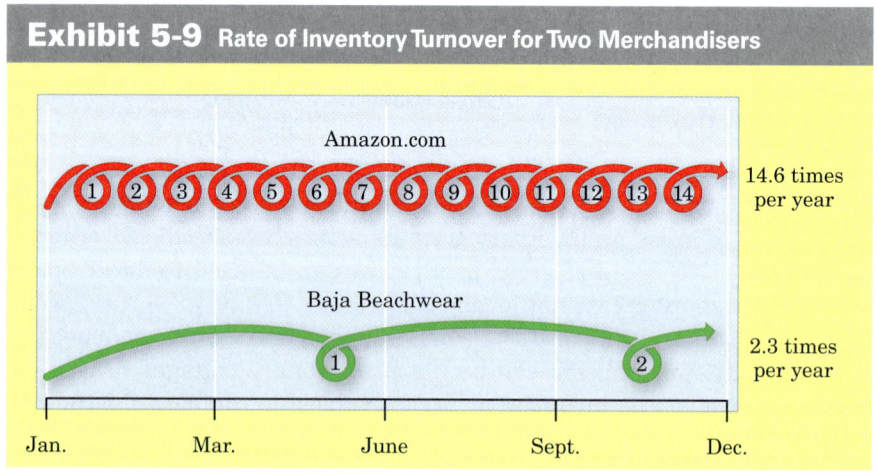

Exhibit 5-9 Rate of Inventory Turnover for Two Merchandisers

---

*The $40,000 beginning inventory balance is found as the ending inventory balance for the prior period.

Demo Doc

Inventory Transaction Analysis (Perpetual System)

Learning Objectives   *2–4*

Peach Rivers Inc. had the following transactions in July 2008:

July 1   Sold $400 of merchandise on account to Sam Smith. The merchandise cost $275 to manufacture. The terms of sale were 2/15, n/eom.

July 3   Purchased $950 of inventory from a supplier on account under the terms 4/10, n/30. Peach was also charged freight in of $50.

July 5   Sold $300 of merchandise on account to Travis Tripp. The merchandise cost $180 to manufacture. The terms of sale were 2/15, n/eom.

July 10   Received payment in full from Sam Smith.

July 12   Paid in full for the goods purchased on July 3.

July 20   Travis Tripp returned 20% of the goods he purchased on July 5. The returned goods were in saleable condition.

July 25   Returned 10% of the goods purchased on July 3 and received a cash refund from the supplier. Freight charges are not refunded.

July 31   Received payment in full from Travis Tripp.

Requirement

1. Journalize these transactions.

Demo Doc Solution

Requirement 1

2 Journalize transactions between the supplier and retailer.

3 Journalize transactions between the retailer and customer.

4 Journalize shipment transactions and identify other selling expenses in a retail business.

Journalize these transactions.

	Part 1	Demo Doc Complete

July 1 Sold $400 of merchandise on account to Sam Smith. The merchandise cost $275 to manufacture. The terms of sale were 2/15, n/eom.

When merchandise is sold (and delivered) to a customer, the company earns sales revenue. By selling merchandise to Sam Smith, Peach has earned sales revenue of $400. The cost of the goods sold is $275 (Peach's cost of manufacturing the merchandise).

Sales Revenue is increased (credit) by $400. Because the customer did not pay in cash, Accounts Receivable is also increased (debit) by $400.

In a related entry, the cost of good sold is recorded. This journal entry results in an increase (debit) of $275 to Cost of Goods Sold (remember, Cost of Goods Sold is an *expense*). Because goods from inventory were given to the customer, the Inventory account is decreased (credit) by $275.

Journal Entry:

Date	Accounts	Post Ref.	Dr.	Cr.
July 1	Accounts Receivable (Asset, ↑; debit)		400	
	Sales Revenue (Revenue, ↑; credit)			400
	Record sales revenue earned.			

Journal Entry:

Date	Accounts	Post Ref.	Dr.	Cr.
July 1	Cost of Goods Sold (Expense, ↑; debit)		275	
	Inventory (Asset, ↓; credit)			275
	Record cost of goods sold.			

Notice that the credit terms of 2/15, n/eom are not relevant right now. The sale is recorded in the same way regardless of the credit terms. However, these terms will be important when the account receivable is collected.

July 3 Purchased $950 of inventory from a supplier on account under the terms 4/10, n/30. Peach was also charged freight in of $50.

The purchase of inventory increases the Inventory account. However, it is not just increased by the purchase price, but also by the freight in charges (because the freight charges are part of the inventory's cost). The total increase (debit) to Inventory is $1,000 ($950 + $50).

Because the purchase was not paid for in cash, Accounts Payable is increased (credit) by $1,000.

Journal Entry:

Date	Accounts	Post Ref.	Dr.	Cr.
July 3	Inventory (Asset, ↑; debit)		1,000	
	Accounts Payable (Liability, ↑; credit)			1,000
	Record inventory purchased on account.			

Notice again that the credit terms are not relevant until the *payment* is made to the supplier.

July 5 **Sold $300 of merchandise on account to Travis Tripp. The merchandise cost $180 to manufacture. The terms of sale were 2/15, n/eom.**

Peach earned sales revenue of $300 because it sold and delivered merchandise to a customer. The cost of the goods sold is $180 (Peach's cost of obtaining or manufacturing the merchandise).

Sales Revenue is increased (credit) by $300. Because the customer did not pay in cash, Accounts Receivable is also increased (debit) by $300.

In a related entry, the cost of good sold is recorded. This journal entry results in an increase of $180 to Cost of Goods Sold (debit). Because goods from inventory were given to the customer, the Inventory account is decreased (credit) by $180. (The sale and the cost of the sale could be recorded in one entry.)

Journal Entry:

Date	Accounts	Post Ref.	Dr.	Cr.
July 5	Accounts Receivable (Asset, ↑; debit)		300	
	Sales Revenue (Revenue, ↑; credit)			300
	Record sales revenue earned.			

Journal Entry:

Date	Accounts	Post Ref.	Dr.	Cr.
July 5	Cost of Goods Sold (Expense, ↑; debit)		180	
	Inventory (Asset, ↓; credit)			180
	Record cost of goods sold.			

July 10 Received payment in full from Sam Smith.

Now that cash is being collected, we must look at the credit terms on the sale.

The payment was received within the 15-day discount period, so Sam is entitled to take a 2% discount. This means that Sam paid cash of $392 [$400 × (100 − 2)%], which settled his account in full.

Cash is increased (debit) by $392 because Peach receives cash. Accounts Receivable is decreased (credit) by the full sales price of $400. The difference relates to the sales discount taken by Sam. The contra-account of Sales Discount is increased (debit) by $8 ($400 × 2%).

Journal Entry:

Date	Accounts	Post Ref.	Dr.	Cr.
July 10	Cash (Asset, ↑; debit) [$400 × (100 − 2%)]		392	
	Sales Discounts (Contra-Revenue, ↑; debit) ($400 × 2%)		8	
	Accounts Receivable (Asset, ↓; credit)			400
	Record cash collected from customer.			

July 12 Paid in full for the goods purchased on July 3.

Now that cash is being paid, we must take the original credit terms into account.

Peach is paying within the discount period, so it is entitled to take a 4% discount. Remember that the discount is *not* taken on the freight charges. The discount must be calculated on the original purchase price and *then* the freight charges must be added:

Original Purchase Price of Goods	$950
Less 4% Discount (4% × $950)	($38)
Net Purchase Price of Goods	$912
Plus Freight Charges	$50
Total Cash Paid	$962
(Total Cost of Inventory Purchased)	

So, Cash is decreased (credit) by $962. Accounts Payable is also decreased (debit) but by the full purchase amount of $1,000. The difference relates to the discount and is treated as a reduction in inventory (because it is a reduction in the cost of the inventory). Inventory is decreased (credit) by $38 (the amount of the discount).

Journal Entry:

Date	Accounts	Post Ref.	Dr.	Cr.
July 12	Accounts Payable (Liability, ↓; debit)		1,000	
	Inventory (Asset, ↓; credit) ($950 × 4%)			38
	Cash (Asset, ↓; credit) ([$950 × (100 − 4%)] + $50)			962
	Record payment of account payable.			

July 20   Travis Tripp returned 20% of the goods he purchased on July 5. The returned goods were in saleable condition.

Travis has not yet paid his account, so his return of the goods will result in a decrease to Accounts Receivable. The original sale was for $300 worth of goods costing $180.

Accounts Receivable is decreased (credit) by $60 (20% × $300). The contra-account of Sales Returns and Allowances is increased (debit) by $60. Travis's Accounts Receivable now has a balance of $240:

ASSETS

**Accounts Receivable—
Travis Tripp**

July 5	300		
		July 20	60
Bal.	240		

In a related entry, we will record the physical return of the goods. Because they are in saleable condition, they will be put back into inventory. Inventory increases (debit) by $36 ($180 × 20%). Because the goods were returned, they are no longer "sold," so the Cost of Goods Sold decreases (credit) by $36.

Journal Entry:

Date	Accounts	Post Ref.	Dr.	Cr.
July 20	Sales Returns and Allowances			
	(Contra-Revenue, ↑ ; debit) ($300 × 20%)		60	
	Accounts Receivable (Asset, ↓ ; credit)			60
	Record customer return.			

Journal Entry:

Date	Accounts	Post Ref.	Dr.	Cr.
July 20	Inventory (Asset, ↑ ; debit) ($180 × 20%)		36	
	Cost of Goods Sold (Expense, ↓ ; credit)			36
	Record goods returned by customer.			

July 25   Returned 10% of the goods purchased on July 3 and received a cash refund from the supplier. Freight charges are not refunded.

Peach returned 10% of the goods and received a cash refund. However, Peach received a discount on this purchase. So the refund will be 10% of the *discounted* purchase price.

From the July 12 transaction, we know that the discounted purchase price for all of the goods was $912. Therefore, by returning 10% of the goods, Peach will receive a refund of $91.20.

Cash is increased (debit) by $91.20, and Inventory is decreased (credit) by $91.20.

Journal Entry:

Date	Accounts	Post Ref.	Dr.	Cr.
July 25	Cash (Asset, ↑; debit) ($912 × 10%)		91.20	
	Inventory (Asset, ↓; credit)			91.20
	Record inventory returned to supplier.			

July 31 Received payment in full from Travis Tripp.

Now we must take the credit terms of the original sale into account.

Travis did not pay within the discount period, so the full amount of the receivable must be paid in cash. As shown in the July 20 transaction, Travis must pay $240.

Cash is increased (debit) by $240, and Accounts Receivable is decreased (credit) by $240.

Journal Entry:

Date	Accounts	Post Ref.	Dr.	Cr.
July 31	Cash (Asset, ↑; debit)		240	
	Accounts Receivable (Asset, ↓; credit)			240
	Record cash collected from customer.			

Part 1	Demo Doc Complete

Accounting in Action

ACCOUNTING FOR A RETAIL BUSINESS

As a retailer, you might be faced with decisions such as the following:

Decision	Guidelines
How do retailers differ from service entities?	• Retailers buy and sell *merchandise inventory*. • Service entities sell *services*.
How do a retailer's financial statements differ statements of a service business?	• Income statement: Shows the *cost of goods sold* from the as a deduction from revenue. • Statements of owner's equity: No difference. • Balance sheet: Includes *inventory*, a current asset.
Which inventory system to use?	• *Perpetual system* shows the current, correct amounts of inventory on hand and the cost of goods sold at all times. • *Periodic system* shows the correct balances of inventory and cost of goods sold only after a physical count of the inventory is taken, which occurs at least once each year.
Which income statement format to use?	• *Single-step format* shows the calculation of net income or net loss by subtracting all expenses from all revenues in a single step. • *Multistep format* shows the calculation of net income or net loss in a series of steps with subtotals for *gross profit* and *operating income*.
How are inventory operations evaluated?	Two key ratios:

$$\text{Gross Profit Precentage} = \frac{\text{Gross Profit}}{\text{Net Sales Revenue}}$$

$$\text{Inventory Turnover} = \frac{\text{Cost of Goods Sold}}{\text{Average Inventory}}$$

Accounting for a Retail Business
Word Power

Compound journal entry A journal entry affecting more than two accounts; an entry that has more than one debit and/or more than one credit.

Cost of goods sold The cost of the inventory that the business has sold to customers.

Credit memorandum A document that supports the return of goods from the customer and the adjustment to the customer's account balance.

Credit terms The payment terms for customers who buy on account.

Debit memorandum A document that supports the return of goods to the supplier and the adjustment to the balance owed to the supplier.

Discount period Period in which the buyer can make early payment for a purchase and receive a discount on that purchase.

eom Credit term specifying that payment for a purchase is due by the end of the month. Also referred to as *n/eom*.

FOB destination Shipping term specifying that title to goods passes to the buyer when the goods are received at buyer's destination; thus, the seller pays the cost of shipping the goods to this destination.

FOB shipping point Shipping term specifying that title to goods passes to the buyer when the goods are shipped at the seller's place of business; thus, the buyer pays the cost of shipping the goods to its location.

Freight The cost of shipping merchandise from the seller to the buyer.

General and administrative expenses Office expenses, such as the salaries of the company president and office employees, depreciation of items used in administration, rent, utilities, and property taxes on the office building.

Gross margin Net sales revenue minus cost of goods sold. Also called gross profit.

Gross margin percentage A measure of profitability equal to gross margin divided by net sales revenue. Also called *gross profit percentage*.

Gross profit Net sales revenue minus cost of goods sold. Also called *gross margin*.

Gross profit percentage A measure of profitability equal to gross profit divided by net sales revenue. Also called *gross margin percentage*.

Income from operations Gross profit minus operating expenses. Also called operating income.

Inventory All the goods purchased for resale to customers in the normal course of merchandising operations. Also called merchandise inventory.

Inventory turnover The ratio of cost of goods sold to average inventory. Measures the number of times a company sells its average level of inventory during a year.

Merchandise inventory All the goods purchased for resale to customers in the normal course of merchandising operations. Also called inventory.

Multistep income statement Income statement format that calculates net income or net loss by listing important subtotals such as gross profit and operating income.

n/30 Credit term specifying that payment for a purchase is due within 30 days after the date of the invoice.

n/eom Credit term specifying that payment for a purchase is due by the end of the month. Also referred to as *eom*.

Net sales revenue Sales revenue less sales discounts and sales returns and allowances.

Operating expenses Expenses of operating a business other than cost of goods sold. Examples include depreciation, rent, salaries, utilities, advertising, delivery expense, property taxes, and supplies expense.

Operating income Gross profit minus operating expenses. Also called income from operations.

Other revenues and expenses Revenues and expenses that fall outside the main operations of a business, such as interest expense and a loss on the sale of long-term assets.

Periodic inventory system An inventory system in which the business does not keep a continuous record of inventory on hand. At the end of the period, a physical count of inventory is taken and determines the inventory owned as well as the cost of the goods sold.

Perpetual inventory system An inventory system in which the business keeps a continuous record of inventory owned and the cost of the goods sold.

Purchase discount Discount received on purchases by paying early cash within a discount period.

Purchase returns and allowances A reduction in the amount owed for a purchase from returning merchandise or accepting damaged goods.

Sales discount Discount granted on sales for the customer's early payment within a discount period; a contra-account to Sales Revenue.

Sales invoice A bill that documents the sale of goods to a business customer.

Sales returns and allowances A reduction in the amount of customer sales from returning merchandise or accepting damaged goods; a contra-account to Sales Revenue.

Sales revenue The amount that a retailer earns from selling its inventory.

Selling expenses Expenses related to advertising and selling products including sales salaries, sales commissions, advertising, depreciation on items used in sales, and delivery expense.

Single-step income statement Income statement format that groups all revenues together and lists all expenses together, subtracting total expenses from total revenues and calculating net income or net loss without computing any subtotals.

Subsidiary ledger An accounting record that contains details, such as a list of customers and the accounts receivable due from each, or a list of suppliers and the accounts payable due to each.

Supply chain The chain of transactions between businesses that supply goods and the customers who ultimately use them.

Title Ownership.

Wholesalers Businesses that buy goods from manufacturers and resell them to retailers.

Quick Check

1. Which account does a retailer, but not a service company, use?

   a. Sales Returns and Allowances
   b. Supplies
   c. Salary Expense
   d. All of the above

2. Which inventory accounting system keeps a running record of inventory and cost of goods sold?

   a. Periodic
   b. Cash basis
   c. Perpetual
   d. Accrual basis

3. Identify the journal entry to record the sale of $500 of goods on account if the cost of these goods is $300.

Journal Entry:

Date	Accounts	Post Ref.	Dr.	Cr.
a.	Accounts Receivable		500	
	Sales Revenue			500
	Costs of Goods Sold		300	
	Inventory			300
b.	Sales Revenue		300	
	Accounts Receivable			300
	Inventory		500	
	Cost of Goods Sold			500
c.	Accounts Receivable		500	
	Sales Revenue			500
	Inventory		300	
	Costs of Good Sold			300
d.	Accounts Receivable		300	
	Sales Revenue			300
	Cost of Goods Sold		500	
	Inventory			500

4. Identify the journal entry to record the receipt of a customer's payment within the discount period if the amount due is $500 and a 2% discount is offered.

Journal Entry:

Date	Accounts	Post Ref.	Dr.	Cr.
a.	Cash		490	
	Sales Discounts		10	
	Accounts Receivable			500
b.	Accounts Payable		500	
	Sales Discounts			10
	Cash			490
c.	Cash		500	
	Sales Discounts			10
	Accounts Receivable			490
d.	Accounts Payable		490	
	Sales Discounts		10	
	Cash			500

5. The journal entry for the return of inventory purchased on account is:

Journal Entry:

Date	Accounts	Post Ref.	Dr.	Cr.
a.	Inventory		500	
	Accounts Receivable			500
b.	Accounts Payable		500	
	Inventory			500
c.	Inventory		500	
	Accounts Payable			500
d.	Accounts Receivable		500	
	Inventory			500

6. YNotUs Company purchased inventory under FOB shipping point for $4,600 and also paid a $400 shipping bill. YNotUs returned half the goods to the seller and took a 2% purchase discount. What is YNotUs's cost of the inventory that it kept?

a. $2,346
b. $2,254
c. $2,746
d. $2,654

7. Which subtotals appear on a multistep income statement but not on a single-step income statement?

    a. Net Income and Operating Expenses
    b. Net Income and Cost of Goods Sold
    c. Operating Expenses and Gross Profit
    d. Cost of Goods Sold and Net Sales Revenue

8. Which of the following would not be included under Selling Expenses on the multistep income statement?

    a. Depreciation Expense, Store Equipment
    b. Advertising Expense
    c. Cost of Goods Sold
    d. Sales Commission Expense

9. Suppose YNotUs Company had sales of $3.5 billion, sales returns of $0.4 billion, and sales discounts of $0.3 billion. Cost of goods sold was $1.8 billion. How much gross profit did YNotUs report?

    a. $1.3 billion
    b. $2.4 billion
    c. $1.0 billion
    d. Cannot be determined from the data given

10. YNotUs Company made net sales of $5.25 billion, and cost of goods sold totaled $3.15 billion. Average inventory was $0.25 billion. What was YNotUs Company's rate of inventory turnover for this period?

    a. 60%
    b. 12.6%
    c. 60 times
    d. 12.6 times

Answers are given after Apply Your Knowledge (p. 283).

Accounting Practice

Short Exercises

S5-1. Match the terms listed on the left with the corresponding accounting definitions listed on the right.

① The supply chain.

_____ **1.** Perpetual inventory system

    a. The chain of transactions between businesses that supply goods and the customers that ultimately use them.

_____ **2.** Inventory

    b. Inventory system that does not keep a running record of all goods owned.

_____ **3.** Supply chain

    c. Inventory system that keeps a running record of all goods owned.

_____ **4.** Periodic inventory system

    d. All goods a company owns and holds for sale in the normal course of operations.

S5-2. Innerscope sells CDs. During May, the business completed these transactions with Best Buy:

③ Journalizing retailer/customer transactions.

May	9	Sold 4,000 CDs to Best Buy on account for $7 each; credit terms were 3/10, n/30. The total cost of these CDs is $16,000.
	11	Best Buy returned 400 CDs that were not part of the original order; the cost of these CDs was $1,600.
	19	Received payment from Best Buy for the balance due on account.

Prepare Innerscope's journal entries for these transactions. How much gross profit did Innerscope earn on these transactions?

S5-3. Sag Harbor sells women's sportswear. During June and July, the business completed these transactions with JCPenney:

③ Journalizing retailer/customer transactions.

June	16	Sold $50,000 of women's sportswear to a JCPenney's store on account under credit terms of 1/15, n/30. The sportswear cost $28,000.
July	1	Received payment from JCPenney.

Record Sag Harbor's journal entries for these transactions. Explanations are not required.

S5-4. Refer to S5-3 and journalize the following transactions for JCPenney. Explanations are not required. What was the net cost of this inventory?

② Journalizing supplier/retailer transactions.

June	16	Purchased $50,000 of women's sportswear on account from Sag Harbor under credit terms of 1/15, n/30.
July	1	Paid Sag Harbor for the sportswear.

S5-5. T.J. Maxx purchases 3,500 sweatshirts on account from Lands' End for $35,000. Credit terms are 3/15, n/30. Journalize the following transactions for T.J. Maxx:

a. Purchase of inventory on May 6.

b. Payment on account, assuming they paid within the discount period on May 16.

(margin note: ② Journalizing supplier/retailer transactions.)

S5-6. Best Buy purchases inventory from a variety of suppliers. Suppose Best Buy buys $300,000 worth of televisions from Sony on credit terms of 2/10, n/eom. Some of the goods are damaged in shipment, so Best Buy returns $75,000 of the merchandise to Sony.

How much must Best Buy pay Sony:

a. If they pay within the discount period?

b. If they pay after the discount period?

(margin note: ② Journalizing supplier/retailer transactions.)

S5-7. Refer to S5-3 and journalize the following transactions for Best Buy. Explanations are not required.

a. Purchase of the goods on April 7, 2008.

b. Return of the damaged goods on April 9, 2008.

c. Payment on April 17, 2008. It may be helpful to post the first two transactions in a T-account for Accounts Payable before journalizing this transaction.

(margin note: ② Journalizing supplier/retailer transactions.)

S5-8. Determine who would have to pay for the shipping costs under each of the following independent situations and determine in which account they would record the costs.

a. JCPenney purchases $50,000 of women's sportswear on account from Sag Harbor with shipping terms FOB shipping point.

b. Famous Footwear purchases $20,000 of sneakers from Nike with shipping terms FOB destination.

(margin note: ④ Journalizing shipment transactions and identifying other selling expenses.)

S5-9. On January 10, 2008, Nike sold 2,000 pairs of sneakers to Famous Footwear for $50,000 on account, credit terms 2/15, n/30. The cost of the sneakers was $15,000. If merchandise is defective, Nike usually allows an allowance on the store's account to encourage the store to keep the merchandise and sell it at a reduced price. On January 14, Nike agreed to a $5,000 allowance for 500 pairs of defective sneakers that Famous Footwear had received. Famous Footwear paid within the discount period.

For these transactions, compute Nike's:

a. Net sales revenue.

b. Gross profit.

(margin note: ⑤ Preparing a retailer's financial statements.)

S5-10. Based on the gross profit computed in S5-9, is it possible for Nike to make a net loss for the period? Explain why or why not.

(margin note: ⑤ Preparing a retailer's financial statements.)

continued.....

S5-11. Baldwin Bikes reported the following data for the month ended January 31, 2008:

Selling and administrative expenses	$ 6,000
Cost of goods sold	9,000
Net sales revenue	15,000

Compute the gross profit percentage. How much gross profit is the company making on every dollar of sales?

S5-12. On January 1, 2008, the inventory account for I. M. Tyred Company had a balance of $14,000. On December 31, 2008, the company's financial statements showed balances of $16,000 for Inventory and $45,000 for Cost of Goods Sold. Compute the 2008 inventory turnover rate for I. M. Tyred.

⑥ Computing gross profit percentage and inventory turnover rate.

⑥ Computing gross profit percentage and inventory turnover rate.

① The supply chain.

② Journalizing supplier/ retailer transactions.

Exercises

E5-13. Complete the following crossword puzzle.

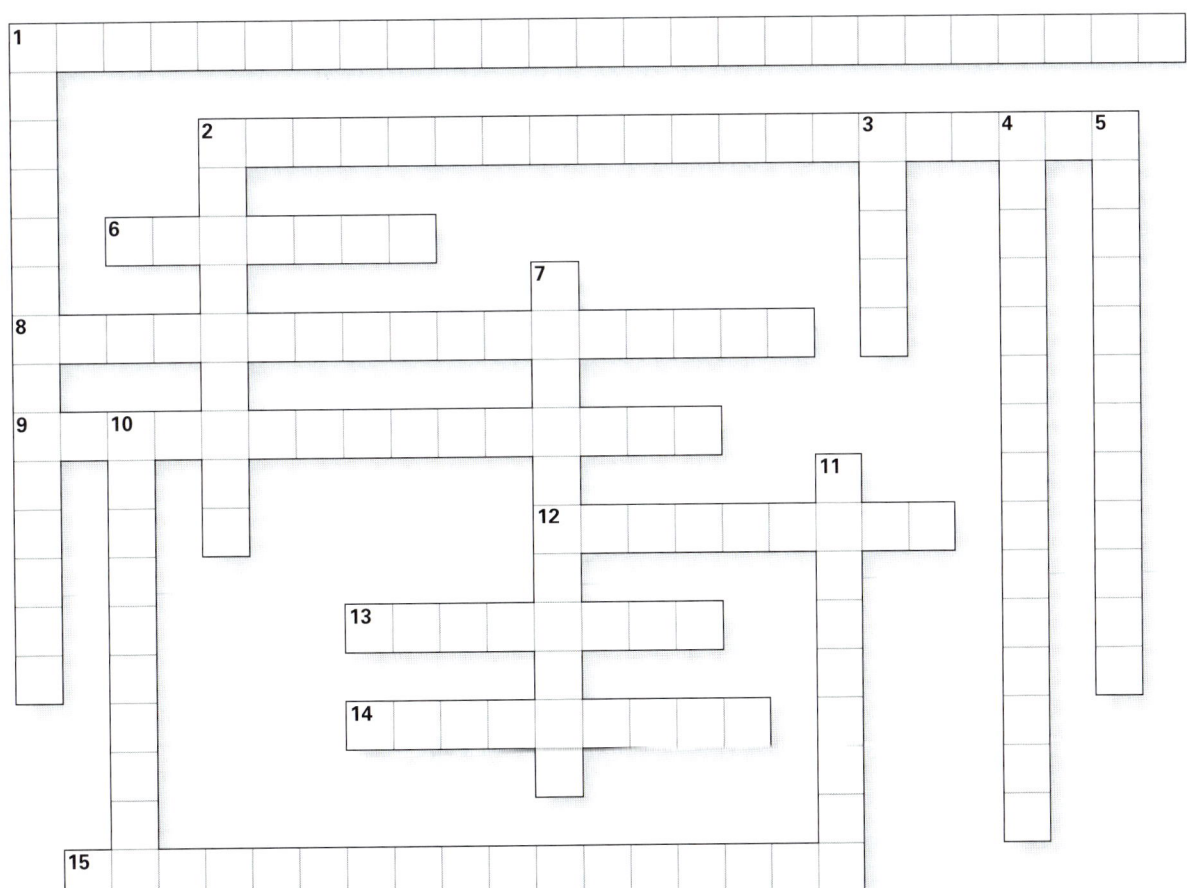

continued.....

3 Journalizing retailer/customer transactions.

5 Preparing a retailer's financial statements.

6 Computing gross profit percentage and inventory turnover rate.

Across:

1. Decreases in the seller's receivables from accepting customers' returns of merchandise or from granting customers an allowance.

2. Gross profit minus operating expenses.

6. A bill that documents the sale of goods to a customer.

8. Ratio of cost of goods sold to average inventory.

9. The cost of the inventory that the business has sold to customers.

12. The inventory system in which the business keeps a running record of inventory and cost of goods sold.

13. The inventory system in which the business does not keep a continuous record of inventory on hand.

14. A format of the income statement that contains subtotals. In addition to net income, it reports gross profit and operating income.

15. Expenses, other than cost of goods sold, that are incurred in operating the business.

Down:

1. Reductions in the amount receivable from a customer offered by the seller as an incentive to the customer for early payment.

2. All the goods that the company owns and expects to sell in the normal course of operations.

3. Inventory would fall under this heading on the balance sheet.

4. Gross profit minus operating expenses.

5. The amount that a retailer earns from selling its inventory.

7. Excess of net sales revenue over cost of goods sold.

10. An income statement format that groups all revenues together and then lists and deducts all expenses together without drawing any subtotals.

11. The buying of goods from suppliers.

3 Journalizing retailer/customer transactions.

E5-14. Journalize the following transactions for I. M. Tyred Company for the month of May:

continued.....

May 3	Sold $3,500 of merchandise to B. Wrested on account with credit terms of 3/10, n/30. The cost of the items sold was $2,100.
May 6	B. Wrested returned $500 of the merchandise he purchased on May 3 because of incorrect sizes. The merchandise had a cost to I .M. Tyred of $300.
May 9	B. Wrested complained that some of the merchandise purchased on May 3 was slightly defective. I. M. Tyred agreed to give B. Wrested a $400 credit memorandum noting that B. Wrested's account has been credited for $400.
May 13	Received payment from B. Wrested for the balance due on account after the return and the allowance.

E5-15. As the proprietor of G. O. Team Sporting Goods, you receive the following invoice from a supplier:

② Journalizing supplier/ retailer transactions.

WIN WEAR INC.
295 Score Boulevard
Buffalo, New York 14202   **Sales Invoice**

Sold to: G. O. Team   Invoice No. 295
        65 Touchdown Lane   Invoice date: April 5, 2008
        Buffalo, New York 14203   Terms: 2/10, n/30 FOB destination

Quantity	Item	Unit Price	Total
50	Team Jerseys	$ 10.00	$ 500.00
50	Helmets	20.00	1,000.00
100	Pendants	6.00	600.00
		Total due	$ 2,100.00

Requirements

1. The company received the invoice on April 7. Record the purchase on account.

2. Too many helmets were ordered by mistake, so 10 were returned to Win Wear Inc. Journalize the return on April 10.

3. Record the April 13 payment of the amount owed.

E5-16. Gemstone Jewels sells jewelry to Silver and Gold Jewelers. During June, the businesses completed the following transactions:

② Journalizing supplier/retailer transactions.

③ Journalizing retailer/customer transactions.

June 18	Gemstone sold $11,000 of jewelry on account to Silver and Gold Jewelers. Terms were 2/15, n/60.
19	Silver and Gold discovered 150 necklaces had broken clasps. They immediately contacted Gemstone and were granted a reduction on the cost of the necklaces. Gemstone faxed them a credit memorandum on June 19, granting them a $500 credit on their account.
30	Silver and Gold paid Gemstone for the June 18 purchase, less the allowance on the necklaces.

continued.....

Requirements

1. Record the transactions in the journal of Gemstone Jewels. The cost of goods sold is 65% of their sales price. Explanations are not required.

2. Record the transactions in the journal of Silver and Gold Jewelers. Explanations are not required.

② Journalizing supplier/retailer transactions.

④ Journalizing shipment transactions.

E5-17. Journalize the following transactions for Bear Office Supplies:

May 2	Purchased $2,000 of goods from Office Depot on account, terms 3/15, n/eom, FOB shipping point. Office Depot paid the $130 shipping cost and added it to Bear's bill.
6	Paid $240 shipping charges for goods sold at the end of April, terms FOB destination.
12	Paid Office Depot for the purchase of May 2, less discount.

② Journalizing supplier/retailer transactions.

③ Journalizing retailer/customer transactions.

④ Journalizing shipment transactions.

E5-18. Journalize the transactions for Uncle Sam's Fireworks Emporium for the month of July. Explanations are not required.

July 2	Purchased $2,400 of inventory on account from Bottle Rockets Ltd. under terms of 3/15, n/eom, FOB shipping point.
5	Returned $500 of defective merchandise purchased on July 2.
7	Paid shipping bill of $30 on previous purchase.
9	Sold inventory on account to Sparkling Sparklers for $4,200. Payment terms were 2/10, n/45, FOB shipping point. These goods cost Uncle Sam's $2,730.
10	Paid amount owed to Bottle Rockets Ltd. on the credit purchase of July 2, less the discount and the return.
11	Granted a sales allowance of $600 to Sparkling Sparklers on the July 9 sale.
19	Received cash from Sparkling Sparklers in full settlement of their debt, less the allowance and the discount.

⑤ Preparing a retailer's financial statements.

E5-19. Family Dollars reported these figures for 2008 and 2009 (in millions):

	2008	2009
Net sales revenue	$38,000	$40,000
Cost of goods sold	7,000	8,000
Total operating expenses	21,000	19,000

For both years, compute Family Dollars'

a. Gross profit.

b. Net income.

c. Which year was more successful? Give your reason.

E5-20. Supply the missing income statement amounts in each of the following situations, assuming no sales returns or allowances have been granted:

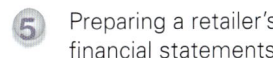
5 Preparing a retailer's financial statements.

Sales	Sales Discounts	Net Sales Revenue	Cost of Goods Sold	Gross Profit
$76,000	$6,000	(a)	$46,000	(b)
$60,000	(c)	$56,000	(d)	$22,000
(e)	$4,000	$85,000	$55,000	(f)
(g)	$2,000	(h)	$82,000	$43,000

E5-21. The trial balance and adjustments data of Monkey Business Pet Shop include the following accounts and balances on December 31, 2008. Use the following data to prepare a single-step income statement, a statement of owner's equity, and a balance sheet for Monkey Business Pet Shop.

5 Preparing a retailer's financial statements.

MONKEY BUSINESS PET SHOP
Worksheet
December 31, 2008

Account Title	Trial Balance Dr.	Trial Balance Cr.	Adjustments Dr.	Adjustments Cr.
Cash	32,000			
Accounts receivable	12,500		(a) 3,500	
Inventory	42,300			
Supplies	3,200			(c) 1,700
Furniture	46,500			
Accumulated depreciation, furniture		12,400		(d) 3,100
Accounts payable		22,600		(f) 2,400
Salary payable				(b) 1,200
Unearned service revenue		12,600	(e) 6,300	
Notes payable, long-term		18,000		
J. Monkey, capital		80,470		
J. Monkey, withdrawals	38,000			
Sales revenue		168,000		(a) 3,500
				(e) 6,300
Sales returns and allowances	5,800			
Cost of goods sold	92,180			
Selling expense	25,090		(f) 2,400	
General and administrative expense	16,500		(c) 1,700	
			(d) 3,100	
			(b) 1,200	
Total	314,070	314,070	18,200	18,200

5   Preparing a retailer's
financial statements.

6   Computing gross
profit percentage
and inventory
turnover rate.

E5-22. Selected amounts from the accounting records of Cuppa Tea Gift Emporium are listed here:

Inventory, May 31, 2008	$ 28,000
Earl Gray, Withdrawals	12,000
Cost of Goods Sold	180,720
General and Administrative Expenses	32,050
Interest Revenue	5,100
Accounts Payable	18,500
Sales Returns and Allowances	3,200
Inventory, May 31, 2007	32,240
Earl Gray, Capital, May 31, 2008	229,600
Sales Discounts	10,600
Accumulated Depreciation, Building	17,800
Sales Revenue	315,000
Selling Expenses	28,700
Unearned Sales Revenue	5,600

Requirements

1. Prepare the business's multistep income statement for the year ended May 31, 2008.

2. Compute the rate of inventory turnover for the year. In 2007, the turnover rate was 5.7 times. Is the turnover rate improving or deteriorating during these two years?

5   Preparing a retailer's
financial statements.

6   Computing gross
profit percentage
and inventory
turnover rate.

E5-23. 1. Prepare Cuppa Tea's single-step income statement for 2008, using the data from E5-22. How does the net income in this single-step income statement compare to that of the multistep statement version in E5-22?

2. Compute the gross profit percentage, and compare it with last year's gross profit percentage of 50%. Does this two-year trend in the gross profit percentage suggest better or worse profitability during the current year?

E5-24. Krunchy Krisp Doughnuts earned sales revenue of $492 million in 2007. Cost of goods sold was $282 million, and net income reached $33.4 million. Total current assets included inventory of $24 million on December 31, 2007. In 2006, ending inventory was $16 million. The managers of Krunchy Krisp need to know the company's gross profit percentage and rate of inventory turnover for 2007. Compute these amounts.

Problems (Group A)

2 Journalizing supplier/retailer transactions.

3 Journalizing retailer/customer transactions.

4 Journalizing shipment transactions.

P5-25A. During April of the current year, the following transactions took place between Chimney Crickets, a retailer of fireplaces and fireplace equipment, and their supplier, Soot Yourself.

April 1	Soot Yourself sold $10,000 worth of merchandise on account to Chimney Crickets on terms of 3/10, n/45, FOB shipping point. Soot Yourself prepaid shipping charges of $220 and included this amount in the invoice total. These goods had a cost to Soot Yourself of $6,500.
4	When Chimney Crickets checked the items received from the purchase of April 1, they realized that they had received too many fireplace inserts. They returned $2,500 of the merchandise to Soot Yourself. Soot Yourself restocked this inventory, which had an original cost of $1,625.
10	Chimney Crickets paid the amount owed to Soot Yourself for the April 1 purchase, less the return and the discount.
25	Chimney Crickets sold $2,500 worth of merchandise to Mimi Cold for cash. This merchandise had a cost to Chimney Crickets of $1,500.

Requirements

1. Journalize these transactions for Chimney Crickets.

2. Journalize these transactions for Soot Yourself.

P5-26A. Sweet Dreams Company, a retailer of beds and mattresses, engaged in the following transactions during September:

2 Journalizing supplier/retailer transactions.

3 Journalizing retailer/customer transactions.

4 Journalizing shipment transactions.

Sept. 4	Purchased inventory for cash, $14,000.
6	Purchased store supplies on credit from C. Paper, terms of n/30, $600.
9	Purchased inventory of $5,500 plus shipping charges of $200 from R. U. Sleepy; credit terms are 2/15, n/60, FOB shipping point.
10	Sold goods for cash, $2,800; Sweet Dreams' cost of these goods was $1,820.
12	After negotiations with R. U. Sleepy, Sweet Dreams received a $1,500 allowance on the inventory purchased on September 9 because the mattress tops were stained.
14	Purchased $4,560 of inventory on credit from T. Sandman, terms of 2/10, n/45, FOB destination.
15	Sold $8,400 of inventory on credit to S. L. Beauty under terms of 3/10, n/30, FOB shipping point. The goods had a cost of $5,460.
16	Paid advertising expense of $250.

continued.....

18	S. L. Beauty returned $1,600 of merchandise from the September 15 sale because Sweet Dreams had shipped incorrect merchandise; the original cost of the merchandise returned was $1,040.
22	Paid R. U. Sleepy for goods purchased on September 9 less the allowance and the discount.
25	After agreeing to allow a discount on a partial payment, Sweet Dreams received payment of $3,000 from S. L. Beauty for the sale on September 15, less the discount.
29	Paid for the store supplies purchased on September 6.

Requirements

1. Journalize the preceding transactions for Sweet Dreams Company.

2. Compute the amount of the receivable on September 30 from S. L. Beauty to whom Sweet Dreams sold merchandise on September 15.

⑤ Preparing a retailer's financial statements.

⑥ Computing gross profit percentage and inventory turnover rate.

P5-27A. The accounting records of Speed Up Auto Parts on August 31, 2008, list the following amounts:

Cost of Goods Sold	$104,000
Sales Discounts	4,600
Equipment	65,200
Salary Payable	2,200
Accounts Payable	19,500
Cam Engine, Withdrawals	31,600
Sales Returns and Allowances	14,300
Selling Expenses	21,400
Cash	15,700
Inventory, August 31, 2007	40,000
Inventory, August 31, 2008	43,200
Sales Revenue	206,500
Notes Payable	6,100
Accumulated Depreciation, Equipment	17,700
Cam Engine, Capital	66,000
General and Administrative Expenses	15,100
Accounts Receivable	6,900

Requirements

1. Prepare a multistep income statement to show the computation of Speed Up Auto Parts' net sales revenue, gross profit, and net income for the year ended August 31, 2008.

continued.....

2. Cam Engine, owner of the business, strives to earn gross profit of $85,000 and net income of $45,000. Did Cam achieve these goals? Explain.

3. Compute the company's gross profit percentage and rate of inventory turnover for 2008.

P5-28A. Selected accounts of Ups A Daisy Florists are listed along with their balances on May 31, 2007.

⑤ Preparing a retailer's financial statements.

Sales Discounts	$ 6,000	Store Equipment	$32,000
Supplies	2,000	Inventory	77,000
Accumulated Depreciation, Store		Notes Payable, Long-Term	64,000
Equipment	6,000	Salary Payable	2,300
Rose Bush, Capital, May 1	76,000	Rose Bush, Withdrawals	20,800
Accounts Payable	25,000	Sales Returns and Allowances ...	7,000
Cash	47,000	Accounts Receivable	36,000
Cost of Goods Sold	58,000	Selling Expenses	38,000
Sales Revenue	$164,000	Interest Payable	4,000
General and Administrative		Unearned Sales Revenue	7,500
Expenses	28,000		
Interest Revenue	3,000		

Requirements

1. Prepare Ups A Daisy Florists' single-step income statement for the month ended May 31, 2007.

2. Prepare Ups A Daisy's classified balance sheet in report format on May 31, 2007. Remember to calculate the May 31, 2007, ending balance of Rose Bush, Capital.

P5-29A. The trial balance and adjustments data of Play Me Video Games at November 30, 2009, follow:

⑤ Preparing a retailer's financial statements.

continued.....

<table>
<thead>
<tr><th colspan="5" align="center">PLAY ME VIDEO GAMES
Worksheet
November 30, 2009</th></tr>
<tr><th rowspan="2">Account Title</th><th colspan="2">Trial Balance</th><th colspan="2">Adjustments</th></tr>
<tr><th>Dr.</th><th>Cr.</th><th>Dr.</th><th>Cr.</th></tr>
</thead>
<tbody>
<tr><td>Cash</td><td>9,100</td><td></td><td></td><td></td></tr>
<tr><td>Accounts receivable</td><td>2,560</td><td></td><td>(a) 2,600</td><td></td></tr>
<tr><td>Inventory</td><td>10,740</td><td></td><td></td><td></td></tr>
<tr><td>Supplies</td><td>9,590</td><td></td><td></td><td>(c) 6,830</td></tr>
<tr><td>Equipment</td><td>88,340</td><td></td><td></td><td></td></tr>
<tr><td>Accumulated depreciation, equipment</td><td></td><td>18,690</td><td></td><td>(d) 8,700</td></tr>
<tr><td>Accounts payable</td><td></td><td>14,910</td><td></td><td>(b) 3,200</td></tr>
<tr><td>Salary payable</td><td></td><td></td><td></td><td>(f) 450</td></tr>
<tr><td>Unearned sales revenue</td><td></td><td>6,000</td><td>(e) 4,500</td><td></td></tr>
<tr><td>Notes payable, long-term</td><td></td><td>22,000</td><td></td><td></td></tr>
<tr><td>C. Pacman, capital</td><td></td><td>60,560</td><td></td><td></td></tr>
<tr><td>C. Pacman, withdrawals</td><td>41,200</td><td></td><td></td><td></td></tr>
<tr><td>Sales revenue</td><td></td><td>231,600</td><td></td><td>(a) 2,600</td></tr>
<tr><td></td><td></td><td></td><td></td><td>(e) 4,500</td></tr>
<tr><td>Sales returns</td><td>4,210</td><td></td><td></td><td></td></tr>
<tr><td>Cost of goods sold</td><td>98,900</td><td></td><td></td><td></td></tr>
<tr><td>Selling expense</td><td>52,900</td><td></td><td>(c) 6,830</td><td></td></tr>
<tr><td></td><td></td><td></td><td>(f) 450</td><td></td></tr>
<tr><td>General and administrative expense</td><td>33,000</td><td></td><td>(d) 8,700</td><td></td></tr>
<tr><td></td><td></td><td></td><td>(b) 3,200</td><td></td></tr>
<tr><td>Interest expense</td><td>3,220</td><td></td><td></td><td></td></tr>
<tr><td></td><td>353,760</td><td>353,760</td><td>26,280</td><td>26,280</td></tr>
</tbody>
</table>

Requirements

1. Use the preceding information to prepare the company's multistep income statement for the year ended November 30, 2009. It is not necessary to complete the worksheet.

2. Compute the gross profit percentage and the inventory turnover rate for 2009. Inventory on hand at November 30, 2008, was $12,680. For 2008, the company's gross profit percentage was 60% and the inventory turnover rate was 7.5 times. Does the two-year trend in these ratios suggest improvement or deterioration in profitability?

6 Computing gross profit percentage and inventory turnover rate.

2 Journalizing supplier/retailer transactions.

3 Journalizing retailer/customer transactions.

4 Journalizing shipment transactions.

Problems (Group B)

P5-30B. During October of the current year, the following transactions took place between Home Station, a retailer of building supplies, and their supplier, Paul Bunyan Lumber.

continued.....

Oct. 4	Paul Bunyan Lumber sold $11,000 worth of merchandise to Home Station on terms of 2/15, n/45, FOB shipping point. Paul Bunyan prepaid shipping charges of $450 and included this amount in the invoice total. These goods cost Paul Bunyan $6,500.
6	Home Station returned $1,500 of the merchandise they received on October 4 to Paul Bunyan Lumber due to an error in the order quantity. Paul Bunyan restocked this inventory, which had an original cost of $975.
17	Home Station paid the amount owed to Paul Bunyan for the October 4 purchase, less the return and the discount.
28	Home Station sold $3,800 worth of merchandise to Bo Window for cash. This merchandise had a cost to Home Station of $2,280.

Requirements

1. Journalize these transactions for Paul Bunyan Lumber.

2. Journalize these transactions for Home Station.

P5-31B. Wet and Wild Pools engaged in the following transactions during June:

June 2	Purchased office supplies for cash, $650.
5	Purchased inventory from H. I. Board on credit terms of 2/10, n/eom, FOB destination, $3,300.
7	Returned $1,100 of the inventory purchased on June 5. It was not the inventory ordered.
9	Sold goods for cash, $660. The cost of these goods was $400.
11	Sold inventory to A. Dolphin on credit terms of 3/10, n/60, $4,600. The cost of the goods was $2,700.
13	Paid the amount owed on account from the purchase of June 5, less the return and the discount.
14	Received defective inventory as a sales return from the June 11 sale, $600. Wet and Wild's cost of the inventory received was $360.
15	Purchased inventory of $8,500 on account from S. Fin. Payment terms were 1/15, n/30, FOB destination.
21	Received cash from A. Dolphin in full settlement of the purchase of June 11, less the return and the discount.
28	Paid S. Fin the amount owed from the purchase on June 15, less the discount.
30	Purchased inventory for cash, $3,200, plus shipping charges of $155.

② Journalizing supplier/retailer transactions.

③ Journalizing retailer/customer transactions.

④ Journalizing shipment transactions.

continued.....

Requirements

1. Journalize the preceding transactions for Wet and Wild Pools.

2. Compute the total sales discount granted during the period.

P5-32B. **P5-32B.** The accounting records of U Make It Craft Shop list the following on December 31, 2007:

Office Equipment	$ 15,250
Accounts Receivable	15,500
Selling Expenses	15,000
Furniture	28,600
Sales Returns and Allowances	4,500
Salary Payable	1,250
Art Easel, Capital	69,295
Sales Revenue	201,000
Accumulated Depreciation, Office Equipment	2,450
Accounts Payable	8,585
Inventory, December 31, 2006	32,850
Inventory, December 31, 2007	32,650
Cash	32,775
Notes Payable	15,830
Accumulated Depreciation, Furniture	11,580
Cost of Goods Sold	110,620
Sales Discounts	3,200
General and Administrative Expenses	27,000
Art Easel, Withdrawals	25,000

Requirements

1. Prepare a multistep income statement to show the computation of U Make It Craft Shop's net sales revenue, gross profit, and net income for the year ended December 31, 2007.

2. Art Easel, owner of the company, strives to earn gross profit of $80,000 and net income of $40,000 each year. Did he achieve these goals?

continued.....

3. Compute the company's gross profit percentage and rate of inventory turnover for 2007.

5-33B. The accounts of the Written Word Book Emporium are listed along with their balances at July 31, 2009.

⑤ Preparing a retailer's financial statements.

Sales Discounts	$ 25,000	Equipment	$ 98,000
Interest Payable	2,300	Inventory	38,000
Accumulated Depreciation, Equipment	24,000	Notes Payable, Long-Term	32,000
		Salary Payable	3,700
M. Novel, Capital, July 1, 2009	92,500	M. Novel, Withdrawals	15,000
Accounts Payable	23,000	Sales Returns and Allowances	20,000
Cash	35,000	Accounts Receivable	22,000
Cost of Goods Sold	600,000	Selling Expenses	$125,000
Sales Revenue	900,000	Supplies	9,500
General and Administrative Expenses	100,000	Unearned Sales Revenue	8,000
Interest Revenue	2,000		

Requirements

1. Prepare the Written Word Book Emporium's single-step income statement for the month ended July 31, 2009.

2. Prepare the Written Word's classified balance sheet in report format at July 31, 2009. Remember to calculate the July 31 ending balance of M. Novel, Capital.

P5-34B. The trial balance and adjustments data of Magic Carpet Company include the following accounts and balances on September 30, 2008:

⑤ Preparing a retailer's financial statements.

⑥ Computing gross profit percentage and inventory turnover rate.

continued.....

MAGIC CARPET COMPANY
Worksheet
September 30, 2008

Account Title	Trial Balance Dr.	Trial Balance Cr.	Adjustments Dr.	Adjustments Cr.
Cash	35,100			
Accounts receivable	25,600		(a) 5,000	
Inventory	30,500			
Supplies	3,900			(c) 1,300
Furniture	28,500			
Accumulated depreciation, furniture		7,400		(d) 1,700
Accounts payable		9,300		(f) 2,000
Salary payable				(b) 3,000
Unearned sales revenue		25,000	(e)18,000	
Notes payable, long-term		18,900		
Jeanie Ride, capital		66,000		
Jeanie Ride, withdrawals	38,700			
Sales revenue		178,000		(a) 5,000
				(e)18,000
Sales returns	11,000			
Cost of goods sold	83,000			
Selling expense`	30,000		(f) 2,000	
General and administrative expense	16,000		(c) 1,300	
			(d) 1,700	
			(b) 3,000	
Interest expense	2,300			
	304,600	304,600	31,000	31,000

Requirements

1. Use the preceding information to prepare the company's multistep income statement for the year ended September 30, 2008. It is not necessary to complete the worksheet.

2. Compute the gross profit percentage and the rate of inventory turnover for 2008. Inventory on hand one year ago, September 30, 2007, was $28,200. For 2007, Magic Carpet Company's gross profit percentage was 50%, and inventory turnover was 2.05 times during the year. Does the two-year trend in these ratios suggest improvement or deterioration in profitability?

for 24/7 practice, visit
www.MyAccountingLab.com

Apply Your Knowledge

Case 1. Kathy Charles was planning to sell her specialty store, so she asked her accountant to prepare financial statements for the most recent fiscal year. The sales for each month were approximately $12,000, but the sales returns were approximately $3,000. Kathy knew that sales returns were a problem, but she did not realize they were so large. In spite of the high sales returns, her store still averaged nearly $4,500 per month in net income.

Her accountant commented on the extremely high amount of returns and told Kathy that potential buyers would probably be concerned with the apparent problem of unhappy customers. Kathy explained that she always provided full refunds to unhappy customers, and thus the cash account had been properly reduced for all refunds given.

The accountant agreed that no misstatement in the cash account had occurred. The problem was the large value of sales returns, which created a significant difference between the sales revenue and the net sales revenue. Kathy then told the accountant to simply exclude sales revenue and sales returns from the income statement and just show net sales revenue as the statement's starting point. She then added that this approach would really make no difference to users of the statement because net income would be the same regardless.

The accountant told Kathy it would be misleading to not provide the sales returns information. Kathy then pointed out that first line of the statement would be "net sales revenue" so potential buyers would see that any sales returns were already "netted out"; thus the income statements would not be misleading. Besides, Kathy noted that many major corporations start their income statements with net sales revenue rather than total sales so she would not be doing anything wrong.

Should Kathy include the sales returns on her income statement? Do you agree with Kathy that it does not matter whether the statement excludes sales return amounts because the net income will be the same? Would it be ethical for Kathy to start her income statements with net sales revenue so potential buyers don't know that some sales returns had occurred? Is it unethical for major corporations to start their income statements with net sales revenue, thereby excluding the sales returns? What should the accountant do?

Case 2. Eric Jordan operated a small retail store that primarily sold model trains. Sales had fallen for the last half of the year, and Eric worried that the bank would revoke the business's revolving line of credit. As a result, Eric did the following:

- Eric used money from the business checking account and bought shares of stock as a short-term investment for the business.

- He sold the vacant lot that the business owned and was going to use as an additional parking lot for future expansion. The business bought the lot many years earlier for $15,000, but sold it for $85,000, realizing a gain on the sale of $70,000.

- The stock purchased as a short-term investment was sold, generating an additional $35,000 of gain for the entity.

Eric was excited that the business net income would be much stronger as a result of these transactions. When Eric told his accountant how the bank would see a strong income statement, his accountant explained that the gains would be included in net income, but not in operating income. Eric asked what effect this difference might make. His accountant explained that:

- Even though net income is important, the operating income is extremely important and looked at more closely than the bottom-line net income. Therefore, the bank would see that the operating income was weakening and that the other revenue of the business actually contributed more to the bottom-line net income.

- The bank would be concerned about the weakening business profit, and even though gains from other activities helped the current bottom line, these gains couldn't be expected to occur again in the future.

Eric asked the accountant whether he could just reclassify the gains as sales because the bottom-line effect would be the same. His accountant did not agree, stating that classifying those gains as sales revenue would be unethical and misleading regardless of whether the bottom-line net income would be the same. Accordingly, the gains must remain in the other revenue category of the income statement.

Eric then asked the accountant to show the $70,000 gain on the sale of the land as a sale revenue because the land was a business asset.

Do you agree with the accountant that the gains should not be reclassified? Why? Does Eric have a valid argument that it really does not matter in which section of the income statement the gains are reported when the bottom-line net income is the same either way? Could the gain on the land sale be included in the sales revenue?

KNOW YOUR BUSINESS

This case will help you to better understand the cost of goods sold and inventory of a retailer as reported in the financial statements. Refer to the Target Balance Sheets, "Consolidated Statements of Financial Position," and Target Income Statements, "Consolidated Results of Operations," in Appendix A. Also, consider the following partial excerpt from the Management Discussion and Analysis (MDA):

> Gross margin rate represents gross margin (sales less cost of sales) as a percent of sales. Cost of sales primarily includes purchases, markdowns, shortage, and other costs associated with our merchandise.

Requirements

1. How does Target compute its gross profit (gross margin)?

2. How much was the cost of sales for 2002, 2003, and 2004? Has the total cost of sales been increasing or decreasing? What does this trend mean?

3. How much inventory did Target have on hand as of January 2005 versus January 2004? Did the inventory increase or decrease? What could this change mean?

4. Compute the gross profit (gross margin) for 2002, 2003, and 2004. Did the gross margin increase or decrease?

5. Compute the gross profit (gross margin) percentage for 2002, 2003, and 2004. Did the percentage increase or decrease? What does this change mean?

For Internet Exercises, Excel in Practice, and additional online activities, go to the Web site www.prenhall.com/pollard.

Quick Check Answers

1. *a* 2. *c* 3. *a* 4. *a* 5. *b* 6. *d* 7. *c* 8. *c* 9. *c* 10. *d*

Appendix 5A

,,,,,,,

Adjusting and Closing the Accounts of a Retailer

A retailer adjusts and closes accounts the same way a service entity does. The worksheet aids the adjusting and closing processes and preparation of the financial statements.

Adjusting Inventory Based on a Physical Count

In a perpetual inventory system, the Inventory account should reflect an accurate cost of inventory at all times; however, theft, damage, and errors occur, which cause the actual number of inventory items on hand to be different from the number shown in the accounting records. For this reason, retail businesses physically count the number of items in inventory at least once a year. The most common time to count inventory is at the end of the fiscal year. The business then adjusts the Inventory account based on the physical count so that it has an accurate value of Inventory, which it can use to prepare financial statements.

Exhibit 5A-1, Baja Beachwear's worksheet for the year ended December 31, 2008, lists a $40,000 balance for Inventory on the trial balance. With no shrinkage due to theft or error, the business should actually have inventory costing $40,000. But on December 31, when Baja Beachwear counts the inventory, the total cost of the goods on hand only amounts to $39,700.

Actual Inventory on Hand	−	Inventory Balance Before Adjustment	=	Adjusting Entry to the Inventory Account
$39,700	−	$40,000	=	Credit of $300

BAJA BEACHWEAR
Worksheet
December 31, 2008

Account Title	Trial Balance Dr.	Trial Balance Cr.	Adjustments Dr.	Adjustments Cr.	Income Statement Dr.	Income Statement Cr.	Balance Sheet Dr.	Balance Sheet Cr.
Cash	3,150						3,150	
Accounts receivable	4,600						4,600	
Inventory	**40,000**			(a) 300			**39,700**	
Supplies	650			(b) 550			100	
Prepaid insurance	1,200			(c) 1,000			200	
Office equipment	32,000						32,000	
Accumulated depreciation, office equipment		2,400		(d) 600				3,000
Accounts payable		40,000						40,000
Unearned sales revenue		2,000	(e) 1,300					700
Wages payable				(f) 400				400
Amy Toms, capital		32,900						32,900
Amy Toms, withdrawals	52,900						52,900	
Sales revenue		170,000		(e) 1,300		171,300		
Sales returns and allowances	3,400				3,400			
Cost of goods sold	**90,000**		(a) 300		**90,300**			
Wage expense	9,800		(f) 400		10,200			
Rent expense	8,400				8,400			
Advertising expense	1,000				1,000			
Delivery expense	200				200			
Depreciation expense, office equipment			(d) 600		600			
Insurance expense			(c) 1,000		1,000			
Supplies expense			(b) 550		550			
	247,300	247,300	4,150	4,150	115,650	171,300	132,650	77,000
Net income					55,650			55,650
					171,300	171,300	132,650	132,650

Note: The Adjusted Trial Balance columns of the worksheet have been omitted for simplicity, so that the adjustments and balances needed for closing entries could be the focus of the worksheet.

Baja Beachwear then records this adjusting entry for inventory shrinkage:

Journal Entry:

Date	Accounts	Post Ref.	Dr.	Cr.
Dec. 31	Cost of Goods Sold		300	
	Inventory ($39,700 – $40,000)			300

This entry brings Inventory and Cost of Goods Sold to their correct balances.

The physical count can also reveal that more inventory is present than the accounting records show, although this is less common. In that case, the adjusting entry debits Inventory and credits Cost of Goods Sold.

Journalizing the Adjusting and Closing Entries

To illustrate a retailer's adjusting and closing process, let's use Baja Beachwear's 2008 worksheet in Exhibit 5A-1. All the accounts new to this chapter, Inventory, Cost of Goods Sold, Sales Revenue, Sales Discounts, and Sales Returns and Allowances, are highlighted for emphasis.

The data used to make the adjustments on the worksheet on December 31, 2008, are:

    a. Inventory on hand, $39,700.

    b. Supplies on hand, $100.

    c. Prepaid insurance expired during the year, $1,000.

    d. Depreciation, $600.

    e. Unearned sales revenue earned during the year, $1,300.

    f. Accrued wage expense, $400.

As you know, the worksheet helps the accountant adjust accounts, prepare the financial statements, and make closing entries. The Exhibit 5A-1 worksheet combines trial balance amounts with the adjustments to determine the balance of the accounts in the Income Statement and Balance Sheet columns.

    Account Title Column The trial balance lists the unadjusted amount for each account. Few accounts will appear without balances and are affected by the adjusting process. Examples include Wages Payable and

Depreciation Expense. Accounts are listed in the order they appear in the ledger.

Trial Balance Columns Examine the Inventory account in the trial balance. Inventory has a balance of $40,000 before the physical count at the end of the year. Any difference between the Inventory amount on the trial balance, $40,000, and the correct amount based on the physical count, $39,700 is debited or credited to Cost of Goods Sold, as we just discussed.

Adjustments Columns The adjustments are similar to those discussed in Chapters 3 and 4. The debit amount of each entry should equal the credit amount, and total debits should equal total credits.

Income Statement Columns The income statement columns in Exhibit 5A-1 show adjusted amounts for the revenues and the expenses. Sales Revenue, for example, has an adjusted balance of $171,300.

The income statement totals indicate a net income or net loss.

- Net income: Total revenues, or credits, > Total expenses, or debits

- Net loss: Total expenses, or debits, > Total revenues, or credits

Baja Beachwear's total credits of $171,300 exceed the total debits of $115,650, so the company earned a net income of $55,650.

Balance Sheet Columns The only new item in the balance sheet columns is Inventory. Remember that the $39,700 balance is determined by the physical count at the end of the period.

Exhibit 5A-2 presents Baja Beachwear's adjusting and closing entries, which are similar to those you have seen previously, except for the inventory adjustment, entry (a). Because of this, explanations have been omitted. The closing entries in the exhibit follow the pattern illustrated in Chapter 4.

- The *first closing entry* transfers the sales revenue amount of $171,300 from the Sales Revenue account to the Income Summary account. We debit the Sales Revenue account to reduce its balance to zero and credit Income Summary to show the increase in equity due to revenue.

- The *second closing entry* credits the contra-revenue account Sales Returns and Allowances, Cost of Goods Sold, and all the expense accounts. The offsetting $115,650 debit to Income Summary represents the amount of total expenses plus the contra-revenues. These amounts come from the debit column of the income statement.

- The *last two closing entries* close net income to the Capital account and also close Withdrawals to the Capital account, just as you saw in Chapter 4.

Exhibit 5A-2 Adjusting and Closing Entries for a Merchandiser

Journal Entry: Adjusting Entries

Date	Accounts	Post Ref.	Dr.	Cr.
Dec. 31	a. Cost of Goods Sold		300	
	Inventory ($39,700 – $40,000)			300
31	b. Supplies Expense ($650 – $100)		550	
	Supplies			550
31	c. Insurance Expense		1,000	
	Prepaid Insurance			1,000
31	d. Depreciation Expense, Office Equipment		600	
	Accumulated Depreciation, Office Equipment			600
31	e. Unearned Sales Revenue		1,300	
	Sales Revenue			1,300
31	f. Wage Expense		400	
	Wages Payable			400

Journal Entry: Closing Entries

Date	Accounts	Post Ref.	Dr.	Cr.
Dec. 31	Sales Revenue		171,300	
	Income Summary			171,300
31	Income Summary		115,650	
	Sales Returns and Allowances			3,400
	Cost of Goods Sold			90,300
	Wage Expense			10,200
	Rent Expense			8,400
	Advertising Expense			1,000
	Delivery Expense			200
	Depreciation Expense, Office Equipment			600
	Insurance Expense			1,000
	Supplies Expense			550
31	Income Summary ($171,300 – $115,650)		55,650	
	Amy Toms, Capital			55,650
31	Amy Toms, Capital		52,900	
	Amy Toms, Withdrawals			52,900

Appendix Accounting Practice

Short Exercises

S5A-35 The balance in the Inventory account of YNotUs Company on December 31 of the current year was $2,850. The physical count of the inventory totaled $2,785. Journalize the adjusting entry that would be made to adjust the Inventory account on December 31.

Adjusting inventory.

S5A-36 The following selected accounts appear on the adjusted trial balance for YNotUs on December 31 of the current year. Journalize the closing entries that should be made at the end of the fiscal year (December 31).

Adjusting and closing entries for a retailer.

Sales Discounts	$ 2,550	General and Administrative Expenses.........	$ 8,550
Inventory	4,845	Supplies......................................	2,150
Y. Not, Capital,		Salary Payable.............................	8,550
December 1.............................	28,000	Y. Not, Withdrawals.....................	12,400
Accounts Payable.......................	895	Sales Returns and Allowances...................	3,550
Cash	14,680	Accounts Receivable.................................	4,950
Cost of Goods Sold......................	24,850	Selling Expenses.........................	5,950
Sales Revenue.............................	43,880		

Exercises

E5A-37 The accounting records of Cuppa Tea Gift Emporium carried the following accounts on May 31, 2008:

Adjusting and closing entries for a retailer.

Inventory, May 31, 2008	$ 28,000
Earl Gray, Withdrawals	12,000
Cost of Goods Sold	180,720
General and Administrative Expenses	32,050
Interest Revenue	5,100
Accounts Payable	18,500
Sales Returns	3,200
Earl Gray, Capital	229,600
Sales Discounts	10,600
Accumulated Depreciation	17,800
Sales Revenue	315,000
Selling Expenses	28,700
Unearned Sales Revenue	5,600

Requirements

1. Journalize all of Cuppa Tea Gift Emporium's closing entries on May 31, 2008.

2. Set up accounts for the Income Summary and Earl Gray, Capital. Post to these accounts and find their ending balances.

E5A-38 The trial balance and adjustments data of Monkey Business Pet Shop
include the following accounts and balances at December 31, 2008:

		MONKEY BUSINESS PET SHOP Worksheet December 31, 2008			

	Trial Balance		Adjustments	
Account Title	**Dr.**	**Cr.**	**Dr.**	**Cr.**
Cash	32,000			
Accounts receivable	12,500		(a) 3,500	
Inventory	42,300		(b) 1,200	
Supplies	3,200			(c) 1,700
Furniture	46,500			
Accumulated depreciation, furniture		12,400		(d) 3,100
Accounts payable		22,600		(f) 2,400
Salary payable				
Unearned service revenue		12,600	(e) 6,300	
Notes payable, long-term		18,000		
J. Monkey, capital		80,470		
J. Monkey, withdrawals	38,000			
Sales revenue		168,000		(a) 3,500
				(e) 6,300
Sales returns	5,800			
Cost of goods sold	92,180			(b) 1,200
Selling expense	25,090		(f) 2,400	
General and administrative expense	14,200		(c) 1,700	
			(d) 3,100	
Interest expense	2,300			
Total	314,070	314,070	18,200	18,200

Requirements

1. Compute the adjusted balance for each account that must be
   closed.

2. Journalize Monkey Business Pet Shop's closing entries on
   December 31, 2008. How much was Monkey Business Pet Shop's
   net income or net loss?

Problems

P5A-39 Wax and Wane Candle Shop's trial balance pertains to December 31,
2007.

continued.....

WAX AND WANE CANDLE SHOP
Trial Balance
December 31, 2007

Account Title	Balance Debit	Balance Credit
Cash	$ 3,850	
Accounts receivable	8,950	
Inventory	77,230	
Store supplies	2,230	
Prepaid insurance	10,800	
Store fixtures	88,430	
Accumulated depreciation, store fixtures		$ 25,340
Accounts payable		28,530
Salary payable		
Interest payable		
Note payable, long-term		37,440
Cindy Stickholder, capital		64,060
Cindy Stickholder, withdrawals	24,000	
Sales revenue		296,880
Cost of goods sold	175,340	
Salary expense	34,280	
Rent expense	15,740	
Utilities expense	6,080	
Depreciation expense		
Insurance expense		
Store supplies expense		
Interest expense	5,320	
Total	$452,250	$452,250

The adjustment data at December 31, 2007, are the following:

a. Prepaid insurance expired during the year, $6,400.

b. Store fixtures have an estimated useful life of five years and are expected to be worthless when they are retired from service.

c. Accrued salaries on December 31, $2,450.

d. Accrued interest expense on December 31, $680.

e. Store supplies on hand on December 31, $1,130.

f. Inventory on hand on December 31, $76,870.

Requirements

Complete Wax and Wane Candle Shop's accounting worksheet for the year ended December 31, 2007. Label adjusting entries by letter.

P5A-40 Refer to the data in problem P5A-39.

Adjusting and closing entries for a retailer.

Requirements

1. Journalize the adjusting and closing entries of Wax and Wane Candle Shop.

2. Determine the December 31, 2007, balance of Candy Stickholder, Capital.

1. Define fraud and describe the different types of fraud in business.

2. Describe an internal control system.

3. Apply internal controls for cash and prepare a bank reconciliation.

4. Record journal entries for the petty cash fund.

5. Report cash on the balance sheet.

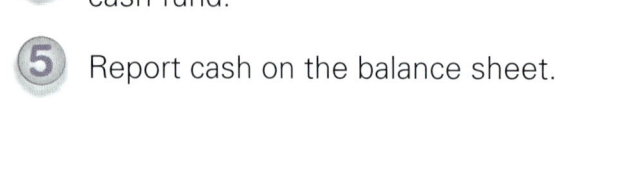

Internal Control and Cash

You are excited about opening your own retail store and selling items you use in your favorite hobby. You identified a target group of customers, selected merchandise, and decided on selling prices. You estimated the sales volume for the first year and determined the location and size of your store as well as the quantity and placement of shelves, displays, and cash registers. You even know the number of people you will hire. You have a good plan, but then your uncle starts asking questions:

- How much cash and inventory do you plan to keep in the store? How are you going to keep it safe?
- What inventory system will you use? What documents do you need to support your transactions? Who will be responsible for using them?
- Who will sign the checks, make the cash deposits, and keep track of the inventory?
- How are you going to know if your employees are trustworthy?

Even the best plan can be destroyed by dishonest suppliers, employees, and customers. For example, unethical suppliers can intentionally overcharge or double-bill for items ordered. Dishonest employees can steal cash or merchandise. Deceitful customers can take goods without paying for them. Protecting yourself from these and other fraudulent actions is vital to the success of you business. How will you defend yourself? ●

Look Back

You have learned about the relationships between suppliers, retailers, and customers, and accounted for transactions between these parties. Further, you have summarized the results of these transactions in financial statements.

Look Ahead

By examining fraudulent business activities, you will understand the importance of internal controls in business as a way of preventing fraud. You will also prepare a bank reconciliation as an important internal control over cash.

In Chapter 5, we discovered how to account for the transactions of a retail business like the store you want to open. We measured the success of the business by preparing both the single-step and multistep versions of the income statement, the statement of owner's equity, the report form of the balance sheet, and by calculating the gross profit percentage and the inventory turnover rate. Understanding the operations of a retailer, we now examine the threats to its success due to unethical behavior, and discover a framework for dealing with these issues. As the most liquid of all assets and therefore the one most susceptible to unethical action, we turn our focus to accounting for cash.

Fraud in Business

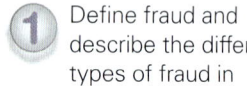

1 Define fraud and describe the different types of fraud in business.

U.S. businesses lose billions of dollars each year due to fraudulent acts. Simply stated, **fraud** involves deceit or trickery that causes financial harm to a business, its stakeholders, or both. Accordingly, the accounting profession believes that fraud includes intentional actions that result in a misstatement of the financial statements.

The Fraud Triangle

For fraud to occur, fraud investigators believe that three factors must be present: **perceived pressure**, **perceived opportunity**, and **rationalization**. Exhibit 6-1 presents the **Fraud Triangle**, which shows the connection of the three factors necessary to commit fraud. To better understand the three factors and how they relate to each other, let's look at situations involving the factors that could lead to the perpetration of fraud.

- *Perceived pressure:* Imagine that an employee feels the need to get cash. Motivations could include:

  - Financial pressure: Maybe the employee has a poor personal credit rating, poor cash management skills, is greedy or addicted to gambling, drugs, alcohol, or expensive relationships.

  - Work-related pressure: Perhaps the employee is dissatisfied with his or her job because of feeling underpaid or overlooked for promotion.

- *Perceived opportunity:* The employee believes an opportunity exists to commit fraud, conceal it, and avoid punishment. Opportunities to commit fraud increase when:

  - The business has weak internal controls to prevent or detect fraud.

  - Monitoring of internal controls by management is ineffective.

  - The business has assets, such as cash, that are particularly susceptible to fraud.

- *Rationalization:* The employee justifies his or her actions and convinces himself or herself that fraud is not wrong. Common rationalizations used by individuals involved in fraud include:
  - "I am only borrowing the money. I will pay it back."
  - "I deserve a pay raise. I should get this anyway."
  - "It's for a good purpose."

Exhibit 6-1 The Fraud Triangle

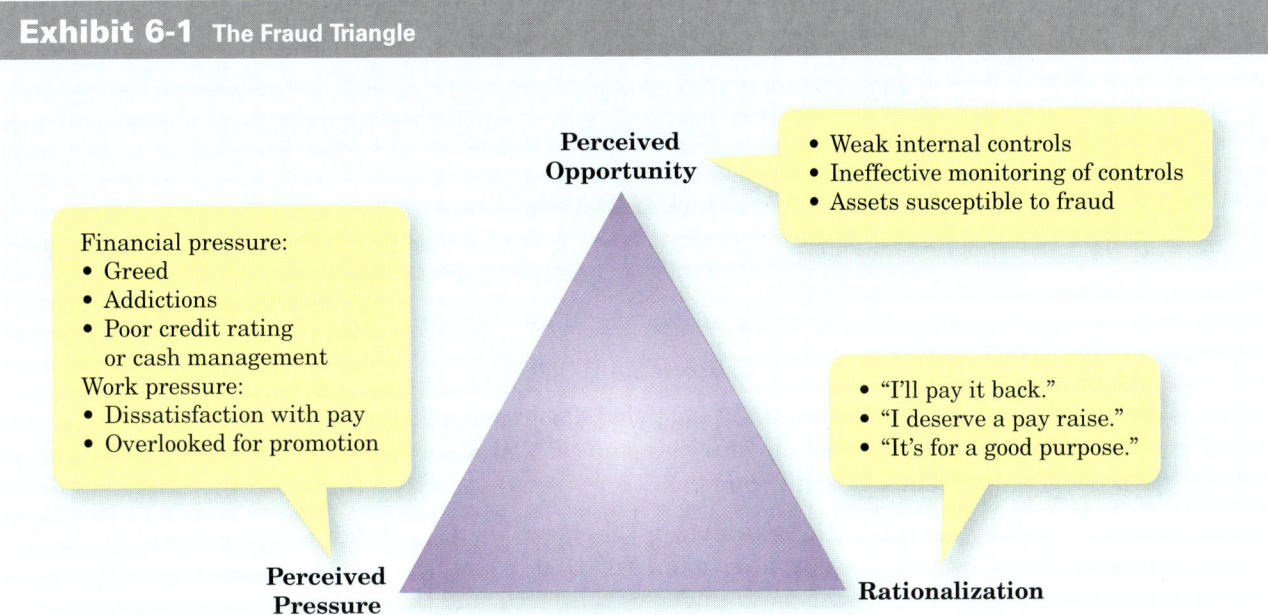

Now let's look at some situations where one of the three factors is missing, and thus, fraud is unlikely to occur:

- *No perceived pressure*: An employee may see an opportunity to steal cash and may even be able to justify taking the cash to replace the raise she believes she deserves, but the individual has all the material wealth that she needs and she likes her job. The employee is not likely to commit fraud because the incentive to do so is low.

- *No perceived opportunity*: An employee may be pressured to steal money to cover a gambling debt and may rationalize that he will repay the company next month; however, the company has good internal controls that would probably reveal the theft. The employee is not likely to commit fraud because he sees no opportunity to engage in fraudulent activity without getting caught.

- *No rationalization*: An employee may desperately need cash and may see a way to steal money without detection, but she cannot find a way to justify taking the money. Ethical values of the employee may inhibit an employee's ability to rationalize fraud.

Fraud

The accounting profession believes that business fraud involves misstated financial statements, so it believes that there are really two types of fraud as follows:

- Misappropriation, or theft, of business assets
- Fraudulent financial reporting caused by falsifying accounting records

Theft of assets is often concealed by misreporting the financial statements, so even this first type of fraud usually involves misstating the financial statement amounts. Fraudulent acts can occur in many forms and can be accomplished by different types of perpetrators. In this chapter, we focus on fraud committed by employees and managers of businesses.

EMPLOYEE EMBEZZLEMENT

Employee embezzlement is employee fraud involving misappropriation of assets, which occurs when employees steal from their employers. Employees can:

- Steal cash, inventory, tools, supplies, or other assets from the employer.
- Establish fake companies and have the employer pay these phony suppliers for goods that are never actually delivered, then intercept and fraudulently cash the checks.
- Take bribes or kickbacks from:
  - Suppliers, to allow for higher purchase prices, nondelivery of goods to the company, or delivery of inferior goods.
  - Customers, to allow for lower sales prices.
- Engage in **disbursement schemes**.

Employee fraud involving disbursement schemes occurs when an employee tricks a company into giving up cash for an invalid reason. Examples of disbursement schemes include:

- **Check tampering:** Employee writes a fraudulent check and makes the check payable to himself. Or, the employee obtains a check intended for an outside party, endorses the check, and then cashes it.
- **Cash register schemes:** Employee gives a false refund for returned merchandise by filling out a refund form, putting it in the cash register, then taking the cash and pocketing it. Another, related scheme happens when the employee accepts cash from the customer for a purchase but does not record the transaction in the cash register, keeping the cash for personal use.
- **Expense schemes:** Employee overbills the company for travel and other business-related expenses, such as lunches, hotels, air travel, parking fees, and cab fares.

MANAGEMENT FRAUD

Management fraud typically involves fraudulent financial reporting by management. This intentional misrepresentation of financial information on the financial statements is driven by greed, such as a manager's desire to receive a larger cash bonus, or pressure to keep his job by showing owners that the business is more profitable than it really is. These pressures, combined with the opportunity to manipulate financial information and the rationalization that an unethical solution is really acceptable, lead managers to commit fraud.

Management fraud occurs because top levels of management are often involved in the fraud themselves. In these cases, the board of directors and auditors are not watching closely. Recently a number of fraudulent financial reporting schemes, such as the ones in which Enron and WorldCom engaged, led to billions of dollars in losses in the form of the decline in stock value and lost retirement monies for thousands of employees.

Fraudulent financial reporting schemes can occur when management:

- Overstates revenues by
  - Overstating receivables related to this revenue that has not been earned.
  - Understating unearned revenue.

- Understates expenses by
  - Overstating the value of equipment, buildings, and other assets or recording assets that do not exist.
  - Understating amounts due to suppliers, employees, creditors, or others.

Organization Accountability for Fraud

Objectives of Internal Control

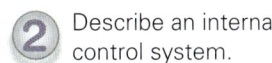

2 Describe an internal control system.

In the first chapter, we talked about organization accountability. The management of an organization is accountable for managing its resources responsibly, thereby reducing the risk of fraud. A business generally can't control the perceived pressure for fraud felt by an employee or an employee's ability to rationalize unethical behavior. Accordingly, the most effective way for a business to prevent fraud is to eliminate the perceived opportunity for an employee to freely steal an asset or for a manager to report false financial information. This opportunity can be reduced through internal controls.

Internal control is a plan, or process, that helps an organization achieve these objectives:

- Safeguard assets and report financial information properly.
- Operate efficiently and effectively.
- Comply with laws and regulations that apply to the organization's operations.

By implementing a plan of internal control, the organization can be accountable to stakeholders and reduce its risk of fraud. Management is responsible for designing and monitoring internal controls that make up the plan. Large companies usually operate with a different internal control system than small companies. Although small companies have a less formal and less structured internal control system, it can still be effective, largely due to the involvement of the owner(s).

Control Activities

Control activities are the policies and procedures of an internal control system. The types of control activities used by an organization vary from firm to firm. Generally, the controls chosen for an entity are based on its control environment, the company's assessment of risk, the size and structure of the company, as well as the nature of its operations. Common control activities include:

- *Separation of duties:* Do not allow any one employee to be responsible for more than one of the following functions:
  - Authorizing transactions
  - Maintaining custody of assets
  - Keeping accounting records

  Assigning an individual with responsibility for more than one of these duties creates an opportunity for fraud. For example, an employee who has access to cash or other assets and can record transactions could steal assets and falsify financial information to hide the theft. Exhibit 6-2 illustrates an organization chart showing the assignment of responsibilities and separation of duties.

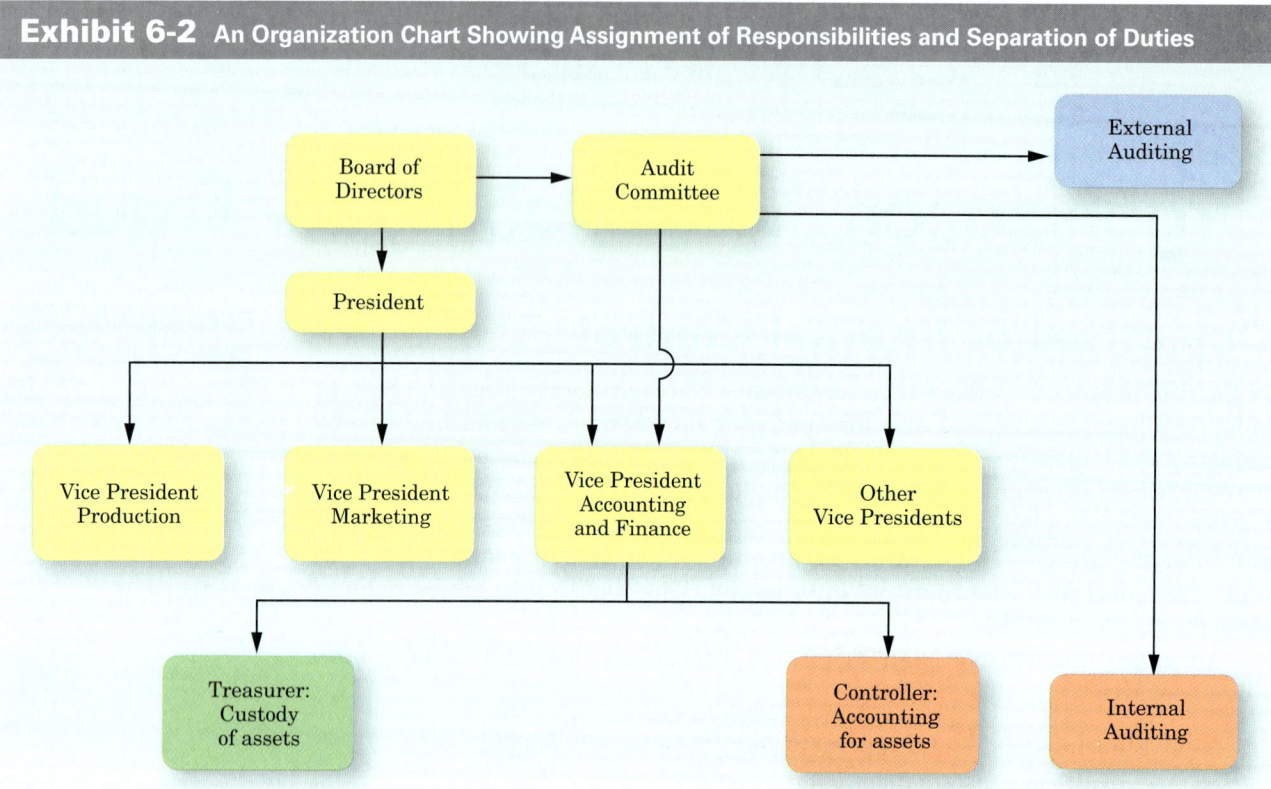

- *Physical safeguards:* Limit the number of employees who have access to the business's assets, such as cash, inventory, and supplies, as well as its financial records. For instance, use cash registers, vaults, and locked storage units to control access to assets. Use passwords to restrict access to computerized accounting records and limit contact with journals and ledgers to the accounting staff. Allowing too many people access to assets and records creates opportunity for fraud and makes it more difficult to find the perpetrator.

- *Proper authorization:* Establish and require appropriate authorization for transactions. For example, in a small business, the owner could review and approve a purchase invoice before a check is written to pay the amount. In a larger company, price lists and credit policies set criteria for credit sales transactions. Good authorization procedures reduce the chance that an unauthorized transaction may occur, thus providing an employee with access to assets.

- *Adequate documents and records:* Implement a system to provide evidence of transactions. An **audit trail**, a trail of business documents and records, evidences the details of business transactions. Documents include checks and invoices, and records include journals and ledgers. Documents should be prenumbered, so gaps in the numbered sequence draw attention. Creating an effective audit trail diminishes the chance that inappropriate activity will go unnoticed.

- *Independent checks on performance:* Assign an employee who does not have access to assets or the accounting records to check for errors and discrepancies. For example, in a small business, the owner can prepare a bank reconciliation to compare the cash reported by the bank to the cash balance reported in the accounting records. In a larger organization, management could compare financial performance measured by net income of the current period to that of prior periods. Reviewing different sets of data reduces the opportunity for fraud to occur without detection.

Exhibit 6-3 provides an overview of the internal control system.

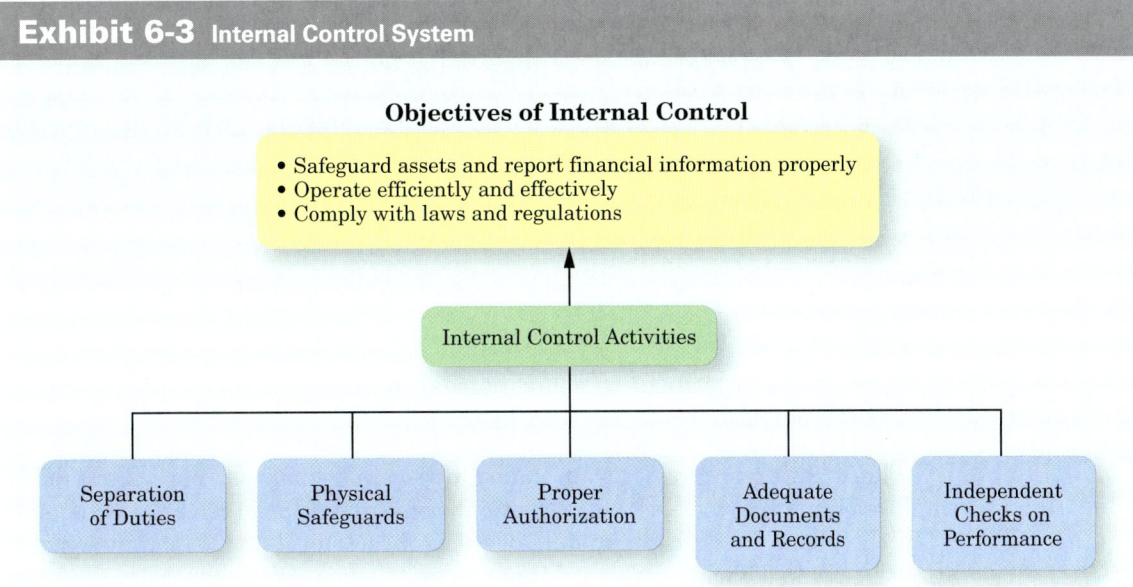

Exhibit 6-3 Internal Control System

Accountability for Internal Control

Audits can validate the accounting records and reports of a business. Hence, consistent with our discussion in Chapter 1, audits involve the examination of the company's financial statements and the accounting system that produces them. To evaluate the system and the reports that it generates, auditors also examine internal controls.

Audits can be internal or external. **Internal audits** are assessments conducted by employees of the business. They check to see that employees are following company policies and procedures, and that operations are running efficiently. Internal auditors also determine whether the company is following applicable legal requirements.

Individuals completely independent of the business perform **external audits**. Recall from Chapter 1 that Certified Public Accountants (CPAs) are the external auditors who perform audits of financial statements. Although *audit* is a term that generally means examination, the accounting meaning of *audit* refers to the assessment of these statements to determine whether they are fairly presented, that is, whether they comply with Generally Accepted Accounting Principles.

Because fraud has occurred so frequently in so many large, publicly owned companies in recent years, a number of regulatory changes have affected accounting and auditing. For example, auditors are now required to assess the possibility of misstatement in the financial statements due to fraud during every audit. Also, in 2002, the U.S. Congress passed the **Sarbanes-Oxley Act**, which requires management of public firms to certify the financial statements of their firms. Further, according to Section 404 of the Act, management must state that they are responsible for establishing and maintaining internal control over financial reporting, and must have the effectiveness of internal controls related to financial reporting assessed by external auditors.

Limitations of Internal Control

Although some reliance may be placed on internal controls to reduce the amount of fraud in a business, an internal control system can provide only reasonable, rather than absolute, assurance that fraud will be prevented or detected. The effectiveness of internal control systems is limited for the following reasons:

- Employees can make mistakes by using poor judgment while following controls, misunderstand policies and procedures, and become tired, careless, or distracted while applying controls.
- Controls can be poorly designed.
- Collusion of two or more people can circumvent controls.
- Management can override controls.
- The cost of implementing some internal controls may exceed the benefits of these controls.

These failures can occur in many different scenarios. For example, an employee can forget to check authorization for the extension of credit to a customer when the phone rings in the middle of the transaction. Collusion can be used in bribery and kickback schemes. Management can override controls, directing accounting staff to record revenue equal to the value of a contract signed but not performed. In small business, the cost of employing enough people for a separation of duties may exceed the benefits of the segregation.

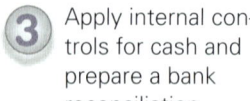

Internal Control for Cash

3 Apply internal controls for cash and prepare a bank reconciliation.

Cash is the most liquid asset of any business because it's the medium of exchange. Also, cash is easy to conceal and has no identifying marks that link it to its owner, making it relatively easy to steal. Further, transactions that affect the cash account also impact other accounts, so misstatement of cash can result in misstatement of other items. As a result, most businesses create specific controls for cash.

Internal Control over Cash Receipts

Companies typically receive cash over the counter and through the mail. Good internal control dictates that all cash receipts should be deposited for safekeeping in the bank quickly. Each source of cash needs its own security measures.

CASH RECEIPTS OVER THE COUNTER

The point-of-sale terminal, the cash register, provides control over the cash receipts for a retail business. Consider a Macy's store. Macy's issues a receipt for each transaction to ensure that every sale is recorded; a customer cannot receive a receipt unless the register records the transaction. When the clerk enters a transaction in the register, the machine records it and the cash drawer opens to receive cash. At the end of the day, a manager checks to see that the proper amount of cash was collected by comparing the cash in the drawer against the machine's record of sales. This step helps prevent theft from cash register schemes.

At the end of the day, or several times a day if business is brisk, the cashier deposits the cash in the bank. If it is impractical to get to the bank, cash may be kept in a locked location within the business such as a vault, although this is not as effective as making a bank deposit. The machine tape then goes to the accounting department so that the journal entry to record the sales can be prepared. These measures, coupled with oversight by a manager, discourage theft.

CASH RECEIPTS BY MAIL

Many companies receive cash by mail, especially if they sell products or services on credit. Exhibit 6-4 shows how companies can control cash received by mail. Generally, an employee who has no other involvement in the sales or collection process, often a mailroom employee, opens all incoming mail and prepares a control listing of amounts received. The mailroom then sends all customer checks to the treasurer, who has the cashier deposit the money in the bank and collect a receipt. The remittance advices, often check stubs, go to the accounting department and serve as a basis for making journal entries to Cash and customer receivable accounts. As a final step, the controller compares the bank deposit amount from the treasurer with the debit to Cash from the accounting department.

The amount of cash received according to the mailroom should match the debit to Cash and should equal the amount deposited in the bank. This procedure ensures that cash receipts are safe in the bank, and the company accounting records are up to date.

Exhibit 6-4 Cash Receipts by Mail

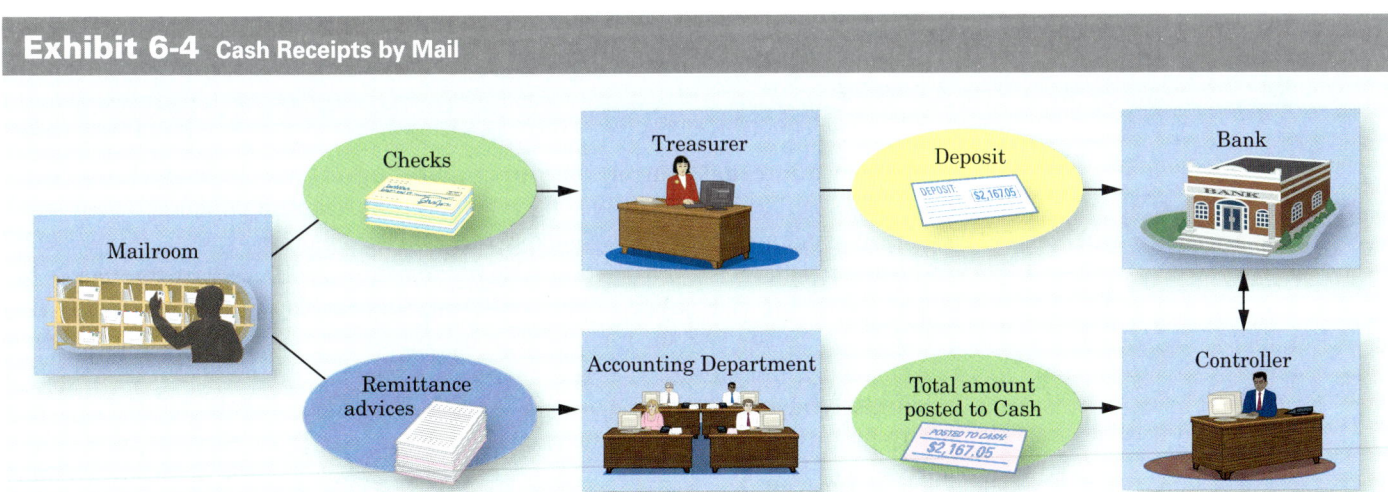

Internal Control over Cash Payments

A good separation of duties between operations and writing checks for cash payments provides internal control over those payments. Also, making payments by check is another important control for several reasons:

- The check provides a written record of the payment.
- An authorized official studies the evidence supporting the payment.
- The official approves the payment by signing the check.

PURCHASE AND PAYMENT PROCESS

To illustrate the internal control over cash payments by check in a company large enough to separate duties, suppose Bicycles Plus buys its inventory from Specialized. This purchase and payment process will differ slightly between companies, but generally the process follows these steps, as shown in Exhibit 6-5:

1. Bicycles Plus faxes a **purchase order** to Specialized, its supplier. By preparing this document, Bicycles Plus is placing an order to buy bicycles.

2. Specialized ships the goods and sends an invoice back to Bicycles Plus.

3. Bicycles Plus receives the bicycles and prepares a **receiving report** as evidence that it got its bikes.

4. After matching the information on these documents, Bicycles Plus sends a **check** to Specialized. By writing the check, Bicycles Plus pays Specialized.

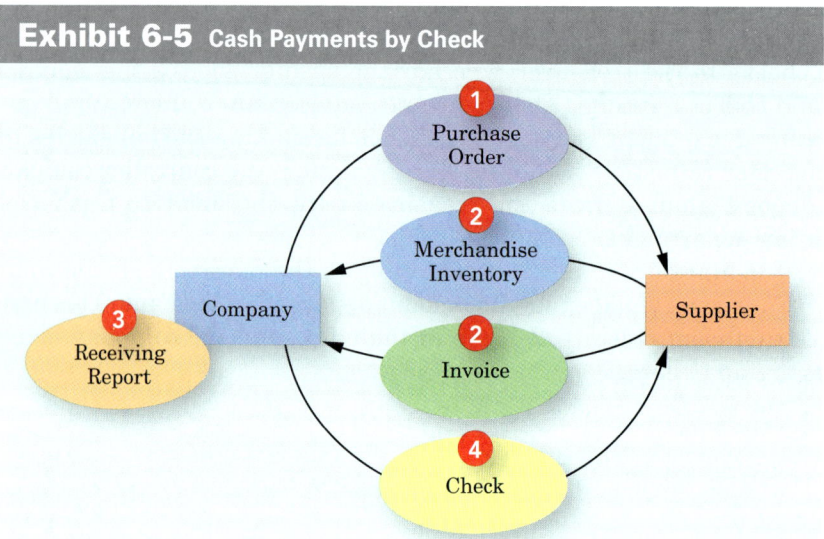

Exhibit 6-5 Cash Payments by Check

For good internal control, the **purchasing agent**, the individual who buys the bikes, should neither receive the goods nor approve the payment. Otherwise, the purchasing agent could buy goods and have them shipped to his home. Or he can receive kickbacks from suppliers by having the supplier bill his employer too much, approving the payment and splitting the excess with the supplier. The **controller**, as the person responsible for the accounting function, should not sign the checks for similar reasons; she could sign a check payable to herself then manipulate the accounting records to hide this improper payment.

Before signing the check, the **treasurer**, who usually assumes responsibility for the custody of cash, should examine each set of documents including the purchase order, receiving report, purchase invoice, and check to prove that they agree. Only then does the company know that:

1. The goods it received were the goods it ordered, as proved by the purchase order and receiving report.

2. It is paying only for the goods ordered and received, as proved by the purchase order, receiving report, invoice, and check.

After payment, the check signer should deface the set of documents, perhaps by punching a hole through the payment packet. Dishonest people have been known to submit the same bill and supporting documents twice for payment; for example, one payment could get sent to the supplier, and the other could be intercepted and fraudulently cashed. This hole or defacement confirms the bill has been paid and prevents the documents from generating a second payment on the same amount due the supplier.

STREAMLINED PAYMENT PROCEDURES

Technology is streamlining payment procedures. **Evaluated receipts settlement (ERS)** compresses the approval process for payment into a single step: comparing the receiving report to the purchase order. If those documents match, the matching proves that the business got the items it ordered. The business then pays the supplier without receiving an invoice.

An even more streamlined process bypasses people and documents altogether. In **electronic data interchange (EDI)**, Wal-Mart's computers communicate directly with the computers of suppliers such as Procter & Gamble and Hershey Foods. When Wal-Mart's inventory of Hershey chocolate candy reaches a low level, the computer sends a purchase order to Hershey. Hershey ships the candy and invoices Wal-Mart electronically. Then an **electronic funds transfer (EFT)** sends Wal-Mart's payment to Hershey via electronic communication.

The Bank Account

Keeping cash in a **bank account** helps a **depositor**, or bank customer, control cash because banks have established practices for safeguarding customers' money. Several documents are used to control cash in a bank account.

- Banks require that customers complete a **signature card** listing each person authorized to sign on an account. This card protects against forgery, because the bank can compare the signature on a check with the signature on the card to see that it is the same, and thus, the payment was properly authorized.

- Banks supply customers with **deposit tickets**, forms used to make bank deposits. The customer completes the deposit ticket by listing the items being deposited and the deposit total. As proof of the transaction, the customer keeps a **deposit receipt**.

- To pay cash, the business writes a check, which tells the bank to pay the designated party a specified amount of money. The three parties to a check include the following:

  - The **maker** who signs the check
  - The **payee** to whom the check is paid
  - The bank that holds the account on which the check is drawn

- Banks send monthly statements to customers. A monthly **bank statement** is a document that reports the changes in the depositor's cash account for a period of time. The statement shows the account's beginning and ending balances, receipts, and payments. Generally the maker's **canceled checks** are included with the statement, although this is becoming less common.

- A **bank reconciliation** is an internal control that identifies and explains the differences between a depositor's cash records and the bank's records of this cash. The bank reconciliation serves as an internal control because this comparison allows the depositor to arrive at the same, correct amount of cash according to both records. Differences between the records arise because of

  - Timing differences between the time when the bank records a transaction and when the depositor records it.
  - Errors made by either the bank or the depositor.

Exhibit 6-6 shows a check drawn by Business Research, Inc., the maker.

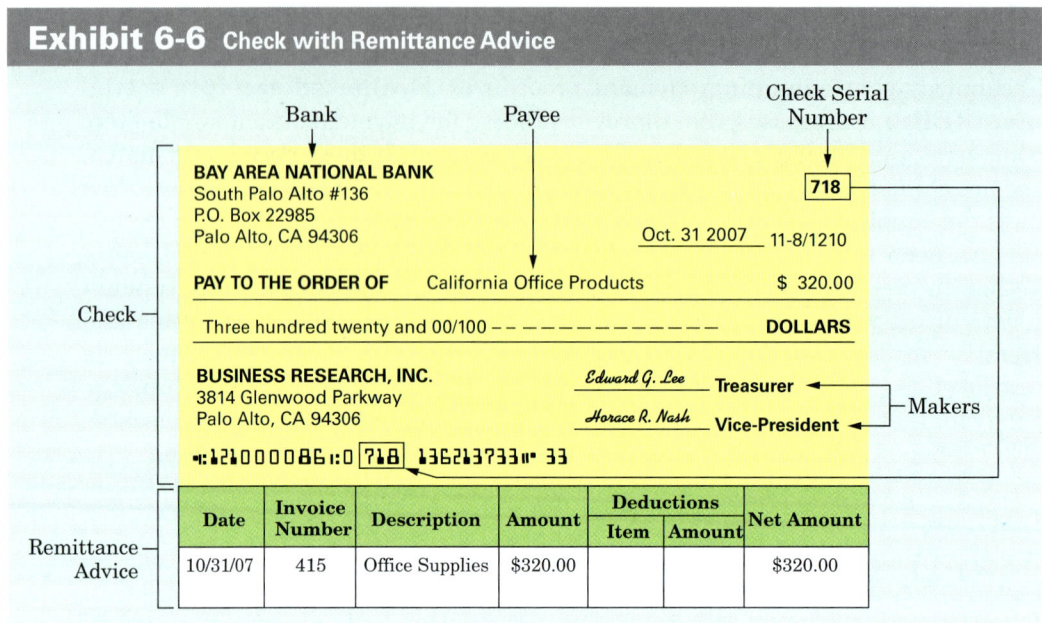

Exhibit 6-6 Check with Remittance Advice

Preparing the Bank Reconciliation

The basic format, showing items that typically appear on a bank reconciliation, is illustrated in Exhibit 6-7. They all cause differences between the bank balance and the **book balance**, the balance according to the company's accounting records. When establishing the procedures for a bank reconciliation, keep in mind our discussion of separation of duties; the person who prepares the bank reconciliation should have no other responsibilities related to cash. Otherwise, the bank reconciler could steal cash and manipulate the reconciliation to conceal the theft.

BANK SIDE OF THE RECONCILIATION

When preparing a bank reconciliation, show the following items on the bank side of the reconciliation:

1. **Deposits in transit** are deposits that the business has recorded but the bank has not. Add deposits in transit to the bank balance.

2. **Outstanding checks** are checks that the business has recorded but the bank has not yet paid. Subtract outstanding checks from the bank balance.

3. Bank errors include the bank recording a deposit or a check that belongs in another bank customer's account. The bank must correct the errors that it has made. Adjust the bank balance for the amount of the error, adding or subtracting as necessary depending on the nature of the error.

BOOK SIDE OF THE RECONCILIATION

Show the following items on the book side of the reconciliation:

1. **Bank collections** are cash collections made by the bank on behalf of the depositor. Many businesses have their customers pay their bank directly. One way customers make payment is through a **lock-box system** in which they send their payments to a business's post office box.

Exhibit 6-7 Summary of a Bank Reconciliation

- Bank collections
- Electronic fund transfers (EFT)
- Interest revenue

- Electronic fund transfers (EFT)
- Nonsufficient funds checks
- Cost of printed checks
- Service charges

Bank Reconciliation			
Bank		**Books**	
Month-end cash balance according to the bank statement	$ XX	Month-end cash balance according to the ledger account	$ XX
Add:		Add:	
Deposits in transit	XX	Additions to bank account not recorded on the books	XX
Bank errors	XX	Book errors	XX
Less:		Less:	
Outstanding checks	(XX)	Deductions to bank account not recorded on the books	(XX)
Bank errors	(XX)	Book errors	(XX)
Adjusted bank balance	$ XX	Adjusted book balance	$ XX

The company has recorded these deposits, but the bank has not yet received them.

The company has recorded these checks, but the bank has not yet paid them.

Bank must correct bank errors.

Company must correct book errors by making journal entries for any reconciling items on the books side of reconciliation.

The bank then collects payments from the box and deposits them in the business's account, thus reducing the chance of theft. Another example is a bank collection of a depositor's note receivable. Because the bank statement is often the first communication that cash was received, the business has not yet recorded the receipt. Add these collections to the book balance.

2. Electronic fund transfers occur when the bank receives or pays cash on the depositor's behalf electronically. Because the bank statement is the first communication of the transactions, adjust the book balance accordingly for the cash receipt or cash payment.

3. Interest revenue may be earned on an account depending on the balance in that account. Add interest revenue to the book balance.

4. **Nonsufficient funds (NSF) checks** are cash receipts of the depositor that have turned out to be worthless because the makers of the checks did not have sufficient funds in their accounts to pay the checks. Subtract these amounts from the book balance to reverse the cash deposit amount made earlier.

5. The cost of printed checks is deducted from an account when new checks are printed. Subtract this cost from the book balance.

6. Service charges are the bank's fees for processing transactions. Subtract these amounts from the book balance.

7. Book errors include mistakes made in recording cash transactions. For example, an error might involve recording a check in the accounting records for a different amount than the check was written. Another mistake might be failing to record a deposit made. Adjust the book balance for the amount of the error, adding or subtracting as necessary depending on the nature of the error.

BANK RECONCILIATION ILLUSTRATED

Exhibit 6-8 is the January bank statement of Business Research, Inc. The summary at the top shows the beginning balance, total deposits, total withdrawals, service charges, and the resulting ending balance. Details of the transactions for the month appear on the statement below this summary. The statement shows that the January 31 bank balance of Business Research, Inc., is $5,875. However, the company's Cash account has a balance of $3,147, as shown in Exhibit 6-9.

The bank reconciliation in Exhibit 6-10 identifies and explains the differences in these balances, thus determining the correct Cash balance at the end of January. Exhibit 6-10, panel A, lists the reconciling items, and panel B shows the completed reconciliation.

Notice that the cash payments appear as one deduction, or credit, to the Cash account in the general ledger to make the process more efficient because businesses often write and record many checks at once.

JOURNALIZING TRANSACTIONS FROM THE RECONCILIATION

The bank reconciliation is an accountant's tool that is separate from the journal and ledger. Even though it identifies any necessary adjustments to these records, preparing a reconciliation does not change the cash or any other balance in the accounting records. To record the transactions into accounts, we must make journal entries and post them to the accounts in the ledger. *All items on the book side of the bank reconciliation require journal entries.*

Exhibit 6-8 Bank Statement

BAY AREA NATIONAL BANK

Business Research, Inc.
3814 Glenwood Parkway
Palo Alto, CA 94306

CHECKING ACCOUNT 136-213733

CHECKING ACCOUNT SUMMARY AS OF 1/31/2008

BEGINNING BALANCE	TOTAL DEPOSITS	TOTAL WITHDRAWALS	SERVICE CHARGES	ENDING BALANCE
6,500	4,362	4,972	15	5,875

DEPOSITS	DATE	AMOUNT
Deposits	4-Jan	1,000
Deposits	4-Jan	112
Deposits	8-Jan	200
EFT-Rent	17-Jan	905
Bank collection	26-Jan	2,115
Interest	31-Jan	30

CHARGES	DATE	AMOUNT
Service charges	31-Jan	15

CHECKS

Number	Amount
956	100
732	3,000
733	160
734	100
735	100
736	1,100

DAILY BALANCE

Date	Balance	Date	Balance
31-Dec	6,500	20-Jan	4,845
4-Jan	7,560	26-Jan	6,960
6-Jan	7,360	31-Jan	5,875
8-Jan	7,560		
10-Jan	7,460		
17-Jan	5,205		

OTHER CHARGES	DATE	AMOUNT
NSF	4-Jan	52
EFT-Insurance	20-Jan	360

MONTHLY SUMMARY

Withdrawals: 8	Minimum Balance: 4,845	Average Balance: 6,085

Exhibit 6-9 Cash Records of Business Research, Inc.

General Ledger:

Cash						Account No. 111
		Post			**Balance**	
Date	**Item**	**Ref.**	**Debit**	**Credit**	**Debit**	**Credit**
2008						
Jan. 1	Balance				6,500	
2		J. 30	1,112		7,612	
7		J. 30	200		7,812	
31		J. 32		6,265	1,547	
31		J. 32	1,600		3,147	

continued . . . . .

Exhibit 6-9 Continued

Cash Payments:

Check No.	Amount	Check No.	Amount
732	$ 3,000	738	$ 320
733	610	739	85
734	100	740	205
735	100	741	460
736	1,100		
737	285	Total	$ 6,265

The journal entries listed here bring the Cash account up-to-date as a result of completing the reconciliation. The letters of the entries correspond to the letters of the reconciling items listed in Exhibit 6-10, Panel A.

Entry (i), the entry for the NSF check, needs explanation. Upon learning that L. Ross's $52 check was not good, Cash must be credited to update the Cash account. Unfortunately, the funds are still receivable from Ross, so Accounts Receivable—L. Ross must be debited to reestablish the amount due from Ross.

Journal Entry:

Date	Accounts	Post Ref.	Dr.	Cr.
Jan. 31	d. Cash		905	
	Rent Revenue			905
	Record receipt of monthly rent.			
31	e. Cash		2,115	
	Notes Receivable			2,000
	Interest Revenue			115
	Record note receivable and interest collected by bank.			
31	f. Cash		30	
	Interest Revenue			30
	Record interest earned on bank balance.			
31	g. Cash		450	
	Accounts payable—Brown Co.			450
	Correct recording of check no. 733.			
31	h. Miscellaneous Expense		15	
	Cash			15
	Record bank service charge.			
31	i. Accounts Receivable—L. Ross		52	
	Cash			52
	Record NSF check returned by bank.			
31	j. Insurance Expense		360	
	Cash			360
	Record payment of monthly insurance premium.			

Exhibit 6-10 Bank Reconciliation

PANEL A—Reconciling Items

a. Deposit in transit: $1,600
b. Bank error: The bank mistakenly deducted $100 for a check written by another company. Add $100 to bank balance because this balance will be $100 higher once the bank fixes its error.
c. Outstanding checks:

Check No.	Amount
737	$285
738	320
739	85
740	205
741	460

d. EFT receipt of rent revenue: $905
e. Bank collection of a note receivable: $2,115, which includes interest revenue of $115
f. Interest revenue earned on bank balance: $30
g. Book error: Check no. 733 for $160 paid to Brown Company on account, was recorded as $610; add $450 to the book balance.
h. Bank service charge: $15
i. NSF check from L. Ross: $52
j. EFT payment of insurance expense: $360

PANEL B—Completed Reconciliation

BUSINESS RESEARCH, INC.
Bank Reconciliation
January 31, 2008

Bank		Books	
Balance, January 31	$ 5,875	Balance, January 31	$ 3,147
Add:		Add:	
a. Deposit of January 31 in transit	1,600	d. EFT receipt of rent revenue	905
b. Correction of bank error	100	e. Bank collection of note receivable, $2,000 plus	
	7,575	interest revenue of $115	2,115
		f. Interest revenue earned on bank balance	30
Less:		g. Correction of book error—overstated our	
c. Outstanding checks		check no. 733 ($610 – $160)	450
No. 737	(285)		6,647
No. 738	(320)	Less:	
No. 739	(85)	h. Service charge	(15)
No. 740	(205)	i. NSF check	(52)
No. 741	(460)	j. EFT payment of insurance expense	(360)
Adjusted bank balance	$ 6,220	Adjusted book balance	$ 6,220

These amounts must agree, or the reconciliation is not complete.

Here is a summary of how to treat the reconciling items encountered most often:

Bank Balance—Always:	Book Balance—Always:
• *Add* deposits in transit.	• *Add* bank collections, interest revenue, and EFT receipts.
• *Subtract* outstanding checks.	• *Subtract* NSF checks, the cost of printed checks, services, charges, and EFT payments.
• *Add* or *subtract* corrections of bank errors.	• *Add* or *subtract* corrections of book errors.

THE BANK RECONCILIATION AS AN INTERNAL CONTROL

The bank reconciliation can be a powerful control device, as the following example illustrates.

Imagine that Vaughn owns apartment complexes that his aunt manages. Vaughn's aunt signs up tenants, collects the monthly rent, arranges custodial work, hires and fires employees, writes the checks, and performs the bank reconciliation. This concentration of duties in one person does not provide internal control for the business. Vaughn's aunt could be stealing from him. Although this suspicion may sound harsh, a reality of business is that employees thought to be trustworthy may be engaging in fraud, even if they are relatives.

So Vaughn exercises some internal controls other than separation of duties over his aunt's activities. Periodically, he drops by his properties to see whether the apartments are in good condition. To control cash, Vaughn relies on the bank reconciliations. On an unpredictable basis, he examines the bank reconciliations prepared by his aunt. He examines every paid check and matches it to the journal entry on the books. Vaughn would know immediately if his aunt were writing checks to herself. Vaughn sometimes prepares his own bank reconciliation to see whether he agrees with his aunt's work. To keep his aunt on her toes, Vaughn lets her know that he periodically reviews her work.

Vaughn also has a simple method for controlling cash receipts. He knows the occupancy level of his apartments; that is, he knows how many apartments are rented. He also knows the monthly rent he charges. He multiplies the number of apartments, say 100, by the monthly rent, which averages $500 per unit, to arrive at expected monthly rent revenue of $50,000. By tracing the $50,000 revenue to the bank statement, Vaughn can tell that his rent money went into his bank account.

Control activities such as these are critical in small businesses. With only a few employees, a separation of duties may not be feasible. The owner should oversee the operations of the business, or the assets can slip away.

Online Banking

Online banking allows businesses to pay bills and view account activity electronically. The company doesn't have to wait until the end of the month to get a bank statement. With online banking, the account can be reconciled at any time and kept current. Exhibit 6-11 shows a page from the account history of Toni Anderson's bank account.

Exhibit 6-11 On-Line Banking—Account History (like a Bank Statement)

Account History for Toni Anderson Checking # 5401-632-9
As of Close of Business 07/27/2008

Account Details

Current Balance $ 4,136.08

Date	Description	Withdrawals	Deposits	Balance
	Current Balance			$ 4,136.08
07/27/08	DEPOSIT		1,170.35	
07/26/08	28 DAYS–INTEREST		2.26	
07/25/08	Check #6131 view image	443.83		
07/24/08	Check #6130 view image	401.52		
07/23/08	EFT PYMT CINGULAR	61.15		
07/22/08	EFT PYMT CITICARD PAYMENT	3,172.85		
07/20/08	Check #6127 view image	550.00		
07/15/08	DEPOSIT		9,026.37	

The account history is like a bank statement since it lists all transactions including deposits, checks, EFT receipts and payments, ATM withdrawals, and interest earned on the bank balance. Because of this, it can be used as a bank statement to reconcile the bank account.

Petty Cash

A business may choose to keep a **petty cash** fund, which is a fund containing a small amount of cash used to pay for minor expenditures, such as the purchase of postage stamps or a shipment of a small package. Cash is easy to steal and the thief is often able to do so without leaving evidence. For this reason, petty cash funds need controls such as the following:

Record journal entries for the petty cash fund.

- Designate a custodian for the petty cash fund to fix responsibility for the fund.
- Establish the fund as an **imprest account** by keeping a specific, fixed amount of cash on hand so that any missing amount can be easily identified.
- Keep the fund in a safe, locked location and only allow the custodian to have access to the fund.
- Support all payments from the fund with a written record documenting the purpose and amount of the payment.

Setting Up the Petty Cash Fund

Businesses establish a petty cash fund by writing a check for the designated amount, usually between $200 and $500, depending on the size and the needs of the business. They typically make the check payable to Petty Cash, cash the check, and place the money in the fund. Every business may have its own form for documenting petty cash payments, but the form is usually signed by the recipient of the petty cash and the custodian to verify the transaction. *The cash in the fund plus the total of the payment forms should equal the fund balance at all times.*

Suppose that Corner Drug Store established a petty cash fund of $300 on October 31. The journal entry to record the creation of the fund is:

Journal Entry:

Date	Accounts	Post Ref.	Dr.	Cr.
Oct. 31	Petty Cash		300	
	Cash			300
	Open the petty cash fund.			

Now imagine that Sam K. Moore, the fund custodian, approved a cash payment to Jeff Snow on November 7 to reimburse Jeff for the $40 of pens he purchased for the store. Sam prepared a record of the disbursement, much like the **petty cash ticket** in Exhibit 6-12, and both he and Jeff signed it. Sam kept the form in the fund as a replacement for the cash taken.

Exhibit 6-12 Petty Cash Ticket

PETTY CASH TICKET

Date Nov. 7, 2008   No. 47

Amount $40.00

For Ink pens

Debit Office Supplies, Acct. No. 145

Received by *Jeff Snow*   Fund Custodian SKM

Replenishing the Petty Cash Fund

Payments deplete the fund, so periodically it must be replenished. On November 30 the petty cash fund of Corner Drug Store holds the following:

- $212 in petty cash
- $88 in petty cash tickets: office supplies, $40; delivery expense, $48

Comparing the $300 cash fund's required balance to the total of cash on hand and petty cash tickets, the petty cash fund can be accounted for as follows:

Fund Balance	$300
Cash on Hand	$212
+ Petty Cash Tickets	88
= Total Accounted for	$300

To replenish the petty cash fund and make the cash on hand equal to $300 again, the company writes a check, payable to Petty Cash, for the $88 spent. The fund custodian cashes this check and puts $88 back in the fund. Now the fund holds $300 cash as required by the imprest system.

The petty cash tickets provide the information necessary to make the journal entry to replenish the fund:

Journal Entry:

Date	Accounts	Post Ref.	Dr.	Cr.
Nov. 30	Office Supplies		40	
	Delivery Expense		48	
	Cash			88
	Replenish the petty cash fund.			

Notice that the journal entry included a credit to Cash, not Petty Cash, because the money to replenish the petty cash fund was taken from the Cash account.

Because of the imprest system, the Petty Cash account keeps its balance, in this case $300, at all times. Petty Cash is debited when

- The petty cash fund is established.
- The petty cash fund imprest balance is increased.

Changing the Petty Cash Fund

Imagine that Corner Drug Store wants to increase the size of its fund from $300 to $500 on December 2. The business writes a $200 check payable to Petty Cash, and the custodian cashes it and places the money in the fund. In this case, the journal entry to record this $200 increase will look like the following:

Journal Entry:

Date	Accounts	Post Ref.	Dr.	Cr.
Dec. 2	Petty Cash		200	
	Cash			200
	Increase the petty cash fund from $300 to $500.			

Reporting Cash on the Balance Sheet

5 Report cash on the balance sheet.

Remember from our discussion of the classified balance sheet in Chapter 4 that Cash is the first asset listed because it's the most liquid. Businesses often have several bank accounts and several petty cash funds, but they customarily combine all cash amounts into a single total. On the balance sheet, this total may be called Cash, or it may be listed as **Cash and Cash Equivalents**.

Cash on the balance sheet includes coin, currency, checks on hand, petty cash, checking accounts, payroll checking accounts, money orders, and traveler's checks. In short, cash consists of anything that a bank will take as a deposit.

Cash equivalents include very liquid, very safe short-term investments that so closely resemble cash that they are included with cash on the balance sheet. These items are liquid because they can readily be converted into cash, and are safe because they have little risk of losing their value. They include time deposits, money market funds, certificates of deposit, and U.S. Treasury bills and Treasury notes. Although Treasury bills and Treasury notes and other cash equivalents can have maturity dates, they are considered cash equivalents if they mature within 90 days of the balance sheet date.

Cash that is restricted should not be reported as a current asset. For example, the bank may require a business to keep a **compensating balance** on deposit as a condition of borrowing money from the bank. If the balance is held as a requirement of a long-term borrowing, then the compensating balance is not included in the cash amount on the balance sheet because it is not available for immediate use.

The balance sheet of Ikard's Part Store reported the following current assets. The store's Cash and Cash Equivalents balance means that the store has $800 available for immediate use.

Ikard's Part Store Balance Sheet December 31, 2008	
Assets	
Current assets:	
Cash and cash equivalents	$ 800
Short-term investments	1,000
Accounts receivable	2,000
Inventory	3,600
Prepaid insurance	400
Total current assets	7,800

Demo Doc

Bank Reconciliations

Learning Objective 3

Chanty Partners had a balance of $5,000 in its Cash account at May 31, 2008. Chanty's bank statement for the month ended May 31, 2008, showed a balance of $4,600. The following differences between Chanty's records and the bank records were found:

a. Chanty had a $2,000 EFT payment on a loan payable. Of this amount, $300 was interest and $1,700 was a principal payment.

b. Outstanding checks totaled $2,400.

c. On May 16, Chanty deposited a check for $250 from a customer. The check was returned for insufficient funds (NSF) in the customer's account.

d. The NSF check described in transaction c resulted in a service fee of $30 charged to Chanty's account.

e. Chanty had deposits in transit of $1,200.

f. Chanty earned interest of $100 on its account.

g. A customer paid its account (total $490) with Chanty via EFT.

h. Chanty accidentally recorded a check written to the Electric Company for $120 as:

Journal Entry:

Date	Accounts	Post Ref.	Dr.	Cr.
May 20	Utilities Expense		210	
	Cash			210
	Record utilities expense.			

Requirements

1. Prepare Chanty's bank reconciliation for the month ended May 31, 2008.

2. Prepare all adjusting journal entries necessary for Chanty as a result of the reconciliation.

Demo Doc Solutions

③ Apply internal controls for cash and prepare a bank reconciliation.

Prepare Chanty's bank reconciliation for the month ended May 31, 2008.

Part 1	Part 2	Demo Doc Complete

Every bank reconciliation has two sides: one for the bank and one for the business doing the reconciliation. The first step is to set up these two sides and fill in the beginning balances.

Bank		Books (Chanty)	
Balance, May 31	$4,600	Balance, May 31	$5,000

Each of the differences between these two records is a reconciling item. The reason a difference exists is because *one side has already recorded the item, while the other has not*. So for each difference (reconciling item), we need to think about which side has recorded the item already and which has not. The side that has *not* yet recorded the item will need to list it on the bank reconciliation (except for errors, which we will address later in this question).

Each side can have items added to the balance or subtracted from the balance. So each side will have an "Add" and a "Less" section:

Bank		Books (Chanty)	
Balance, May 31	$4,600	Balance, May 31	$5,000
Add:		Add:	
Less:		Less:	

Now we must go through each item and determine where to put it on the reconciliation.

a. Chanty had a $2,000 EFT payment on a loan payable. Of this amount, $300 was interest and $1,700 was a principal payment.

EFT payments are made automatically by the bank, which means that the bank has already recorded this item. However, Chanty has not recorded it. We need to put this $2,000 payment on Chanty's side of the reconciliation.

Will this item increase or decrease Chanty's Cash account? It is a payment Chanty is making, so it will decrease Cash and needs to be subtracted on the reconciliation.

Bank		Books (Chanty)	
Balance, May 31	$4,600	Balance, May 31	$5,000
Add:		Add:	
Less:		Less:	
		EFT payment on loan payable	(2,000)

b. Outstanding checks totaled $2,400.

These outstanding checks were written by Chanty, but they have not been cashed yet at the bank. Chanty has recorded them but the bank has not.

Will this item increase or decrease Chanty's bank account? Checks are payments of cash to other people or businesses, so they will decrease the bank account. The outstanding checks will be subtracted on the reconciliation.

Bank		Books (Chanty)	
Balance, May 31	$4,600	Balance, May 31	$5,000
Add:		Add:	
Less:		Less:	
Outstanding checks	(2,400)	EFT payment on loan payable	(2,000)

c. On May 16, Chanty deposited a check for $250 from a customer. The check was returned for insufficient funds (NSF) in the customer's account.

When Chanty deposited the check, it increased the Cash account. However, the check was NSF and these funds were never deposited to Chanty's bank account. The bank knows about this NSF and has already recorded it, but Chanty has not.

Will this item increase or decrease Chanty's Cash account? The cash deposit never occurred, so when it is reversed in Chanty's books, it decreases Cash. It is subtracted on the reconciliation.

Bank		Books (Chanty)	
Balance, May 31	$4,600	Balance, May 31	$5,000
Add:		Add:	
Less:		Less:	
Outstanding checks	(2,400)	EFT payment on loan payable	(2,000)
		NSF check	(250)

d. The NSF check described in transaction c resulted in a service fee of $30 charged to Chanty's account.

The bank charged the fee and already recorded it. Chanty must now record the fee.

Will this item increase or decrease Chanty's bank account? Fees are expenses to Chanty and will decrease the bank account. It will be subtracted on the reconciliation.

Bank		Books (Chanty)	
Balance, May 31	$4,600	Balance, May 31	$5,000
Add:		Add:	
Less:		Less:	
Outstanding checks	(2,400)	EFT payment on loan payable	(2,000)
		NSF check	(250)
		Service fees	(30)

e. Chanty had deposits in transit of $1,200.

These deposits in transit were made by Chanty, but they have not been recorded yet at the bank.

Will these deposits increase or decrease Chanty's bank account? Deposits increase a bank account. This item will be added on the reconciliation.

Bank		Books (Chanty)	
Balance, May 31	$4,600	Balance, May 31	$5,000
Add:		Add:	
Deposits in transit	1,200		
Less:		Less:	
Outstanding checks	(2,400)	EFT payment on loan payable	(2,000)
		NSF check	(250)
		Service fees	(30)

f. Chanty earned interest of $100 on its account.

The interest is calculated and recorded by the bank. Chanty has not yet recorded this item.

Will interest increase or decrease Chanty's Cash account? Interest earned is revenue to Chanty, so it increases its Cash and is added on the reconciliation.

Bank		Books (Chanty)	
Balance, May 31	$4,600	Balance, May 31	$5,000
Add:		Add:	
Deposits in transit	1,200	Interest earned on bank balance	100
Less:		Less:	
Outstanding checks	(2,400)	EFT payment on loan payable	(2,000)
		NSF check	(250)
		Service fees	(30)

g. A customer paid its account (total $490) with Chanty via EFT.

EFT collections are recorded automatically by the bank. The customer paid Chanty, which means that the bank collected the cash on Chanty's behalf. The bank has already recorded this item, but Chanty has not.

Will this EFT collection increase or decrease Chanty's Cash account? The collection is a deposit, so it will increase Chanty's bank account. It will be added on the reconciliation.

Bank		Books (Chanty)	
Balance, May 31	$4,600	Balance, May 31	$5,000
Add:		Add:	
Deposits in transit	1,200	Interest earned on bank balance	100
		EFT collection from customer	490
Less:		Less:	
Outstanding checks	(2,400)	EFT payment on loan payable	(2,000)
		NSF check	(250)
		Service fees	(30)

h. Chanty accidentally recorded a check written to the Electric Company for $120 as:

Journal Entry:

Date	Accounts	Post Ref.	Dr.	Cr.
May 20	Utilities Expense		210	
	Cash			210
	Record utilities expense.			

This reconciling item is not the same as the others. The other items were legitimate differences that needed to be recorded, but this item is an error. *Errors are corrected by the side that made them.*

In this case, the check was written for $120, but the journal entry accidentally recorded the wrong amount of $210. Because the payment amount was recorded incorrectly, $90 ($210 – $120) too much was recorded as an expense. This extra $90 must be reversed by Chanty.

The original entry to record the payment decreased the Cash account, so reversing some of that entry will increase the Cash account. So the difference is added on the reconciliation.

Bank		Books (Chanty)	
Balance, May 31	$4,600	Balance, May 31	$5,000
Add:		Add:	
Deposits in transit	1,200	Interest earned on bank balance	100
		EFT collection from customer	490
		Correction of error	90
Less:		Less:	
Outstanding checks	(2,400)	EFT payment on loan payable	(2,000)
		NSF check	(250)
		Service fees	(30)

Now that we have gone through all of the reconciling items, we must add a title and total up both sides of the reconciliation.

Chanty Partners
Bank Reconciliation
May 31, 2008

Bank		Books (Chanty)	
Balance, May 31	$4,600	Balance, May 31	$5,000
Add:		Add:	
Deposits in transit	1,200	Interest earned on bank balance	100
		EFT collection from customer	490
		Correction of error	90
Less:		Less:	
Outstanding checks	(2,400)	EFT payment on loan payable	(2,000)
		NSF check	(250)
		Service fees	(30)
Adjusted bank balance	$3,400	Adjusted book balance	$3,400

The two adjusted balances are the same, which indicates that we have found all of the reconciling items.

Requirement 2

Prepare all adjusting journal entries necessary for Chanty as a result of the reconciliation.

Part 1	Part 2	Demo Doc Complete

Every item on Chanty's side of the reconciliation is a journal entry that must be recorded to adjust Chanty's Cash account to its correct balance.

a. Chanty had a $2,000 EFT payment on a loan payable. Of this amount, $300 was interest and $1,700 was a principal payment.

The interest portion of the payment is an increase to Interest Expense (a debit), while the principal is a payment of the loan itself, causing a decrease to the Loan Payable account (a debit). Because the payment is subtracted from Chanty's reconciliation, we know that it decreases Cash (a credit).

Journal Entry:

Date	Accounts	Post Ref.	Dr.	Cr.
May 31	Interest Expense (Expense, ↑; debit)		300	
	Loan Payable (Liability, ↓; debit)		1,700	
	Cash (Asset, ↓; credit)			2,000
	Record payment of principal and interest			
	on loan payable.			

b. Outstanding checks totaled $2,400.

Checks that have not yet cleared the bank do not require an adjustment by Chanty. This adjustment will be made by the *bank* as the checks are processed.

c. On May 16, Chanty deposited a check for $250 from a customer. The check was returned for insufficient funds (NSF) in the customer's account.

When Chanty recorded the deposit, it decreased (credited) the Accounts Receivable asset and increased (debited) Cash. Because the deposit was not valid due to insufficient funds, the Accounts Receivable must be reinstated, or increased (debit), and Cash must be decreased (credit).

Journal Entry:

Date	Accounts	Post Ref.	Dr.	Cr.
May 31	Accounts Receivable (Asset, ↑; debit)		250	
	Cash (Asset, ↓; credit)			250
	Record NSF check from customer.			

d. The NSF check described in item c resulted in a service fee of $30 charged to Chanty's account.

The service fee is an expense for Chanty. It increases (debit) Miscellaneous Expense. Because the fee is subtracted from Chanty's reconciliation, we know that it decreases Cash (a credit).

Journal Entry:

Date	Accounts	Post Ref.	Dr.	Cr.
May 31	Miscellaneous Expense (Expense, ↑; debit)		30	
	Cash (Asset, ↓; credit)			30
	Record bank service charge.			

e. Chanty had deposits in transit of $1,200.

Deposits that have not yet been recorded by the bank do not require an adjustment by Chanty. This adjustment will be made by the *bank* as the deposits are processed.

f. Chanty earned interest of $100 on its account.

The interest earned is interest revenue. It is an increase to Interest Revenue (a credit). Because it is added to Chanty's reconciliation, we know that it increases Cash (a debit).

Journal Entry:

Date	Accounts	Post Ref.	Dr.	Cr.
May 31	Cash (Asset, ↑; debit)		100	
	Interest Revenue (Revenue, ↑; credit)			100
	Record interest revenue earned on bank account.			

g. A customer paid its account (total $490) with Chanty via EFT.

When a collection is made from a customer that owes Chanty money, Accounts Receivable is decreased (a credit). Because it is added to Chanty's reconciliation, we know that Cash is increased (a debit).

Journal Entry:

Date	Accounts	Post Ref.	Dr.	Cr.
May 31	Cash (Asset, ↑; debit)		490	
	Accounts Receivable (Asset, ↓; credit)			490
	Record cash collected from customer.			

h. Chanty accidentally recorded a check written to the Electric Company for $120 as:

Journal Entry:

Date	Accounts	Post Ref.	Dr.	Cr.
May 20	Utilities Expense		210	
	Cash			210
	Record utilities expense.			

The incorrect entry originally debited Utilities Expense and credited Cash. Because $90 of this entry is being reversed, the exact opposite entry must be made. We credit Utilities Expense and debit Cash.

Journal Entry:

Date	Accounts	Post Ref.	Dr.	Cr.
May 31	Cash (Asset, ↑; debit)		90	
	Utilities Expense (Expense, ↓; credit)			90
	Correct error.			

Part 1	Part 2	Demo Doc Complete

Accounting in Action

INTERNAL CONTROL AND CASH

Successful businesses need good internal control including procedures to prevent the loss of assets such as cash and to promote accurate financial reporting. Here are some deci-

sions you might encounter while establishing a system of internal control and accounting for cash in your business:

Decision	Guidelines
What is fraud? What are the two types?	Fraud is *deceit or trickery causing financial* harm. The accounting profession believes that fraud involves *intentional actions that result in a misstatement of the financial statements*. The two types are: • Misappropriation of assets • Fraudulent financial reporting
What is the difference between employee fraud and management fraud?	*Employee embezzlement* can include stealing cash or other assets, taking of kickbacks from suppliers or customers, or submitting a false document that results in payment from the employer as in check tampering, cash register schemes, and expense schemes. *Management fraud* involves the manipulation of financial information so that the business looks more profitable than it really is. Managers may record revenues prematurely or fictitiously, or understate expenses.
Why does a business need internal controls?	Internal controls *reduce the risk of fraud* by setting policies and procedures that help the business: • Safeguard assets and report financial information properly • Operate efficiently and effectively • Comply with applicable laws and regulations
What control activities need to exist in a business?	• Separation of duties • Physical safeguards • Proper authorization procedures • Adequate documents and records • Independent checks on performance
Why reconcile the Cash account?	Reconcile Cash to bring into agreement • The balance according to the bank • The balance according to the books, or accounting records, of the business and thus *determine the correct amount of cash owned*.
Why do differences appear in the cash balance per the bank and the cash balance per books?	Differences result from • *Timing differences* from items recorded on one set of records but not yet on the other • *Errors* in the records made by the bank or by the company

Decision

How do I prepare a bank reconciliation?

Guidelines

Adjust the bank and book balances to bring them into agreement:

Adjusted bank balance = Bank balance + Deposits in transit − Outstanding checks ± Bank errors

Adjusted book balance = Book balance + Bank collections ± EFT transfers + Interest revenue − NSF checks − Cost of printed checks − Service charges ± Book errors

To determine the correct cash balance, the adjusted bank balance must equal the adjusted book balance.

Review

Internal Control and Cash
Word Power

Audit trail A trail of business documents and records that provides evidence of transactions.

Bank account An amount held on deposit at a bank used to execute cash transactions.

Bank collection Collection of money by the bank on behalf of a depositor.

Bank reconciliation A document that identifies and explains the differences between a depositor's record of a cash account and a bank's record of the same cash account.

Bank statement A document the bank prepares to report the changes in the depositor's cash account for a period of time: shows the beginning bank account balance, lists the month's cash transactions, and shows the ending bank account balance.

Book balance The balance in a company's bank account according to the company's accounting records, or books.

Cancelled checks Checks written and paid.

Cash Coin, currency, checks, petty cash, checking accounts, payroll accounts, money orders, traveler's checks, and anything the bank will accept as a deposit.

Cash and Cash Equivalents The balance sheet item used to describe cash and items so closely resembling cash that they are presented as cash.

Cash equivalents Highly liquid, highly safe investments that so closely resemble cash they may be shown with cash on the balance sheet.

Cash register schemes A fraud scheme in which an employee falsely documents a refund for returned merchandise and takes the cash refund amount, or accepts cash from a customer but does not record the sale transaction in the cash register.

Check A document that instructs a bank to pay the designated person or business a specified amount of money.

Check tampering A fraud scheme in which an employee writes a fraudulent check and makes the check payable to herself or himself, or obtains a check intended for an outside party, endorses the check, and then cashes it.

Compensating balance An amount held on deposit as a condition of borrowing money from a bank.

Control activities The policies and procedures of an internal control system.

Controller The individual in an organization responsible for the accounting system and financial statements.

Depositor A bank customer; one who holds a bank account.

Deposit receipt A document that proves a deposit was made.

Deposit ticket A document used to make a deposit to a bank account.

Deposit in transit A deposit recorded by the company but not yet by its bank.

Disbursement schemes A form of employee embezzlement in which an employee tricks a company into giving up cash for an invalid reason. Examples include check tampering, cash register schemes, and expense schemes.

Electronic data interchange (EDI) Direct electronic communication between suppliers and retailers.

Electronic funds transfer (EFT) System that transfers cash by electronic communication rather than by paper documents.

Employee embezzlement Fraud where employees steal from employers by taking assets, bribes, or kickbacks, or engaging in disbursement schemes to steal cash.

Evaluated receipts settlement (ERS) System in which payments to suppliers are automatically generated based on a matching of the purchase order and receiving report.

Expense schemes A fraud scheme in which an employee overbills the company for travel and other business-related expenses, such as lunches, hotels, air travel, parking fees, and cab fares.

External audit An audit of financial statements performed by Certified Public Accountants (CPAs).

Fraud Deceit or trickery involving intentional actions that cause harm to a business, its stakeholders, or both; according to the accounting profession, fraud results in misstatements of the financial statements.

Fraud triangle The combination of perceived pressure, perceived opportunity, and rationalization necessary to commit fraud.

Imprest account Establishment of a fixed balance in an account; a way to account for petty cash by maintaining a constant balance in the petty cash account, where the cash plus payment tickets always equal this constant balance.

Internal audit Assessment of a company's compliance with laws and regulations, operations, and policies and procedures performed by employees of the company.

Internal control The organizational plan and all related measures to safeguard assets, report financial information properly, operate efficiently and effectively, and comply with applicable laws and regulations.

Lock-box system A system in which customers send payments to a post office box of a business; the bank collects payments from the box and deposits them to the business's account.

Maker The party who signs a check, thus directing the bank to make payment to the payee.

Management fraud Management's intentional misstatement of the financial statements, driven by greed or the pressure to keep a job by showing owners that the business is more profitable than it really is.

Nonsufficient funds (NSF) check A check drawn against a bank account that has insufficient money to pay the check.

Outstanding check A check that has been issued by a company and recorded on its books but has not yet been paid by its bank.

Payee The party to a check to whom the bank makes payment.

Perceived opportunity An element of the fraud triangle in which the employee believes a chance exists to commit fraud, conceal it, and avoid punishment.

Perceived pressure An element of the fraud triangle in which the employee is motivated to obtain cash or other assets.

Petty cash Fund containing a small amount of cash that is used to pay for minor expenditures.

Petty cash ticket A form used to document expenditures from a petty cash fund.

Purchase order A document showing details of merchandise being ordered from a supplier.

Purchasing agent The individual in an organization responsible for buying items for that organization.

Rationalization An element of the fraud triangle in which the employee justifies his or her actions and convinces himself or herself that fraud is not wrong.

Receiving report A document evidencing the receipt of goods purchased.

Sarbanes-Oxley Act A law passed in 2002 by the U.S. Congress in response to recent, large-scale fraud in publicly owned companies.

Signature card Document used by a bank to identify authorized signers on a bank account.

Treasurer The individual in an organization responsible for the custody of assets such as cash.

Quick Check

1. Which of the following is necessary for fraud to occur?

   a. Perceived pressure
   b. Perceived opportunity
   c. Rationalization
   d. All three are necessary

2. On what element of the fraud triangle do most organizations usually focus their fraud prevention efforts?

   a. Perceived pressure
   b. Perceived opportunity
   c. Rationalization
   d. All three are targeted

3. Darice Goodrich receives cash from customers as part of her job duties. Her other duty is to post the receipts to customer accounts receivable. Based on these duties, her company has weak:

   a. Ethics
   b. Fraud triangle
   c. Separation of duties
   d. Disbursement schemes

4. Internal control is:

   a. The act of stealing a business's assets
   b. The preparation of fraudulent financial statements
   c. The process that helps a business achieve its objectives, such as operating efficiently and effectively
   d. The reconciliation of the bank's cash balance to the book's cash balance

5. The document that identifies and explains all differences between the company's record of cash and the bank's record of that cash is:

   a. Bank reconciliation
   b. Bank collection
   c. Bank statement
   d. Electronic fund transfer

6. Which item(s) appears as a reconciling item(s) to the book balance in a bank reconciliation?

   a. Outstanding checks
   b. Deposits in transit
   c. Both a and b
   d. None of the above

7. Which item(s) appears as a reconciling item(s) to the bank balance in a bank reconciliation?

    a. Outstanding checks
    b. Deposits in transit
    c. Both a and b
    d. None of the above

8. On its books, Navarro Company's Cash account shows an ending balance of $770. The bank statement for the current period shows a $20 service charge and an NSF check for $100. A $250 deposit is in transit, and outstanding checks total $400. What is Navarro's adjusted book balance for Cash?

    a. $530
    b. $650
    c. $680
    d. $1,050

9. After performing a bank reconciliation, journal entries are required for:

    a. All items on the bank side of the reconciliation
    b. All items on the book side of the reconciliation
    c. All items on the reconciliation
    d. No items from the reconciliation because the Cash account needs no adjustment

10. Separation of duties is important for internal control over:

    a. Cash receipts
    b. Cash payments
    c. Neither of the above
    d. Both a and b

Answers are given after Apply Your Knowledge (p. 347).

Accounting Practice

Short Exercises

1 Fraud and its different types.

S6-1. Identify each of the following as an example of a perceived pressure (P), perceived opportunity (O), or rationalization (R) in the fraud triangle:

  P   Job dissatisfaction

  ____   1. Greed

  ____   2. "It's for a good purpose."

  ____   3. Weak internal control

  ____   4. Gambling addiction

1 Fraud and its different types.

S6-2. Indicate by letters the type of fraud committed:

Check tampering (CT)

Cash register scheme (CR)

Expense scheme (E)

Bribe (B)

Fraudulent financial reporting (F)

  CT   Employee writes a fraudulent check making it payable to herself.

  ____   1. At the end of the year, the chief financial officer for Electra International recorded $100,000 in sales that had not been made.

  ____   2. Carrie is a cashier at a local restaurant. Once a day, she leaves the cash register open and does not record the sale in the cash register when she takes the customer's cash.

  ____   3. Harry's major customer in Iowa asked Harry to take 20% off of the sales price on the next shipment of jeans to their stores. In return, they will give him part of the money saved from the reduced sales price. Harry agrees to lower the price.

  ____   4. Frank Farmer, owner of Farmer Real Estate, asked the accountant to ignore any depreciation that should be recorded on assets owned.

  ____   5. Judson submits a cash reimbursement for a cab ride he never took.

2 Internal control.

S6-3. Indicate by letters which of the following control activities match with the following descriptions:

Separation of duties (SD)

Physical safeguards (PS)

continued . . . . .

Proper authorization (PA)

Adequate documents and records (ADR)

Independent checks on performance (ICP)

_____ 1. Preparation of a bank reconciliation

_____ 2. Locking inventory in a warehouse

_____ 3. Password protection of accounting software

_____ 4. Establishment of price lists

_____ 5. Not allowing the accounts payable clerk to sign checks

S6-4. Review the internal controls over cash receipts by mail. Exactly what is accomplished by the final step in the process, performed by the controller?

③ Applying internal controls for cash and preparing a bank reconciliation.

S6-5. A purchasing agent for Westgate Wireless receives the goods that he purchased and also approves payment for the goods. How could this purchasing agent cheat his company?

③ Applying internal controls for cash and preparing a bank reconciliation.

S6-6. For each of the following, indicate whether the item is an adjustment to the bank balance or the book balance:

③ Applying internal controls for cash and preparing a bank reconciliation.

_____ 1. Bank service charge

_____ 2. Deposit in transit

_____ 3. Bank collection of amount due from customer

_____ 4. Interest revenue on bank balance

_____ 5. Outstanding check

S6-7. For each of the following items, indicate whether the item increases the book balance (+), decreases the book balance (−), or has no effect (NE) on the book balance of Slater Meats:

③ Applying internal controls for cash and preparing a bank reconciliation.

_____ 1. An NSF check received from a customer

_____ 2. Bank service charge

_____ 3. Deposit in transit

_____ 4. Bank collection of a $500 note receivable

_____ 5. Interest revenue on bank balance

_____ 6. Outstanding checks

_____ 7. A check for $15 recorded as $51

S6-8. The Cash account of Mee Auto Services showed a balance of $2,500 on March 31, 2008. Outstanding checks totaled $900 and a March 31 deposit of $200 was still in transit. The bank statement, which came from Alamo Bank, listed a March 31 balance of $3,900. Included in the bank balance was a collection of $710 on account from Sandra Owens, a customer who
continued . . . . .

③ Applying internal controls for cash and preparing a bank reconciliation.

paid the bank directly. The bank statement also showed a $20 service charge and $10 of interest revenue that Mee earned on its bank balance. Prepare Mee Auto Service's bank reconciliation at March 31.

③ Applying internal controls for cash and preparing a bank reconciliation.

S6-9. After preparing Mee Auto Service's bank reconciliation in S6-8, make the necessary journal entries arising from the bank reconciliation. Date each entry March 31 and include an explanation with each entry.

④ Recording journal entries for petty cash.

S6-10. Record the following petty cash transactions of Handy Dan in the journal; explanations are not required.

Nov.	1	Established a petty cash fund with a $100 balance.
	30	The petty cash fund had $33 in cash and $67 in petty cash tickets that were issued to pay for postage. Replenished the fund with cash.

④ Recording journal entries for petty cash.

S6-11. Record the following petty cash transactions of Xeno Corp. in the journal; explanations are not required.

June	1	Established a petty cash fund with a $200 balance.
	30	The petty cash fund had $26 in cash and $174 in petty cash tickets that were issued to pay for office supplies ($104) and entertainment expense ($70). Replenished the fund with $174.

⑤ Reporting cash on the balance sheet.

S6-12. Prepare the current assets section of the balance sheet as of December 31, 2008, for Lipton, Inc., using the following information:

Accounts receivable	$63,000	Inventory	$55,500
Petty cash	500	Money market funds	15,000
Cash in bank accounts	22,000	Certificates of deposit	10,000

Exercises

① Fraud and its different types.

E6-13. Look at each of the following employees of Agetro's Restaurant. Which of the elements of the fraud triangle apply: perceived pressure (P), perceived opportunity (O), or rationalization (R)?

  R   As the bartender puts $100 in tips in his pocket, he thinks, "Nobody will get hurt."

  ____   1. Tina uses the stolen money to pay for her mother's high medical bills.

  ____   2. Hector knows he will be fired if he doesn't record some fictitious sales.

  ____   3. Roxanne, the night shift manager, knows that upper management does not monitor internal control.

  ____   4. Leo, a waiter, drove to work in a BMW and bragged about his recent vacation to the French Riviera.

  ____   5. Victoria, a cashier for the past five years, was caught stealing cash. When questioned about the theft, she said that she had not received a promotion and deserved more pay.

E6-14. Identify each of the following as an internal control objective (O), an internal control activity (A), or a limitation of internal control (L).

2 Internal control.

_____ 1. Separation of duties

_____ 2. Collusion

_____ 3. Proper authorization

_____ 4. Report financial information properly

_____ 5. Independent checks on performance

_____ 6. Management override

_____ 7. Complies with laws and regulations

_____ 8. Adequate documents and records

_____ 9. Poor design

_____ 10. Operates efficiently and effectively

E6-15. Hazel's Video Store maintains the following policies with regard to purchases of new videotapes at each of its branch stores. Indicate by letter which of the following control procedures applies to each of the following policies:

2 Internal control.

a. Proper authorization

b. Adequate documents and records

c. Physical safeguards

d. Independent checks on performance

e. Separation of duties

_____ 1. Every day, all checks written are recorded in the accounting records, using the information on the check stubs.

_____ 2. Once each month, a person from the home office visits each branch to examine the receipt of videos in the accounting records and to compare the inventory of tapes with the accounting records.

_____ 3. Purchases of new tapes must be authorized by purchase order in the home office and paid for by the treasurer in the home office. Receiving reports are prepared in each branch and sent to the home office.

_____ 4. The purchasing agent prepares the purchase invoice. When the goods are received and counted, the purchase invoice and count sheet go to the owner, who authorizes payment. The accountant writes the check, and then the owner signs it and mails it.

_____ 5. The company maintains passwords that limit access to its computerized accounting records.

E6-16. The following situations suggest a strength or a weakness in internal control. Identify each as strength or weakness, and give the reason for your answer.

a. Top managers delegate all internal control procedures to the accounting department.

b. The accounting department orders merchandise and approves invoices for payment.

c. Cash received over the counter is controlled by the sales clerk, who rings up the sale and places the cash in the register. The sales clerk matches the total recorded by the register to each day's cash sales.

d. The officer who signs checks need not examine the payment packet because he is confident the amounts are correct.

E6-17. Identify the missing internal control in the following situations. Select from these activities:

- Timely deposit of receipts

- Separation of duties

- Adequate documents and records

- Job rotation

a. While reviewing the records of Discount Pharmacy, you find that the same employee orders merchandise and approves invoices for payment.

b. Business is slow at Fun City Amusement Park on Tuesday, Wednesday, and Thursday nights. To reduce expenses, the owner decides not to use a ticket taker on those nights. The ticket seller is told to keep the tickets as a record of the number sold.

c. The same trusted employee has served as cashier for 10 years.

d. When business is brisk, Stop-n-Go deposits cash in the bank several times during the day. The manager at one store wants to reduce the time employees spend delivering cash to the bank, so he starts a new policy: Cash will build up over the weekends, and the total will be deposited on Monday.

e. At a grocery store, the manager decides to reduce paperwork. She eliminates the requirement that the receiving department prepare a receiving report.

E6-18. Classify each of the following items as a(n):

Addition to the book balance (+ Book)

Subtraction from the book balance (− Book)

continued . . . . .

Addition to the bank balance (+ Bank)

Subtraction from the bank balance (– Bank)

____ 1. Outstanding checks

____ 2. Deposits in transit

____ 3. NSF check

____ 4. Bank collection of our note receivable

____ 5. Interest earned on bank balance

____ 6. Bank service charge

____ 7. Book error: We credited Cash for $200. The correct amount of the check was $2,000.

____ 8. Bank error: The bank decreased our account for a check written by another customer.

E6-19. Calculate the answers for the missing data:

3 Applying internal controls for cash and preparing a bank reconciliation.

Bank			Books	
Balance, March 31		(a)	Balance, March 31	$335
Add:			Add:	
Deposit in transit	300		Bank collection	(c)
	800		Interest revenue	10
				570
Less:			Less:	
Outstanding checks	– (250)		Service charge	(d)
Adjusted bank balance		(b)	Adjusted book balance	$550

E6-20. Calculate the answers for the missing data:

3 Applying internal controls for cash and preparing a bank reconciliation.

Bank			Books	
Balance, January 31	$1,000		Balance, January 31	(c)
Add:			Add:	
Deposit in transit	600		Bank collection	425
		(a)	Interest revenue	15
				(d)
Less:			Less:	
Outstanding checks		(b)	Service charge	(30)
Adjusted bank balance	$1,200		Adjusted book balance	$1,200

E6-21. Mary Fox's checkbook lists the following:

Date	Check No.	Item	Check	Deposit	Balance
12/1					$ 1,000
3	785	Target	$ 75		925
14	786	Pizza Hut	15		910
15	787	Go Gas	30		880
15		Paycheck		$650	1,530
22	788	Cash	200		1,330
23	789	Wal-Mart	150		1,180
29	790	Minter Properties	600		580
30		Paycheck		640	1,220

Fox's December bank statement shows the following:

Balance, December 1				$1,000
Deposits:				650
Checks:	No.	Amount		
	785	$75		
	786	15		
	787	30		
	788	200		(320)
Other Charges:				
	Service charge		$15	(15)
Balance, December 31				$1,315

Prepare Fox's bank reconciliation on December 31, 2008. How much cash does Fox actually have on December 31?

E6-22. Dirk Cole's checkbook lists the following:

Date	Check No.	Item	Check	Deposit	Balance
9/1					$ 1,425
5	922	Mesilla Kitchen	$ 22		1,403
10		Dividends received		$115	1,518
14	923	Best Products	25		1,493
15	924	Fina	60		1,433
19	925	Cash	200		1,233
27	926	Staples	175		1,058
29	927	Hobart Properties	1,000		58
30		Paycheck		4,095	4,153

continued . . . . .

Cole's September bank statement shows the following:

Balance, September 1				$ 1,425
Deposits:				115
Checks:	No.	Amount		
	922	$22		
	923	25		
	924	70*		
	925	200		(317)
Other Charges:				
Printed checks			$20	
Service charge			15	(35)
Balance, September 30				$ 1,188

*This amount is correct for check no. 924.

Prepare Cole's bank reconciliation on September 30, 2008. How much cash does Cole actually have on September 30?

E6-23. Goddard Picture Frames received the January 31, 2007, bank statement from State National Bank, and the statement shows an ending balance of $1,000. Listed on the statement are an EFT rent collection of $500, a service charge of $15, NSF checks totaling $65, and a $10 charge for printed checks. In reviewing the cash records, Goddard's bookkeeper identifies outstanding checks totaling $525 and a deposit in transit of $2,700. During January, Goddard recorded a $300 check by debiting Salary Expense and crediting Cash for $30. Goddard's Cash account shows a January 31 balance of $3,035. Prepare the bank reconciliation on January 31.

③ Applying internal controls for cash and preparing a bank reconciliation.

E6-24. Using the data from E6-23, make the journal entries Goddard should record on January 31. Include an explanation for each entry.

③ Applying internal controls for cash and preparing a bank reconciliation.

E6-25. Jamie's Music School created a $200 imprest petty cash fund on March 1. During the month, the fund custodian authorized and signed petty cash tickets as follows:

④ Recording journal entries for petty cash.

Petty Cash

Ticket No.	Item	Account Debited	Amount
1	Delivery of programs to customers	Delivery Expense	$ 20
2	Mail package	Postage Expense	40
3	Newsletter	Supplies Expense	44
4	Key to closet	Miscellaneous Expense	16
5	Computer diskettes	Supplies Expense	30

continued . . . . .

a. Record the journal entry to create the petty cash fund.

b. Assuming that the cash in the fund totals $50 on March 31, make the journal entry to replenish the petty cash fund.

Recording journal entries for petty cash.

E6-26. Hazelnut maintains an imprest petty cash fund of $150. On November 30, the fund holds $10 cash, and petty cash tickets for office supplies, $90, and delivery expense, $50.

a. Record the journal entry to establish the petty cash fund on November 1.

b. Make the journal entry to replenish the petty cash fund.

c. What is the petty cash balance on November 1? What is the petty cash balance on November 30 after the petty cash fund has been replenished?

Problems (Group A)

Internal control.

P6-27A. Each of the following situations has an internal control weakness.

a. Betty Grable has been your trusted employee for 30 years. She performs all cash-handling and accounting duties. Ms. Grable just purchased a new Lexus and a new home in an expensive suburb. As owner of the company you wonder how she can afford these luxuries because you pay her only $35,000 a year and she has no sources of outside income.

b. Sanchez Hardwoods, a private company, falsified sales and inventory figures in order to get an important loan. The loan went through, but Sanchez later went bankrupt and couldn't repay the bank.

c. The office supply company where Champ's Sporting Goods purchases its business forms recently notified Champs that their documents were no longer going to be prenumbered. Alex Champ, the owner, replied that he never uses the receipt numbers anyway.

d. Discount stores such as Target make most of their sales in cash, with the remainder in credit card sales. To reduce expenses, one store manager allows the cashiers to record sales in the accounting records.

1. Identify the missing internal control in each situation. Answers include audit, documentation, and separation of duties.

2. Identify the possible problem caused by each control weakness. Answers include theft and unreliable financial statements.

3. Propose a solution to each internal control problem.

P6-28A. The May 2009 cash records of Nielson, Inc., follow:

③ Applying internal controls for cash and preparing a bank reconciliation.

Cash Receipts (CR)		Cash Payments (CP)	
Date	**Cash Debit**	**Check No.**	**Cash Credit**
May 4	$2,716	1416	$ 8
9	544	1417	775
14	896	1418	88
17	367	1419	126
31	2,037	1420	970
		1421	200
		1422	2,267

Nielson's Cash account shows the balance of $6,171 on May 31. On May 31, Nielson received the following bank statement:

Bank Statement for May			
Beginning Balance			$4,045
Deposits and other additions			
May 1		$ 625 EFT	
5		2,716	
10		544	
15		896	
18		367	
31		1,000 BC	6,148
Checks and other deductions			
May 8		$ 441 NSF	
15	(Check no. 1416)	8	
19		340 EFT	
22	(Check no. 1417)	775	
29	(Check no. 1418)	88	
31	(Check no. 1419)	216	
31		25 SC	(1,893)
Ending Balance			$8,300

Explanations: BC—bank collection; EFT—electronic funds transfer; NSF—nonsufficient funds check; SC—service charge.

Additional data for the bank reconciliation:

a. The EFT deposit was a receipt of rent revenue. The EFT debit was payment of insurance expense.

b. The NSF check was received from a customer.

c. The $1,000 bank collection was for a note receivable.

d. The correct amount of check 1419 is $216. Nielson mistakenly recorded the check for $126.

continued . . . . .

Requirements

Prepare Nielson's bank reconciliation at May 31, 2009.

(3) Applying internal controls for cash and preparing a bank reconciliation.

P6-29A. The May 31, 2007, bank statement of Blake's Hamburger just arrived from First State Bank. To prepare the bank reconciliation, you gather the following data:

a. The May 31 bank balance is $12,209.

b. The bank statement includes two charges for NSF checks from customers. One is for $67 and the other is for $192.

c. The following checks are outstanding at May 31:

Check No.	Amount
616	$402
802	74
806	36
809	161
810	229
811	48

d. Blake's collects from a few customers by EFT. The May bank statement lists a $200 EFT deposit.

e. The bank statement includes two special deposits: $900, for rental revenue, and $16, the interest revenue Blake's earned on its bank balance during May.

f. The bank statement lists $7 for the bank service charge.

g. On May 31, Blake's treasurer deposited $381, but this deposit does not appear on the bank statement.

h. The bank statement includes a $410 deduction for a check written by Danson Freight rather than Blake's Hamburger. Blake's notified the bank of this bank error.

i. Blake's Cash account shows a balance of $11,200 on May 31.

Requirements

1. Prepare the bank reconciliation for May 31.

2. Record the entries called for by the reconciliation. Include an explanation for each entry.

(4) Recording journal entries for petty cash.

P6-30A. On July 1, Chi Kong creates a petty cash fund with an imprest balance of $300. During July, Elise Sautter, the fund custodian, signs the following petty cash tickets:

continued .....

Petty Cash Ticket Number	Item	Amount
101	Office supplies	$86
102	Cab fare for executive	25
103	Delivery of package across town	17
104	Dinner money for president and a potential customer	90

On July 31, prior to replenishment, the fund contains these tickets plus cash of $82. The accounts affected by petty cash payments are Office Supplies Expense, Travel Expense, Delivery Expense, and Entertainment Expense.

Requirements

1. Record the journal entry to create the petty cash fund.

2. Record the journal entry to replenish the petty cash fund on July 31.

3. Make the August 1 entry to increase the fund balance to $350. Include an explanation, and briefly describe what the custodian does when the balance is increased.

Problems (Group B)

P6-31B. Each of the following situations has an internal control weakness.

 Internal control.

a. The sales manager likes to take potential customers out to lunch. However, he sometimes takes out family and friends and charges the company for their meals. At the end of the month he pads his expense report to include the meals with his family and friends. He does not provide support for these expenses. He always receives a check to reimburse the full amount on his expense report.

b. Taco King opened a restaurant in Taos. The owner purchased one cash register. Six people have access to the cash register during the day. Every night when the manager counts the cash in the drawer and compares it to the cash receipts tape, she finds the cash drawer to be short $20 to $50.

c. Aimee Atkins worked for Michael Riggs, MD, for many years. Atkins performs all accounting duties, including opening the mail, making the bank deposits, writing checks, and preparing the bank reconciliation. Riggs trusts Atkins completely.

d. Herbert Williams is the manager of a local car wash. His secretary submits the tickets for repayment from the petty cash fund and no one questions her about the validity of the tickets.

e. In evaluating internal control over cash payments, an auditor learns that the purchasing agent is responsible for purchasing diamonds for use in the company's manufacturing process. The purchasing agent also approves the invoices for payment and signs the checks.

continued . . . . .

1. Identify the missing internal control in each situation. Choices include documentation, physical safeguards, independent checks, and separation of duties.
2. Identify the possible problem caused by each control weakness. Answers include theft and unreliable financial statements.
3. Propose a solution to each internal control problem.

③ Applying internal controls for cash and preparing a bank reconciliation.

P6-32B. The cash records of Jungle Gymnastics for April 2009 follow:

Cash Receipts (CR)		Cash Payments (CP)	
Date	**Cash Debit**	**Check No.**	**Cash Credit**
Apr. 2	$ 4,170	3113	$ 890
8	500	3114	140
10	550	3115	1,930
16	2,180	3116	660
22	1,850	3117	1,470
29	1,060	3118	1,000
30	330	3119	630
		3120	1,670
		3121	100
		3122	2,410

Jungle's cash account shows a balance of $13,640 at April 30. On April 30, Jungle Gymnastics received the following bank statement:

Bank Statement for April			
Beginning Balance			$13,900
Deposits and other additions			
Apr. 1		$ 300 EFT	
4		4,170	
9		500	
12		550	
17		2,180	
22		1,300 BC	
23		1,850	10,850
Checks and other deductions			
Apr. 7	(Check no. 3113)	$ 890	
13	(Check no. 3115)	1,390	
14		900 NSF	
15	(Check no. 3114)	140	
18	(Check no. 3116)	660	
21		200 EFT	
26	(Check no. 3117)	1,470	
30	(Check no. 3118)	1,000	
30		20 SC	(6,670)
Ending Balance			$18,080

Explanations: EFT—electronic funds transfer; BC—bank collections: NSF—nonsufficient funds check; SC—service charge.

continued . . . . .

Additional data for the bank reconciliation:

a. The EFT deposit was a receipt of rent revenue. The EFT debit was an insurance payment.

b. The NSF check was received from a customer.

c. The $1,300 bank collection was for a note receivable.

d. The correct amount of check number 3115 is $1,390. Jungle Gymnastics mistakenly recorded the check for $1,930.

Requirements

Prepare the Jungle Gymnastics' bank reconciliation on April 30.

P6-33B. The August 31, 2007, bank statement of Darla's Dance Studio just arrived from Union Bank. To prepare Darla's bank reconciliation, you gather the following data:

③ Applying internal controls for cash and preparing a bank reconciliation.

a. Darla's Cash account shows a balance of $2,420 on August 31.

b. The bank statement includes two NSF checks from customers: $395 and $193.

c. Darla's pays rent expense, $750, and insurance expense, $290, each month by EFT.

d. Darla's Dance Studio's outstanding checks on August 31 include the following.

Check No.	Amount
237	$ 49
288	141
291	578
293	11
294	609
295	8
296	101

e. The bank statement includes a deposit of $1,200, collected on a note receivable by the bank.

f. The bank statement shows that Darla earned $18 of interest on its bank balance during August.

g. The bank statement lists a $10 bank service charge.

continued.....

h. On August 31, Darla deposited $316, but this deposit does not appear on the bank statement.

i. The bank statement includes a $300 deposit that Darla did not make. The bank erroneously credited Darla's account for another customer's deposit.

j. The August 31 bank balance shown on Darla's bank statement is $3,481.

Requirements

1. Prepare the bank reconciliation for Darla's Dance Studio on August 31, 2007.

2. Record the journal entries that bring the book balance of Cash into agreement with the adjusted book balance on the reconciliation. Include an explanation for each entry.

 Recording journal entries for petty cash.

P6-34B. Suppose that on June 1, Cool Gyrations, a disk jockey service, creates a petty cash fund with an imprest balance of $300. During June, Carol King, fund custodian, signs the following petty cash tickets:

Petty Cash Ticket Number	Item	Amount
1	Postage for package received	$ 18
2	Decorations and refreshments for office party	13
3	Two boxes of floppy disks	20
4	Printer cartridges	27
5	Dinner money for sales manager entertaining a customer	50

On June 30, prior to replenishment, the fund contains these tickets plus cash of $172. The accounts affected by petty cash payments are Office Supplies Expense, Entertainment Expense, and Postage Expense.

Requirements

1. Record the journal entry to create the petty cash fund.

2. Record the journal entry to replenish the petty cash fund on June 30.

3. Make the entry on July 1 to increase the fund balance to $350. Include an explanation, and briefly describe what the custodian does when the balance is increased.

for 24/7 practice, visit www.MyAccountingLab.com

Apply Your Knowledge

BE ON GUARD

Case 1. Rex Banner is the manager of a Stop Mart convenience store. He has been employed by the company for 12 years, the last 9 years of which was as a store manager. Rex applied for a promotion to regional manager, which oversees all 30 locations, but was once again denied promotion. Had he been promoted, the regional manager salary would have given Rex $14,000 more per year.

Rex was upset and decided that if the company would not give him the additional compensation he deserved then he would give himself a raise at the expense of the company. He knew that whenever he hired a new employee, the required paperwork sent to the corporate headquarters was simply filed without being reviewed. Thus, Rex completed all the company employment forms for a fictitious new employee he named "Sam Jones." He figured that, when the company was notified by the Social Security Administration that the Social Security number for "Sam Jones" was fraudulent, Rex would simply report that the employee had just quit and that Rex had no way to contact him. Rex's scheme involved the following actions:

- He put "Sam" on the schedule.
- Every week, he submitted a signed time card for "Sam" along with all the other legitimate employee time cards.
- Every two weeks when Rex received the employee paychecks, he pulled "Sam's" paycheck and hid it in his briefcase.
- He then cashed the paycheck for "Sam" and enjoyed the extra money.

While Rex's actions are clearly unethical, were they justified, given that he was again denied a promotion and therefore undercompensated? Will Rex be caught? Does the company bear some responsibility too? If the company required direct deposit of its employee paychecks, could this type of fraud be prevented? Can you recommend any other procedures the company could adopt that would help to prevent Rex's fraud?

Case 2. Mary Rel was hired as the new store manager for the Bargain Bin. The store used four cash registers, and 10 cashiers worked various shifts in the store. Store operations include the following procedures:

- At the start of each shift, a cashier counts the beginning cash balance in the drawer, which is supposed to be $550.
- A the end of each shift, the cashier then
  - Counts the ending cash balance in the drawer and adds to it any amounts dropped in the safe
  - Completes the shift cash form that reconciles the cash received to the total register sales tape.
  - Reports any difference between the cash on hand and the cash that should be on hand based on receipts.

As a manager, Mary was responsible for preparing the cash drawers for each shift. She decided to test the honesty of the cashiers so she added an additional

$50 to the beginning balance of one cash drawer. Mary planned to look at the shift cash form to see whether the cashier reported the extra $50 that was part of the beginning balance or just reported the $550 expected balance, taking the $50 for personal use.

Mary also tested her assistant manager. She gave him the bank deposit bag containing $5,246.24, but included a deposit ticket that was exactly $100 less, listing $5,146.24 as the deposit amount. Mary wanted to see whether the assistant manager would report the extra $100 in the deposit bag.

Mary planned to never let her employees or even her assistant manager know that she had tested them; instead she would just say that she made a simple mistake in counting the cash if they questioned her.

Should Mary distrust her employees? Is it ethical for a manager to test employees without their knowledge? Should Mary ever inform the employees that they had been tested? Was it unethical for Mary to test an assistant manager?

KNOW YOUR BUSINESS

The annual report of Target in Appendix A contains financial statements and related footnotes as well as a management analysis and discussion of the business. Footnotes, the financial disclosures that accompany the financial statements, provide important information about the company. In this case, you will understand the responsibilities of both management and the independent auditors for the annual report content. Knowing the importance of strong internal controls and knowing the role of controls in achieving reliable financial reporting, you will also understand who is responsible for implementing and maintaining the internal control environment. You will further grasp the respective roles of both management and the auditors in the company's internal control system. Finally, you will be able to determine the amount of cash and cash equivalents available to the company as reported in the financial statements.

Refer to the Target Annual Report in Appendix A. You will need to find and then read the following reports:

- Report of Management on the Financial Statements
- Report of Independent Registered Public Accounting Firm on Consolidated Financial Statements
- Report of Management on Internal Control
- Report of Independent Registered Public Accounting Firm on Internal Control over Financial Reporting
- Report of Audit Committee

Requirements

1. Who is responsible for the information in the annual report? How was this responsibility fulfilled? Which company officers signed their names?
2. Who were the independent auditors? Under what standards did they conduct their audit? What was their opinion of the audited financial statements?

3. Who is responsible for establishing and maintaining adequate internal control over financial reporting? Is the effectiveness of the internal controls ever reviewed? Do you think that internal control procedures are necessary? Why?

4. Do the auditors have any responsibility with respect to the internal controls? What was the auditor's opinion regarding the management assessment of internal control effectiveness? What role did the audit committee have in the financial reporting?

5. Which financial statement(s) can you use to determine the amount of cash and cash equivalents Target had as of January 2005? How much cash and cash equivalents did Target have as of January 2005? Was this figure more or less that the total as of January 2004?

For Internet Exercises, Excel in Practice, and additional online activities, go to the Web site www.prenhall.com/pollard.

Quick Check Answers

1. *d* 2. *b* 3. *c* 4. *c* 5. *a* 6. *d* 7. *c* 8. *b* 9. *b* 10. *d*

1. Describe the types of sales and receivables and discuss the related internal controls.

2. Use the direct write-off method to account for uncollectible receivables.

3. Use the allowance method to account for uncollectible receivables.

4. Account for notes receivable.

5. Calculate the quick ratio and days' sales in receivables.

Receivables

Let's say you own a business that sells water sports equipment. Some customers are willing to pay cash at the time of sale. Others use their bank cards, credit cards, or debit cards. A few have even asked you to sell on credit.

You love getting the cash at the time of sale. You can also work with credit card companies and banks, because they give you cash quickly and collect cash from your customers later. But you're not too sure about extending credit to some of your customers. Can you wait 30 days to get your money? Will you have to delay payment of your own bills until cash is received?

Most businesses face this situation, and there are both advantages and disadvantages to extending credit to customers. The main advantage of selling on credit is expanding your customer base. For example, Ford and General Motors originally sold cars for cash. Over the years these companies increased car sales by extending credit to many of their customers. More customers mean more sales and probably greater net income for the business. The main disadvantage, however, is that you have to wait to receive cash and, alas, some customers never pay you. This is one of the unpleasant costs of running a business. ●

Look Back

You have studied fraudulent business activities and the importance of internal controls in business. Further, you have learned how to prepare a bank reconciliation as an important internal control over cash, and seen how cash is reported on the balance sheet.

Look Ahead

You will learn about internal controls for receivables. Using two methods of estimating uncollectible receivables, you will discover how to account for receivables and report them on the balance sheet.

In Chapter 6, you learned about fraudulent business activities and gained a better understanding of internal controls as a way of addressing the risk of fraud. You discovered that preparing a bank reconciliation can be a way of maintaining control over cash. Further, you found that an imprest account can control petty cash. As we've focused on accounting for cash as the most liquid asset, you saw how cash and cash equivalents are reported on the balance sheet. In this chapter, we will examine different types of sales and receivables and the accounting for these items. We continue to discuss internal controls and learn about controls related to other current assets, accounts and notes receivable. We will also explain how companies account for customers who don't pay the receivables due from buying goods or services on credit. We will use two methods to estimate uncollectible accounts receivable, and account for notes receivable transactions. Finally, we will see how to report receivables on the balance sheet and calculate two important measures of liquidity, the quick ratio and days' sales in receivables.

Sales and Receivables

 Describe the types of sales and receivables and discuss the related internal controls.

In Chapter 1, we learned about organizations that sell services. In Chapter 5, we introduced you to relationships between retailers and customers as part of the supply chain involving a retail business. Regardless of whether the business is selling services or goods, companies find it hard to turn customers away so they often agree to make sales on credit. But businesses prefer not to do business with customers who don't pay their bills on time. In this chapter, we look at the challenges that many businesses face to attract and keep the right customers, provide internal controls to protect cash collections from customers, track amounts due from these customers, and estimate resulting bad debts.

Types of Sales

Recall that liquidity, a primary goal of businesses, means having enough cash to pay bills on time. Selling goods or providing services can provide a steady inflow of cash to pay for the operating expenses of a business.

As a small business owner, how would you like to receive cash from your customers? As shown in Exhibit 7-1, you have several choices:

CASH SALES

Cash sales are the easiest type to track because customers give currency or a check at the time of sale. The business does not need to keep records of the individual customers. Recording a cash sale requires increasing the Cash account and increasing the Sales Revenue account for the amount of the sale. Although cash sales are easy to account for, businesses may limit their sales potential by not providing options for customers to buy now and pay later.

BANK CREDIT CARD SALES

One alternative that helps businesses attract more customers is the acceptance of bank credit cards, sometimes called bank cards. Bank credit cards are a form of

Exhibit 7-1 Types of Sales

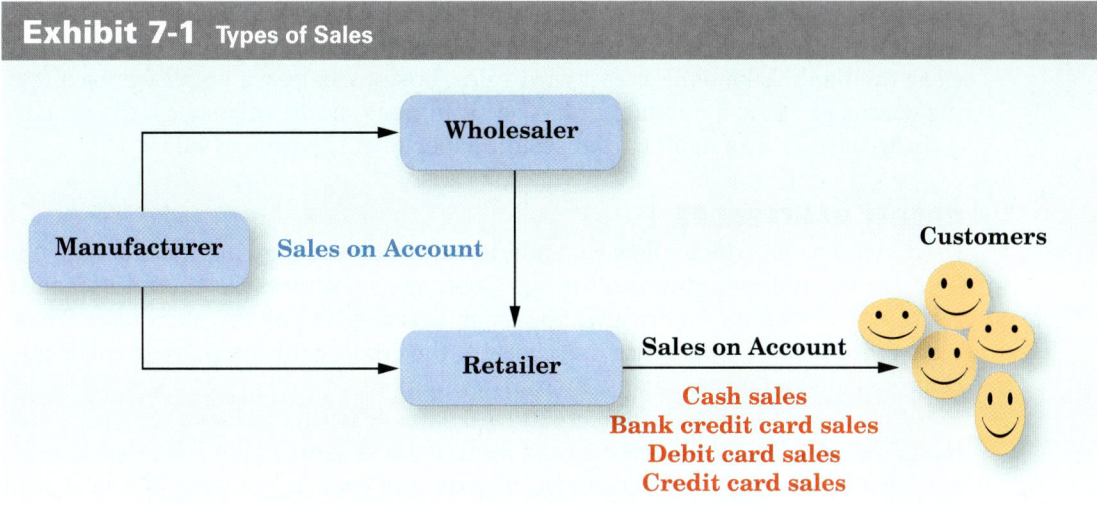

credit cards issued by most banks, which allow customers to buy now and pay the bank later. VISA and MasterCard are the two main examples. Retailers taking a bank credit card as payment do not have to worry about collecting the cash or keep accounts receivable records because the bank issuing the cards bears the responsibility of collecting the amounts due from the customers.

Bank credit card purchases are reported on a monthly statement prepared by the bank, and cardholders write one check to the bank to pay the amount due. The retailer accepting the card typically pays the bank a small service fee to cover the processing costs. The retailer records the cost as a credit card expense at the time of sale.

For example, when an Exxon station makes a sale and takes a VISA card in payment, the station essentially collects cash for the sale. The cash received is usually less than the full amount of the sale because the bank deducts its service fee. Suppose the Exxon station sells $150 of fuel to a family vacationing in a motor home. The station takes a VISA card for the sale, and the bank that issued the card charges a 2% service fee. The Exxon station records the bank credit card sale as follows:

Journal Entry:

Date	Accounts	Post Ref.	Dr.	Cr.
	Cash		147	
	Credit/Debit Card Expense ($150 × 0.02)		3	
	Sales Revenue			150
	Record a bank credit card sale.			

DEBIT CARD SALES

Businesses can also attract customers by accepting debit card payments rather than cash. Debit cards allow the debit card users the freedom to pay for purchases without carrying cash or writing a check. They also offer advantages to retailers because retailers collect the cash from the bank and don't need records of accounts receivable.

At Target or Kroger or Wal-Mart, the buyer "swipes" the card through a special terminal, and the buyer's bank balance is automatically decreased. Target's cash is increased immediately, without the retailer having to deposit a check and wonder whether sufficient funds are in the account to pay it so that the check will clear the bank. Like bank credit card sales, businesses pay a small fee for allowing customers to use a debit card. Also as in bank credit card sales, the retailer records the cost as a debit card discount expense at the time of sale.

CREDIT CARD SALES

Credit card sales, which allow customers to buy now and pay later, are common in both traditional and online retailing. Customers will present the retailer with credit cards such as American Express or Discover to pay for purchases. These credit card owners then write one check to the credit card company to cover purchases made and reported on a monthly statement.

Retailers also benefit from credit card sales. They do not have to check a customer's credit rating. The credit card company has already done so. Retailers do not have to keep accounts receivable records, and they do not have to collect cash from customers.

However, these benefits do not come free because the retailer must pay a small fee for accepting these cards, just as it does for accepting bank credit cards and debit cards. The seller receives less than the full amount of the sale because the credit card company charges a fee of 1% to 5% of the sale. The retailer then records this fee related to the sale as a credit card expense.

Suppose you and your family have lunch at a Red Lobster restaurant. You pay the bill, $100, with a Discover card. Red Lobster's entry to record the $100 sale, subject to the credit card company's 3% discount, is:

Journal Entry:

Date	Accounts	Post Ref.	Dr.	Cr.
	Cash		97	
	Credit/Debit Card Expense ($100 × 0.03)		3	
	Sales Revenue			100
	Record a credit card sale.			

SALES ON ACCOUNT

Cash, bank credit card, debit card, and credit card sales are common methods of sales in a retail, business-to-customer environment. In Chapter 5, we discussed sales of merchandise on account, which can occur in a retailer-to-customer environment such as Dillard's Department Stores. However, this happens more commonly in a supplier-to-retailer environment where one business is a customer to another business. As illustrated in Exhibit 7-1 the following supplier/retailer/customer relationships provide opportunities for sales on account:

- Manufacturers sell to wholesalers

- Manufacturers sell to retailers

- Wholesalers sell to retailers

- Retailers sell to customers

When businesses agree to sell on credit, sales increase, but so does the risk of not being able to collect what is owed as a result of these sales. Accordingly, companies bear the risk of **bad debts**, or **uncollectible accounts**, which occur when a customer does not pay for goods or services rendered. Regardless of its size, a business must manage its customer relationships to avoid bad debts. To attract customers who pay their bills on time, a business can do the following:

- Choose its customers carefully. Establish a credit policy for accepting new customers including:

  - Credit application

  - Credit check from a credit rating agency such as Dun and Bradstreet for businesses or TRW for individual customers

  - Credit references from businesses that sell to the new customer and banks that have accounts with the new customer

- Enforce a credit policy for existing customers:

  - Explain payment times and penalties for early or late payment.

  - Follow up on overdue accounts. Send statements and reminders of payment due dates.

  - Use a series of overdue notices to remind them of payment date.

  - Set an absolute date when the account goes to a collection agency to obtain payment.

  - Consider accepting notes receivable in lieu of accounts receivable for some customers.

Sales on account create receivables. Let's look at the types of receivables that businesses can have.

Types of Receivables

The two major types of receivables are accounts receivable and notes receivable. Remember from Chapter 1 that a business's accounts receivable are current assets that reflect the amounts due from customers for credit sales of goods or services. Also recall from Chapter 2 that notes receivable are written promises for future collection of cash.

As we saw in Chapter 5, businesses keep a subsidiary ledger of the receivable due from each customer, as illustrated here. Accounts Receivable in the general ledger serves as a **control account** because it summarizes, or *controls*, the total of the receivables from all customers. The information on the individual customer accounts within the subsidiary ledger provides information for preparing monthly billing statements. The total of the customer account balances in the subsidiary ledger should equal the balance of the Accounts Receivable control account. If not, an error exists in the records.

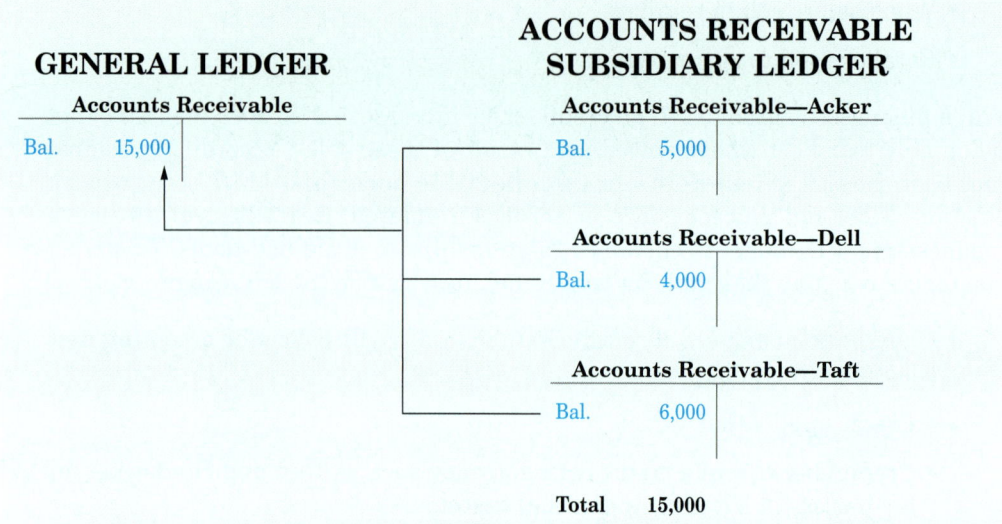

Notes receivable are more formal than accounts receivable. The debtor promises in writing to pay the creditor a definite sum at a future date, and a promissory note, discussed in Chapter 2, serves as the evidence of this pledge. When we discussed the classified balance sheet in Chapter 5, we saw that notes receivable due within one year or less are current, or short-term, assets, while those due beyond one year are long-term.

For notes collected in periodic installments, the portion due within one year is a current asset, and the remainder is long-term; even though both portions relate to the same note, they are shown in different sections of the asset portion of the balance sheet. For example, General Motors may hold a $6,000 note receivable from you, but only the $2,000 due from you this year is a current asset to GM. The remaining $4,000 is a long-term receivable. Receivables are often reported as shown in Exhibit 7-2, and are highlighted for emphasis.

Exhibit 7-2 Assets with Receivables Highlighted

EXAMPLE COMPANY
Balance Sheet
Date

Assets		
Current Assets:		
Cash		$ X,XXX
Accounts receivable	$ X,XXX	
Less: Allowances for uncollectible accounts	(XXX)	X,XXX
Notes receivable, short-term		X,XXX
Interest receivable		X,XXX
Inventory		X,XXX
Prepaid expenses		X,XXX
Total current assets		X,XXX
Investments:		
Investments		X,XXX
Notes receivable, long-term		X,XXX
Total investments		X,XXX
Fixed assets:		
Property, plant, and equipment		X,XXX
Total assets		$ X,XXX

Internal Control over Receivables

Businesses that sell on credit receive most cash receipts by mail. Because of the amount of these receipts, internal control over collections is important, and a critical element of internal control is the separation of duties. As we discussed in Chapter 6, no one person should be responsible for more than one of the following tasks: authorizing transactions, maintaining custody of assets, or keeping accounting records. Let's see how a lack of separation in duties can be a problem:

> Snowden Supply Co. is family-owned and takes pride in the loyalty of its workers. Most company employees have been with the Snowdens for years. The company makes 90% of its sales on account.

> The office staff consists of a bookkeeper and a supervisor. The bookkeeper maintains the accounts receivable subsidiary ledger. He also makes the daily bank deposit. The supervisor prepares monthly financial statements and special reports.

Can you spot the internal control weakness here? The bookkeeper has access to the accounts receivable records and also has custody of the cash. The bookkeeper could forge the endorsement on a check received by the business, deposit it in his bank account, and remove the record of the customer's account. Unless someone reviews the bookkeeper's work, the theft may go undetected.

How can Snowden Supply correct this control weakness? They could redistribute duties so that the bookkeeper does not handle cash. Only the remittance advices should go to the bookkeeper to indicate which customer accounts to credit. Or, use of a bank lockbox could achieve the same result. In a lockbox system, customers would send cash to the lockbox and Snowden Supply's bank would then deposit the cash in the company's bank account.

Managing the Collection of Receivables

Most large companies have a credit department to evaluate potential customers. The extension of credit requires a balancing act. The company doesn't want to lose sales to good customers, but it also wants to avoid selling to customers who do not pay their bills. *Uncollectible receivables become an expense of doing business on credit*, which reduces net income.

For good internal control over credit management, separation of duties is again important. The credit department should have no access to cash. For example, a credit employee who handles cash might pocket money received from a customer. The employee could then label the customer's account as uncollectible, authorizing the company to remove it from the accounting records. The company would stop billing that customer, and the employee would have covered the theft.

The main issues in controlling and managing receivables and a plan of action for each issue follow:

Issue	Action
• Extend credit only to customers most likely to pay.	Require a credit application, run a credit check, and request credit references on prospective customers.

• Prevent the perceived opportunity to commit fraud.	Design the internal control system to separate
	    • credit (authorization),
	    • cash-handing (custody), and
	    • accounting duties (record keeping)
	and keep employees from stealing cash collected from customers.

• Maximize cash flow by pursuing collection from customers.	Enforce credit policies for existing customers.

The Direct Write-Off Method

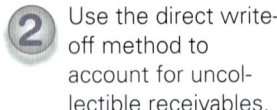

2 Use the direct write-off method to account for uncollectible receivables.

As we mentioned earlier, credit sales will allow a business to attract more customers, but may also result in drawing some customers that will never pay the amount that they owe the business. These uncollectible accounts create an **uncollectible accounts expense** for the seller, and this account is a selling expense that reduces operating income for the year. The amount of this expense varies from year to year. The problem with accounting for uncollectible accounts is that, at the time of sale, it is not known which receivable amounts will never be paid; if it was known, these customers would not be allowed to make credit purchases and would instead have to pay cash at the time of the sale.

One way of accounting for uncollectible accounts is the **direct write-off method**. Under this method, the decision to **write off** a customer's account receivable as uncollectible occurs when the business knows with certainty that the customer will not pay.

Let's look at an example using the direct write-off method. Julia's Cleaning Supply sold $2,000 of merchandise on credit to Nini Co. Julia's Cleaning Supply attempted to collect the amount due from Nini, and finally decided that Nini will never pay. At this point, Julia wrote off Nini's account receivable by debiting Uncollectible Accounts Expense and crediting Nini's Account Receivable, as follows:

Journal Entry:

Date	Accounts	Post Ref.	Dr.	Cr.
Jan. 2	Uncollectible Accounts Expense		2,000	
	Accounts Receivable—Nini Co.			2,000
	Write off an account receivable.			

Occasionally, a customer becomes willing and able to pay on an account that has been written off. In these cases, the receivable account is reinstated and then the cash received is recorded. Let's assume that Nini Co. was able to pay the $2,000 to Julia's Cleaning Supply on July 22. To account for this recovery, Julia's makes two journal entries to reverse the earlier write-off and record the cash collection, as follows:

Journal Entry:

Date	Accounts	Post Ref.	Dr.	Cr.
July 22	Accounts Receivable—Nini Co.		2,000	
	Uncollectible Accounts Expense			2,000
	Reinstated an account receivable.			
22	Cash		2,000	
	Accounts Receivable—Nini Co.			2,000
	Record collection on account.			

This method is simple to use because the company does not make any entry for the uncollectible account until it is known that the account is, in fact, uncollectible. However, it is not widely used because it is not considered acceptable according to Generally Accepted Accounting Principles. The problem is that it does not record the uncollectible account expense in the same period as the sales revenue generated from the credit sale. Remember from Chapter 1 that expenses are the value of resources used to produce revenue; in Chapter 3 we found that they must be matched against the revenues they generate by recording both in the same accounting period.

The Allowance Method

Most companies use the **allowance method** to account for uncollectible accounts. Under this method, the income statement matches Uncollectible Accounts Expense against the revenue that the credit sales created. It also allows the balance sheet to show the amount of accounts receivable realistically expected to be collected in the future. When the allowance method is used:

3 Use the allowance method to account for uncollectible receivables.

1. The amount of uncollectible accounts receivable is estimated.

2. The current estimate of uncollectible accounts receivable is debited to Uncollectible Accounts Expense and credited to **Allowance for Uncollectible Accounts**, which is a contra-asset account. This entry is recorded as an adjusting entry at the end of the period.

3. When a customer's account receivable balance is written off, the amount is debited to Allowance for Uncollectible Accounts and credited to Accounts Receivable.

Exhibit 7-3 provides an overview of the customer activity that can occur when a business has credit sales and uses the allowance method to manage uncollectible accounts.

Exhibit 7-3 Customer Activity Involving Credit Sales and the Allowance Method

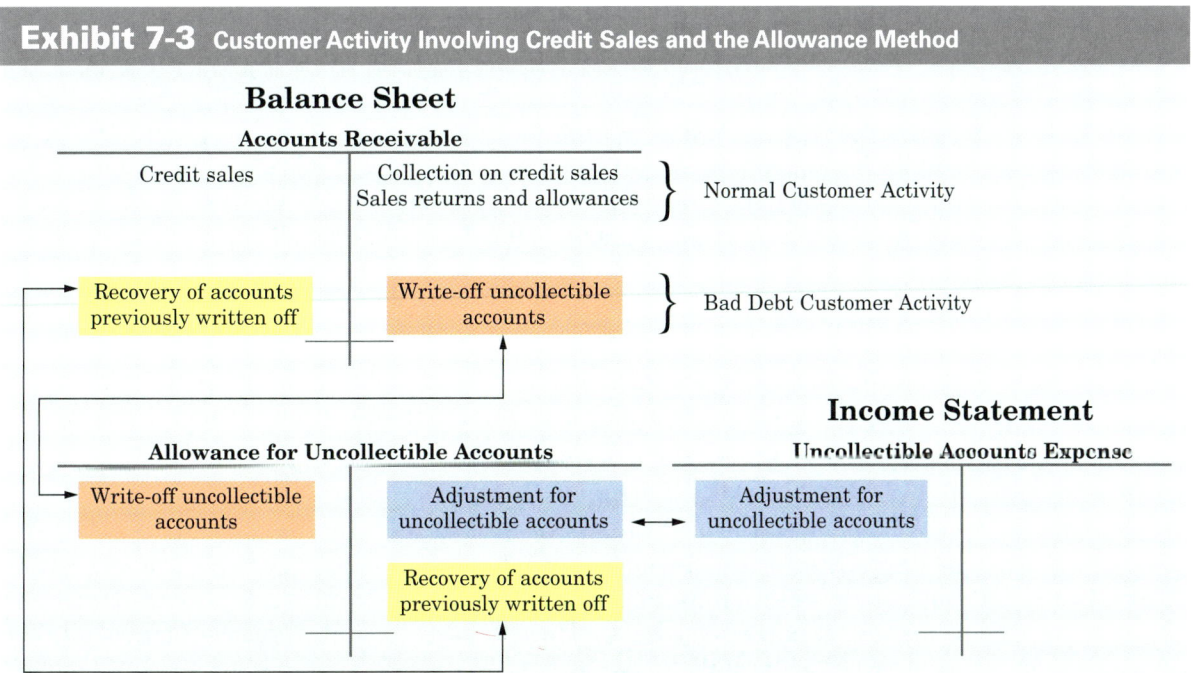

The Allowance for Uncollectible Accounts shows the amount of receivables the business expects *not* to collect. In this way, it serves as a cushion for the business, ready to absorb the amount of uncollectible accounts that will surely happen, despite sound credit policies. Subtracting the Allowance for Uncollectible Accounts from Accounts Receivable yields the net amount that the business expects to collect, also called **net realizable value** of the accounts receivable, or net receivables.

For example, if a business has $28,000 in Accounts Receivable at the end of the year, and $4,000 is not expected to be collected, the balance sheet would show the following:

Balance Sheet	
Accounts receivable	$28,000
Less: Allowance for uncollectible accounts	(4,000)
Accounts receivable, net	$24,000

Another way to report receivables on the balance sheet follows:

Accounts receivable, net allowance for uncollectible accounts, $4,000	$24,000

The income statement can report Uncollectible Accounts Expense as a selling expense, as follows:

Income Statement	
Selling expenses:	
Uncollectible accounts expense	$3,400

Notice that the amount of the uncollectible account expense doesn't necessarily equal the amount of the allowance for uncollectible accounts. Some of the allowance may have already been used to absorb uncollectible accounts or may be left over from a prior periods' sales yet to be discovered as uncollectible.

Estimating Uncollectibles

How are uncollectible accounts estimated? Companies use past experience. Under the allowance method, two basic methods are used to estimate uncollectibles:

PERCENT-OF-SALES METHOD
The **percent-of-sales method** computes uncollectible accounts expense as a percentage of **net credit sales**. Net credit sales are equal to total credit sales less the related sales discounts and sales returns and allowances. We will simply call it credit sales in this chapter. This method is also called the **income-statement approach** because it focuses on Uncollectible Accounts Expense, an account that appears on the income statement.

Assume it is December 31, 2007, and the accounts of Polly's Pretty Petals have these balances before the year-end adjustments:

Accounts Receivable			Allowance for Uncollectible Accounts	
Bal.	120,000		Bal.	500

Prior to any adjustments, net receivables total $119,500 ($120,000 − $500). This amount is more than the business realistically expects to collect from customers. Based on prior experience, the credit department estimates that the expense of the current year's uncollectible accounts is 2% of net credit sales, which were $500,000 for 2007. The adjusting entry to record uncollectible accounts expense for 2007 and to update the Allowance for Uncollectible Accounts is:

Journal Entry:

Date	Accounts	Post Ref.	Dr.	Cr.
Dec. 31	Uncollectible Accounts Expense ($500,000 × 0.02)		10,000	
	Allowance for Uncollectible Accounts			10,000
	Record estimate of uncollectible accounts expense			
	for the year.			

Now the accounts are ready for reporting in the 2007 financial statements.

Accounts Receivable			Allowance for Uncollectible Accounts	
Bal.	120,000		Bal.	500
			Adj.	10,000
Uncollectible Accounts Expense			Bal.	10,500
Adj.	10,000			

Customers owe the business $120,000, and now the Allowance for Uncollectible Accounts is realistic. The balance sheet will report accounts receivable at the net amount of $109,500 ($120,000 − $10,500). The income statement will report 2007's Uncollectible Accounts Expense of $10,000, along with the other operating expenses for the period.

AGING METHOD

The second popular approach for estimating uncollectibles is the **aging method**. This method is also called the **balance-sheet approach** because it focuses on accounts receivable, which appears on the balance sheet. In the aging approach, the accountant completes two steps:

STEP 1

Calculate the balance needed in the Allowance for Uncollectible Accounts at the end of the period.

- Group individual accounts based on their age, and calculate the total amount of accounts receivable for each group: 1–30 days, 31–60 days, 61–90 days, or over 90 days.

- Multiply the total for each group by a percentage representing the estimated portion of that total that will never be collected. The older the group, the higher percentage of the balance that will likely not be collected; in other words, the longer it has been since a customer made a credit purchase, the less likely it is that the customer will pay the amount due. The result will be the dollar amount of each category expected to be uncollectible.

- Calculate the balance needed in the Allowance for Uncollectible Accounts at the end of the period by adding the estimated uncollectible amounts for each group together.

STEP 2

Calculate the uncollectible accounts expense. Compare the ending balance of the Allowance for Uncollectible Accounts before adjustment to the amount needed, as calculated in step 1. The difference is the amount of the adjustment to Allowance for Uncollectible Accounts and Uncollectible Accounts Expense.

For example, Ross Builders Supply groups its accounts receivable into 30-day periods, as Exhibit 7-4 shows:

Exhibit 7-4 Aging the Accounts Receivable of Ross Builders Supply

		Age of Account				
Customer Name		**1–30 Days**	**31–60 Days**	**61–90 Days**	**Over 90 Days**	**Total Balance**
T-Bar-M Co.		$ 20,000				$ 20,000
Chicago Pneumatic Parts		10,000				10,000
Sarasota Pipe Corp.			$13,000	$10,000		23,000
Oneida, Inc.				3,000	$1,000	4,000
Other accounts		70,000	12,000	2,000	2,000	86,000
Totals		$100,000	$25,000	$15,000	$3,000	$143,000
Estimated percentage uncollectible		× 0.1%	× 1%	× 5%	× 90%	
Required balance for Allowance for Uncollected Accounts		$100 +	$250	$750	$2,700	$3,800

Ross's Accounts Receivable total of $143,000 is shown at the far right of the exhibit. As step 1, calculate the required allowance for these receivables by first multiplying the total for each group of receivables by the estimated percentage uncollectible for that group. Then add these amounts together to get the required ending balance for the Allowance account. Of $143,000 in Accounts Receivable, the aging schedule estimates that Ross will *not* collect $3,800.

For step two, now compute the amount of the uncollectible accounts expense. The Accounts Receivable and Allowance for Uncollectible Accounts appear as follows *before the year-end adjustment*:

Accounts Receivable			Allowance for Uncollectible Accounts		
Bal.	143,000			Bal.	1,100

To update the allowance, Ross compares the $1,100 balance currently in the Allowance account to the $3,800 balance calculated in the aging schedule. He makes an adjusting entry to record *the difference* as an Uncollectible Accounts Expense:

Journal Entry:

Date	Accounts	Post Ref.	Dr.	Cr.
Dec. 31	Uncollectible Accounts Expense ($3,800 – $1,100)		2,700	
	Allowance for Uncollectible Accounts			2,700
	Record estimate of uncollectible accounts expense			
	for the year.			

Now the balance sheet can report receivables at the amount that Ross expects to collect from customers, $139,200 ($143,000 – $3,800), as follows:

Accounts Receivable		Allowance for Uncollectible Accounts	
Bal. 143,000		Bal. 1,100	
		Adj. 2,700	
		Bal. 3,800	

The net amount of accounts receivable, $139,200, is the net realizable value because it is the amount Ross expects to realize, or collect, in cash.

Exhibit 7-5 summarizes the two approaches to the allowance method. Know that both methods are acceptable because both result in matching uncollectible accounts expense against the sales of the period. Also, both methods involve *estimating* uncollectible accounts since the actual amount cannot be known at the time of the sale. Notice, though, the fundamental difference in approach between these two methods: The percent-of-sales method focuses on the amount that should be recorded as Uncollectible Accounts Expense and *added to* the Allowance for Uncollectible Accounts balance based on credit sales. In contrast, the aging method concentrates on what the balance of the Allowance for Uncollectible Accounts *needs to be* according to the aging schedule.

Now compare the allowance method to the direct write-off method (see Exhibit 7-6).

WRITING OFF UNCOLLECTIBLE ACCOUNTS

Imagine that, in early 2007, Ross Builders Supply collects on most of its $143,000 accounts receivable and records the cash receipts as follows:

Journal Entry:

Date	Accounts	Post Ref.	Dr.	Cr.
Jan.–Mar.	Cash		123,000	
	Accounts Receivable			123,000
	Record collections on account.			

Also suppose that, after repeated attempts to collect, Ross's credit department determines that Ross cannot collect a total of $1,200 from customers Andrews, $900, and Jones, $300. Under the allowance method, Ross then writes off the receivables from these delinquent customers as follows:

Exhibit 7-5 Comparison of Two Allowance Methods

	Allowance Method for Estimating Uncollectible Accounts Receivable	
	Percent-of-Sales	**Aging of Accounts Receivable**
Approach to estimating uncollectible accounts.	Income Statement—What percentage of credit sales for the year will not be collected?	Balance Sheet—What percentage of customer balances at year-end will not be collected?
Information needed to estimate uncollectible accounts.	• Net Credit Sales • Estimated percentage of net credit sales considered uncollectible (based on historical information)	• Balance of accounts 30, 60, 90+ days unpaid. • Estimated percentage of balances considered uncollectible for each time range (based on historical information)
Calculation of estimated Uncollectible Accounts Expense.	Uncollected Accounts Expense = % x Net Credit Sales	Step 1. Calculate Allowance balance needed according to analysis at year-end: $\quad$ % × 1–30 days $\qquad$ \$ XX + % × 31–60 days $\qquad$ XX + % × 61–90 days $\qquad$ XX + % × Over 90 days $\qquad$ XX Allowance for Uncollectible Accounts balance needed $\quad$ \$XXX Step 2. Calculate Uncollectible Accounts Expense Allowance balance needed from step 1 $\quad$ \$ XXX $-$ Unadjusted Allowance balance $\quad$ at the end of the period $\qquad$ $-$ XXX = Uncollectible Accounts Expense $\quad$ \$ XX
Adjusting journal entry to record uncollectible account expense. Accounts are the same, but the amounts are different.	$\qquad\qquad\qquad\qquad\qquad\qquad$ Dr. $\quad$ Cr. Uncollectible Accounts Expense $\quad$ XX $\quad$ Allowance for Uncollectible Accounts $\qquad$ XX	$\qquad\qquad\qquad\qquad\qquad\qquad$ Dr. $\quad$ Cr. Uncollectible Accounts Expense $\quad$ XX $\quad$ Allowance for Uncollectible Accounts $\qquad$ XX

Exhibit 7-6 Comparison of Allowance Method to Direct Write-Off Method

Journal Entries	Allowance Method	Direct Write-Off Method
Adjusting journal entry to estimate uncollectible accounts.	$\qquad\qquad\qquad\qquad\qquad\qquad$ Dr. $\quad$ Cr. Uncollectible Accounts Expense $\quad$ XX $\quad$ Allowance for Uncollectible Accounts $\qquad$ XX Net income decreases; total assets decrease	No adjusting entry is made because no Allowance account is used
Write off uncollectible accounts	Allowance for Uncollectible Accounts $\quad$ XX $\quad$ Accounts Receivable $\qquad$ XX No effect on net income or total assets	$\qquad\qquad\qquad\qquad\qquad\qquad$ Dr. $\quad$ Cr. Uncollectible Accounts Expense $\quad$ XX $\quad$ Accounts Receivable $\qquad$ XX Net income decreases; total assets decrease
Recover account balance previously written off Receive cash from customer	Accounts Receivable $\quad$ XX $\quad$ Allowance for Uncollectible Accounts $\qquad$ XX Cash $\quad$ XX $\quad$ Accounts Receivable $\qquad$ XX No effect on net income or total assets	Accounts Receivable $\quad$ XX $\quad$ Uncollectible Accounts Expense $\qquad$ XX Cash $\quad$ XX $\quad$ Accounts Receivable $\qquad$ XX Net income increases, total assets increase

The write-off of uncollectible receivables has no impact on total assets, liabilities, or equity, because an asset account, Accounts Receivable, and a contra-asset account, Allowance for Uncollectible Accounts, are both decreased by the same amount; the total change in assets is zero.

Journal Entry:

Date	Accounts	Post Ref.	Dr.	Cr.
Mar. 31	Allowance for Uncollectible Accounts		1,200	
	Accounts Receivable—Andrews			900
	Accounts Receivable—Jones			300
	Write off uncollectible accounts.			

RECOVERY OF ACCOUNTS PREVIOUSLY WRITTEN OFF

When an account receivable is written off as uncollectible, the receivable does not cease to exist. The customer still owes the money, but the business stops pursuing collection and writes off the account. Some companies turn delinquent receivables over to an attorney and recover some of the cash through a process called **recovery of an uncollectible account**.

Let's see how to record the recovery of an account previously written off under the allowance method. Recall that on March 31, 2007, Ross Builders Supply wrote off the $900 receivable from customer Andrews. It is now November 4, and Ross unexpectedly receives $900 from Andrews. To account for this recovery, Ross makes two journal entries to reverse the earlier write-off and record the cash collection, as follows:

Journal Entry:

Date	Accounts	Post Ref.	Dr.	Cr.
Nov. 4	Accounts Receivable—Andrews		900	
	Allowance for Uncollectible Accounts			900
	Reinstate account receivable.			
4	Cash		900	
	Accounts Receivable—Andrews			900
	Record collection on account.			

Notes Receivable

Overview

Notes receivable are more formal than accounts receivable because, for a note receivable, the debtor signs a promissory note as evidence of the debt. Terms used to account for notes follow:

④ Account for notes receivable.

- As we defined in Chapter 2, a promissory note is a written promise to pay a specified amount of money at a future date.

- The **maker** of the note is the party who signs the note and promises to pay the required amount; the maker of the note is also known as the **debtor**.

- The **payee** of the note is the party to whom the maker promises future payment; the payee of the note is the **creditor**.
- The **principal** is the amount loaned by the payee and borrowed by the maker of the note.
- **Interest** is the fee for using money. It is revenue earned by the payee for loaning the money; it is an expense incurred by the maker as the cost of borrowing the money.
- The **interest period** is the time span of the note during which interest is computed. It extends from the original date of the note to the maturity date. It is also referred to as the **note term**, or simply **time**.
- The **interest rate** is the percentage rate of interest specified by the note. Interest rates are almost always stated for a period of one year. For example, a 9% note means that the amount of interest for *one year* is 9% of the note's principal amount.
- The **maturity date** of the note is the date when final payment of the note is due. It is also called the **due date**.
- The **maturity value** of the note is the sum of the principal plus interest due at maturity.

Exhibit 7-7 illustrates a promissory note.

Exhibit 7-7 A Promissory Note

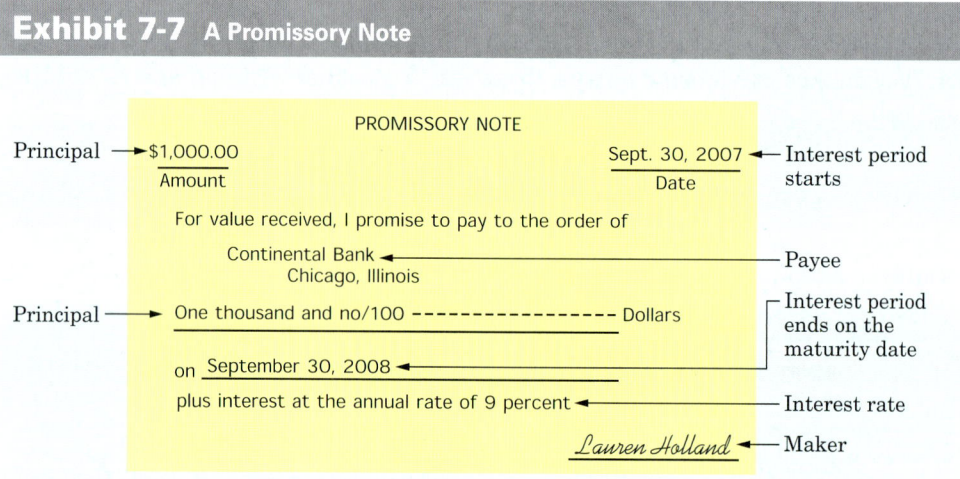

IDENTIFYING THE MATURITY DATE

Some notes specify the maturity date, as shown in Exhibit 7-7. Other notes state the period of the note in days or months. When the period is given in months, the note's maturity date falls on the same day of the month as the date the note was issued. For example, a six-month note dated February 16 matures on August 16.

When the period is given in days, the maturity date is determined by counting the days from the date of issue. A 120-day note dated September 14, 2007, for instance, matures on January 12, 2008, as shown here:

Month	Number of Days	Total Days
Sept. 2007	30 − 14 = 16	16
Oct. 2007	31	47
Nov. 2007	30	77
Dec. 2007	31	108
Jan. 2008	12	120

In counting the days remaining for a note, remember to count the maturity date and to omit the date the note was issued.

COMPUTING INTEREST ON A NOTE

The formula for computing the amount of interest on a note is:

Amount of Interest   =   Principal   ×   Interest Rate   ×   Time

Using the data in Exhibit 7-7, Continental Bank, as the payee, computes interest revenue for one year as shown here. The time element is one because the note's term is one year.

Amount of Interest	=	Principal	×	Interest Rate	×	Time
$90		$1,000		0.09		1 year

The formula for computing the maturity value of a note is:

Maturity Value   =   Principal   +   Interest

Using the data in Exhibit 7-7, Continental Bank computes the maturity value of the note as:

Maturity Value	=	Principal	+	Interest
$1,090		$1,000		$90

When the term of a note is stated in months, we compute the interest based on the 12-month year. Interest on a $2,000 note at 15% for three months is computed as:

Amount of Interest	=	Principal	×	Interest Rate	×	Time
$75		$2,000		0.15		3/12

When the term of a note is stated in days, we generally compute interest based on a 360-day year rather than on a 365-day year. A 360-day year eliminates some rounding, and is consistent with actual practice in most cases. The interest on a $5,000 note at 12% for 60 days can be computed as

Amount of Interest	=	Principal	×	Interest Rate	×	Time
$100		$5,000		0.12		60/360

Keep in mind that interest rates are stated as annual rates. Therefore, the time in the interest formula should also be expressed in terms of a year.

Accounting for Notes Receivable

RECORDING NOTES RECEIVABLE IN EXCHANGE FOR CASH

Consider the note shown in Exhibit 7-7. After Lauren Holland signs the note, Continental Bank gives her $1,000 cash. The bank's entry to record the loan is:

Journal Entry:

Date	Accounts	Post Ref.	Dr.	Cr.
Sept. 30, 2007	Notes Receivable—L. Holland		1,000	
	Cash			1,000
	Record loan supported by note.			

At maturity, the bank collects $1,090 from Holland, which includes the original principal and the calculated interest. Continental's entry to record the collection is:

Journal Entry:

Date	Accounts	Post Ref.	Dr.	Cr.
Sept. 30, 2008	Cash ($1,000 + $90)		1,090	
	Notes Receivable—L. Holland			1,000
	Interest Revenue ($1,000 × 0.09 × 1)			90
	Record collection of loan supported by note.			

Because the bank is in the business of loaning money, it must track a number of notes receivable separately. Thus, the Notes Receivable general ledger account is supported by a subsidiary ledger listing each note. The journal entry recording the note indicates the name of the person signing the note; in other words, it includes the name of the maker. It specifies that the L. Holland account in the subsidiary ledger needs increasing at the same time the Notes Receivable general ledger account is increased for the making of the note. Both L. Holland's account in the subsidiary ledger and the Notes Receivable account in the general ledger are reduced when the note is paid.

RECORDING NOTES RECEIVABLE IN EXCHANGE FOR GOODS

Some companies sell goods in exchange for notes receivable. Suppose that on October 20, 2008, General Electric sells household appliances for $15,000 to Hoffman Builders. Hoffman signs a 90-day promissory note at 10% annual interest. General Electric's entries to record the sale, excluding the entry to record the cost of goods sold, and collection from Hoffman are:

Journal Entry:

Date	Accounts	Post Ref.	Dr.	Cr.
Oct. 20, 2008	Notes Receivable—Hoffman Builders		15,000	
	Sales Revenue			15,000
	Record sale made for note receivable.			

Journal Entry:

Date	Accounts	Post Ref.	Dr.	Cr.
Jan 18, 2009	Cash ($15,000 + $375)		15,375	
	Notes Receivable—Hoffman Builders			15,000
	Interest Revenue ($15,000 × 0.10 × 90/360)			375
	Record collection of note receivable.			

RECORDING NOTES RECEIVABLE IN EXCHANGE FOR ACCOUNTS RECEIVABLE

A company may accept a note receivable from a customer who fails to pay an account receivable. The customer signs a promissory note, becoming the maker, and gives it to the payee. Suppose MiniGolf cannot pay Loman Supply. Loman may accept a one-year, $2,400 note receivable, with 9% interest, from MiniGolf on October 1, 2008. Loman's entry is:

Journal Entry:

Date	Accounts	Post Ref.	Dr.	Cr.
Oct. 1, 2008	Notes Receivable—MiniGolf		2,400	
	Accounts Receivable—MiniGolf			2,400
	Record note received for account.			

October 1, 2009, when the note is due, Loman records the receipt of the payment.

Journal Entry:

Date	Accounts	Post Ref.	Dr.	Cr.
Oct. 1, 2009	Cash ($2,400 + $216)		2,616	
	Notes Receivable—MiniGolf			2,400
	Interest Revenue ($2,400 × 0.09 × 1)			216
	Record collection of note receivable.			

Accruing Interest Revenue

A note receivable may be outstanding at the end of an accounting period. Recall that interest revenue is earned over time, not just when cash is received. Thus, the interest revenue earned on the note up to year-end is part of that year's earnings and represents accrued revenue. To record this accrued revenue, we will create and increase the asset, Interest Receivable, and increase a revenue account, Interest Revenue, much like the entry we made to accrue service revenue earned but not yet received in Chapter 3. Exhibit 7-8 illustrates accruing interest revenue for the following example.

Let's continue with the Loman Supply note receivable from MiniGolf. Loman Supply's accounting period ends December 31. How much of the total interest revenue does Loman earn in 2008? How much does it earn in 2009?

Loman will earn three months' interest in 2008, for October, November, and December. In 2009, Loman will earn nine months' interest, for January through September. On December 31, 2008, Loman will make the following adjusting entry to accrue interest revenue:

Journal Entry:

Date	Accounts	Post Ref.	Dr.	Cr.
Dec. 31, 2008	Interest Receivable ($2,400 × 0.09 × 3/12)		54	
	Interest Revenue			54
	Accrue interest revenue.			

Then, on the maturity date, Loman collects the principal and interest as follows:

Journal Entry:

Date	Accounts	Post Ref.	Dr.	Cr.
Oct. 1, 2009	Cash ($2,400 + $54 + $162)		2,616	
	Notes Receivable—MiniGolf			2,400
	Interest Receivable ($2,400 × 0.09 × 3/12)			54
	Interest Revenue ($2,400 × 0.90 × 9/12)			162
	Record collection of note receivable.			

The entries for accrued interest at December 31, 2008, and for collection at October 1, 2009, assign the correct amount of interest to each year.

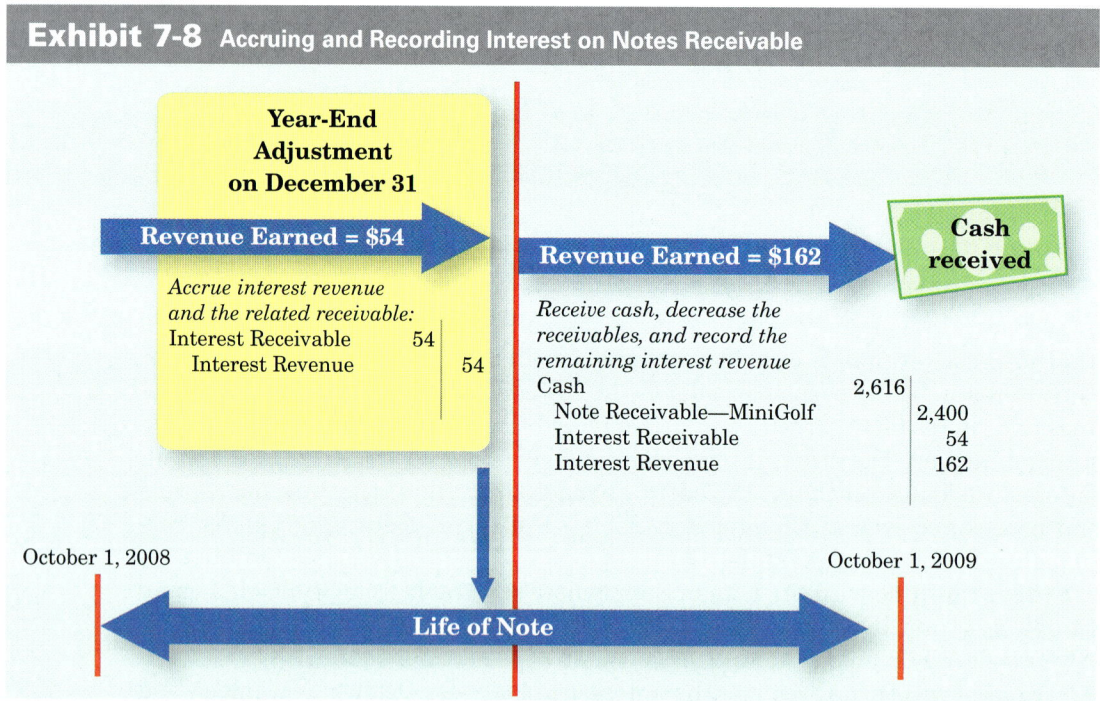

Exhibit 7-8 Accruing and Recording Interest on Notes Receivable

Dishonored Notes Receivable

If the maker of a note does not pay at maturity, the maker **dishonors**, or **defaults** on, the note. Because the term of the note has expired, the note agreement is no longer in force. But the payee still has a claim against the maker. In this case, the payee will transfer the amount of the note plus interest from Notes Receivable to Accounts Receivable. Suppose Anderson Jewelers has a 6-month, 10% note receivable for $1,200 from L. Ellis, and on the February 3 maturity date, L. Ellis defaults. Anderson Jewelers records the default as follows:

Journal Entry:

Date	Accounts	Post Ref.	Dr.	Cr.
Feb. 3	Accounts Receivable—L. Ellis ($1,200 + $60)		1,260	
	Notes Receivable—L. Ellis			1,200
	Interest Revenue ($1,200 × 0.10 × 6/12)			60
	Record a dishonored note receivable.			

Anderson will then pursue collection from Ellis as an account receivable.

More Ratios for Decision Making

The balance sheet lists assets in order of liquidity:

 Calculate the quick ratio and days' sales in receivables.

- Cash comes first because it is the most liquid asset.

- Short-term investments appear next because they are almost as liquid as cash.

- Current receivables are less liquid than short-term investments because the company must collect the receivables; hence, they appear next on the balance sheet.

- Merchandise inventory is less liquid than receivables because, to generate cash, the goods must first be sold, so they follow the other current assets.

- Prepaid expenses generally appear next because they are the least liquid.

Quick Ratio

A stringent measure of a company's ability to pay its current liabilities is the **quick ratio**, often called the **acid-test ratio**. The quick ratio reveals how well the entity can pay all its current liabilities by comparing **quick assets** to current liabilities. The formula for the quick ratio is:

$$\text{Quick Ratio} = \frac{\text{Cash} + \frac{\text{Short-Term}}{\text{Investments}} + \frac{\text{Net Current}}{\text{Receivables}}}{\text{Total Current Liabilities}}$$

Let's assume that the Ronald Corp. has the following current asset information for December 31, 2008: cash, $4,400; short-term investments, $1,400; and net current receivables, $2,400. Current liabilities are $3,900. The quick ratio for Ronald Corp. is calculated as follows:

$$\frac{\$4,400 + \$1,400 + \$2,400}{\$3,900} = 2.10$$

The higher the quick ratio, the more able the business is to pay its current liabilities. Ronald's quick ratio of 2.10 means that Ronald has $2.10 of quick assets to pay each $1 of current liabilities, which is an extremely strong position.

What is an acceptable quick ratio? The answer depends on the industry. Wal-Mart operates smoothly with a quick ratio of less than 0.20. Several things make this low ratio possible: Wal-Mart collects cash rapidly and has almost no receivables. The quick ratios for most department stores cluster around 0.80, while travel agencies average 1.10. In general, a quick ratio of 1.00 is considered safe.

Days' Sales in Receivables

After making a credit sale, the next step is to collect the resulting receivables. **Days' sales in receivables**, also called the **collection period**, indicates how many days it takes to collect the average level of receivables. The shorter the collection period, the quicker the organization can get and use its cash. The longer the collection period, the less cash is available for operations. Days' sales in receivables can be computed in two steps:

STEP 1

$$\text{One Day's Sales} = \frac{\text{Net Sales (or Total Revenues)}}{365 \text{ days}}$$

STEP 2

$$\frac{\text{Days' Sales in Average}}{\text{Accounts Receivable}} = \frac{\text{Average Net Accounts Receivable}}{\text{One Day's Sales}} = \frac{\left(\dfrac{\text{Beginning Net}}{\text{Receivables}} + \dfrac{\text{Ending Net}}{\text{Receivables}}\right) \div 2}{\text{One Day's Sales}}$$

For example, Johnson Supply provided the following information from the 2007 financial statements: net sales, $10,800; beginning net receivables, $2,500; and ending net receivables, $2,400. The days' sales in receivables for Johnson Supply is calculated by first computing the one day's sales. Johnson Supply finds that one day's sales averages to $29.6 per day. Next, the company must figure the average days' sales, and it sees that it has 83 days' sales in average accounts receivable. Johnson reached this numbers as follows:

STEP 1

One days' sales

$$\frac{\$10,800}{365} = \$29.6 \text{ per Day}$$

STEP 2

$$\frac{\text{Days' Sales in Average}}{\text{Accounts Receivable}} = \frac{(\$2,500 + \$2,400)/2}{\$29.6} = 83 \text{ Days}$$

The firm could also use the following formula to calculate the days' sales in average accounts receivable:

$$\frac{\text{Days' Sales in}}{\text{Average Receivables}} = \frac{\text{Average Net Receivables}}{\text{Net Sales}} \times 365$$

$$\frac{\text{Days' Sales in}}{\text{Average Receivables}} = \frac{\$2,450}{\$10,800} \times 365 = 83 \text{ Days}$$

The days' sales in receivables, or the length of the collection period, depends on the credit terms of the sale. For example, sales made on terms of net 30 should be collected within approximately 30 days. When a discount, such as 2/10, n/30, is offered, the collection period may be shorter. Credit terms of net 45 result in a longer collection period.

You have already discovered how to calculate other ratios, such as the gross profit percentage and inventory turnover rate, that provide insight into a business's performance. Investors and creditors do not evaluate a company on the basis of one or two ratios. Instead, they analyze all the information available. Then they stand back and ask, "What is our overall impression of this company?" Accounting is the system that produces the information to make this assessment possible.

Demo Doc

Accounts Receivable

Learning Objective   3

Pendant Corp. had Accounts Receivable of $10,000 and an Allowance for Uncollectible Accounts of $500 at January 1, 2008. During 2008, Pendant had the following transactions:

a. **Made credit sales of $35,000.**

b. **Collected $38,000 of cash from customers.**

c. **Accounts receivable in the amount of $480 were determined to be uncollectible and were written off.**

d. **Previously written-off receivables in the amount of $60 were unexpectedly collected in cash.**

Requirements

1. Journalize these transactions. Post these entries to the Accounts Receivable and Allowance for Uncollectible Accounts T-accounts.

2. Assume that Pendant estimates that 1.5% of all credit sales will eventually result in uncollectible accounts expense. Journalize the uncollectible accounts expense for 2008. What are the Allowance for Uncollectible Accounts and Net Accounts Receivable balances at December 31, 2008?

3. Ignoring Requirement 2, assume instead that Pendant estimates that 2% of Accounts Receivable less than 60 days old and 10% of Accounts Receivable 60 or more days old will never be collected. Of Pendant's receivables, $4,000 are less than 60 days old at December 31, 2008. Journalize the uncollectible accounts expense for 2008. What are the Allowance for Uncollectible Accounts and net Accounts Receivable balances at December 31, 2008?

Demo Doc Solutions

Requirement 1

Journalize these transactions. Post these entries to the Accounts Receivable and Allowance for Uncollectible Accounts T-accounts.

Part 1	Part 2	Part 3	Demo Doc Complete

a. Made credit sales of $35,000.

Credit sales are revenue and are recorded just like any other kind of revenue. Sales Revenue is increased by $35,000 (credit). Because the sales were on credit (that is, not paid in cash), Accounts Receivable is also increased by $35,000 (debit).

③ Use the allowance method to account for uncollectible receivables.

Journal Entry:

Date	Accounts	Post Ref.	Dr.	Cr.
	Accounts Receivable (Asset, ↑; debit)		35,000	
	Sales Revenue (Revenue, ↑; credit)			35,000
	Record sales revenue earned.			

Accounts Receivable

Bal.	10,000		
a.	35,000		
Bal.	45,000		

Allowance for Uncollectible Accounts

		Bal.	500
		Bal.	500

b. Collected $38,000 of cash from customers.

When cash is collected from customers, Cash is increased by $38,000 (debit) and Accounts Receivable is decreased by $38,000 (credit).

Journal Entry:

Date	Accounts	Post Ref.	Dr.	Cr.
	Cash (Asset, ↑; debit)		38,000	
	Accounts Receivable (Asset, ↓; credit)			38,000
	Record cash collected from customer.			

	Accounts Receivable					Allowance for Uncollectible Accounts		
Bal.	10,000	b.	38,000				Bal.	500
a.	35,000							
Bal.	7,000						Bal.	500

c. Accounts receivable in the amount of $480 were determined to be uncollectible and were written off.

If the receivables are uncollectible, then they are no longer valid assets (they no longer have any future benefits). This means that Accounts Receivable is decreased by $480 (credit).

The Allowance for Uncollectible Accounts is Pendant's estimate of the receivables that will not be collected. We have now identified some receivables that are uncollectible. By removing these receivables, the allowance now only estimates the *remaining unidentified* accounts that are uncollectible. So the allowance is also decreased by $480 (debit).

In other words, *both* the receivables *and* the allowance are decreased.

Journal Entry:

Date	Accounts	Post Ref.	Dr.	Cr.
	Allowance for Uncollectible Accounts (Contra-Asset, ↓; debit)		480	
	Accounts Receivable (Asset, ↓; credit)			480
	Write off uncollectible accounts receivable.			

	Accounts Receivable					Allowance for Uncollectible Accounts		
Bal.	10,000	b.	38,000	c.		480	Bal.	500
a.	35,000	c.	480					
Bal.	6,520						Bal.	20

Notice that by decreasing *both* the Accounts Receivable and the Allowance for Uncollectible Accounts, we keep *net* accounts receivable *the same*:

	Before Write-off	After Write-off	
Accounts Receivable	$7,000	$6,520	*Total receivables*
– Allowance for Uncollectible Accounts	(500)	(20)	*Amount we do not expect to collect*
= Accounts Receivable, Net	$6,500	$6,500	*Amount we do expect to collect*

The amount of receivables that we *do* expect to collect has remained the same. It is not affected by identifying customers who will not pay.

d. Previously written-off receivables in the amount of $60 were unexpectedly collected in cash.

If an account is written off, as in transaction **c**, it is removed from the accounting records. If it is subsequently collected, it must first be put back into the accounting records.

To reinstate the receivable, we must reverse the entry that removed the account. In other words, we must write the entry *backwards*.

The entry to write off accounts receivable debits the allowance and credits the accounts receivable (as in transaction **c**). To reverse this entry, we must do the opposite: credit the allowance and debit the receivables by $60.

Once this journal entry has been made, the cash collection is recorded as usual. Accounts Receivable is decreased by $60 (credit) and Cash is increased by $60 (debit).

Journal Entry:

Date	Accounts	Post Ref.	Dr.	Cr.
	Accounts Receivable (Asset, ↑; debit)		60	
	Allowance for Uncollectible Accounts (Contra-Asset, ↑; credit)			60
	Reinstate accounts receivable previously written off.			

Journal Entry:

Date	Accounts	Post Ref.	Dr.	Cr.
	Cash (Asset, ↑; debit)		60	
	Accounts Receivable (Asset, ↓; credit)			60
	Record cash collected from customer.			

	Accounts Receivable				Allowance for Uncollectible Accounts		
Bal.	10,000	b.	38,000	c.	480	Bal.	500
a.	35,000	c.	480			d.	60
d.	60	d.	60				
Bal.	6,520					Bal.	80

Requirement 2

Assume that Pendant estimates that 1.5% of all credit sales will eventually result in uncollectible accounts expense. Journalize the uncollectible accounts expense for 2008. What are the Allowance for Uncollectible Accounts and Net Accounts Receivable balances at December 31, 2008?

Part 1	**Part 2**	Part 3	Demo Doc Complete

The key phrase in this question is *1.5% of all credit sales*. It tells us that Pendant is using the percent-of-sales method to determine its Allowance for Uncollectible Accounts. In other words:

$$\% \text{ of Sales} = \text{Uncollectible Accounts Expense}$$

The percent-of-sales method is an income statement approach. The sales *and* the uncollectible accounts expense calculated are *both* on the income statement.

From transaction **a**, we know that credit sales were $35,000 for the year.

$$1.5\% \text{ of Credit Sales} = \text{Uncollectible Accounts Expense}$$
$$1.5\% \times \$35,000 = \$525$$

The uncollectible accounts expense must be recorded in a journal entry. Uncollectible Accounts Expense is increased by $525 (debit). This expense is our estimate of the increase in uncollectible receivables. So our estimate of the receivables we will not collect is going up. Allowance for Uncollectible Accounts is also increased (credit) by $525.

Journal Entry:

Date	Accounts	Post Ref.	Dr.	Cr.
	Uncollectible Accounts Expense (Expense, ↑; debit)		525	
	Allowance for Uncollectible Accounts (Contra-Asset, ↑; credit)			525
	Record uncollectible accounts expense for the year.			

	Accounts Receivable				Allowance for Uncollectible Accounts		
Bal.	10,000	b.	38,000	c.	480	Bal.	500
a.	35,000	c.	480			d.	60
d.	60	d.	60			Req. 2	525
Bal.	6,520					Bal.	605

The net Accounts Receivable is calculated as in transaction **c**.

Accounts Receivable	$6,520
– Allowance for Uncollectible Accounts	(605)
= Accounts Receivable, Net	$5,915

Requirement 3

Ignoring Requirement 2, assume instead that Pendant estimates that 2% of accounts receivable less than 60 days old and 10% of accounts receivable 60 or more days old will never be collected. Of Pendant's receivables, $4,000 are less than 60 days old at December 31, 2008. Journalize the uncollectible accounts expense for 2008. What are the Allowance for Uncollectible Accounts and net Accounts Receivable balances at December 31, 2008?

Part 1	Part 2	**Part 3**	Demo Doc Complete

The key phrases in this question are *2% of accounts receivable* and *10% of accounts receivable*. They tell us that Pendant is using the accounts receivable aging method to determine its allowance for uncollectible accounts. In other words:

% of Accounts Receivable =
Ending Balance in Allowance for Uncollectible Accounts

The accounts receivable aging method is a balance sheet approach. Accounts receivable and the Allowance for Uncollectible Accounts are both on the balance sheet.

The balance in Accounts Receivable after transaction **d** is $6,520. If $4,000 of this balance is less than 60 days old, then $2,520 ($6,520 – $4,000) is 60 or more days old.

% of Accounts Receivable =
Ending Balance in Allowance for Uncollectible Accounts
$(2\% \times \$4,000) + (10\% \times \$2,520) = \$332$

The ending balance in Allowance for Uncollectible Accounts should be $332.

Allowance for Uncollectible Accounts

c.	480	Bal.	500
		d.	60
		Req. 3	x
		Bal.	332

What do we need to do to bring the Allowance account to a balance of $332? We must credit the Allowance by x (see T-account). We can calculate x as:

$$500 + 60 + x - 480 = 332$$
$$x = 252$$

Accounts Receivable					Allowance for Uncollectible Accounts		
Bal.	10,000	b.	38,000	c.	480	Bal.	500
a.	35,000	c.	480			d.	60
d.	60	d.	60			Req. 3	252
Bal.	6,520					Bal.	332

So we must have a journal entry that increases the allowance by $252 (credit). This increase is an additional cost to the business of uncollectible accounts, so we must also increase the Uncollectible Accounts Expense by $252 (debit).

Journal Entry:

Date	Accounts	Post Ref.	Dr.	Cr.
	Uncollectible Accounts Expense (Expense, ↑; debit)		252	
	Allowance for Uncollectible Accounts (Contra-Asset, ↑; credit)			252
	Record uncollectible account expense for the year.			

The net Accounts Receivable is calculated as in transaction **c**:

Accounts Receivable	$6,520
− Allowance for Uncollectible Accounts	(332)
= Accounts Receivable, Net	$6,188

Part 1	Part 2	Part 3	Demo Doc Complete

Accounting in Action

Suppose you want to open your own business and make sales on account as well as for cash. What actions would you take to account for receivables?

Decision	**Guidelines**
How to make sales?	Make
	• *Cash* sales
	• *Bank credit card* sales
	• *Debit card* sales
	• *Credit card* sales
	• *Sales on account*

If I make sales on account, how much of my receivables will I collect?

Less than the full amount of the receivables because we cannot collect from some customers; the amount we realistically expect to collect is the *net realizable value*, or the net accounts receivable.

How do I report receivables at their net realizable value?

1. Use the *allowance method* to account for uncollectible receivables. Set up an allowance for uncollectible accounts

2. Estimate uncollectibles by either of these methods:

   a. *Percent-of-sales method* (income-statement approach)
   b. *Aging method* (balance-sheet approach)

3. Write off uncollectible receivables as they prove uncollectible.

4. $$\begin{array}{c} \text{Net Accounts} \\ \text{Receivable} \end{array} = \begin{array}{c} \text{Accounts} \\ \text{Receivable} \end{array} - \begin{array}{c} \text{Allowance for} \\ \text{Uncollectible Accounts} \end{array}$$

Accounts Receivable	$XXX
Less: Allowance for Uncollectible Accounts	(X)
Accounts Receivable, Net	$ XX

How do I report receivables on the balance sheet?

Can I account for uncollectible receivables in another way?

The *direct write-off method* uses no allowance for uncollectible accounts. It simply writes off a customer's account receivable when it proves uncollectible. This method is not acceptable according to GAAP unless the uncollectible amounts are insignificant.

How to account for other receivables?

How do I compute amounts related to notes receivable?

Notes receivable are written promises of future payment.

• *Interest* = Principal × Interest Rate × Time
• *Maturity Value* = Principal + Interest

How do I evaluate a company's financial position?

• $$\text{Quick Ratio} = \frac{\text{Cash} + \begin{array}{c}\text{Short-Term} \\ \text{Investments}\end{array} + \begin{array}{c}\text{Net Current} \\ \text{Receivables}\end{array}}{\text{Total Current Liabilities}}$$

• $$\begin{array}{c}\text{Day's Sales in} \\ \text{Average Accounts Receivable}\end{array} = \frac{\begin{array}{c}\text{Average Net} \\ \text{Accounts Receivable}\end{array}}{\text{One Day's Sales}}$$

Review

Receivables
Word Power

Acid-test ratio Ratio that reveals how well the entity can pay its current liabilities. Also called the quick ratio.

Aging method Method of estimating uncollectible accounts that focuses on accounts receivable; the accountant calculates the end-of-the-period allowance balance needed according to the aging of the receivable accounts. Also called the *balance-sheet approach*.

Allowance for Uncollectible Accounts A contra-asset account that holds the estimated amount of uncollectible accounts receivable.

Allowance method The method of accounting for uncollectible accounts that estimates these amounts and uses an allowance account so that the balance sheet shows the amount of accounts receivable expected to be collected in the future.

Bad debts Receivable amounts due that are never collected. Also called uncollectible accounts.

Balance-sheet approach Method of estimating uncollectible accounts that focuses on accounts receivable; the accountant calculates the end-of-the-period allowance balance needed according to the aging of the receivable accounts. Also called the *aging method*.

Collection period The number of days it takes to collect the average level of receivables. Also called the *days' sales in receivables*.

Control account An account in the general ledger that summarizes the details of an account balance.

Creditor The entity to whom the debtor promises future payment. Also called the *payee of a note*.

Days' sales in receivables The number of days it takes to collect the average level of receivables. Also called the *collection period*.

Debtor The entity that promises future payment; also called the *maker of a note*.

Default Failure of the maker to pay the note at maturity. Also called *dishonor*.

Direct write-off method The method of accounting for uncollectible accounts that writes off a customer's account as an uncollectible when the business knows the customer will not pay.

Dishonor Failure of the maker to pay the note at maturity. Also called *default*.

Due date The date when final payment of the note is due. Also called the *maturity date*.

Income-statement approach Method of estimating uncollectible accounts that focuses on net credit sales. Also called the *percent-of-sales method*.

Interest The fee for using money; revenue to the creditor for loaning money; expense to the debtor for borrowing money.

Interest period The time span of the note during which interest is computed; it extends from the original date of the note to the maturity date. Also called *note term*, or *time*.

Interest rate The percentage rate of interest specified by the note; almost always stated for a period of one year.

Maker The entity that promises future payment; Also called the *debtor*.

Maturity date The date when final payment of the note is due. Also called the *due date*.

Maturity value The sum of the principal plus interest due at maturity.

Net credit sales The total credit sales less sales discounts and sales returns and allowances related to the credit sales.

Net realizable value The net amount that the business expects to collect; the net realizable value of receivables is calculated by subtracting Allowance for Uncollectible Accounts from Accounts Receivable.

Note term The time span of the note during which interest is computed; it extends from the original date of the note to the maturity date. Also called the *interest period*, or *time*.

Payee The entity to whom the debtor promises future payment. Also called the creditor.

Percent-of-sales method Method of estimating uncollectible accounts that focuses on net credit sales. Also called the *income-statement approach*.

Principal The amount loaned by the payee and borrowed by the maker of the note.

Quick assets Highly liquid assets used to calculate the quick ratio, including cash and cash equivalents, short-term investments, and accounts receivable, net.

Quick ratio Ratio that reveals how well the entity can pay its current liabilities. Also called the *acid-test ratio*.

Recovery of an uncollectible account Collection of cash from an account previously written off.

Time The time span of the note during which interest is computed; it extends from the original date of the note to the maturity date. Also called the *interest period*, or *note term*.

Uncollectible accounts Receivable amounts due that are never collected. Also called *bad debts*.

Uncollectible accounts expense Selling expense caused by uncollectible accounts that reduce operating income.

Write off Removing a customer's receivable from the accounting records because it is considered uncollectible.

Quick Check

1. According to good internal controls, the person who handles cash can also:

   a. Account for cash receipts from customers
   b. Account for cash payments
   c. Issue credits to customers for merchandise returned
   d. None of the above

2. Uncollectible accounts are the same as:

   a. Bad debts
   b. Notes receivable
   c. Both a and b
   d. None of the above

3. Which method of estimating uncollectible receivables focuses on net credit sales?

   a. Aging approach
   b. Percent-of-sales approach
   c. Net realizable value approach
   d. All of the above

4. Your business uses the allowance method to account for uncollectible receivables. At the beginning of the year, Allowance for Uncollectible Accounts had a credit balance of $1,100. During the year you recorded Uncollectible Accounts Expense of $2,000 and wrote off bad receivables of $2,100. What is your year-end balance in Allowance for Uncollectible Accounts?

   a. $1,000
   b. $2,000
   c. $3,100
   d. $3,200

5. Your ending balance of Accounts Receivable is $20,000. Use the data in the preceding question to compute the net realizable value of Accounts Receivable at year-end. Or, stated differently, determine the net receivables to report on your year-end balance sheet.

   a. $18,000
   b. $19,000
   c. $20,000
   d. $21,000

6. What is wrong with the direct write-off method of accounting for uncollectibles?

   a. The direct write-off method does not set up an allowance for uncollectible accounts.
   b. The direct write-off method does not use an allowance for uncollectible accounts and thus overstates assets on the balance sheet.

c. The direct write-off method does not match expenses against revenues very well.

d. All of the above.

7. On December 31, you have a $10,000 note receivable from a customer. Interest of 8% has also accrued for six months on the note. What will your financial statements report for this situation?

a. Nothing, because you haven't received the cash yet.

b. Balance sheet will report the note receivable of $10,000.

c. Balance sheet will report the note receivable of $10,000 and interest receivable of $400.

d. Income statement will report a note receivable of $10,000.

8. Return to the data in the preceding question. What will be the income statement report for this situation?

a. Nothing, because you haven't received the cash yet

b. Interest revenue of $400

c. Note receivable of $10,000

d. Both b and c

9. At year-end, your business has cash of $10,000, receivables of $40,000, inventory of $50,000, and prepaid expenses totaling $5,000. Liabilities of $60,000 must be paid within the next year. What is your quick ratio?

a. 0.83

b. 1.67

c. 1.75

d. Cannot be determined from the data given

10. Return to the data in the preceding question. A year ago receivables stood at $60,000, and sales for the current year total $730,000. How many days did it take you to collect your average level of receivables?

a. 45

b. 35

c. 25

d. 20

Answers are given after Apply Your Knowledge (p. 403).

Accounting Practice

Short Exercises

S7-1. What duty must be withheld from a company's credit department in order to safeguard the company's cash? If the credit department does this job, what can a dishonest credit department employee do to hurt the company?

S7-2. Suppose the Fina station near the Alamo in San Antonio, Texas, had these transactions on a busy Saturday in April:

American Express credit card sales	$10,000
VISA bank card sale	8,000

Suppose American Express charges merchants 4% and VISA charges 3%. Record these sale transactions for the Fina station.

S7-3. Bly Paper Company included the following items in its financial statements as of December 31, 2009:

Allowance for		Sales Revenue	$140,000
Uncollectible Accounts	$ 1,500	Other Assets	4,000
Cash	12,000	Cost of Goods Sold and	
Accounts Receivable	26,000	Other Expenses	125,000
Accounts Payable	10,250	Notes Payable	33,000

1. How much net income did Bly earn for the year?

2. Show how Bly reported receivables on its classified balance sheet.

S7-4. During its first year of operations, Atlas Travel earned revenue of $400,000 on account. Industry experience suggests that Atlas Travel's uncollectible accounts will amount to 2% of revenues. On December 31, 2007, accounts receivable total $90,000. The company uses the allowance method to account for uncollectibles.

1. Journalize Atlas Travel's uncollectible accounts expense using the percent-of-sales method.

2. Show how Atlas should report accounts receivable on its balance sheet on December 31, 2007. Follow the reporting format illustrated in Exhibit 7-2.

S7-5. This exercise continues the situation of S7-4, in which Atlas Travel ended 2007 with accounts receivable of $90,000 and an Allowance for

continued.....

Uncollectible Accounts of $8,000. During 2008, Atlas Travel completed these transactions:

- Service revenue on account, $600,000

- Collections on account, $580,000

- Write-offs of uncollectibles, $15,000

- Uncollectible accounts expense, 2% of service revenue

Journalize Atlas Travel's 2008 transactions.

S7-6. Gorav Dental Group started 2007 with Accounts Receivable of $120,000 and an Allowance for Uncollectible Accounts of $6,000. During 2007, Gorav Dental completed these transactions:

a. Credit sales, $400,000

b. Collections on account, $320,000

c. Write-offs of uncollectibles, $15,000

d. At December 31, the aging of accounts receivable showed that Gorav will probably *not* collect $5,000 of its accounts receivable.

Journalize Gorav's 2007 transactions. Prepare a T-account for the Allowance for Uncollectible Accounts to show your computation of uncollectible accounts expense for the year.

③ Using the allowance method.

S7-7. Limo.com had the following balances on December 31, 2008, before the year-end adjustments:

③ Using the allowance method.

Accounts Receivable	Allowance for Uncollectible Accounts
104,000	1,300

The aging of receivables yields these data:

	Age of Accounts				
	1–30 Days	31–60 Days	61–90 Days	Over 90 Days	Total Receivables
Accounts receivable.....	$70,000	$20,000	$10,000	$4,000	$104,000
Estimate percentage uncollectible............	× 1%	× 2%	× 5%	× 50%	

Journalize Limo's entry to adjust the allowance account to its correct balance on December 31, 2008.

2 Using the direct write-off method.

S7-8. Antonio Galvan, an attorney, uses the direct write-off method to account for uncollectible receivables. On August 31, Galvan's accounts receivable were $8,000. During September, he earned service revenue of $20,000 on account and collected $22,000 from clients on account. He also wrote off uncollectible receivables of $2,000. What is Galvan's balance of Accounts Receivable on September 30? Does he expect to collect this entire amount? Why or why not?

4 Accounting for notes receivable.

5 Calculating the quick ratio and days' sales in receivables.

S7-9. Match the term with its definition by placing the corresponding letter in the space provided:

a. Maker of a note

b. Payee of a note

c. Dishonor of a note

d. Quick ratio

e. Days' sales in receivables

_____ **1.** Failure of a note's maker to pay a note receivable at maturity

_____ **2.** The entity that promises to pay the amount required by the note agreement; the debtor

_____ **3.** Tells how well the entity could pay its current liabilities

_____ **4.** The entity to receive future payment from a note; the creditor

_____ **5.** Tells how many days' sales it takes to collect the average level of receivables

4 Accounting for notes receivable.

S7-10. For each of the following notes receivable, compute the amount of interest revenue earned during 2005. Use a 360-day year, and round to the nearest dollar.

	Principal	Interest Rate	Interest Period During 2005
Note 1	$100,000	8%	6 months
Note 2	30,000	12%	75 days
Note 3	20,000	9%	60 days
Note 4	50,000	10%	3 months

4 Accounting for notes receivable.

S7-11. Bank of America lent $100,000 to Christine Kleuters on a 90-day, 8% note. Record the following transactions for Bank of America (explanations are not required):

1. Lending the money on June 12.

2. Collecting the principal and interest at maturity. Specify the date. For the computation of interest, use a 360-day year.

S7-12. On September 30, 2008, Bank of America loaned $1,000, at 6% interest, for 6 months to Robert Foster. The accounting year of Bank of America ends on December 31, 2008. Journalize Bank of America's lending money on September 30, 2008. Also calculate accrued interest revenue on December 31, 2008, and record the adjusting entry.

④ Accounting for notes receivable.

S7-13. Calculate the quick assets and the quick ratio for each of the following companies:

⑤ Calculating the quick ratio and days' sales in receivables.

	Jaxon	Kilborn
Cash	$ 10,000	$ 25,000
Short-term investments	5,000	15,000
Net receivables	45,000	52,000
Total quick assets		
Current liabilities	$ 45,000	$ 100,000
Quick ratio		

S7-14. Calculate day's sales in receivables for the following two companies; include answers for steps 1 and 2.

⑤ Calculating the quick ratio and days' sales in receivables.

	Moore	Noel
Step 1.		
Net sales	$ 73,000	$ 45,625
Divide by 365 days	365	365
One day's sales		
Step 2.		
Net accounts receivable, beginning	$ 12,000	$ 23,000
Add: Net accounts receivable, ending	13,000	21,000
Divide by 2	2	2
Average net accounts receivable		
Average net accounts receivable (Step 2)		
Divide by one day's sales (Step 1)		
Days' sales in receivables		

Exercises

② Using the direct write-off method.

E7-15. Match the term with its definition by placing the corresponding letter in the space provided:

③ Using the allowance method.

a. Creditor   c. Receivables

b. Debtor   d. Uncollectible accounts expense

④ Accounting for notes receivable.

continued.....

e. Allowance method

h. Aging method

f. Allowance for
Uncollectible Accounts

i. Direct write-off method

g. Percent-of-sales method

__c__ Example: Monetary claims against a business or an individual

_____ **1.** A contra-account, related to accounts receivable, which holds
the estimated amount of uncollectible receivables

_____ **2.** A method of accounting for uncollectible receivables in which
the company waits until a specific customer's account receivable
is uncollectible before recording uncollectible accounts expense

_____ **3.** A method of recording receivable losses on the basis of estimates instead of waiting to see which customers the company
will not collect from

_____ **4.** The party to a credit transaction who sells goods or a service
and obtains a receivable

_____ **5.** A way to estimate uncollectible accounts by analyzing individual accounts receivable according to the length of time
they have been receivable

_____ **6.** The party to a credit transaction who makes a purchase and
has a payable

_____ **7.** Cost to the seller of credit sales; arises from the failure to collect from credit customers

_____ **8.** A method of estimating uncollectible receivables that calculates uncollectible accounts expense based on net credit sales

① The types of sales and
receivables and related
internal controls.

E7-16. Claire Billiot, the office manager of a local office supply company, is
designing its internal control system. Billiot proposes the following
procedures for credit checks on new customers, sales on account, cash
collections, and write-offs of uncollectible receivables:

a. The credit department runs a credit check on all customers who
apply for credit. When an account proves uncollectible, the credit
department authorizes the write-off of the account receivable.

b. Cash receipts come into the credit department, which separates
the cash received from the customer remittance slips. The credit
department lists all cash receipts by customer name and amount of
cash received.

c. The cash goes to the treasurer for deposit in the bank. The remittance
slips go to the accounting department for recording of the collections.

d. The controller compares the daily deposit slip to the total amount
of the collections recorded. Both amounts must agree.

continued.....

For each of the four procedures, indicate whether the procedure includes an internal control weakness. Explain how employee fraud could occur because of the weakness. What can Claire do to strengthen the internal control system?

E7-17. Rice Automotive ended December 2008 with Accounts Receivable of $30,000 and Allowance for Uncollectible Accounts of $1,500. During January 2009, Rice Automotive completed the following transactions:

3 Using the allowance method.

- Sales of $180,000, which included $120,000 in credit sales and $60,000 of cash sales

- Cash collections on account, $90,000

- Write-offs of uncollectible receivables, $1,200

- Uncollectible accounts expense, estimated as 2% of credit sales

Requirements

1. Prepare journal entries to record sales, collections, write-offs of uncollectibles, and uncollectible accounts expense by the percent-of-sales method.

2. Calculate the ending balances in Accounts Receivable, Allowance for Uncollectible Accounts, and net Accounts Receivable at January 31. How much does Rice Automotive expect to collect?

E7-18. Refer to E7-17.

2 Using the direct write-off method.

Requirements

1. Record Uncollectible Accounts Expense for January using the direct write-off method.

2. What accounts receivable amount does Rice Automotive report on its January 31 balance sheet under the direct write-off method? Does it expect to collect the full amount?

E7-19. On December 31, 2008, the Accounts Receivable balance of Alterations Express is $300,000. The Allowance for Uncollectible Accounts has a $3,900 credit balance. Alterations prepares the following aging schedule for its accounts receivable:

3 Using the allowance method.

	Age of Accounts			
	1–30 Days	31–60 Days	61–90 Days	Over 90 Days
Accounts receivable	$140,000	$80,000	$70,000	$10,000
Estimated percentage uncollectible......	0.5%	1.0%	6.0%	50%

continued.....

1. Journalize the year-end adjusting entry for uncollectible accounts on the basis of the aging schedule. Calculate the resulting ending balance of the Allowance account based on the account aging. Show the T-account for the Allowance on December 31, 2008.

2. Show how Alterations Express will report Accounts Receivable on its December 31, 2008, balance sheet.

③ Using the allowance method.

E7-20. House Depot made credit sales of $500,000 during 2008. Experience indicates that Uncollectible Accounts Expense is 1% of credit sales.

On December 31, 2008, House Depot's Accounts Receivable balance is $130,000, and Allowance for Uncollectible Accounts is $1,600 before the year-end adjustment.

Record uncollectible accounts expense for 2008. Then report House Depot's receivables, net of the allowance, on December 31, 2008.

④ Accounting for notes receivable.

E7-21. Match the term with its definition by placing the corresponding letter in the space provided:

a. Interest   f. Maturity value

b. Interest period   g. Payee of the note

c. Interest rate   h. Principal

d. Maker of the note   i. Promissory note

e. Maturity date

_____ 1. A written promise to pay a specified amount of money at a particular future date

_____ 2. The date when final payment of the note is due; also called the due date

_____ 3. The percentage rate of interest specified by the note for one year

_____ 4. The entity to whom the maker promises future payment

_____ 5. The period of time during which interest is computed

_____ 6. The amount loaned out by the payee and borrowed by the maker of the note

_____ 7. The sum of the principal plus interest due at maturity

_____ 8. The entity that signs the note and promises to pay the required amount

_____ 9. The revenue to the payee for loaning money; the expense to the debtor

E7-22. On April 30, 2007, Citibank loaned $100,000 to Grant Hughes on a one-year, 6% note.

④ Accounting for notes receivable.

Requirements

1. Compute the interest for the years ended December 31, 2007, and 2008, on the Hughes note.

2. Which party has a

   a. Note receivable?

   b. Note payable?

   c. Interest revenue?

   d. Interest expense

3. How much in total would Hughes pay the bank if he pays off the note early—say, on November 30, 2007?

E7-23. Journalize the following transactions of Cramer, Inc., which ends its accounting year on June 30:

④ Accounting for notes receivable.

Apr.	1	Loaned $20,000 cash to R. Simpson on a one-year, 8% note.
June	6	Sold goods to Friday Corp., receiving a 90-day, 10% note for $3,000.
	30	Made a single compound entry to accrue interest revenue on both notes. Use a 360-day year for interest computations.

E7-24. Record the following transactions in the journal of Brooks Jewelry:

① The types of sales and receivables and related internal controls.

④ Accounting for notes receivable.

2008		
Feb.	12	Recorded VISA bank card sales of $60,000, less a 2% discount.
May	1	Loaned $20,000 to J. Lim on a one-year, 6% note.
Dec.	31	Accrued interest revenue on the J. Lim note.
2009		
May	1	Collected the maturity value of the J. Lim note.

E7-25. Gorman Enterprises sells on account. When a customer account becomes four months old, Gorman converts the account to a note receivable. During 2008, Gorman completed these transactions:

④ Accounting for notes receivable.

June	29	Sold goods on account to I. Happy, $10,000.
Nov.	1	Received a $10,000, 60-day, 9% note from I. Happy in satisfaction of his past-due account receivable.
Dec.	31	Collected the I. Happy note at maturity.

continued.....

Requirements

Record the transactions in Gorman's journal.

E7-26. Refer to E7-25. During 2009, Gorman completed these transactions:

④ Accounting for notes receivable.

May 14	Sold goods on account to A. Karsen, $1,200.
Sept. 1	Received a $1,200, 60-day, 8% note from A. Karsen in satisfaction of her past-due account receivable.
Oct. 31	A. Karsen dishonored the note.

Requirements

Record the transactions in Gorman's journal.

⑤ Calculating the quick ratio and days' sales in receivables.

E7-27. Calculate the quick assets and the quick ratio for each of the following companies:

	A	B	C	D
Cash	$ 92,000	$ 64,000	$ 23,000	$ 107,000
Short-term investments	70,000	28,000	15,000	53,000
Net receivables	125,000	110,000	52,000	140,000
Total quick assets				
Current liabilities	$ 205,000	$ 101,000	$ 60,000	$ 350,000
Quick ratio				

Which of the companies should be concerned about their liquidity?

⑤ Calculating the quick ratio and days' sales in receivables.

E7-28. Calculate days' sales in receivables for Hybrid Tech for 2004 through 2007; include the answers for steps 1 and 2.

	2004	2005	2006	2007
Step 1.				
Net sales	$ 73,000	$ 80,300	$ 88,330	$ 100,010
Divide by 365 days	365	365	365	365
One day's sales				

continued.....

Step 2.

Net accounts receivable, beginning	$ 12,000	$ 13,000	$ 17,800	$ 25,760
Add: Net accounts receivable, ending	13,000	17,800	25,760	18,080
Divide by 2	2	2	2	2
Average net accounts receivable				
Average net accounts receivable (Step 2)				
Divide by one day's sales (Step 1)				
Days' sales in receivables				

E7-29. Vision Equipment reported the following items on February 28, 2008 (amounts in thousands, with last year's amounts also given as needed):

⑤ Calculating the quick ratio and days' sales in receivables.

Accounts Payable......................	$ 449	Accounts Receivable, Net:	
Cash...	215	February 28, 2008......................	$ 220
Inventory:		February 28, 2007......................	150
February 28, 2008................	190	Cost of Goods Sold.........................	1,200
February 28, 2007................	160	Short-Term Investments...............	165
Net Credit Sales.......................	1,930	Other Current Assets....................	90
Long-Term Assets....................	410	Other Current Liabilities..............	145
Long-Term Liabilities..............	10		

Compute Vision Equipment's (a) quick ratio and (b) days' sales in average receivables for 2008. Evaluate each ratio value as strong or weak. Assume Vision Equipment sells on terms of net 30.

E7-30. Hughes Computer sells on account. Recently, Hughes reported these figures (in millions of dollars):

⑤ Calculating the quick ratio and days' sales in receivables.

	2006	**2005**
Net sales..	$31,168	$31,188
Receivables at end of year...........	2,269	2,424

Requirements

1. Compute Hughes's average collection period on receivables during 2006.

2. Suppose Hughes's normal credit terms for a sale on account are "net 30 days." How well does Hughes' collection period compare to the company's credit terms? Are the results of the comparison good or bad for Hughes? Explain.

Problems (Group A)

② Using the direct write-off method.

③ Using the allowance method.

P7-31A. On August 31, Pro Tennis Equipment had a $200,000 debit balance in Accounts Receivable. During September, Pro Tennis made sales of $500,000, all on credit. Other data for September include:

- Collections on account, $550,000

- Write-offs of uncollectible receivables, $11,000

Requirements

1. Record sales and collections on account. Then record September's uncollectible accounts expense and write-offs of customer accounts using the allowance method. Show all September activity in T-accounts for Accounts Receivable, Allowance for Uncollectible Accounts, and Uncollectible Accounts Expense. The August 31 unadjusted balance in Allowance for Uncollectible Accounts was $3,000. Uncollectible Accounts Expense was estimated at 2% of credit sales.

2. Suppose Pro Tennis Equipment used a different method to account for uncollectible receivables. Record sales and collections on account. Then record uncollectible accounts expense for September using the direct write-off method. Post to T-accounts for Accounts Receivable and Uncollectible Accounts Expense and show their balances on September 30.

3. What amount of uncollectible accounts expense would Pro Tennis Equipment report on its September income statement under each of the two methods? Which amount better matches expenses with revenue? Give your reason.

4. What amount of net accounts receivable would Pro Tennis Equipment report on its September 30 balance sheet under each of the two methods? Which amount is more realistic? Give your reason.

③ Using the allowance method.

P7-32A. Regents Supply completed the following transactions during 2008 and 2009:

2008		
Dec.	31	Estimated that Uncollectible Accounts Expense for the year was 3/4 of 1% on credit sales of $400,000, and recorded that amount.
	31	Made the closing entry for Uncollectible Accounts Expense.
2009		
Jan.	17	Sold inventory to Abe Gomez, $600, on account. Ignore cost of goods sold.
June	29	Wrote off the Abe Gomez account as uncollectible after repeated efforts to collect from him.

continued.....

Aug. 6 Received $200 from Abe Gomez, along with a letter stating his intention to pay within 30 days. Reinstated his account in full.

Sept. 4 Received the balance due from Abe Gomez.

Dec. 31 Made a compound entry to write off the following accounts as uncollectible: Bernard Clark, $700; Marie Montrose, $300; and Terry Forman, $600.

31 Estimated that Uncollectible Accounts Expense for the year was 2/3 of 1% on credit sales of $480,000, and recorded that amount as expense.

31 Made the closing entry for Uncollectible Accounts Expense.

Requirements

1. Open ledger accounts for Allowance for Uncollectible Accounts and Uncollectible Accounts Expense. These accounts have beginning balances of $0.

2. Record the transactions in the journal, and post to the two ledger accounts; remember to update the account balances but ignore posting references.

3. The December 31, 2009, balance of Accounts Receivable is $139,000. Show how Accounts Receivable would be reported on the balance sheet at that date.

P7-33A. The Bailey Insurance Agency received the following notes during 2008:

④ Accounting for notes receivable.

Note	Date	Principal Amount	Interest Rate	Term
(1)	Dec. 23	$13,000	9%	1 year
(2)	Nov. 30	12,000	12%	6 months
(3)	Dec. 7	9,000	10%	30 days

Requirements

1. Identifying each note by number, compute interest using a 360-day year, and determine the due date and maturity value of each note.

2. Journalize a single adjusting entry on December 31, 2008, to record accrued interest revenue on all three notes. Explanations are not required.

3. For note (1), journalize the collection of principal and interest at maturity. Explanations are not required.

P7-34A. Record the following transactions in the journal of Bingham Phone Accessories. Explanations are not required.

④ Accounting for notes receivable.

continued.....

2007		
Dec.	19	Received a $3,000, 60-day, 12% note on account from Arnold Collins.
	31	Made an adjusting entry to accrue interest on the Collins note.
	31	Made a closing entry for interest revenue.
2008		
Feb.	17	Collected the maturity value of the Collins note.
June	1	Loaned $10,000 cash to Electra Mann, receiving a 6-month, 11% note.
Oct.	31	Received a $1,500, 60-day, 12% note from Mark Phillips on his past-due account receivable.
Dec.	1	Collected the maturity value of the Electra Mann note.
	30	Mark Phillips dishonored his note at maturity; wrote off the note receivable as uncollectible, debiting Allowance for Uncollectible Accounts.

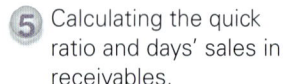

5 Calculating the quick ratio and days' sales in receivables.

P7-35A. The comparative financial statements of Bien Taco Restaurants for 2006, 2005, and 2004 include the following selected data:

	(In Thousands)		
	2006	**2005**	**2004**
Balance Sheet			
Current assets:			
Cash	$82	$80	$60
Short-term investments	140	174	122
Receivables, net of allowance for uncollectible accounts of $6, $6, and $5 respectively	257	265	218
Inventory	429	341	302
Prepaid expenses	21	27	46
Total current assets	929	887	748
Total current liabilities	$680	$700	$600
Income Statement			
Sales revenue	$5,189	$4,995	$4,206
Cost of goods sold	2,734	2,636	2,418

Requirements

1. Compute these ratios for 2006 and 2005:

   a. Quick ratio

   b. Days' sales in receivables

2. Write a memo explaining to the company owner which ratios improved from 2005 to 2006, which ratios deteriorated, and which item in the financial statements changed and caused changes in some ratios? Discuss whether this change conveys a favorable or an unfavorable impression about the company.

Problems (Group B)

P7-36B. On February 28, Hobby Lobby had an $80,000 debit balance in Accounts Receivable. During March, Hobby Lobby made sales of $450,000, all on credit. Other data for March include:

2 Using the direct write-off method.

3 Using the allowance method.

- Collections on account, $426,000.

- Write-offs of uncollectible receivables, $4,000.

Requirements

1. Record sales and collections on account. Then record March's uncollectible accounts expense and write-offs of customer accounts using the allowance method. Show all March activity in T-accounts for Accounts Receivable, Allowance for Uncollectible Accounts, and Uncollectible Accounts Expense. The February 28 unadjusted balance in Allowance for Uncollectible Accounts was $2,000. Uncollectible Accounts Expense was estimated at 2% of credit sales.

2. Suppose Hobby Lobby used a different method to account for uncollectible receivables. Record sales and collections on account. Then record Uncollectible Accounts Expense for March using the direct write-off method. Post to T-accounts for Accounts Receivable and Uncollectible Accounts Expense and show their balances on March 31.

3. What amount of Uncollectible Accounts Expense would Hobby Lobby report on its March income statement under each of the two methods? Which amount better matches expense with revenue? Give your reason.

4. What amount of net accounts receivable would Hobby Lobby report on its March 31 balance sheet under each of the two methods? Which amount is more realistic? Give your reason.

3 Using the allowance method.

P7-37B. Computer Learning Systems completed the following selected transactions during 2006 and 2007:

2006		
Dec.	31	Estimated that Uncollectible Accounts Expense for the year was 2/3 of 1% on credit sales of $450,000 and recorded that amount as expense.
	31	Made the closing entry for Uncollectible Accounts Expense.
2007		
Feb.	4	Sold inventory to Marian Hager, $1,500 on account. Ignore cost of goods sold.
July	1	Wrote off Marian Hager's account as uncollectible after repeated efforts to collect from her.

continued.....

Oct.	19	Received $500 from Marian Hager, along with a letter stating her intention to pay within 30 days. Reinstated Hager's account in full.
Nov.	15	Received the balance due from Marian Hager.
Dec.	31	Made a compound entry to write off the following accounts as uncollectible: Kay Brown, $800; Tim Sanders, $500; and Anna Chan, $1,200.
	31	Estimated that Uncollectible Accounts Expense for the year was 2/3 of 1% on credit sales of $585,000 and recorded the expense.
	31	Made the closing entry for Uncollectible Accounts Expense.

Requirements

1. Open ledger accounts for Allowance for Uncollectible Accounts and Uncollectible Accounts Expense. These accounts have a beginning balance of $0.

2. Record the transactions in the journal, and post to the two ledger accounts; remember to update account balances but ignore posting references.

3. The December 31, 2007, balance of Accounts Receivable is $164,500. Show how Accounts Receivable would be reported on the balance sheet at that date.

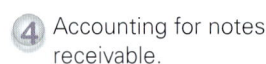 Accounting for notes receivable.

P7-38B. Lincoln Bank loaned money and received the following notes during 2008:

Note	Date	Principal Amount	Interest Rate	Term
(1)	Dec. 1	$12,000	9%	1 year
(2)	Oct. 31	11,000	12%	3 months
(3)	Nov. 19	15,000	10%	60 days

Requirements

1. Identifying each note by number, compute interest using a 360-day year, and determine the due date and maturity value of each note.

2. Journalize a single adjusting entry on December 31, 2008, to record accrued interest revenue on all three notes. Explanations are not required.

3. For note (1), journalize the collection of principal and interest at maturity. Explanations are not required.

P7-39B. Record the following transactions in the journal of Power Vitamins. Explanations are not required.

④ Accounting for notes receivable.

2006

Dec. 21 Received a $2,800, 30-day, 10% note on account from Joe Fritz.

31 Made an adjusting entry to accrue interest on the Fritz note.

31 Made a closing entry for interest revenue.

2007

Jan. 20 Collected the maturity value of the Fritz note.

Sept. 14 Loaned $6,000 cash to Broadman Investors, receiving a three-month, 13% note.

30 Received a $1,600, 60-day, 16% note from Chuck Post on his past-due account receivable.

Nov. 29 Chuck Post dishonored his note at maturity; wrote off the note as uncollectible, debiting Allowance for Uncollectible Accounts.

Dec. 14 Collected the maturity value of the Broadman Investors note.

P7-40B. The comparative financial statements of Scoopy's Ice Cream for 2008, 2007, and 2006 include the data shown here:

⑤ Calculating the quick ratio and days' sales in receivables.

	(In Millions)		
	2008	**2007**	**2006**
Balance Sheet			
Current assets:			
Cash	$27	$26	$ 22
Short-term investments	93	101	69
Receivables, net of allowance for uncollectible accounts of $7, $6, and $4 respectively	146	154	127
Inventory	454	383	341
Prepaid expenses	32	31	25
Total current assets	752	695	584
Total current liabilities	$400	$416	$ 388
Income Statement			
Sales revenue	$2,671	$2,505	$1,944
Cost of goods sold	1,380	1,360	963

continued.....

Requirements

1. Compute these ratios for 2008 and 2007:

   a. Quick ratio

   b. Days' sales in receivables

2. Write a memo explaining to the company owner which ratios improved from 2007 to 2008 and which ratios deteriorated. Which item in the financial statements changed and caused some ratios to improve and others to deteriorate? Discuss whether this change conveys a favorable or an unfavorable sign about the company.

**for 24/7 practice, visit
www.MyAccountingLab.com**

Apply Your Knowledge

Case 1. Ed Casey is the owner of Casey's Collectibles. The business uses the accrual method of accounting and recognizes sales revenue in the period in which the sale is made. As a result, the Accounts Receivable balance at year-end was $92,480, which was net of the Allowance for Uncollectible Accounts of $1,260. Ed was completing the year-end financial statements for the business in order to apply for a much needed business loan when he saw a letter from a district court. The letter was to inform him as proprietor of Casey's Collectibles that Charlie Smith had declared bankruptcy. As it turned out, Charlie was Ed's largest customer and his account receivable balance was $34,295, which the bankruptcy notification letter stated was never going to be paid. When Ed looked over the account receivable aging schedule he saw that Charlie's account was more than 90 days past due, and even though Ed had been suspicious, he still hoped that Charlie would pay his account balance. Ed looked at his balance sheet and thought that if he wrote off Charlie's account, the bank would become concerned about all of the accounts receivable listed. He then thought that had he not been so quick to open the mail, he would have not known that Charlie was bankrupt, and the balance sheet he was about to present to the bank would be fine. Knowing how potentially damaging this new information could be, Ed decided to just ignore it for the moment and simply go ahead with the balance sheet he had originally planned to give to the bank.

Should Ed provide the bank with a new balance sheet that reflects this new information? Would Ed have been fine with the original balance sheet had he simply waited to open his mail? Are any ethical issues involved with updating financial statement information for subsequent events? Did Ed not properly use the allowance method as he only had a balance for doubtful accounts totaling $1,260? Would Ed need to inform the bank had the bankruptcy letter been from a customer with an account receivable balance of $120?

Case 2. Bob and Larry were finishing the financial statements for their business when they saw the net income for the year was not going to be as large as they had hoped. Concerned that the bank would question the lower reported net income, Bob suggested that they reduce the percentage used to estimate uncollectible accounts for the current year from 5% of credit sales to 1% of credit sales. Larry quickly pointed out that for the last seven years; the bad debts always approximated 5% of the total credit sales. Bob then said that the key was simply that an "estimate" was used to compute the bad debt expense, so why not simply change the percentage from the "5% estimate" to a "1% estimate"? Larry was concerned because the change was not due to new business information; rather it was due to pressure to increase the current year profit by reducing the amount of bad debt expense currently included in the income statement. He told Bob that the current year credit sales were $6,587,000 and the Uncollectible Accounts Expense should be 5% or $329,350, not 1% or $65,870, because they could expect that over the next fiscal year approximately $329,000 of Accounts Receivable would end up as uncollectible. Bob pointed out, however, that by only using a 1% estimate the current year net income would be much larger since the amount of Uncollectible Account Expense would only be $65,870 instead of the larger $329,350. He also noted that the Allowance account would also be reduced so the Net Accounts Receivable on the balance sheet would be larger as well. Besides, Bob told Larry that they could worry about it in the next fiscal year. Larry told

Bob that the bank would find out what they had done, to which Bob said there would be no problem; they could just say they made a mistake in their estimate.

Would it be unethical to change the percentage used to compute the current year Uncollectible Accounts Expense? Would it be acceptable to change the percentage amount if the change was disclosed? Would it be acceptable if they compromised and used 3%? If they had used a new screening method to determine the creditworthiness of customers and, as a result, they were certain that the bad debts would be drastically reduced, could they change the percentage amount used? What do you think would happen if they used the 1% of credit sales for the current year financial statements? What would you recommend?

KNOW YOUR BUSINESS

This case will address the accounts receivable that resulted from sales on account. Target uses accrual accounting and therefore recognizes revenues in the period earned rather than in the period when the cash is received. Although many of the sales transactions are sales made for cash, other sales transactions are made on credit. As you learned, an allowance needs to be made for uncollectible accounts because sales booked in the current period may not be collected in the next accounting period. Therefore, the related uncollectible account expense is included in the current period. Refer to the Target Corporation financial statements in Appendix A. Also, consider the following partial excerpts from the first footnote, Summary of Accounting Policies:

Accounts Receivable
Accounts receivable are recorded net of an allowance for expected losses. The allowance, recognized in an amount equal to the anticipated future write-offs based on delinquencies, risk scores, aging trends, industry risk trends, and our historical experience, was $387 million at January 29, 2005, and $352 million at January 31, 2004.

Use of Estimates
The preparation of our financial statements, in conformity with accounting principles generally accepted in the United States (GAAP), requires management to make estimates and assumptions that affect the reported amounts in the financial statements and accompanying notes. Actual results may differ from those estimates.

Requirements

1. Who is responsible for establishing the estimated amount of uncollectible accounts? Are estimated amounts allowed under GAAP? Is the estimate used simply a guess?

2. What was the Accounts Receivable balance as of January 2005? What was the Accounts Receivable balance as of January 2004? Did the amount of accounts receivable increase or decrease during the year? What is the possible significance of the change in the accounts receivable balance?

continued.....

3. Did you notice that the Accounts Receivable balances included on the balance sheets are stated at "net"? Can you determine the total amount of Accounts Receivable Target had as of January 2005? Did the amount of the Allowance for Uncollectible Accounts increase or decrease? Why did the amount of the Allowance account change?

4. Can you find the Uncollectible Accounts Expense for the 2004 fiscal year that ended January 29, 2005? (*Hint*: Look at the Consolidated Statements of Cash Flows.) Can you compute the amount of accounts receivable Target wrote off during the fiscal year ended January 29, 2005? How does this amount compare to the previous year? How do you feel about the amount of Uncollectible Accounts Expense Target recognized?

For Internet Exercises, Excel in Practice, and additional online activities, go to the Web site www.prenhall.com/pollard.

Quick Check Answers

1. *d* 2. *a* 3. *b* 4. *a* 5. *b* 6. *d* 7. *c* 8. *b* 9. *a* 10. *c*

LEARNING OBJECTIVES

8

1. Describe inventory and discuss the related internal controls.

2. Compute inventory costs using first-in, first-out (FIFO), last-in, first-out (LIFO), and average cost methods and journalize inventory transactions.

3. Compare the effects of the different costing methods on the financial statements.

4. Apply the lower-of-cost-or-market (LCM) rule to value inventory.

5. Report inventory on the balance sheet and measure the effect of inventory errors.

6. Estimate ending inventory by the gross profit method.

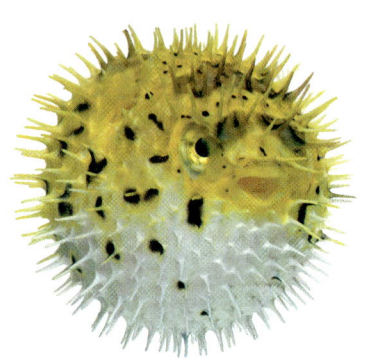

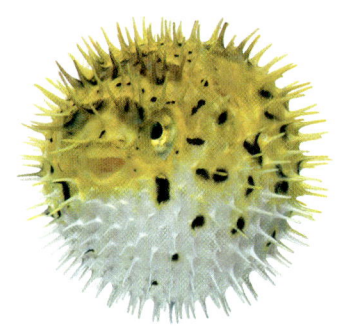

Inventory

Let's continue with the idea that you own a business that sells water sports equipment. You have a great location, lots of space, and good employees. You work with more than 15 suppliers to purchase the best in water sports equipment and accessories for your customers. Your company's balance sheet shows 30% of your assets are held in the form of inventory. You don't want to lose any inventory to theft, because you know the losses could lead your business into bankruptcy. You have a responsibility to manage the inventory, but how do you do it?

All manufacturers, wholesalers, and retailers face the possibility of losing inventory to employee theft, shoplifting, and other causes. Retailers want to prevent these losses, and internal controls for inventory can do so. In addition to protecting inventory, retailers need to make sure that the value of inventory is properly reflected on the balance sheet. ●

Look Back

You learned about internal controls for cash and receivables. You also used the two methods of estimating uncollectible receivables to account for receivables and report them on the balance sheet.

Look Ahead

You will study internal controls for inventory and see how to compute inventory cost using three different costing methods. Building on Chapter 5, you will learn more about reporting inventory and cost of goods sold.

In previous chapters, you understood internal controls and their importance. We discussed which controls can prevent the risk of loss in cash and receivables, and we talked about how to account for those assets and present them on the balance sheet. In this chapter, we turn our attention to another important asset, inventory, and the controls that can reduce the risk of inventory loss. We will also consider different methods of calculating the cost of inventory and the related cost of goods sold. We will examine the effect of the different costing methods, and see the impact that errors in accounting for inventory and cost of goods sold can have on the financial statements. Finally, we will look at how to value inventory correctly and estimate inventory value when necessary.

Inventory

① Describe inventory and discuss the related internal controls.

Types of Inventory

In addition to cash and receivables, management has a responsibility to protect inventory and to properly report it and cost of goods sold in the financial statements. Let's begin our consideration of inventory by examining the assets that a company can hold as inventory during the accounting period.

As we mentioned in Chapter 5, inventory represents the goods that a business owns and has available to sell to its customers; it is the products that the business holds for sale as part of its normal operations. Wholesalers and retailers have an inventory of goods available for resale, while manufacturers have inventory of **raw materials** to be used in production, **work in process** of partially completed goods, and **finished goods** ready to sell. These inventories will be discussed in a later chapter. Even though service, retail, and manufacturing businesses may have inventories of supplies for office, janitorial, and other use, these inventories are accounted for as supplies; recall from Chapter 5 that Inventory is the account used to hold the cost of goods available for sale, not for use, by the business.

Inventory is a current asset usually listed after receivables on the balance sheet. In a perpetual inventory system discussed in Chapter 5, retailers track the related cost of goods sold appearing on the income statement by recording activity in this account and the merchandise inventory account as it occurs. Manufacturers calculate the cost of goods manufactured by analyzing the activity in the raw materials and work in process inventory accounts, and calculate the cost of goods sold by analyzing the activity in the finished goods inventory account. Accounting for inventory in a manufacturing company will be covered in another chapter.

In this chapter, we focus on managing and accounting for inventory in retail businesses. This inventory represents a key asset for retailers; it is probably the business's largest current asset, as well as the center of merchandising transactions. Accordingly, it requires special internal controls to protect it from the risk of loss.

Inventory Shrinkage

In recent years, a number of major retail businesses filed for bankruptcy due to inventory losses. Billions of dollars in sales are lost each year due to inventory shrinkage. **Inventory shrinkage** is the loss of inventory; it is the difference between actual inventory value and the inventory value recorded in the accounting records. Each loss decreases the inventory value as well as net income. Exhibit 8-1 shows the sources of inventory shrinkage. Anyone can be involved in shrinkage, including employees, customers, managers, and suppliers:

- *Employee theft*: Employee theft of goods can occur when the store is opened or closed.

- *Customer shoplifting*: Customer theft of goods can occur during store hours.

- *Administrative error*: Loss from poor purchasing decisions, poor physical organization, and poor inventory management can result in damage, spoilage, spillage, or obsolescence, or errors in counting inventory.

- *Vendor fraud*: Vendors can charge excessive prices for merchandise or accept payment for merchandise that is never received.

Exhibit 8-1 Sources of Inventory Shrinkage		
Source	**% of Loss***	**$ Lost**
Employee Theft	48	$15.1 billion
Shoplifting	31	$ 9.7 billion
Administrative Error	15	$ 4.8 billion
Vendor Fraud	5	$ 1.7 billion
Total Inventory Shrinkage		**$31.3 billion**

*Total does not equal 100% due to rounding.
Source: National Retail Security Survey, November 2002 (based on 2001 retail sales and inventory shrinkage).

Inventory is an easy target for theft because many retailers don't keep continuous track of the quantity of items on hand. To prevent inventory shrinkage, businesses need sound internal controls.

Internal Controls over Inventory

The objectives of internal controls for inventory are to ensure inventory is physically safe and secure, reasonably well organized, not obsolete, properly recorded, and properly valued. Exhibit 8-2 provides a summary of some key internal control procedures for inventory.

Additionally, a retailer can prevent losses in other ways related to employee management:

- Obtain reference checks on employees.

- Educate employees on the costs of inventory shrinkage.

- Give employee discounts in order to monitor employee purchases.

- Reward employees who recover goods from shoplifters or identify fellow employees who are stealing.

Exhibit 8-2 Key Internal Control Procedures for Inventory

Control Activities	Internal Control Procedures: Inventory
Separation of duties	• Individuals who have access to inventory items should not maintain inventory records. • Individuals authorizing transactions should not record them.
Physical safeguards	• Restrict access to inventory items, including keys to the store. • Leave no employee alone in the store. • Physically count inventory on a regular basis, at least once a year. • Use electronic security systems, security mirrors, and video cameras to monitor activity.
Independent checks on performance	• Reconcile physical counts to counts reflected in accounting records by someone who does not handle inventory or inventory records. • Review and analyze relevant data such as inventory turnover, shrinkage, and sales trends. • Inspect garbage for evidence of stolen inventory before garbage is dumped.
Proper authorization	• Individual approving inventory transactions should not have access to inventory.
Adequate documents and records	• Maintain perpetual records of inventory. • Document purchase and sale transactions.

Physical safeguards put in place are critical for preventing employee theft, shoplifting, and loss due to damage, spoilage, or spillage. To get an accurate measure of inventory losses, retailers will count inventory. Most retailers count inventory only once a year at the end of the fiscal year because a physical count of inventory is costly and time consuming; however, more frequent inventory counts could help the retailer detect theft sooner. For example, the Outback Steakhouse managers reconcile a daily count of uncooked steaks to the number of steaks that should be on hand based on their accounting records. If the numbers do not agree, the managers can address the problem immediately.

A physical inventory count determines the amount of inventory actually owned and a number of commonly used procedures help ensure the accuracy of the count. It usually occurs when the store is closed. Individuals assigned to the count can use maps of inventory locations, prenumbered count sheets, ink pens, and may count in pairs. The count may also involve prewritten inventory instructions and tags to identify merchandise to be counted, and is typically supervised. To save time and increase objectivity for the count, an outside inventory-taking firm may be used to take counts instead of, or in addition to, employees.

The actual inventory count derived from the physical inventory is used to determine the inventory account balance on the balance sheet as well as the related cost of goods sold on the income statement, adjusting accounting records as necessary for any shrinkage. If the entity has its financial statements audited, a representative of the audit firm will probably be present at the count to take test counts and determine whether inventory instructions are being adequately followed. This allows the auditor to evaluate whether inventory and cost of goods sold are fairly presented in the statements.

Inventory Costing Methods

As we mentioned earlier, the objectives of internal controls for inventory include ensuring proper recording and valuation of inventory. With this purpose in mind, we will now look at methods for calculating the cost of inventory, and we will review the journal entries to record inventory activity.

Inventory Cost Flows

The Inventory account is a current asset with a normal debit balance. Remember from Chapter 5 that, in a perpetual inventory system, purchases of goods for resale increase the balance of the Inventory account, while sales of goods to customers decrease the account's balance. The Inventory account also reflects purchase discounts, purchase returns and allowances, and shipping costs related to the purchase of goods:

Inventory			
Bal.	XX		
Purchases	XX	Purchase Discounts	XX
Shipping	XX	Purchase Returns and Allowances	XX
		Sales	XX
Bal.	XX		

Also recall from Chapter 5 that, in a perpetual inventory system, companies determine the number of units in inventory from inventory accounting records verified by a physical count. The physical count provides an internal control over the number of units on hand.

Ending Inventory $=$ Number of Units on Hand $\times$ Unit Cost

Cost of Goods Sold $=$ Number of Units Sold $\times$ Unit Cost

The cost of the inventory flows through the Inventory account as items are purchased and sold. The cost of the units on hand in inventory at the beginning of the period are added to the net cost of units purchased for the period to determine the **cost of goods available for sale**. The objective of tracking the inventory cost is to assign the cost of the goods available for sale to the following categories:

- Units sold, which, as recorded in Cost of Goods Sold, is subtracted from net sales revenue on the income statement to arrive at gross profit

- Units on hand, or unsold, which, as inventory, are current assets on the balance sheet

Let's follow the November inventory activity for suede jackets sold by Adler's Outfitters, using the following information:

2 Compute inventory costs using first-in, first-out (FIFO), last-in, first-out (LIFO), and average cost methods and journalize inventory transactions.

Nov.	1	One jacket is on hand, unsold from the previous month.
	5	Purchased six jackets.
	15	Sold four jackets.
	26	Purchased seven jackets.
	30	Sold eight jackets.
	30	Two jackets are on hand, unsold.

During November, Adler had 14 suede jackets available for sale: 1 unit on hand in beginning inventory plus 13 units purchased. Of the 14 jackets available for sale, Adler sold 12 jackets and still had two jackets on hand, or unsold, at the end of the month. What would be the cost of the goods sold for the month and the ending inventory balance for that month, if we assume that each jacket costs $40 to purchase from a coat manufacturer?

Inventory

Nov. 1 Beginning balance (1 × $40)	40		
5 Purchased (6 × $40)	240	Nov. 15 Sold (4 × ?)	??
26 Purchased (7 × $40)	280	30 Sold (8 × ?)	??
Nov. 30 Ending balance (2 × ?)	?		

In this example, Adler paid $40 for all 14 jackets available for sale. So we use the $40 unit cost to calculate the cost of suede jackets sold of $480 ($40 × 12 jackets sold) and the cost of jackets unsold in ending inventory of $80 ($40 × 2 jackets unsold). Let's look at the inventory account after these calculations have been made:

Inventory

Nov. 1 Beginning balance (1 × $40)	40		
5 Purchased (6 × $40)	240	Nov. 15 Sold (4 × $40)	160
26 Purchased (7 × $40)	280	30 Sold (8 × $40)	320
Nov. 30 Ending balance (2 × $40)	80		

As you can see, the cost of goods available for sale is $560 ($40 + $240 + $280). The cost of goods sold is $480 ($160 + $320) and the ending balance of Inventory is $80. The sum of the cost of goods sold and the ending inventory balance is $560 ($480 + $80), which equals the cost of goods available for sale. By adding together the cost of goods sold and goods unsold, we can check to see that all of the costs have been assigned.

If you sell only one item, this method is a simple way to calculate the cost of goods sold and the ending balance of the Inventory account. What about a company such as Dollar General or Wal-Mart who has to keep track of thousands of products? Managers must watch for theft, and accountants need to establish inventory cost and the cost of goods sold. In addition, the cost to buy merchandise almost always changes over time. For example, electronics become cheaper and energy fuel becomes more expensive. When price changes happen, how do we assign the cost of goods available for sale to the goods sold and unsold? Exhibit 8-3 illustrates the objective of calculating inventory costs.

Different costing methods help the accountant assign the cost of goods available for sale. The four costing methods allowed by GAAP include the following:

1. **Specific-unit-cost method**

2. **Average cost method**

3. **First-in, first-out (FIFO) method**

4. **Last-in, first-out (LIFO) method**

A company can, according to GAAP, use any of these methods to account for its inventory.

The specific-unit-cost method is also called the **specific-identification method**. This method values inventory according to the specific cost of each unit of inventory. Some businesses deal in items that differ from unit to unit, such as automobiles, jewels, and real estate. For instance, a Chevrolet dealer may have two vehicles, a "stripped-down" model that costs $26,000 and a "loaded" model that costs $29,000. If the dealer sells the loaded model, the cost of goods sold is $29,000, the cost of that specific unit. Suppose the stripped-down auto is the only unit left in inventory at the end of the period; ending inventory is $26,000, the dealer's cost of that particular car.

Amazon.com uses the specific-unit-cost method to account for its inventory, but very few other companies do because this method is time consuming and sometimes nearly impossible to carry out. A company may make many purchases of identical goods and the unit cost of the goods may change over time, especially in an inflationary economy. Hence, it may difficult, if not impossible, to determine which goods are sold and which remain on hand in inventory at the end of the period.

Consider different types of inventory that need tracking. In the case of cars, specific-identification is done fairly easily because each vehicle is large, has its own unique features, and is identified with a vehicle identification number. Other items that aren't so simply identified, such as plain white T-shirts or packages of ballpoint pens, can still use the specific-identification method if some marker such as a computer chip placed inside the product labels the items. Clearly, this method is lengthy and expensive; accordingly, it is rarely used.

So, we will shift our attention to the more popular inventory costing methods. Let's see how to compute inventory amounts under the FIFO, LIFO, and average cost methods. We will use the following transaction data for all the illustrations:

Adler's Outfitters Suede Jacket		Number of Units	Unit Cost
Nov. 1	Beginning inventory	1	$40
5	Purchase	6	$45
15	Sale	4	
26	Purchase	7	$50
30	Sale	8	

As we check out the different costing methods, keep in mind that the objective of all three methods is to assign the cost of goods available for sale to the cost of goods sold and ending inventory, as shown in Exhibit 8-3.

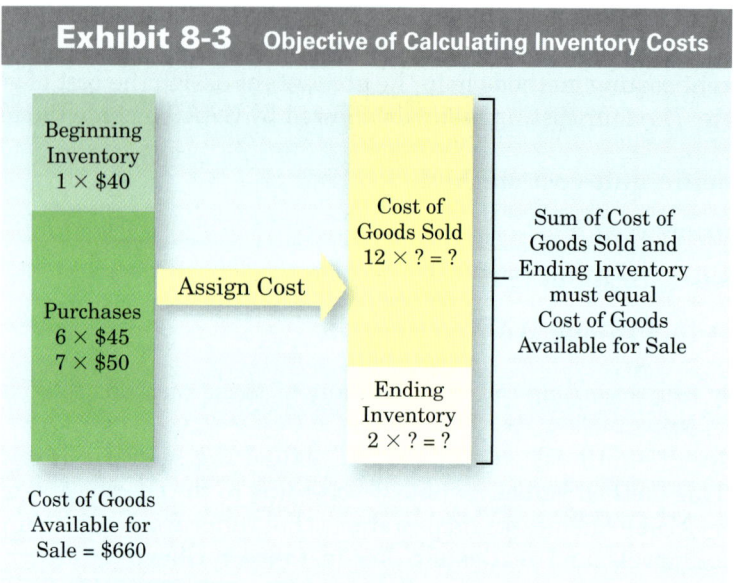

Exhibit 8-3 Objective of Calculating Inventory Costs

Beginning Inventory
$1 \times \$40$

Purchases
$6 \times \$45$
$7 \times \$50$

Cost of Goods Available for Sale = $660

Assign Cost

Cost of Goods Sold
$12 \times ? = ?$

Ending Inventory
$2 \times ? = ?$

Sum of Cost of Goods Sold and Ending Inventory must equal Cost of Goods Available for Sale

As we shall see, the various inventory costing methods produce different values for ending inventory and cost of goods sold. Let's begin with the FIFO method.

First-In, First-Out (FIFO) Method

Assume that Adler's Outfitters uses the FIFO method to account for its inventory. FIFO costing is consistent with the physical movement of inventory for most companies. Under FIFO, the first inventory costs incurred by Adler each period are the first costs to be assigned to cost of goods sold. *Simply put, FIFO assumes that the first inventory items owned are the first inventory items sold.* FIFO leaves in ending inventory the last, the most recent, costs incurred. Exhibit 8-4 illustrates the flow of costs using FIFO, which supports the FIFO perpetual inventory record in Exhibit 8-5.

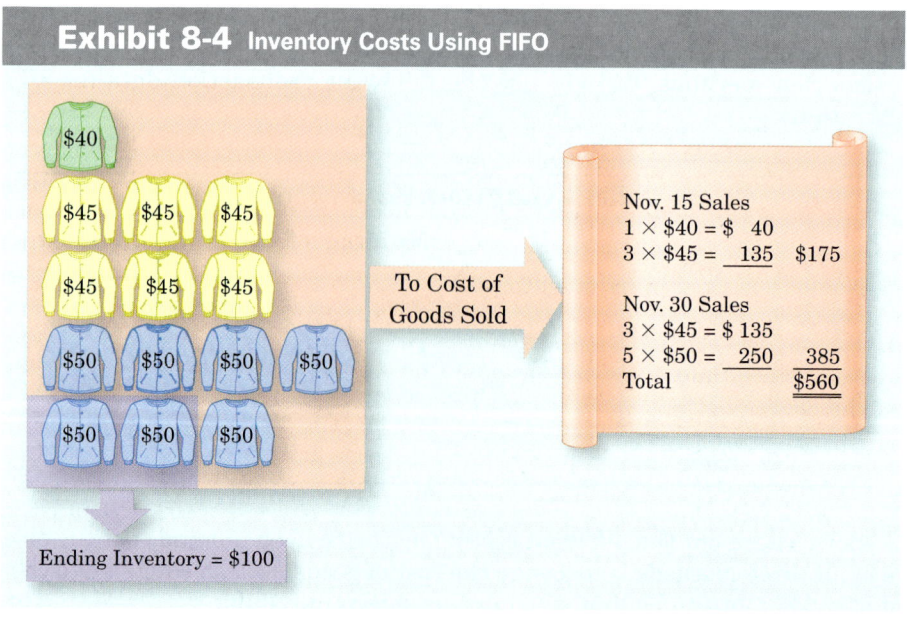

Exhibit 8-4 Inventory Costs Using FIFO

To Cost of Goods Sold

Nov. 15 Sales
$1 \times \$40 = \$\ \ 40$
$3 \times \$45 = \underline{\ \ \ 135}\ \ \ \$175$

Nov. 30 Sales
$3 \times \$45 = \$135$
$5 \times \$50 = \underline{\ \ \ 250}\ \ \ \ \underline{385}$
Total $\underline{\underline{\$560}}$

Ending Inventory = $100

Exhibit 8-5 Perpetual Inventory Record: FIFO

Suede Jackets

	Purchases			Cost of Goods Sold			Inventory on Hand		
Date	Quantity	Unit Cost	Total Cost	Quantity	Unit Cost	Total Cost	Quantity	Unit Cost	Total Cost
Nov. 1							1	$40	$ 40
5	6	$45	$270				1	$40	$ 40
							6	$45	$270
15				1	$40	$ 40			
				3	$45	$135	3	$45	$135
26	7	$50	$350				3	$45	$135
							7	$50	$350
30				3	$45	$135			
				5	$50	$250	2	$50	$100
30	13		$620	12		$560	2		$100

Adler began November with one suede jacket that cost $40. After the November 5 purchase, the inventory on hand consists of seven units: 1 at $40 plus 6 at $45. On November 15, Adler sold four units. Under FIFO, the first unit sold is costed at the oldest cost, $40 per unit. The next three units sold come from the group that cost $45 per unit. That leaves three units in inventory on hand, and those units cost $45 each. The remainder of the inventory record follows the same pattern.

The FIFO monthly summary on November 30 is:

- Cost of goods sold: 12 units that cost a total of $560. Look for this amount in Exhibit 8-4 and in the last row of the cost of goods sold columns of the perpetual inventory record in Exhibit 8-5.

- Ending inventory: 2 units that cost a total of $100. Look for this amount in Exhibit 8-4 and in the last row of the inventory on hand columns of the perpetual inventory record in Exhibit 8-5.

If Adler used the FIFO method, it would measure cost of goods sold and inventory in this manner to prepare its financial statements. Notice that the sum of the cost of goods sold and ending inventory equal cost of goods available for sale, $660 ($560 + $100).

Last-In, First-Out (LIFO) Method

Now imagine that Adler uses the LIFO method instead of FIFO. Under the LIFO method, the last, most recent costs incurred are the first costs assigned to the cost of goods sold. *Thus, LIFO assumes that the last inventory items owned are the first inventory items sold.* Ending inventory's cost comes from the oldest, earliest costs of the period. LIFO costing does not follow the actual flow of goods for most companies, but it doesn't have to match; *the point of choosing an inventory costing method is to allow businesses to make assumptions about which goods are sold and which remain in inventory so they don't have to track each item.* When costs are increasing, LIFO often results in the highest cost of goods sold, and the lowest income tax, the main advantage of LIFO. Exhibit 8-6 illustrates the assignment of costs using LIFO, which supports the LIFO perpetual inventory record in Exhibit 8-7.

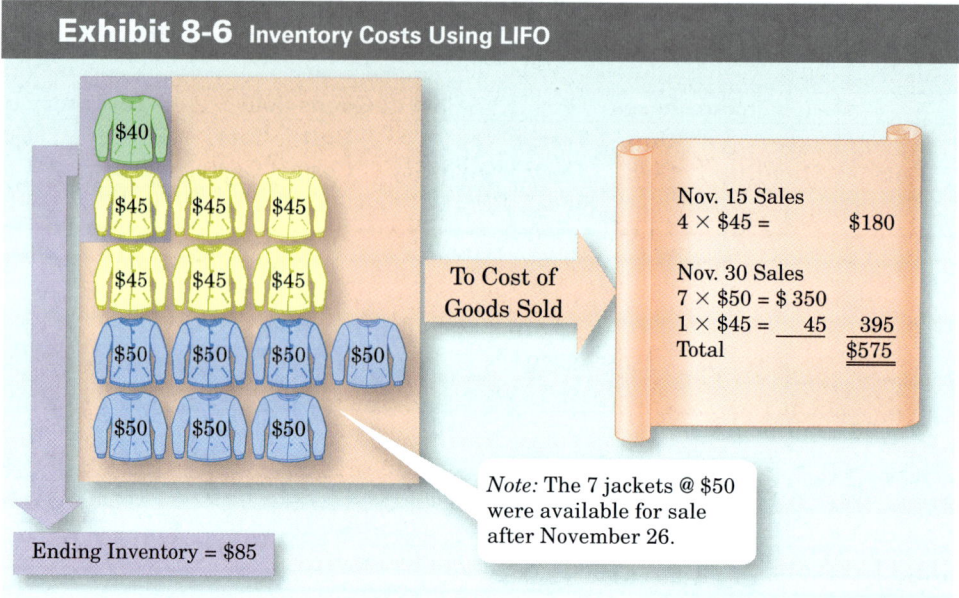

Exhibit 8-6 Inventory Costs Using LIFO

Nov. 15 Sales
4 × $45 = $180

Nov. 30 Sales
7 × $50 = $ 350
1 × $45 = 45   395
Total $575

To Cost of Goods Sold

Note: The 7 jackets @ $50 were available for sale after November 26.

Ending Inventory = $85

Again, Adler had one suede jacket at the beginning of November. After the purchase on November 5, Adler holds seven units of inventory: 1 at $40 plus 6 at $45. Adler then sells four units on November 15. Under LIFO, the cost of goods sold always comes from the latest purchase. That leaves three suede jackets in inventory on November 15: 1 at $40 plus 2 at $45. The purchase of seven units on November 26 adds a new $50 layer to inventory. Then the sale of eight units on November 30 peels back units in LIFO order.

The LIFO monthly summary on November 30 is:

- Cost of goods sold: 12 units that cost a total of $575. Look for this amount in Exhibit 8-6 and in the last row of the cost of goods sold columns of the perpetual inventory record in Exhibit 8-7.

Exhibit 8-7 Perpetual Inventory Record: LIFO

Suede Jackets

Date	Purchases Quantity	Unit Cost	Total Cost	Cost of Goods Sold Quantity	Unit Cost	Total Cost	Inventory on Hand Quantity	Unit Cost	Total Cost
Nov. 1							1	$40	$ 40
5	6	$45	$270				1	$40	$ 40
							6	$45	$270
15				4	$45	$180	1	$40	$ 40
							2	$45	$ 90
26	7	$50	$350				1	$40	$ 40
							2	$45	$ 90
							7	$50	$350
30				7	$50	$350			
				1	$45	$ 45	1	$40	$ 40
							1	$45	$ 45
30	13		$620	12		$575	2		$ 85

• Ending inventory: 2 units that cost a total of $85. Look for this amount in Exhibit 8-6 and in the last row of the inventory on hand columns of the perpetual inventory record and Exhibit 8-7.

If Adler used the LIFO method, Adler could measure cost of goods sold and inventory in this manner to prepare its financial statements. Notice that the sum of the cost of goods sold and ending inventory equal cost of goods available for sale, $660 ($575 + $85).

Average Cost Method

Suppose Adler's Outfitters uses the average cost method to account for its inventory of suede jackets. *With this method, the business computes a new, weighted average cost per unit after each purchase* based on the number of items purchased at each price. Ending inventory and cost of goods sold are then based on the average cost per unit. Exhibit 8-8 shows a perpetual inventory record for the average cost method. We round average unit cost to the nearest cent and total cost to the nearest dollar.

The new average unit cost on November 5 is based on the cost of the unit on hand at the beginning of November plus the cost of the 6 units purchased on November 5:

		Number of Units	Unit Cost	Total Cost
Nov. 1	Beginning inventory	1	$40	$40
5	Purchase	6	$45	$270
Total		7		$310

Total Cost of Inventory on Hand	÷	Number of Units on Hand	=	Average Cost per Unit
$310		7 Units		$44.29

The goods sold on November 15 are then costed out at $44.29 per unit. Adler then computes a new average cost after the November 26 purchase.

The average cost monthly summary on November 30 is:

• Cost of goods sold: 12 units that cost a total of $563. Look for this amount in the last row of the cost of goods sold columns of the perpetual inventory record.

• Ending inventory: 2 units that cost a total of $97. Look for this amount in the last row of the inventory on hand columns of the perpetual inventory record.

If Adler used the average cost method, it would use these amounts to prepare its financial statements. Notice that the sum of the cost of goods sold and ending inventory equal the cost of goods available for sale, $660 ($563 + $97).

Exhibit 8-8 Perpetual Inventory Record: Average Cost

Suede Jackets

Date	Purchases Quantity	Purchases Unit Cost	Purchases Total Cost	Cost of Goods Sold Quantity	Cost of Goods Sold Unit Cost	Cost of Goods Sold Total Cost	Inventory on Hand Quantity	Inventory on Hand Unit Cost	Inventory on Hand Total Cost
Nov. 1							1	$40.00	$ 40
5	6	$45	$270				7	$44.29	$310
15				4	$44.29	$177	3	$44.29	$133
26	7	$50	$350				10	$48.30	$483
30				8	$48.30	$386	2	$48.30	$ 97
30	13		$620	12		$563	2		$ 97

Journalizing Inventory Transactions

Now, let's look at the journal entries to record inventory transactions for November using the following information:

- All purchases and sales in November were made on account.
- The sales price of a suede jacket charged to a customer was $80.

The journal entries to record the purchases and sales of inventory on account are the same, regardless of the costing method chosen. *The differences occur when we move the cost of the jackets sold from the inventory account to the cost of goods sold* as shown in Exhibit 8-9.

Exhibit 8-9 Comparison of Journal Entries for the Inventory Costing Methods

	Date	Accounts	FIFO Dr.	FIFO Cr.	LIFO Dr.	LIFO Cr.	Average Cost Dr.	Average Cost Cr.
Purchase inventory on account (6 jackets @ $45 each)	Nov. 5	Inventory	270		270		270	
		Accounts Payable		270		270		270
Sold 4 jackets for $80 each	15	Accounts Receivable	320		320		320	
		Sales Revenue		320		320		320
	15	Cost of Goods Sold	175		180		177	
		Inventory		175		180		177
Purchased inventory on account (7 jackets @ $50 each)	26	Inventory	350		350		350	
		Accounts Payable		350		350		350
Sold 8 jackets for $80 each	30	Accounts Receivable	640		640		640	
		Sales Revenue		640		640		640
	30	Cost of Goods Sold	385		395		386	
		Inventory		385		395		386

Comparing FIFO, LIFO, and Average Cost

Exhibit 8-10 compares the FIFO, LIFO, and average cost methods of costing inventory assuming that, over time, inventory costs are increasing. Different methods have different benefits. FIFO is the most popular inventory costing method, LIFO is next most popular, and average cost ranks third.

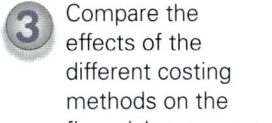 **3** Compare the effects of the different costing methods on the financial statements.

Exhibit 8-10 Comparison of Inventory Costing Methods When Costs are Increasing		
Inventory Costing Method	**Description**	**Benefit**
First-In, First-Out (FIFO)	Cost of goods sold has older, lower costs. Ending inventory has the newer, higher costs.	Most closely matches actual flow of goods in most cases. Maximizes net income. Use method to attract investors or borrow money.
Last-In, First-Out (LIFO)	Cost of goods sold has newer, higher costs. Ending inventory has the older, lower costs.	Minimizes net income and income tax and minimizes ending inventory. Use method to reduce income tax and cash needed to pay tax.
Average Cost	Averages costs in ending inventory and cost of goods sold.	A "middle-ground solution" for reporting net income and inventory and paying income tax.

Exhibit 8-11 summarizes the results of the three inventory methods as used for Adler's Outfitters. It shows Sales Revenue, Cost of Goods Sold, and Gross Profit for FIFO, LIFO, and average cost. All data come from Exhibits 8-5, 8-7, and 8-8.

Exhibit 8-11 shows that FIFO produces the lowest cost of goods sold and the highest gross profit. Net income is also the highest under FIFO when inventory costs are rising. Many companies use this method when they want to report high income in order to attract investors and borrow on attractive terms.

LIFO results in the highest cost of goods sold and the lowest gross profit. It lets companies pay the lowest income taxes when inventory costs are rising. Low tax payments conserve a company's cash, but the downside of LIFO is that the company reports low net income.

Exhibit 8-11 Comparative Results for FIFO, LIFO, and Average Cost			
	FIFO	**LIFO**	**Average Cost**
Sales revenue	$960	$960	$960
Cost of goods sold	560	575	563
Gross profit	$400	$385	$397

The average cost method generates gross profit, income tax, and net income amounts that fall between the extremes of FIFO and LIFO. Companies that seek a "middle-ground" solution, therefore, use the average cost method for inventory.

Valuing Inventory Using Lower-of-Cost-or-Market (LCM)

 4 Apply the lower-of-cost-or-market (LCM) rule to value inventory.

Remember the Pentium 3 processor and videotapes? Retailers who sell electronics face a decrease in the value of inventory. Industries affected by technology for computers, calculators, televisions, and other electronic equipment may have to write down the value of their inventory due to constant changes in technology. For other businesses, changes in customer preference for items such as clothing, furniture, and vehicles will cause the value of the inventory for these items to decrease.

When the cost of replacing these items is lower than the historical cost, the price of the items at the time of purchase, the **lower-of-cost-or-market rule (LCM)** applies. LCM requires businesses to report inventory in the financial statements at whichever is lower, the historical cost, or the market value of each inventory item. For inventory, market value generally means current replacement cost, that is, the cost to replace the inventory on hand at that point in time.

The lower-of-cost-or-market method is an example of an important accounting principle, **conservatism**. Conservatism in accounting means reporting items in the financial statements at amounts that lead to the most cautious immediate results. Conservatism appears in accounting guidelines in such statements as:

- "Anticipate no gains, but provide for all probable losses."

- "If in doubt, record an asset at the lowest reasonable amount and a liability at the highest reasonable amount."

- "When there's a question, record an expense rather than an asset."

The goal is for financial statements to report realistic figures.

If the replacement cost of inventory is less than its historical cost, we write down the inventory value by decreasing inventory and increasing cost of goods sold. In this way, net income is decreased in the period in which the decrease in market value occurred.

Let's look at the process of valuing inventory according to lower-of-cost-or-market for the inventory in Exhibit 8-12.

- Prepare a table listing each inventory item, its quantity, unit cost, and market value.

- Calculate the total cost and total market value for each item. Inventory Item 122A, for example, has a total cost of $2,000 (40 units × $50 cost per unit) and a total market value of $2,080 (40 units × $52 market value per unit).

- Place the lower of the cost or market value for each item in the "Lower of C or M" column, which is $2,000 for item 122A.

- Add the amounts in each column to obtain the total cost, total market value, and total lower-of-cost-or-market amounts.

- Adjust the inventory balance to reflect the lower-of-cost-or-market amount. The total cost is $14,800 and the total LCM amount is $14,425, so a journal entry is made to reduce the inventory amount by the difference of $375 ($14,800 − $14,425).

Exhibit 8-12 Calculating Inventory Value Using Lower-of-Cost-or-Market Method

Inventory Item	Inventory Quantity	Unit Cost	Unit Market Value	Total		Lower of C or M
				Cost	Market	
122A	40	$ 50	$ 52	$ 2,000	$ 2,080	$ 2,000
134CD	75	$ 80	$ 75	6,000	5,625	5,625
165MZ	68	$100	$101	6,800	6,868	6,800
				$14,800	$14,573	$14,425

Application of the LCM rule is a continuation of the process of valuing inventory. Businesses will record inventory transactions, attaching a cost to each inventory item sold by the specific-identification, FIFO, LIFO, or average cost method and arriving at a total value for ending inventory and cost of goods sold. They will then compare the cost of each item in ending inventory to its market value, and value each at the lower figure. In this way, businesses report conservative values for inventory and net income.

Reporting Inventory on the Balance Sheet

Several accounting principles have special relevance to inventory. Conservatism, discussed previously, is one of them. Now, we will look at the other principles related to accounting for inventory.

 Report inventory on the balance sheet and measure the effect of inventory errors.

Most businesses will report inventory on the balance sheet at the lower-of-cost-or-market value; however, others will use the concept of **materiality** to decide whether inventory needs to be written down to its current replacement cost. The materiality concept states that a company must perform strictly proper accounting *only* for items that are significant for the business's financial statements. Information is significant, or in accounting terminology, *material,* when its presentation in the financial statements would cause someone to change a decision; stated differently, a material amount is one large enough to make a difference to a user of the financial statements. For example, if the lower-of-cost-or-market comparison in Exhibit 8-12 resulted in a difference between total cost and total LCM of $3, the company would have been appropriate in ignoring any adjustment to inventory for the $3. Hence, the materiality concept frees accountants from having to report every account in strict accordance with GAAP, yet still report items properly.

The **full disclosure** principle holds that a company's financial statements should report enough information for outsiders to make knowledgeable decisions about the company. To provide this information, accountants typically include a set of disclosures or **footnotes** to accompany the financial statements. As we discussed in Chapter 1, a company should report relevant, reliable, and comparable information about its economic affairs; the preparation of disclosures helps accomplish this goal.

With respect to inventory, the disclosure principle means stating the method being used to value inventory. Suppose a banker is comparing two companies, one using LIFO and the other FIFO. When prices are rising, the FIFO company reports higher net income, but only because it uses the FIFO inventory costing method. Without knowledge of the accounting methods the companies are using, the banker could lend money to the wrong business, or lend the wrong amount of money to each.

Financial Statement Presentation of Inventory

As we mentioned earlier, inventory is a current asset often listed after receivables on the balance sheet. In addition to showing the inventory amount, a business must disclose the costing method used (specific-identification, FIFO, LIFO, or average cost) and the valuation of inventory at the lower-of-cost-or-market value. For example:

Balance Sheet	
Current assets:	
Inventory, at market (which is lower than FIFO cost)	$2,200

Companies often disclose LCM in notes to their financial statements, as shown here:

NOTE 2: Statement of Significant Accounting Policies:

Inventory. Inventory is carried at the *lower of cost or market*. Cost is determined using the first-in, first-out method.

The **consistency** principle states that businesses should use the same accounting methods and procedures from period to period. Consistency helps investors compare a company's financial statements from one period to the next.

Suppose you are analyzing a company's net income pattern over a two-year period when costs are rising. If the company switched from LIFO to FIFO during that time, then its net income increased dramatically, but only as a result of the change in inventory method. Not knowing about the change, you might believe that the company's income increased because of improved operations. Therefore, companies must report any changes in the accounting methods they use and they generally must retrospectively apply the impact of the change as an adjustment to beginning owner's equity, unless it is impractical to do so. Investors need this information to make wise decisions about the company.

Effects of Inventory Errors

Business managers are accountable for accurately reporting the value of inventory at the end of the period. An accurate count of the inventory items on hand helps managers calculate the inventory's value. However, errors in the inventory count can and do occur due to:

- Human error
  - Incorrectly counting inventory
  - Double counting inventory; for example, counting it in one location and then moving it to another location to be counted again
  - Not counting one section of the storeroom or excluding incoming goods shipped FOB shipping point
- Failure to recognize obsolete or damaged goods, resulting in failure to write down their value accordingly

Some of these errors are perhaps made intentionally and thus may represent fraudulent activities, so internal controls are necessary to ensure an accurate count of inventory.

What is the impact of a counting error? Remember that even in a perpetual inventory system, a count of inventory is necessary to verify the record of inventory on the books. So, a wrong count, a count that disagrees with the accounting records of inventory, will result in making a journal entry to adjust the balance in the Inventory account. Because cost of goods available for sale is divided between those goods on hand at the end of the period and those goods sold, this adjustment will also affect the Cost of Goods Sold account.

As the period 1 segment of Exhibits 8-13 and 8-14 show, an error in the ending inventory creates an error in the cost of goods sold. Further, the cost of goods sold is subtracted from net sales revenue to obtain gross profit, so the resulting gross profit and net income will also be wrong.

Let's assume that ending inventory is really $10,000 for each of the three periods. Look at Exhibit 8-13, and compare period 1's ending inventory, which is overstated, with period 3, which is correct. Period 1 *should* look exactly like

Exhibit 8-13 Inventory Errors: An Example

Period 1		Period 2		Period 3	
$10,000	Actual ending inventory	$15,000	*Beginning* inventory	$10,000	*Beginning* inventory
5,000	Adjustment to bring inventory	(5,000)	Adjustment to bring inventory	0	Adjustment to bring inventory
	to amount *miscounted*		to amount counted		to amount counted
	(Overstatement)				
$15,000	Miscounted *ending* inventory	$10,000	Counted *ending* inventory	$10,000	Counted *ending* inventory

Income Statement	Period 1:		Period 2:		Period 3:	
Sales revenue	$100,000		$100,000		$100,000	
Cost of goods sold	25,000	*(Understatement)*	35,000	*(Overstatement)*	30,000	
Gross profit	75,000		65,000		70,000	
Correct gross profit	70,000		70,000		70,000	
Error in gross profit, and hence, net income	$ 5,000		$ (5,000)		$ 0	

period 3. Look at Exhibit 8-13 to see the effect of assigning too much cost to Inventory.

- If we incorrectly assign too much cost to Inventory instead of Cost of Goods Sold ($15,000 rather than the correct, actual balance of $10,000),

- Then Cost of Goods Sold gets a smaller portion ($25,000 rather than the correct balance of $30,000) in error, and thus,

- Inventory is overstated and Cost of Goods sold is understated by $5,000.

Recall from Chapter 4 that Inventory, as an asset, is a permanent account that carries its balance over to the next period. So, one period's ending inventory becomes the next period's beginning inventory. Thus, the error in ending inventory carries over into the next period. See how these overstatements and understatements affect the next period in Exhibit 8-13.

As shown, the error cancels out after two periods. The overstatement of Cost of Goods Sold in period 2 offsets the understatement for period 1, as illustrated in Exhibit 8-14. Thus, total gross profit for the two periods combined is correct. These effects are summarized in Exhibit 8-15.

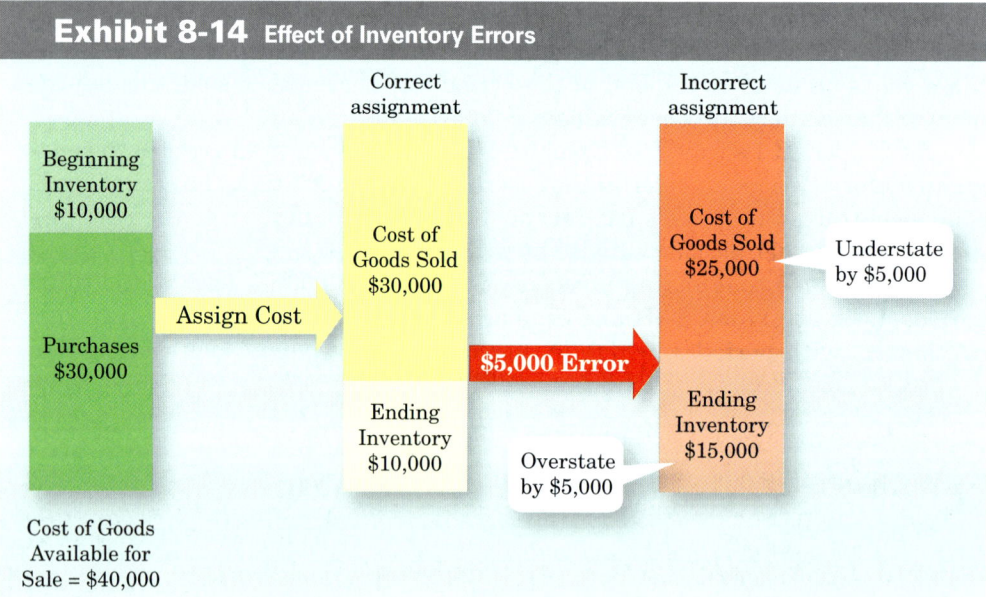

Exhibit 8-14 Effect of Inventory Errors

Exhibit 8-15 Effects of Inventory Errors

	Period 1		Period 2	
Inventory Error	**Cost of Goods Sold**	**Gross Profit and Net Income**	**Cost of Goods Sold**	**Gross Profit and Net Income**
Period 1 Ending Inventory *Overstated*	Understated	Overstated	Overstated	Understated
Period 1 Ending Inventory *Understated*	Overstated	Understated	Understated	Overstated

Using the Gross Profit Method to Estimate Ending Inventory

Often a business must estimate the value of its inventory. Suppose the company suffers a fire loss. To collect insurance, it must estimate the cost of the inventory destroyed, that is, it must estimate the ending inventory.

The **gross profit method** estimates inventory by using the pattern of cost assignment:

6 Estimate ending inventory by the gross profit method.

  Beginning Inventory
+ Purchases (Net of Discounts and Returns and Allowances, Plus Shipping Costs)
= Cost of Goods Available for Sale
− Ending Inventory
= Cost of Goods Sold

Rearranging ending inventory and cost of goods sold helps to estimate ending inventory. Let's look at an example. We can estimate ending inventory through the following steps and amounts, as shown in Exhibits 8-16 and 8-17:

STEP 1

Calculate the cost of goods available for sale. Add the beginning balance of inventory and the net cost of purchases for the accounting period ($14,000 + $66,000 = $80,000).

STEP 2

Estimate the cost of goods sold. Remember calculating the gross profit percentage in Chapter 5? The historical profit percentage of a business can be used to estimate the current period's gross profit. Calculate the estimated gross profit by multiplying the net sales revenue by the historical gross profit percentage ($100,000 × 40% = $40,000). Subtract the estimated gross profit from the net sales revenue to get the estimated cost of goods sold ($100,000 − $40,000 = $60,000).

STEP 3

Estimate the ending inventory. Subtract estimated cost of goods sold from the cost of goods available for sale ($80,000 − $60,000 = $20,000).

Exhibit 8-16 Gross Profit Method of Estimating Inventory (amounts assumed)		
Beginning inventory		$14,000
+ Purchases (net)		66,000
Step 1. = Cost of goods available for sale		80,000
Step 2. Estimated cost of goods sold:		
Net sales revenue	$100,000	
− Estimated gross profit of 40% ($100,000 × 40%)	(40,000)	
= Estimated cost of goods sold		(60,000)
Step 3. Estimated ending inventory		$20,000

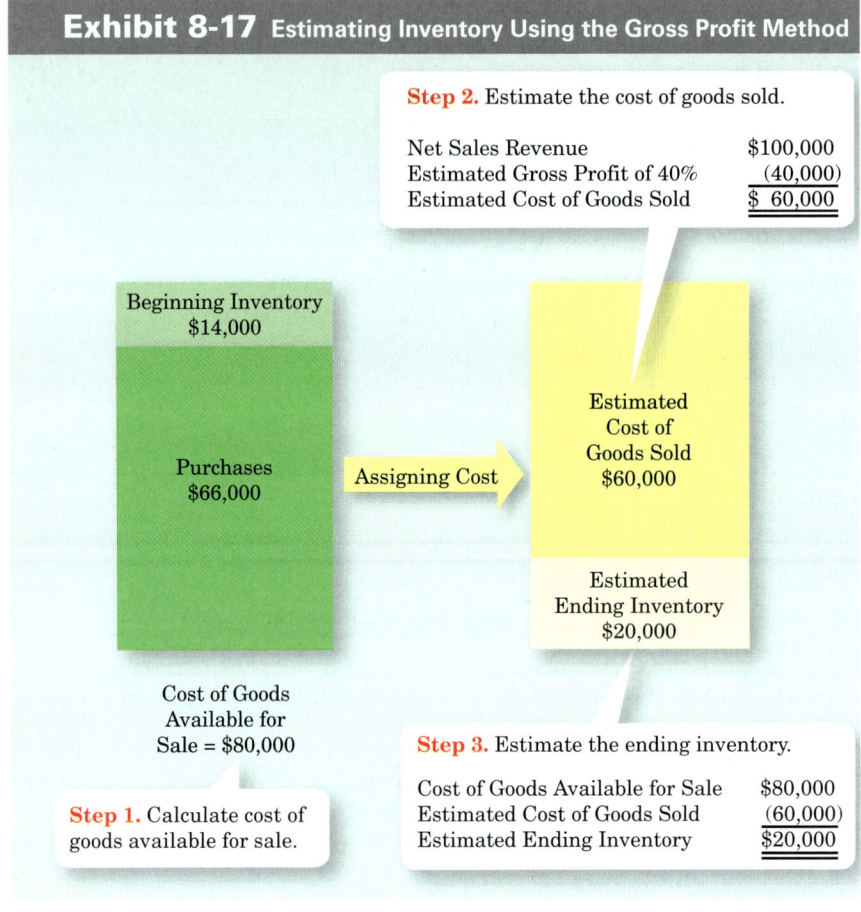

Exhibit 8-17 Estimating Inventory Using the Gross Profit Method

Step 2. Estimate the cost of goods sold.

Net Sales Revenue	$100,000
Estimated Gross Profit of 40%	(40,000)
Estimated Cost of Goods Sold	$ 60,000

Beginning Inventory
$14,000

Purchases
$66,000

Assigning Cost

Estimated
Cost of
Goods Sold
$60,000

Estimated
Ending Inventory
$20,000

Cost of Goods
Available for
Sale = $80,000

Step 1. Calculate cost of goods available for sale.

Step 3. Estimate the ending inventory.

Cost of Goods Available for Sale	$80,000
Estimated Cost of Goods Sold	(60,000)
Estimated Ending Inventory	$20,000

Demo Doc

Inventory Costing

Learning Objective 2

Chancellor Industries had the following inventory information for 2008:

Jan. 1	**Beginning inventory was 100 units costing $2 per unit.**
Mar. 1	**Purchased 50 units at $2.30 per unit.**
May 1	**Sold 80 units.**
July 1	**Purchased 45 units at $3 per unit.**
Sept. 1	**Sold 90 units.**
Nov. 1	**Purchased 25 units at $3.20 per unit.**
Dec. 31	**Performed year-end inventory count.**

Requirements

1. Assuming that no inventory shrinkage occurs, how many units remain in Chancellor's inventory at December 31, 2008?

2. Calculate Chancellor's cost of goods sold for 2008 and the value of Chancellor's inventory at December 31, 2008, under the following costing methods:

   a. FIFO
   b. LIFO
   c. Average cost

Demo Doc Solutions

Requirement 1

2 Computing inventory costs using first-in, first-out (FIFO), last-in, first-out (LIFO), and average cost methods and journalize inventory transactions.

Assuming that no inventory shrinkage occurs, how many units remain in Chancellor's inventory at December 31, 2008?

Part 1	Part 2	Part 3	Part 4	Demo Doc Complete

Inventory flows in and out of the warehouse in the following pattern:

Number of Units in Beginning Inventory
+ Number of Units Purchased
− Number of Units Sold
Number of Units in Ending Inventory

We are told that beginning inventory consisted of 100 units. Inventory purchases are 120 units (50 units in March + 45 units in July + 25 units in November). Chancellor sold 170 units (80 units in May + 90 units in September). If we put these numbers into the formula, we get the following result:

100 Units in Beginning Inventory
+ 120 Units Purchased
− 170 Units Sold
50 Units in Ending Inventory

Requirement 2

Calculate Chancellor's cost of goods sold for 2008 and the value of Chancellor's inventory at December 31, 2008, under the following costing methods:

a. **FIFO**
b. **LIFO**
c. **Average cost**

Part 1	Part 2	Part 3	Part 4	Demo Doc Complete

a. FIFO

We must set up a record to keep track of our inventory under FIFO (see Exhibit 8-7, p. 414). The first entry is the amount of the beginning inventory of 100 units costing $2 per unit. This number is the amount of inventory Chancellor had (that is, the inventory *on hand*) at January 1, 2008.

Under the Inventory on Hand section of the table, we put in a quantity of 100 units at a cost of $2 each for a total cost of $200 (100 × $2).

Date	Purchases Quantity	Purchases Unit Cost	Purchases Total Cost	Cost of Goods Sold Quantity	Cost of Goods Sold Unit Cost	Cost of Goods Sold Total Cost	Inventory on Hand Quantity	Inventory on Hand Unit Cost	Inventory on Hand Total Cost
Jan. 1							100	$2	$200

The first inventory transaction is the purchase of 50 units for $2.30 each on March 1. On the next line of the table in the Purchases section, we put in a quantity of 50 units at a cost of $2.30 each for a total of $115 (50 × $2.30).

Date	Purchases Quantity	Purchases Unit Cost	Purchases Total Cost	Cost of Goods Sold Quantity	Cost of Goods Sold Unit Cost	Cost of Goods Sold Total Cost	Inventory on Hand Quantity	Inventory on Hand Unit Cost	Inventory on Hand Total Cost
Jan. 1							100	$2.00	$200
Mar. 1	50	$2.30	$115				?	?	?

We now have *both* the original 100 units *and* the new 50 units in inventory, so we copy these amounts in the Inventory on Hand section of the table.

Date	Purchases Quantity	Purchases Unit Cost	Purchases Total Cost	Cost of Goods Sold Quantity	Cost of Goods Sold Unit Cost	Cost of Goods Sold Total Cost	Inventory on Hand Quantity	Inventory on Hand Unit Cost	Inventory on Hand Total Cost
Jan. 1							100	$2.00	$200
Mar. 1	50	$2.30	$115				100	$2.00	$200
							50	$2.30	$115

The next transaction was the sale of 80 units on May 1. Under FIFO, we assume that we sell the *first* units in (that is, the *oldest* units on hand). The oldest units we have are the original 100 units costing $2 each from beginning inventory. The 80 we sold must have come from this group. Therefore, 80 units costing $2 each were sold for a total of $160 (80 × $2). We put this information into the Cost of Goods Sold section of the table.

Date	Purchases Quantity	Purchases Unit Cost	Purchases Total Cost	Cost of Goods Sold Quantity	Cost of Goods Sold Unit Cost	Cost of Goods Sold Total Cost	Inventory on Hand Quantity	Inventory on Hand Unit Cost	Inventory on Hand Total Cost
Jan. 1							100	$2.00	$200
Mar. 1	50	$2.30	$115				100	$2.00	$200
							50	$2.30	$115
May 1				80	$2.00	$160	?	?	?

Of the original 100 units in beginning inventory, only 20 (100 − 80) are left. These units cost $2 each for a total of $40 (20 × $2). We also still have the 50 units purchased on March 1 for $2.30 each (total $115). We put this information into the Inventory on Hand section of the table.

Date	Purchases Quantity	Unit Cost	Total Cost	Cost of Goods Sold Quantity	Unit Cost	Total Cost	Inventory on Hand Quantity	Unit Cost	Total Cost
Jan. 1							100	$2.00	$200
Mar. 1	50	$2.30	$115				100	$2.00	$200
							50	$2.30	$115
May 1				80	$2.00	$160	20	$2.00	$ 40
							50	$2.30	$115

On July 1, another purchase was made for 45 units at $3 per unit for a total cost of $135 (45 × $3). We put this information into the Purchases section of the table.

After this purchase, we now have the 20 units left from beginning inventory *and* the 50 units purchased March 1 *and* these 45 new units in inventory. We copy these amounts into the Inventory on Hand section of the table.

Date	Purchases Quantity	Unit Cost	Total Cost	Cost of Goods Sold Quantity	Unit Cost	Total Cost	Inventory on Hand Quantity	Unit Cost	Total Cost
Jan. 1							100	$2.00	$200
Mar. 1	50	$2.30	$115				100	$2.00	$200
							50	$2.30	$115
May 1				80	$2.00	$160	20	$2.00	$ 40
							50	$2.30	$115
July 1	45	$3.00	$135				20	$2.00	$ 40
							50	$2.30	$115
							45	$3.00	$135

The next transaction is the sale of 90 units on September 1. Under FIFO, we assume that we sell the *oldest* units. The oldest units on hand are the remaining 20 from beginning inventory costing $2 each for a total of $40. These units must have been sold. We put these units into the Cost of Goods Sold section of the table.

	Purchases			Cost of Goods Sold			Inventory on Hand		
Date	Quantity	Unit Cost	Total Cost	Quantity	Unit Cost	Total Cost	Quantity	Unit Cost	Total Cost
Jan. 1							100	$2.00	$200
Mar. 1	50	$2.30	$115				100	$2.00	$200
							50	$2.30	$115
May 1				80	$2.00	$160	20	$2.00	$ 40
							50	$2.30	$115
July 1	45	$3.00	$135				20	$2.00	$ 40
							50	$2.30	$115
							45	$3.00	$135
Sept. 1				20	$2.00	$ 40	?	?	?

However, 20 units is not enough. Of the 90 units were sold, we found the oldest 20 units. We have 90 − 20 = 70 more units to record. The next oldest units are the 50 units costing $2.30 each for a total of $115. These units must also have been sold. We put these units into the Cost of Goods Sold section of the table.

	Purchases			Cost of Goods Sold			Inventory on Hand		
Date	Quantity	Unit Cost	Total Cost	Quantity	Unit Cost	Total Cost	Quantity	Unit Cost	Total Cost
Jan. 1							100	$2.00	$200
Mar. 1	50	$2.30	$115				100	$2.00	$200
							50	$2.30	$115
May 1				80	$2.00	$160	20	$2.00	$ 40
							50	$2.30	$115
July 1	45	$3.00	$135				20	$2.00	$ 40
							50	$2.30	$115
							45	$3.00	$135
Sept. 1				20	$2.00	$ 40	?	?	?
				50	$2.30	$115			

These additional 50 units are still not enough. We need another 70 − 50 = 20 for this sale. These 20 units must have come from the next oldest group of inventory: the 45 units costing $3 each purchased July 1. We sold only 20 of these units, so in the Cost of Goods Sold section of the table, we put in an additional 20 units at $3 each for a total of $60 (20 × $3).

Date	Purchases			Cost of Goods Sold			Inventory on Hand		
	Quantity	Unit Cost	Total Cost	Quantity	Unit Cost	Total Cost	Quantity	Unit Cost	Total Cost
Jan. 1							100	$2.00	$200
Mar. 1	50	$2.30	$115				100	$2.00	$200
							50	$2.30	$115
May 1				80	$2.00	$160	20	$2.00	$ 40
							50	$2.30	$115
July 1	45	$3.00	$135				20	$2.00	$ 40
							50	$2.30	$115
							45	$3.00	$135
Sept. 1				20	$2.00	$ 40	?	?	?
				50	$2.30	$115			
				20	$3.00	$ 60			

Notice that 20 + 50 + 20 = 90, which is the total number of units sold on September 1.

After this purchase, 45 − 20 = 25 units purchased on July 1 at $3 each (for a total of $75 = 25 × $3) are left. We copy these amounts in the Inventory on Hand section of the table.

Date	Purchases			Cost of Goods Sold			Inventory on Hand		
	Quantity	Unit Cost	Total Cost	Quantity	Unit Cost	Total Cost	Quantity	Unit Cost	Total Cost
Jan. 1							100	$2.00	$200
Mar. 1	50	$2.30	$115				100	$2.00	$200
							50	$2.30	$115
May 1				80	$2.00	$160	20	$2.00	$ 40
							50	$2.30	$115
July 1	45	$3.00	$135				20	$2.00	$ 40
							50	$2.30	$115
							45	$3.00	$135
Sept. 1				20	$2.00	$ 40	?	?	?
				50	$2.30	$115			
				20	$3.00	$ 60	25	$3.00	$ 75

In the last transaction on November 1, 25 units costing $3.20 each for a total of $80 (25 × $3.20) were purchased. We put this information into the Purchases section of the table.

After this purchase, we now have the 25 units left from the July 1 purchase *and* these 25 new units in inventory. We copy these amounts in the Inventory on Hand section of the table.

| | Purchases | | | Cost of Goods Sold | | | Inventory on Hand | | |
Date	Quantity	Unit Cost	Total Cost	Quantity	Unit Cost	Total Cost	Quantity	Unit Cost	Total Cost
Jan. 1							100	$2.00	$200
Mar. 1	50	$2.30	$115				100	$2.00	$200
							50	$2.30	$115
May 1				80	$2.00	$160	20	$2.00	$ 40
							50	$2.30	$115
July 1	45	$3.00	$135				20	$2.00	$ 40
							50	$2.30	$115
							45	$3.00	$135
Sept. 1				20	$2.00	$ 40	?	?	?
				50	$2.30	$115			
				20	$3.00	$ 60	25	$3.00	$ 75
Nov. 1	25	$3.20	$ 80				25	$3.00	$ 75
							25	$3.20	$ 80

We have now input all of the transactions into the table. The last thing to do is total the transactions.

As shown in Requirement 1, the units purchased should total up to 120 units. This calculation is verified as:

$$50 + 45 + 25 = 120$$

Adding up the Total Cost column of the Purchases section gives us:

$$\$115 + \$135 + \$80 = \$330$$

As shown in Requirement 1, the units sold should total up to 170 units. This calculation is verified as:

$$80 + 20 + 50 + 20 = 170$$

Adding up the Total Cost column of the Cost of Goods Sold section gives us:

$$\$160 + \$40 + \$115 + \$60 = \$375$$

In Requirement 1, we calculated that the ending inventory was 50 units. This calculation is verified as:

$$25 + 25 = 50$$

Adding up the Total Cost in the last row of the Inventory on Hand section gives us:

$$\$75 + \$80 = \$155$$

Date	Purchases Quantity	Purchases Unit Cost	Purchases Total Cost	Cost of Goods Sold Quantity	Cost of Goods Sold Unit Cost	Cost of Goods Sold Total Cost	Inventory on Hand Quantity	Inventory on Hand Unit Cost	Inventory on Hand Total Cost
Jan. 1							100	$2.00	$200
Mar. 1	50	$2.30	$115				100	$2.00	$200
							50	$2.30	$115
May 1				80	$2.00	$160	20	$2.00	$ 40
							50	$2.30	$115
July 1	45	$3.00	$135				20	$2.00	$ 40
							50	$2.30	$115
							45	$3.00	$135
Sept. 1				20	$2.00	$ 40	?	?	?
				50	$2.30	$115			
				20	$3.00	$ 60	25	$3.00	$ 75
Nov. 1	25	$3.20	$ 80				25	$3.00	$ 75
							25	$3.20	$ 80
Dec. 31	120		$330	170		$375	50		$155

Notice that we end with 50 units of inventory (as calculated at the beginning of the question).

Let's double-check to see whether we calculated everything correctly. We know that:

Cost of Goods Sold = Beginning Inventory + Inventory Purchases − Ending Inventory

So in this question:

$$\$375 = (100 \text{ units} \times \$2 \text{ per unit}) + \$330 - \$155 \ \sqrt{} \ \text{Correct!}$$

b. LIFO

Part 1	Part 2	**Part 3**	Part 4	Demo Doc Complete

We must create a table to keep track of the inventory under LIFO. As we did for the FIFO table, the first entry is to record the beginning inventory of 100 units costing $2 each for a total of $200 (100 × $2).

Date	Purchases Quantity	Purchases Unit Cost	Purchases Total Cost	Cost of Goods Sold Quantity	Cost of Goods Sold Unit Cost	Cost of Goods Sold Total Cost	Inventory on Hand Quantity	Inventory on Hand Unit Cost	Inventory on Hand Total Cost
Jan. 1							100	$2.00	$200

The first purchase of 50 units on March 1 is input in the same way as was done for the FIFO table. Inventory now contains the original 100 units of beginning inventory and these new 50 units.

	Purchases			Cost of Goods Sold			Inventory on Hand		
Date	Quantity	Unit Cost	Total Cost	Quantity	Unit Cost	Total Cost	Quantity	Unit Cost	Total Cost
Jan. 1							100	$2.00	$200
Mar. 1	50	$2.30	$115				100	$2.00	$200
							50	$2.30	$115

On May 1, 80 units were sold. Under LIFO, we assume the units *last* in are sold: We are selling the *newest* units we have. The newest units are the 50 units purchased on March 1. These units must have been sold. The 50 units cost $2.30 each for a total of $115.

	Purchases			Cost of Goods Sold			Inventory on Hand		
Date	Quantity	Unit Cost	Total Cost	Quantity	Unit Cost	Total Cost	Quantity	Unit Cost	Total Cost
Jan. 1							100	$2.00	$200
Mar. 1	50	$2.30	$115				100	$2.00	$200
							50	$2.30	$115
May 1				50	$2.30	$115			

However, these 50 units are not enough. Another 80 − 50 = 30 units were sold. These units must have come from the next newest group of units: the beginning inventory of 100 units costing $2 each. Of these 100 units, 30 must have been sold for a total cost of $60 (30 × $2).

The other 70 units from beginning inventory at a total cost of $140 (70 × $2) remain in inventory.

	Purchases			Cost of Goods Sold			Inventory on Hand		
Date	Quantity	Unit Cost	Total Cost	Quantity	Unit Cost	Total Cost	Quantity	Unit Cost	Total Cost
Jan. 1							100	$2.00	$200
Mar. 1	50	$2.30	$115				100	$2.00	$200
							50	$2.30	$115
May 1				50	$2.30	$115			
				30	$2.00	$ 60	70	$2.00	$140

The next transaction is the purchase on July 1 of 45 units costing $3 each for a total of $135. The purchase information (in the Purchases section of the table) is entered in the same way as it was for the FIFO table.

Inventory now holds the 70 units costing $2 each and the new purchase of 45 units costing $3 each. This information is entered into the Inventory on Hand section of the table.

Date	Purchases			Cost of Goods Sold			Inventory on Hand		
	Quantity	Unit Cost	Total Cost	Quantity	Unit Cost	Total Cost	Quantity	Unit Cost	Total Cost
Jan. 1							100	$2.00	$200
Mar. 1	50	$2.30	$115				100	$2.00	$200
							50	$2.30	$115
May 1				50	$2.30	$115			
				30	$2.00	$ 60	70	$2.00	$140
July 1	45	$3.00	$135				70	$2.00	$140
							45	$3.00	$135

90 units were sold on September 1. Under LIFO, we assume that we sell the *newest* 90 units. The newest units are the 45 units costing $3 each that were purchased in July. These units must have been sold.

However, these 45 units are not enough. Another 90 − 45 = 45 units were sold. These units must have come from the next newest group of inventory: the 70 units costing $2 each. Of this group, 45 units costing $2 each for a total of $90 (45 × 2) were sold.

All of this information is put into the Cost of Goods Sold section of the table.

Date	Purchases			Cost of Goods Sold			Inventory on Hand		
	Quantity	Unit Cost	Total Cost	Quantity	Unit Cost	Total Cost	Quantity	Unit Cost	Total Cost
Jan. 1							100	$2.00	$200
Mar. 1	50	$2.30	$115				100	$2.00	$200
							50	$2.30	$115
May 1				50	$2.30	$115			
				30	$2.00	$ 60	70	$2.00	$140
July 1	45	$3.00	$135				70	$2.00	$140
							45	$3.00	$135
Sept. 1				45	$3.00	$135	?	?	?
				45	$2.00	$ 90			

After this transaction, $70 - 45 = 25$ units costing $2 (for a total of $25 \times \$2 = \$50$) remain in inventory. This information is put into the Inventory on Hand section of the table.

Date	Purchases Quantity	Purchases Unit Cost	Purchases Total Cost	Cost of Goods Sold Quantity	Cost of Goods Sold Unit Cost	Cost of Goods Sold Total Cost	Inventory on Hand Quantity	Inventory on Hand Unit Cost	Inventory on Hand Total Cost
Jan. 1							100	$2.00	$200
Mar. 1	50	$2.30	$115				100	$2.00	$200
							50	$2.30	$115
May 1				50	$2.30	$115			
				30	$2.00	$ 60	70	$2.00	$140
July 1	45	$3.00	$135				70	$2.00	$140
							45	$3.00	$135
Sept. 1				45	$3.00	$135			
				45	$2.00	$ 90	25	$2.00	$ 50

The last transaction is the purchase on November 1 of 25 units costing $3.20 each for a total of $80. The purchase information (in the Purchases section of the table) is entered in the same way as it was for the FIFO table.

The 25 units costing $2 each and the new purchase of 25 units costing $3.20 each are in inventory. This information is entered into the Inventory on Hand section of the table.

Date	Purchases Quantity	Purchases Unit Cost	Purchases Total Cost	Cost of Goods Sold Quantity	Cost of Goods Sold Unit Cost	Cost of Goods Sold Total Cost	Inventory on Hand Quantity	Inventory on Hand Unit Cost	Inventory on Hand Total Cost
Jan. 1							100	$2.00	$200
Mar. 1	50	$2.30	$115				100	$2.00	$200
							50	$2.30	$115
May 1				50	$2.30	$115			
				30	$2.00	$ 60	70	$2.00	$140
July 1	45	$3.00	$135				70	$2.00	$140
							45	$2.00	$135
Sept. 1				45	$3.00	$135			
				45	$2.00	$ 90	25	$2.00	$ 50
Nov. 1	25	$3.20	$ 80				25	$2.00	$ 50
							25	$3.20	$ 80

We have now input all of the transactions into the table. The last thing to do is total the transactions.

The Purchases section is the same as in the FIFO table and so the totals are also the same.

As shown in Requirement 1, the units sold should total up to 170 units. This calculation is verified as:

$$50 + 30 + 45 + 45 = 170$$

Adding up the Total Cost column of the Cost of Goods Sold section gives us:

$$\$115 + \$60 + \$135 + \$90 = \$400$$

In Requirement 1, we calculated that the ending inventory was 50 units. This calculation is verified as:

$$25 + 25 = 50$$

Adding up the Total Cost in the last row of the Inventory on Hand section gives us:

$$\$50 + \$80 = \$130$$

Date	Purchases Quantity	Unit Cost	Total Cost	Cost of Goods Sold Quantity	Unit Cost	Total Cost	Inventory on Hand Quantity	Unit Cost	Total Cost
Jan. 1							100	$2.00	$200
Mar. 1	50	$2.30	$115				100	$2.00	$200
							50	$2.30	$115
May 1				50	$2.30	$115			
				30	$2.00	$ 60	70	$2.00	$140
July 1	45	$3.00	$135				70	$2.00	$140
							45	$3.00	$135
Sept. 1				45	$3.00	$135			
				45	$2.00	$ 90	25	$2.00	$ 50
Nov. 1	25	$3.20	$ 80				25	$2.00	$ 50
							25	$3.20	$ 80
Dec. 31	120		$330	170		$400	50		$130

Notice that we end with 50 units of inventory (as calculated at the beginning of the question).

Let's check to see whether we calculated everything correctly. We know that:

Cost of Goods Sold = Beginning Inventory + Inventory Purchases − Ending Inventory

So in this question:

$$\$400 = (100 \text{ units} \times \$2 \text{ per unit}) + \$330 - \$130 \sqrt{} \text{ Correct!}$$

c. Average Cost

Part 1   Part 2   Part 3   **Part 4**   Demo Doc Complete

We must create a table to keep track of the inventory under average cost. As we did for the FIFO and LIFO tables, the first entry is to record the beginning inventory of 100 units costing $2 each for a total of $200 (100 × $2).

Date	Purchases Quantity	Unit Cost	Total Cost	Cost of Goods Sold Quantity	Unit Cost	Total Cost	Inventory on Hand Quantity	Unit Cost	Total Cost
Jan. 1							100	$2.00	$200

The first purchase of 50 units on March 1 is input in the same way as was done for the FIFO and LIFO tables.

Date	Purchases Quantity	Unit Cost	Total Cost	Cost of Goods Sold Quantity	Unit Cost	Total Cost	Inventory on Hand Quantity	Unit Cost	Total Cost
Jan. 1							100	$2.00	$200
Mar. 1	50	$2.30	$115						

Once a purchase is made, the average cost per unit of the inventory must be calculated.

$$\text{Total Cost of Inventory on Hand} \div \text{Number of Units on Hand} = \text{Average Cost per Unit}$$

The inventory on hand is the beginning inventory (100 units costing $200) and the March 1 purchase of 50 units costing $115.

$$\frac{\$200 + \$115}{100 + 50} = \text{Average Cost per Unit}$$

$$\frac{\$315}{150} = \$2.10$$

So now inventory contains 100 + 50 = 150 units costing $2.10 each for a total of $315 ($200 + $115 *or* 150 × $2.10). We put this information into the Inventory on Hand section of the table.

Date	Purchases Quantity	Unit Cost	Total Cost	Cost of Goods Sold Quantity	Unit Cost	Total Cost	Inventory on Hand Quantity	Unit Cost	Total Cost
Jan. 1							100	$2.00	$200
Mar. 1	50	$2.30	$115				150	$2.10	$315

On May 1, 80 units are sold. The units in inventory have an average cost of $2.10 each, so the units sold have a cost of $2.10 each as well for a total of $168 (80 × $2.10). This information is put into the Cost of Goods Sold section of the table.

This transaction leaves 150 − 80 = 70 units in inventory at $2.10 each for a total of $147 (70 × $2.10). This information is put into the Inventory on Hand section of the table.

Date	Purchases Quantity	Unit Cost	Total Cost	Cost of Goods Sold Quantity	Unit Cost	Total Cost	Inventory on Hand Quantity	Unit Cost	Total Cost
Jan. 1							100	$2.00	$200
Mar. 1	50	$2.30	$115				150	$2.10	$315
May 1				80	$2.10	$168	70	$2.10	$147

On July 1, another purchase of 45 units costing $3 each for a total of $135 is made. With a new purchase, we must now recalculate the average cost per unit of inventory.

$$\text{Total Cost of Inventory on Hand} \div \text{Number of Units on Hand} = \text{Average Cost per Unit}$$

The inventory on hand is the previous inventory of 70 units costing $147 and the July 1 purchase of 45 units costing $135.

$$\frac{\$147 + \$135}{70 + 45} = \text{Average Cost per Unit}$$

$$\frac{\$282}{115} = \$2.45$$

So now 70 + 45 = 115 units, costing $2.45 each for a total of $282 ($147 + $135 or 115 × $2.45), remain in inventory (remember to round to the nearest dollar). We put this information into the Inventory on Hand section of the table.

Date	Purchases Quantity	Unit Cost	Total Cost	Cost of Goods Sold Quantity	Unit Cost	Total Cost	Inventory on Hand Quantity	Unit Cost	Total Cost
Jan. 1							100	$2.00	$200
Mar. 1	50	$2.30	$115				150	$2.10	$315
May 1				80	$2.10	$168	70	$2.10	$147
July 1	45	$3.00	$135				115	$2.45	$282

On September 1, 90 units are sold. The units in inventory have an average cost of $2.45 each, so the units sold have a cost of $2.45 each as well for a total of $221 (90 × $2.45). This information goes into the Cost of Goods Sold section of the table.

Inventory now consists of 115 − 90 = 25 units costing $2.45 each for a total of $61 (25 × $2.45). This information is put into the Inventory on Hand section of the table.

Date	Purchases			Cost of Goods Sold			Inventory on Hand		
	Quantity	Unit Cost	Total Cost	Quantity	Unit Cost	Total Cost	Quantity	Unit Cost	Total Cost
Jan. 1							100	$2.00	$200
Mar. 1	50	$2.30	$115				150	$2.10	$315
May 1				80	$2.10	$168	70	$2.10	$147
July 1	45	$3.00	$135				115	$2.45	$282
Sept. 1				90	$2.45	$221	25	$2.45	$ 61

On November 1, another purchase of 25 units costing $3.20 each for a total of $80 is made. With a new purchase, we must now recalculate the average cost per unit of inventory.

$$\frac{\text{Total Cost of}}{\text{Inventory on Hand}} \div \frac{\text{Number of}}{\text{Units on Hand}} = \frac{\text{Average Cost}}{\text{per Unit}}$$

The inventory on hand is the previous inventory of 25 units costing $61 and the November 1 purchase of 25 units costing $80.

$$\frac{\$61+\$80}{25+25} = \text{Average Cost per Unit}$$

$$\frac{\$141}{50} = \$2.82$$

So now 25 + 25 = 50 units, costing $2.82 each for a total of $141 ($61 + $80), remain in inventory. We put this information into the Inventory on Hand section of the table.

Date	Purchases			Cost of Goods Sold			Inventory on Hand		
	Quantity	Unit Cost	Total Cost	Quantity	Unit Cost	Total Cost	Quantity	Unit Cost	Total Cost
Jan. 1							100	$2.00	$200
Mar. 1	50	$2.30	$115				150	$2.10	$315
May 1				80	$2.10	$168	70	$2.10	$147
July 1	45	$3.00	$135				115	$2.45	$282
Sept. 1				90	$2.45	$221	25	$2.45	$ 61
Nov. 1	25	$3.20	$ 80				50	$2.82	$141

We have now input all of the transactions into the table. The last thing to do is total the transactions.

The Purchases section is the same as in the FIFO and LIFO tables and so the totals are also the same.

As shown in Requirement 1, the units sold should total up to 170 units. This calculation is verified as:

$$80 + 90 = 170$$

Adding up the Total Cost column of the Cost of Goods Sold section gives us:

$$\$168 + \$221 = \$389$$

The totals for inventory on hand have already been calculated and are shown on the last line of that section.

	Purchases			Cost of Goods Sold			Inventory on Hand		
Date	Quantity	Unit Cost	Total Cost	Quantity	Unit Cost	Total Cost	Quantity	Unit Cost	Total Cost
Jan. 1							100	$2.00	$200
Mar. 1	50	$2.30	$115				150	$2.10	$315
May 1				80	$2.10	$168	70	$2.10	$147
July 1	45	$3.00	$135				115	$2.45	$282
Sept. 1				90	$2.45	$221	25	$2.45	$ 61
Nov. 1	25	$3.20	$ 80				50	$2.82	$141
Dec. 31	120		$330	170		$389	50		$141

Notice that we end with 50 units of inventory (as calculated at the beginning of the question).

Let's check to see whether we calculated everything correctly. We know that:

Cost of Goods Sold = Beginning Inventory + Inventory Purchases − Ending Inventory

So in this question:

$$\$389 = (100 \text{ units} \times \$2 \text{ per unit}) + \$330 - \$141 \checkmark \text{ Correct!}$$

Part 1	Part 2	Part 3	Part 4	Demo Doc Complete

Accounting in Action

INVENTORY

If you owned a retail store that sells inventory, how would you safeguard your goods? What actions would you take to account for inventory?

Decision	Guidelines
How can inventory be protected against loss?	• Separate persons with access to inventory from record-keeping of inventory transactions from authorization of transactions • Restrict access to inventory, leave no one alone with goods, use security systems • Physically count inventory regularly and reconcile counts to inventory records • Review and analyze inventory data such as inventory turnover rate • Use perpetual inventory system and documents to evidence inventory transactions
How is cost of inventory determined?	• *Specific-unit cost*: Inventory items are specifically labeled or identified • *First-in, first-out (FIFO)*: The first inventory costs incurred are the first costs to be assigned to cost of goods sold • *Last-in, first-out (LIFO)*: The last inventory costs incurred are the first costs to be assigned to cost of goods sold • *Average cost*: After each purchase of inventory, a new weighted average cost per unit is computed

What is the effect of the different costing methods?	When prices are rising:
	
	  • FIFO reports the highest ending inventory and lowest cost of goods sold
	  • LIFO reports the lowest ending inventory and highest cost of goods sold
	  • Average cost averages the cost of ending inventory items and cost of goods sold

What is the effect of an overstatement of ending inventory?	If ending inventory is overstated, then
	
	  • Cost of goods sold is understated
	  • Gross profit is overstated
	  • Net income is overstated

How many periods are affected by misstatement?	Because ending inventory for one period becomes beginning inventory for the next, *the inventory, cost of goods sold, gross profit, and net income of two periods is misstated*

How do I estimate the cost of ending inventory?	Using the *Gross Profit Method*
	    Step 1. Calculate cost of goods available for sale
	    Step 2. Estimate cost of goods sold
	    Step 3. Estimate ending inventory

Review

Inventory

Word Power

Average cost method Inventory costing method where, after each purchase of inventory, a new weighted average cost per unit is computed and is used to value ending inventory and cost of goods sold.

Conservatism Accounting principle that states that a business must report all items in the financial statements at amounts that lead to the most cautious immediate results.

Consistency Accounting principle that states that a business should use the same accounting methods and procedures from period to period.

Cost of goods available for sale The cost of inventory on hand at the beginning of the period plus the net cost of inventory purchased during the period.

Finished goods Inventory of goods ready to sell.

First-in, first-out (FIFO) method Inventory costing method in which the first inventory costs incurred are the first costs to be assigned to cost of goods sold; FIFO leaves in ending inventory the last, the most recent, costs incurred.

Footnotes Disclosures that accompany the financial statements.

Full disclosure Accounting principle that states that a company's financial statements should report enough information for users to make knowledgeable decisions about the company.

Gross profit method A way of estimating inventory by estimating gross profit, using estimated gross profit to estimate

cost of goods sold, and using estimated cost of goods sold to estimate ending inventory.

Inventory shrinkage The loss of inventory.

Last-in, first-out (LIFO) method Inventory costing method in which the last inventory costs incurred are the first costs to be assigned to cost of goods sold; LIFO leaves in ending inventory the first, the oldest, costs incurred.

Lower-of-cost-or-market (LCM) rule Rule that a business must report inventory in the financial statements at whichever is lower, the historical cost or the market value, of each inventory item.

Materiality Accounting principle that states that a company must perform strictly proper accounting *only* for items that are significant for the business's financial statements. Information is significant, or material, when its presentation in the financial statements would cause someone to change a decision.

Raw materials Inventory items used in the production of goods.

Specific-identification method Inventory costing method in which a business uses the specific cost of each unit of inventory; also called the *specific-unit-cost method*.

Specific-unit-cost method Inventory costing method in which a business uses the specific cost of each unit of inventory; also called the *specific-identification method*.

Work in process Inventory of partially completed goods.

Quick Check

1. The chain store, The Limited, Inc., made sales of $9,363 million, and ended the year with inventory totaling $966 million. Cost of goods sold was $6,110 million. Total operating expenses were $2,734 million. How much net income did The Limited earn for the year?

   a. $519 million
   b. $3,253 million
   c. $5,663 million
   d. $6,629 million

2. Which inventory costing method assigns to ending inventory the latest, the most recent, costs incurred during the period?

   a. Specific-unit cost
   b. First-in, first-out (FIFO)
   c. Last-in, first-out (LIFO)
   d. Average cost

3. Hardings began June with 10 units of inventory that cost a total of $190. During June, Hardings purchased and sold goods as follows:

June 8	Purchase..................	30 units @ $20
14	Sale.....................	25 units @ $40
22	Purchase.................	20 units @ $22
27	Sale.....................	30 units @ $40

   Assume Hardings uses the FIFO inventory method and the perpetual inventory system. How much is Hardings' cost of goods sold for the transaction on June 14?

   a. $790
   b. $1,000
   c. $500
   d. $490

4. After the purchase on June 22, what is Hardings' cost of the inventory on hand?

   a. $300
   b. $440
   c. $740
   d. $720

5. Hardings' journal entry(s) on June 14 is:

Journal Entry:

Date	Accounts	Post Ref.	Dr.	Cr.
a.	Accounts Receivable		490	
	Inventory			490
b.	Costs of Goods Sold		1,000	
	Inventory			1,000
c.	Costs of Goods Sold		490	
	Inventory			490

d. Both b and c

6. Which inventory costing method results in the lowest net income during a period of rising inventory costs?

a. Specific-unit cost
b. First-in, first-out (FIFO)
c. Last-in, first-out (LIFO)
d. Average cost

7. Suppose Hardings used the average cost method and the perpetual inventory system. Use the data in question 3 to compute the cost of the company's inventory on hand at June 14. Round unit cost to the nearest cent.

a. $19
b. $20
c. $19.75
d. $26.33

8. Which of the following is most closely tied to accounting conservatism?

a. Consistency principle
b. Full disclosure principle
c. Materiality concept
d. Lower-of-cost-or-market method

9. At December 31, 2008, McAdam Company overstated ending inventory by $40,000. How does this error affect cost of goods sold and net income for 2005?

a. Overstates cost of goods sold and understates net income
b. Understates cost of goods sold and overstates net income
c. Overstates both cost of goods sold and net income
d. Leaves both cost of goods sold and net income

10. Suppose Adler's Outfitters suffered a fire loss and needs to estimate the cost of the goods destroyed. Beginning inventory was $100,000, purchases totaled $600,000, and sales came to $1,000,000. Adler's normal gross profit percentage is 45%. Use the gross profit method to estimate the cost of the inventory lost in the fire.

   a. $150,000
   b. $250,000
   c. $300,000
   d. $350,000

Answers are given after Apply Your Knowledge (p. 459).

Accounting Practice

Short Exercises

⑤ Reporting inventory and measuring the effect of errors.

S8-1. Match the terms with the definitions.

a. Conservatism

b. Consistency

c. Full disclosure

d. Materiality

____ 1. A company must perform strictly proper accounting only for items that are significant to the business's financial statements

____ 2. Reporting the least favorable figures in the financial statements

____ 3. A business's financial statements must report enough information for users to make knowledgeable decisions about the company

____ 4. A business should use the same accounting methods and procedures from period to period

① Inventory and related internal controls.

S8-2. For each of the following, indicate whether the item would be inventory for a retailer (R), a manufacturer (M), or accounted for as Supplies (S).

____ 1. Finished goods inventory

____ 2. Janitorial supplies

____ 3. Merchandise inventory

____ 4. Office supplies inventory

____ 5. Raw materials

____ 6. Work in process inventory

② Computing inventory costs.

S8-3. Adler's Outfitters began June with four pairs of gloves costing $10 per pair. During June, the store completed the following inventory transactions:

June 15	Purchased six pairs of gloves at $15 per pair on account
20	Sold seven pairs of gloves at $30 per pair on account

Assuming that Adler uses the FIFO method to calculate the cost of inventory for the company's perpetual inventory system:

1. Calculate the cost of goods sold for the June 20 transaction.

2. How many pairs of gloves are on hand at June 30? Calculate the cost of ending inventory at June 30.

S8-4. Refer to the information in S8-3. Prepare the journal entries to record the purchase and sale of gloves for June using the LIFO method.

② Computing inventory costs.

S8-5. Refer to the information in S8-3. Assuming Adler uses the average cost method to calculate the cost of inventory for the company's perpetual system:

② Computing inventory costs.

1. Calculate the cost of goods sold for the June 20 transaction.

2. Calculate the cost of ending inventory on June 30.

S8-6. Study Exhibit 8-11 and answer these questions in your own words:

③ Comparing the effects of the different costing methods.

1. Why does FIFO produce the lowest cost of goods sold during a period of rising prices?

2. Why does LIFO produce the highest cost of goods sold during a period of rising prices?

S8-7. Explain in your own words which inventory method results in the highest and the lowest cost of ending inventory. Assume that prices are rising.

③ Comparing the effects of the different costing methods.

S8-8. Ross, Inc., gathered the following information for inventory on December 31, 2007. Calculate the value of inventory using lower-of-cost-or-market by completing the following table:

④ Applying the lower-of-cost-or-market rule.

Inventory Item	Inventory Quantity	Unit Cost	Unit Market Value	Total Cost	Total Market	Lower of C or M
L14A	5	$2,000	$1,990			
M72R	18	$ 600	$ 605			
P4XY	22	$ 75	$ 74			
Q19T	9	$ 120	$ 118			

S8-9. Assume Adler's Outfitters uses a perpetual inventory system and the FIFO method to value its inventory. Adler is preparing monthly financial statements on November 30. Assume that Adler's chief financial officer determines that the current replacement cost of the ending inventory is $90. Report the inventory on the balance sheet.

⑤ Reporting inventory and measuring the effect of errors.

S8-10. Borov Corporation's inventory data for the year ended December 31, 2007 was:

⑤ Reporting inventory and measuring the effect of errors.

continued.....

Beginning inventory	$ 40,000
Add: Purchases	250,000
Cost of goods available for sale	290,000
Less: Ending inventory	(90,000)
Cost of goods sold	$200,000

If the ending inventory is overstated by $50,000, what is the correct ending inventory? By how much is cost of goods sold misstated? Is it overstated or understated?

⑤ Reporting inventory and measuring the effect of errors.

S8-11. Refer back to Borov's inventory data in S8-10. How would the inventory error affect Borov's cost of goods sold and gross profit for the year ended December 31, 2008?

⑥ Estimating ending inventory.

S8-12. Edgar Company began the year with inventory of $350,000. Inventory purchases for the year totaled $1,600,000. Edgar managers estimate that cost of goods sold for the year will be $1,800,000. How much is Edgar's estimated cost of ending inventory? Use the gross profit method.

⑥ Estimating ending inventory.

S8-13. Prime Roofing began the year with inventory of $50,000 and purchased $160,000 of goods during the year. Sales for the year are $300,000, and Prime's gross profit percentage is 40% of sales. Compute Prime's estimated cost of ending inventory by the gross profit method.

Exercises

① Inventory and related internal controls.

E8-14. Match the internal control procedures for inventory with the following examples:

Proper authorization (A)

Adequate documents and records (D)

Independent checks on performance (I)

Physical safeguards (P)

Separation of duties (S)

_____ 1. Restrict access to inventory

_____ 2. Individuals authorizing purchases should not record payments

_____ 3. Reconcile physical counts to total counts reflected in accounting records by using someone who does not handle or record purchases

_____ 4. Physically count inventory on a regular basis

continued.....

_____ 5. Store manager approves payment of inventory purchases

_____ 6. Maintain perpetual records of inventory

_____ 7. Use video cameras and electronic security systems to watch employees and customers

E8-15. Indicate true or false for the following statements.

① Inventory and related internal controls.

_____ 1. One way to prevent shrinkage is to reward employees who identify fellow employees who are stealing.

_____ 2. Retailers count merchandise inventory at least once a year.

_____ 3. Maps and prenumbered count sheets help ensure an accurate count

_____ 4. The best time to count the inventory is during the day while customers are shopping.

_____ 5. Inspecting garbage for evidence of stolen inventory is not an internal control procedure for inventory.

E8-16. The Music Cottage carries a large inventory of hand drums and other musical instruments. The Music Cottage uses the FIFO method and a perpetual inventory system. Company records indicate the following for a particular line of hand drums:

② Computing inventory costs.

			Number of Units	Unit Cost
July	1	Balance	5	$70
	6	Sale	3	
	8	Purchase	10	$80
	17	Sale	4	
	30	Sale	5	

Requirements

Prepare a perpetual inventory record for the hand drums. Then determine the amounts Music Cottage should report for ending inventory and cost of goods sold by the FIFO method.

E8-17. After preparing the FIFO perpetual inventory record in E8-16, journalize Music Cottage's June 8 purchase of inventory on account and cash sale on July 17, assuming the sale price of each hand drum was $150.

② Computing inventory costs.

E8-18. Refer to The Music Cottage inventory data in E8-16. Assume that The Music Cottage uses the LIFO cost method. Prepare The Music Cottage's perpetual inventory record for the hand drums on the LIFO basis. Then identify the cost of ending inventory and cost of goods sold for the month.

② Computing inventory costs.

E8-19. Refer to the Music Cottage inventory data in E8-16. Assume that Music Cottage uses the average cost method. Prepare Music Cottage's perpetual inventory record for the hand drums on the average cost basis. Round average cost per unit to the nearest cent and all other amounts to the nearest dollar.

2 Computing inventory
costs.

E8-20. Accounting records for Niebuhr Hardware yield the following data for the year ended December 31, 2008 (amounts in thousands):

5 Reporting inventory
and measuring the
effect of errors.

Inventory, December 31, 2007	$ 37,000
Purchases of inventory (on account)	310,000
Sales of inventory—80% on account; 20% for cash (cost $285,000)	440,000
Inventory, December 31, 2008	?

Requirements

1. Journalize Niehbuhr's inventory transactions in the perpetual system. Show all amounts in thousands.

2. Report ending inventory on the balance sheet, and sales, cost of goods sold, and gross profit on the income statement (amounts in thousands).

2 Computing inventory
costs.

E8-21. Assume that a toy store bought and sold a video game during December as follows:

3 Comparing the
effects of the
different costing
methods.

Beginning inventory	10 units @ $20
Sale	6 units
Purchase...	15 units @ $22
Sale	14 units

Using the perpetual inventory system, compute the cost of ending inventory under (a) FIFO and (b) LIFO. Which method results in a higher cost of ending inventory? A higher cost of goods sold?

2 Computing inventory
costs.

E8-22. Assume that Casey's Carpet Store completed the following perpetual inventory transactions for a line of carpet:

Beginning inventory	20 rolls @ $200
Purchase...	8 rolls @ $300
Sale	15 rolls @ $500

continued.....

Compute cost of goods sold and gross profit under (a) FIFO, (b) LIFO, and (c) average cost (round average cost per unit to the nearest cent).

E8-23. Ingram, Inc., gathered the following information for inventory on December 31, 2008. Calculate the value of inventory using lower-of-cost-or-market by completing the following table:

4 Applying the lower-of-cost-or-market rule.

Inventory Item	Inventory Quantity	Unit Cost	Unit Market Value	Total Cost	Total Market	Lower of C or M
IG101	100	$ 30	$ 28			
KB284	60	$ 15	$ 14			
MR276	48	$ 70	$ 72			
NI982	15	$ 40	$ 41			
PR1086	72	$105	$104			

E8-24. Namaste Foods reports inventory at the lower of cost or market. Prior to releasing its March 2007 financial statements, Namaste's preliminary income statement appears as follows:

4 Applying the lower-of-cost-or-market rule.

NAMASTE FOODS
Income Statement
Month Ended March 31, 2007

Sales revenue	$118,000
Cost of goods sold	45,000
Gross profit	73,000

Namaste's ending inventory account balance is $17,000. However, it has determined that the replacement cost of this inventory is $16,000.

Requirements

Prepare a revised income statement to apply the lower-of-cost-or-market method. Also show the relevant portion of Namaste's balance sheet at March 31, 2007.

E8-25. Refer to the data for Namaste in E8-24. Assume that the ending inventory amount was miscounted and the LCM value of $16,000 is incorrect. Determine the correct amounts of cost of goods sold and gross profit if Namaste's:

5 Reporting inventory and measuring the effect of errors.

a. Ending inventory is overstated by $3,000

b. Ending inventory is understated by $3,000

Reporting inventory and measuring the effect of errors.

E8-26. Strong Tools reported the following comparative income statement for the years ended September 30, 2009, and 2008.

STRONG TOOLS		
Income Statements		
Years Ended September 30, 2009 and 2008		
	2009	**2008**
Sales revenue	$140,000	$120,000
Cost of goods sold	70,000	65,000
Gross profit	70,000	55,000
Operating expenses	30,000	25,000
Net income	$ 40,000	$ 30,000

During 2009, accountants for the company discovered that ending 2008 inventory was overstated by $4,000. Prepare the corrected comparative income statement for the two-year period, complete with a heading for the statement. What was the effect of the error on net income for the two years combined? Explain your answer.

6 Estimating ending inventory.

E8-27. Assume that the accounting records for Amana microwaves show the following:

Beginning inventory	$ 150,000
Net purchases.....................................	800,000
Net sales	1,000,000
Gross profit rate.................................	30%

Suppose this inventory, stored in Miami, was lost in a hurricane. Estimate the amount of the loss to Amana. Use the gross profit method.

6 Estimating ending inventory.

E8-28. Gleason, Inc., began January with inventory of $47,500. During January, the business made net purchases of $37,600 and had net sales of $60,000. For the past several years, Gleason's gross profit has been 40% of sales. Use the gross profit method to estimate the cost of the ending inventory for the monthly financial statements.

Problems (Group A)

2 Computing inventory costs.

P8-29A. The Ski Shop began February with an inventory of 50 ski vests that cost a total of $1,500, with each costing $30. The store purchased and sold merchandise on account as follows:

Purchase 1	60 vests @ $35
Sale 1	100 vests @ $60
Purchase 2	80 vests @ $40
Sale 2	70 vests @ $70

continued.....

Assume that Ski Shop uses the FIFO cost method. Cash payments on account totaled $5,100. Operating expenses were $2,400; the store paid two-thirds in cash and recorded the rest as accounts payable.

Requirements

1. Prepare a perpetual inventory record, at FIFO cost, for this merchandise.

2. Make journal entries to record the store's transactions.

P8-30A. Refer to the Ski Shop situation in P8-29A. Keep all the data unchanged, but assume that Ski Shop actually uses the average cost method.

② Computing inventory costs.

Requirements

1. Prepare a perpetual inventory record at average cost. Round average unit cost to the nearest cent and all other amounts to the nearest dollar.

2. Prepare a multistep income statement for Ski Shop for the month of February.

P8-31A. Spring Garden Supply, which uses the LIFO method, began March with 50 units of inventory that cost $15 each. During March, Spring Garden Supply completed these inventory transactions:

② Computing inventory costs.

			Number of Units	Unit Cost	Unit Sale Price
March	2	Purchase	12	$20	
	8	Sale	40		$36
	17	Purchase	24	$25	
	22	Sale	31		$40

Requirements

1. Prepare a perpetual inventory record for Spring Garden Supply's merchandise.

2. Determine the cost of goods sold for March.

3. Compute gross profit for March.

P8-32A. Gordon's Drug has been plagued with lackluster sales, and some of the company's merchandise is gathering dust. It is now December 31, 2007. Assume the current replacement cost of Gordon's ending inventory is $700,000 below what Gordon paid for the goods, which was $3,900,000. Before any adjustments at the end of the period, assume the Cost of Goods Sold account has a balance of $22,400,000.

What action should Gordon take in this situation, if any? Give any journal entry required. At what amount should Gordon report Inventory on the balance sheet? At what amount should the company report Cost of Goods Sold on the income statement? Discuss the accounting principle or concept that is most relevant to this situation.

P8-33A. The accounting records of Taco Cabana Mexican Restaurant show these data (in thousands):

	2008	2007	2006
Net sales revenue	$210	$165	$170
Cost of goods sold	120	110	105
Gross profit	90	55	65
Operating expenses	74	38	46
Net income	$ 16	$ 17	$ 19

In early 2009, internal auditors discovered that the ending inventory for 2006 was understated by $8 (thousands).

Requirements

1. Show corrected income statements for the three years.

2. State whether each year's net income as reported here is understated or overstated. For each incorrect figure, indicate the amount of the understatement or overstatement.

P8-34A. Baca Motors estimates its inventory by the gross profit method when preparing monthly financial statements. For the past two years, gross profit has averaged 25% of net sales. Assume further that the company's inventory records reveal the following data (amounts in thousands):

Inventory, March 1	$ 292
Transactions during March:	
Purchases..	6,585
Purchase discounts....................................	149
Purchase returns.......................................	8
Sales...	8,657
Sales returns	17

continued.....

1. Estimate the March 31, 2009, inventory using the gross profit method.

2. Prepare the March income statement through gross profit for Baca Motors.

Problems (Group B)

P8-35B. KayBee purchases inventory in crates, so each unit of inventory is a crate of toys. Assume a department began July with an inventory of 20 units that cost a total of $1,200, with each costing $60. During the month, the department purchased and sold merchandise on account as follows:

② Computing inventory costs.

Purchase 1	30 units @ $65
Sale 1	40 units @ $100
Purchase 2	70 units @ $70
Sale 2	75 units @ $110

KayBee uses the LIFO cost method. Cash payments on account totaled $6,300. Department operating expenses for the month were $3,600. The department paid two-thirds in cash, with the rest recorded as accounts payable.

Requirements

1. Prepare a perpetual inventory record, at LIFO cost, for this merchandise.

2. Make journal entries to record the department's transactions.

② Computing inventory costs.

P8-36B. Refer to the KayBee situation in Problem 8-35B. Keep all the data unchanged, but assume that KayBee uses the average cost method.

Requirements

1. Prepare a perpetual inventory record at average cost. Round average unit cost to the nearest cent and all other amounts to the nearest dollar.

2. Prepare a multistep income statement for the KayBee department for the month of July.

P8-37B. A clothing outlet store, which uses the FIFO method, began October with 50 coats in inventory that cost $40 each. During October, the store completed these inventory transactions:

② Computing inventory costs.

continued.....

		Number of Units	Unit Cost	Unit Sale Price
Oct. 3	Sale	40		$70
8	Purchase	80	$44	
21	Sale	70		$73
30	Purchase	20	$48	

Requirements

1. Prepare a perpetual inventory record for the coat inventory.

2. Determine the store's cost of goods sold for October.

3. Compute gross profit for October.

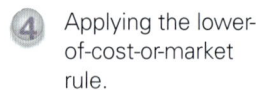

Applying the lower-of-cost-or-market rule.

P8-38B. The Army/Navy Surplus Store experienced lackluster sales, and some of the company's merchandise is gathering dust. It is now December 31, 2008, and the current replacement cost of the ending inventory is $650,000 below what Army/Navy actually paid for the goods, which was $4,900,000. Before any adjustments at the end of the period, the company's Cost of Goods Sold account has a balance of $29,600,000.

What action should the Army/Navy Surplus Store take in this situation, if any? Give any journal entry required. At what amount should Army/Navy report Inventory on the balance sheet? At what amount should the company report Cost of Goods Sold on the income statement? Discuss the accounting principle or concept that is most relevant to this situation.

Reporting inventory and measuring the effect of errors.

P8-39B. The Bermuda Company books show the following data (in thousands). In early 2008, internal auditors found that the ending inventory for 2005 was overstated by $8 (thousands).

	2007	2006	2005
Net sales revenue	$360	$285	$244
Cost of goods sold	190	125	145
Gross profit	170	160	99
Operating expenses	113	109	76
Net income	$ 57	$ 51	$ 23

Requirements

1. Show corrected income statements for the three years.

2. State whether each year's net income as reported here is understated or overstated. For each incorrect figure, indicate the amount of the understatement or overstatement.

P8-40B. The Toy Factory estimates its inventory by the gross profit method when preparing monthly financial statements. The gross profit has averaged 40% of net sales. Assume that the company's inventory records reveal the following data (amounts in thousands):

6 Estimating ending inventory.

Inventory, July 1	$ 367
Transactions during July:	
Purchases	3,789
Purchase discounts	26
Purchase returns	12
Sales	6,430
Sales returns	30

Requirements

1. Estimate the July 31, 2008, inventory using the gross profit method.

2. Prepare the Toy Factory's July income statement through gross profit.

for 24/7 practice, visit www.MyAccountingLab.com

Apply Your Knowledge

Case 1. Robert Jordan was the owner of The Antique Store. He had applied for a business loan from the bank and was reviewing the year-end inventory figures that would be shown on the balance sheet. The total cost of the inventory was $185,000 but Robert knew that it was worth more. He told his accountant that, of the 12 major categories of inventory, he believed 10 of the categories held inventory with values that should be reported higher than their original cost because they were worth more than their purchase prices. Robert then provided a schedule showing the total inventory valued at $368,000. In response, his accountant explained that inventory must be reported at the lower-of-cost-or-market value, and even though 10 of the inventory categories may have a market value that was higher than cost, the inventory could not be reported above the historical cost. The accountant then asked about the other two categories. Robert stated that the current market value for those categories was actually $12,000 lower than the reported cost. The accountant explained that conservatism would require the total inventory be reported at the lower of cost or market, and accordingly, the amount on the balance sheet should be $173,000 to reflect the $12,000 lower value. Robert became upset and said it was unfair—lowering the total inventory value would also lower the total owner's equity because assets equal liabilities plus owner's equity. His accountant said that GAAP required the lower of either cost or market to provide financial statement users with a more conservative financial position. Robert then insisted on using the current values; he felt that not showing the most up-to-date inventory values would be misleading. The accountant would not go along with Robert's plan because he felt it would be unethical.

What ethical concern does the accountant have? Should the inventory be shown at a value even lower than historical cost? Does Robert have a valid argument when he says that, by not showing inventory at the current market value, the financial statements are misleading? Could Robert show the inventory at the current market value and add a footnote explaining what the total inventory originally cost? Do you have any suggestions?

Case 2. Madge and Cindy both owned retail shops in the city and they were discussing their latest year-end results. As it turned out, they both operated similar businesses with about the same volume of sales; however, Cindy reported a much larger net income than Madge. Upon further investigation Madge found out that Cindy used the FIFO method of inventory costing whereas Madge used the LIFO method. As prices rose sharply, Madge included the higher-cost inventory purchases in her cost of goods sold, which resulted in a lower gross profit and a lower net income. Madge was concerned because she and Cindy were both selling their businesses, and potential buyers might prefer Cindy's business because it appeared more profitable. Further, Madge worried because, under LIFO, the older, lower-cost purchases were reported on her balance sheet as the ending inventory. Thus, her reported balance sheet inventory was lower than Cindy's reported inventory. Cindy, on the other hand, was reporting the ending inventory on her balance sheet at the recent higher costs and thus had a higher reported inventory amount. Madge complained to her accountant that her business looked worse compared to Cindy's even though both businesses were essentially the same except for the method of inventory costing they used. Given the situation, Madge told her accountant to change the inventory method used from LIFO to

FIFO so the financial statements would portray her business more favorably and it would make it more comparable to Cindy's business.

Can Madge change the method of inventory used from LIFO to FIFO? Are any ethical issues involved? Is Madge's reason for wanting to change inventory methods valid? Wouldn't a potential buyer be able to see that both businesses were essentially the same except for the impact of the inventory methods used? What other thoughts do you have?

KNOW YOUR BUSINESS

This case addresses the inventory of Target Corporation. You know that inventory of a merchandiser, such as Target, is the goods that the merchandiser has available for sale to its customers. Further, you recall that several acceptable methods, including LIFO or FIFO, are available to account for inventory. You also know that inventory is classified as a current asset, and for large merchandisers such as Target, the inventory may be a large component of the total current assets. Refer to the Target Corporation financial statements in Appendix A. Also, consider the following partial excerpt from the Inventory footnote included in the annual report:

Inventory

Substantially all of our inventory and the related cost of sales are accounted for under the retail inventory accounting method using the last-in, first-out (LIFO) basis. Inventory is stated at the lower of LIFO cost or market. Inventory also includes a LIFO provision that is calculated based on inventory levels, markup rates and internally generated retail price indices.

Requirements

1. What was the percentage of inventory compared to the total current assets as of January 2005? What is the significance of this percentage? Was the ending inventory a larger or smaller portion of the total current assets compared to the beginning inventory?

2. What method of inventory did Target use? Did Target use conservatism in valuing its inventory? Do you think the reported results would be different if Target used the FIFO method? What safeguards do you think Target has in place to protect its inventory?

For Internet Exercises, Excel in Practice, and additional online activities, go to the Web site www.prenhall.com/pollard.

Quick Check Answers

1. *a* 2. *b* 3. *d* 4. *c* 5. *c* 6. *c* 7. *c* 8. *d* 9. *b* 10. *a*

Comparing the Perpetual and Periodic Inventory Systems

Inventory Costing in a Periodic System

We described the periodic inventory system briefly in Chapter 5. Accounting is simpler in a periodic system because the company keeps no continuous, running record of inventory on hand. The only way to determine the ending inventory and cost of goods sold in a periodic system is to count the goods at the end of the accounting period, usually at the end of the year. The periodic system works well for a business that sells many, relatively inexpensive items because the cost of keeping perpetual records outweighs the control offered by the continuous records. In a small company, the owner can instead control inventory by visual inspection.

This appendix illustrates how the periodic system works. Accounting in a periodic system is similar to a perpetual system, except:

1. The periodic system uses four additional accounts to track certain transactions, rather than including these activities in a single Inventory account as is the procedure for a perpetual inventory system:

   - *Purchases:* This account holds the cost of inventory as it is purchased and carries a debit balance.
   - *Purchase Discounts:* This contra-account carries a credit balance because it offsets the purchase costs with any discounts received for making payments on purchases within the discount period.
   - *Purchase Returns and Allowances:* This contra-account carries a credit balance because it offsets the purchase costs with the costs of any returns or allowances on damaged goods.
   - *Freight-In:* This account carries a debit balance because it reflects the additional costs of shipping goods that are included in inventory.
   - Net purchases is thus calculated by combining the balances in these accounts. Purchase Discounts and Purchase Returns and Allowances reduce Purchases, while Freight-In increases it.

2. The end-of-period entries are more extensive in the periodic system because we must remove the beginning inventory balance and replace it with the cost of the ending inventory. This appendix illustrates this process.

3. Cost of goods sold in a periodic inventory system is computed by the following formula using the amounts shown:

Beginning inventory (ending inventory of the preceding period)..........	$ 5,000
Add: Net purchases (often abbreviated as Purchases)...........................	20,000*
Cost of goods available for sale..	25,000
Less: Ending inventory (ending inventory of the current period).........	(7,000)
Cost of goods sold	$18,000
*Net purchases (using amounts shown):	
Purchases...	$21,000
Less: Purchase discounts	(2,000)
Purchase returns and allowances	(5,000)
Add: Freight in..	6,000
Net purchases	$20,000

The application of the various costing methods, FIFO, LIFO, and average cost, in a periodic inventory system follows the pattern illustrated earlier for the perpetual system. To show how the periodic inventory system works, we use the same Adler's Outfitters data as we used for the perpetual system, as follows:

Adler's Outfitters Suede Jacket			
		Number of Units	**Unit Cost**
Nov. 1	Beginning inventory	1	$40
5	Purchase	6	$45
15	Sale	4	
26	Purchase	7	$50
30	Sale	8	
30	Ending inventory	2	$?

First-In, First-Out (FIFO) Method

Adler's Outfitters could use the FIFO costing method with a periodic inventory system. The FIFO computations follow:

Beginning inventory (1 unit @ $40)...	$ 40
Add: Purchases (6 units @ $45 + 7 units @ $50)	620
Cost of goods available for sale (14 units)..	660
Less: Ending inventory (2 units @ $50)...	(100)
Cost of goods sold (12 units)...	$560

Cost of goods available is always the sum of beginning inventory plus purchases. Under FIFO, the ending inventory comes from the latest, the most recent, purchases, which cost $50 per unit. Ending inventory is therefore $100, and cost of goods sold is $560. These amounts are exactly the same as we saw for FIFO in the perpetual system in Exhibit 8-5.

Fewer journal entries are used in the periodic system because Adler would record a sale with only a single entry. For example, Adler's sale of four suede jackets for $80 each is recorded as follows:

Journal Entry:

Date	Accounts	Post Ref.	Dr.	Cr.
Nov. 15	Accounts Receivable (4 × $80)		320	
	Sales Revenue			320

No adjustment to Cost of Goods Sold or Inventory is recorded in the periodic system at the time of sale.

Last-In, First-Out (LIFO) Method

The LIFO method fits well with a periodic inventory system. Adler's LIFO computations follow:

Beginning inventory (1 unit @ $40)	$ 40
Add: Purchases (6 units @ $45 + 7 units @ $50)..............	620
Cost of goods available for sale (14 units)........................	660
Less: Ending inventory (1 unit @ $40 + 1 unit @ $45)	(85)
Cost of goods sold (12 units)	$575

Under LIFO, the ending inventory comes from the earliest units obtained, the single beginning unit that cost $40 plus one of the units purchased for $45. Ending inventory is therefore $85, and cost of goods sold is $575. These amounts are the same as we saw for the perpetual system in Exhibit 8-7. In some cases, the LIFO amounts can differ between the perpetual and the periodic systems.

Average Cost Method

In the average cost method, we compute a single average cost per unit for the entire period as follows:

Cost of Goods Available for Sale		Number of Units Available for Sale		Average Cost per Unit for the Entire Period
$660	÷	14 units	=	$47.14

This average cost per unit is then used to compute the ending inventory and cost of goods sold as follows:

Beginning inventory (1 unit @ $40)...	$ 40
Add: Purchases (6 units @ $45 + 7 units @ $50)....................	620
Cost of goods available for sale (14 units @ average cost of $47.14)..	660
Less: Ending inventory (2 units @ $47.14).............................	(94)
Cost of goods sold (12 units @ $47.14)....................................	$566

Ending inventory and cost of goods sold under the periodic system differ from the amounts in a perpetual system. Why? Because under the perpetual system, a new average cost is computed after each purchase. But the periodic system uses a single average cost that is determined at the end of the period.

Exhibit 8A-1 provides a side-by-side comparison of the two inventory accounting systems using the amounts assumed for the Exhibit. It gives the journal entries, the T-accounts, and all financial statement effects of both inventory systems.

In the periodic system, the purchase of inventory is *not* recorded in the Inventory account. Instead, purchases are recorded in the Purchases account, which is an expense (see transaction 1 in the exhibit, right column). A sale transaction includes *no* cost of goods sold entry (transaction 2). How, then, does the business record inventory and cost of goods sold?

Transactions 3a and 3b give the end-of-period entries to update the Inventory account and record Cost of Goods Sold. Transaction 3c closes the Purchases account into Cost of Goods Sold to complete the periodic process.

Panel B of the exhibit shows the financial statements under both systems.

Exhibit 8A-1 Comparing the Perpetual and Periodic Inventory Systems

PANEL A—Recording in the Journal and Posting to the Accounts

Perpetual System	Dr.	Cr.	Periodic System	Dr.	Cr.
1. Credit purchases of $560,000:			**1. Credit purchases of $560,000:**		
Inventory	560,000		Purchases	560,000	
Accounts Payable		560,000	Accounts Payable		560,000
2. Credit sales of $900,000 (cost $540,000):			**2. Credit sales of $900,000:**		
Accounts Receivable	900,000		Accounts Receivable	900,000	
Sales Revenue		900,000	Sales Revenue		900,000
Cost of Goods Sold	540,000		**3. End-of-period adjusting entries to**		
Inventory		540,000	**update Inventory and record Cost**		
3. End-of-period adjusting entries:			**of Goods Sold:**		
No entries required. Both Inventory and			**a. Transfer the cost of beginning inventory**		
Cost of Goods Sold are up-to-date unless			**($100,000) to Cost of Goods Sold:**		
an adjustment is necessary as a result of			Cost of Goods Sold	100,000	
physical inventory count.			Inventory (beginning balance)		100,000
			b. Record the cost of ending inventory		
			($120,000) based on a physical count:		
			Inventory (ending balance)	120,000	
			Cost of Goods Sold		120,000
			c. Transfer the cost of purchases to		
			Cost of Goods Sold:		
			Cost of Goods Sold	560,000	
			Purchases		560,000

Inventory and Cost of Goods Sold Accounts

Inventory		Cost of Goods Sold	
100,000*	540,000	540,000	
560,000			
120,000			

Inventory and Cost of Goods Sold Accounts

Inventory		Cost of Goods Sold	
100,000*	100,000	100,000	120,000
120,000		560,000	
120,000		540,000	

* Beginning Inventory was $100,000.

PANEL B—Reporting in the Financial Statements

Perpetual System			Periodic System		
Income Statement					
Sales revenue		$900,000	Sales revenue		$900,000
Cost of goods sold		540,000	Cost of goods sold:		
Gross profit		360,000	Beginning inventory	$100,000	
			Add: Purchases	560,000	
			Cost of goods available for sale	660,000	
			Less: Ending inventory	(120,000)	
			Cost of goods sold		540,000
			Gross profit		360,000
Balance Sheet					
Current assets:			Current assets:		
Inventory		120,000	Inventory		120,000

Appendix Assignments

Short Exercises

S8A-41 Ivy Shirts uses a periodic inventory system. Ivy completed the following inventory transactions during April:

Inventory costing a in periodic system: FIFO and LIFO.

Apr.	1	Purchased 10 shirts @ $40
	7	Sold 6 shirts for $70 each
	13	Sold 2 shirts for $80 each
	21	Purchased 3 shirts @ $50

Compute Ivy's ending inventory and cost of goods sold under both LIFO and FIFO. Compute gross profit under both methods. Which method results in more gross profit?

S8A-42 Ivy Shirts uses a periodic inventory system. Use the Ivy Shirts data in S8-41A to compute ending inventory and cost of goods sold under the average cost method. Round average unit cost to the nearest cent.

Inventory costing in a periodic system: Average cost.

Exercises

E8A-43 The periodic inventory records of Quilts Galore indicate the following on October 31:

Inventory costing in a periodic system: FIFO, LIFO, average cost and specific-unit cost.

Oct.	1	Beginning inventory....................................	9 units @ $160
	8	Purchase	4 units @ $160
	15	Purchase	12 units @ $170
	26	Purchase	3 units @ $176

The physical inventory on October 31 counts eight units on hand.

Requirements

Compute ending inventory and cost of goods sold, using each of the following methods:

1. Specific-unit cost, assuming four $170 units and four $160 units are on hand

2. Average cost

3. First-in, first-out

4. Last-in, first-out

Problems (Group A)

P8A-44 Baby's World began December with 140 units of inventory that cost $75 each. During December, the store made the following purchases:

Inventory costing in a periodic system: FIFO, LIFO, and average cost.

Dec. 3	217 @ $79
12	95 @ $82
18	210 @ $83
24	248 @ $87

The store uses the periodic inventory system, and the physical count on December 31 indicates that 229 units of inventory are on hand.

Requirements

1. Determine the ending inventory and cost-of-goods-sold amounts for the December financial statements under the average cost, FIFO, and LIFO methods. Round average cost per unit to the nearest cent and all other amounts to the nearest dollar.

2. Sales revenue for December totaled $90,000. Compute Baby World's gross profit for December under each method.

3. Which method will result in the lowest income taxes for Baby's World? Why? Which method will result in the highest net income for Baby's World? Why?

Inventory costing in a periodic system: FIFO.

P8A-45 Heath Hardware Company, which uses a periodic inventory system, began 2007 with 6,000 units of inventory that cost a total of $30,000. During 2007, Heath purchased merchandise on account as follows:

Purchase 1 (10,000 units costing)	$ 60,000
Purchase 2 (20,000 units costing)	$140,000

continued.....

At year-end, the physical count indicated 5,000 units of inventory on hand.

Requirements

1. How many units did Heath sell during the year? The sale price per unit was $10. Determine Heath's sales revenue for the year.

2. Compute cost of goods sold by the FIFO method. Then determine gross profit for the year.

LEARNING OBJECTIVES

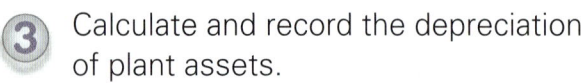

1 Define and describe the life cycle of long-term assets.

2 Calculate and record the acquisition of plant assets.

3 Calculate and record the depreciation of plant assets.

4 Calculate and record the disposal of plant assets.

5 Calculate and record the depletion of natural resources.

6 Account for intangible assets.

7 Report long-term assets on the balance sheet.

Long-Term Assets: Plant Assets and Intangibles

Think about the resources you use every day. In your home, you rely on appliances and equipment, such as electric razors, hair dryers, microwave ovens, refrigerators, vacuum cleaners, and heating/cooling systems, to make your life easier. Once you leave the house, you probably depend on a car, truck, or SUV to get you to work or school. Throughout the day, you likely use computers, cell phones, iPods, and PDAs. In addition, you may own your own home and may even have a recreational vehicle. All of these items that you own, use, and enjoy are considered your assets, and some of them will last more than a year.

Just as you use resources to live your life more efficiently and enjoyably, businesses also acquire resources for long-term use. For example, FedEx owns a huge fleet of delivery trucks throughout the world. In addition to tracking the cost of these trucks, FedEx spreads this cost over time as the trucks make deliveries. Eventually, FedEx will retire, sell, or exchange these trucks for new ones. These activities impact the financial position of FedEx and must be shown in its financial statements. ●

Look Back

You have learned about internal controls for cash, receivables, and inventory. You have also seen how to account for each, and how to report them on the balance sheet.

Look Ahead

You will calculate and record the acquisition, use, and disposal of plant assets. You will also account for intangible assets and learn how to present long-term assets on the balance sheet.

In the last few chapters, you examined current assets such as cash, accounts receivable, notes receivable, and inventory. You discovered the internal controls necessary to protect these assets and witnessed the unique issues associated with accounting for each. For example, you estimated uncollectibles, calculated interest on notes, and valued inventory according to the LCM rule. Further, you saw how to report each of these accounts on the balance sheet.

In this chapter, we continue our conversation about assets and turn our attention to the different long-term assets that support business operations. These items may be found in service, retail, or manufacturing businesses. Businesses own land, buildings, equipment, and even natural resources such as oil, timber, or minerals. Companies may also possess intangible assets, such as patents or trademarks. Like current assets, these long-term assets present accounting challenges. Accordingly, in this chapter we look at how to accomplish proper accounting and reporting of their acquisition, use, and disposal.

Long-Term Assets

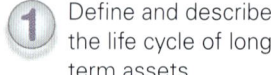 Define and describe the life cycle of long-term assets.

You learned about current assets that businesses convert to cash, sell, or use up within a year. Although businesses utilize cash, receivables due from customers, and inventory to operate during the year, these entities also invest in expensive resources that will be useful for a long time. Recall from Chapter 3 that long-term assets are resources owned by a business and employed for more than one year. These assets support daily operations and are not held for sale to customers. Long-term assets include the following:

- Plant assets: Long-lived, tangible assets used in the operations of the business. Examples include land, land improvements, buildings, equipment, furniture, and fixtures, as well as **natural resources**, such as ore deposits and timber.
- **Intangible assets**: Long-lived resources without physical form that represent rights, such as patents, copyrights, trademarks, trade names, and franchises.

Over time, a business acquires, uses, and disposes of long-term assets. Exhibit 9-1 summarizes the major activities that affect long-term assets.

Long-term assets may either be donated to or purchased by a business. As the asset is used, a portion of its cost is expensed against the revenues earned from its use. The following expenses relate to long-term assets:

- Depreciation, as we discussed in Chapter 3, is the allocation of the cost of assets such as buildings, equipment, and machinery, to expense over their useful life.
- **Depletion** is the allocation of the cost of natural resources to expense over their useful life.

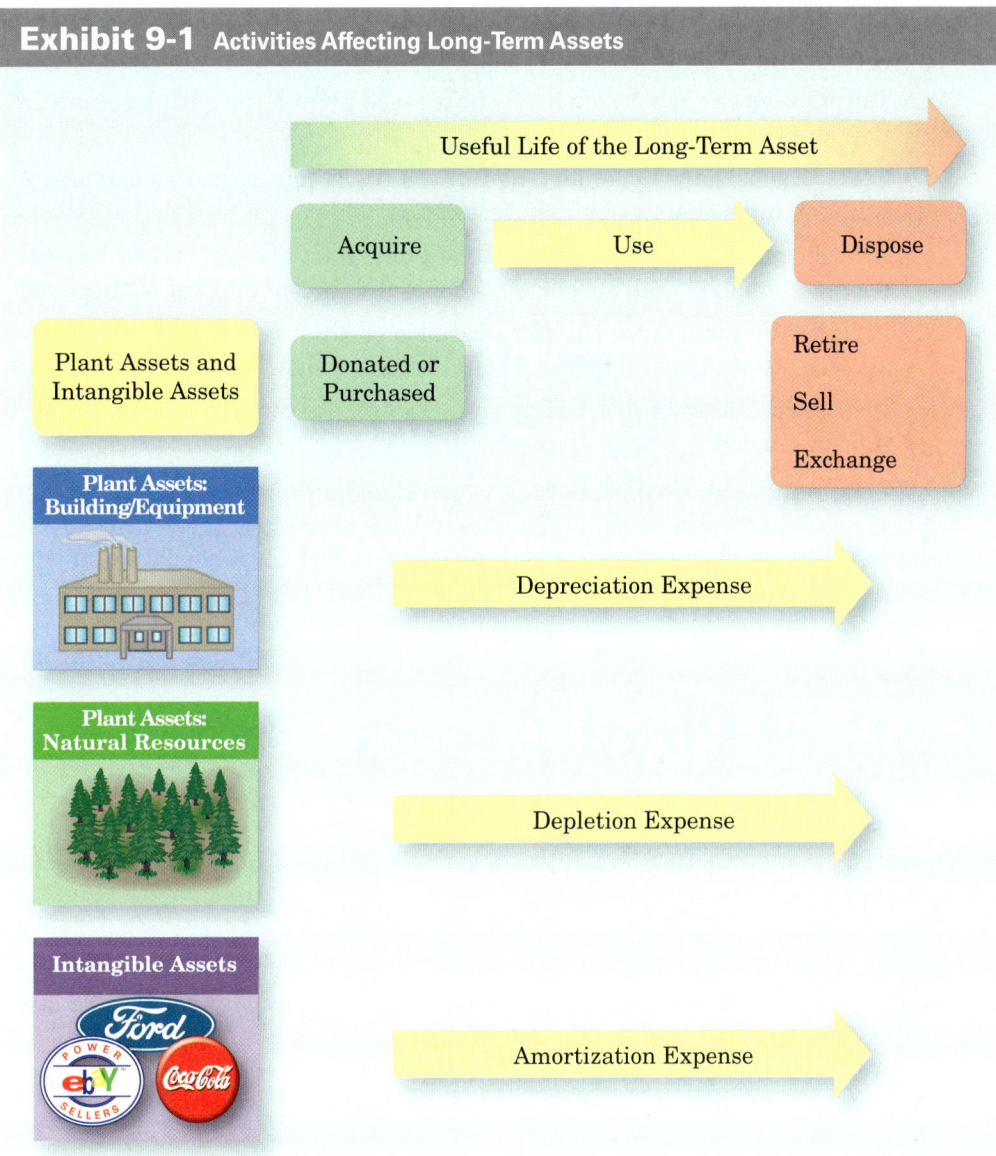

Exhibit 9-1 Activities Affecting Long-Term Assets

- **Amortization** is the allocation of the cost of intangible assets to expense over their useful life.

Businesses may decide to dispose of a long-term asset before, or at the end of, its useful life. To determine whether the disposal of an asset generates a gain or loss and thus affects net income, the accountant compares the cash or trade-in value received to the book value of the asset. Also mentioned in Chapter 3, the book value is the portion of the asset's original cost that has not been used or expensed; it is the cost of the asset less its accumulated depreciation. The book value of an asset represents the value of the asset *on the books*, in other words, in the accounting records; it is thus measured against the amount received during disposal of the asset to determine any gain or loss on the asset's disposition.

Organizational accountability applies to long-term assets as well as current ones. Business managers are responsible for developing internal controls for long-term assets. These assets are often expensive, and some long-term assets such as computers are easy to steal, so the following internal controls are important. In addition to the general internal control activities examined in previous chapters, some specifics apply:

- Tag or otherwise label each newly purchased plant asset with an identification number.
- Create a subsidiary ledger for long-term assets, listing each asset and its identification number, date of purchase, location, and person responsible for it.
- In each plant asset's account in the subsidiary ledger, record the cost, depreciation data, and subsequent disposal date and amount of the asset.
- Periodically make sure the total balance of all asset subsidiary accounts agrees with the general ledger account balances shown on the balance sheet.
- Inspect each asset at least once a year, noting its condition and whether it remains in use.

In the remainder of this chapter, we will compute and record the costs to acquire, use, and dispose of long-term assets. We will see how these transactions, including gains and losses recognized on disposals, affect the financial statements.

Measuring the Cost of Plant Assets

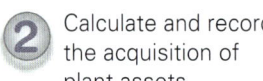

2 Calculate and record the acquisition of plant assets.

The cost principle mentioned in Chapter 1 says that an asset should be carried on the balance sheet at its historical cost, the amount actually paid for the asset. The general rule for measuring cost is to include all amounts paid to acquire the asset and make it ready for its intended use. The types of costs differ between the various plant assets, so we discuss each asset type individually. Exhibit 9-2 summarizes the costs of plant assets.

Exhibit 9-2 Costs of Plant Assets

Land
- Purchase price
- Brokerage commission
- Survey and legal fees
- Unpaid taxes
- Costs to clear land
- Costs to remove buildings

Land Improvements
- Purchase price
- Examples:
  - Fencing
  - Paving
  - Sprinkler systems
  - Lighting
  - Signs

Building
- Construction costs
  - Architectural fees
  - Building permits
  - Material, labor, and overhead
- Purchase price
  - Brokerage commission
  - Legal fees
  - Unpaid taxes
  - Renovation and repair costs

Furniture/Fixtures
- Purchase price, less discounts
- Transportation costs
- Sales tax

Equipment/Machinery
- Purchase price, less discounts
- Transportation costs
- Insurance while in transit
- Sales tax
- Commission
- Installation costs
- Testing equipment

Land and Land Improvements

The cost of land generally includes its purchase price, brokerage commission, survey and legal fees, and any unpaid property taxes the purchaser pays. It also includes the cost of clearing the land and removing any unwanted buildings. As mentioned in Chapter 3, the cost of land is not depreciated because it is never really exhausted. The cost does *not* include fencing, paving, sprinkler systems, and lighting. These plant assets, called **land improvements**, are recorded separately because they are subject to depreciation.

Imagine that High Range Manufacturing signed a $500,000 note payable to purchase land on January 1. High Range also paid $40,000 in delinquent property taxes, $8,000 in transfer taxes, $5,000 to remove an old building, and a $1,000 survey fee. What is the cost of this land? All of the costs incurred to bring the land to its intended use are part of the land's cost.

High Range's entry to record the purchase of the land follows:

Journal Entry:

Date	Accounts	Post Ref.	Dr.	Cr.
Jan. 1	Land		554,000	
	Notes Payable			500,000
	Cash			54,000
	Record purchase of land.			

We say that High Range **capitalized** the cost of the land at $554,000. In other words, the company debited an asset account, Land, for $554,000.

On July 1, High Range paid $260,000 for fences, paving, lighting, and signs on the property. The following entry records the cost of these land improvements:

Journal Entry:

Date	Accounts	Post Ref.	Dr.	Cr.
July 1	Land Improvements		260,000	
	Cash			260,000
	Record land improvements.			

Land and Land Improvements are two entirely separate asset accounts. The costs of land improvements are depreciated over the assets' useful lives.

Buildings, Equipment, Machinery, Furniture, and Fixtures

A business may hire a contractor to construct a building, or it may buy a building already built. The costs to construct a building include fees, permits, and the cost of material, labor, and overhead. When an existing building is purchased, its cost can include many of the items mentioned in our discussion of land, such as commissions, legal fees, and unpaid taxes, plus other costs such as those needed to repair and renovate the building for its intended use.

The cost of equipment and machinery includes purchase price less any discounts, shipping charges, insurance while in transit, sales and other taxes, purchase commission, installation costs, and the cost of testing the asset before it is used.

Furniture and fixtures consist of desks, chairs, file cabinets, and display racks. The cost of furniture and fixtures includes the basic cost of each asset less any discounts, plus all other costs to get the assets ready for use, such as transportation costs and sales tax. Nearly all companies have furniture and fixtures.

A Lump-Sum (Basket) Purchase of Assets

A company may purchase several assets as a group, in a **basket purchase**, for a single price. For example, a company may pay one price for land, land improvements, and a building. For accounting purposes, the company must identify the cost of each asset because each is used, or depreciated, differently, and land is not depreciated at all. The total cost of the assets purchased is divided among the assets according to their relative appraised, or market, values. This allocation technique is called the **relative-sales-value method**.

Assume that, on May 1, Steinborn purchased land and a building for its main office. The combined purchase price of the land and the building was $2.8 million. An appraisal indicated that the land's market value was $300,000 and that the building's market value was $2.7 million, making the total appraised value equal to $3 million.

To allocate the total purchase price between these two assets, first figure the ratio of each asset's market value to the total market value of both assets combined. Once the ratio of each asset's market value to the total is known, use this ratio to allocate the total purchase price between the two assets as shown here:

Asset	Market Value	Percentage of Total Market Value		Total Purchase Price		Cost of Each Asset
Land	$ 300,000	$300,000/$3,000,000 = 10%	×	$2,800,000	=	$ 280,000
Building	2,700,000	$2,700,000/$3,000,000 = 90%	×	$2,800,000	=	2,520,000
Total	$3,000,000	100%				$2,800,000

The land valued at $300,000 was 10% of the total market value. The building's market value was 90% of the total. The cost of the land was determined as $280,000, and the cost of the building was computed as $2,520,000. Steinborn paid cash, so the entry to record the purchase is:

Journal Entry:

Date	Accounts	Post Ref.	Dr.	Cr.
May 1	Land		280,000	
	Building		2,520,000	
	Cash			2,800,000
	Record purchase of land and a building.			

Capital Expenditures

Even after an asset has been purchased, it may be necessary to spend money on it. Businesses buy resources for use in daily operations. These expenditures may be consumed over more than one period and treated as an asset.

Conversely, they may be consumed in the current period and treated as an expense.

Expenditures that increase the asset's capacity or efficiency or that extend the asset's useful life are called **capital expenditures** because they result in the capitalization, or increase, of an asset. For example, GM's purchase of a robot and American Airlines' purchase of a Boeing 767 are capital expenditures. Also, the cost of a major overhaul that makes an asset's useful life longer is a capital expenditure. Repair work that generates a capital expenditure is called an **extraordinary repair**. Capital expenditures and extraordinary repairs are both recorded by increasing assets.

Other expenditures do not extend an asset's efficiency, life, or capacity, but merely maintain the asset in working order. These costs are recorded as expenses and immediately subtracted from the revenue they produced. Examples include the costs of repainting a truck, repairing a fender, and replacing tires. These costs of **ordinary repairs** are debited to an expense account such as Repair Expense or Maintenance Expense.

The distinction between capital and maintenance expenditures requires judgment. Does the cost improve the capacity, efficiency, or the life expectancy of the asset? If so, it represents a capital expenditure. Or does it only maintain the asset in good condition, and thus should be journalized as an expense? Exhibit 9-3 illustrates the distinction between capital expenditures and expenses for several delivery-truck expenditures.

Exhibit 9-3 Delivery-Truck Expenditures: Capital Expenditure or Expense?	
Capital Expenditure: Record as an Asset	**Expense:** Record as an Expense
Extraordinary repairs:	*Ordinary repairs:*
Major engine overhaul	Repair of transmission or engine
Modification for new use	Oil change, lubrication, etc.
Addition to storage capacity	Replacement of tires or windshield
	Paint job

The decision to capitalize or expense a particular expenditure strongly affects the way net income is reported. The general guidelines for capitalizing a cost are to capitalize all costs that provide a future benefit for the business, and expense all others; however, business managers may be motivated to report higher or lower amounts of income and thus be tempted to not properly follow the guidelines. On one hand, if they want to save money by decreasing income taxes, managers will want to expense all costs in order to decrease taxable income. For example, if the purchase of a $100,000 machine is incorrectly expensed in year one, expenses are overstated and net income and assets are both understated.

On the other hand, many companies that ignored the general guidelines have gotten into trouble by capitalizing costs that were really expenses. Remember discussing fraudulent financial reporting in Chapter 6? Some companies made their financial statements look better than the facts warranted by overstating assets or recording those that didn't exist instead of properly recording costs as expenses. Capitalizing an expense will understate expenses and overstate both net income and assets.

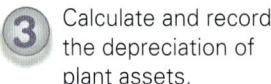

Measuring Plant Asset Depreciation

3 Calculate and record the depreciation of plant assets.

As we saw previously, depreciation is the allocation of an asset's cost to expense over its useful life. Recognizing depreciation expense matches the portion of the asset cost used in the period against the revenue earned by the asset in that period. Exhibit 9-4 shows the purchase and subsequent depreciation of a Boeing 767 jet by United Airlines.

Exhibit 9-4 Depreciation and Matching Expense with Revenue

Boeing 767
Cost, $40 million

Estimated useful life, 20 years

Match

Annual revenue generated, $9 million

Annual depreciation expense, $2 million
$40 million/20 years = $2 million per year

Depreciation is an expense that reflects the wear and tear or the obsolescence of plant assets. For example, depreciation of a car reflects the wear and tear, or usage, of the car. But other assets, such as computers, software, and other electronic equipment, may become obsolete before they wear out. An asset is obsolete when another asset can do the job much more efficiently. Thus, an asset's useful life may be shorter than its physical life. Accountants usually depreciate computers over a short period, perhaps two to four years, even though the computers can continue working much longer. In all cases, the asset's cost is depreciated over the period that the asset is truly useful.

Depreciation of a plant asset is based on three factors:

1. Cost is the amount paid to acquire the asset and get it ready for use. This factor is known because it relates to an event that already happened.

2. Useful life is the *estimated* length of service of an asset. Useful life may be expressed in years, units of output, miles, or another measure of productivity. For example, a building's life is stated in years, a bookbinding machine in the number of books it can bind, and a delivery truck in miles.

3. **Residual value**, also called **salvage value**, is the *estimated* cash value of a plant asset at the end of its useful life. Imagine that a machine's useful life is seven years. After seven years, the company expects to sell the machine as scrap metal. The expected cash receipt is the machine's estimated residual value. The estimated residual value of the asset is excluded from the amount of cost depreciated because the business expects to receive this amount at the end. If the asset has no residual value, then the business depreciates the full cost of the asset. Cost minus residual value is called **depreciable cost**.

You may have an idea of *depreciation* that is different from the accounting meaning of this term. For example, have you ever heard someone say that a car depreciates thousands of dollars as soon after purchase as it's driven off the dealer's lot? That comment means that the car may have lost thousands of its market value, not that it has used that much of its cost. Keep in mind the following as you learn about depreciation:

- Depreciation is not a process of adjusting the recorded value of the asset to its market value.

- Depreciation does not mean that the business sets aside cash to replace an asset when it is used up. Depreciation has nothing to do with establishing a cash fund.

Depreciation Methods

Three major methods exist for computing depreciation. These methods allocate different amounts of depreciation to each period, but they all result in the same total depreciation for the asset because they all need to account for the same depreciable cost.[1] All are acceptable methods according to GAAP, just as FIFO, LIFO, and average cost are acceptable inventory cost methods. Because depreciation is based on an *estimate* of how much of an asset's value is used during the period, it is acceptable that the different methods estimate this use differently. Let's illustrate depreciation for an Orbit Airways baggage-handling truck purchased on January 1, 2005.

Depreciation Factor	Amount
Cost of Truck	$41,000
Less: Residual Value	(1,000)
Depreciable Cost	$40,000
Useful Life:	
Years	5 years
Units-of-Production	100,000 Miles

STRAIGHT-LINE (SL) METHOD

The **straight-line (SL) method** allocates an equal amount of depreciation to each year of a plant asset's use. Depreciable cost is divided by useful life in years to determine annual depreciation. The calculation of SL depreciation applied to the Orbit Airways truck is the following:

$$\text{Straight-Line Depreciation} = \frac{\text{Cost} - \text{Residual Value}}{\text{Useful Life, in Years}} = \frac{\$41,000 - \$1,000}{5}$$

$$= \$8,000 \text{ per Year}$$

Because straight-line depreciation remains the same in each year of the asset's life, depreciation under this method can also be expressed as a rate that can be applied to depreciable cost:

Straight-Line Depreciation Rate = 1/Years of Useful Life = 1/5 = 20%

The entry to record each year's depreciation is:

---

[1] We omit the sum-of-years'-digits method because only 7 of 600 companies in a recent poll used it.

Journal Entry:

Date	Accounts	Post Ref.	Dr.	Cr.
Dec. 31	Depreciation Expense, Truck		8,000	
	Accumulated Depreciation, Truck			8,000
	Record depreciation on truck using the straight-line method.			

A straight-line depreciation schedule for the truck includes the asset's depreciation rate, depreciable cost, yearly depreciation expense, accumulated depreciation, and book value, which is cost less accumulated depreciation, as shown in Exhibit 9-5.

Exhibit 9-5 Straight-Line Depreciation for a Truck

Date	Asset Cost	Depreciation Rate		Depreciable Cost		Depreciation Expense	Accumulated Depreciation	Book Value
Jan. 1, 2005	$41,000							$41,000
Dec. 31, 2005		0.20	×	$40,000	=	$8,000	$ 8,000	33,000
Dec. 31, 2006		0.20	×	40,000	=	8,000	16,000	25,000
Dec. 31, 2007		0.20	×	40,000	=	8,000	24,000	17,000
Dec. 31, 2008		0.20	×	40,000	=	8,000	32,000	9,000
Dec. 31, 2009		0.20	×	40,000	=	8,000	40,000	1,000

As an asset is used, accumulated depreciation increases and the asset's book value decreases, as shown in the Accumulated Depreciation and Book Value columns in Exhibit 9-5. At the end, the asset is said to be fully depreciated because the book value of the asset in its final year of depreciation is equal to its residual value.

UNIT-OF-PRODUCTION (UOP) METHOD

The **units-of-production (UOP) method** allocates a fixed amount of depreciation to each unit of output produced by a plant asset:

$$\frac{\text{Units-of-Production}}{\text{Depreciation per Unit of Output}} = \frac{\text{Cost} - \text{Residual Value}}{\text{Useful Life, in Units of Production}}$$

$$= \frac{\$41,000 - \$1,000}{100,000 \text{ Miles}}$$

$$= \$0.40 \text{ per Mile}$$

Assume that this truck is likely to be driven 20,000 miles the first year, 30,000 the second, 25,000 the third, 15,000 the fourth, and 10,000 during the fifth. The amount of UOP depreciation each year varies according to the number of units the asset produces. Exhibit 9-6 shows the UOP depreciation schedule for this asset.

Exhibit 9-6 Units-of-Production Depreciation for a Truck

Date	Asset Cost	Depreciation for the Year			Accumulated Depreciation	Book Value
		Depreciation Per Unit	Number of Units	Depreciation Expense		
Jan. 1, 2005	$41,000					$41,000
Dec. 31, 2005		$0.40 ×	20,000 =	$ 8,000	$ 8,000	33,000
Dec. 31, 2006		0.40 ×	30,000 =	12,000	20,000	21,000
Dec. 31, 2007		0.40 ×	25,000 =	10,000	30,000	11,000
Dec. 31, 2008		0.40 ×	15,000 =	6,000	36,000	5,000
Dec. 31, 2009		0.40 ×	10,000 =	4,000	40,000	1,000

DOUBLE-DECLINING BALANCE (DDB) METHOD

The **double-declining-balance (DDB) method** is an **accelerated depreciation method** because it records more depreciation near the start of a plant asset's life than at the end of its life, unlike the straight-line method. Although other accelerated methods are available, double-declining-balance is the one often used. This method multiplies the plant asset's decreasing book value by a constant percentage that is double, or 2 times, the straight-line depreciation rate. DDB depreciation amounts can be computed in two steps:

1. Compute the straight-line depreciation rate per year. A 5-year asset has a straight-line rate of 1/5, or 20% per year. A 10-year asset has a straight-line rate of 1/10, or 10% per year, and so on. Compute the DDB rate by doubling the straight-line rate. The DDB rate for a 5-year asset is 40% (20% × 2) per year. For a 10-year asset, the DDB rate is 20% (10% × 2).

2. Compute DDB depreciation for each year. Multiply the asset's book value at the beginning of each year by the DDB rate until book value equals residual value, which usually occurs in the last year of an asset's life. The first-year depreciation for the truck is

$$\text{DDB Depreciation for the First Year} = \text{Asset Book Value at the Beginning of the Year} \times \text{DDB Rate}$$

$$\$16,400 = \$41,000 \times 0.40$$

The same approach is used to compute DDB depreciation for all later years, except for the final year. Final-year depreciation is the amount needed to bring the asset to its residual value. In the DDB depreciation schedule, Exhibit 9-7, final-year depreciation is $4,314, book value of $5,314 less the $1,000 residual value.

Exhibit 9-7 Double-Declining-Balance Depreciation for a Truck

Date	Asset Cost	Depreciation for the Year			Accumulated Depreciation	Book Value
		DDB Depreciation Rate	Book Value	Depreciation Expense		
Jan. 1, 2005	$41,000					$41,000
Dec. 31, 2005		0.40 ×	$41,000 =	$16,400	$16,400	24,600
Dec. 31, 2006		0.40 ×	24,600 =	9,840	26,240	14,760
Dec. 31, 2007		0.40 ×	14,760 =	5,904	32,144	8,856
Dec. 31, 2008		0.40 ×	8,856 =	3,542	35,686	5,314
Dec. 31, 2009				4,314	40,000	1,000

The DDB method differs from the other methods in two ways:

- Residual value is ignored at the start of the asset's life. In the first year, depreciation is computed on the asset's full cost.

- Final-year depreciation is the amount needed to bring the asset to residual value. Final-year depreciation is a "plug" figure; the residual value is known, and we work backwards to determine what the depreciation expense must be in this last year.

Many companies change to the straight-line method during the next-to-last year of the asset's life. Let's use this plan to compute annual depreciation for 2008 and 2009. In Exhibit 9-7, book value at the end of 2007 is $8,856, so depreciable cost is $7,856 after subtracting the residual value of $1,000. Depreciable cost can be spread evenly over the last two years, recording $3,928 in each year ($7,856 ÷ 2 remaining years).

Comparing Depreciation Methods

Let's compare the depreciation methods just discussed. As shown, annual amounts vary by method, but total depreciation of $40,000 is the same for all methods.

	Depreciation per Year		
			Accelerated Method
Year	Straight-Line	Units-of-Production	Double-Declining-Balance
2005	$ 8,000	$ 8,000	$16,400
2006	8,000	12,000	9,840
2007	8,000	10,000	5,904
2008	8,000	6,000	3,542
2009	8,000	4,000	4,314
Total	$40,000	$40,000	$40,000

Exhibit 9-8 shows which methods are best for different types of assets. Currently, the straight-line depreciation method is most popular. Exhibit 9-9 graphs annual depreciation for the three methods.

Exhibit 9-8 Comparison of Depreciation Methods for Different Types of Assets

Depreciation Method	Use method for assets that:	So that depreciation is recorded:
Straight-line	Generate revenue evenly over time	Equally over each period
Units-of-production	Depreciate due to wear and tear, rather than obsolescence	Only when an asset is used (more use causes greater depreciation)
Double-declining-balance	Produce more revenue in early years	With higher amounts in early years to match expense against those periods' greater revenue

- Straight-line depreciation is flat because annual depreciation is an even amount in all periods.

- Units-of-production depreciation follows no pattern because annual depreciation varies depending on the use of the asset.

- DDB depreciation is greater in the first year and less in the later years of the asset's life.

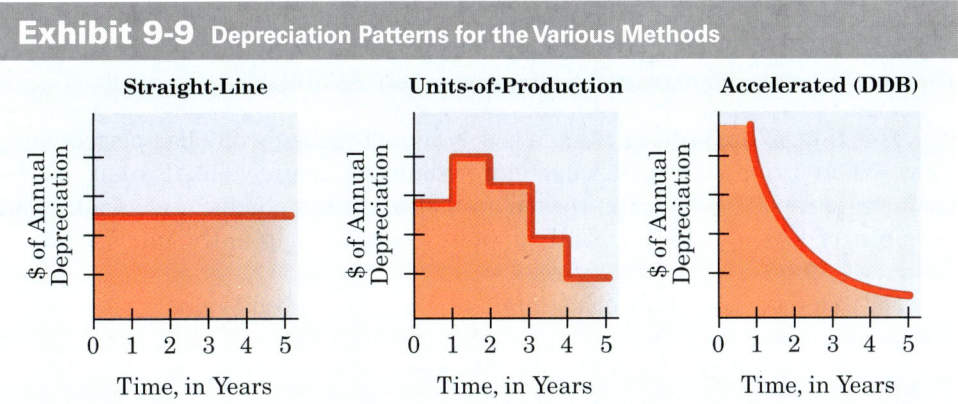

Exhibit 9-9 Depreciation Patterns for the Various Methods

Other Issues in Accounting for Plant Assets

DEPRECIATION FOR PARTIAL YEARS

Companies purchase plant assets whenever they need them. They don't typically wait until the beginning of an accounting period. Therefore, companies often develop policies for partial years of asset ownership. Suppose Linens 'n Things purchases a building on April 1 for $500,000. The building's estimated useful life is 20 years, with an estimated residual value of $80,000. How does Linens 'n Things compute depreciation for the first year ended December 31?

Many companies compute partial-year depreciation by first calculating a full year's depreciation. They then multiply full-year depreciation by the fraction of the year that they used the asset. Under the straight-line method, the year's depreciation for the Linens 'n Things building is $15,750, computed as follows:

$$\text{Full-Year Depreciation} = \frac{\$500,000 - \$80,000}{20 \text{ Years}} = \$21,000$$
$$\text{Partial-Year Depreciation} = \quad \$21,000 \times 9/12 \quad = \$15,750$$

What if the company bought the asset on April 18? One policy is to record no depreciation for the month on assets purchased after the 15th of that month. This policy also records a full month's depreciation on assets bought on or before the 15th. In that case, the year's depreciation would be $14,000 for eight months ($21,000 × 8/12).

Partial-year depreciation is computed under the other depreciation methods in the same way, by applying the appropriate portion of the year that the asset is used to the depreciation amount for the whole year. Most companies use computerized systems to account for fixed assets. Such systems automatically calculate the depreciation expense for each period.

CHANGING THE USEFUL LIFE OF A PLANT ASSET

Estimating the useful life of a plant asset poses an accounting challenge because it involves guessing at the future of an asset. As time passes and the asset is used, the business may change its estimated useful life based on experience and new information. Walt Disney Company made such a change in its accounting estimate. Disney refigured depreciation for theme-park assets. The following note in Disney's financial statements reports this change in estimate:

Note 5:

. . . [T]he Company extended the estimated useful lives of certain theme park . . . assets based upon . . . engineering studies. The effect of this change was to decrease depreciation by approximately $8 million.

This type of accounting change is common because no one has perfect foresight. When a company makes such an accounting change, GAAP requires the business to report the nature, reason, and effect of the change. Let's look at an example of Disney depreciating a hotdog stand originally purchased on January 1, 2005.

For a change in accounting estimate, the remaining book value of the asset is spread over the asset's remaining life. Assume that Disney World purchased a hotdog stand costing $40,000. Disney originally believed the asset had an eight-year life with no residual value. Using the straight-line method, Disney recorded depreciation of $5,000 each year ($40,000/8 years).

After using the hotdog stand for two years, accumulated depreciation reached $10,000. The asset's remaining depreciable book value, cost less accumulated depreciation less residual value, is $30,000 ($40,000 − $10,000 − $0). At the beginning of 2007, Disney management believed the hotdog stand will remain useful for 10 more years. The company recomputed depreciation as follows:

$$\frac{\text{Revised}}{\text{SL Depreciation}} = \frac{\text{Cost} - \text{Accumulated Depreciation} - \text{New Residual Value}}{\text{Estimated Remaining Useful Life in Years}}$$

$$= \frac{\$40,000 - \$10,000 - \$0}{10 \text{ Years}}$$

$$= \$3,000 \text{ per Year}$$

Beginning in 2007, the annual depreciation entry based on the new useful life is:

Journal Entry:

Date	Accounts	Post Ref.	Dr.	Cr.
Dec. 31	Depreciation Expense, Hotdog Stand		3,000	
	Accumulated Depreciation, Hotdog Stand			3,000
	Record revised depreciation using the			
	straight-line method.			

USING FULLY DEPRECIATED PLANT ASSETS

A fully depreciated asset is one that has reached the end of its estimated useful life. The company may continue using this fully depreciated asset, but no more depreciation is recorded for the asset. In this situation, the asset account and its accumulated depreciation remain on the books; this is how the business recognizes that it still owns and probably still uses the item. The company will sell or dispose of a plant asset when it is no longer useful.

DEPRECIATION AND INCOME TAXES

Most companies use straight-line depreciation for their financial statements, but they use a different depreciation method for income taxes. For tax purposes, most companies use an accelerated method.

Suppose you manage the United Airlines operation at Chicago O'Hare International Airport. The IRS allows the DDB depreciation method, and you prefer accelerated to straight-line depreciation because it provides the most depreciation expense as quickly as possible. The accelerated depreciation decreases your net income and your immediate tax payments and thus conserves your cash. You can then invest the cash and earn more income. This strategy is common.

To understand how depreciation affects cash flow, recall our earlier depreciation of the Orbit Airways truck: First-year depreciation is $8,000 under the straight-line method and $16,400 under double-declining-balance. Which tax deduction would you prefer? You would choose DDB depreciation because it gives you a greater tax deduction and saves cash.

A special depreciation method called the Modified Accelerated Cost Recovery System (MACRS) is used for income tax purposes. Under MACRS, assets are divided into classes by asset life. MACRS depreciation is computed by the double-declining-balance method, the 150%-declining-balance method, or the straight-line method. Under 150% DB, the annual depreciation rate is computed by multiplying the straight-line rate by 1.50, rather than by 2, as for DDB. For a 20-year asset, the straight-line rate is 0.05 (1/20, or 0.05), so the annual MACRS depreciation rate is 0.075 (0.05 × 1.50).

Disposing of a Plant Asset

Eventually, an asset stops being useful. The asset may be worn out or obsolete, and accordingly, the owner disposes of it. To account for the disposal properly, we first update the depreciation on the asset. We can then measure the asset's final book value accurately and calculate any gain or loss that may result from the disposition.

 Calculate and record the disposal of plant assets.

To illustrate, Orbit Airways disposed of a storage building involving the following information:

Depreciation Factor	Amount
Cost of Building	$36,000
Less: Residual Value	(6,000)
Depreciable Cost	$30,000
Divided by Useful Life	÷ 10 Years
SL Depreciation	= $3,000
Times Years Used	× 8
Accumulated Depreciation	= $24,000

To dispose of the asset on April 30, we update the depreciation expense for the storage building. Partial-year depreciation must be recorded for four months, from January 1, 2008, to the sale date on April 30. The straight-line depreciation entry is:

Journal Entry:

Date	Accounts	Post Ref.	Dr.	Cr.
Apr. 30	Depreciation Expense, Building			
	($3,000 × 4/12)		1,000	
	Accumulated Depreciation, Building			1,000
	Record 4 months' depreciation using the			
	straight-line method.			

Now the Building and the Accumulated Depreciation, Building, accounts appear as follows:

Building				Accumulated Depreciation, Building	
Bal.	36,000			Bal.	24,000
				Adj.	1,000
				Bal.	25,000

The book value of the building at this point is:

$$\text{Cost} - \text{Accumulated Depreciation} = \text{Book Value}$$

$$\$36,000 - \$25,000 = \$11,000$$

When recording the disposal of a plant asset, the business must do the following:

- Remove the balances in the asset account and its accumulated depreciation account.

  - Assets accounts have debit balances, so to remove the value of the asset sold, the asset account is credited.

  - Accumulated Depreciation accounts, as contra-asset accounts, have credit balances; to remove the accumulated depreciation on the asset sold, the accumulated depreciation account is debited.

- Record a gain or loss if the cash or trade-in value received differs from the asset's book value. Gains and losses are reported on the income statement.

  - A loss occurs when the cash or trade-in value received is less than the book value of the asset. Losses decrease net income and, like expenses, are recorded with debits.

  - A gain occurs when the cash or trade-in value received is greater than the book value of the asset. Gains increase net income, and like revenues, are recorded with credits.

- Record the value of any cash received if the asset was sold.

- Record the value of any new asset obtained if the old asset was exchanged in trade, and also record any cash payment made in addition to the trade-in value of the asset exchanged.

Let's look at how to record the entries for the three ways to dispose of an asset.

Selling a Plant Asset

Imagine that Orbit Airways sells the storage building for $6,000, $11,000, and $16,000 in cash. Exhibit 9-10 illustrates the calculations necessary to record the sale:

Exhibit 9-10 Sale of an Asset

	Loss on Sale	No Loss or Gain on Sale	Gain on Sale
Cash received	$ 6,000	$11,000	$ 16,000
Less: Book value	(11,000)	(11,000)	(11,000)
Gain (loss) on sale	$ (5,000)	$ –	$ 5,000

If Orbit sells the storage building for:

- $6,000 cash, they will suffer a loss on the sale because cash received is less than their book value of $11,000.

- $11,000 cash, they will have no gain or loss on the sale.

- $16,000 cash, they will have a gain on the sale because the cash received is greater than their book value of $11,000.

Referring to the calculations in Exhibit 9-10, let's see the journal entries Orbit would make to record the sale of the building under each of the three scenarios.
Sale of building for $6,000:

Journal Entry:

Date	Accounts	Post Ref.	Dr.	Cr.
Apr. 30	Cash		6,000	
	Accumulated Depreciation, Building		25,000	
	Loss on Sale of Building		5,000	
	Building			36,000
	Record the sale of the storage building for $6,000 cash.			

Sale of building for $11,000:

Journal Entry:

Date	Accounts	Post Ref.	Dr.	Cr.
Apr. 30	Cash		11,000	
	Accumulated Depreciation, Building		25,000	
	Building			36,000
	Record the sale of the storage building for $11,000 cash.			

Sale of building for $16,000:

Journal Entry:

Date	Accounts	Post Ref.	Dr.	Cr.
Apr. 30	Cash		16,000	
	Accumulated Depreciation, Building		25,000	
	Building			36,000
	Gain on Sale of Building			5,000
	Record the sale of the storage building for $16,000 cash.			

Exchanging Plant Assets

Businesses often exchange old plant assets for newer, more efficient assets. The most common exchange transaction is the trade-in of an asset for a similar type of new asset. In these trades, no gains are recognized because the business still owns the same type of asset that it owned before the trade. The cost of the new asset becomes the book value of the old asset plus any cash paid in the exchange.

For example, a pizza restaurant traded in a five-year-old delivery car for a newer model on July 1. The old pizza delivery car cost $9,000, has accumulated depreciation of $8,000, and a book value of $1,000. If the pizza restaurant trades in the old auto and pays cash of $10,000:

$$\text{Cost of a New Car} = \text{Cash Paid} + \text{Book Value of Old Car}$$
$$\$11,000 = \$10,000 + \$1,000$$

The exchange would be recorded as follows:

Journal Entry:

Date	Accounts	Post Ref.	Dr.	Cr.
July 1	Delivery Car (new)		11,000	
	Accumulated Depreciation, Delivery Car (old)		8,000	
	Delivery Car (old)			9,000
	Cash			10,000
	Record the trade of delivery cars.			

Retiring a Plant Asset

Sometimes a business is unable to sell or exchange an asset and must instead retire it without receiving cash or a trade-in value in return.

To dispose of a fully depreciated asset, let's assume we have three computers with a total cost of $6,000. The accumulated depreciation is $6,000. To retire these computers on December 31, the journal entry would be:

Journal Entry:

Date	Accounts	Post Ref.	Dr.	Cr.
Dec. 31	Accumulated Depreciation, Equipment		6,000	
	Equipment			6,000
	Record the retirement of three computers.			

To dispose of partially depreciated assets, we will record a loss equal to the book value of the assets. Using the preceding illustration, let's assume the computers costing $6,000 have accumulated depreciation of $5,500 on July 1. Disposal of these computers generates a loss, as follows:

Journal Entry:

Date	Accounts	Post Ref.	Dr.	Cr.
July 1	Accumulated Depreciation, Equipment		5,500	
	Loss on Retirement of Equipment		500	
	Equipment			6,000
	Record the retirement of three computers.			

Accounting for Natural Resources

Natural resources are plant assets and are usually listed below Property, Plant, and Equipment on the balance sheet. Examples include iron ore, oil, natural gas, and timber. Natural resources are like inventories in the ground such as oil or on top of the ground such as timber. The acquisition cost of the natural resource is recorded as an asset. As the natural resources are extracted and sold, a portion of their cost is expensed through depletion. **Depletion expense** is that portion of the cost of natural resources that is used in a particular period. Account for depletion as follows:

 Calculate and record the depletion of natural resources.

- Compute depletion over the asset's estimated useful life using the units-of-production method.

- Record depletion in Depletion Expense and Accumulated Depletion, a contra-asset account similar to Accumulated Depreciation.

Depletion expense is computed by the units-of-production formula, and natural resources usually have no residual value. Suppose, for example, Kent Oil paid $100,000 for an oil well holding an estimated 10,000 barrels of oil.

$$\frac{\text{Depletion}}{\text{Expense}} = \frac{\text{Cost} - \text{Residual Value}}{\text{Estimated Total Units of Natural Resource}} \times \text{Number of Units Removed}$$

For Kent, the depletion rate would be $10 per barrel ($100,000/10,000 barrels). If 3,000 barrels are extracted and sold during 2008, then depletion is $30,000 (3,000 barrels × $10 per barrel). The depletion entry for 2008 is:

Journal Entry:

Date	Accounts	Post Ref.	Dr.	Cr.
Dec. 31	Depletion Expense, Oil		30,000	
	Accumulated Depletion, Oil			30,000
	Record depletion.			

If 4,500 barrels are removed and sold next year, depletion would be $45,000 (4,500 barrels × $10 per barrel).

Accounting for Intangible Assets

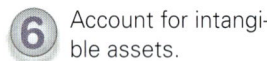 **6** Account for intangible assets.

Rather than having physical form, intangible assets provide benefit to their owners because they convey special rights. The acquisition cost of an intangible asset is recorded as an asset. Intangible assets are listed after the plant assets on the balance sheet. The cost of the intangible asset is transferred to expense through amortization, the systematic reduction of the intangible asset's carrying value on the books. Account for most intangible assets as follows:

- Compute amortization over the asset's estimated useful life, usually by the straight-line method. Obsolescence often shortens an intangible's useful life.

- The residual value of most intangibles is zero.

- **Amortization expense** for an intangible asset can be recorded directly against the asset account without using a separate account for accumulated amortization.

Some intangibles have indefinite lives because it may be hard for a company to determine how long their benefits last. For these assets, the company records no systematic amortization each period. Instead, it accounts for any decrease in the value of the intangible, as we shall see for goodwill.

Patents

A **patent** is a federal government grant giving the holder the exclusive 20-year right to produce and sell an invention. The invention may be a product or a process, for example, the Dolby noise-reduction process. Like any other asset, a patent may be purchased. Suppose General Electric Company (GE) pays $200,000 to acquire a patent on January 1. GE believes this patent's useful life is five years. Amortization expense is $40,000 per year ($200,000/5 years). The entry to record amortization is:

Journal Entry:

Date	Accounts	Post Ref.	Dr.	Cr.
Dec. 31	Amortization Expense, Patents		40,000	
	Patents			40,000
	Record amortization of the patent.			

At the end of the first year, GE will report this patent at $160,000, $200,000 minus the first year's amortization of $40,000; next year it will report it at $120,000, and so on.

Copyrights

A **copyright** is the exclusive right to reproduce and sell a book, musical composition, film, or other work of art, or intellectual property. Copyrights also protect computer software programs, such as Microsoft® Windows and the Microsoft® Excel spreadsheet. Issued by the federal government, a copyright extends 70 years beyond the author's life.

A company may pay a large sum to purchase an existing copyright. For example, the publisher Simon & Schuster may pay $1 million for the copyright on a popular novel. Most copyrights have short useful lives.

Trademarks and Trade Names

Trademarks and **trade names** are assets that represent distinctive products or services, such as the CBS "eye" and NBC's peacock. Legally protected slogans include Chevrolet's "Like a Rock" and Avis Rent A Car's "We try harder." The cost of a trademark or trade name is amortized over its useful life.

Franchises and Licenses

Franchises and **licenses** are privileges granted by a private business or a government to sell products or services under specified conditions. The Green Bay Packers football organization is a franchise granted by the National Football League. McDonald's restaurants and Holiday Inn hotels are popular business franchises. The acquisition cost of a franchise or license is amortized over its useful life.

Goodwill

The term **goodwill** in accounting has a specific meaning, which is perhaps different from how it is used in everyday life. In accounting, goodwill is the excess of the cost to purchase another company over the market value of the net assets purchased, where net assets are equal to total assets minus total liabilities.

As Wal-Mart expands into Mexico, suppose it acquires Mexana Company at a cost of $10 million on January 1. The sum of the market values of Mexana's assets is $9 million and its liabilities total $1 million, so Mexana's net assets total $8 million. In this case, Wal-Mart paid $2 million for goodwill, computed as follows:

Purchase Price to Acquire Mexana Company		$10 million
Market Value of Mexana Company's Assets	$ 9 million	
Less: Mexana Company's Liabilities	(1 million)	
Less: Market Value of Mexana Company's Net Assets..		(8 million)
Goodwill		$ 2 million

Wal-Mart's entry to record the purchase of Mexana Company, including the goodwill that Wal-Mart purchased, would be:

Journal Entry:

Date	Accounts	Post Ref.	Dr.	Cr.
Jan. 1	Assets (Cash, Receivables, Inventories, Plant Assets, all at market value)		9,000,000	
	Goodwill		2,000,000	
	Liabilities			1,000,000
	Cash			10,000,000
	Record purchase of Mexana Company.			

Goodwill has some special features:

- Goodwill is recorded only by a company that purchases another company. An outstanding reputation may create extra value or goodwill for a company, but that company never records goodwill for its own business. Instead, goodwill is recorded *only* by the acquiring entity when it buys another company, because it is the willingness of an entity to pay extra for goodwill that proves it exists.

- According to GAAP, goodwill is *not* amortized. Instead, the company measures the current value of its purchased goodwill each year. If the goodwill increases in value, the company does not record it because this extra goodwill was not purchased. On the other hand, if goodwill's value decreases, then the company records a loss and reduces the value of goodwill. For example, suppose Wal-Mart's goodwill, purchased in the Mexana acquisition, is worth only $1,500,000 at the end of the first year. In that case, Wal-Mart would make this entry:

Journal Entry:

Date	Accounts	Post Ref.	Dr.	Cr.
Dec. 31	Loss on Goodwill		500,000	
	Goodwill			500,000
	Record loss on goodwill.			

Wal-Mart would then report this goodwill at its current value of $1,500,000 ($2,000,000 – $500,000).

Presenting Long-Term Assets on the Balance Sheet

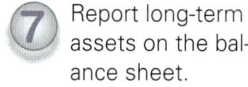

7 Report long-term assets on the balance sheet.

The use of long-term assets in business operations affects the income statement and the balance sheet. The income statement can include depreciation, depletion, and amortization expense, as well as gains and losses on disposal of assets, and loss on goodwill. Footnotes to the financial statements will describe the methods used to compute depreciation, depletion, and amortization.

As we mentioned in Chapter 4, current assets appear first on a classified balance sheet. Following these assets, businesses will include a section, often called "Property, Plant, and Equipment," that includes the original cost, accumulated depreciation, and book value of assets such as land, buildings, and equipment. The original cost, accumulated depletion, and book value of natural resources will follow. Some businesses will choose to show the net amount, the book value, on the balance sheet and include a footnote showing the costs and accumulated depreciation or depletion for each asset group.

When a business has an intangible asset, the balance sheet will show the amount after the Property, Plant, and Equipment section of the assets. The footnotes to the financials will include a description of the intangible asset and its estimated useful life. Exhibit 9-11 illustrates the presentation of long-term assets:

Exhibit 9-11 Plant and Intangible Assets on the Balance Sheet

Total current assets		$880,000
Property, plant, and equipment:		
Land		120,000
Buildings	$800,000	
Equipment	160,000	
Total plant and equipment	960,000	
Less: Accumulated depreciation, buildings and equipment	(410,000)	550,000
Oil	$380,000	
Less: Accumulated depletion, oil	(80,000)	300,000
Property, plant, and equipment, net		970,000
Goodwill	350,000	

Demo Doc

Depreciation and Disposal of Depreciable Assets

Learning Objectives   3, 4

Jensen, Inc., purchased a color laser printer for $100,000 on January 1, 2008. The printer was expected to last for 6 years and to print 180,000 pages during that time. The printer has a residual value of $10,000.

Jensen printed 50,000 pages in 2008, 20,000 in 2009, and 40,000 in 2010.

Requirements

1. Prepare a depreciation table showing depreciation calculations for the years 2008, 2009, and 2010 under the following depreciation methods: (a) straight-line, (b) units-of-production, and (c) double-declining-balance.

2. On May 1, 2011, Jensen sold the printer for $60,000 cash. Assume that Jensen was using the straight-line method of depreciation. Journalize all transactions on this date.

Demo Doc Solutions

Requirement 1

Prepare a depreciation table showing depreciation calculations for the years 2008, 2009, and 2010 under the following depreciation methods: (a) straight-line, (b) units-of-production, and (c) double-declining-balance.

Part 1	Part 2	Demo Doc Complete

Straight-Line

Refer to the straight-line depreciation table as shown in Exhibit 9-5 (p. 478). On the printer's purchase date (January 1, 2008), the printer's cost of $100,000 must be input. Because no depreciation has been taken yet, the book value is the same as the original cost.

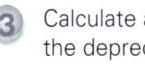

3 Calculate and record the depreciation of plant assets.

		Depreciation for the Year				
Date	Asset Cost	Depreciation Rate	Depreciable Cost	Depreciation Expense	Accumulated Depreciation	Book Value
Jan. 1, 2008	$100,000					$100,000

Remember that:

$$\text{Straight-Line Depreciation} = \frac{\text{Cost} - \text{Residual Value}}{\text{Useful Life, in Years}} = \frac{\$100,000 - \$10,000}{6}$$

$$= \$15,000 \text{ per Year}$$

The depreciable cost of the printer is cost − residual value = $90,000 ($100,000 − $10,000). So for each year, the depreciation expense will be:

$$\$90,000 \times 1/6 = \$15,000$$

		Depreciation for the Year					
Date	Asset Cost	Depreciation Rate		Depreciable Cost		Depreciation Expense	Accumulated Depreciation	Book Value
Jan. 1, 2008	$100,000							$100,000
Dec. 31, 2008		1/6	×	$90,000	=	$15,000		
Dec. 31, 2009		1/6	×	90,000	=	15,000		
Dec. 31, 2010		1/6	×	90,000	=	15,000		

Accumulated depreciation is all of the depreciation expense that has *ever* been taken. So, to calculate accumulated depreciation, we take the previous year's accumulated depreciation and add on the current year's accumulated depreciation.

The first year of the printer's life is 2008 so in that year no prior depreciation has accumulated. Therefore, accumulated depreciation at December 31, 2008, is the same as the depreciation expense for 2008: $15,000.

For 2009, the accumulated depreciation is the December 31, 2008, accumulated depreciation plus the 2009 depreciation expense. So accumulated depreciation at December 31, 2009, is:

$$\$15,000 + \$15,000 = \$30,000$$

For 2010, the accumulated depreciation is the December 31, 2009, accumulated depreciation plus the 2010 depreciation expense. So accumulated depreciation at December 31, 2010, is:

$$\$30,000 + \$15,000 = \$45,000$$

Date	Asset Cost	Depreciation for the Year				Accumulated Depreciation	Book Value
		Depreciation Rate		Depreciable Cost	Depreciation Expense		
Jan. 1, 2008	$100,000						$100,000
Dec. 31, 2008		1/6	×	$90,000	=	$15,000	$15,000	
Dec. 31, 2009		1/6	×	90,000	=	15,000	30,000	
Dec. 31, 2010		1/6	×	90,000	=	15,000	45,000	

The book value of the printer is its cost minus its accumulated depreciation. So to calculate the book value for each year, subtract the accumulated depreciation from the total cost of $100,000.

Book Value at December 31, 2008 = $85,000 ($100,000 − $15,000)
Book Value at December 31, 2009 = $70,000 ($100,000 − $30,000)
Book Value at December 31, 2010 = $55,000 ($100,000 − $45,000)

Date	Asset Cost	Depreciation for the Year				Accumulated Depreciation	Book Value
		Depreciation Rate		Depreciable Cost	Depreciation Expense		
Jan. 1, 2008	$100,000						$100,000
Dec. 31, 2008		1/6	×	$90,000	=	$15,000	$15,000	85,000
Dec. 31, 2009		1/6	×	90,000	=	15,000	30,000	70,000
Dec. 31, 2010		1/6	×	90,000	=	15,000	45,000	55,000

Units-of-Production

Refer to the units-of-production depreciation table as shown in Exhibit 9-6 (p. 479). As with straight-line, the cost and starting book value of the printer are both $100,000.

Date	Asset Cost	Depreciation for the Year			Accumulated Depreciation	Book Value
		Depreciation Per Unit	Number of Units	Depreciation Expense		
Jan 1, 2008	$100,000					$100,000

Remember that:

$$\text{Units-of-Production Depreciation per Unit of Output} = \frac{\text{Cost} - \text{Residual Value}}{\text{Useful Life, in Units of Production}}$$

$$= \frac{\$100{,}000 - \$10{,}000}{180{,}000 \text{ Pages}}$$

$$= \$0.50 \text{ per Page}$$

Each year, the depreciation expense is calculated as the depreciation cost per page multiplied by the number of pages printed.

2008 Depreciation Expense = $0.50 Depreciation Expense per Page
                            × 50,000 Pages Printed
                          = $25,000

2009 Depreciation Expense = $0.50 Depreciation Expense per Page
                            × 20,000 Pages Printed
                          = $10,000

2010 Depreciation Expense = $0.50 Depreciation Expense per Page
                            × 40,000 Pages Printed
                          = $20,000

| Date | Asset Cost | Depreciation for the Year | | | Accumulated Depreciation | Book Value |
		Depreciation Per Unit	Number of Units	Depreciation Expense		
Jan. 1, 2008	$100,000					$100,000
Dec. 31, 2008		$0.50	× 50,000 =	$25,000		
Dec. 31, 2009		0.50	× 20,000 =	10,000		
Dec. 31, 2010		0.50	× 40,000 =	20,000		

Accumulated depreciation and book value are calculated in the same manner as was used for straight-line.

Accumulated Depreciation = Accumulated Depreciation from the Prior Year +
                           Depreciation Expense from the Current Year

Book Value = Cost − Accumulated Depreciation = $100,000 − Accumulated Depreciation

Accumulated Depreciation at December 31, 2008 = $0 + $25,000 = $25,000
Book Value at December 31, 2008 = $100,000 − $25,000 = $75,000

Accumulated Depreciation at December 31, 2009 = $25,000 + $10,000 = $35,000
Book Value at December 31, 2009 = $100,000 − $35,000 = $65,000

Accumulated Depreciation at December 31, 2010 = $35,000 + $20,000 = $55,000
Book Value at December 31, 2010 = $100,000 − $55,000 = $45,000

		Depreciation for the Year				
Date	Asset Cost	Depreciation Per Unit	Number of Units	Depreciation Expense	Accumulated Depreciation	Book Value
Jan. 1, 2008	$100,000					$100,000
Dec. 31, 2008		$0.50	× 50,000 =	$25,000	$25,000	75,000
Dec. 31, 2009		0.50	× 20,000 =	10,000	35,000	65,000
Dec. 31, 2010		0.50	× 40,000 =	20,000	55,000	45,000

Double-Declining-Balance

Refer to the double-declining-balance (DDB) depreciation table as shown in Exhibit 9-7 (p. 479). As with straight-line and units-of-production, the cost and starting book value of the printer are both $100,000.

		Depreciation for the Year				
Date	Asset Cost	DDB Depreciation Rate	Book Value	Depreciation Expense	Accumulated Depreciation	Book Value
Jan. 1, 2008	$100,000					$100,000

The depreciation rate is double the straight-line rate, or 2/Years of useful life.

$$\text{DDB Depreciation Rate} = \frac{2}{\text{Years of Useful Life}} = \frac{2}{6 \text{ Years}} = 1/3$$

Each year, the depreciation rate is multiplied by the book value of the printer *at the beginning of the year*. So for 2008, the depreciation expense is:

$$\$100,000 \times 1/3 = \$33,333$$

Accumulated depreciation and book value at the end of the year are calculated as under straight-line and units-of-production.

Accumulated Depreciation at December 31, 2008 = $0 + $33,333 = $33,333
Book Value at December 31, 2008 = $100,000 − $33,333 = $66,667

		Depreciation for the Year				
Date	Asset Cost	DDB Depreciation Rate	Book Value	Depreciation Expense	Accumulated Depreciation	Book Value
Jan. 1, 2008	$100,000					$100,000
Dec. 31, 2008		1/3	× $100,000 =	$33,333	$33,333	66,667

Depreciation expense for 2009 is the book value of the printer *at the beginning* of 2009 multiplied by the depreciation rate. So for 2009, the depreciation expense is:

$$\$66,667 \times 1/3 = \$22,222$$

Accumulated Depreciation at December 31, 2009 = $33,333 + $22,222 = $55,555

Book Value at December 31, 2009 = $100,000 − $55,555 = $44,445

| | | Depreciation for the Year | | | | |
Date	Asset Cost	DDB Depreciation Rate	Book Value	Depreciation Expense	Accumulated Depreciation	Book Value
Jan. 1, 2008	$100,000					$100,000
Dec. 31, 2008		1/3	× $100,000	= $33,333	$33,333	66,667
Dec. 31, 2009		1/3	× 66,667	= 22,222	55,555	44,445

Depreciation expense for 2010 is the book value of the printer *at the beginning* of 2010 multiplied by the depreciation rate. So for 2010, the depreciation expense is:

$$\$44,445 \times 1/3 = \$14,815$$

Accumulated Depreciation at December 31, 2010 = $55,555 + $14,815 = $70,370

Book Value at December 31, 2010 = $100,000 − $70,370 = $29,630

| | | Depreciation for the Year | | | | |
Date	Asset Cost	DDB Depreciation Rate	Book Value	Depreciation Expense	Accumulated Depreciation	Book Value
Jan. 1, 2008	$100,000					$100,000
Dec. 31, 2008		1/3	× $100,000	= $33,333	$33,333	66,667
Dec. 31, 2009		1/3	× 66,667	= 22,222	55,555	44,445
Dec. 31, 2010		1/3	× 44,445	= 14,815	70,370	29,630

Requirement 2

On May 1, 2011, Jensen sold the printer for $60,000 cash. Assume that Jensen was using the straight-line method of depreciation. Journalize all transactions on this date.

Part 1	Part 2	Demo Doc Complete

Before Jensen can record the disposal of the printer, it must update the depreciation on the printer. Depreciation represents use of an asset and because the asset was used for four months of 2011 (January, February, March, and April), four months of depreciation expense must be recorded.

 Calculate and record the disposal of plant assets.

From Requirement 1, we know that the annual depreciation expense on the printer under the straight-line method is $15,000 per year (12 months). To adjust for only four months we must multiply by the fraction of 4/12.

Depreciation Expense for 2011:

$$\$15,000 \times 4/12 = \$5,000$$

This depreciation expense must now be recorded in a journal entry. Depreciation Expense is increased (debit) by $5,000, and Accumulated Depreciation is increased (credit) by $5,000.

Journal Entry:

Date	Accounts	Post Ref.	Dr.	Cr.
May 1	Depreciation Expense, Printer		5,000	
	Accumulated Depreciation, Printer			5,000
	Record 4 months' depreciation on printer using the straight-line method.			

Now that this journal entry is made, we can calculate the balance in Accumulated Depreciation immediately before the disposal.

The transactions that have affected the Accumulated Depreciation account are the depreciation expense recorded in each year (2008, 2009, 2010, and 2011). We can add the 2011 depreciation expense to the Accumulated Depreciation balance from the prior year (2010).

Printer

Dec. 31, 2010 Bal. 100,000	
May 1, 2011 Bal. 100,000	

Accumulated Depreciation, Printer

	Dec. 31, 2010 Bal. 45,000
	May 1, 2011 5,000
	May 1, 2011 Bal. 50,000

Now we are ready to journalize the disposal of the printer.

Jensen is receiving cash, so Cash increases (debit) by the $60,000 of cash received.

The printer is being sold, so the Printer asset will be decreased (credit) by its original cost of $100,000 (the amount in the printer T-account).

If the printer is sold, it no longer makes sense to have the accumulated depreciation on the printer. This account must be removed as well. Remember that Accumulated Depreciation is a contra-account, and so it goes wherever its associated asset goes. If we remove the printer from the accounting records, then the accumulated depreciation on that printer goes with it and is removed as well. We will therefore decrease Accumulated Depreciation (debit) by its balance of $50,000.

So far for the journal entry we have:

Journal Entry:

Date	Accounts	Post Ref.	Dr.	Cr.
May 1	Cash		60,000	
	Accumulated Depreciation, Printer		50,000	
	?????			?????
	Printer			100,000

The remaining portion of the journal entry is the gain or loss on the sale of the printer. The amount of the gain or loss is the amount required to balance the journal entry. So far, the total debits in this entry are $110,000 ($60,000 + $50,000), and the total credits are $100,000. So a credit of $10,000 ($110,000 − $100,000) is needed to balance the entry.

Because the balancing amount is a credit, it is *similar* to revenue in that it will increase net income (be a positive number on the income statement). Therefore it is a gain, so we will credit Gain on Sale of Printer for $10,000.

Journal Entry:

Date	Accounts	Post Ref.	Dr.	Cr.
May 1	Cash		60,000	
	Accumulated Depreciation, Printer		50,000	
	Gain on Sale of Printer			10,000
	Printer			100,000
	Record sale of printer.			

Part 1	Part 2	Demo Doc Complete

Accounting in Action

LONG-TERM ASSETS: PLANT ASSETS AND INTANGIBLES

Suppose you buy a Curves International franchise and invest in Nautilus and other fitness equipment. What actions would you take to account for plant and intangible assets?

Decision	Guidelines
What types of long-term assets are involved?	• *Plant assets*, including land, land improvements, buildings, equipment, furniture, fixtures, *and natural resources*
	• *Intangible assets* such as patents, copyrights, trademarks, trade names, franchises, licenses, and goodwill
What events are accounted for?	Account for asset
	• *Acquisition*
	• *Use*
	• *Disposal*
How do I record acquisition of assets? How do I record asset use?	Capitalize all costs that prepare the asset for its intended use Compute depreciation:
	• *SL Depreciation* = (Cost – Residual Value)/Useful Life in Years
	• *UOP Depreciation* = [(Cost – Residual Value)/Useful Life in Units] × Units Produced for the Year
	• *DDB Depreciation* = Asset's Book Value at Beginning of Year × DDB Rate; DDB Rate = 2 × SL Rate
How do I account for disposal of assets?	• Remove the balances in the asset account and its accumulated depreciation account
	• Record a gain or loss if the cash or trade-in value received differs from the asset's book value
	• Record any cash received in a sale
	• Record any cash paid in an exchange, and any asset received in the exchange
How do I account for natural resources?	Record *depletion* expense for the portion of the cost of natural resources that is used in a particular period
How do I account for intangibles?	Record *amortization* for the systematic reduction of the intangible asset's carrying value

Review

Long-Term Assets: Plant Assets and Intangibles
Word Power

Accelerated depreciation method Depreciation method that records more depreciation near the start of an asset's useful life than the straight-line method does.

Amortization The allocation of the cost of an intangible assets to expense over their useful life.

Amortization expense Systematic reduction of the intangible asset's carrying value on the books.

Basket purchase Purchase of two or more assets for one price.

Capital expenditure Expenditure that increases the capacity or efficiency of an asset or extends its useful life.

Capitalize To record as an asset.

Copyright Exclusive right to reproduce and sell a book, musical composition, film, other work of art, intellectual property, or computer program. Issued by the federal government, a copyright extends 70 years beyond the author's life.

Depletion The allocation of the cost of natural resources to expense over their useful life.

Depletion expense Portion of a natural resource's cost used in a particular period. Computed in the same way as units-of-production depreciation.

Depreciable cost The cost of a plant asset minus its residual value.

Double-declining-balance (DDB) method An accelerated depreciation method that computes annual depreciation by multiplying the plant asset's decreasing book value by a constant percent that is two times the straight-line rate.

Extraordinary repair Repair work that generates a capital expenditure.

Franchises Privileges granted by a private business or a government to sell a product or service under specified conditions; also called *licenses*.

Goodwill Excess of the cost of an acquired company over the sum of the market values of its net assets.

Intangible assets Long-lived resources without physical form that represent rights.

Land improvements Plant assets representing improvements to land.

Licenses Privileges granted by a private business or a government to sell a product or service under specified conditions; also called franchises.

Natural resources Plant assets existing in or on land.

Ordinary repair Repair work that maintains the plant asset in working order.

Patent A federal government grant giving the holder the exclusive right to produce and sell an invention for 20 years.

Relative-sales-value method Allocation technique that divides the total cost of a basket purchase of assets according to their relative sales value.

Residual value Estimated cash value of a plant asset at the end of its useful life; also called *salvage value*.

Salvage value Estimated cash value of a plant asset at the end of its useful life; also called *residual value*.

Straight-line (SL) method Depreciation method that allocates an equal amount of depreciation to each year of a plant asset's useful life.

Trademark Asset that represents distinctive identifications of a product or service; also called a *trade name*.

Trade name Asset that represents distinctive identifications of a product or service; also called a *trademark*.

Units-of-production (UOP) method Depreciation method that allocates a fixed amount of depreciation to each unit of output produced by a plant asset.

Quick Check

1. Which cost is not recorded as part of the cost of a building?

   a. Construction materials, labor, and overhead
   b. Annual building maintenance
   c. Real estate commission paid to buy the building
   d. Earthmoving for the building's foundation

2. Orbit Airways bought two used Boeing 707 airplanes. Each plane was worth $35 million, but Orbit bought the combination for $60 million. How much is Orbit's cost of each plane?

   a. $30 million
   b. $35 million
   c. $60 million
   d. $70 million

3. How should a capital expenditure be recorded?

   a. Debit capital
   b. Debit an expense
   c. Debit a liability
   d. Debit an asset

4. Which depreciation method usually produces the most depreciation in the first year?

   a. Straight-line
   b. Units-of-production
   c. Double-declining-balance
   d. All produce the same amount of depreciation for the first year

5. A FedEx airplane costs $50 million and is expected to fly 500 million miles during its 10-year life. Residual value is expected to be zero because the plane was used when acquired. If the plane travels 20 million miles the first year, how much depreciation should FedEx record under the units-of-production method?

   a. $2 million
   b. $5 million
   c. $10 million
   d. Cannot be determined from the data given

6. Which depreciation method is generally preferable for income tax purposes? Why?

   a. Straight-line, because it is simplest
   b. Units-of-production, because it best tracks the asset's use

c. Double-declining-balance, because it gives the most total depreciation over the asset's life

d. Double-declining-balance, because it gives the fastest tax deductions for depreciation

7. A copy machine cost $40,000 when new and has accumulated depreciation of $37,000. Suppose Kinko's junks this machine, receiving nothing in return. What is the result of the disposal transaction?

a. Gain of $3,000
b. Loss of $3,000
c. Gain of $37,000
d. Loss of $40,000

8. Using information from the preceding question, suppose Kinko's sold the machine for $5,000. What is the result of this disposal transaction?

a. Gain of $2,000
b. Loss of $2,000
c. Gain of $3,000
d. Gain of $5,000

9. Which method is typically used to compute depletion?

a. Depletion method
b. Straight-line method
c. Units-of-production method
d. Double-declining-balance method

10. Which intangible asset is recorded only as part of the acquisition of another company?

a. Copyright
b. Patent
c. Franchise
d. Goodwill

Answers are given after Apply Your Knowledge (p. 519).

Accounting Practice

Short Exercises

1 Describing long-term assets.

S9-1. Identify each of the following assets as a plant asset (P) or an intangible asset (I):

_____ 1. Franchises

_____ 2. Ore deposits

_____ 3. Buildings

_____ 4. Furniture

_____ 5. Patents

_____ 6. Copyrights

_____ 7. Trademarks

_____ 8. Land improvements

1 Describing long-term assets.

S9-2. Identify each of the following as land (L) or land improvements (LI):

_____ 1. Survey fees

_____ 2. Fencing

_____ 3. Lighting

_____ 4. Clearing land

_____ 5. Parking lot

2 Calculating and recording acquisition cost.

S9-3. Johnson purchased land having a current market value of $80,000, a building with a market value of $64,000, and equipment with a market value of $16,000. Journalize the lump-sum purchase of the three assets purchased for a total cost of $120,000 in exchange for a note payable.

2 Calculating and recording acquisition cost.

S9-4. Orbit Airways repaired one of its Boeing 767 aircraft at a cost of $600,000, which Orbit paid in cash. Orbit erroneously capitalized this cost as part of the cost of the plane.

1. Journalize both the incorrect entry the accountant made to record this transaction and the correct entry that the accountant should have made.

2. How will this accounting error affect Orbit's net income? Ignore depreciation.

3 Calculating and recording depreciation.

S9-5. At the beginning of the year, Orbit Airways purchased a used Boeing aircraft at a cost of $45 million. Orbit expects the plane to remain useful for five years (3 million miles) and to have a residual value of $5 million. Orbit expects the plane to be flown 750,000 miles the first year.

1. Compute Orbit's first-year depreciation on the plane using the following methods:

   a. Straight-line

   b. Units-of-production

   c. Double-declining-balance

2. Show the airplane's book value at the end of the first year under the straight-line method.

S9-6. At the beginning of the year, Orbit Airways purchased a used Boeing aircraft at a cost of $45 million. Orbit expects the plane to remain useful for five years (3 million miles) and to have a residual value of $5 million. Orbit expects the plane to be flown 750,000 miles the first year and 1.5 million miles the second year. Compute second-year depreciation on the plane using the following methods:

        ③ Calculating and recording depreciation.

   a. Straight-line

   b. Units-of-production

   c. Double-declining-balance

S9-7. On March 31, 2008, Orbit Airways purchased a used Boeing aircraft at a cost of $45 million. Orbit expects to fly the plane for five years and to have a residual value of $5 million. Compute Orbit's depreciation on the plane for the year ended December 31, 2008, using the straight-line method.

        ③ Calculating and recording depreciation.

S9-8. Big Boy's Hot Dogs purchased a hotdog stand for $40,000 with an estimated useful life of eight years, and no residual value. Suppose that after using the hotdog stand for four years, the company determines that the asset will remain useful for only two more years. Record Big Boy's depreciation on the hotdog stand for year 5 by the straight-line method.

        ③ Calculating and recording depreciation.

S9-9. Orbit Airways purchased a baggage-handling truck for $41,000. Suppose Orbit sold the truck on December 31, 2008, for $28,000 cash, after using the truck for two full years and accumulating depreciation of $16,000. Make the journal entry to record Orbit's sale of the truck.

        ④ Calculating and recording disposal.

S9-10. Kent Oil, a small Texas oil company, holds huge reserves of oil and gas assets. Assume that at the end of 2008, Kent's cost of mineral assets totaled approximately $18 million, representing 2.4 million barrels of oil and gas reserves in the ground.

        ⑤ Calculating and recording depletion.

   1. Which depletion method does Kent use to compute its annual depletion expense for the minerals removed from the ground?

   2. Suppose Kent removed 0.8 million barrels of oil during 2009. Record Kent's depletion expense for 2009.

S9-11. When one media company buys another, goodwill is often the most costly asset acquired. World Media paid $700,000 to acquire *The Dandy Dime*, a weekly advertising paper. At the time of the acquisition, *The Dandy Dime's* balance sheet reported total assets of $1,200,000 and liabilities of $600,000. The fair market value of *The Dandy Dime's* assets was $800,000.

1. How much goodwill did World Media purchase as part of the acquisition of *The Dandy Dime?*

2. Journalize World Media's acquisition of *The Dandy Dime*.

S9-12. Keystone Applications paid $500,000 to acquire a patent on software. After readying the software for production, Keystone's sales revenue for the first year of the patent use totaled $2 million. Cost of goods sold was $200,000, and selling expenses were $400,000. All these transactions occurred during 2008. Keystone expects the patent to have a useful life of five years. Prepare Keystone Applications' single-step income statement for the year ended December 31, 2008.

Exercises

E9-13. For each of the following long-term assets, identify the type of expense that will be incurred to allocate the asset's cost as depreciation expense (DR), depletion expense (DL), amortization expense (A), or none of these (NA).

____ 1. Franchises

____ 2. Land

____ 3. Buildings

____ 4. Furniture

____ 5. Patents

____ 6. Copyrights

____ 7. Trademarks

____ 8. Land improvements

____ 9. Gold ore deposits

E9-14. Bozeman Systems purchased land, paying $80,000 cash as a down payment and signing a $120,000 note payable for the balance. In addition, Bozeman paid delinquent property tax of $2,100, title insurance costing $2,500, and a $10,400 charge for leveling the land and removing an unwanted building. The company constructed an office building on the land at a cost of $800,000. It also paid $51,000 for a fence around the

continued.....

property, $15,000 for the company sign near the entrance, and $6,000 for special lighting of the grounds. Determine the cost of the company's land, land improvements, and building. Which of the assets will Bozeman depreciate?

E9-15. Lynch Brothers manufactures conveyor belts. Early in January 2007, Lynch constructed its own building at a materials, labor, and overhead cost of $900,000. Lynch also paid for architect fees and building permits of $72,000.

② Calculating and recording acquisition cost.

Requirements

1. How much should Lynch record as the cost of the building in 2007?

2. Record Lynch's transactions related to the construction of the building.

E9-16. Tonya's Tanning Salon bought three tanning beds in a $10,000 lump-sum purchase. An independent appraiser valued the tanning beds as follows:

② Calculating and recording acquisition cost.

Tanning Bed	Appraised Value
1	$3,000
2	5,000
3	4,000

Tonya's paid $5,000 in cash and signed a note payable for $5,000. Record the purchase in the journal, identifying each tanning bed's cost by number in a separate Tanning Bed account. Round decimals to three places.

E9-17. Classify each of the following expenditures as a capital expenditure (CAP) or an expense related to machinery (EXP):

② Calculating and recording acquisition cost.

a. Purchase price

b. Ordinary recurring repairs to keep the machinery in good working order

c. Lubrication of the machinery before it is placed in service

d. Periodic lubrication after the machinery is placed in service

e. Major overhaul to extend useful life by three years

f. Sales tax paid on the purchase price

g. Transportation and insurance while machinery is in transit from seller to buyer

h. Installation

continued.....

i. Training of personnel for initial operation of the machinery

j. Income tax paid on income earned from the sale of products manufactured by the machinery

(3) Calculating and recording depreciation.

E9-18. Jessica Brooks just slept through the class in which Professor Dominguez explained the concept of depreciation. Because the next test is scheduled for Wednesday, Brooks telephones Hanna Svensen to get her notes from the lecture. Svensen's notes are concise: "Depreciation—Sounds like Greek to me." Brooks next tries Tim Lake, who says he thinks depreciation is what happens when an asset wears out. David Coe is confident that depreciation is the process of building up a cash fund to replace an asset at the end of its useful life. Explain the concept of depreciation for Brooks. Evaluate the explanations of Lake and Coe. Be specific.

(3) Calculating and recording depreciation.

E9-19. Memorial Medical Center bought equipment on January 2, 2006, for $30,000. The equipment was expected to remain in service for four years and to perform 1,000 operations. At the end of the equipment's useful life, Memorial estimates that its residual value will be $6,000. The equipment performed 100 operations the first year, 300 the second year, 400 the third year, and 200 the fourth year. Prepare a schedule of depreciation expense per year for the equipment under the three depreciation methods. After two years under double-declining-balance depreciation, the company switched to the straight-line method. Show your computations.

Which method tracks the wear and tear on the equipment most closely? Which method would Memorial prefer to use for income-tax purposes in the first years of the equipment's life? Explain in detail why a taxpayer prefers this method.

(3) Calculating and recording depreciation.

E9-20. LHD Freight purchased a building for $700,000 and depreciated it on a straight-line basis over a 40-year period. The estimated residual value was $100,000. After using the building for 15 years, LHD realized that wear and tear on the building would force the company to replace it before 40 years. Starting with the 16th year, LHD began depreciating the building over a revised total life of 30 years and increased the estimated residual value to $175,000. Record depreciation expense on the building for years 15 and 16.

(3) Calculating and recording depreciation.

(4) Calculating and recording disposal.

E9-21. On January 2, 2007, Bright Lights purchased showroom fixtures for $10,000 cash, expecting the fixtures to remain in service for five years. Bright Lights has depreciated the fixtures on a straight-line basis, with zero residual value. On September 30, 2008, Bright Lights sold the fixtures for $5,000 cash. Record both the depreciation expense on the fixtures for 2008 and the sale of the fixtures on September 30, 2008.

(4) Calculating and recording disposal.

E9-22. Assume that Henson Corporation's comparative balance sheet reported these amounts:

continued.....

		December 31	
		2007	2006
Property:			
Plant and Equipment		$600,000	$595,000
Less: Accumulated Depreciation		(145,000)	(135,000)
Net Plant and Equipment		$455,000	$460,000

Requirements

Assume that on January 2, 2008, Henson sold 1/10 of its plant and equipment for $75,500 in cash. Journalize this transaction for Henson.

E9-23. Mesilla Valley Transport (MVT) is a large trucking company. MVT uses the units-of-production (UOP) method to depreciate its trucks. In 2006, MVT acquired a Mack truck costing $350,000 with a useful life of 10 years or 1 million miles. Estimated residual value was $100,000. The truck was driven 80,000 miles in 2006, 120,000 miles in 2007, and 160,000 miles in 2008. After 40,000 miles in 2009, MVT traded in the Mack truck for a less-expensive Freightliner and paid cash of $50,000. Determine MVT's cost of the new Freightliner truck. Journal entries are not required.

③ Calculating and recording depreciation.

④ Calculating and recording disposal.

E9-24. Asarco Mining paid $398,500 for the right to extract mineral assets from a 200,000-ton mineral deposit. In addition to the purchase price, Asarco also paid a $500 filing fee, a $1,000 license fee to the state of Colorado, and $60,000 for a geological survey of the property. Because the company purchased the rights to the minerals only, the company expected the asset to have zero residual value when fully depleted. During the first year, Asarco removed 40,000 tons of minerals. Using the Mineral Assets account, make journal entries to record:

⑤ Calculating and recording depletion.

a. Purchase of the minerals

b. Payment of fees and other costs

c. Depletion for the first year

E9-25. *Part 1.* Millennium Printing manufactures high-speed printers. Millennium recently paid $1 million for a patent on a new laser printer. Although it gives legal protection for 20 years, the patent is expected to provide a competitive advantage for only 8 years. Using the straight-line method of amortization, make journal entries to record (a) the purchase of the patent and (b) amortization for year 1.

⑥ Accounting for intangible assets.

Part 2. After using the patent for 4 years, Millennium learns at an industry trade show that another company is designing a more-efficient printer. On the basis of this new information, Millennium decides,

continued.....

starting with year 5, to amortize the remaining cost of the patent over 2 remaining years, giving the patent a total useful life of 6 years. Record amortization for year 5.

6 Accounting for intangible assets.

E9-26. Rutherford Corp. aggressively acquired other companies. Assume that Rutherford purchased Lancer, Inc., for $11 million cash. The market value of Lancer, Inc., assets is $15 million, and it has liabilities of $10 million.

Requirements

1. Compute the cost of goodwill purchased by Rutherford.

2. Record the purchase of Lancer, Inc., by Rutherford.

2 Calculating and recording acquisition cost.

E9-27. Assume that early in year 1, Mariposa purchased equipment at a cost of $500,000. Management expects the equipment to remain in service five years, with zero residual value. Mariposa uses the straight-line depreciation method. Through an accounting error, Mariposa accidentally expensed the entire cost of the equipment at the time of purchase.

Requirements

Prepare a schedule to show the overstatement or understatement in the following items at the end of each year over the five-year life of the equipment.

1. Equipment, net

2. Net income

7 Reporting long-term assets.

E9-28. At the end of 2008, Zeman Corp. had total assets of $25 million and total liabilities of $13 million. Included in the assets were property, plant, and equipment with a cost of $9 million and accumulated depreciation of $3 million. During 2008, Zeman earned total revenues of $20 million and had total expenses of $17 million. Show how Zeman Corp. reported property, plant, and equipment on its balance sheet on December 31, 2008. What was the book value of property, plant, and equipment on that date?

7 Reporting long-term assets.

E9-29. At the end of 2007, Farley Foods had total assets of $460,000 and total liabilities of $330,000. Included among the assets were property, plant, and equipment with a cost of $500,000 and accumulated depreciation of $200,000. During 2007, Farley earned total revenues of $270,000 and had total expenses of $280,000. Show how Farley Foods would report property, plant, and equipment on its balance sheet on December 31, 2007.

2 Calculating and recording acquisition cost.

3 Calculating and recording depreciation.

Problems (Group A)

P9-30A. Gegax Manufacturing incurred the following costs in acquiring land, making land improvements, and constructing and furnishing a new building.

continued.....

a. Purchase price of four acres of land	$200,000
b. Additional dirt and earthmoving	8,100
c. Fence around the boundary of the property	17,600
d. Attorney fee for title search on the land	1,000
e. Unpaid property taxes on the land to be paid by Gegax	5,900
f. Company signs at the front of the property	4,400
g. Building permit for the building	500
h. Architect's fee for the design of the building	22,500
i. Labor to construct the building	709,000
j. Materials used to construct the building	224,000
k. Landscaping	6,400
l. Parking lot and concrete walks	29,700
m. Lights for the parking lot and walkways	10,300
n. Salary of construction supervisor (85% to building; 15% to parking lot and concrete walks)	40,000
o. Furniture for the building	107,100
p. Transportation and installation of furniture	2,100

Gegax depreciates buildings over 40 years, land improvements over 20 years, and furniture over 8 years, all on a straight-line basis with zero residual value.

Requirements

1. Set up columns for Land, Land Improvements, Building, and Furniture. Show how to account for each cost by listing the cost under the correct account. Determine the total cost of each asset.

2. All construction was complete and assets were placed in service on May 1. Record partial-year depreciation for the year ended December 31. Round to the nearest dollar.

P9-31A. Regal Freightway provides freight service. The company's balance sheet includes Land, Buildings, and Motor-Carrier Equipment. Regal uses a separate accumulated depreciation account for each depreciable asset. During 2007, Regal completed the following transactions:

② Calculating and recording acquisition cost.

③ Calculating and recording depreciation.

continued.....

④ Calculating and recording disposal.	Jan. 1	Traded in motor-carrier equipment with accumulated depreciation of $90,000 (cost of $130,000) for similar new equipment with a cash cost of $176,000. Regal received a trade-in allowance of $70,000 on the old equipment and paid the remainder in cash.
	July 1	Sold a building that cost $550,000 and had accumulated depreciation of $250,000 through December 31 of the preceding year. Depreciation is computed on a straight-line basis. The building has a 40-year useful life and a residual value of $50,000. Regal received $100,000 cash and a $600,000 note receivable.
	Oct. 31	Purchased land and a building for a cash payment of $300,000. An independent appraisal valued the land at $115,000 and the building at $230,000.
	Dec. 31	Recorded depreciation as follows:
		New motor-carrier equipment has an expected useful life of 1 million miles and an estimated residual value of $26,000. Depreciation method is the units-of-production method. During the year, Regal drove the truck 150,000 miles.
		Depreciation on buildings is straight-line. The new building has a 40-year useful life and a residual value equal to $20,000.

Requirements

Record the transactions in Regal Freightway's journal.

② Calculating and recording acquisition cost.

③ Calculating and recording depreciation.

P9-32A. On January 3, 2004, Jose Rojo, Inc., paid $224,000 for equipment used in manufacturing automotive supplies. In addition to the basic purchase price, the company paid $700 transportation charges, $100 insurance for the equipment while in transit, $12,100 sales tax, and $3,100 for a special platform on which to place the equipment in the plant. Rojo management estimates that the equipment will remain in service five years and have a residual value of $20,000. The equipment will produce 50,000 units the first year, with annual production decreasing by 5,000 units during each of the next four years (i.e., 45,000 units in year 2, 40,000 units in year 3, and so on for a total of 200,000 units). In trying to decide which depreciation method to use, Rojo requested a depreciation schedule for each of the three depreciation methods (straight-line, units-of-production, and double-declining-balance).

Requirements

1. For each depreciation method, prepare a depreciation schedule showing asset cost, depreciation expense, accumulated depreciation, and asset book value. For the units-of-production method, round depreciation per unit to three decimal places.

2. Rojo prepares financial statements using the depreciation method that reports the highest income in the early years of asset use. For

continued.....

income tax purposes, the company uses the depreciation method that minimizes income taxes in the early years. Consider the first year Rojo uses the equipment. Identify the depreciation methods that meet Rojo's objectives, assuming the income tax authorities permit the use of any method.

P9-33A. Benny's Restaurants acquired Hungry Boy Diners. The financial records of Hungry Boy included the following:

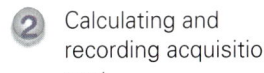

⑥ Accounting for intangible assets.

Book value of assets	$2.4 million
Market value of assets	2.7 million
Liabilities	2.2 million

Requirements

1. Make the journal entry to record Benny's purchase of Hungry Boy for $3 million cash, including any goodwill.

2. How should Benny's account for this goodwill after acquiring Hungry Boy? Explain in detail.

P9-34A. Wright Oil Company's balance sheet includes three assets: Natural Gas, Oil, and Coal. Suppose Wright paid $2.8 million cash for the right to work a mine with an estimated 100,000 tons of coal. Assume the company paid $60,000 to remove unwanted buildings from the land and $45,000 to prepare the surface for mining. Further, assume that Wright signed a $30,000 note payable to a company that will return the land surface to its original condition after the mining ends. During the first year, Wright removed 40,000 tons of coal, which it sold on account for $39 per ton. Operating expenses for the first year totaled $252,000, all paid in cash.

⑤ Calculating and recording depletion.

Requirements

1. Record all of Wright's transactions, including depletion, for the year.

2. Prepare the company's income statement for its coal operations for the year.

Problems (Group B)

P9-35B. Seaside Apartments incurred the following costs to acquire land, make land improvements, and construct and furnish an apartment building:

② Calculating and recording acquisition cost.

continued.....

a. Purchase price of three acres of land...	$150,000
b. Delinquent real estate taxes on the land to be paid by Seaside Apartments...	3,700
c. Additional dirt and earthmoving...	5,100
d. Title insurance on the land acquisition...	1,000
e. Fence around the boundary of the property......................................	44,200
f. Building permit for the apartment building....................................	200
g. Architect's fee for the design of the building...................................	32,000
h. Signs near the approaches to the property.......................................	20,900
i. Materials used to construct the building...	814,000
j. Labor to construct the building...	737,400
k. Parking lots and concrete walks on the property.............................	17,500
l. Lights for the parking lot and walkways..	8,900
m. Salary of construction supervisor (90% to building; 10% to parking lot and concrete walks)...	55,000
n. Furniture..	123,500
o. Transportation of furniture from seller to the building..................	1,100
p. Landscaping..	9,000

Seaside depreciates buildings over 40 years, land improvements over 20 years, and furniture over 8 years, all on a straight-line basis with zero residual value.

Requirements

1. Set up columns for Land, Land Improvements, Apartment Building, and Furniture. Show how to account for each cost by listing the cost under the correct account. Determine the total cost of each asset.

2. All construction was complete and the assets were placed in service on March 31. Record partial-year depreciation for the year ended December 31. Round to the nearest dollar.

P9-36B. Lesko Manufacturing's balance sheet reports Land, Buildings, Office Equipment, Assembly Equipment, and Finishing Equipment, with a separate accumulated depreciation account for each depreciable asset. During 2007, Lesko completed the following transactions:

continued.....

| May 1 | Purchased assembly and finishing equipment. Total cost was $80,000, paid in cash. An independent appraisal valued the assembly equipment at $90,000 and the finishing equipment at $10,000. | 4 Calculating and recording disposal. |

May 1 Purchased assembly and finishing equipment. Total cost was $80,000, paid in cash. An independent appraisal valued the assembly equipment at $90,000 and the finishing equipment at $10,000.

July 30 Traded in old office equipment with book value of $11,000 (cost of $96,000 and accumulated depreciation of $85,000) for new office equipment with a cost of $88,000. The seller gave Lesko a trade-in allowance of $20,000 on the old equipment, and Lesko paid the remainder in cash.

Sept. 1 Sold a building that cost $475,000 (accumulated depreciation of $350,000 through December 31 of the preceding year). Depreciation is computed on a straight-line basis. The building had a 30-year useful life and a residual value of $47,500. Lesko received $200,000 cash.

Dec. 31 Recorded depreciation as follows:

Assembly equipment and finishing equipment are depreciated by the straight-line method over a five-year life with zero residual value.

New office equipment is depreciated straight-line over seven years with a $9,000 residual value.

Requirements

Record the transactions in the journal of Lesko Manufacturing.

2 Calculating and recording acquisition cost.

P9-37B. On January 2, 2008, Holguin Supplies purchased a used trailer at a cost of $63,000. Before placing the trailer in service, the company spent $2,200 painting it, $800 replacing tires, and $4,000 overhauling the chassis. Holguin management estimates that the trailer will remain in service for six years and have a residual value of $14,200. The trailer's annual mileage is expected to be 18,000 miles in each of the first four years and 14,000 miles in each of the next two years—100,000 miles in total. In deciding which depreciation method to use, Manuel Holguin, the general manager, requests a depreciation schedule for each of the depreciation methods (straight-line, units-of-production, and double-declining-balance).

3 Calculating and recording depreciation.

Requirements

1. Prepare a depreciation schedule for each depreciation method, showing asset cost, depreciation expense, accumulated depreciation, and asset book value. For the units-of-production method, round depreciation per mile to three decimal places.

2. Holguin prepares financial statements using the depreciation method that reports the highest net income in the early years of

continued.....

asset use. For income-tax purposes, however, the company uses the depreciation method that minimizes income taxes in the early years. Consider the first year that Holguin uses the trailer. Identify the depreciation methods that meet the general manager's objectives, assuming the income tax authorities permit the use of any of the methods.

6 Accounting for intangible assets.

P9-38B. UniComm provides communication services. Assume that UniComm purchased goodwill as part of the acquisition of CityComm, which had these figures:

Book value of assets	$575,000
Market value of assets	906,000
Liabilities	406,000

Requirements

1. Make the journal entry to record UniComm's purchase of CityComm for $1 million cash.

2. How should UniComm account for goodwill after acquiring CityComm? Explain in detail.

5 Calculating and recording depletion.

P9-39B. Tri-State, Inc., operates a pipeline that provides natural gas. The company's balance sheet includes the asset Oil and Gas Properties.

Suppose Tri-State paid $7 million cash for oil and gas reserves with an estimated 500,000 barrels of oil. Assume the company paid $550,000 for additional geological tests of the property and $450,000 to prepare for drilling. During the first year of production, Tri-State removed 70,000 barrels of oil, which it sold on credit for $20 per barrel. Operating expenses related to this project totaled $185,000, all paid in cash.

Requirements

1. Record all of Tri-State's transactions, including depletion, for the year.

2. Prepare the company's income statement for this oil and gas project for the first year.

for 24/7 practice, visit www.MyAccountingLab.com

Apply Your Knowledge

Case 1. Larry Johnson owns Larry's Limousine, which operates a fleet of limousines and shuttle buses. Upon reviewing the most recent financial statements, he became confused over the recent decline in net income. He called his accountant and asked for an explanation. The accountant told Larry that the numerous repairs and maintenance expenses, such as oil changes, cleaning, and minor engine repairs, had totaled up to a large amount. Further, because several drivers were involved in accidents, the fleet insurance premiums had also risen sharply. Larry told his accountant to simply capitalize all the expenses related to the vehicles rather than expensing them. These capitalized repair costs could then be depreciated over the next 10 or 20 years. By capitalizing those expenses, the net income would be higher, as would property and equipment assets; therefore, both the income statement and balance sheet would look better. His accountant, however, disagreed because the costs were clearly routine maintenance and because they did not extend the fleet's useful life. Larry then told his accountant that the estimated useful life of the vehicles needed to be changed from 5 years to 20 years to lower the amount of depreciation expense. His accountant responded that capitalizing costs that should be expensed and extending the estimated lives of assets just to increase the reported net income was unethical and wrong. Larry said that it was his business and therefore demanded that the financial statements be changed to show more net income. As a result, the accountant told Larry to pick up his files and find another accountant. What ethical concerns did the accountant have? If the total amount of repairs and maintenance were so large, couldn't a case be made that the amount should be capitalized? Is it unethical to change the estimated life of an asset? Was it unethical for the accountant to sever the business relationship? Do you have any suggestions?

Case 2. Table Corporation purchased Chairs Unlimited for $10 million. The fair market value of Chairs' net assets at the time was $8 million, so Table Corporation recorded $2 million of goodwill. Also included in the purchase was a patent valued at $1 million with an estimated remaining life of 10 years. To comply with GAAP, the goodwill was not amortized, but the patent was amortized over the remaining 10-year life. However, the Chairs Unlimited business was not as profitable as anticipated and as a result, the accountant for Table Corporation stated that the goodwill needed to be written off. Further, the accountant discovered that the remaining life of the patent was only 6 years and that it should be amortized over the remaining 6-year life rather than the 10-year life originally estimated. The CEO became concerned because these adjustments would cause net income to be extremely low for the year. As a result, he told the accountant to wait before writing off the goodwill because of the possibility that the purchase could be profitable in the future. Also, he argued, the life of the patent should be left alone because it was originally based upon what was thought to be a 10-year life. After much debate, the CEO then agreed with the accountant as long as the amount of goodwill was not completely written off in the current year. What ethical concerns are involved? Should the accountant change the amortizable life of an intangible asset? Should the accountant completely write off the goodwill account in the current year? Does the CEO's concern for higher net income create any ethical problems when the accountant agrees to not completely write off the goodwill? Do you have any other thoughts?

This case addresses the long-term assets of Target Corporation. The majority of these assets consists of the property and equipment, and the intangible assets. You will not only see and understand the classification and presentation of these assets, but also the related depreciation and amortization expense. In the text, you learned how most long-term tangible assets used in business are capitalized and depreciated over their estimated useful lives. Further, you learned that certain intangible assets with capitalized costs are amortized over time. In addition, you know that land is not depreciated and goodwill is not amortized, yet these assets can be found on most corporate financial statements. You will now have an opportunity to see the impact of the long-term assets on the financials. Refer to the Target Corporation financial statements in Appendix A. Also, consider the following partial excerpts from the footnotes included in the annual report.

PROPERTY AND EQUIPMENT

Property and equipment are recorded at cost, less accumulated depreciation. Depreciation is computed using the straight-line method over estimated useful lives. Depreciation expense for the years 2004, 2003, and 2002 was $1,232 million, $1,068 million, and $942 million, respectively. Accelerated depreciation methods are generally used for income tax purposes. Repair and maintenance costs were $453 million, $393 million, and $355 million in 2004, 2003, and 2002, respectively.

Estimated useful lives by major asset category are as follows:

Asset	Life (in Years)
Buildings and improvements	8–39
Fixtures and equipment	4–15
Computer hardware and software	4

OTHER NONCURRENT ASSETS

Other noncurrent assets as of January 29, 2005, and January 31, 2004, consist of the following:

	2004	2003
Prepaid pension expense	$ 711	$ 580
Cash value of life insurance	439	363
Goodwill and intangible assets	206	229
Other	155	205
Total	$ 1,511	$ 1,377

GOODWILL AND INTANGIBLE ASSETS

Goodwill and intangible assets are recorded within other noncurrent assets at cost less accumulated amortization. Amortization is computed on intangible assets with definite useful lives using the straight-line method over estimated useful lives that range from 3 to 15 years. Amortization expense for the years 2004, 2003, and 2002 was $27 million, $30 million, and $25 million, respectively. On January 29, 2005, and January 31, 2004, goodwill and intangible assets by major classes were as follows:

(millions)	Goodwill		Leasehold Acquisition Costs		Other		Total	
	2004	2003	2004	2003	2004	2003	2004	2003
Gross assets	**$80**	$80	**$185**	$182	**$201**	$200	**$466**	$462
Accumulated amortization	**(20)**	(20)	**(52)**	(34)	**(188)**	(179)	**(260)**	(233)
Net goodwill and intangible assets	**$60**	$60	**$133**	$148	**$13**	$21	**$206**	$229

Requirements

1. What was the balance of net property and equipment on January 29, 2005? What was the balance of net property and equipment on January 31, 2004? Did the amount of ending net property and equipment increase or decrease? What is the possible significance of the change in the net property and equipment account balance?

2. What methods of depreciation were used by Target? What were the estimated useful lives? Where are the goodwill and other intangible assets located? What was the method of amortization used by Target? What estimated lives did Target use for amortization of the intangible assets?

3. What was the percentage of net property and equipment compared to the total assets on January 29, 2005? What was the percentage of net property and equipment compared to the total assets on January 31, 2004? Did the percentage increase or decrease during the year? What is the significance, if any, of this change in percentage?

4. What was the depreciation expense for each of the three fiscal years? How does the depreciation expense in 2004 compare with the change in accumulated depreciation during the year? Why do you suppose the amounts differ? What was the total amortization expense for each of the three fiscal years?

5. Can you find the depreciation and amortization expense on the cash flow statements? Was the total amount increasing or decreasing for the three fiscal years presented? Are the amounts you found the same on the income statements? Why would this figure be found on both financial statements?

For Internet Exercises, Excel in Practice, and additional online activities, go to the Web site www.prenhall.com/pollard.

Quick Check Answers

1. *b* 2. *a* 3. *d* 4. *c* 5. *a* 6. *d* 7. *b* 8. *a* 9. *c* 10. *d*

LEARNING OBJECTIVES

1. Account for current liabilities of known amount.

2. Account for estimated and contingent liabilities.

3. Calculate the current ratio and working capital.

4. Calculate payroll amounts.

5. Describe the payroll process.

6. Record basic payroll transactions.

7. Report current liabilities on the balance sheet.

10

Current Liabilities and Payroll

Upon graduation, you decide to put your business degree to good use and open your own fitness club. Your facility and staff are ready, so you open your doors and welcome your first customers. As the first few weeks and months roll by, you are engrossed in the day-to-day operations of the business. You buy supplies, such as towels from vendors, hire a cleaning service, and purchase an inventory of workout wear. You accept membership subscriptions from customers; the amounts they pay for these subscriptions will allow them to work out in your club for the next 3, 6, or 12 months, depending on the amount of their payment. Not to be forgotten, you also pay your employees.

All businesses incur current liabilities as part of their routine operations. They buy supplies and inventory on account, and even purchase services on account, too. They receive advance payments for goods and services to be provided later. They collect sales tax on merchandise purchases that their customers make, and record amounts due for employees' pay and payroll taxes due to government agencies. ●

Look Back

In previous chapters, you have seen how to account for both current and long-term assets, and how internal controls safeguard the items that businesses own. You also saw how to report them on the balance sheet.

Look Ahead

You will now examine how businesses keep track of current liabilities, obligations due within one year. You will check out the accounting for liabilities of known amounts as well as those that must be estimated, and determine the proper treatment for potential liabilities. You will also learn about accounting for the payroll process.

In previous chapters, you saw how businesses acquire the resources they need to operate. You discovered how to account for cash, receivables, inventory such as workout wear, and long-term assets such as the equipment that might be used in a fitness club. You also became familiar with internal controls that protect these things.

In this chapter, we will examine the accounting for the current liabilities that enable daily operations. We will distinguish between liabilities of known amounts and those that are estimated or contingent. We will view accounting for credit purchases, short-term notes, and sales tax owed to the government. We will also record the related liability for expenses incurred but not yet paid and track unearned revenue amounts. Finally, we will account for the liabilities associated with payroll and see how current liabilities are reported in the financial statements.

Current Liabilities of Known Amount

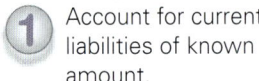 Account for current liabilities of known amount.

Recall from Chapter 1 that liabilities represent debts or obligations owed to others outside the business. Businesses may owe money for goods or services purchased on account. Businesses may also have the obligation to provide a good or service in the future or to repay principal and interest on loans received earlier. Payroll, payroll taxes, and sales tax also represent amounts due from most companies.

Accounts Payable

Amounts owed for products or services purchased on account are accounts payable, and are backed by the general reputation and credit standing of the debtor. Businesses increase the balance of accounts payable every time they purchase products or services on account. They decrease the balance of accounts payable as they make cash payments on the amounts they owe to their suppliers.

Imagine that Bob's Sporting Goods purchases baseball equipment from its supplier, Baseballs-R-Us, in anticipation of the upcoming season. As we saw in Chapter 5, to record the purchase of inventory on account, Bob's increases Inventory, an asset, and also increases Accounts Payable, a liability, as follows:

Journal Entry:

Date	Accounts	Post Ref.	Dr.	Cr.
Oct. 19	Inventory		600	
	Accounts Payable—Baseballs-R-Us			600
	Record purchase of inventory on account.			

Then, to pay the liability, Bob's decreases Accounts Payable and Cash:

Journal Entry:

Date	Accounts	Post Ref.	Dr.	Cr.
Nov. 12	Accounts Payable—Baseballs-R-Us		600	
	Cash			600
	Record payment on account.			

Short-Term Notes Payable and Interest Payable

Short-term notes provide a common way of obtaining operating funds or making purchases. Short-term notes payable are promissory notes that must be paid within one year. Interest payable represents the interest that is due on such notes.

To record the purchase of inventory in exchange for a short-term note, companies increase Inventory and Notes Payable, Short-Term. If the note won't be paid until the next fiscal year, they accrue the interest at year-end. This matches interest expense against the revenues resulting from sale of the inventory financed through the note. Interest incurred on the note since the time of signing is recorded by increasing both Interest Expense and Interest Payable. Recall from our coverage of notes receivable in Chapter 7 that interest is calculated using the following formula:

$$\text{Amount of Interest} = \text{Principal} \times \text{Interest Rate} \times \text{Time}$$

Suppose that, on September 30, 2007, Bob's signs a one-year, 10% note payable to Sporting Goods Inc. for the purchase of additional sporting equipment inventory. The journal entry to record the note is:

Journal Entry:

Date	Accounts	Post Ref.	Dr.	Cr.
Sept. 30, 2007	Inventory		8,000	
	Notes Payable, Short-Term—			
	Sporting Goods Inc.			8,000
	Record purchase of inventory for note			
	payable.			

At fiscal year-end, Bob's makes the following entry to record accrued interest for three months:

Journal Entry:

Date	Accounts	Post Ref.	Dr.	Cr.
Dec. 31, 2007	Interest Expense ($8,000 × .10 × 3/12)		200	
	Interest Payable			200
	Record 3 months' interest on note payable.			

Bob's balance sheet at December 31, 2007, reports the note payable of $8,000 and interest payable of $200 as current liabilities because they will be paid within the year. The income statement for 2007 reports interest expense of $200. Both the balance sheet and the income statement are partially illustrated as follows:

BOB'S SPORTING GOODS		BOB'S SPORTING GOODS	
Balance Sheet		**Income Statement**	
December 31, 2007		Year Ended December 31, 2007	
Liabilities		**Expenses**	
Current liabilities:		Interest expense	$200
Note payable, short-term	$8,000		
Interest payable	200		

Interest expense of $200 was correctly allocated to 2007. Interest expense for the nine months of the loan in 2008 will be $600. At maturity, Bob's will pay the full year's interest on the note of $800, and will have correctly divided the total expense between the two different time periods in which it belongs, $200 for three months of interest in 2007 and $600 for nine months of interest in 2008.

To record the payment of the note in 2008, Bob's will decrease Notes Payable, Short-Term and Interest Payable, increase Interest Expense to record the period's interest of $600, and decrease Cash for the total of the principal and interest amounts.

Journal Entry:

Date	Accounts	Post Ref.	Dr.	Cr.
Sept. 30, 2008	Notes Payable, Short-Term—Sporting Goods Inc.		8,000	
	Interest Payable		200	
	Interest Expense ($8,000 × .10 × 9/12)		600	
	Cash ($8,000 + $200 + $600)			8,800
	Record payment of principal and interest on note payable.			

Sales Tax Payable

Most states levy sales tax on retail sales. The easiest way for the states to collect the tax is to require retailers to serve as collection agents and collect the sales tax from the customer in addition to the price of the item sold. The retailers keep track of the sales tax collected and then pay it to the state at regular intervals. In this way, sales tax represents a liability to retailers; they have collected tax that is paid by the consumer but is *owed* to the state government.

As retailers collect the sales tax at the time of sale, they increase the current liability, Sales Tax Payable. Then the retailers pay the collected sales taxes to the state government and decrease Sales Tax Payable. Exhibit 10-1 illustrates the distribution of cash collections for Pete's Pizza.

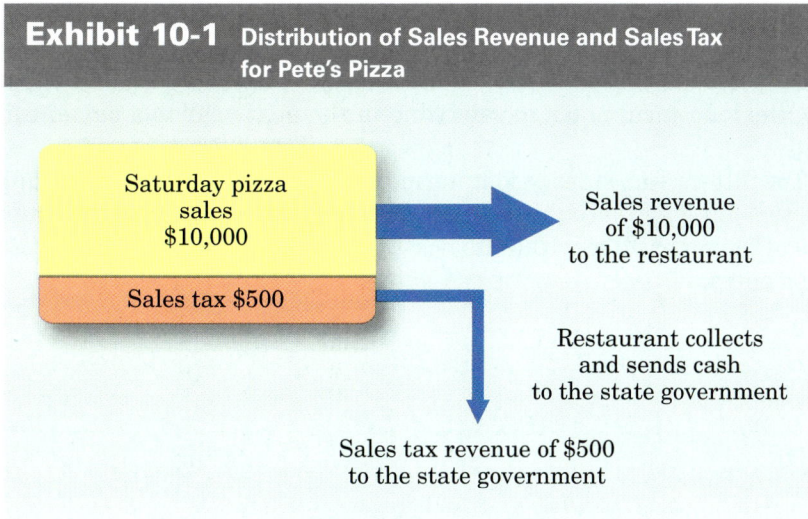

Exhibit 10-1 Distribution of Sales Revenue and Sales Tax for Pete's Pizza

Suppose on March 3, Saturday's sales at a Pete's Pizza total $10,000. The business collects an additional 5% in sales tax, which would equal $500 ($10,000 × 0.05). The business increases Cash for the full amount of cash received, increases Sales Revenue for the value of the pizza sold, and increases Sales Tax Payable to show the amount of tax owed to the state:

Journal Entry:

Date	Accounts	Post Ref.	Dr.	Cr.
Mar. 3	Cash ($10,000 + $500)		10,500	
	Sales Tax Payable			500
	Sales Revenue			10,000
	Record pizza sales for cash.			

Later, Pete's Pizza prepares a special sales tax report summarizing the sales activities and the sales tax due for the reporting period. The tax form and a check for the sales tax due are mailed to the state government. Assuming that Pete's collected $9,700 in sales tax for the quarter ending March 31, Pete will record the payment of $9,700 sales tax by reducing Sales Tax Payable and Cash:

Journal Entry:

Date	Accounts	Post Ref.	Dr.	Cr.
Mar. 31	Sales Tax Payable		9,700	
	Cash			9,700
	Record payment of sales tax collected.			

Current Portion of Long-Term Notes Payable

Some long-term notes payable and bonds payable are paid in installments. As we said in Chapter 4, the **current portion of long-term notes payable** is the amount of the principal payable within one year, a current liability. The remaining portion of the long-term debt is a long-term liability. At the end of the fiscal year, the company may make an adjusting entry to shift the installment of the long-term notes payable due in the next year to a current liability account.

If Tot Sitters Inc. signs a long-term note payable to Childcraft Equipment Co. for the purchase of equipment to be used in its childcare business, and $10,000 of the note is due within its next fiscal year, the company may record the following entry:

Journal Entry:

Date	Accounts	Post Ref.	Dr.	Cr.
Dec. 31	Notes Payable, Long-Term—Childcraft Equipment Co.		10,000	
	Current Portion of Notes Payable			10,000
	Transfer current portion of notes payable.			

Accrued Expenses

As we mentioned in Chapter 3, accruals are revenues earned or expenses incurred before cash has been exchanged. **Accrued expenses**, such as salary, tax, and the interest we accounted for earlier in the chapter, are also called **accrued liabilities** because recording these amounts increases both expenses and liabilities. As in the case of interest, accrued expenses arise when an expense is matched against the revenue it produced in one time period, but the payment of the expense is made in a later period.

Payroll, which is also called **employee compensation**, can be a major expense for a business. For service organizations, such as CPA firms and travel agencies, payroll is *the* major expense because it consists of the employee costs of providing the services. Payroll expense for salaries or wages usually causes an accrued liability at year-end because employees have earned salaries and wages that won't be paid until the end of the next pay period. The end of a pay period rarely coincides with the end of the company's fiscal year, which means such amounts must be accrued. We show how to account for payroll expenses and liabilities later in the chapter.

Unearned Revenues

Also remember from Chapter 3 that another term for unearned revenues is *deferred revenues*. By receiving cash from customers before earning the revenue, the business has an obligation to provide goods or services to the customer. Let's consider an example. Business 2.0 sells three-year magazine subscriptions and collects cash in advance. By receiving cash before earning the revenue, Business 2.0 has a liability to provide magazines during the next three years. The liability account used to record this obligation is called Unearned Subscription Revenue.

Assume that Business 2.0 charges $60 for a three-year subscription. To record the cash received in advance from 10 customers, Business 2.0 increases Cash and Unearned Subscription Revenue for $600 ($60 × 10 customers):

Journal Entry:

Date	Accounts	Post Ref.	Dr.	Cr.
Jan. 1	Cash		600	
	Unearned Subscription Revenue			600
	Record cash received for three-year			
	subscriptions in advance of providing magazines.			

During 2007, Business 2.0 produces and delivers one year's, or one-third, of the total magazines due and earns $200 ($600 × 1/3) of the revenue. Business 2.0 will record the revenue earned during this year by decreasing Unearned Subscription Revenue and increasing Subscription Revenue:

Journal Entry:

Date	Accounts	Post Ref.	Dr.	Cr.
Dec. 31	Unearned Subscription Revenue		200	
	Subscription Revenue			200
	Record subscription revenue earned.			

At the end of 2007, Business 2.0 still owes its subscribers $400 in magazines ($600 − $200).

Estimated and Contingent Liabilities

A business may know that a liability exists but not know the exact amount owed. This liability must be reported on the balance sheet. A prime example is a liability called Estimated Warranty Payable, which is common for companies that manufacture products.

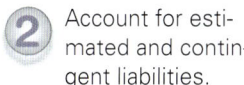 **2** Account for estimated and contingent liabilities.

Estimated Warranty Payable

Many companies guarantee their products against defects under warranty agreements. Ninety-day warranties and one-year warranties are common. If the product fails to perform within that time period, the customer may return it for repair or for a refund.

The matching principle says to record **warranty expense** in the same period that the revenue from the sale of the product is recorded. Therefore, the warranty expense occurs at the time of the sale, not at the time that the warranty claim is made by the customer. However, a challenge arises because, at the time of the sale, the company does not know the exact amount of warranty expense that will be incurred because it does not know how many products will fail to perform. Businesses handle this issue by estimating warranty expense and the related liability according to past experience with the product.

Assume that Maytag made appliance sales of $200,000, subject to product warranties. Maytag estimates that 3% of its products will require warranty payments. To record the sale, Maytag increases Accounts Receivable and Sales Revenue. At the time of the sale, Maytag also records the estimate of 3% for warranty payments as an increase to Warranty Expense and Estimated Warranty Payable. Ignoring the cost of the appliances sold, the journal entries follow:

Journal Entry:

Date	Accounts	Post Ref.	Dr.	Cr.
June 20	Accounts Receivable		200,000	
	Sales Revenue			200,000
	Record sales on account.			
	Warranty Expense ($200,000 × 0.03)		6,000	
	Estimated Warranty Payable			6,000
	Record estimated warranty expense.			

Assume that Maytag's warranty payments total $5,800 for the year. Maytag makes this journal entry to reduce liabilities and assets:

Journal Entry:

Date	Accounts	Post Ref.	Dr.	Cr.
Dec. 31	Estimated Warranty Payable		5,800	
	Cash			5,800
	Record payment of warranty claims.			

Maytag's expense on the income statement is the estimated amount of $6,000, not the $5,800 actually paid. After paying for these warranties, Maytag's liability account has a credit balance of $200 ($6,000 − $5,800).

Contingent Liabilities

A **contingent liability** is not an actual liability. Instead, it is a potential liability that depends on a *future* event. For example, Merck & Co., Inc., is a pharmaceutical company currently being sued over its Vioxx painkiller. Plaintiffs in the suits believe that Vioxx is linked to the deaths of persons who took Vioxx for pain relief. Merck thus faces a contingent liability, which may or may not become an actual liability. If the lawsuits' outcomes could hurt Merck, it would be unethical for Merck to withhold knowledge of the litigation from the users of its financial statements.

Another example of a contingent liability is the **cosigning** of a note payable by one company on behalf of another company. For example, if Company A cosigns a note payable for Company B, then Company A has a contingent liability for the note until the note comes due. If Company B pays the note, the contingent liability ceases to exist. If it does not pay the note, Company A must pay

Company B's debt, and Company A's contingent liability becomes a real obligation to pay the amount owed.

Companies must record contingent liabilities if the situation meets two criteria. A liability must be recorded for a contingency when

- It is probable that the company will be liable, and
- The amount of the liability can be reasonably estimated.

Businesses use judgment in determining whether the two criteria are met. To assess the likelihood that they will become liable, entities use past experience and consult their attorneys. For example, Merck lost in three of six Vioxx cases to date, and it may use this information to determine the probability that it will be held accountable in future suits. To estimate the amount of the liability, businesses use historical data adjusted for new information. Again, Merck might estimate the amount of its potential future liability by examining the dollar amount of the judgments in the suits it lost. In the case of a contingency for a cosigned note, the amount of the liability can more easily be estimated as the amount of the note principal plus interest.

The accounting profession divides contingent liabilities into three categories according to each category's likelihood that the contingency will cause a loss, and therefore, a liability. The three categories of contingent liabilities, along with how to report them, are shown in Exhibit 10-2.

Exhibit 10-2 Three Categories of Contingent Liabilities

Likelihood That the Contingency Will Become an Actual Liability	How to Report the Contingency
Remote	Ignore. *Example:* A frivolous lawsuit.
Reasonably possible	Describe the situation in a footnote to accompany the financial statements. *Example:* The company is the defendant in a significant lawsuit and the outcome could go either way.
Probable, and the amount of the loss can be estimated	Record an expense and a liability based on estimated amounts. *Example:* The company is the defendant in a significant lawsuit; legal counsel believes the outcome will be unfavorable to the company.

Exhibit 10-3 summarizes the transactions that affect various liability accounts.

Exhibit 10-3 Transactions Affecting Liabiliy Accounts

Liability Account	When to Increase the Liability ⬆	When to Decrease the Liability ⬇
Accounts Payable	Purchase goods or services on account	Pay on account
Short-Term Notes Payable	Sign note	Pay note

continued.....

Exhibit 10-3 (continued. . . .)		
Interest Payable	Adjust at year-end for interest incurred but not paid	Pay interest
Sales Tax Payable	Collect cash from customer at time of sale	Pay state government
Current Portion of Long-Term Notes Payable	Adjust at year-end for amount due within the next year	Pay note
Accrued Liabilities	Adjust at year-end for amount incurred but not paid	Pay salaries, interest, taxes, etc.
Unearned Revenue	Collect cash from customer at time of sale	Deliver goods or services
Estimated Warranty Payable	Sell product	Make warranty payments, perform warranty work, or replace product

More Ratios for Decision Making

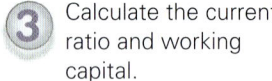 **3** Calculate the current ratio and working capital.

Accounting is designed to provide information for decision making by stakeholders. For example, a bank considering lending money to a company must predict whether the company can repay the loan. If the business already has a lot of debt, repayment is less certain than if it doesn't owe too much money. Two of the most widely used decision aids in assessing the short-term liquidity of a business are the **current ratio** and the measure of **working capital**.

The current ratio measures a company's ability to pay its current liabilities by comparing those liabilities against current assets. It is computed as follows:

$$\text{Current Ratio} = \text{Current Assets/Current Liabilities}$$

A company prefers to have a high current ratio because that means it has plenty of current assets to pay current liabilities. An increasing current ratio over time indicates improvement in a company's ability to pay current debts. A rule of thumb is that a strong current ratio is 1.50, which indicates that the company has $1.50 in current assets for every $1.00 in current liabilities. Hence, a company with a current ratio of 1.50 would probably have little trouble paying its current liabilities. A current ratio of 1.00 is considered low.

A related measure is working capital.

$$\text{Working Capital} = \text{Current Assets} - \text{Current Liabilities}$$

Working capital also measures a company's ability to meet short-term obligations with current assets. A positive result indicates that the business has more current assets than it has current liabilities, and thus shows that current assets could pay current liabilities. A negative result indicates the opposite; current liabilities are greater than the current assets of the entity.

Accounting for Payroll

Large companies typically go through a formal process of hiring employees. When a new employee begins work, the payroll process begins. Businesses that hire employees need to properly account for employee compensation in order to comply with federal and state law. Accordingly, an accounting system should include a process that ensures the correct and timely payments to the following:

4 Calculate payroll amounts.

- Employees for work performed

- The federal and state governments for taxes due from employees and employers

- Third parties for employee benefits and charitable contributions

Employee compensation for work performed can take many forms:

- A **salary** is a set amount of pay for a period of time such as a year, month, or week. For example, an employee may earn a salary of $48,000 per year, and another may earn $1,000 per week. The standard workweek for most businesses is 40 hours.

- **Wages** are pay amounts stated at an hourly rate, such as $10 per hour, times the number of hours worked. The hours worked will vary among employees and may even vary from pay period to pay period for the same employee.

- A **commission** is pay stated as a percentage of a sale amount, such as 5% commission on a sale. For example, a realtor selling $100,000 of real estate would earn a $5,000 commission (5% × $100,000).

- A **bonus** is pay for exceptional performance over and above the base salary, wage, or commission. The bonus is often paid in a single amount after year-end for performance during that year.

Gross Pay and Net Pay

Businesses need to compute and account for two amounts of employee pay. **Gross pay** is the total amount of salary, wages, commission, and bonus earned by the employee during a pay period. Gross pay is the amount of pay before taxes or any other amounts are deducted. Gross pay is the expense to the employer for the employee's efforts.

In addition to regular earnings, gross pay may include overtime pay for an employee who works extra hours. For businesses involved in interstate commerce, overtime earnings must be computed according to a federal law called the **Fair Labor Standards Act**. The act says that most employees must be paid at least one and a half times their regular pay rate for any hours they work over 40 in one workweek. For example, Joe Lewis earns $15 per hour, so when he works more than 40 hours, he earns a rate of $22.50 ($15.00 × 1.5) for each hour of overtime. For working 42 hours during a week, he earns $645, computed as follows:

Regular Pay: $15 × 40 Hours	$600
Overtime Pay: $22.50 × 2 Hours	45
Gross Pay	$645

Net pay, also called, **take-home pay**, is the amount of pay the employee gets to keep. Take-home pay equals gross pay minus all deductions for taxes and other employee-related items. Net or take-home pay is the amount of earnings that the employee actually receives.

Employee Payroll Deductions

The federal government requires businesses, as employers, to act as collection agents for employee taxes. Thus, employers subtract taxes and other amounts from employee gross pay to determine net pay. These amounts withheld from an employee's pay are called **deductions**. Some deductions, such as taxes, are required; others, including union dues, insurance premiums, charitable contributions, and other amounts withheld at the employee's request, are optional. Payroll deductions become the liability of employers, who collect the funds withheld then pay the government and other outside parties.

EMPLOYEE INCOME TAX

Federal law requires individuals to pay income tax on a pay-as-you-go basis, so employers must withhold income tax from their employees' pay. The amount of income tax deducted from gross pay is called **income tax withheld**. The amount of income tax withheld depends on the employee's gross pay, filing status, and number of **withholding allowances** the employee claims.

At the beginning of employment, an employee files Internal Revenue Service (IRS) **Form W-4, Employee's Withholding Allowance Certificate**, with his or her employer to indicate the number of allowances claimed. Each allowance lowers the amount of tax withheld. Generally, an employee may claim a withholding allowance for himself or herself, one for his or her spouse, and one for each of his or her dependents, such as a child. Based on the information submitted in the W-4, the employer determines the amount of federal income tax that needs to be withheld by consulting an IRS publication called Circular E, Employer's Tax Guide, also known as Publication 15.

Exhibit 10-4 shows a W-4 for R. C. Dean, who claims four allowances on line 5.

Exhibit 10-4 Form W-4

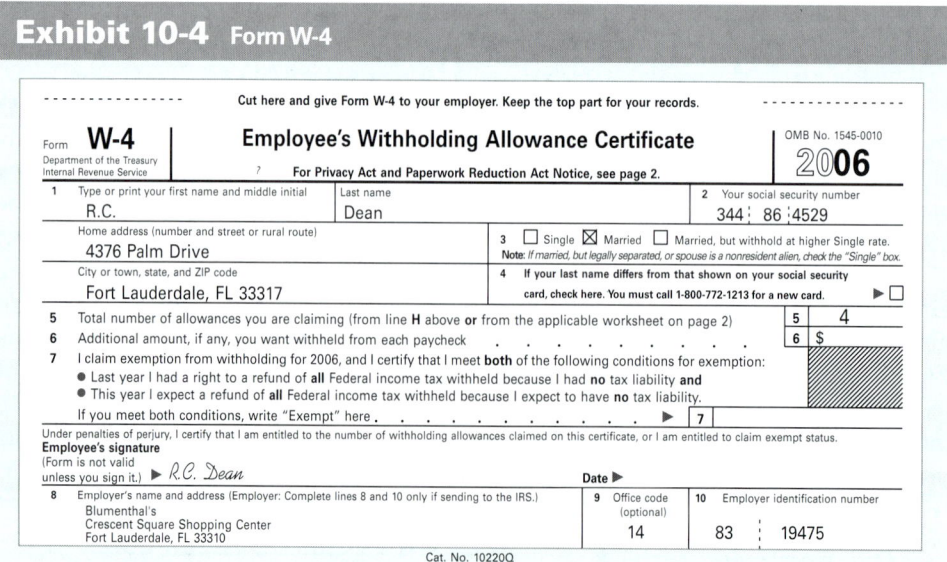

SOCIAL SECURITY (FICA) TAX

The **Federal Insurance Contributions Act (FICA)**, also known as the **Social Security Act**, created the **social security tax**, which is used to provide retirement, disability, and medical benefits. The law requires employers to withhold social security (FICA) tax from employees' paychecks and has two components:

1. Old age, survivors', and disability insurance (OASDI)

2. Health insurance, or Medicare

The OASDI and Medicare tax rates and the OASDI wage base amount are set by the federal government and may increase some in each calendar year. For 2006, the OASDI tax rate of 6.2% is applied to the first $94,200 of employee gross earnings in a year. Therefore, the maximum OASDI tax that an employee paid in 2006 was $5,840.40 ($94,200 × 0.062). The Medicare portion of the FICA tax applies to all employee gross earnings. For 2006, the tax rate was 1.45% of every dollar that an employee earned. An employee thus paid a combined FICA tax rate of 7.65% (6.2% + 1.45%) of the first $94,200 of annual earnings, plus 1.45% of earnings above $94,200.

Assume that, in 2006, Rex Jennings earned gross pay of $52,800 prior to December. Jennings's salary for December was $4,800. How much FICA tax was withheld from Jennings's December paycheck? Because his earnings for the year to date were well below the OASDI limit of $94,200, all of the $4,800 he earned in December was subject to both OASDI and Medicare tax. The computation follows:

2006 OASDI Tax Wage Base Limit	$94,200
Jennings' 2006 Gross Earnings Prior to December	(52,800)
Amount below OASDI Tax Wage Base Limit	$41,400
Jennings' December Gross Earnings below the OASDI Wage Base Limit	$4,800
Combined FICA Tax Rate	×.0765
FICA Tax Withheld from Jennings' December Pay Check	$367.20

Optional Deductions

As a convenience to employees, many companies make payroll deductions and disburse cash according to employee instructions. Deductions for retirement savings plans, gifts to charitable organizations such as the United Way and Habit for Humanity, insurance payments, and union dues are some common examples. Like taxes withheld, these amounts represent liabilities to employers until they are turned over to the appropriate parties.

Exhibit 10-5 summarizes the relationship between gross pay, deductions withheld from an employee's paycheck, and net pay.

Employer Payroll Taxes

Payroll taxes that employers pay increase the cost of employee compensation, and thus represent an expense to the employer in addition to the cost of the compensation itself. They also are liabilities that the employer owes to the federal and state governments until paid. Employers must pay at least three payroll taxes:

1. Social Security (FICA) Tax: The Social Security system is funded by equal contributions from employees and employers. Thus, employers must pay the same amount of tax on behalf of employees that the employees pay. The wage base limit and tax rates already discussed apply to employers, too; in 2006 for example, employers paid an OASDI tax at a rate of 6.2% on the wages employees earned below $94,000, and paid a Medicare tax rate of 1.45% on all earnings of employees.

2. **State Unemployment Tax (SUTA)**: This state tax funds unemployment compensation and is mandated by the federal government.

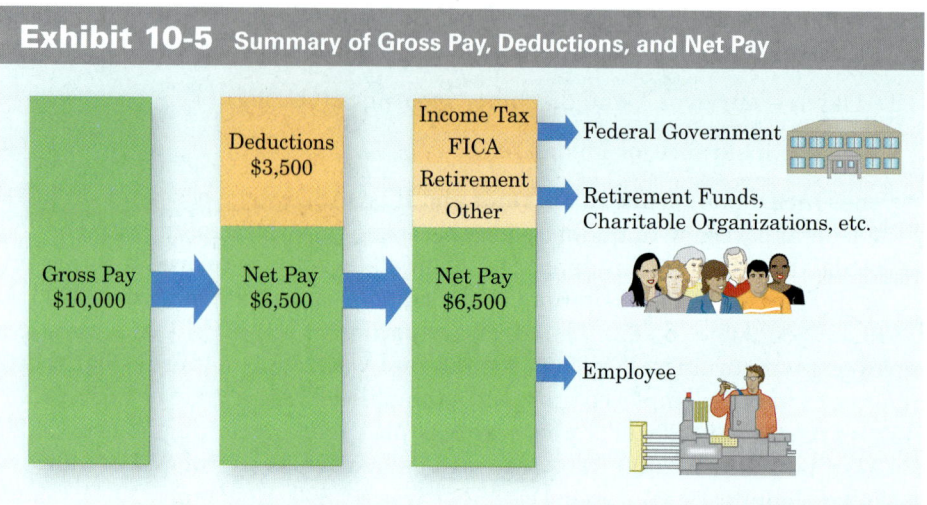

Exhibit 10-5 Summary of Gross Pay, Deductions, and Net Pay

3. **Federal Unemployment Tax (FUTA)**: The same federal law that created social security also created an unemployment tax and requires all states, territories, and the District of Columbia to run unemployment compensation programs. In 2006, employers paid FUTA tax at a rate of 6.2% on wages earned by employees up to a wage base limit of $7,000. However, the federal government allows employers to take a tax credit for SUTA tax against this tax, up to a maximum credit of 5.4%. This allowance typically results in employers paying a tax rate of 5.4% to the state, plus 0.8% to the federal government.

Other Payroll Considerations

Our discussion to this point centered on the computation of payroll amounts based on federal payroll laws, such as the Fair Labor Standards Act and the FICA law that created social security and unemployment tax. You need to know that states also pass laws governing payroll. These laws can vary significantly from one state to another and create differences in the way that employers need to account for payroll. For example, in 2005, 43 states required employees to pay state income tax, so employers in these 43 states needed to withhold state income tax from their employees' paychecks. Further, states have laws that sometimes overlap federal law. Businesses located in California, for instance, must not only comply with federal law in computing and paying overtime pay, but must also follow the state law that applies, too. Although they are too diverse for discussion here, be aware that all laws, whether federal, state, or local, must be followed in properly accounting for payroll costs.

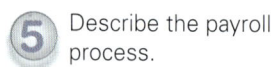

The Payroll Process

5 Describe the payroll process.

The payroll process, which begins with the hiring of employees, requires many documents, including the W-4 form that employees complete upon hire. Employers keep the forms and wage or salary information for employees in employees' personnel files. These data, along with information from time sheets or time cards, are used to continue the payroll process through computation of employee gross pay, deduction amounts, and net pay. See Exhibit 10-6.

Exhibit 10-6 Overview of the Payroll Process

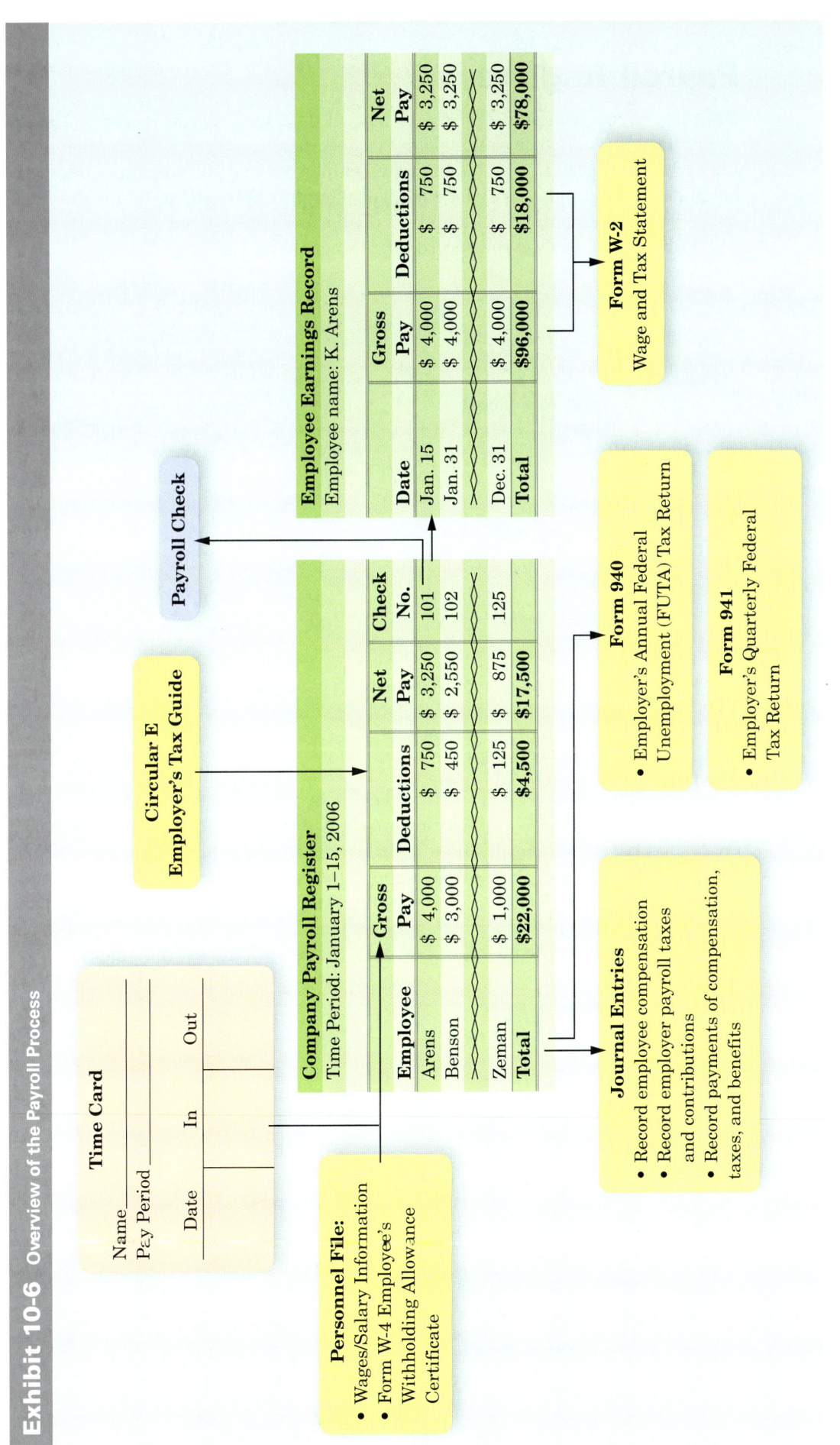

Time Card

Name_____
Pay Period_____

Date	In	Out

Personnel File:
- Wages/Salary Information
- Form W-4 Employee's Withholding Allowance Certificate

**Circular E
Employer's Tax Guide**

Payroll Check

Company Payroll Register
Time Period: January 1–15, 2006

Employee	Gross Pay	Deductions	Net Pay	Check No.
Arens	$ 4,000	$ 750	$ 3,250	101
Benson	$ 3,000	$ 450	$ 2,550	102
Zeman	$ 1,000	$ 125	$ 875	125
Total	**$22,000**	**$4,500**	**$17,500**	

Employee Earnings Record
Employee name: K. Arens

Date	Gross Pay	Deductions	Net Pay
Jan. 15	$ 4,000	$ 750	$ 3,250
Jan. 31	$ 4,000	$ 750	$ 3,250
Dec. 31	$ 4,000	$ 750	$ 3,250
Total	**$96,000**	**$18,000**	**$78,000**

Journal Entries
- Record employee compensation
- Record employer payroll taxes and contributions
- Record payments of compensation, taxes, and benefits

Form 940
- Employer's Annual Federal Unemployment (FUTA) Tax Return

Form 941
- Employer's Quarterly Federal Tax Return

Form W-2
Wage and Tax Statement

Payroll Register

Each pay period, companies organize payroll data in a special record called the **payroll register**. The payroll register is a document containing information about the current pay period's payroll, listing all employees and showing gross pay, withholding amounts, and net pay for each. The payroll register serves as a check register because it shows the check numbers of all checks used to pay payroll.

Exhibit 10-7 is a payroll record for Blumenthal's.

Exhibit 10-7 Blumenthal's Payroll Register

Week Ended: December 31, 2006

| Employee | Hours | Gross Pay | | | Deductions | | | | | Net Pay | |
		Straight-Time	Overtime	Total Salary Expense	Federal Income Tax	FICA Tax	Habitat for Humanity	Total	Amount	Check No.
Chen, W. L.	40	500.00		500.00	71.05	38.25	2.50	111.80	388.20	1621
Dean, R. C.	46	400.00	90.00	490.00	59.94	37.49	2.00	99.43	390.57	1622
Ellis, M.	41	560.00	21.00	581.00	86.14	44.45		130.59	450.41	1623
Trimble, E. A.†	40	2,360.00		2,360.00	663.22		15.00	678.22	1,681.78	1641
Total		**13,940.00**	**714.00**	**14,654.00**	**3,367.76**	**861.94**	**150.00**	**4,379.70**	**10,274.30**	

†The business deducted no FICA tax from E. A. Trimble. She has already earned more than $94,200.

Payroll Checks

Most companies pay employees by check or by electronic fund transfer (EFT), sometimes referred to as automatic deposit. A paycheck has an attachment that details the payroll amounts. These figures come from the payroll register such as the one in Exhibit 10-7. Exhibit 10-8 shows payroll check number 1622, issued to R. C. Dean for net pay of $390.57. If the employee authorizes the company to make deposits directly to his or her own bank account, the employer still furnishes the employee with the attachment, or pay stub, that shows the payroll amounts.

Exhibit 10-8 Payroll Check

Blumenthal's
Payroll Account
Fort Lauderdale, FL   1622

                                                12/31   2006

Pay to the
Order of   R. C. Dean $ 390.57

Three hundred ninety & 57/100 .... **Dollars**

Republic Bank
Fort Lauderdale
Florida 33310
                                    Anna Figaro
●A111900031A 0787C50000454C   **Treasurer**

| Pay | | | Deductions | | | | Net Pay | Check No. |
Straight time	Overtime	Gross	Income tax	FICA	United Way	Total		
400.00	90.00	490.00	59.94	37.49	2.00	99.43	390.57	1622

Employee Earnings Record

Employers must file payroll tax returns with the federal and state governments. One important return, **Form 941, Employer's Quarterly Federal Tax Return**, details total employee compensation, the amount of federal income tax withheld, as well as total FICA taxes owed on compensation. This report must be filed no later than one month after the end of a quarter. Another important form that must be filed is **Form 940, Employer's Annual Federal Unemployment (FUTA)Tax Return,** an annual return showing compensation related to federal unemployment tax, and the tax due on this compensation.

Employers must also provide employees with **Form W-2, Wage and Tax Statement**, at the end of the calendar year. Exhibit 10-9 shows the W-2 for employee R. C. Dean. Employers prepare these statements and give copies to employees, the Social Security Administration, and the state government. Dean uses the W-2 to prepare his income tax return.

Exhibit 10-9 Employee Wage and Tax Statement, Form W-2

a Control number 2222 | Void ☐ | For Official Use Only ▶ OMB No. 1545-0008

b Employer identification number 83-19475	1 Wages, tips, other compensation 23,210.00	2 Federal income tax withheld 1,946.72
c Employer's name, address, and ZIP code Blumenthal's Crescent Square Shopping Center Fort Lauderdale, FL 33310-1234	3 Social security wages 23,210.00	4 Social security tax withheld 1,439.02
	5 Medicare wages and tips 23,210.00	6 Medicare tax withheld 336.55
	7 Social security tips	8 Allocated tips
d Employee's social security number 344-86-4529	9 Advance EIC payment	10 Dependent care benefits
e Employee's name (first, middle initial, last) R.C. Dean	11 Nonqualified plans	12 Benefits included in box 1
4376 Palm Drive Fort Lauderdale, FL 33317	13 See instrs. for box 13	14 Other
f Employee's address and ZIP code	15 Statutory employee ☐ Deceased ☐ Pension plan ☐ Legal rep. ☐ Deferred compensation ☐	

16 State Employer's state ID no.	17 Sate wages, tips, etc	18 State income tax	19 Locality name	20 Local wages, tips, etc	21 Local income tax

Form **W-2** Wage and Tax Statement **2006**

Copy A For Social Security Administration—Send this entire page with Form W-3 to the Social Security Administration; photocopies are **not** acceptable.

Cat. No. 10134D

Department of the Treasury—Internal Revenue Service
For Privacy Act and Paperwork Reduction Act Notice, see separate instructions.

To keep track of the information necessary to prepare the W-2s and employer tax returns, businesses maintain a payroll record in addition to the payroll register. This record is called the **employee earnings record**, and shows payroll information for one employee; an earnings record is kept for each person that the business employees. Exhibit 10-10 shows the earnings record of R. C. Dean for the last two weeks of 2006.

Internal Control over Payroll

Two main types of internal controls are used in the payroll process. One set deals with ensuring the efficiency of the payroll process and the other protects disbursements of pay.

Exhibit 10-10 Employee Earnings Record for 2003

EMPLOYEE NAME AND ADDRESS:

DEAN, R. C.
4376 PALM DRIVE
FORT LAUDERDALE, FL 33317

SOCIAL SECURITY NO.: 344-86-4529
MARITAL STATUS: MARRIED
WITHHOLDING EXEMPTIONS: 4
PAY RATE: $400 PER WEEK
JOB TITLE: SALESPERSON

| Week Ended | Hrs. | Gross Pay | | | | Deductions | | | | Net Pay | |
		Straight-Time	Over-time	Total	To Date	Federal Income Tax	FICA Tax	United Way Charity	Total	Amount	Check No.
Dec. 24	48	400.00	120.00	520.00	22,720.00	66.75	39.78	2.00	108.53	411.47	1598
Dec. 31	46	400.00	90.00	490.00	23,210.00	59.94	37.49	2.00	99.43	390.57	1622
Total		20,800.00	2,410.00	23,210.00		1,946.72	1,775.57	104.00	3,826.29	19,383.71	

EFFICIENCY

Reconciling the bank account can be time-consuming because of many outstanding payroll checks. To reduce the number of outstanding checks for the payroll bank account, many companies actually use two bank accounts for payroll transactions. They pay the payroll from one bank account one month and from the other payroll account the next month. This way they can reconcile each account every other month, which makes the reconciliation process faster and smoother.

Payroll transactions are ideal for computer processing. Employee payroll data are stored in a file. The computer makes all pay and deduction calculations, prints the payroll register and the paychecks, and updates employee earnings records electronically. Also, because of the time and effort involved in accounting for payroll, many companies, such as ADP, Paychex, and Ceridian, handle payroll processes for other businesses and charge a fee for this service.

SAFEGUARDING PAYROLL DISBURSEMENTS

Owners and managers of small businesses can monitor their payrolls by personal contact with employees. Large corporations cannot. A particular risk is that a paycheck may be written to a fictitious person and cashed by a dishonest employee. To guard against this and other crimes, large businesses typically adopt strict internal control policies for payrolls.

The duties of hiring and firing employees should be separated from payroll accounting and from passing out paychecks. Issuing paychecks to employees with a photo ID ensures that only actual employees receive pay. A formal timekeeping system helps ensure that employees actually worked the number of hours claimed. Employees may punch time cards at the start and end of the workday to prove their attendance and number of hours worked.

Separation of duties does play a critical role in a sound internal control system, so companies should have separate departments for the following payroll functions:

- Human resources hires and fires employees.

- Payroll maintains employee earnings records.

- Accounting records all transactions.

- The treasurer distributes paychecks to employees.

Payroll Entries

Businesses continue the payroll process by recording payroll transactions. The payroll register serves as a key source of information necessary to record the three types of payroll transactions that occur on a regular basis.

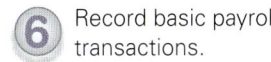

6 Record basic payroll transactions.

Record Employee Compensation

Employers record the expense of compensating employees as well as the liabilities for amounts withheld from compensation. The payroll register serves as the source of the information necessary to make these journal entries.

To illustrate, let's assume that AgriChem employs five employees. First, it records the journal entry for May's monthly gross payroll of $10,000. Withholding deductions include employee income tax of $1,200, FICA tax of $765 ($10,000 × 0.0765), and contributions to Habitat for Humanity of $140. AgriChem increases Salary Expense for the gross pay of $10,000, increases liability accounts for amounts deducted, and increases Salary Payable for the net pay amount as follows:

Journal Entry:

Date	Accounts	Post Ref.	Dr.	Cr.
May 31	Salary Expense		10,000	
	Employee Income Tax Payable			1,200
	FICA Tax Payable			765
	Payable to Habitat for Humanity			140
	Salary Payable			7,895
	Record May payroll.			

Record Employer Payroll Taxes and Contributions to Employee Benefits

Remember that employers are obligated to pay social security and unemployment taxes. The tax amounts are also an expense of the employer because they add to the cost of having employees. Employers may choose to pay for health insurance, contribute to retirement plans, or provide other incentives to obtain and motivate employees. Again, these expenses are related to employees' work. Here are the calculations for the AgriChem's May employer payroll taxes:

FICA Tax Payable ($10,000 × 0.0765)	$ 765
State Unemployment Tax Payable ($10,000 × 0.054)	540
Federal Unemployment Tax Payable ($10,000 × 0.008)	80
Total Payroll Tax Expense	$1,385

AgriChem increases Payroll Tax Expense for the total tax amounts, and increases liabilities as follows:

Journal Entry:

Date	Accounts	Post Ref.	Dr.	Cr.
May 31	Payroll Tax Expense		1,385	
	FICA Tax Payable			765
	State Unemployment Tax Payable			540
	Federal Unemployment Tax Payable			80
	Record May employer payroll taxes.			

Employers must also record the company's contributions to employee benefits. AgriChem pays for health and life insurance on its employees, a common practice. It also pays cash into a retirement plan for the benefit of employees after they retire. The following entry records AgriChem's liability for these amounts:

Journal Entry:

Date	Accounts	Post Ref.	Dr.	Cr.
May 31	Health Insurance Expense		800	
	Life Insurance Expense		200	
	Retirement Expense		500	
	Employee Benefits Payable			1,500
	Record May employer-paid employee benefits.			

Record Payments of Compensation, Taxes, and Benefits

Most employers must record at least three cash payments for payrolls.

NET PAY TO EMPLOYEES

When companies pay employees, they decrease Salary Payable and Cash. Using AgriChem's data in the previous section, the company would make the following entry to record the cash payment for the May payroll:

Journal Entry:

Date	Accounts	Post Ref.	Dr.	Cr.
May 31	Salary Payable		7,895	
	Cash			7,895
	Record payment of May payroll.			

PAYROLL TAXES AND OTHER DEDUCTIONS

Employers must send the government two sets of payroll taxes: those withheld from employees' pay and those paid by the employer. Due dates vary depending on the tax being paid and the amount of the tax, but the payment itself is illustrated here, assuming that all amounts are paid at the end of the payroll period. Based on the AgriChem data in the previous section, the business would decrease the liability accounts and Cash:

Journal Entry:

Date	Accounts	Post Ref.	Dr.	Cr.
May 31	Employee Income Tax Payable		1,200	
	FICA Tax Payable ($765 × 2)		1,530	
	Payable to Habitat for Humanity		140	
	State Unemployment Tax Payable		540	
	Federal Unemployment Tax Payable		80	
	Cash			3,490
	Record payment of May payroll taxes			
	and other deductions.			

BENEFITS

Employers that pay for employees' insurance coverage and retirement plans need to write checks to fulfill these obligations. If the total cash payment for these benefits is $1,500, AgriChem reduces the payable account and Cash:

Journal Entry:

Date	Accounts	Post Ref.	Dr.	Cr.
May 31	Employee Benefits Payable		1,500	
	Cash			1,500
	Record payment of May payroll benefit amounts.			

‧‧‧‧‧‧ Reporting Current Liabilities

At the end of each accounting period, companies report all of their current liabilities on the balance sheet. At December 31, 2006, Hamburg Homes had the current liabilities shown in Exhibit 10-11. Hamburg combines all payroll liabilities under a single heading, Compensation, Tax, and Benefits Payable.

 Report current liabilities on the balance sheet.

  Management can fraudulently report liabilities. As discussed in Chapter 6, managers may be tempted to show a higher level of income in order to raise money from investors, obtain a bank loan, or to just keep their job by making the company look more successful than it is. Thus, managers may be tempted to overlook some expenses and liabilities at the end of the accounting period and deliberately not make necessary accruals. For example, a company can fail to accrue

Exhibit 10-11	Current Liabilities on the Balance Sheet
Current liabilities:	
Accounts payable	$ 6,400
Compensation, tax, and benefits payable	3,800
Unearned revenue	4,500
Other accrued liabilities	5,700
Total current liabilities	$20,400

estimated warranty expense, which would cause total liabilities and expenses to be understated and net income to be overstated.

Contingent liabilities pose a particularly big challenge to ethical financial reporting. Because contingencies are potential liabilities, not real liabilities, they are easy to overlook. However, a contingent liability can be an amount material to the financial position of a business. Failure to recognize contingent liabilities that should be recorded as liabilities misstates both the balance sheet and income statement. Misleading information can harm stakeholders. Falsifying financial statements can also ruin the reputation of a company and can land the perpetrator in prison.

Demo Doc

Known and Estimated Current Liabilities

Learning Objectives 1, 2

Alexander Inc. began operations on January 1, 2008, selling personal music players. Each player comes with a one-year warranty included in the selling price. Alexander also sells digital songs that owners can download and play back on their players. Customers prepay $100 for 100 songs and can download them whenever they wish.

During 2008, Alexander had the following information:

Sales Revenue from Sale of Music Players Sold to Customers....	$100,000
Manufacturing Cost of Music Players Sold to Customers	$ 40,000
Sales Tax Rate (sales tax charged on player sales only).............	7%
Music Downloads Purchased by Customers	20,000 songs
Songs Downloaded by Customers	6,000 songs
Repairs Made to Players Under Warranty	$ 1,200

Alexander estimates that the repairs they will have to make to music players under the warranty provided will cost 2% of the selling price. Alexander has contracted with a local repair shop to service any players required for upfront cash payment.

At December 31, 2008, Alexander estimated that of the remaining prepaid music downloads, 10,000 songs would be downloaded in 2009, with the rest downloaded in 2010.

Requirements

1. Journalize the following transactions:

   a. The sale of all music players in 2008 (assume cash sales)

   b. Payment of the year's sales taxes to the state government

   c. The sale of music downloads in 2008 (assume cash sales)

   d. Song downloads in 2008

   e. Repairs made under warranty in 2008

2. Are the following liabilities current or long-term for Alexander?

   a. Sales Tax Payable

   b. Unearned Music Downloads Revenue

   c. Estimated Warranty Payable

Demo Doc Solutions

Requirement 1

① Account for current liabilities of known amount.

② Account for estimated and contingent liabilities.

Journalize the following transactions:

Part 1	Part 2	Demo Doc Complete

a. The sale of all music players in 2008 (assume cash sales)

When the players are sold, a number of accounts are affected. First, Alexander must record the sales revenue and cash collected. We are told in the problem that $100,000 of music players were sold, so Sales Revenue—Players increases (credit) by $100,000.

Cash also increases, but is $100,000 the *only* amount the customers paid? No, in addition to selling price, customers must also pay sales tax when they buy a player. The total cash paid by customers was $107,000 [$100,000 + ($100,000 × 7%)]. So Cash is increased (debit) by $107,000.

The extra $7,000 ($100,000 × 7%) collected by Alexander *does not belong* to Alexander. It belongs to the state government. Because Alexander is now holding money that does not belong to the company, Alexander must pay it to its rightful owner. A future payment (or *obligation*) is a liability. Alexander must record (credit) a Sales Tax Payable of $7,000.

Journal Entry:

Date	Accounts	Post Ref.	Dr.	Cr.
	Cash ($100,000 × 1.07)		107,000	
	Sales Revenue—Players			100,000
	Sales Tax Payable ($100,000 × 7%)			7,000
	Record sales for cash.			

In addition to recording the sales revenue, Alexander must record the cost of the players. The players cost $40,000 to manufacture, so we must record (debit) Cost of Goods Sold for $40,000. As the players are sold, Inventory is also decreased (credit) by $40,000.

Journal Entry:

Date	Accounts	Post Ref.	Dr.	Cr.
	Cost of Goods Sold		40,000	
	Inventory			40,000
	Record cost of sales.			

One other issue must be addressed when recording the sales of the players: the warranties included in the selling price. Warranty costs are recorded *at the time of sale* to have proper matching (the expense of the warranty is recorded *at the same time* as the sales revenue).

Alexander estimates that the warranty costs will be 2% of selling price, so Alexander must record (debit) Warranty Expense for $2,000 ($100,000 × 2%). Alexander is now *obligated* to pay for these repairs when customer players break down. In accounting, *a future obligation is a liability*. So Alexander must record an Estimated Warranty Payable liability (credit) of $2,000.

Journal Entry:

Date	Accounts	Post Ref.	Dr.	Cr.
	Warranty Expense ($100,000 × 0.02)		2,000	
	Estimated Warranty Payable			2,000
	Record estimated warranty expense.			

b. Payment of the year's sales taxes to the state government

The sales taxes must be sent to the state government. When this payment is made, Sales Tax Payable is decreased (debit) by $7,000 and Cash is decreased (credit) by $7,000.

Journal Entry:

Date	Accounts	Post Ref.	Dr.	Cr.
	Sales Tax Payable		7,000	
	Cash			7,000
	Record payment of sales tax collected.			

Notice that this entry is nearly identical to the entry to record payment of general accounts payable because the transaction is nearly identical: that of a liability being paid in cash.

c. The sale of music downloads in 2008 (assume cash sales)

The customer pays for the music downloads before they receive them. In other words, Alexander has received the cash but not provided the songs yet. So, *for Alexander, this is a liability* of unearned revenue. Alexander has an *obligation* (a liability) to provide these songs to the customer.

Alexander *has not yet earned* the download revenue because they have not yet provided the songs to customers. Revenue will be earned as customers download their songs.

With 20,000 songs prepaid for $1 per song, we must record Unearned Music Downloads Revenue (credit) of $20,000 (20,000 × $1). We must also record an increase in Cash (debit) of $20,000.

Journal Entry:

Date	Accounts	Post Ref.	Dr.	Cr.
	Cash		20,000	
	Unearned Music Downloads Revenue			20,000
	Record cash received for music downloads in advance of providing songs.			

d. Song downloads in 2008

Once songs are downloaded, Alexander earns the revenue from the sale of the songs. Then, they record Sales Revenue—Music Downloads of $6,000 (6,000 × $1). Because Alexander is now meeting its obligation to its customers by providing songs, the Unearned Music Downloads Revenue account is decreased (debit) by $6,000.

Journal Entry:

Date	Accounts	Post Ref.	Dr.	Cr.
	Unearned Music Downloads Revenue		6,000	
	Sales Revenue—Music Downloads (6,000 × $1)			6,000
	Record downloads revenue earned.			

After this transaction is recorded, the Unearned Revenue and related Sales Revenue accounts are as follows:

Unearned Music Downloads Revenue		Sales Revenues—Music Downloads	
	Downloads Prepaid 20,000		6,000
Songs Downloaded 6,000			
	Dec. 31 Bal. 14,000		

e. Repairs made under warranty in 2008

When repairs are made under warranty, Alexander's obligation to pay for these repairs is being met. This causes Estimated Warranty Payable to decrease (debit) by $1,200.

The repairs are being paid for in cash, so Cash is also decreased (credit) by $1,200.

Journal Entry:

Date	Accounts	Post Ref.	Dr.	Cr.
	Estimated Warranty Payable		1,200	
	Cash			1,200
	Record payment of warranty claims.			

Notice that warranty expense is *not* affected by this transaction! The expense was *already* recorded back when the players were sold (see transaction **a**). To record warranty expense now would be double-counting.

After this transaction is recorded, the warranty-related accounts are as follows:

Estimated Warranty Payable			Warranty Expense	
	Players Sold	2,000	2,000	
Repairs Made 1,200				
	Dec. 31 Bal.	800		

Requirement 2

Are the following liabilities current or long-term for Alexander?

Part 1	Part 2	Demo Doc Complete

① Account for current liabilities of known amount.

② Account for estimated and contingent liabilities.

a. Sales Tax Payable

Governments usually do not want to wait long for their money. Most sales taxes are remitted to the government within one month of being collected (often sooner). In this example, Alexander already remitted the 2008 sales before the end of the year. A real company could send sales tax collections to the state government once a month.

Because sales tax liabilities are paid well within one year, the Sales Tax Payable account is a current liability.

b. Unearned Music Downloads Revenue

The prepaid music downloads are unearned revenue. But when will that revenue be earned? In 2008, 6,000 songs were downloaded, and Alexander expects that another 10,000 will be downloaded in 2009, with the remaining 4,000 songs (20,000 – 6,000 – 10,000) being downloaded in 2010.

At December 31, 2008, Alexander has an Unearned Music Downloads Revenue liability of $14,000 for 14,000 songs (see transaction **d**). Of this $14,000, $10,000 is a current liability (because it will be earned during the next year of 2009 as songs are downloaded) and $4,000 is a long-term liability (for songs downloaded after 2009).

c. Estimated Warranty Payable

Warranties can cover many years, so it is possible that an Estimated Warranty Payable liability could have both current and long-term portions (as Alexander's Unearned Revenue does). However, the warranties Alexander provides are only one year long, so we know that all obligations under the warranty will be met within one year. Therefore the entire Estimated Warranty Payable is a current liability.

Part 1	Part 2	Demo Doc Complete

Accounting in Action

Suppose you manage a CompUSA store near your college and employ 10 people. What decisions must you make to account for liabilities and payroll properly?

Decision	Guidelines

What are the basic categories of current liabilities?

- Current liabilities of *known amount*
- Current liabilities that must be *estimated*
- *Contingent*, or potential, current liabilities

How do you evaluate current liabilities?

Compute:
- *Current ratio*
- *Working capital*

What payroll amounts do you calculate?

Gross pay
  − *Employee payroll deductions*
  - *Employee income tax*
  - *Social security (FICA) tax*
  - Optional deductions
= *Net, or take-home, pay*
Employer taxes
  - *Social security (FICA) tax*
  - *State unemployment tax (SUTA)*
  - *Federal unemployment tax (FUTA)*

What are the key elements of the payroll process?

- *Form W-4, Employee's Withholding Allowance Certificate*
- *Payroll register*
- *Payroll checks*
- *Employer tax returns, Forms 940 and 941*
- *Employee earnings record*
- *Form W-2, Wage and Tax Statement*

How do you record payroll?

Record:
- Employee compensation and deductions
- Employer payroll taxes and contributions to employee benefits
- Payment of compensation, taxes, and benefits
  - Net pay
  - Payroll taxes and other deductions
  - Benefits

Review

Current Liabilities and Payroll
Word Power

Accrued expense An expense that the business has incurred but not yet paid; also called *accrued liability*.

Accrued liability An expense that the business has incurred but not yet paid; also called *accrued expense*.

Bonus Pay for exceptional performance over and above the base salary, wage, or commission.

Commission Pay stated as a percentage of a sale amount.

Contingent liability A potential liability that is dependent on a future event.

Cosign To sign a note payable with the borrower on behalf of the borrower; if the borrower fails to pay, the cosigner is responsible for paying the principal and interest of the note.

Current portion of long-term notes payable Amount of the principal that is payable within one year and must be shown as a current liability.

Current ratio The ratio of current assets to current liabilities; a key measure of liquidity.

Deductions Amounts withheld from employees' gross pay.

Employee compensation A major expense of businesses with employees; also called *payroll*.

Employee earnings record Payroll record that contains the pay information of an employee.

Fair Labor Standards Act Federal law that regulates overtime pay.

Federal Insurance Contributions Act (FICA) Federal law that created the social security tax as well as the unemployment tax; also called the *Social Security Act*.

Federal unemployment tax (FUTA) Federal tax, paid by employers, that provides unemployment compensation.

Form W-2, Wage and Tax Statement Internal Revenue Service form prepared by employers used to report employee earnings and withholdings for a calendar year.

Form W-4, Employee's Withholding Allowance Certificate Internal Revenue Service form completed by employees upon hire to report marital status and withholding allowances.

Form 940, Employer's Annual Federal Unemployment (FUTA) Tax Return Internal Revenue Service form prepared by employers annually to report earnings subject to unemployment tax and the amount of the unemployment tax on those earnings.

Form 941, Employer's Quarterly Federal Tax Return Internal Revenue Service form prepared by employers quarterly to report employee compensation, the amount of federal income tax withheld, and FICA taxes owed on compensation.

Gross pay Total amount of salary, wages, commission, bonus, or any other employee compensation before taxes and other deductions.

Income tax withheld Amount of income tax deducted from gross pay.

Net pay Gross pay minus all deductions; also called take-home pay.

Payroll A major expense of businesses with employees; also called *employee compensation*.

Payroll register Payroll record that contains information about a pay period.

Salary A set amount of pay for a period of time such as a year, month, or week.

Social Security Act Federal law that created the social security tax as well as the unemployment tax.; also called the *Federal Insurance Contributions Act (FICA)*.

Social security tax Federal Insurance Contributions Act (FICA) tax, which is withheld from employees' pay and paid by the employer.

State unemployment tax (SUTA) State tax, mandated by the federal government and paid by employers, that provides unemployment compensation.

Take-home pay Gross pay minus all deductions; also called *net pay*.

Wage A pay amount stated at an hourly rate.

Warranty expense Expense of selling a product with a warranty that guarantees the product against defects.

Withholding allowances Allowances claimed for self, spouse, and dependents, which reduce the amount of income tax withheld from gross pay.

Working capital The excess of current assets over current liabilities; a key measure of liquidity.

Quick Check

1. Known liabilities of uncertain amounts should be

    a. Estimated and accrued when they occur
    b. Ignored; record them when paid
    c. Reported on the income statement
    d. Described in the notes to the financial statements

2. On January 1, 2006, you borrowed $10,000 on a five-year, 8% note payable. At December 31, 2007, you should record

    a. Note payable of $10,000
    b. Nothing ; the note has already been recorded
    c. Interest payable of $800
    d. Cash receipt of $10,000

3. Your company sells $100,000 of goods and you collect sales tax of 3%. What current liability does the sale create?

    a. Accounts Payable of $3,000
    b. Unearned Revenue of $3,000
    c. Sales Revenue of $103,000
    d. Sales Tax Payable of $3,000

4. At December 31, your company owes employees for three days of the five-day workweek. The total payroll for the week is $8,000. What journal entry should you make at December 31?

    a. Nothing, because you will pay the employees on Friday

Journal Entry:

Date	Accounts	Post Ref.	Dr.	Cr.
b.	Salary Expense		8,000	
	Salary Payable			8,000
c.	Salary Expense		4,800	
	Salary Payable			4,800
d.	Salary Expense		3,200	
	Cash			3,200

5. How is unearned revenue shown on a classified balance sheet?

    a. Receivable
    b. Current liability
    c. Revenue
    d. Current asset

6. Sony owed Estimated Warranty Payable of $1,000 at the end of 2006. During 2007, Sony made sales of $100,000 and expects product warranties to cost the company 3% of the sales. During 2007, Sony paid $2,500 for warranties. What is Sony's Estimated Warranty Payable at the end of 2007?

a. $1,500
b. $2,500
c. $3,000
d. $3,500

7. Payroll expenses of the employer include

a. Salaries and wages
b. Employee benefits paid by the employer
c. Employer payroll taxes
d. All of the above

8. What is the most that an employee paid the federal government for OASDI tax during 2006?

a. $5,840.40
b. $94,200
c. Nothing. The employer paid it
d. There is no limit

9. What document does an employer give to each employee at the end of the year to report annual earnings and taxes paid?

a. Payroll register
b. Form 941
c. Form W-2
d. Form W-4

10. The foundation of internal control over payrolls is

a. Paying the correct amount of payroll tax
b. Accurately computing gross pay, deductions, and net pay
c. Filing government tax forms on time
d. Separating payroll duties

Answers are given after Apply Your Knowledge (p. 567).

Accounting Practice

Short Exercises

1 Accounting for current liabilities of known amount.

S10-1. On June 30, 2007, Harper Co. purchased $9,000 of inventory for a one-year, 9% note payable. Journalize the following for the company:

1. Accrual of interest expense on December 31, 2007

2. Payment of the note plus interest on June 30, 2008

1 Accounting for current liabilities of known amount.

S10-2. Refer to the data in S10-1. What amounts would Harper Co. report for the note payable and the related interest payable on its balance sheet at December 31, 2007, and on its income statement for the year ended December 31, 2007?

2 Accounting for estimated and contingent liabilities.

S10-3. Lake Country Boats guarantees its boats for three years or 36,000 miles, whichever comes first. Past experience of other boat makers indicates that Lake Country can expect that warranty costs will equal 5% of sales. Assume that in its first year Lake Country Boats made sales totaling $600,000, receiving cash for 30% of sales and notes receivable for the remainder. Warranty payments totaled $25,000 during the year.

1. Record the sales, warranty expense, and warranty payments for Lake Country Boats.

2. Post relevant portions of the journal entries to the Estimated Warranty Payable T-account. At the end of the first year, how much in estimated warranty payable does Lake Country owe its customers?

2 Accounting for estimated and contingent liabilities.

S10-4. Refer to the data given in S10-3. What amount of warranty expense will Lake Country report during its first year of operations? Does the warranty expense for the year equal the year's cash payments for warranties? Which accounting principle addresses this situation? Explain how this accounting principle applies to warranty expense.

2 Accounting for estimated and contingent liabilities.

S10-5. Harley-Davidson, Inc., the motorcycle manufacturer, included the following note (adapted) in its annual report:

Notes to Consolidated Financial Statements

7: Commitments and Contingencies (Adapted)

The Company self-insures its product liability losses in the United States up to $3 million.

Catastrophic coverage is maintained for individual claims in excess of $3 million up to $25 million.

1. Why are these liabilities considered contingent?

2. How can a contingent liability become a real liability for Harley-Davidson?

S10-6. Gene Oldham is paid $600 for a 40-hour week and time-and-a-half for hours above 40.

④ Calculating payroll amounts.

1. Compute Oldham's gross pay for working 50 hours during the first week of February.

2. Oldham's income tax withholding is 10% of total pay. His only payroll deductions are payroll taxes. Compute Oldham's net pay for the week, using a 7.65% FICA tax rate and assuming his total earnings are still below $94,200 for the year.

S10-7. Refer to S10-6. Oldham's employer, Bobby King Golf Company, pays all employer payroll taxes plus benefits for employee retirements at 5% of total pay, health insurance of $60 per employee per month, and disability insurance of $8 per employee per month. Compute Bobby King's total expense of employing Gene Oldham for the 50 hours that he worked during the first week of February. Assume that Oldham has made less than $7,000. Carry amounts to the nearest cent.

④ Calculating payroll amounts.

S10-8. Refer to S10-6 and S10-7. Record the following for Bobby King Golf Company:

⑥ Recording payroll transactions.

1. Employee compensation

2. Employer payroll taxes and contributions to employee benefits

S10-9. Suppose you work for an accounting firm all year and earn a monthly salary of $8,000. No overtime is paid. Your withheld income taxes consume 15% of gross pay. In addition to payroll taxes, you elect to contribute 5% monthly to your retirement plan. Your employer also deducts $200 monthly for your co-payment of the health insurance premium. Compute your net pay for November. Use a 7.65% FICA tax rate, and assume that total earnings for the year are still less than $94,200.

④ Calculating payroll amounts.

S10-10. The following information was taken from Harper Company's payroll register for the month of June.

⑥ Recording payroll transactions.

Employee Earnings:	
Regular employee earnings........................	$17,500.00
Overtime pay..	7,500.00
Gross employee earnings...........................	$25,000.00
Deductions and Net Pay:	
Income tax withheld..................................	$ 2,300.00
FICA tax...	1,912.50
Charitable contributions	400.00
Medical insurance......................................	700.00
Total deductions..	5,312.50
Net pay	$19,687.50
Account Debited:	
Salary Expense	$25,000.00

Prepare the journal entry to record employee compensation.

5 Describing the payroll process.

S10-11. What are some of the important elements of good internal control to safeguard payroll disbursements?

7 Reporting current liabilities.

S10-12. Hi Range Sports' payroll register for the week ended December 31, 2007, included these totals:

		Withholding Deductions				
	Federal		Habitat			
Gross Pay	Income Tax	FICA Tax	for Humanity	Total	Net Pay
$ 8,000	$ 750	$ 612	$ 110	$ 1,472	$ 6,528

In addition to the payroll liabilities shown, Hi Range Sports has the following current liabilities at December 31, 2007:

Accounts Payable	$44,000
FICA Tax Payable (employer portion)	612

Prepare the current liabilities section of Hi Range's balance sheet at December 31, 2007. List current liabilities in descending order, starting with the largest first, including the payroll liabilities. Show total current liabilities.

3 Calculating the current ratio and working capital.

S10-13. Using the current liability amounts from S10-12 and assuming that current assets total $62,000, calculate the following for Hi Range Sports:

1. Current ratio

2. Working capital

Exercises

1 Accounting for current liabilities of known amount.

E10-14. Make journal entries to record the following transactions. Explanations are not required.

Mar. 31	Recorded cash sales of $200,000 for the month, plus sales tax of 4% collected for the state of Illinois.
Apr. 6	Sent March sales tax to the state.

1 Accounting for current liabilities of known amount.

E10-15. Record the following note payable transactions of Lisbon Corp. in the company's journal. Explanations are not required.

2006	
May 1	Purchased equipment costing $15,000 by issuing a one-year, 6% note payable.
Dec. 31	Accrued interest on the note payable.

continued.....

2007	
May 1	Paid the note payable at maturity.

E10-16. Ozark Publishing Company completed the following transactions during 2007:

① Accounting for current liabilities of known amount.

Nov. 1	Sold a six-month subscription, collecting cash of $180, plus sales tax of 5%.
Dec. 15	Remitted the sales tax to the state of Illinois.
31	Made the necessary adjustment at year-end to record the amount of subscription revenue earned during the year.

Journalize these transactions. Explanations are not required. Then report the liability on the company's balance sheet at December 31, 2007.

E10-17. The accounting records of Osgood Carpets included the following at December 31, 2007:

② Accounting for estimated and contingent liabilities.

Estimated Warranty Payable	
	Bal. 3,000

In the past, Osgood's warranty expense has been 6% of sales. During 2008, Osgood made sales of $200,000 and paid $10,000 to satisfy warranty claims.

Requirements

1. Journalize Osgood's warranty expense and cash payments made to satisfy warranty claims during 2008. Explanations are not required.

2. What balance of Estimated Warranty Payable will Osgood report on its balance sheet at December 31, 2008?

E10-18. Lydia Gomez manages the women's sportswear department of Los Mariposas Department Store. She earns a base monthly salary of $750 plus a 10% commission on her personal sales. Through payroll deductions, Gomez donates $25 per month to a charitable organization, and she authorizes Los Mariposas to deduct $20 monthly for her health insurance. Tax rates on Gomez's earnings are 10% for income tax, 6.2% of the first $94,200 for OASDI tax, and 1.45% for Medicare tax. During the first 11 months of the year, she earned $87,000.

④ Calculating payroll amounts.

Requirements

Compute Gomez's gross pay and net pay for December, assuming her sales for the month are $80,000.

4 Calculating payroll amounts.

6 Recording payroll transactions.

E10-19. Mel Morgan works as a cook for an Applebee's diner. His regular pay rate is $10 per hour, with time-and-a-half for hours in excess of 40 per week. Morgan's payroll deductions include withheld income tax of 7% of total earnings, FICA tax of 7.65% of total earnings, and a weekly deduction of $5 for a charitable contribution to United Way. Assume his total earnings for the year to date are less than $94,200.

Requirements

Assuming Morgan worked 50 hours during the week, (a) compute his gross pay and net pay for the week and (b) make a journal entry to record employee compensation for Morgan's work, including payroll deductions. Explanations are not required.

4 Calculating payroll amounts.

6 Recording payroll transactions.

E10-20. The records of Friendly Food Service show the following figures:

Employee Earnings	
Regular earnings	$ (a)
Overtime pay	5,100
Total employee earnings	88,994
Deductions and Net Pay	
Withheld income tax	$ 9,300
FICA tax	(b)
Charitable contributions	(c)
Medical insurance	1,372
Total deductions	18,880
Net pay	70,114
Account Debited	
Salary Expense	$ (d)

Requirements

Determine the missing amounts on lines (a) through (d).

4 Calculating payroll amounts.

6 Recording payroll transactions.

E10-21. Picacho Hills Golf Course incurred total salary expense of $92,000 for December. The pro shop's payroll taxes include employer FICA tax of 7.65% in addition to state unemployment tax of 5.4% and federal unemployment tax of 0.8%. Of the total salaries, $90,000 is subject to OASDI tax, and $9,000 is subject to unemployment tax. Also, the store provides the following benefits for employees: health insurance, $2,060; life insurance, $350; and retirement benefits, 6% of salary expense.

Requirements

Record Picacho Hills' employer payroll taxes and its expenses for employee benefits. Explanations are not required.

E10-22. Jupiter Technologies has annual salary expense of $600,000. In addition, Jupiter incurs payroll tax expense equal to 9% of the total payroll. At December 31, Jupiter owes salaries of $4,000 and FICA and other payroll taxes of $1,000. Jupiter will pay these amounts early next year.

7 Reporting current liabilities.

Requirements

Show what Jupiter will report for these amounts on its income statement and year-end balance sheet.

E10-23. Carruthers Medical Group borrowed $3 million on January 2, 2006, by issuing a 9% long-term note payable that must be paid in three equal annual installments plus interest each January 2.

1 Accounting for current liabilities of known amount.

Requirements

Insert the appropriate amounts to show how Carruthers would report its current and long-term liabilities.

	December 31		
	2006	2007	2008
Current Liabilities:			
Current Portion of Long-Term Note Payable ... $ _____	$ _____	$ _____	
Interest Payable... _____	_____	_____	
Long-Term Liabilities:			
Long-Term Note Payable.................................... _____	_____	_____	

E10-24. Assume that Wilson Sporting Goods completed these selected transactions during December 2007:

7 Reporting current liabilities.

    a. Sales of $500,000 are subject to estimated warranty cost of 3%.

    b. Champs, a chain of sporting goods stores, ordered $9,000 of tennis and golf equipment. With its order, Champs sent a check for $9,000 in advance. Wilson will ship the goods on January 3, 2008.

    c. The December payroll of $200,000 is subject to employee-withheld income tax of 9%, FICA tax of 7.65%, state unemployment tax of 5.4%, and federal unemployment tax of 0.8%. On December 31, Wilson pays employees but accrues all tax amounts.

Requirements

Report each item at its correct amount on Wilson's balance sheet at December 31, 2007. Show total current liabilities.

E10-25. Using the information from E10-24 and assuming that Wilson has current assets of $150,000, calculate its (a) current ratio and (b) working capital.

Problems (Group A)

③ Calculating the current
ratio and working
capital.

① Accounting for current
liabilities of known
amount.

② Accounting for esti-
mated and contingent
liabilities.

P10-26A. The following transactions of My Dollar stores occurred during 2006 and 2007:

2006		
Feb.	3	Purchased equipment for $10,000, signing a six-month, 9% note payable.
	28	Recorded the week's sales of $51,000, one-third for cash, and two-thirds on account. All sales amounts are subject to a 5% sales tax.
Mar.	7	Sent last week's sales tax to the state.
Apr.	30	Borrowed $100,000 on a four-year, 9% note payable that calls for annual payment of interest each April 30.
Aug.	3	Paid the six-month, 9% note at maturity.
Nov.	30	Purchased inventory at a cost of $7,200, signing a three-month, 8% note payable for that amount.
Dec.	31	Accrued warranty expense, which is estimated at 3% of total sales of $260,000.
	31	Accrued interest on all outstanding notes payable. Accrue interest for each note separately.

2007		
Feb.	28	Paid off the 8% inventory note, plus interest, at maturity.
Apr.	30	Paid the interest for one year on the long-term note payable.

Requirements

Record the transactions in the company's journal. Explanations are not required.

④ Calculating payroll
amounts.

⑥ Recording payroll
transactions.

P10-27A. Alicia Summers is a vice president at Harbor State Bank in Boston. During 2007, she worked for the bank all year at a $6,500 monthly salary. She also earned a year-end bonus equal to 15% of her annual salary.

Summers's federal income tax withheld during 2007 was $820 per month, plus $2,480 on her bonus check. State income tax withheld came to $60 per month, plus $80 on the bonus. The FICA tax withheld was 7.65% of the first $94,200 of annual earnings. Summers authorized the following payroll deductions: United Way contribution of 1% of total earnings and life insurance of $20 per month.

Harbor State Bank incurred payroll tax expense on Summers for FICA tax of 7.65% of the first $94,200 in total annual earnings. The bank also paid state unemployment tax of 5.4% and federal unemployment tax of 0.8% on the first $7,000 in annual earnings. The bank provided Summers with the following benefits: health insurance at a cost of $40 per month, and retirement benefits of $4,000 for 2007.

continued.....

Requirements

1. Compute Summers's gross pay, payroll deductions, and net pay during 2007.

2. Compute the bank's total 2007 payroll expense for Summers.

3. Prepare the bank's summary journal entries to record:

   a. Summers' total earnings for the year, her payroll deductions, and her net pay. Debit Salary Expense and Executive Bonus Compensation Expense as appropriate. Credit appropriate liability accounts for the payroll deductions and Cash for net pay.

   b. Employer payroll taxes for Summers.

   c. Benefits provided to Summers.

Round all amounts to the nearest dollar. Explanations are not required.

P10-28A. The Emerson Technology ledger at September 30, 2008, the company's fiscal year end, includes the following account balances before adjusting entries:

1 Accounting for current liabilities of known amount.

6 Recording payroll transactions.

7 Reporting current liabilities.

Accounts Payable..	$ 88,200
Current Portion of Long-Term Notes Payable.........	_____
Interest Payable...	_____
Salary Payable..	_____
Employee Payroll Taxes Payable.............................	_____
Employer Payroll Taxes Payable.............................	_____
Unearned Rent Revenue...	3,900
Long-Term Notes Payable.......................................	100,000

The additional data needed to develop the adjusting entries at September 30 are as follows:

a. The long-term notes payable is payable in annual installments of $50,000, with the next installment due on January 31, 2009. On that date, Emerson will also pay one year's interest at 6.6%. Interest was last paid on January 31, 2008.

b. Gross salaries for the last payroll of the fiscal year were $4,300. Of this amount, employee payroll taxes were $950.

c. Employer payroll taxes on this payroll were $890.

d. On August 1, the company collected six months' rent of $3,900 in advance.

Requirements

1. Open the listed accounts and insert their unadjusted September 30 balances.

continued.....

2. Journalize and post the September 30 adjusting entries to the accounts opened. Label adjusting entries by letter.

3. Prepare the liabilities section of Emerson Technology's balance sheet at September 30, 2008. Show total current liabilities and total liabilities.

④ Calculating payroll amounts.

⑥ Recording payroll transactions.

P10-29A. The payroll records of a Diesel Recon district office provided the following information for the weekly pay period ended December 29, 2006:

Employee	Hours Worked	Weekly Earnings Rate	Federal Income Tax	Health Insurance	Earnings Through Previous Week
Clay Hipp...............	43	$ 400	$ 74	$ 16	$17,060
Tim LeMann..........	46	480	90	10	22,300
Lena North............	48	1,400	319	46	86,200
Karen York............	40	240	32	6	3,410

All employees are paid time-and-a-half their regular rate for hours worked in excess of 40 per week. Round all amounts to the nearest dollar. Show your computations. Explanations are not required for journal entries.

Requirements

1. Enter the appropriate information in a payroll register similar to Exhibit 10-7. In addition to the deductions listed, the employer also withholds FICA tax: 7.65% of the first $94,200 of each employee's annual earnings.

2. Record the employee compensation for the pay period.

3. Assume that the first payroll check is number 178, paid to Clay Hipp. Record the check numbers in the payroll register. Also, prepare the journal entry to record payment of net pay to the employees.

4. The employer's payroll taxes include FICA of 7.65% of the first $94,200 of each employee's annual earnings. The employer also pays unemployment taxes of 6.2%, 5.4% for the state and 0.8% for the federal government, on the first $7,000 of each employee's annual earnings. Record the employer's payroll taxes in the journal.

① Accounting for current liabilities of known amount.

② Accounting for estimated and contingent liabilities.

⑦ Reporting current liabilities.

P10-30A. Following are pertinent facts about events during the current year at Greely Snowboards.

a. December sales totaled $404,000, and Greely collected sales tax of 5%. The sales tax will be sent to the state of Washington early in January.

continued.....

b. Greely owes $75,000 on a long-term note payable. At December 31, 6% interest for the year plus $25,000 of principal are payable within one year.

c. On August 31, Greely signed a six-month, 6% note payable to purchase a machine costing $80,000. The note requires payment of principal and interest at maturity.

d. Sales of $909,000 were covered by the Greely product warranty. At January 1, estimated warranty payable was $11,300. During the year, Greely recorded warranty expense of $27,900 and paid warranty claims of $30,100.

e. On October 31, Greely received cash of $2,400 in advance for the rent on a building. This rent will be earned evenly over six months.

Requirements

For each item, indicate the account and the related amount to be reported as a current liability on Greely's December 31 balance sheet.

Problems (Group B)

P10-31B. The following transactions of Groban Accessories occurred during 2007 and 2008:

① Accounting for current liabilities of known amount.

② Accounting for estimated and contingent liabilities.

2007		
Jan. 9	Purchased equipment at a cost of $20,000, signing a six-month, 8% note payable for that amount.
29	Recorded the week's sales of $40,000, three-fourths on account, and one-fourth for cash. Sales amounts are subject to a 6% state sales tax.
Feb. 5	Sent last week's sales tax to the state.
28	Borrowed $200,000 on a four-year, 9% note payable that calls for annual installment payments of $50,000 principal plus interest.
July 9	Paid the six-month, 8% note at maturity.
Nov. 30	Purchased inventory for $3,000, signing a six-month, 10% note payable.
Dec. 31	Accrued warranty expense, which is estimated at 3% of total sales of $650,000.
31	Accrued interest on all outstanding notes payable. Accrue interest for each note separately.

2008	
Feb. 28	Paid the first installment and interest for one year on the long-term note payable.
May 31	Paid off the 10% note plus interest at maturity.

continued.....

Requirements

Round all amounts to the nearest dollar. Explanations are not required.

④ Calculating payroll amounts.

⑥ Recording payroll transactions.

P10-32B. Brenda Stevens is vice president of Finance for Interstate Leasing. During 2008, she worked for the company all year at a $6,625 monthly salary. She also earned a year-end bonus equal to 10% of her annual salary.

Stevens's federal income tax withheld during 2008 was $737 per month, plus $1,007 on her bonus check. State income tax withheld came to $43 per month, plus $27 on the bonus. The FICA tax withheld was 7.65% of the first $94,200 in annual earnings. Stevens authorized the following payroll deductions: United Way contribution of 1% of total earnings and life insurance of $19 per month.

Interstate incurred payroll tax expense on Stevens for FICA tax of 7.65% of the first $94,200 in annual earnings. The company also paid state unemployment tax of 5.4% and federal unemployment tax of 0.8% on the first $7,000 in annual earnings. In addition, Interstate provides Stevens with health insurance at a cost of $35 per month and retirement benefits of $7,000 for 2008.

Requirements

1. Compute Stevens's gross pay, payroll deductions, and net pay for 2008.

2. Compute Interstate's total 2008 payroll expense for Brenda Stevens.

3. Prepare Interstate's summary journal entries to record the following (explanations are not required):

   a. Stevens's total earnings for the year, her payroll deductions, and her net pay. Debit Salary Expense and Executive Bonus Compensation Expense as appropriate. Credit appropriate liability accounts for the payroll deductions and Cash for net pay.

   b. Employer payroll taxes on Stevens.

   c. Benefits provided to Stevens.

① Accounting for current liabilities of known amount.

⑥ Recording payroll transactions.

⑦ Reporting current liabilities.

P10-33B. The ledger of Red Brick Investments at June 30, 2008, the end of the company's fiscal year, includes the following account balances before adjusting entries:

Accounts Payable	$105,520
Current Portion of Long-Term Notes Payable	_____
Interest Payable	_____
Salary Payable	_____

continued.....

Employee Payroll Taxes Payable					_____
Employer Payroll Taxes Payable					_____
Unearned Rent Revenue					6,000
Long-Term Notes Payable					200,000

The additional data needed to develop the adjusting entries at June 30 are as follows:

a. The long-term notes payable is payable in annual installments of $40,000 with the next installment due on July 31. On that date, Red Brick will also pay one year's interest at 9%. Interest was last paid on July 31 of the preceding year.

b. Gross salaries for the last payroll of the fiscal year were $5,044. Of this amount, employee payroll taxes were $1,088.

c. Employer payroll taxes on this payroll were $876.

d. On February 1, the company collected one year's rent of $6,000 in advance.

Requirements

1. Open the listed accounts and insert the unadjusted June 30 balances.

2. Journalize and post the June 30 adjusting entries to the accounts opened. Identify adjusting entries by letter.

3. Prepare the liabilities section of the balance sheet at June 30, 2008. Show total current liabilities and total liabilities.

P10-34B. Assume that the payroll records of a district sales office of PetCo provided the following information for the weekly pay period ended December 29, 2006:

④ Calculating payroll amounts.

⑥ Recording payroll transactions.

Employee	Hours Worked	Hourly Earnings Rate	Federal Income Tax	United Fund Contributions	Earnings Through Previous Week
Larry Fist............	42	$40	$278	$35	$87,474
Felicia Green.......	47	8	87	4	23,154
Joe Oster.............	40	11	64	4	4,880
Sara Tate.............	46	35	288	8	86,600

Employees are paid time-and-a-half their regular rate for hours over 40 per week. Round all amounts to the nearest dollar. Show your computations. Explanations are not required for journal entries.

continued.....

1. Enter the appropriate information in a payroll register similar to Exhibit 10-7. In addition to the deductions listed, the employer also takes out FICA tax: 7.65% of the first $94,200 of each employee's annual earnings.

2. Record the employee compensation for the period.

3. Assume that the first payroll check is number 319, paid to Larry Fist. Record the check numbers in the payroll register. Also, prepare the journal entry to record payment of net pay to the employees.

4. The employer's payroll taxes include FICA tax of 7.65% of the first $94,200 of each employee's earnings. The employer also pays unemployment taxes of 6.2%, 5.4% for the state and 0.8% for the federal government, on the first $7,000 of each employee's annual earnings. Record the employer's payroll taxes in the journal.

① Accounting for current liabilities of known amount.

② Accounting for estimated and contingent liabilities.

⑦ Reporting current liabilities.

P10-35B. Following are pertinent facts about Falcon Jet's transactions during the current year.

a. On November 30, Falcon received cash of $6,000 in advance for the rent on a building. This rent will be earned evenly over three months.

b. December sales totaled $110,000, and Falcon collected a state sales tax of 7%. This amount will be sent to the state of Tennessee early in January.

c. Falcon owes $100,000 on a long-term note payable. At December 31, 6% interest on the full note and $20,000 of the principal are payable within one year.

d. Sales of $400,000 were covered by Falcon's product warranty. At January 1, estimated warranty payable was $8,000. During the year, Falcon recorded warranty expense of $22,000 and paid warranty claims of $24,000.

e. On September 30, Falcon signed a six-month, 9% note payable to purchase equipment costing $30,000. The note requires payment of principal and interest at maturity.

Requirements

For each item, indicate the account and the related amount to be reported as a current liability on Falcon's December 31 balance sheet.

Apply Your Knowledge

BE ON GUARD

Case 1. Alex met with his accountant to discuss the financial statements his business was submitting to the bank for a much needed loan. The accountant expressed concern over the total amount of current liabilities. Alex did not understand why his accountant was concerned because the total assets were $9,864,000 and the total liabilities were only $1,745,000, resulting in total equity of $8,119,000. The problem, the accountant believed, was in the classifications of the assets and liabilities. Even though the total assets were nearly $10 million, only $312,000 was current compared to $1,630,000 of current liabilities. The accountant said that the bankers would be worried because current assets available were less than the amount needed to cover the liabilities due within the next fiscal year. Alex still did not understand the problem; after all, his business had more total assets than total liabilities. His accountant showed him a current ratio of .19 to 1.00 ($312,000/$1,630,000), which meant that for every dollar of current liabilities there was only 19 cents of current assets. Alex then said he could simply sell off some equipment if necessary to pay any current liabilities that came due. His accountant explained that banks want to see how well businesses can meet current obligations without resorting to selling long-term assets. Given the situation, Alex told the accountant to simply reclassify the current liabilities to noncurrent and eliminate the problem. His accountant objected, stating that it would be unethical and misleading to reclassify the current liabilities. Alex could only see that all liabilities were obligations regardless of their due dates, and his total assets were plainly sufficient to cover liabilities.

What ethical concerns did the accountant have? Would it be acceptable to reclassify some of the current liabilities? Does Alex have a valid point that the business has sufficient assets available to cover all the liabilities? Could some of the noncurrent assets be reclassified as current to demonstrate liquidity? Do you have any suggestions?

Case 2. The Transmission Shop was the largest company in the state specializing in rebuilding automobile transmissions. Every transmission rebuilt by the business was covered by a six-month warranty. The owner, Ron Wood, was meeting with his accountant to go over the yearly financial statements. In reviewing the balance sheet, Ron became puzzled by the large amount of current liabilities being reported, so he asked his accountant to explain them. The accountant said that most of the current liabilities were the result of accruals, such as the estimated warranty payable, some additional wages payable, and interest accrued on the note owed to the bank. The employees were not actually paid until the first week of the new year, so some of their wages had to be recorded and properly matched against revenues in the current period. Also, several months of interest expense had to be accrued on a bank loan, but the largest amount of the accrued liabilities was due to the estimated warranty expense. Ron asked whether the wages payable and the interest payable could be removed because they would be paid off shortly after the year ended. The accountant stated that accrued liabilities had to be properly recognized in the current accounting period, and thus they could not be removed. Ron agreed but then asked about the large accrued liability based upon the estimated warranty amounts. Again, the accountant stated that in previous years actual warranty cost had been about 5% of the total sales and therefore in the current year the estimate was accrued at 5%. Ron then informed the accountant that a new conditioning lubricant had been added to each transmission rebuilt, which dramatically reduced the amount of rebuilt transmissions being returned under warranty. As a result, Ron strongly felt that the warranty estimate should be reduced to only 2% of total sales and thereby the accrued warranty liability and related expense would also be reduced. The accountant argued that the only reason Ron wanted to reduce the estimated percentage was to improve the financial statements, which would be unethical and inappropriate.

What is the impact of accrued liabilities on the financial statements? Should the accrued liabilities for wages and interest payable be removed from the balance sheet? Does Ron have a valid reason for wanting to reduce the estimated warranty liability? Are the concerns expressed by the accountant valid? What ethical issues are involved?

KNOW YOUR BUSINESS

This case focuses on the current liabilities of the Target Corporation. Current liabilities are those obligations that will become due and payable within the next year or operating cycle, whichever is longer. Simply put, those financial obligations that must be currently addressed are classified as current liabilities. It is important to properly classify and report these liabilities because they affect liquidity. We will now consider the current liabilities of Target. Refer to the Target Corporation financial statements found in Appendix A. Also, consider the following partial excerpts from the footnotes included in the annual report.

Accounts Payable

Our accounting policy is to reduce accounts payable when checks to vendors clear the bank from which they were drawn. Outstanding checks included in accounts payable were $992 million and $966 million at year-end 2004 and 2003, respectively.

Accrued Liabilities

Accrued liabilities as of January 29, 2005, and January 31, 2004, consist of the following:

	2004	2003
Wages and benefits	$ 412	$ 369
Taxes payable*	287	245
Gift card liability	214	169
Other	720	505
Total	$1,633	$1,288

*Taxes payable consist of real estate, employee withholdings, and sales tax liabilities. Gift card liability represents the amount of gift cards that have been issued but have not been presented for redemption.

Requirements

1. What was the balance of the total current liabilities at January 29, 2005? What was the balance of the total current liabilities at January 31, 2004?

Did the amount of ending total current liabilities increase or decrease? What seems to be the reason for the change in total current liabilities?

2. Which current liability was the largest at both the beginning and at the end of the year? What was the percentage of that liability compared to the total amount of current liabilities? How much was the total change? Why do you think the amount changed? What other observations do you have regarding the current liabilities?

3. Look at the beginning balance of accrued liabilities at January 31, 2004, and the ending balance of accrued liabilities at January 29, 2005. Then look at the footnote that provides the breakdown of the total accrued liabilities. Did the balances of all the accrued liabilities increase or decrease? What was the percentage change? What are accrued liabilities and why would they be included in the current liability section? Can you explain what the gift card liability is?

4. Read the accounts payable footnote. What is the meaning of this footnote? Why would Target provide this disclosure? How would the financial statements change if Target simply reduced the cash account and accounts payable balances by the amount of outstanding checks? What are your thoughts?

5. Look at the provision for income taxes, the income tax expense, on the Consolidated Results of Operations. Was the amount of income tax expense in 2004 larger than the previous year? Now look at the income taxes payable in the current liabilities. Did the amounts increase or decrease? Why aren't these amounts the same? Explain the relationship between income tax expense and income taxes payable.

For Internet Exercises, Excel in Practice, and additional online activities, go to the Web site www.prenhall.com/pollard.

Quick Check Answers

1. *a* 2. *c* 3. *d* 4. *c* 5. *b* 6. *a* 7. *d* 8. *a* 9. *c* 10. *d*

Appendix A

Selected Financial Information from Target Corporation

ˏˏ˒˒˒˒˒ˌ
Know Your Business

As mentioned in the introduction of the first Know Your Business case in Chapter 1, studying the Annual Report of Target Corporation is "designed to familiarize you with the financial reporting of a real company to further your understanding of the chapter material you are learning." A key word in that introduction is *"real."* Checking out Target's financial facts will demonstrate that *the material you are learning is relevant to life outside the classroom.* Throughout this case you will see, for example, that:

- The financial statements prepared by Target include the very same elements that you will master:
    - The income statement, called the "Consolidated Statements of Operations" by Target
    - The statement of owner's equity, called the "Consolidated Statements Shareholders' Investment" by Target
    - The balance sheet, called the "Consolidated Statements of Financial Position" by Target
    - The statement of cash flows, called the "Consolidated Statements of Cash Flows" by Target

- Assets *really do* equal liabilities plus owners' equity

- Auditors attest to the fairness of the statements and adequacy of the system of internal control

- Accounting information is relevant, reliable, and comparable

Further, the data contained in the Target pages is standard information available for publicly held companies. What if you want to invest in another company, or maybe even work for one? Know that studying Target will provide you with the real-life, hands-on experience you need to examine any entity in which you are interested.

The following pages include Target's financial statements, accompanying notes, and auditor reports from the 2004 and 2005 Annual Reports. For additional information contained in Target's Annual Reports for these years, please go to www.Target.com.

Have fun!

Selected Financial Information for Target Corporation 2005

The Income Statement

CONSOLIDATED STATEMENTS OF OPERATIONS

(millions, except per share data)	2005	2004	2003
Sales	$51,271	$45,682	$40,928
Net credit card revenues	1,349	1,157	1,097
Total revenues	52,620	46,839	42,025
Cost of sales	34,927	31,445	28,389
Selling, general and administrative expenses	11,185	9,797	8,657
Credit card expenses	776	737	722
Depreciation and amortization	1,409	1,259	1,098
Earnings from continuing operations before interest expense and income taxes	4,323	3,601	3,159
Net interest expense	463	570	556
Earnings from continuing operations before income taxes	3,860	3,031	2,603
Provision for income taxes	1,452	1,146	984
Earnings from continuing operations	2,408	1,885	1,619
Earnings from discontinued operations, net of taxes of $46 and $116	—	75	190
Gain on disposal of discontinued operations, net of taxes of $761	—	1,238	—
Net earnings	$ 2,408	$ 3,198	$ 1,809
Basic earnings per share			
Continuing operations	$ 2.73	$ 2.09	$ 1.78
Discontinued operations	—	.08	.21
Gain from discontinued operations	—	1.37	—
Basic earnings per share	$ 2.73	$ 3.54	$ 1.99
Diluted earnings per share			
Continuing operations	$ 2.71	$ 2.07	$ 1.76
Discontinued operations	—	.08	.21
Gain from discontinued operations	—	1.36	—
Diluted earnings per share	$ 2.71	$ 3.51	$ 1.97
Weighted average common shares outstanding			
Basic	882.0	903.8	911.0
Diluted	889.2	912.1	919.2

See Notes to Consolidated Financial Statements throughout pages 28-39.

The Balance Sheet

CONSOLIDATED STATEMENTS OF FINANCIAL POSITION

(millions, except footnotes)	January 28, 2006	January 29, 2005
Assets		
Cash and cash equivalents	$ 1,648	$ 2,245
Accounts receivable, net	5,666	5,069
Inventory	5,838	5,384
Other current assets	1,253	1,224
Total current assets	14,405	13,922
Property and equipment		
Land	4,449	3,804
Buildings and improvements	14,174	12,518
Fixtures and equipment	3,219	2,990
Computer hardware and software	2,214	1,998
Construction-in-progress	1,158	962
Accumulated depreciation	(6,176)	(5,412)
Property and equipment, net	19,038	16,860
Other non-current assets	1,552	1,511
Total assets	$34,995	$32,293
Liabilities and shareholders' investment		
Accounts payable	$ 6,268	$ 5,779
Accrued liabilities	2,193	1,633
Income taxes payable	374	304
Current portion of long-term debt and notes payable	753	504
Total current liabilities	9,588	8,220
Long-term debt	9,119	9,034
Deferred income taxes	851	973
Other non-current liabilities	1,232	1,037
Shareholders' investment		
Common stock (a)	73	74
Additional paid-in-capital	2,121	1,810
Retained earnings	12,013	11,148
Accumulated other comprehensive income	(2)	(3)
Total shareholders' investment	14,205	13,029
Total liabilities and shareholders' investment	$34,995	$32,293

(a) *Authorized 6,000,000,000 shares, $.0833 par value; 874,074,850 shares issued and outstanding at January 28, 2006; 890,643,966 shares issued and outstanding at January 29, 2005.*

Preferred Stock *Authorized 5,000,000 shares, $.01 par value; no shares were issued or outstanding at January 28, 2006 or January 29, 2005.*

See Notes to Consolidated Financial Statements throughout pages 28-39.

The Statement of Cash Flows

CONSOLIDATED STATEMENTS OF CASH FLOWS

(millions)	2005	2004	2003
Operating activities			
Net earnings	$ 2,408	$ 3,198	$ 1,809
Earnings from and gain on disposal of discontinued operations, net of taxes	—	(1,313)	(190)
Earnings from continuing operations	2,408	1,885	1,619
Reconciliation to cash flow			
Depreciation and amortization	1,409	1,259	1,098
Share-based compensation expense	93	60	57
Deferred income taxes	(122)	233	208
Bad debt provision	466	451	476
Loss on disposal of property and equipment, net	70	59	41
Other non-cash items affecting earnings	(50)	73	10
Changes in operating accounts providing/(requiring) cash:			
Accounts receivable originated at Target	(244)	(209)	(279)
Inventory	(454)	(853)	(579)
Other current assets	(28)	(37)	(196)
Other non-current assets	(24)	(147)	(166)
Accounts payable	489	823	721
Accrued liabilities	351	319	85
Income taxes payable	70	(91)	74
Other	17	(17)	19
Cash flow provided by operations	4,451	3,808	3,188
Investing activities			
Expenditures for property and equipment	(3,388)	(3,068)	(2,738)
Proceeds from disposals of property and equipment	58	56	67
Change in accounts receivable originated at third parties	(819)	(690)	(538)
Proceeds from sale of discontinued operations	—	4,881	—
Cash flow (required for)/provided by investing activities	(4,149)	1,179	(3,209)
Financing activities			
Decrease in notes payable, net	—	—	(100)
Additions to long-term debt	913	10	1,200
Reductions of long-term debt	(527)	(1,487)	(1,179)
Dividends paid	(318)	(272)	(237)
Repurchase of stock	(1,197)	(1,290)	(48)
Stock option exercises	172	146	36
Share-based compensation tax benefit	59	69	25
Other	(1)	—	(10)
Cash flow required for financing activities	(899)	(2,824)	(313)
Cash flows of discontinued operations (Revised) (a)			
(Required for)/provided by operations	—	(549)	545
Required for investing activities	—	(44)	(248)
Required for financing activities	—	(33)	(5)
Net cash (required for)/provided by discontinued operations	—	(626)	292
Net (decrease)/increase in cash and cash equivalents	(597)	1,537	(42)
Cash and cash equivalents at beginning of year	2,245	708	750
Cash and cash equivalents at end of year	$ 1,648	$ 2,245	$ 708

(a) We have revised this statement for 2004 and 2003 to separately disclose the operating, investing and financing portions of the cash flows attributable to our discontinued operations. We had previously reported these amounts on a combined basis.

Amounts presented herein are on a cash basis and therefore may differ from those shown in other sections of this Annual Report. Consistent with the provisions of SFAS No. 95, "Statement of Cash Flows," cash flows related to accounts receivable are classified as either an operating activity or an investing activity, depending on their origin.

Cash paid for income taxes was $1,448 million, $1,742 million and $781 million during 2005, 2004 and 2003, respectively. Cash paid for interest (net of interest capitalized) was $468 million, $480 million and $542 million during 2005, 2004 and 2003, respectively.

See Notes to Consolidated Financial Statements throughout pages 28-39.

The Statement of Owners' Equity

CONSOLIDATED STATEMENTS OF SHAREHOLDERS' INVESTMENT

(millions, except footnotes)	Common Stock Shares	Stock Par Value	Additional Paid-in Capital	Retained Earnings	Accumulated Other Comprehensive Income/(Loss)	Total
February 1, 2003	909.8	$76	$1,400	$ 8,017	$ 4	$ 9,497
Consolidated net earnings	—	—	—	1,809	—	1,809
Other comprehensive loss	—	—	—	—	(1)	(1)
Total comprehensive income						1,808
Dividends declared	—	—	—	(246)	—	(246)
Repurchase of stock	(1.5)	—	—	(57)	—	(57)
Issuance of stock for ESOP	0.6	—	17	—	—	17
Stock options and awards	2.9	—	113	—	—	113
January 31, 2004	911.8	76	1,530	9,523	3	11,132
Consolidated net earnings	—	—	—	3,198	—	3,198
Other comprehensive loss	—	—	—	—	(6)	(6)
Total comprehensive income						3,192
Dividends declared	—	—	—	(280)	—	(280)
Repurchase of stock	(28.9)	(3)	—	(1,293)	—	(1,296)
Stock options and awards	7.7	1	280	—	—	281
January 29, 2005	890.6	74	1,810	11,148	(3)	13,029
Consolidated net earnings	—	—	—	2,408	—	2,408
Other comprehensive income	—	—	—	—	1	1
Total comprehensive income						2,409
Dividends declared	—	—	—	(334)	—	(334)
Repurchase of stock	(23.1)	(2)	—	(1,209)	—	(1,211)
Stock options and awards	6.6	1	311	—	—	312
January 28, 2006	**874.1**	**$73**	**$2,121**	**$12,013**	**$(2)**	**$14,205**

In June 2004, our Board of Directors authorized the repurchase of $3 billion of our common stock. In November 2005, our Board increased the aggregate authorization by $2 billion, for a total authorization of $5 billion. We expect the repurchase of our common stock to be made primarily in open market transactions, subject to market conditions, and anticipate completion of the aggregate program in the next two to three years. In 2005, we repurchased a total of 23.1 million shares of our common stock for a total investment of $1,197 million ($51.88 per share).

Junior Preferred Stock Rights In 2001, we declared a distribution of preferred share purchase rights which expire in September 2006. Terms of the plan provide for a distribution of one preferred share purchase right for each outstanding share of our common stock. Each right will entitle shareholders to buy one twelve-hundredth of a share of a new series of junior participating preferred stock at an exercise price of $125.00, subject to adjustment. The rights will be exercisable only if a person or group acquires ownership of 20 percent or more of our common stock or announces a tender offer to acquire 30 percent or more of our common stock.

Dividends Dividends declared per share were $.38, $.31 and $.27 in 2005, 2004 and 2003, respectively.

See Notes to Consolidated Financial Statements throughout pages 28-39.

NOTES TO CONSOLIDATED FINANCIAL STATEMENTS

1. Summary of Accounting Policies

Organization Target Corporation (the Corporation or Target) operates large-format general merchandise discount stores in the United States. Our credit card operation represents an integral component of our core retail business. We also operate Target.com, an online business. We operate as a single business segment.

Consolidation The consolidated financial statements include the balances of the Corporation and its subsidiaries after elimination of material intercompany balances and transactions. All material subsidiaries are wholly owned.

Use of Estimates The preparation of our consolidated financial statements, in conformity with U.S. generally accepted accounting principles (GAAP), requires management to make estimates and assumptions affecting reported amounts in the consolidated financial statements and accompanying notes. Actual results may differ from those estimates.

Fiscal Year Our fiscal year ends on the Saturday nearest January 31. Unless otherwise stated, references to years in this report relate to fiscal years rather than to calendar years. Fiscal years 2005, 2004 and 2003 each consisted of 52 weeks.

Reclassifications Certain prior year amounts have been reclassified to conform to the current year presentation.

Share-Based Compensation We adopted the provisions of Statement of Financial Accounting Standards No.123R, "Share-Based Payment" (SFAS No.123R), in 2004 under the modified retrospective transition method. Therefore, all prior period financial statements have been restated to recognize compensation cost in the amounts previously reported in the Notes to Consolidated Financial Statements under the provisions of SFAS No.123. SFAS No.123R requires that all share-based compensation be accounted for using a fair-value-based method. In 2005, the FASB issued additional guidance on SFAS No.123R in the form of Staff Positions (FSPs). FSP 123(R)-2 clarifies that a share-based compensation award is considered "granted" (and fair value should be estimated) when the employer and its employees have a mutual understanding of the key terms and conditions of the award, and further clarifies that this mutual understanding is presumed to exist at the date the award is approved by the Board of Directors or management with relevant authority, assuming certain conditions are met. We applied this guidance to our share-based awards upon issuance of the FSP.

SFAS No.123R requires companies to determine the amount of an additional paid-in capital (APIC) pool that would be available to absorb deferred tax asset write-offs by calculating the net excess tax benefits credited to APIC as if the company had always been following the provisions of SFAS No.123R. FSP 123(R)-3 provides an elective transition alternative for calculating the beginning balance of the APIC pool, which we have elected to adopt. Our practice with regard to awards that were not fully vested upon our adoption of SFAS No.123R is to treat the entire amount of such awards as partially vested for purposes of calculating the beginning balance of the APIC pool.

Generally, in accordance with SFAS No.123R, we recognize compensation expense for awards on a straight-line basis over the four-year vesting period. However, in certain circumstances under our share-based compensation plans, we allow for the vesting of employee awards to continue post-employment. Accordingly, for awards granted subsequent to our adoption of SFAS No.123R and to the extent those awards continue to vest post-employment because the employee met certain age and service requirements at the date of grant, we accelerate expense recognition, such that the value of the award is fully expensed over the employee's service period instead of over the explicit vesting period. Awards granted prior to the adoption of SFAS No.123R continue to be expensed over the explicit vesting period in accordance with SEC guidelines. Information related to outstanding stock options, performance shares and restricted stock is disclosed in Note 26, pages 35-36.

Derivative Financial Instruments SFAS No.133, "Accounting for Derivative Instruments and Hedging Activities," as amended, defines derivatives and requires that they be carried at fair value on the balance sheet. It also provides for hedge accounting when certain conditions are met. Our derivative instruments are primarily interest rate swaps which hedge the fair value of certain debt by effectively converting interest from a fixed rate to a floating rate. These instruments qualify for hedge accounting and the associated assets and liabilities are recorded in the Consolidated Statements of Financial Position. The change in market value of an interest rate swap as well as the offsetting change in market value of the hedged debt is recognized into earnings in the current period. Ineffectiveness would result when changes in the market value of the hedged debt are not completely offset by changes in the market value of the interest rate swap. There was no ineffectiveness recognized in 2005, 2004 or 2003 related to these instruments. Further information related to interest rate swaps is disclosed in Note 21, page 33.

2. Revenues

Revenues are recognized as sales occur and are net of expected returns. Total revenues do not include sales tax as we consider ourselves a pass-through conduit for collecting and remitting sales taxes. Commissions earned on sales generated by leased departments are included within sales and were $14 million in 2005, $14 million in 2004 and $13 million in 2003.

Revenue from gift card sales is recognized at redemption of the gift card. Our gift cards do not have expiration dates. Based on historical redemption rates, a certain percentage of gift cards will never be redeemed, which is referred to as "breakage." Estimated breakage revenue is recognized as the remaining gift card values are redeemed.

Net credit card revenues are recognized according to the contractual provisions of each applicable credit card agreement. If an account is written-off, any uncollected finance charges or late fees are recorded as a reduction of net credit card revenues. Target retail store sales charged to our credit cards totaled $3,655 million, $3,269 million and $3,006 million in 2005, 2004 and 2003, respectively.

3. Cost of Sales and Selling, General and Administrative (SG&A) Expenses

The following illustrates the primary costs classified in each major expense category:

Cost of Sales	SG&A Expenses
Total cost of products sold including:	Payroll and benefit costs
• Freight expenses associated with moving merchandise from our vendors to our distribution centers and our retail stores	Occupancy and operating costs of retail, distribution, and corporate facilities
• Vendor income that is not reimbursement of specific, incremental and identifiable costs	Advertising offset by vendor income that is a reimbursement of specific, incremental and identifiable costs
Inventory shrink	Other administrative costs
Markdowns	
Shipping and handling expenses	
Terms cash discount	

The methodology behind the classification of expenses varies across the retail industry.

4. Consideration Received from Vendors

We receive consideration for a variety of vendor-sponsored programs, such as volume rebates, markdown allowances, promotions and advertising and for our compliance programs, referred to as "vendor income." Vendor income reduces either our inventory costs or SG&A expenses based on application of EITF Issue No. 02-16, "Accounting by a Customer (Including a Reseller) for Certain Consideration Received from a Vendor," as amended by EITF Issue No. 03-10, "Application of Issue 02-16 by Resellers to Sales Incentives Offered to Consumers by Manufacturers." Promotional and advertising allowances are intended to offset our costs of promoting and selling the vendor's merchandise in our stores. Under our compliance programs, vendors are charged for merchandise shipments that do not meet our requirements ("violations"), such as late or incomplete shipments. These allowances are recorded when violations occur.

5. Advertising Costs

Advertising costs are expensed at first showing of the advertisement and were $1,028 million, $888 million and $872 million for 2005, 2004 and 2003, respectively. Advertising vendor income that offset advertising expenses was approximately $110 million, $72 million and $58 million for 2005, 2004 and 2003, respectively. Newspaper circulars and media broadcast made up the majority of our advertising costs in all three years.

6. Discontinued Operations

We completed the sale of our Marshall Field's and Mervyn's businesses during 2004. In accordance with SFAS No. 144, "Accounting for the Impairment or Disposal of Long-Lived Assets," the financial results of Marshall Field's and Mervyn's are reported as discontinued operations.

No financial results of discontinued operations are included for the year ended January 28, 2006. For the years ended January 29, 2005 and January 31, 2004, total revenues included in discontinued operations were $3,095 million and $6,138 million, respectively, and earnings from discontinued operations were $75 million and $190 million, net of taxes of $46 million and $116 million, respectively. In addition, we recorded a gain on the sale of discontinued operations of $1,238 million, net of taxes of $761 million, during the year ended January 29, 2005.

There were no assets or liabilities of Marshall Field's or Mervyn's included in our Consolidated Statements of Financial Position at January 28, 2006 or January 29, 2005.

7. Earnings per Share

Basic earnings per share (EPS) is net earnings divided by the average number of common shares outstanding during the period. Diluted EPS includes the incremental shares assumed to be issued on the exercise of stock options and the potentially issuable performance shares.

(millions, except per share data)	Basic EPS			Diluted EPS		
	2005	2004	2003	**2005**	2004	2003
Net earnings	**$2,408**	$3,198	$1,809	**$2,408**	$3,198	$1,809
Basic weighted average common shares outstanding	**882.0**	903.8	911.0	**882.0**	903.8	911.0
Stock options and performance shares	**—**	—	—	**7.2**	8.3	8.2
Weighted average common shares outstanding	**882.0**	903.8	911.0	**889.2**	912.1	919.2
Earnings per share	**$ 2.73**	$ 3.54	$ 1.99	**$ 2.71**	$ 3.51	$ 1.97

Our diluted EPS calculation excludes any shares related to stock options for which the effect would have been antidilutive. There were no material antidilutive shares issuable upon exercise excluded from the dilutive EPS calculations at January 28, 2006, January 29, 2005 and January 31, 2004, respectively.

8. Other Comprehensive Income/(Loss)

Other comprehensive income/(loss) includes revenues, expenses, gains and losses that are excluded from net earnings under GAAP and are recorded directly to shareholders' investment. In 2005, 2004 and 2003, other comprehensive income/(loss) primarily included gains and losses on certain hedge transactions and the change in our minimum pension liability, net of related taxes.

9. Cash Equivalents

Cash equivalents include highly liquid investments with an original maturity of three months or less from the time of purchase. We carry these investments at cost, which approximates market value. These investments were $1,172 million and $1,732 million in 2005 and 2004, respectively. Also included in cash equivalents are proceeds due from credit and debit card transactions with settlement terms of less than five days. Credit and debit card receivables included within cash equivalents were $285 million and $242 million, respectively, for 2005 and 2004.

10. Accounts Receivable

Accounts receivable are recorded net of an allowance for expected losses. The allowance, recognized in an amount equal to the anticipated future write-offs based on delinquencies, risk scores, aging trends, industry risk trends and our historical experience, was $451 million at January 28, 2006 and $387 million at January 29, 2005. Substantially all accounts continue to accrue finance charges until they are written off. Accounts are written off when they become 180 days past due.

In 2004, we chartered Target Bank for the purpose of issuing credit cards to qualified businesses, as our Target National Bank charter does not allow for the issuance of commercial credit cards.

As a method of providing funding for our accounts receivable, we sell on an ongoing basis all of our consumer credit card receivables to Target Receivables Corporation (TRC), a wholly-owned bankruptcy remote subsidiary. TRC then transfers the receivables to the Target Credit Card Master Trust (the Trust), which from time to time will sell debt securities to third parties, either directly or through a related trust. These debt securities represent undivided interests in the Trust assets. TRC has also retained an undivided interest in the Trust's assets that are not represented by the debt securities sold to third parties and a 2 percent undivided interest in the Trust assets that is held by Target National Bank, a wholly-owned subsidiary of Target which also services receivables. TRC uses the proceeds from the sale of debt securities and its share of collections on the receivables to pay the purchase price of the receivables to Target.

The accounting guidance for such transactions, SFAS No.140, "Accounting for Transfers and Servicing of Financial Assets and Extinguishments of Liabilities (a replacement of SFAS No.125)," requires the inclusion of the receivables within the Trust and any debt securities issued by the Trust, or a related trust, in our Consolidated Statements of Financial Position. Notwithstanding this accounting treatment, the receivables transferred to the Trust are not available to general creditors of Target. Upon termination of the securitization program and repayment of all debt securities issued from time to time by the Trust, or a related trust, any remaining assets could be distributed to Target in a liquidation of TRC.

11. Inventory

Substantially all of our inventory and the related cost of sales are accounted for under the retail inventory accounting method using the last-in, first-out (LIFO) method. Inventory is stated at the lower of LIFO cost or market. The LIFO provision is calculated based on inventory levels, markup rates and internally-measured retail price indices. We have not recorded any material LIFO provision in 2005 or 2004.

We routinely enter into arrangements with certain vendors whereby we do not purchase or pay for merchandise until that merchandise is ultimately sold to a guest. Revenues under this program are included in the sales line in the Consolidated Statements of Operations, but the merchandise received under the program is not included in our Consolidated Statements of Financial Position because of the simultaneous timing of our purchase and sale of this inventory. Sales made under these arrangements totaled $872 million, $357 million and $142 million for 2005, 2004 and 2003, respectively.

In 2005, we adopted SFAS No.151, "Inventory Costs, an amendment of ARB No.43, Chapter 4," which clarifies that abnormal amounts of idle facilities expense, freight, handling costs and spoilage are to be recognized as current period charges and provides guidance on the allocation of overhead. This adoption did not have a material impact on our net earnings, cash flows or financial position.

12. Other Current Assets

(millions)	January 28, 2006	January 29, 2005
Vendor income and other receivables	$ 560	$ 428
Deferred taxes	344	344
Other	349	452
Total	$1,253	$1,224

In addition to vendor income, other receivables relate primarily to pharmacy receivables and merchandise sourcing services provided to third parties.

13. Property and Equipment

Property and equipment are recorded at cost, less accumulated depreciation. Depreciation is computed using the straight-line method over estimated useful lives. Depreciation expense for the years 2005, 2004 and 2003 was $1,384 million, $1,232 million and $1,068 million, respectively. Accelerated depreciation methods are generally used for income tax purposes. Repair and maintenance costs were $474 million, $453 million and $393 million in 2005, 2004 and 2003, respectively, and are expensed as incurred.

Estimated useful lives by major asset category are as follows:

Asset	Life (in years)
Buildings and improvements	8–39
Fixtures and equipment	4–15
Computer hardware and software	4

In accordance with SFAS No.144, "Accounting for the Impairment or Disposal of Long-Lived Assets," all long-lived assets are reviewed when events or changes in circumstances indicate that the asset's carrying value may not be recoverable. No material impairments were recorded in 2005, 2004 or 2003 as a result of the tests performed.

In March 2005, the FASB issued FASB Interpretation No. 47, "Accounting for Conditional Asset Retirement Obligations, an interpretation of FASB Statement No.143" (FIN 47). The primary purpose of FIN 47 is to clarify that an entity is required to recognize a liability for the fair value of a conditional asset retirement obligation when incurred if the liability's fair value can be reasonably estimated. FIN 47 is effective no later than the end of fiscal years ending after December 15, 2005. The adoption of this guidance did not have a material impact on our net earnings, cash flows or financial position.

14. Other Non-Current Assets

(millions)	January 28, 2006	January 29, 2005
Prepaid pension expense	$ 752	$ 733
Cash value of life insurance	524	446
Goodwill and intangible assets	183	206
Other	93	126
Total	$1,552	$1,511

15. Goodwill and Intangible Assets

Goodwill and intangible assets are recorded within other non-current assets at cost less accumulated amortization. Goodwill and intangible assets by major classes were as follows:

(millions)	Goodwill Jan. 28, 2006	Goodwill Jan. 29, 2005	Leasehold Acquisition Costs Jan. 28, 2006	Leasehold Acquisition Costs Jan. 29, 2005	Other Jan. 28, 2006	Other Jan. 29, 2005	Total Jan. 28, 2006	Total Jan. 29, 2005
Gross asset	$ 80	$ 80	$ 182	$ 185	$ 205	$ 201	$ 467	$ 466
Accumulated amortization	(20)	(20)	(70)	(52)	(194)	(188)	(284)	(260)
Net goodwill and intangible assets	$ 60	$ 60	$ 112	$ 133	$ 11	$ 13	$ 183	$ 206

Amortization is computed on intangible assets with definite useful lives using the straight-line method over estimated useful lives that range from three to 29 years. Amortization expense for the years 2005, 2004 and 2003 was $25 million, $27 million and $30 million, respectively. The estimated aggregate amortization expense of our definite-lived intangible assets for each of the five succeeding fiscal years is as follows:

(millions)	2006	2007	2008	2009	2010
Amortization expense	$23	$20	$19	$19	$17

We have goodwill and certain intangible assets that are not amortized but instead are subject to an annual impairment test. Discounted cash flow models are used in determining fair value for the purposes of the required annual impairment analysis. No material impairments were recorded in 2005, 2004 and 2003 as a result of the tests performed.

During 2004, goodwill with an approximate carrying value of $63 million was disposed of as part of the Marshall Field's transaction.

16. Accounts Payable

Our accounting policy is to reduce accounts payable when checks to vendors clear the bank from which they were drawn. Outstanding checks included in accounts payable were $645 million and $992 million at year-end 2005 and 2004, respectively.

17. Accrued Liabilities

(millions)	January 28, 2006	January 29, 2005
Wages and benefits	$ 506	$ 422
Taxes payable	366	287
Gift card liability	294	214
Other	1,027	710
Total	$2,193	$1,633

Taxes payable consist of real estate, employee withholdings and sales tax liabilities. Gift card liability represents the amount of gift cards that have been issued but have not been redeemed, net of estimated breakage.

18. Commitments and Contingencies

At January 28, 2006, our obligations included notes and debentures of $9,771 million (further discussed in Note 19, page 32), the present value of capital lease obligations of $101 million and total future payments of operating leases with total contractual lease payments of $3,097 million, including certain options for lease term extension that are expected to be exercised in the amount of $1,421 million and $122 million of legally binding minimum lease payments for stores that will open in 2006 (see additional detail in Note 22, pages 33-34). In addition, real estate obligations, including commitments for the purchase, construction, or remodeling of real estate and facilities, were approximately $838 million at January 28, 2006. Purchase obligations, which include all legally binding contracts such as firm commitments for inventory purchases, merchandise royalties, purchases of equipment, marketing-related contracts, software acquisition/license commitments and service contracts and were $1,431 million at January 28, 2006. In the normal course of business we issue purchase orders to purchase inventory, which represent authorizations to purchase and are cancelable by their terms. We do not consider purchase orders to be firm inventory commitments. We also issue letters of credit in the ordinary course of business which are not firm commitments as they are conditional on the purchase order not being cancelled. If under certain circumstances, and at our sole discretion, we choose to cancel a purchase order, we may be obligated to reimburse the vendor for unrecoverable outlays incurred prior to cancellation. Standby letters of credit, which relate primarily to the portion of our insurance claims for which we have retained the risk, totaled $104 million at January 28, 2006.

The terms of a significant portion of the Visa/MasterCard antitrust litigation settlement were finalized during 2005. Consequently, we recorded a $27 million ($.02 per share) gain for our share of the proceeds, which we expect to collect during fiscal 2006. We also expect to receive an additional, smaller payment; however, the amount and timing of that payment are not certain at this time. Accordingly, no additional gain was recorded at January 28, 2006.

We are exposed to claims and litigation arising in the ordinary course of business and use various methods to resolve these matters in a manner that we believe serves the best interest of our shareholders and other constituents. We believe the amounts provided in our consolidated financial statements are adequate in light of the probable and estimable liabilities. Our policy is to disclose pending lawsuits and other known claims that may have a material adverse impact on our results of operations, cash flows or financial condition. We do not believe any of the currently identified claims and litigated matters meet this criterion.

19. Notes Payable and Long-Term Debt

We obtain short-term financing throughout the year under our commercial paper program, which is a form of notes payable. Information on this program is as follows:

Notes Payable

(dollars in millions)	2005	2004
Notes payable outstanding at year-end	$ —	$ —
Maximum amount outstanding during the year	$ 994	$1,422
Average amount outstanding during the year	$ 77	$ 55
Weighted-average interest rate	4.0%	1.3%

At January 28, 2006, a committed unsecured credit facility totaling $1.6 billion was in place through a group of banks at specified rates. This 2005 facility replaced our two previous committed credit agreements and is scheduled to expire in June 2010. No balances were outstanding at any time during 2005 or 2004 under any of these agreements.

On November 9, 2005, TRC issued to the public, through the Target Credit Card Owner Trust 2005-1, $900 million of debt backed by credit card receivables. This issue of receivable-backed securities has an expected maturity of five years and a floating interest rate set at 1-month LIBOR plus 0.06 percent. Refer to Note 10, page 30, for further discussion of our accounts receivable financing program. The total amount of long-term debt backed by credit card receivables was $1,650 million at January 28, 2006 and $750 million at January 29, 2005. We did not repurchase any significant amount of long-term debt during 2005.

In 2004, we issued no long-term debt and we called or repurchased $542 million of long-term debt with an average remaining life of 24 years and weighted average interest rate of 7.0 percent, resulting in a pre-tax loss of $89 million (approximately $.06 per share), reflected in net interest expense.

Our debt portfolio, including swap valuation adjustments, was as follows:

Long-Term Debt

	January 28, 2006		January 29, 2005	
(dollars in millions)	Rate *(a)*	Balance	Rate *(a)*	Balance
Notes and debentures:				
Due 2005–2009	5.6%	$4,249	4.1%	$4,818
Due 2010–2014	5.8	3,840	6.2	2,954
Due 2015–2019	5.5	240	3.3	234
Due 2020–2024	9.3	213	9.3	212
Due 2025–2029	6.7	325	6.7	325
Due 2030–2032	6.6	904	6.6	904
Total notes and debentures *(b)*	5.9%	9,771	5.2%	9,447
Capital lease obligations		101		91
Less: current portion		(753)		(504)
Long-term debt		$9,119		$9,034

(a) Reflects the weighted average stated interest rate as of year-end, including the impact of interest rate swaps.

(b) The estimated fair value of total notes and debentures, using a discounted cash flow analysis based on our incremental interest rates for similar types of financial instruments, was $10,229 million at January 28, 2006 and $10,171 million at January 29, 2005.

Required principal payments on total notes and debentures over the next five years, excluding capital lease obligations and fair market value adjustments recorded in long-term debt, are:

(millions)	2006	2007	2008	2009	2010
Required principal payments	$751	$1,321	$1,451	$751	$2,236

Most of our long-term debt obligations contain certain covenants related to secured debt levels. In addition, our credit facility contains a debt leverage covenant. We are, and expect to remain, in compliance with these covenants.

20. Net Interest Expense

(millions)	2005	2004	2003
Interest expense on debt	$524	$509	$543
Interest expense on capital leases	8	9	9
Loss on debt repurchase	—	89	15
Capitalized interest	(42)	(18)	(8)
Interest income	(27)	(19)	(3)
Net interest expense	$463	$570	$556

21. Interest Rate Swaps

Our accounting policy for derivative financial instruments is discussed in Note 1 on page 28.

At January 28, 2006 and January 29, 2005, interest rate swaps were outstanding in notional amounts totaling $3,300 million and $2,850 million, respectively. The increase in swap exposure was executed to convert more of our fixed-rate debt to floating-rate debt to minimize the effect on our earnings of changes in interest rates, given that the majority of interest rates on our credit card receivables re-price based on the changes in the prime rate.

During 2005, we entered into four interest rate swaps with notional amounts of $250 million, $350 million, $325 million and $225 million. We also terminated an interest rate swap with a notional amount of $200 million, resulting in a gain of $24 million that will be amortized into net interest expense over the remaining 13-year life of the hedged debt. During 2004, we entered into two interest rate swaps with notional amounts of $200 million and two interest rate swaps with notional amounts of $250 million. We also terminated an interest rate swap with a notional amount of $200 million, resulting in a loss of $16 million that will be amortized into net interest expense over the remaining 14-year life of the hedged debt. In 2005 and 2004, the gains and losses amortized into net interest expense for terminated swaps were not material to our results of operations.

Interest Rate Swaps

(dollars in millions)

| Maturity | Notional Amount Outstanding at | | Receive Fixed | Pay Floating Rate at (a) | |
	Jan. 28, 2006	Jan. 29, 2005		Jan. 28, 2006	Jan. 29, 2005
Feb. 2005	$ —	$ 500	7.5%	—%	2.4%
May 2006	550	550	4.6	4.8	3.3
Mar. 2008	250	—	3.9	4.4	—
Mar. 2008	250	250	3.8	4.4	2.4
Oct. 2008	500	500	4.4	4.8	3.2
Oct. 2008	250	250	3.8	4.4	2.5
Nov. 2008	200	200	3.9	4.4	2.4
Jun. 2009	400	400	4.4	4.8	3.3
Jun. 2009	350	—	4.2	4.5	—
Aug. 2010	325	—	4.8	4.5	—
Aug. 2010	225	—	4.5	4.5	—
May 2018	—	200	5.8	—	3.3
	$3,300	$2,850			

(a) Reflects floating interest rate as of the respective year-end.

The weighted average life of the interest rate swaps was approximately 2.7 years at January 28, 2006.

The fair value of outstanding interest rate swaps and unamortized gains/(losses) from terminated interest rate swaps was $(21) million at January 28, 2006 and $45 million at January 29, 2005. There was no ineffectiveness recognized in 2005, 2004 or 2003 related to these instruments.

22. Leases

We lease certain retail locations, warehouses, distribution centers, office space, equipment and land. Assets held under capital leases are included in property and equipment and lease payments are charged to depreciation and net interest expense over the life of the lease. Operating lease rentals are expensed on a straight-line basis over the life of the lease. Rent expense is recognized beginning with the earlier of the date when we become legally obligated for the rent payments or the date when we take possession of the property. At the inception of a lease, we determine the lease term by assuming the exercise of those renewal options that are reasonably assured because of the significant economic penalty that exists for not exercising those options. The exercise of lease renewal options is at our sole discretion. The expected lease term is used to determine whether a lease is capital or operating and is used to calculate straight-line rent expense. Additionally, the useful life of buildings and leasehold improvements are limited by the expected lease term. Our amortization of leasehold improvements is consistent with the guidance issued by the EITF in 2005 in Issue No. 05-6, "Determining the Amortization Period for Leasehold Improvements Purchased after Lease Inception or Acquired in a Business Combination," which requires that leasehold improvements purchased after the beginning of the initial lease term be amortized over the shorter of the assets' useful lives or a term that includes the original lease term plus any renewals that are reasonably assured at the date the leasehold improvements are purchased. Therefore, our adoption of this guidance did not have an impact in our net earnings, cash flows or financial position.

Rent expense on buildings, which is included in selling, general and administrative expenses, includes percentage rents based on a percentage of retail sales over contractual levels. Total rent expense was $154 million in 2005, $240 million in 2004 and $150 million in 2003. Refer to Note 29, page 39 for discussion of the 2004 lease accounting adjustment. Certain leases require us to pay real estate taxes, insurance, maintenance and other operating expenses associated with the leased premises. These amounts are not included in rent expense but are classified in selling, general and administrative expenses consistent with similar costs for owned locations. Most long-term leases include options to renew, with terms varying from one to 50 years. Certain leases also include options to purchase the property.

Future minimum lease payments required under noncancelable lease agreements existing at January 28, 2006, were:

Future Minimum Lease Payments

(millions)	Operating Leases	Capital Leases
2006	$137	$12
2007	132	12
2008	123	13
2009	114	13
2010	107	13
After 2010	2,484	160
Total future minimum lease payments	$3,097 (a)	223
Less: Interest (b)		(122)
Present value of minimum capital lease payments		$101 (c)

(a) Total contractual lease payments include certain options to extend lease terms, in the amount of $1,421 million, that are expected to be exercised because the investment in leasehold improvements is significant and also includes $122 million of legally binding minimum lease payments for stores that will open in 2006.

(b) Calculated using the interest rate at inception for each lease.

(c) Includes current portion of $2 million.

23. Income Taxes

We account for income taxes under the asset and liability method. We have recognized deferred tax assets and liabilities for the estimated future tax consequences attributable to differences between the financial statement carrying amounts of existing assets and liabilities and their respective tax bases. Deferred tax assets and liabilities are measured using enacted income tax rates in effect for the year in which those temporary differences are expected to be recovered or settled. The effect on deferred tax assets and liabilities of a change in tax rate is recognized into income in the period that includes the enactment date. In the Consolidated Statements of Financial Position, the current deferred tax asset balance is the net of all current deferred tax assets and current deferred tax liabilities. The non-current deferred tax liability is the net of all non-current deferred tax assets and non-current deferred tax liabilities.

To determine our quarterly provision for income taxes, we use annual effective tax rates based on expected annual income and statutory tax rates, adjusted for discrete tax events that occur during the quarter.

Reconciliation of tax rates is as follows:

Tax Rate Reconciliation

	2005	2004	2003
Federal statutory rate	**35.0%**	35.0%	35.0%
State income taxes, net of federal tax benefit	**3.3**	3.3	3.3
Dividends on ESOP stock	**(0.2)**	(0.2)	(0.2)
Work opportunity tax credits	**(0.2)**	(0.2)	(0.2)
Other	**(0.3)**	(0.1)	(0.1)
Effective tax rate	**37.6%**	37.8%	37.8%

The components of the provision for income taxes were:

Income Tax Provision: Expense

(millions)	2005	2004	2003
Current			
Federal	**$1,361**	$ 908	$ 669
State/other	**213**	144	107
	1,574	1,052	776
Deferred			
Federal	**(110)**	83	184
State/other	**(12)**	11	24
	(122)	94	208
Total	**$1,452**	$1,146	$ 984

The components of the net deferred tax asset/(liability) were:

Net Deferred Tax Asset/(Liability)

(millions)	January 28, 2006	January 29, 2005
Gross deferred tax assets		
Deferred and other compensation	$ 399	$ 332
Self-insured benefits	217	179
Accounts receivable valuation allowance	167	147
Inventory	1	47
Postretirement health care obligation	39	38
Other	151	128
	974	871
Gross deferred tax liabilities		
Property and equipment	(1,080)	(1,136)
Pension	(287)	(268)
Deferred credit card income	(103)	(87)
Other	(11)	(9)
	(1,481)	(1,500)
Total	$ (507)	$ (629)

During the year ended January 29, 2005, $566 million of the proceeds attributable to the real properties sold in the Marshall Field's and Mervyn's dispositions were used to acquire replacement properties which will be used in our business. $373 million of the gain related to the sold real properties was deferred for income tax purposes as allowed by Section 1031 of the Internal Revenue Code until such time as the replacement properties are disposed.

24. Other Non-Current Liabilities

(millions)	January 28, 2006	January 29, 2005
Deferred compensation	$ 596	$ 528
Worker's compensation and general liability	362	317
Other	274	192
Total	$1,232	$1,037

25. Share Repurchase

In June 2004, our Board of Directors authorized the repurchase of $3 billion of our common stock. In November 2005, our Board increased the aggregate authorization by $2 billion, for a total authorization of $5 billion. In 2005, we repurchased 23.1 million shares at an average price per share of $51.88, for a total investment of $1,197 million. Since June 2004, we have repurchased a total of 51.6 million shares at an average price per share of $47.95, for a total investment of $2,473 million. We expect to complete the aggregate program in the next two to three years.

26. Share-Based Compensation

Our accounting policy for share-based compensation is discussed in Note 1 on page 28.

We maintain a long-term incentive plan for key employees and non-employee members of our Board of Directors. Our long-term incentive plan allows us to grant equity-based compensation awards, including stock options, performance share awards, restricted stock awards, or a combination of awards. A majority of granted awards are non-qualified stock options that vest annually in equal amounts over a four-year period. These options generally expire no later than 10 years after the date of the grant. Options granted to the non-employee members of our Board of Directors become exercisable after one year and have a 10-year term. We have issued performance share or performance share unit awards annually since January 2003. These awards represent shares potentially issuable in the future based upon the attainment of performance criteria including compound annual growth rates in revenue and EPS. The number of unissued common shares reserved for future grants under the share-based compensation plans was 47,659,572 at January 28, 2006 and 51,560,249 at January 29, 2005.

Share-Based Compensation Awards

	Stock Options						Performance Shares
	Total Outstanding			Currently Exercisable			
(options and shares in thousands)	Number of Options	Exercise Price(a)	Intrinsic Value(b)	Number of Options	Exercise Price(a)	Intrinsic Value(b)	Potentially Issuable
February 1, 2003	34,787	$25.73	$204	21,931	$20.89	$204	552(c)
Granted	4,638	38.34					573(d)
Canceled/forfeited	(407)	34.77					—
Exercised	(2,859)	12.58					—
January 31, 2004	36,159	$28.28	$363	23,689	$24.48	$326	1,125
Granted	4,072	49.12					629(e)
Canceled/forfeited	(513)	35.32					(73)
Exercised/earned	(7,727)	20.95					(73)
January 29, 2005	31,991	$32.59	$540	22,102	$28.79	$458	1,608
Granted	4,057	53.94					597(f)
Canceled/forfeited	(691)	40.67					(252)
Exercised	(6,643)	26.58					—
January 28, 2006	28,714	$36.82	$505	19,229	$31.64	$438	1,953(g)

(a) Weighted average.

(b) Represents stock price appreciation subsequent to the grant date, in millions.

(c) Awards are earned based on performance during four years ending February 3, 2007.

(d) Awards are earned based on performance during four years ending February 2, 2008.

(e) Awards are earned based on performance during three years ending February 2, 2008.

(f) Awards are earned based on performance during three years ending January 31, 2009.

(g) Approximately 34 percent of these potentially issuable performance shares, if and when earned, will be paid in cash or deferred through a credit to the deferred compensation accounts of the participants in an amount equal to the value of any earned performance shares.

Nonvested Options and Performance Share Awards

(options and shares in thousands)	Stock Options	Weighted Average Fair Value at Grant Date	Performance Shares Potentially Issuable	Weighted Average Fair Value at Grant Date
Nonvested at January 30, 2005	9,889	$11.83	1,608	$38.84
Granted	4,057	16.85	597	53.96
Vested/earned (a)	(3,774)	11.75	—	—
Cancelled/forfeited	(687)	11.78	(252)	39.28
Nonvested at January 28, 2006	9,485	$14.01	1,953	$44.55

(a) Based on the explicit vesting period.

The Black-Scholes model was used to estimate the fair value of the options at grant date based on the assumptions noted in the following table. Volatility represents an average of market quotes for implied volatility of 5.5-year options on Target stock. The expected life is estimated based on analysis of options already exercised and any foreseeable trends or changes in behavior. The risk-free interest rate is an interpolation of the relevant U.S. Treasury security maturities as of each applicable grant date. The assumptions disclosed below represent a weighted average of the assumptions used for all of our stock option grants throughout the year.

Valuation of Share-Based Compensation

	2005	2004	2003
Stock option valuation assumptions:			
Dividend yield	0.7%	0.7%	0.8%
Volatility	27%	22%	29%
Risk-free interest rate	4.4%	3.8%	3.0%
Expected life in years	5.5	5.5	5.0
Grant date weighted-average fair value	$16.85	$13.10	$11.04
Performance share grant date weighted-average fair value	$53.96	$49.43	$38.25
Compensation expense recognized in Statements of Operations (millions) (a)	$ 93	$ 60	$ 57
Related income tax benefit (millions)	$ 37	$ 23	$ 22
Compensation realized by employees upon option exercises (millions)	$180	$201	$ 72
Related income tax benefit (millions)	$ 71	$ 77	$ 28

(a) Represents the total fair value of options vested and performance shares earned.

As of January 28, 2006, there was $102 million of total unrecognized compensation expense related to nonvested stock options. That cost is expected to be recognized over a weighted average period of 1.4 years. The weighted average remaining life of currently exercisable options is 4.6 years, while total outstanding options have a weighted average remaining life of six years. Future compensation expense related to performance shares depends on future performance and could range from a credit of $39 million for previously recognized amounts up to a maximum of $50 million of expense assuming full payout under all outstanding awards.

27. Defined Contribution Plans

Employees who meet certain eligibility requirements can participate in a defined contribution 401(k) plan by investing up to 80 percent of their compensation, as limited by statute or regulation. Generally, we match 100 percent of each employee's contribution up to 5 percent of total compensation. Our contribution to the plan is initially invested in Target Corporation common stock. These amounts are free to be diversified by the employee three years after initial eligibility in the plan.

In addition, we maintain non-qualified, unfunded deferred compensation plans for highly-compensated employees whose participation in our 401(k) plan is limited by statute or regulation. These employees choose from a menu of crediting rate alternatives which are the same as the investment choices in our 401(k) plan. We credit an additional 2 percent per year to the accounts of active employees, in part to recognize the risks inherent to their participation in a plan of this nature. We also maintain a frozen non-qualified, unfunded plan for certain officers in which deferred compensation earns returns tied to market levels of interest rates plus an additional 6 percent return as determined by the plan's terms. We control some of our risk of offering the non-qualified plans through investing in vehicles that offset a substantial portion of our economic exposure to the returns of those plans. These investment vehicles are marked to market with the

related gains and losses recognized in the Consolidated Statements of Operations in the period they occur. At times, adjusting our position in these investment vehicles includes repurchasing shares of Target common stock. In 2005, 2004 and 2003, these repurchases totaled 1.5 million, 0.8 million and 1.5 million shares, respectively.

(millions)	2005	2004	2003
401(k) Defined Contribution Plan			
401(k) matching contributions	$118	$118	$117
Non-Qualified Deferred Compensation Plans			
Benefits expense	$ 64	$ 63	$ 86
Related investments	(34)	(40)	(58)
Net expense	$ 30	$ 23	$ 28

In 2005, 2004 and 2003, certain retired executives accepted our offer to exchange our obligation to them under certain frozen non-qualified plans for cash or deferrals in our current non-qualified deferred compensation plan. These exchange transactions resulted in expense of $7 million, $17 million, and $17 million, respectively. We expect lower future expenses as a result of these transactions.

Expenses for Marshall Field's and Mervyn's employees are included in the table above to the extent we retained the related assets and obligations of their plans subsequent to the 2004 divestiture of those businesses.

28. Pension and Postretirement Health Care Benefits

We have a qualified defined benefit pension plan covering all U.S. employees who meet age and service requirements. We also have unfunded non-qualified pension plans for employees with qualified plan compensation restrictions. Benefits are provided based on years of service and the employee's compensation. During fiscal 2004, we merged our three qualified U.S. pension plans into one plan. This merger did not have a material impact on the financial results of the plan. Upon retirement employees also become eligible for certain health care benefits if they meet minimum age and service requirements and agree to contribute a portion of the cost.

We recorded a reduction in our accumulated post-retirement benefit obligation of $7 million in 2004 as a result of the Medicare Prescription Drug, Improvements and Modernization Act of 2003. In addition, the expense amounts shown in the table below for 2004 reflect a $1 million reduction due to the amortization of the actuarial gain and reduction in interest cost due to the effects of the Act.

In 2005, certain non-qualified pension and survivor benefits owed to current officers were exchanged for cash or deferrals in our current non-qualified deferred compensation plan, which resulted in expense of $11 million. The effect of these exchange transactions is included in the pension tables below. There were no such exchange transactions during 2004 or 2003.

Obligations and Funded Status

(millions)	Pension Benefits				Postretirement Health Care Benefits	
	Qualified Plans		Non-qualified Plans			
	2005	2004	2005	2004	2005	2004
Change in Projected Benefit Obligation						
Benefit obligation at beginning of measurement period (a)	$1,515	$1,333	$ 34	$ 29	$ 107	$ 123
Service cost	66	78	1	1	2	3
Interest cost	85	82	2	2	6	7
Actuarial loss	55	68	4	4	3	(6)
Benefits paid	(94)	(65)	(5)	(3)	(13)	(13)
Plan amendments	(1)	19	(3)	1	—	(7)
Benefit obligation at end of measurement period	$1,626	$1,515	$ 33	$ 34	$ 105	$ 107
Change in Plan Assets						
Fair value of plan assets at beginning of measurement period	$1,698	$1,405	$ —	$ —	$ —	$ —
Actual return on plan assets	174	157	—	—	—	—
Employer contribution	67	201	5	3	13	13
Benefits paid	(94)	(65)	(5)	(3)	(13)	(13)
Fair value of plan assets at end of measurement period	$1,845	$1,698	$ —	$ —	$ —	$ —
Funded status	$ 219	$ 183	$(33)	$(34)	$(105)	$(107)
Unrecognized actuarial loss	561	584	16	15	8	6
Unrecognized prior service cost	(32)	(39)	—	2	—	—
Net amount recognized	$ 748	$ 728	$(17)	$(17)	$ (97)	$(101)

(a) Measurement date is October 31 of each year.

Amounts recognized in the Consolidated Statements of Financial Position consist of:

(millions)	Pension Benefits				Postretirement Health Care Benefits	
	Qualified Plans		Non-qualified Plans			
	2005	2004	2005	2004	2005	2004
Prepaid benefit cost	$ 752	$ 733	$ —	$ —	$ —	$ —
Accrued benefit cost	(9)	(11)	(22)	(24)	(97)	(101)
Intangible assets	—	—	—	2	—	—
Accumulated OCI	5	6	5	5	—	—
Net amount recognized	$ 748	$ 728	$(17)	$(17)	$ (97)	$(101)

Net Pension and Postretirement Health Care Benefits Expense

(millions)	Pension Benefits			Postretirement Health Care Benefits		
	2005	2004	2003	2005	2004	2003
Service cost benefits earned during the period	$ 67	$ 79	$ 74	$ 2	$ 3	$ 2
Interest cost on projected benefit obligation	87	84	75	6	7	8
Expected return on assets	(137)	(122)	(114)	—	—	—
Recognized losses	43	36	18	1	1	1
Recognized prior service cost	(5)	(7)	(7)	—	—	—
Settlement/curtailment charges	—	1	—	—	(7)	—
Total	$ 55	$ 71	$ 46	$ 9	$ 4	$11

The amortization of any prior service cost is determined using the straight-line method over the average remaining service period of employees expected to receive benefits under the plan. As a result of freezing the benefits for Marshall Field's and Mervyn's team members at the time of their respective dispositions and retaining the related assets and obligations of the plans, we were required to record curtailment charges in 2004. These charges are also included in the gain on disposal of discontinued operations in the Consolidated Statements of Operations.

Other information related to defined benefit pension plans is as follows:

(millions)	2005	2004
Accumulated benefit obligation (ABO) for all plans (a)	$1,534	$1,501
Projected benefit obligation for pension plans with an ABO in excess of plan assets (b)	46	49
Total ABO for pension plans with an ABO in excess of plan assets	41	45
Fair value of plan assets for pension plans with an ABO in excess of plan assets	3	5

(a) The present value of benefits earned to date assuming no future salary growth.

(b) The present value of benefits earned to date by plan participants, including the effect of assumed future salary increases.

Assumptions

Weighted average assumptions used to determine benefit obligations at October 31:

	Pension Benefits		Postretirement Health Care Benefits	
	2005	2004	2005	2004
Discount rate	5.75%	5.75%	5.75%	5.75%
Average assumed rate of compensation increase	3.50%	2.75%	n/a	n/a

Weighted average assumptions used to determine net periodic benefit cost for years ended October 31:

	Pension Benefits		Postretirement Health Care Benefits	
	2005	2004	**2005**	2004
Discount rate	**5.75%**	6.25%	**5.75%**	6.25%
Expected long-term rate of return on plan assets	**8.00%**	8.00%	**n/a**	n/a
Average assumed rate of compensation increase	**2.75%**	3.25%	**n/a**	n/a

The discount rate used to measure net periodic benefit cost each year is the rate as of the beginning of the year (i.e. the prior measurement date). With an essentially stable asset allocation over the following time periods, our annualized rate of return on qualified plans' assets has averaged 5.1 percent, 9.9 percent and 11.5 percent for the 5-year, 10-year and 15-year periods, respectively, ending October 31, 2005.

An increase in the cost of covered health care benefits of 10 percent was assumed for 2005. The rate is assumed to be 9 percent in 2006 and is reduced by 1 percent annually to 5 percent in 2010 and thereafter.

A 1 percent change in assumed health care cost trend rates would have the following effects:

	1% Increase	1% Decrease
Effect on total of service and interest cost components of net periodic postretirement health care benefit cost	$ —	$ —
Effect on the health care component of the postretirement benefit obligation	$ 5	$ (4)

Additional Information

Our pension plan weighted average asset allocations at October 31, 2005 and 2004 by asset category were as follows:

Asset Category

	2005	2004
Domestic equity securities	**36%**	37%
International equity securities	**20**	21
Debt securities	**26**	26
Other	**18**	16
Total	**100%**	100%

Our asset allocation strategy for 2006 targets 35 percent in domestic equity securities, 20 percent in international equity securities, 25 percent in debt securities and 20 percent in other assets. Equity securities include our common stock in amounts substantially less than 1 percent of total plan assets at October 31, 2005 and 2004. Other assets include private equity, mezzanine and distressed debt and timber and less than a 5 percent allocation to real estate. Our expected long-term rate of return assumptions as of October 31, 2005 were 8.5 percent, 8.5 percent, 5 percent and 10 percent for domestic equity securities, international equity securities, debt securities and other assets, respectively.

Contributions

Given the qualified pension plan's funded position, we are not required to make any contributions in 2006, although we may choose to make discretionary contributions of up to $80 million. We expect to make contributions in the range of $5 million to $15 million to our post-retirement health care benefit plan in 2006.

Estimated Future Benefit Payments

Benefit payments by the plans, which reflect expected future service as appropriate, are expected to be paid as follows:

(millions)	Pension Benefits	Postretirement Health Care Benefits
2006	$ 64	$11
2007	72	12
2008	80	13
2009	86	13
2010	90	14
2011–2015	$540	$79

29. Quarterly Results (Unaudited)

Due to the seasonal nature of our business, fourth quarter operating results typically represent a substantially larger share of total year revenues and earnings because it includes the holiday shopping season. We follow the same accounting policies for preparing quarterly and annual financial data. The table below summarizes quarterly results for 2005 and 2004:

(millions, except per share data)	First Quarter		Second Quarter		Third Quarter		Fourth Quarter		Total Year	
	2005	2004	2005	2004	2005	2004	2005	2004	2005	2004
Total revenues	$11,477	$10,180	$11,990	$10,556	$12,206	$10,909	$16,947	$15,194	$52,620	$46,839
Gross margin	$ 3,615	$ 3,140	$ 3,839	$ 3,268	$ 3,829	$ 3,300	$ 5,061	$ 4,529	$16,344	$14,237
Earnings from continuing operations	$ 494	$ 392	$ 540	$ 360	$ 435	$ 324	$ 939	$ 809	$ 2,408	$ 1,885
Earnings from discontinued operations, net of taxes of $25, $19, $2 and $46	$ —	$ 40	$ —	$ 31	$ —	$ 4	$ —	$ —	$ —	$ 75
Gain/(loss) on disposal of discontinued operations, net of taxes of $650, $132, $(21) and $761 (a)	$ —	$ —	$ —	$ 1,019	$ —	$ 203	$ —	$ 16	$ —	$ 1,238
Net earnings (b)	$ 494	$ 432	$ 540	$ 1,410	$ 435	$ 531	$ 939	$ 825	$ 2,408	$ 3,198
Basic earnings per share (c)										
Continuing operations	$ .56	$ .43	$ .61	$ .40	$ .49	$ .36	$ 1.07	$ .91	$ 2.73	$ 2.09
Discontinued operations	$ —	$ .04	$ —	$ .03	$ —	$ —	$ —	$ —	$ —	$ .08
Gain from discontinued operations	$ —	$ —	$ —	$ 1.12	$ —	$ .23	$ —	$ .01	$ —	$ 1.37
Basic earnings per share (b)	$ .56	$ .47	$ .61	$ 1.55	$ .49	$ .59	$ 1.07	$ .92	$ 2.73	$ 3.54
Diluted earnings per share (c)										
Continuing operations	$ .55	$ .43	$ .61	$ .39	$ .49	$ .36	$ 1.06	$ .90	$ 2.71	$ 2.07
Discontinued operations	$ —	$ .04	$ —	$ .03	$ —	$ —	$ —	$ —	$ —	$ .08
Gain from discontinued operations	$ —	$ —	$ —	$ 1.11	$ —	$ .23	$ —	$ .01	$ —	$ 1.36
Diluted earnings per share (b)	$ .55	$ .47	$ .61	$ 1.53	$ .49	$ .59	$ 1.06	$ .91	$ 2.71	$ 3.51
Dividends declared per share (c)	$ .08	$ .07	$ .10	$ .08	$ .10	$ .08	$ .10	$ .08	$ .38	$ .31
Closing common stock price										
High	$ 52.50	$ 45.63	$ 59.98	$ 46.43	$ 57.80	$ 50.02	$ 58.85	$ 52.43	$ 59.98	$ 52.43
Low	$ 46.41	$ 38.59	$ 46.28	$ 40.80	$ 50.84	$ 40.42	$ 52.61	$ 48.50	$ 46.28	$ 38.59

(a) Minor tax adjustments related to the dispositions of Marshall Field's and Mervyn's were recorded in fourth quarter 2004.

(b) Target adjusted its method of accounting for leases related to a specific category of owned store locations on leased land, which resulted in a non-cash adjustment, primarily attributable to an increase in the straight-line rent accrual, of $65 million ($.04 per share) in the fourth quarter of 2004.

(c) Per share amounts are computed independently for each of the quarters presented. The sum of the quarters may not equal the total year amount due to the impact of changes in average quarterly shares outstanding.

Report of Management on the Financial Statements

Management is responsible for the consistency, integrity and presentation of the information in the Annual Report. The consolidated financial statements and other information presented in this Annual Report have been prepared in accordance with accounting principles generally accepted in the United States and include necessary judgments and estimates by management.

To fulfill our responsibility, we maintain comprehensive systems of internal control designed to provide reasonable assurance that assets are safeguarded and transactions are executed in accordance with established procedures. The concept of reasonable assurance is based upon recognition that the cost of the controls should not exceed the benefit derived. We believe our systems of internal control provide this reasonable assurance.

The Board of Directors exercised its oversight role with respect to the Corporation's systems of internal control primarily through its Audit Committee, which is comprised of four independent directors. The Committee oversees the Corporation's systems of internal control, accounting practices, financial reporting and audits to assess whether their quality, integrity and objectivity are sufficient to protect shareholders' investments. The Committee's report appears on this page.

In addition, our consolidated financial statements have been audited by Ernst & Young LLP, independent registered public accounting firm, whose report also appears on this page.

Robert J. Ulrich
Chairman of the Board and
Chief Executive Officer
March 29, 2006

Douglas A. Scovanner
Executive Vice President and
Chief Financial Officer

Report of Independent Registered Public Accounting Firm on Consolidated Financial Statements

The Board of Directors and Shareholders
Target Corporation

We have audited the accompanying consolidated statements of financial position of Target Corporation and subsidiaries as of January 28, 2006 and January 29, 2005, and the related consolidated statements of operations, cash flows, and shareholders' investment for each of the three years in the period ended January 28, 2006. These financial statements are the responsibility of the Corporation's management. Our responsibility is to express an opinion on these financial statements based on our audits.

We conducted our audits in accordance with the standards of the Public Company Accounting Oversight Board (United States). Those standards require that we plan and perform the audit to obtain reasonable assurance about whether the financial statements are free of material misstatement. An audit includes examining, on a test basis, evidence supporting the amounts and disclosures in the financial statements. An audit also includes assessing the accounting principles used and significant estimates made by management, as well as evaluating the overall financial statement presentation. We believe that our audits provide a reasonable basis for our opinion.

In our opinion, the financial statements referred to above present fairly, in all material respects, the consolidated financial position of Target Corporation and subsidiaries at January 28, 2006 and January 29, 2005, and the consolidated results of their operations and their cash flows for each of the three years in the period ended January 28, 2006, in conformity with U.S. generally accepted accounting principles.

We also have audited, in accordance with the standards of the Public Company Accounting Oversight Board (United States), the effectiveness of the Corporation's internal control over financial reporting as of January 28, 2006, based on criteria established in *Internal Control – Integrated Framework*, issued by the Committee of Sponsoring Organizations of the Treadway Commission and our report dated March 29, 2006, expressed an unqualified opinion thereon.

Minneapolis, Minnesota
March 29, 2006

Ernst + Young LLP

Report of Management on Internal Control

Our management is responsible for establishing and maintaining adequate internal control over financial reporting, as such term is defined in Exchange Act Rules 13a-15(f). Under the supervision and with the participation of our management, including our chief executive officer and chief financial officer, we assessed the effectiveness of our internal control over financial reporting as of January 28, 2006, based on the framework in *Internal Control – Integrated Framework*, issued by the Committee of Sponsoring Organizations of the Treadway Commission. Based on our assessment, we conclude that the Corporation's internal control over financial reporting is effective based on those criteria.

Our management's assessment of the effectiveness of our internal control over financial reporting as of January 28, 2006, has been audited by Ernst & Young LLP, independent registered public accounting firm, whose report also appears on this page.

Robert J. Ulrich
Chairman of the Board and
Chief Executive Officer
March 29, 2006

Douglas A. Scovanner
Executive Vice President and
Chief Financial Officer

Report of Independent Registered Public Accounting Firm on Internal Control over Financial Reporting

The Board of Directors and Shareholders
Target Corporation

We have audited management's assessment, included in the accompanying Report of Management on Internal Control, that Target Corporation and subsidiaries maintained effective internal control over financial reporting as of January 28, 2006, based on criteria established in *Internal Control – Integrated Framework*, issued by the Committee of Sponsoring Organizations of the Treadway Commission (the COSO criteria). The Corporation's management is responsible for maintaining effective internal control over financial reporting and for its assessment of the effectiveness of internal control over financial reporting. Our responsibility is to express an opinion on management's assessment and an opinion on the effectiveness of the Corporation's internal control over financial reporting based on our audit.

We conducted our audit in accordance with the standards of the Public Company Accounting Oversight Board (United States). Those standards require that we plan and perform the audit to obtain reasonable assurance about whether effective internal control over financial reporting was maintained in all material respects. Our audit included obtaining an understanding of internal control over financial reporting, evaluating management's assessment, testing and evaluating the design and operating effectiveness of internal control, and performing such other procedures as we considered necessary in the circumstances. We believe that our audit provides a reasonable basis for our opinion.

A company's internal control over financial reporting is a process designed to provide reasonable assurance regarding the reliability of financial reporting and the preparation of financial statements for external purposes in accordance with generally accepted accounting principles. A company's internal control over financial reporting includes those policies and procedures that (1) pertain to the maintenance of records that, in reasonable detail, accurately and fairly reflect the transactions and dispositions of the assets of the company, (2) provide reasonable assurance that transactions are recorded as necessary to permit preparation of financial statements in accordance with generally accepted accounting principles and that receipts and expenditures of the company are being made only in accordance with authorizations of management and directors of the company, and (3) provide reasonable assurance regarding prevention or timely detection of unauthorized acquisition, use, or disposition of the company's assets that could have a material effect on the financial statements.

Because of its inherent limitations, internal control over financial reporting may not prevent or detect misstatements. Also, projections of any evaluation of effectiveness to future periods are subject to the risk that controls may become inadequate because of changes in conditions or that the degree of compliance with the policies or procedures may deteriorate.

In our opinion, management's assessment that Target Corporation and subsidiaries maintained effective internal control over financial reporting as of January 28, 2006, is fairly stated, in all material respects, based on the COSO criteria. Also, in our opinion, the Corporation maintained, in all material respects, effective internal control over financial reporting as of January 28, 2006, based on the COSO criteria.

We also have audited, in accordance with the standards of the Public Company Accounting Oversight Board (United States), the consolidated statements of financial position of Target Corporation and subsidiaries as of January 28, 2006 and January 29, 2005, and the related consolidated statements of operations, cash flows and shareholders' investment for each of the three years in the period ended January 28, 2006, of Target Corporation and subsidiaries and our report dated March 29, 2006, expressed an unqualified opinion thereon.

Minneapolis, Minnesota
March 29, 2006

Ernst + Young LLP

Report of Audit Committee

The Audit Committee met six times during fiscal 2005 to review the overall audit scope, plans for internal and independent audits, the Corporation's systems of internal control, emerging accounting issues, audit fees and benefit plans. The Committee also met individually with the independent auditors, without management present, to discuss the results of their audits. The Committee encourages the internal and independent auditors to communicate closely with the Committee.

Audit Committee results were reported to the full Board of Directors and the Corporation's annual financial statements were reviewed and approved by the Board of Directors before issuance. The Audit Committee also recommended to the Board of Directors that the independent auditors be reappointed for fiscal 2006, subject to the approval of the shareholders at the annual meeting.

March 29, 2006

Selected Financial Information for Target Corporation 2004

The Income Statement

CONSOLIDATED RESULTS OF OPERATIONS

(millions, except per share data)	2004	2003	2002
Sales	$45,682	$40,928	$36,519
Net credit card revenues	1,157	1,097	891
Total revenues	46,839	42,025	37,410
Cost of sales	31,445	28,389	25,498
Selling, general and administrative expense	9,797	8,657	7,505
Credit card expense	737	722	629
Depreciation and amortization	1,259	1,098	967
Earnings from continuing operations before interest expense and income taxes	3,601	3,159	2,811
Net interest expense	570	556	584
Earnings from continuing operations before income taxes	3,031	2,603	2,227
Provision for income taxes	1,146	984	851
Earnings from continuing operations	$ 1,885	$ 1,619	$ 1,376
Earnings from discontinued operations, net of $46, $116 and $152 tax	$ 75	$ 190	$ 247
Gain on disposal of discontinued operations, net of $761 tax	$ 1,238	$ —	$ —
Net earnings	$ 3,198	$ 1,809	$ 1,623
Basic earnings per share			
Continuing operations	$ 2.09	$ 1.78	$ 1.52
Discontinued operations	$ 0.08	$ 0.21	$ 0.27
Gain from discontinued operations	$ 1.37	$ —	$ —
Basic earnings per share	$ 3.54	$ 1.99	$ 1.79
Diluted earnings per share			
Continuing operations	$ 2.07	$ 1.76	$ 1.51
Discontinued operations	$ 0.08	$ 0.21	$ 0.27
Gain from discontinued operations	$ 1.36	$ —	$ —
Diluted earnings per share	$ 3.51	$ 1.97	$ 1.78
Weighted average common shares outstanding:			
Basic	903.8	911.0	908.0
Diluted	912.1	919.2	914.3

See Notes to Consolidated Financial Statements throughout pages 28-37.

The Balance Sheet

CONSOLIDATED STATEMENTS OF FINANCIAL POSITION

(millions)	January 29, 2005	January 31, 2004
Assets		
Cash and cash equivalents	$ 2,245	$ 708
Accounts receivable, net	5,069	4,621
Inventory	5,384	4,531
Other current assets	1,224	1,000
Current assets of discontinued operations	—	2,092
Total current assets	13,922	12,952
Property and equipment		
Land	3,804	3,312
Buildings and improvements	12,518	11,022
Fixtures and equipment	4,988	4,577
Construction-in-progress	962	969
Accumulated depreciation	(5,412)	(4,727)
Property and equipment, net	16,860	15,153
Other non-current assets	1,511	1,377
Non-current assets of discontinued operations	—	1,934
Total assets	$32,293	$31,416
Liabilities and shareholders' investment		
Accounts payable	$ 5,779	$ 4,956
Accrued liabilities	1,633	1,288
Income taxes payable	304	382
Current portion of long-term debt and notes payable	504	863
Current liabilities of discontinued operations	—	825
Total current liabilities	8,220	8,314
Long-term debt	9,034	10,155
Deferred income taxes	973	632
Other non-current liabilities	1,037	917
Non-current liabilities of discontinued operations	—	266
Shareholders' investment		
Common stock*	74	76
Additional paid-in-capital	1,810	1,530
Retained earnings	11,148	9,523
Accumulated other comprehensive income	(3)	3
Total shareholders' investment	13,029	11,132
Total liabilities and shareholders' investment	$32,293	$31,416

* **Common Stock** *Authorized 6,000,000,000 shares, $.0833 par value; 890,643,966 shares issued and outstanding at January 29, 2005; 911,808,051 shares issued and outstanding at January 31, 2004.*

   Preferred Stock *Authorized 5,000,000 shares, $.01 par value; no shares were issued or outstanding at January 29, 2005 or January 31, 2004.*

See Notes to Consolidated Financial Statements throughout pages 28-37.

The Statement of Cash Flows

CONSOLIDATED STATEMENTS OF CASH FLOWS

(millions)	2004	2003	2002
Operating activities			
Net earnings	$ 3,198	$ 1,809	$ 1,623
Earnings from and gain on disposal of discontinued operations, net of tax	1,313	190	247
Earnings from continuing operations	1,885	1,619	1,376
Reconciliation to cash flow:			
Depreciation and amortization	1,259	1,098	967
Deferred tax provision	233	208	208
Bad debt provision	451	476	391
Loss on disposal of fixed assets, net	59	41	54
Other non-cash items affecting earnings	133	67	179
Changes in operating accounts providing/(requiring) cash:			
Accounts receivable originated at Target	(209)	(279)	(454)
Inventory	(853)	(579)	(370)
Other current assets	(37)	(196)	13
Other non-current assets	(147)	(166)	(136)
Accounts payable	823	721	545
Accrued liabilities	319	85	3
Income taxes payable	(78)	99	(80)
Other	(17)	19	29
Cash flow provided by operations	3,821	3,213	2,725
Investing activities			
Expenditures for property and equipment	(3,068)	(2,738)	(3,040)
Proceeds from disposals of fixed assets	56	67	32
Change in accounts receivable originated at third parties	(690)	(538)	(1,768)
Proceeds from sale of discontinued operations	4,881	—	—
Cash flow provided by/(required for) investing activities	1,179	(3,209)	(4,776)
Financing activities			
Decrease in notes payable, net	—	(100)	—
Additions to long-term debt	10	1,200	3,116
Reductions of long-term debt	(1,487)	(1,179)	(1,098)
Dividends paid	(272)	(237)	(218)
Repurchase of stock	(1,290)	(48)	(3)
Stock option exercises	146	36	27
Other	56	(10)	(20)
Cash flow (required for)/provided by financing activities	(2,837)	(338)	1,804
Net cash (required)/provided by discontinued operations	(626)	292	508
Net increase/(decrease) in cash and cash equivalents	1,537	(42)	261
Cash and cash equivalents at beginning of year	708	750	489
Cash and cash equivalents at end of year	$ 2,245	$ 708	$ 750

Amounts presented herein are on a cash basis and therefore may differ from those shown in other sections of this Annual Report. Consistent with the provisions of SFAS No. 95, "Statement of Cash Flows," cash flows related to accounts receivable are classified as either Provided by Operations or From Investing Activities, depending on their origin.

Cash paid for income taxes was $1,742 million, $781 million and $853 million during 2004, 2003 and 2002, respectively. Cash paid for interest (including interest capitalized) was $498 million, $550 million and $526 million during 2004, 2003 and 2002, respectively.

See Notes to Consolidated Financial Statements throughout pages 28-37.

The Statement of Owner's Equity

CONSOLIDATED STATEMENTS OF SHAREHOLDERS' INVESTMENT

(millions, except footnotes)	Common Stock Shares	Stock Par Value	Additional Paid-in Capital	Retained Earnings	Accumulated Other Comprehensive Income	Total
February 2, 2002	905.2	$75	$1,193	$ 6,628	$ —	$ 7,896
Consolidated net earnings	—	—	—	1,623	—	1,623
Other comprehensive income	—	—	—	—	4	4
Total comprehensive income						1,627
Dividends declared	—	—	—	(218)	—	(218)
Repurchase of stock	(.5)	—	—	(16)	—	(16)
Issuance of stock for ESOP	3.0	1	105	—	—	106
Stock options and awards	2.1	—	102	—	—	102
February 1, 2003	909.8	76	1,400	8,017	4	9,497
Consolidated net earnings	—	—	—	1,809	—	1,809
Other comprehensive income	—	—	—	—	(1)	(1)
Total comprehensive income						1,808
Dividends declared	—	—	—	(246)	—	(246)
Repurchase of stock	(1.5)	—	—	(57)	—	(57)
Issuance of stock for ESOP	0.6	—	17	—	—	17
Stock options and awards	2.9	—	113	—	—	113
January 31, 2004	911.8	76	1,530	9,523	3	11,132
Consolidated net earnings	—	—	—	3,198	—	3,198
Other comprehensive income	—	—	—	—	(6)	(6)
Total comprehensive income						3,192
Dividends declared	—	—	—	(280)	—	(280)
Repurchase of stock	(28.9)	(3)	—	(1,293)	—	(1,296)
Issuance of stock for ESOP	—	—	—	—	—	—
Stock options and awards	7.7	1	280	—	—	281
January 29, 2005	890.6	$74	$1,810	$11,148	$(3)	$13,029

Common Stock *Authorized 6,000,000,000 shares, $.0833 par value; 890,643,966 shares issued and outstanding at January 29, 2005; 911,808,051 shares issued and outstanding at January 31, 2004; 909,801,560 shares issued and outstanding at February 1, 2003.*

In June of 2004, our Board of Directors authorized the repurchase of $3 billion of our common stock. The repurchase of our common stock is expected to be made primarily in open market transactions, subject to market conditions, and is expected to be completed over two to three years. This authorization replaced our previous repurchase programs that were authorized by our Board of Directors in January 1999 and March 2000. In 2004, we repurchased a total of 29 million shares of our common stock at a total cost of approximately $1,290 million ($44.68 per share).

Preferred Stock *Authorized 5,000,000 shares, $.01 par value; no shares were issued or outstanding at January 29, 2005, January 31, 2004 or February 1, 2003.*

Junior Preferred Stock Rights *In 2001, we declared a distribution of preferred share purchase rights. Terms of the plan provide for a distribution of one preferred share purchase right for each outstanding share of our common stock. Each right will entitle shareholders to buy one twelve-hundredth of a share of a new series of junior participating preferred stock at an exercise price of $125.00, subject to adjustment. The rights will be exercisable only if a person or group acquires ownership of 20 percent or more of our common stock or announces a tender offer to acquire 30 percent or more of our common stock.*

Dividends *Dividends declared per share were $0.31, $0.27 and $0.24 in 2004, 2003 and 2002, respectively.*

See Notes to Consolidated Financial Statements throughout pages 28-37.

NOTES TO CONSOLIDATED FINANCIAL STATEMENTS

Summary of Accounting Policies

Organization Target Corporation operates large-format general merchandise discount stores in the United States and a much smaller, rapidly growing on-line business. Additionally, our credit card operations represent an integral component of our retail business.

Consolidation The financial statements include the balances of the Corporation and its subsidiaries after elimination of material inter-company balances and transactions. All material subsidiaries are wholly owned.

Use of Estimates The preparation of our financial statements, in conformity with accounting principles generally accepted in the United States (GAAP), requires management to make estimates and assumptions that affect the reported amounts in the financial statements and accompanying notes. Actual results may differ from those estimates.

Fiscal Year Our fiscal year ends on the Saturday nearest January 31. Unless otherwise stated, references to years in this report relate to fiscal years rather than to calendar years. Fiscal years 2004, 2003 and 2002 each consisted of 52 weeks.

Reclassifications Certain prior year amounts have been reclassified to conform to the current year presentation.

Stock-based Compensation In December 2004, the Financial Accounting Standards Board finalized Statement of Financial Accounting Standards No. 123R, "Share-Based Payment" (SFAS No. 123R). SFAS No. 123R eliminates accounting for share-based compensation transactions using the intrinsic value method prescribed in APB Opinion No. 25, "Accounting for Stock Issued to Employees," and requires instead that such transactions be accounted for using a fair-value-based method. We adopted SFAS No. 123, "Accounting for Stock-Based Compensation," in accordance with the prospective transition method prescribed in SFAS No. 148, "Accounting for Stock-Based Compensation – Transition and Disclosure" in the first quarter of 2003. Therefore, the fair value based method has been applied prospectively to awards granted subsequent to February 1, 2003 (the last day of our 2002 fiscal year). We have elected to adopt the provisions of SFAS No. 123R in 2004 under the modified retrospective transition method. All prior period financial statements have been restated to recognize compensation cost in the amounts previously reported in the Notes to Consolidated Financial Statements under the provisions of SFAS No. 123. Information related to outstanding stock options and performance shares is disclosed on pages 33-34.

Revenues

The contribution to revenue from sales is recognized when the sales occur and are net of expected returns. Revenue from gift card sales is recognized upon redemption of the gift card. Commissions earned on sales generated by leased departments are included within sales and were $46 million in 2004, $32 million in 2003 and $19 million in

2002. Net credit card revenues are comprised of finance charges and late fees from credit card holders, as well as third-party merchant fees earned from the use of our Target Visa credit card. Net credit card revenues are recognized according to the contractual provisions of each applicable credit card agreement. If an account is written-off, any uncollected finance charges or late fees are recorded as a reduction of credit card revenue. The amount of our retail sales charged to our credit cards was $3,269 million, $3,006 million and $2,980 million in 2004, 2003 and 2002, respectively.

Consideration Received from Vendors

We receive income for a variety of vendor-sponsored programs such as volume rebates, markdown allowances, promotions and advertising, and for our compliance programs. Promotional and advertising allowances are intended to offset our costs of promoting and selling the vendor's merchandise in our stores and are recognized when we incur the cost or complete the promotion. Under our compliance programs, vendors are charged for merchandise shipments that do not meet our requirements, such as late or incomplete shipments, and we record these allowances when the violation occurs. Vendor income either reduces our inventory costs or our operating expenses based on the requirements of Emerging Issues Task Force (EITF) Issue No. 02-16, "Accounting by a Customer (Including a Reseller) for Certain Consideration Received from a Vendor" as discussed below.

In the first quarter of 2003, we adopted EITF No. 02-16 which resulted in the reclassification of certain vendor income items from operating expenses to inventory purchases and recognized into income as the vendors' merchandise is sold. The guidance was applied on a prospective basis only as required by EITF No. 02-16. This guidance had no material impact on sales, cash flows or financial position for any period.

In the fourth quarter of 2003, we adopted EITF No. 03-10, "Application of Issue 02-16 by Resellers to Sales Incentives Offered to Consumers by Manufacturers," which amends EITF No. 02-16. In accordance with EITF No. 03-10, if certain criteria are met, consideration received from a vendor for honoring the vendor's sales incentives offered directly to consumers (i.e. manufacturer's coupons) should not be recorded as a reduction of the cost of the reseller's purchases from the vendor. The adoption of EITF No. 03-10 did not have a material impact on net earnings, cash flows or financial position.

Buying, Occupancy and Distribution Expenses

Buying expenses primarily consist of salaries and expenses incurred by our merchandising operations, while occupancy expenses primarily consist of rent, property taxes and other operating costs of our retail, distribution and headquarters facilities. Buying and occupancy expenses classified in selling, general and administrative expenses were $1,421 million, $1,213 million and $1,063 million in 2004, 2003 and 2002, respectively. In addition, we recorded $1,035 million, $910 million and $789 million of depreciation expense for our retail, distribution and headquarters facilities in 2004, 2003 and 2002, respectively.

Advertising Costs

Advertising costs, included in selling, general and administrative expense, are expensed at first showing of the advertisement and were $888 million, $872 million and $666 million for 2004, 2003 and 2002, respectively. Advertising vendor income used to reduce advertising expenses was approximately $72 million, $58 million and $173 million for 2004, 2003 and 2002, respectively. Television and radio broadcast and newspaper circulars make up the majority of our advertising costs in all three years.

Discontinued Operations

On March 10, 2004, we began a review of strategic alternatives for our Marshall Field's and Mervyn's businesses, which included but was not limited to the possible sale of one or both as ongoing businesses to existing retailers or other qualified buyers.

On June 9, 2004, we agreed to sell Marshall Field's and the Mervyn's stores located in Minnesota to The May Department Store Company (May). We completed the sale of Marshall Field's on July 31, 2004 and the sale of the Minnesota Mervyn's stores on August 24, 2004. May acquired total assets and liabilities with a net carrying value of $1,563 million in exchange for $3,240 million cash consideration, resulting in a gain on the sale of $1,677 million or $1.14 per share.

On July 29, 2004, we agreed to sell the remaining Mervyn's retail stores and distribution centers to an investment consortium including Sun Capital Partners, Inc., Cerberus Capital Management, L.P., and Lubert-Adler/Klaff and Partners, L.P. and to sell Mervyn's credit card receivables to GE Consumer Finance, a unit of General Electric Company, for total cash consideration of $1,641 million. This sale transaction was completed as of August 28, 2004, resulting in a gain of $322 million or $.22 per share.

In accordance with SFAS No. 144, "Accounting for the Impairment or Disposal of Long-Lived Assets," the financial results of Marshall Field's and Mervyn's are reported as discontinued operations for all periods presented.

In connection with the sale of Marshall Field's, May is purchasing transition support services from us until the end of first quarter 2005. We are providing transition services to the buyer of Mervyn's for a fee until the earlier of August 2007 or the date on which an alternative long-term solution for providing these services is in place. The fees received for providing these services exceed our marginal costs, but when an allocable share of our fixed costs is included, the consideration received is essentially equal to our total costs.

The financial results included in discontinued operations were as follows:

(millions)	January 29, 2005	January 31, 2004	February 1, 2003
Revenue	$3,095	$6,138	$6,507
Earnings from discontinued operations before income taxes	121	306	399
Earnings from discontinued operations, net of $46, $116 and $152 tax, respectively	75	190	247
Gain on sale of discontinued operations, net of $761 tax	1,238	—	—
Total income from discontinued operations, net of tax	$1,313	$ 190	$ 247

There were no assets or liabilities of Marshall Field's or Mervyn's included in our Consolidated Statements of Financial Position at January 29, 2005. The major classes of assets and liabilities of discontinued operations in the Consolidated Statements of Financial Position on January 31, 2004 were as follows:

(millions)	January 31, 2004
Cash and cash equivalents	$ 8
Accounts receivable, net	1,155
Inventory	812
Other	117
Current assets of discontinued operations	**$2,092**
Property and equipment, net	**$1,816**
Other	118
Non-current assets of discontinued operations	**$1,934**
Accounts payable	$ 492
Accrued liabilities	330
Current portion of long-term debt and notes payable	3
Current liabilities of discontinued operations	**$ 825**
Long-term debt	$ 62
Deferred income taxes	—
Other	204
Non-current liabilities of discontinued operations	**$ 266**

Earnings per Share

Basic earnings per share (EPS) is net earnings divided by the average number of common shares outstanding during the period. Diluted EPS includes the incremental shares that are assumed to be issued on the exercise of stock options.

(millions, except per share data)	Basic EPS			Diluted EPS		
	2004	2003	2002	2004	2003	2002
Net earnings	$3,198	$1,809	$1,623	$3,198	$1,809	$1,623
Basic weighted average common shares outstanding	903.8	911.0	908.0	903.8	911.0	908.0
Stock options	—	—	—	8.3	8.2	6.3
Weighted average common shares outstanding	903.8	911.0	908.0	912.1	919.2	914.3
Earnings per share	$ 3.54	$ 1.99	$ 1.79	$ 3.51	$ 1.97	$ 1.78

The shares related to stock options shown above do not include shares issuable upon exercise of approximately 4.5 million and 13.2 million at January 31, 2004 and February 1, 2003, respectively, because the effect would have been antidilutive. There were no antidilutive shares issuable upon exercise at January 29, 2005.

Other Comprehensive Income

Other comprehensive income includes revenues, expenses, gains and losses that are excluded from net earnings under GAAP. In 2004 and 2003, other comprehensive income primarily included gains and losses on certain hedge transactions and the change in our minimum pension liability, net of related taxes.

Cash Equivalents

Cash equivalents represent short-term investments with a maturity of three months or less from the time of purchase and were $1,732 million, $244 million and $357 million in 2004, 2003 and 2002, respectively. The increase of $1,488 in 2004 compared to 2003 is primarily due to investment of the remaining proceeds at year end from the divestitures of Marshall Field's and Mervyn's.

Accounts Receivable

Accounts receivable are recorded net of an allowance for expected losses. The allowance, recognized in an amount equal to the anticipated future write-offs based on delinquencies, risk scores, aging trends, industry risk trends and our historical experience, was $387 million at January 29, 2005 and $352 million at January 31, 2004.

Through our special purpose subsidiary, Target Receivables Corporation (TRC), we transfer, on an ongoing basis, substantially all of our receivables to the Target Credit Card Master Trust (the Trust) in return for certificates representing undivided interests in the Trust's assets. TRC owns the undivided interest in the Trust's assets, other than the Trust's assets securing the financing transactions entered into by the Trust and the 2 percent of Trust assets held by Target National Bank (TNB). TNB is a wholly owned subsidiary of the Corporation that also services receivables. SFAS No. 140 "Accounting for Transfers and Servicing of Financial Assets and Extinguishments of Liabilities (a replacement of SFAS No. 125)" is the accounting guidance applicable to such transactions. SFAS No. 140 requires that we include the receivables within the Trust and any debt securities issued by the Trust in our Consolidated Statement of Financial Position. Notwithstanding this accounting treatment, the receivables within the Trust are owned by our wholly-owned, bankruptcy remote subsidiary, TRC, and thus are not available to general creditors of Target.

Inventory

Substantially all of our inventory and the related cost of sales are accounted for under the retail inventory accounting method using the last-in, first-out (LIFO) basis. Inventory is stated at the lower of LIFO cost or market. Inventory also includes a LIFO provision that is calculated based on inventory levels, markup rates and internally generated retail price indices. Our only accumulated LIFO reserve relates to Target Commercial Interiors and is immaterial to our consolidated financial statements. Because we have experienced price deflation recently, we have not recorded a LIFO provision for Target Stores.

Other Current Assets

Other current assets as of January 29, 2005 and January 31, 2004 consist of the following:

	2004	2003
Vendor income and other receivables	$ 428	$ 391
Deferred taxes	344	236
Other	452	373
Total	$1,224	$1,000

In addition to vendor income, other receivables relate primarily to pharmacy receivables and merchandise sourcing services provided to third parties.

Property and Equipment

Property and equipment are recorded at cost, less accumulated depreciation. Depreciation is computed using the straight-line method over estimated useful lives. Depreciation expense for the years 2004, 2003 and 2002 was $1,232 million, $1,068 million and $942 million, respectively. Accelerated depreciation methods are generally used for income tax purposes. Repair and maintenance costs were $453 million, $393 million and $355 million in 2004, 2003 and 2002, respectively.

Estimated useful lives by major asset category are as follows:

Asset	Life (in years)
Buildings and improvements	8–39
Fixtures and equipment	4–15
Computer hardware and software	4

In accordance with SFAS No. 144, "Accounting for the Impairment or Disposal of Long-Lived Assets," all long-lived assets are reviewed when events or changes in circumstances indicate that the carrying value of the asset may not be recoverable. We review assets at the lowest level for which there are identifiable cash flows, which is usually at the store level. The carrying amount of the store assets is compared to the expected undiscounted future cash flows to be generated by those assets over the estimated remaining useful life of the store. Cash flows are projected for each store based upon historical results and expectations. In cases where the expected future cash flows and fair value are less than the carrying amount of the assets, those stores are considered impaired and the assets are written down to fair value. Fair value is based on appraisals or other reasonable methods to estimate fair value. Impairment losses are included in depreciation expense for assets held and in use and included within selling, general and administrative expense on assets classified as held for sale. No impairments were recorded in 2004 or 2003 as a result of the tests performed.

Other Non-current Assets

Other non-current assets as of January 29, 2005 and January 31, 2004 consist of the following:

	2004	2003
Prepaid pension expense	$ 711	$ 580
Cash value of life insurance	439	363
Goodwill and intangible assets	206	229
Other	155	205
Total	$1,511	$1,377

Goodwill and Intangible Assets

Goodwill and intangible assets are recorded within other non-current assets at cost less accumulated amortization. Amortization is computed on intangible assets with definite useful lives using the straight-line method over estimated useful lives that range from three to fifteen years. Amortization expense for the years 2004, 2003 and 2002 was $27 million, $30 million and $25 million, respectively. At January 29, 2005 and January 31, 2004, goodwill and intangible assets by major classes were as follows:

(millions)	Goodwill 2004	2003	Leasehold Acquisition Costs 2004	2003	Other 2004	2003	Total 2004	2003
Gross asset	$80	$80	$185	$182	$201	$200	$466	$462
Accumulated amortization	(20)	(20)	(52)	(34)	(188)	(179)	(260)	(233)
Net goodwill and intangible assets	$60	$60	$133	$148	$ 13	$ 21	$206	$229

As required, we adopted SFAS No. 142, "Goodwill and Other Intangible Assets," during the first quarter of 2002. In 2004, 2003 and 2002, the adoption of this statement reduced annual amortization expense of certain intangible assets by approximately $5 million (less than $.01 per share). The estimated aggregate amortization expense of our definite-lived intangible assets for each of the five succeeding fiscal years, 2005 to 2009, is expected to be $24 million, $22 million, $20 million, $19 million and $19 million, respectively. During 2004, goodwill with an approximate carrying value of $63 million was sold as part of the Marshall Field's transaction. There was no goodwill included in the Mervyn's sale transaction that also occurred in 2004.

Discounted cash flow models were used in determining fair value for the purposes of the required annual goodwill impairment analysis. No impairments were recorded in 2004, 2003 and 2002 as a result of the tests performed.

Accounts Payable

Our accounting policy is to reduce accounts payable when checks to vendors clear the bank from which they were drawn. Outstanding checks included in accounts payable were $992 million and $966 million at year-end 2004 and 2003, respectively.

Accrued Liabilities

Accrued liabilities as of January 29, 2005 and January 31, 2004 consist of the following:

	2004	2003
Wages and benefits	$ 412	$ 369
Taxes payable	287	245
Gift card liability	214	169
Other	720	505
Total	$1,633	$1,288

Taxes payable consist of real estate, employee withholdings and sales tax liabilities. Gift card liability represents the amount of gift cards that have been issued but have not been presented for redemption.

Commitments and Contingencies

At January 29, 2005, our obligations included notes and debentures of $9,447 million (discussed in detail under Notes Payable and Long-term Debt below), the present value of capital lease obligations of $91 million and total future payments of operating leases with total contractual lease payments of $3,049 million, including certain options to extend the lease term that are expected to be exercised in the amount of $1,415 million (discussed in detail under Leases on page 32). In addition, commitments for the purchase, construction, lease or remodeling of real estate, facilities and equipment were approximately $544 million at year-end 2004. Merchandise royalty

commitments of approximately $102 million are due during the five-year period ending in 2009. Throughout the year, we enter into various commitments to purchase inventory. In addition to the accounts payable reflected in our Consolidated Statements of Financial Position on page 25, we had commitments with various vendors for the purchase of inventory as of January 29, 2005. These purchase commitments are cancelable by their terms.

We expect to receive a share of the proceeds from the $3 billion Visa/MasterCard antitrust litigation settlement, as we are a member of the class action lawsuit. However, the amount and timing of the payment are not certain at this time.

We are exposed to claims and litigation arising out of the ordinary course of business and use various methods to resolve these matters in a manner that we believe serves the best interest of our shareholders and other constituents. Our policy is to disclose pending lawsuits and other known claims that we expect may have a material impact on our results of operations, cash flows or financial condition. Other than the matter discussed above, we do not believe any of the currently identified claims and litigated matters meet this criterion, either individually or in the aggregate.

Notes Payable and Long-term Debt

At January 29, 2005, no notes payable were outstanding. The average amount of notes payable outstanding during 2004 was $55 million at a weighted average interest rate of 1.3 percent. In 2004, notes payable balances fluctuated significantly during the year due to seasonal financing needs, proceeds from sale of Marshall Field's and Mervyn's and other factors. On July 28, 2004, our short-term borrowing reached $1,422 million, its highest level for the year.

At January 31, 2004, no notes payable were outstanding. The average amount of notes payable outstanding during 2003 was $377 million at a weighted average interest rate of 1.2 percent. On October 31, 2003, our short-term borrowing reached $1,409 million, its highest level for the year.

At January 29, 2005, two committed credit agreements totaling $1,600 million were in place through a group of 25 banks at specified rates. Of these credit lines, an $800 million credit facility expires in June 2005 and includes a one-year term-out option to June 2006. The remaining $800 million credit facility expires in June 2008. There were no balances outstanding at any time during 2004 or 2003 under these agreements.

In 2004, we issued no long-term debt. We called or repurchased $542 million of long-term debt with an average remaining life of 24 years and a weighted average interest rate of 7.0 percent, resulting in a pre-tax loss of $89 million (approximately $.06 per share), reflected in interest expense.

In 2003, we issued $500 million of long-term debt maturing in 2008 at 3.38 percent, $200 million of long-term debt maturing in 2018 at 4.88 percent and $500 million of long-term debt maturing in 2013 at 4.00 percent. We also called or repurchased $297 million of long-term debt with an average remaining life of 20 years and a weighted average interest rate of 7.8 percent, resulting in a pre-tax loss of $15 million (approximately $.01 per share), reflected in interest expense.

The portion of long-term debt secured by credit card receivables was $750 million at January 29, 2005. On January 31, 2004, we had $1,500 million of long-term debt secured by credit card receivables, $750 million of which was classified as current portion of long-term debt.

At year-end, our debt portfolio, including adjustments related to swap transactions discussed in the following derivatives section, was as follows:

Notes Payable and Long-term Debt

(millions)	January 29, 2005 Rate*	January 29, 2005 Balance	January 31, 2004 Rate*	January 31, 2004 Balance
Notes payable	—%	$ —	—%	$ —
Notes and debentures:				
Due 2004–2008	4.0	4,045	3.1	4,953
Due 2009–2013	5.9	3,726	5.8	3,795
Due 2014–2018	3.3	234	2.3	227
Due 2019–2023	9.3	213	9.3	214
Due 2024–2028	6.7	325	6.7	400
Due 2029–2033	6.6	904	6.7	1,300
Total notes payable, notes and debentures**	5.2%	$9,447	4.7%	$10,889
Capital lease obligations		91		129
Less: current portion		(504)		(863)
Notes payable and long-term debt		$9,034		$10,155

Reflects the weighted average stated interest rate as of year-end, including the impact of interest rate swaps.

**The estimated fair value of total notes payable, notes and debentures, using a discounted cash flow analysis based on our incremental interest rates for similar types of financial instruments, was $10,171 million at January 29, 2005 and $11,681 million at January 31, 2004.*

Required principal payments on long-term debt over the next five years, excluding capital lease obligations, are $501 million in 2005, $751 million in 2006, $1,321 million in 2007, $1,451 million in 2008 and $751 million in 2009.

Derivatives

Our derivative instruments are primarily interest rate swaps which hedge the fair value of certain debt by effectively converting interest from a fixed rate to a variable rate. We also hold derivative instruments to manage our exposure to risks associated with the effect of equity market returns on our non-qualified defined contribution plans as discussed on page 34.

At January 29, 2005 and January 31, 2004, interest rate swaps were outstanding in notional amounts totaling $2,850 million and $2,150 million, respectively. The change in market value of an interest rate swap as well as the offsetting change in market value of the hedged debt is recognized into earnings in the current period. Ineffectiveness would result when changes in the market value of the hedged debt are not completely offset by changes in the market value of the interest rate swap. There was no ineffectiveness recognized in 2004 or 2003 related to these instruments. The fair value of outstanding interest rate swaps and net unamortized gains from terminated interest rate swaps was $45 million at January 29, 2005 and $97 million at January 31, 2004.

During 2004, we entered into two interest rate swaps with notional amounts of $200 million and two interest rate swaps with notional amounts of $250 million. We also terminated an interest rate swap with a notional amount of $200 million, resulting in a loss of $16 million that will be amortized into expense over the remaining life of the hedged debt. During 2003, we entered into interest rate swaps with notional amounts of $200 million, $500 million and $400 million.

We also terminated an interest rate swap with a notional amount of $400 million, resulting in a gain of $24 million that will be amortized into income over the remaining life of the hedged debt. In 2004 and 2003, the gains and losses amortized into income for terminated swaps were not material to our results of operations.

Interest Rate Swaps Outstanding at Year-end
(millions)

January 29, 2005 Notional Amount	January 29, 2005 Receive Fixed	January 29, 2005 Pay Floating*	January 31, 2004 Notional Amount	January 31, 2004 Receive Fixed	January 31, 2004 Pay Floating*
$500	7.5%	2.4%	$500	7.5%	1.2%
200	5.8	3.3	—	—	—
550	4.6	3.3	550	4.6	1.3
500	4.4	3.2	500	4.4	1.2
400	4.4	3.3	400	4.4	1.4
200	3.9	2.4	—	—	—
250	3.8	2.5	—	—	—
250	3.8	2.4	—	—	—
—	—	—	200	4.9	1.1
$2,850			$2,150		

Reflects floating interest rate accrued at the end of the year.

The weighted average life of the interest rate swaps was approximately 3 years at January 29, 2005.

Leases

Assets held under capital leases are included in property and equipment and are charged to depreciation and interest over the life of the lease. Operating leases are not capitalized and lease rentals are expensed on a straight-line basis over the life of the lease. Rent expense on buildings, classified in selling, general and administrative expense, includes percentage rents that are based on a percentage of retail sales over contractual levels. Total rent expense was $240 million in 2004, $150 million in 2003 and $150 million in 2002. Most of the long-term leases include options to renew, with terms varying from one to 50 years. Certain leases also include options to purchase the property.

Future minimum lease payments required under noncancelable lease agreements existing at January 29, 2005, were:

Future Minimum Lease Payments

(millions)	Operating Leases	Capital Leases
2005	$146	$12
2006	142	12
2007	137	13
2008	117	13
2009	102	12
After 2009	2,405	127
Total future minimum lease payments	$3,049***	$189
Less: Interest*		(98)
Present value of minimum capital lease payments		$91**

Calculated using the interest rate at inception for each lease.

**Includes current portion of $3 million.*

***Total contractual lease payments include certain options to extend lease terms, in the amount of $1,415, that are expected to be exercised because the investment in leasehold improvement is significant.*

Income Taxes

Reconciliation of tax rates is as follows:

Tax Rate Reconciliation

	2004	2003	2002
Federal statutory rate	35.0%	35.0%	35.0%
State income taxes, net of federal tax benefit	3.3	3.3	3.4
Dividends on ESOP stock	(0.2)	(0.2)	(0.2)
Work opportunity tax credits	(0.2)	(0.2)	(0.2)
Other	(0.1)	(0.1)	0.2
Effective tax rate	37.8%	37.8%	38.2%

The components of the provision for income taxes were:

Income Tax Provision: Expense

(millions)	2004	2003	2002
Current:			
Federal	$ 908	$ 669	$ 550
State	144	107	93
	1,052	776	643
Deferred:			
Federal	83	184	185
State	11	24	23
	94	208	208
Total	$1,146	$ 984	$ 851

The components of the net deferred tax asset/(liability) were:

Net Deferred Tax Asset/(Liability)

(millions)	January 29, 2005	January 31, 2004
Gross deferred tax assets:		
Deferred compensation	$ 332	$ 297
Self-insured benefits	179	143
Accounts receivable valuation allowance	147	133
Inventory	47	44
Postretirement health care obligation	38	42
Other	128	53
	871	712
Gross deferred tax liabilities:		
Property and equipment	(1,136)	(806)
Pension	(268)	(218)
Other	(96)	(84)
	(1,500)	(1,108)
Total	$ (629)	$ (396)

In the Consolidated Statement of Financial Position, the current deferred tax asset balance is the net of all current deferred tax assets and current deferred tax liabilities. The non-current deferred tax liability is the net of all non-current deferred tax assets and non-current deferred tax liabilities.

Approximately $566 million of the proceeds attributable to the real properties sold in the Marshall Field's and Mervyn's dispositions were used to acquire replacement properties which will be used in our business. Approximately $371 million of the gain related to the sold real properties was deferred for income tax purposes as required by Section 1031 of the Internal Revenue Code until such time as the replacement properties are disposed.

Other Non-current Liabilities

Other non-current liabilities as of January 29, 2005 and January 31, 2004 consist of the following:

	2004	2003
Deferred compensation	$ 528	$464
Worker's compensation and general liability	317	286
Other	192	167
Total	$1,037	$917

Share Repurchase

In June 2004, our Board of Directors authorized the repurchase of $3 billion of our common stock, which we expect to complete over two to three years. This authorization replaced our previous repurchase programs that were authorized by our Board of Directors in January 1999 and March 2000. We repurchased 29 million shares at an average price per share of $44.68 during 2004, at a total cost of $1,290 million.

Stock-based Compensation

We maintain a long-term incentive plan for key employees and non-employee members of our Board of Directors. Our long-term incentive plan allows for the grant of equity-based compensation awards, including stock options, performance share awards, restricted stock awards, or a combination of awards. A majority of the awards are non-qualified stock options that vest annually in equal amounts over a four-year period. Therefore, in accordance with SFAS No. 123R, we recognize compensation expense for these awards on a straight-line basis over the four-year vesting period. These options generally expire no later than ten years after the date of the grant. Options granted to the non-employee members of our Board of Directors vest after one year and have a ten-year term. Performance share awards represent shares issuable in the future based upon attainment of specified levels of future financial performance. We use a three or four year performance measurement period for performance share awards. The number of unissued common shares reserved for future grants under the stock-based compensation plans was 51,560,249 at January 29, 2005 and 19,279,658 at January 31, 2004.

Options and Performance Share Awards Outstanding

	Options						Performance Shares
	Total Outstanding			Currently Exercisable			
(options and shares in thousands)	Number of Options	Average Price*	Average Life**	Number of Options	Average Price*	Average Life**	Potentially Issuable
February 2, 2002	31,315	$24.07	5.7	17,629	$17.04	5.7	—
Granted	6,096	30.60					552
Canceled	(561)	35.55					
Exercised	(2,063)	12.22					
February 1, 2003	34,787	$25.73	5.5	21,931	$20.89	5.4	552
Granted	4,638	38.34					573
Canceled	(407)	34.77					
Exercised	(2,859)	12.58					
January 31, 2004	36,159	$28.28	6.2	23,689	$24.48	5.2	1,125
Granted	4,072	49.12					629
Canceled/forfeited	(513)	35.32					(73)
Exercised/earned	(7,727)	20.95					(73)
January 29, 2005	**31,991**	**$32.59**	**5.8**	**22,102**	**$28.79**	**5.3**	**1,608**

*Weighted average exercise price.

**Weighted average contractual life remaining in years.

Total compensation expense related to stock-based compensation, which is the total fair value of shares vested was $60 million, $57 million and $49 million, during 2004, 2003 and 2002, respectively. The weighted-average grant date fair value of options granted during 2004, 2003 and 2002 was $13.10, $11.04 and $10.07, respectively. The total intrinsic value of options (the amount by which the stock price exceeded the strike price of the option on the date of exercise) that were exercised during 2004, 2003 and 2002 was $201 million, $72 million and $66 million, respectively.

Nonvested Options and Performance Share Awards

	Weighted Average		Weighted Average	
(options and shares in thousands)	Stock Options	Fair Value at Grant Date	Performance Shares	Fair Value at Grant Date
Nonvested at February 1, 2004	12,470	$11.07	1,125	$34.33
Granted	4,072	13.10	419	49.43
Vested/earned	(6,237)	11.25	(73)	34.44
Forfeited/cancelled	(416)	11.00	(73)	34.44
Nonvested at January 29, 2005	**9,889**	**$11.83**	**1,398**	**$38.84**

As of January 29, 2005, there was $104 million of total unrecognized compensation expense related to nonvested share-based compensation arrangements granted under our plans. That cost is expected to be recognized over a weighted-average period of 1.5 years.

We have elected to adopt the provisions of SFAS No. 123R in 2004 under the modified retrospective transition method. The beginning balances of deferred taxes, paid-in capital and retained earnings for 2003 have been restated by $54 million, $143 million and $90 million, respectively, to recognize compensation cost for fiscal years 1996 through 2002 in the amounts previously reported in the Notes to Consolidated Financial Statements under the provisions of SFAS No. 123. The requirements of SFAS No. 123R are discussed on page 23.

The Black-Scholes model was used to estimate the fair value of the options at grant date based on the following assumptions:

	2004	2003	2002
Dividend yield	.7%	.8%	.8%
Volatility	22%	29%	35%
Risk-free interest rate	3.8%	3.0%	3.0%
Expected life in years	5.5	5.0	5.0

Defined Contribution Plans

Employees who meet certain eligibility requirements can participate in a defined contribution 401(k) plan by investing up to 80 percent of their compensation. Highly compensated employees, however, are further limited by federal law and related regulation. Subject to these limits, we match 100 percent of each employee's contribution up to 5 percent of total compensation. Our contribution to the plan is initially invested in Target Corporation common stock but once vested after a period of three years the amounts are free to be diversified. Benefits expense related to these matching contributions was $118 million, $117 million and $111 million in 2004, 2003 and 2002, respectively.

In addition, we maintain other non-qualified, unfunded plans that allow participants who are otherwise limited by qualified plan statutes or regulations. They can defer compensation including remaining company match amounts, and earn returns tied to the results of either our 401(k) plan investment choices, including Target stock, or in the case of a frozen plan, market levels of interest rates, plus an additional return determined by the terms of each plan. We recognized benefits expense for these non-qualified plans of $63 million and $86 million in 2004 and 2003, respectively, and income of $20 million in 2002. We manage the risk of offering these retirement savings plans through a variety of activities, which include investing in vehicles that offset a substantial portion of our exposure to these returns. Including the impact of these related investments, net benefits expense from these plans was $23 million, $28 million, and $16 million in 2004, 2003, and 2002, respectively. We adjusted our position in some of the investment vehicles resulting in the repurchase of 0.8 million, 1.5 million and 0.5 million shares of our common stock in 2004, 2003 and 2002, respectively.

In 2004 and 2003, certain retired executives accepted our offer to exchange our obligation to them under our frozen non-qualified plan for cash or deferrals in our current non-qualified plans, which resulted in expense of $17 million in both years. Additionally, during 2002, certain non-qualified pension and survivor benefits owed to current executives were exchanged for deferrals in our current non-qualified plans and certain retired executives accepted our offer to exchange our obligation to them in our frozen non-qualified plan for deferrals in our current plans. These exchanges resulted in expense of $33 million. We expect lower future expenses as a result of these transactions because they were designed to be economically neutral or slightly favorable to us.

Participants in our non-qualified plans deferred compensation of $33 million, $42 million and $35 million in 2004, 2003 and 2002, respectively.

Pension and Postretirement Health Care Benefits

We have a qualified defined benefit pension plan that covers all U.S. employees who meet certain age, length of service and hours worked per year requirements. We also have unfunded non-qualified pension plans for employees who have qualified plan compensation restrictions. Benefits are provided based upon years of service and the employee's compensation. Retired employees also become eligible for certain health care benefits if they meet minimum age and service requirements and agree to contribute a portion of the cost. Prior to the end of 2004, but after the measurement date, we merged our three qualified U.S. pension plans into one plan. The expected impact of this merger on future accounting results is immaterial.

The Medicare Prescription Drug, Improvements and Modernization Act of 2003 (the Act) was signed into law in December 2003. As a result of the Act we recorded a reduction in our accumulated postretirement benefit obligation of $7 million in 2004. In addition, the expense amounts shown in the table below reflect a $1 million reduction due to the amortization of the actuarial gain and reduction in interest cost due to the effects of the Act.

Obligations and Funded Status at October 31, 2004

| | Pension Benefits | | | | Postretirement Health Care Benefits | |
| | Qualified Plans | | Non-qualified Plans | | | |
(millions)	2004	2003	2004	2003	2004	2003
Change in Benefit Obligation						
Benefit obligation at beginning of measurement period	$1,333	$1,078	$29	$23	$123	$116
Service cost	78	73	1	1	3	2
Interest cost	82	74	2	2	7	8
Actuarial loss	68	164	4	6	(6)	7
Benefits paid	(65)	(56)	(3)	(3)	(13)	(10)
Plan amendments	19	—	1	—	(7)	—
Settlement	—	—	—	—	—	—
Benefit obligation at end of measurement period	$1,515	$1,333	$34	$29	$107	$123
Change in Plan Assets						
Fair value of plan assets at beginning of measurement period	$1,405	$1,058	$ —	$ —	$ —	$ —
Actual return on plan assets	157	203	—	—	—	—
Employer contribution	201	200	3	3	13	10
Benefits paid	(65)	(56)	(3)	(3)	(13)	(10)
Fair value of plan assets at end of measurement period	$1,698	$1,405	$ —	$ —	$ —	$ —
Funded status	$ 183	$ 72	$(34)	$(29)	$(107)	$(123)
Unrecognized actuarial loss	584	587	15	12	6	12
Unrecognized prior service cost	(39)	(65)	2	3	—	1
Net amount recognized	$ 728	$ 594	$(17)	$(14)	$(101)	$(110)

Amounts recognized in the Statements of Financial Position consist of:

| | Pension Benefits | | | | Postretirement Health Care Benefits | |
| | Qualified Plans | | Non-qualified Plans | | | |
(millions)	2004	2003	2004	2003	2004	2003
Prepaid benefit cost	$733	$600	$ —	$ —	$ —	$ —
Accrued benefit cost	(11)	(6)	(24)	(20)	(101)	(110)
Intangible assets	—	—	2	3	n/a	n/a
Accumulated OCI	6	—	5	3	n/a	n/a
Net amount recognized	$728	$594	$(17)	$(14)	$(101)	$(110)

The accumulated benefit obligation for all defined benefit pension plans was $1,501 million and $1,237 million at October 31, 2004 and 2003, respectively. The projected benefit obligation, accumulated benefit obligation and fair value of plan assets for the pension plans with an accumulated benefit obligation in excess of plan assets were $49 million, $45 million and $5 million, respectively, as of October 31, 2004 and $34 million, $30 million and $1 million, respectively, as of October 31, 2003.

Net Pension and Postretirement Health Care Benefits Expense

| | Pension Benefits | | | Postretirement Health Care Benefits | | |
(millions)	2004	2003	2002	2004	2003	2002
Service cost benefits earned during the period	$ 79	$ 74	$ 58	$ 3	$ 2	$ 2
Interest cost on projected benefit obligation	84	75	75	7	8	8
Expected return on assets	(122)	(114)	(108)	—	—	—
Recognized losses	36	18	10	1	1	1
Recognized prior service cost	(7)	(7)	1	—	—	—
Settlement/curtailment charges	1	—	(12)	(7)	—	—
Total	$ 71	$ 46	$ 24	$ 4	$11	$11

The amortization of any prior service cost is determined using a straight-line amortization of the cost over the average remaining service period of employees expected to receive benefits under the plan. Curtailment gains recorded in 2004 were a result of the sale of Marshall Field's and Mervyn's. These curtailment gains are included in the gain on disposal of discontinued operations as a result of freezing the benefits for Marshall Field's and Mervyn's employees and retaining the related assets and obligations of the plans.

Assumptions

Weighted average assumptions used to determine benefit obligations at October 31:

	Pension Benefits		Postretirement Health Care Benefits	
	2004	2003	**2004**	2003
Discount rate	**5.75%**	6.25%	**5.75%**	6.25%
Average assumed rate of compensation increase	**2.75%**	3.25%	**n/a**	n/a

Weighted average assumptions used to determine net periodic benefit cost for years ended October 31:

	Pension Benefits		Postretirement Health Care Benefits	
	2004	2003	**2004**	2003
Discount rate	**6.25%**	7.00%	**6.25%**	7.00%
Expected long-term rate of return on plan assets	**8.00%**	8.50%	**n/a**	n/a
Average assumed rate of compensation increase	**3.25%**	4.00%	**n/a**	n/a

Our rate of return on qualified plans' assets has averaged 4.9 percent and 10.2 percent per year over the 5-year and 10-year periods, respectively, ending October 31, 2004 (our measurement date).

An increase in the cost of covered health care benefits of 6 percent was assumed for 2004. The rate is assumed to be 10 percent in 2005 and is reduced by 1 percent annually to 5 percent in 2010 and thereafter. The health care cost trend rate assumption may have a significant effect on the amounts reported.

A one percent change in assumed health care cost trend rates would have the following effects:

	1% Increase	1% Decrease
Effect on total of service and interest cost components of net periodic postretirement health care benefit cost	$—	$—
Effect on the health care component of the postretirement benefit obligation	$ 4	$ (4)

Additional Information

Our pension plan weighted average asset allocations at October 31, 2004 and 2003 by asset category are as follows:

Asset Category

	2004	2003
Equity securities	**58%**	56%
Debt securities	**26**	26
Other	**16**	18
Total	**100%**	100%

Our asset allocation strategy for 2005 targets 55 percent in equity securities, 25 percent in debt securities and 20 percent in other assets. Equity securities include our common stock in amounts substantially less than 1 percent of total plan assets at October 31, 2004 and 2003. Other assets include private equity, mezzanine and distressed debt and timber and less than a 5 percent allocation to real estate. Our expected long-term rate of return assumptions as of October 31, 2004 are 8.5 percent, 5 percent and 10 percent for equity securities, debt securities and other assets, respectively.

Contributions

Given the qualified pension plans' funded position, we are not required to make any contributions in 2005. In similar situations in the past, we have chosen to make discretionary contributions for various purposes, including minimizing Pension Benefit Guaranty Corporation premium payments and maintaining the fully-funded status of the plans. In 2005, such discretionary contributions could range from $0 to $50 million. We expect to make contributions in the range of $5 million to $15 million to our other postretirement benefit plans in 2005.

Estimated Future Benefit Payments

The following benefit payments, which reflect expected future service, as appropriate, are expected to be paid:

(millions)	Pension Benefits	Postretirement Health Care Benefits
2005	$ 59	$ 8
2006	62	8
2007	66	8
2008	70	9
2009	75	9
2010–2014	$476	$53

Quarterly Results (Unaudited)

Due to the seasonal nature of our business, fourth quarter operating results typically represent a substantially larger share of total year revenues and earnings due to the inclusion of the holiday shopping season. The same accounting policies are followed in preparing quarterly financial data as are followed in preparing annual data. The table below summarizes results by quarter for 2004 and 2003:

(millions, except per share data)	First Quarter		Second Quarter		Third Quarter		Fourth Quarter		Total Year	
	2004	2003	**2004**	2003	**2004**	2003	**2004**	2003	**2004**	2003
Total revenues	$10,180	$8,928	$10,556	$9,594	$10,909	$9,827	$15,194	$13,676	$46,839	$42,025
Gross margin	$ 3,140	$2,706	$ 3,268	$2,874	$ 3,300	$2,909	$ 4,529	$ 4,050	$14,237	$12,539
Earnings from continuing operations	$ 392	$ 313	$ 360	$ 322	$ 324	$ 262	$ 809	$ 722	$ 1,885	$ 1,619
Earnings from discontinued operations, net of $25, $18, $19, $18, $2, $18, $62, $46 and $116 tax	$ 40	$ 29	$ 31	$ 29	$ 4	$ 31	$ —	$ 101	$ 75	$ 190
Gain/(loss) on disposal of discontinued operations, net of $650, $132, $(21), and $761 tax (c)	$ —	$ —	$ 1,019	$ —	$ 203	$ —	$ 16	$ —	$ 1,238	$ —
Net earnings (a) (b)	$ 432	$ 342	$ 1,410	$ 351	$ 531	$ 293	$ 825	$ 823	$ 3,198	$ 1,809
Basic earnings per share (d)										
Continuing operations	$ 0.43	$ 0.34	$ 0.40	$ 0.35	$ 0.36	$ 0.29	$ 0.91	$ 0.79	$ 2.09	$ 1.78
Discontinued operations	$ 0.04	$ 0.03	$ 0.03	$ 0.03	$ —	$ 0.03	$ —	$ 0.11	$ 0.08	$ 0.21
Gain from discontinued operations	$ —	$ —	$ 1.12	$ —	$ 0.23	$ —	$ 0.01	$ —	$ 1.37	$ —
Basic earnings per share (a) (b)	$ 0.47	$ 0.37	$ 1.55	$ 0.38	$ 0.59	$ 0.32	$ 0.92	$ 0.90	$ 3.54	$ 1.99
Diluted earnings per share (d)										
Continuing operations	$ 0.43	$ 0.34	$ 0.39	$ 0.35	$ 0.36	$ 0.29	$ 0.90	$ 0.79	$ 2.07	$ 1.76
Discontinued operations	$ 0.04	$ 0.03	$ 0.03	$ 0.03	$ —	$ 0.03	$ —	$ 0.11	$ 0.08	$ 0.21
Gain from discontinued operations	$ —	$ —	$ 1.11	$ —	$ 0.23	$ —	$ 0.01	$ —	$ 1.36	$ —
Diluted earnings per share (a) (b)	$ 0.47	$ 0.37	$ 1.53	$ 0.38	$ 0.59	$ 0.32	$ 0.91	$ 0.90	$ 3.51	$ 1.97
Dividends declared per share (d)	$ .070	$ .060	$ .080	$ .070	$ .080	$ .070	$ .080	$ .070	$ .310	$ .270
Closing common stock price (e)										
High	$ 45.63	$33.44	$ 46.43	$39.82	$ 50.02	$41.54	$ 52.43	$ 40.15	$ 52.43	$ 41.54
Low	$ 38.59	$26.06	$ 40.80	$33.06	$ 40.42	$37.55	$ 48.50	$ 37.05	$ 38.59	$ 26.06

(a) Net earnings for first, second and third quarter of 2004 and all four quarters of 2003 has been adjusted to reflect the impact of the SFAS No. 123R restatement for those periods. The amount of the restatement was $6 million for each of the three quarters in 2004 and $8 million for each of the four quarters in 2003. The restatement impact on per share amounts for each respective quarter was all less than $0.01 per share.

(b) Target adjusted its method of accounting for leases related to a specific category of owned store locations on leased land which resulted in a non-cash adjustment, primarily attributable to an increase in the straight-line rent accrual, of $65 million ($0.04 per share) in the fourth quarter of 2004.

(c) Minor tax adjustments related to the dispositions of Marshall Field's and Mervyn's were recorded in fourth quarter 2004.

(d) Per share amounts are computed independently for each of the quarters presented. The sum of the quarters may not equal the total year amount due to the impact of changes in average quarterly shares outstanding.

(e) Our common stock is listed on the New York Stock Exchange and Pacific Exchange. At March 21, 2005, there were 18,030 registered shareholders and the closing common stock price was $50.28 per share.

Report of Management on the Financial Statements

Management is responsible for the consistency, integrity and presentation of the information in the Annual Report. The consolidated financial statements and other information presented in this Annual Report have been prepared in accordance with accounting principles generally accepted in the United States and include necessary judgments and estimates by management.

To fulfill our responsibility, we maintain comprehensive systems of internal control designed to provide reasonable assurance that assets are safeguarded and transactions are executed in accordance with established procedures. The concept of reasonable assurance is based upon recognition that the cost of the controls should not exceed the benefit derived. We believe our systems of internal control provide this reasonable assurance.

The Board of Directors exercised its oversight role with respect to the Corporation's systems of internal control primarily through its Audit Committee, which is comprised of four independent directors. The Committee oversees the Corporation's systems of internal control, accounting practices, financial reporting and audits to assess whether their quality, integrity and objectivity are sufficient to protect shareholders' investments. The Committee's report appears on this page.

In addition, our consolidated financial statements have been audited by Ernst & Young LLP, independent registered public accounting firm, whose report also appears on this page.

Robert J. Ulrich
Chairman of the Board and
Chief Executive Officer
March 25, 2005

Douglas A. Scovanner
Executive Vice President and
Chief Financial Officer

Report of Independent Registered Public Accounting Firm on Consolidated Financial Statements
The Board of Directors and Shareholders
Target Corporation

We have audited the accompanying consolidated statements of financial position of Target Corporation and subsidiaries as of January 29, 2005, and January 31, 2004, and the related consolidated results of operations, cash flows and shareholders' investment for each of the three years in the period ended January 29, 2005. These financial statements are the responsibility of the Corporation's management. Our responsibility is to express an opinion on these financial statements based on our audits.

We conducted our audits in accordance with the standards of the Public Company Accounting Oversight Board (PCAOB) (United States). Those standards require that we plan and perform the audit to obtain reasonable assurance about whether the financial statements are free of material misstatement. An audit includes examining, on a test basis, evidence supporting the amounts and disclosures in the financial statements. An audit also includes assessing the accounting principles used and significant estimates made by management, as well as evaluating the overall financial statement presentation. We believe that our audits provide a reasonable basis for our opinion.

In our opinion, the financial statements referred to above present fairly, in all material respects, the consolidated financial position of Target Corporation and subsidiaries at January 29, 2005, and January 31, 2004, and the consolidated results of their operations and their cash flows for each of the three years in the period ended January 29, 2005, in conformity with U.S. generally accepted accounting principles.

We also have audited, in accordance with the standards of the PCAOB (United States), the effectiveness of the Corporation's internal control over financial reporting as of January 29, 2005, based on criteria established in Internal Control – Integrated Framework issued by the Committee of Sponsoring Organizations of the Treadway Commission, and our report dated March 25, 2005, expressed an unqualified opinion thereon.

As discussed in the Stock-based Compensation note to the financial statements, effective February 1, 2004, the Corporation adopted Statement of Financial Accounting Standards No. 123 (revised 2004), "Share-Based Payment" using the modified retrospective transition method.

Minneapolis, Minnesota
March 25, 2005

Ernst & Young LLP

Report of Management on Internal Control

Our management is responsible for establishing and maintaining adequate internal control over financial reporting, as such term is defined in Exchange Act Rules 13a-15(f). Under the supervision and with the participation of our management, including our chief executive officer and chief financial officer, we assessed the effectiveness of our internal control over financial reporting as of January 29, 2005 based on the framework in Internal Control – Integrated Framework issued by the Committee of Sponsoring Organizations of the Treadway Commission. Based on our assessment we conclude that the Corporation's internal control over financial reporting is effective based on those criteria.

Our management's assessment of the effectiveness of our internal control over financial reporting as of January 29, 2005 has been audited by Ernst & Young LLP, an independent registered public accounting firm, as stated in their report which is included herein.

Robert J. Ulrich
Chairman of the Board and
Chief Executive Officer
March 25, 2005

Douglas A. Scovanner
Executive Vice President and
Chief Financial Officer

Report of Independent Registered Public Accounting Firm on Internal Control over Financial Reporting
The Board of Directors and Shareholders
Target Corporation

We have audited management's assessment, included in the accompanying Report of Management on Internal Control, that Target Corporation and subsidiaries maintained effective internal control over financial reporting as of January 29, 2005, based on criteria established in Internal Control – Integrated Framework issued by the Committee of Sponsoring Organizations of the Treadway Commission (the COSO criteria). The Corporation's management is responsible for maintaining effective internal control over financial reporting and for its assessment of the effectiveness of internal control over financial reporting. Our responsibility is to express an opinion on management's assessment and an opinion on the effectiveness of the Corporation's internal control over financial reporting based on our audit.

We conducted our audit in accordance with the standards of the Public Company Accounting Oversight Board (PCAOB) (United States). Those standards require that we plan and perform the audit to obtain reasonable assurance about whether effective internal control over financial reporting was maintained in all material respects. Our audit included obtaining an understanding of internal control over financial reporting, evaluating management's assessment, testing and evaluating the design and operating effectiveness of internal control, and performing such other procedures as we considered necessary in the circumstances. We believe that our audit provides a reasonable basis for our opinion.

A company's internal control over financial reporting is a process designed to provide reasonable assurance regarding the reliability of financial reporting and the preparation of financial statements for external purposes in accordance with generally accepted accounting principles. A company's internal control over financial reporting includes those policies and procedures that (1) pertain to the maintenance of records that, in reasonable detail, accurately and fairly reflect the transactions and dispositions of the assets of the company; (2) provide reasonable assurance that transactions are recorded as necessary to permit preparation of financial statements in accordance with generally accepted accounting principles, and that receipts and expenditures of the company are being made only in accordance with authorizations of management and directors of the company; and (3) provide reasonable assurance regarding prevention or timely detection of unauthorized acquisition, use, or disposition of the company's assets that could have a material effect on the financial statements.

Because of its inherent limitations, internal control over financial reporting may not prevent or detect misstatements. Also, projections of any evaluation of effectiveness to future periods are subject to the risk that controls may become inadequate because of changes in conditions, or that the degree of compliance with the policies or procedures may deteriorate.

In our opinion, management's assessment that Target Corporation and subsidiaries maintained effective internal control over financial reporting as of January 29, 2005, is fairly stated, in all material respects, based on the COSO criteria. Also, in our opinion, the Corporation maintained, in all material respects, effective internal control over financial reporting as of January 29, 2005, based on the COSO criteria.

We also have audited, in accordance with the standards of the PCAOB (United States), the consolidated statements of financial position of Target Corporation and subsidiaries as of January 29, 2005, and January 31, 2004, and the related consolidated results of operations, cash flows, and shareholders' investment for each of the three years in the period ended January 29, 2005, of Target Corporation and subsidiaries, and our report dated March 25, 2005, expressed an unqualified opinion thereon.

Minneapolis, Minnesota
March 25, 2005

Ernst & Young LLP

Report of Audit Committee

The Audit Committee met six times during fiscal 2004 to review the overall audit scope, plans for internal and independent audits, the Corporation's systems of internal control, emerging accounting issues, audit fees and benefit plans. The Committee also met individually with the independent auditors, without management present, to discuss the results of their audits. The Committee encourages the internal and independent auditors to communicate closely with the Committee.

The Audit Committee reviewed and approved the Corporation's annual financial statements and recommended to the full Board of Directors that they be included in the Annual Report. The Audit Committee also recommended to the Board of Directors that the independent auditors be reappointed for fiscal 2005, subject to the approval of the shareholders at the annual meeting.

March 25, 2005

Appendix B

Accounting Information Systems

LEARNING OBJECTIVES

1 Describe an effective accounting information system.

2 Use the sales journal, the cash receipts journal, and the accounts receivable ledger.

3 Use the purchases journal, the cash payments journal, and the accounts payable ledger.

4 Explain the role of the general journal when special journals are used.

Effective Accounting Information Systems

Good personnel are critical to business success. Employees must be both competent and honest. Design features also make the accounting system run efficiently. A good system, whether computerized or manual, must have

 Describe an effective accounting information system.

- Control
- Compatibility
- Flexibility
- Good cost/benefit relationship

Features of Effective Systems

Managers must *control* operations, or the company will lose focus. *Internal controls*, as introduced in Chapter 6, safeguard assets, promote proper financial reporting, eliminate waste, and facilitate compliance with laws and regulations. For example, in companies such as FedEx, Target, and Intel, managers control cash disbursements to avoid theft through unauthorized payments. VISA, MasterCard, and Discover keep accounts receivable records to ensure that they collect cash on time.

A *compatible* system is one that works smoothly with the company's personnel and organizational structure. An example is Bank of America, which is organized as a network of branch offices. Bank of America's top managers track revenues in each region where the bank does business. They must analyze loans in different geographic regions. If revenues in Texas are lagging, managers can focus on their Texas banks. They may move some top managers to their banks in Dallas or Houston.

Organizations change over time. They develop new products, sell off unprofitable operations, and acquire new ones. Changes in the business may require a new accounting system. A well-designed system is *flexible* if it accommodates changes in the organization. Consider Monsanto Company's acquisition of the pharmaceuticals firm Searle, which features Nutrasweet. Monsanto's accounting system was flexible enough to fold Searle/Nutrasweet into Monsanto.

Control, compatibility, and flexibility cost money. Managers want a system that gives the most benefit at the least cost. This is a favorable *cost/benefit relationship*. Most small companies use off-the-shelf computerized accounting packages, and the smallest businesses might not computerize at all. But large companies, such as the brokerage firm Edward Jones, have specialized information needs. Custom programming is a must. The benefits, in terms of good information, far outweigh the costs. The result? Better decisions.

Components of a Computerized System

A computerized accounting system has three basic components:

- Hardware
- Software
- Company personnel

Hardware is the electronic equipment including the computers, disk drives, monitors, and printers, and the network that connects them. Most systems require a **network** to link different computers sharing the same information. In a networked system, the **server** stores the program and the data. With a network, a PriceWaterhouseCoopers auditor in London can work on the data of a client in Sydney, Australia. The result is a speedier audit for the client.

Software is the set of programs that drives the computer. Accounting software reads, edits, and stores transaction data. It also generates the reports managers use to run the business. Many software packages operate independently. For example, a company that owns a chain of gas stations may be only partly computerized. This small business may use software for employee payrolls. Other parts of the accounting system may not be automated.

For large enterprises, such as Hershey Foods and Caterpillar, Inc., the accounting software is integrated into the company's **database**, or computerized storehouse of information.

How Computerized and Manual Systems Work

Computerized accounting systems have replaced manual systems in many organizations, even in small businesses such as your neighborhood pharmacy. The three stages of data processing (inputs, processing, and outputs) are shown in Exhibit B-1.

Inputs represent data from source documents, such as fax orders received from customers, sales receipts, and bank statements. Inputs are usually grouped by type. For example, a firm would enter cash-sale transactions separately from sales on account.

In a manual system, *processing* includes analyzing and journalizing transactions, posting to the accounts, and preparing the trial balance and financial statements. A computerized system also processes transactions, but handles the intermediate steps of journalizing, posting, and preparing the trial balance and statements electronically.

Outputs are the reports used for decision making, including the financial statements. Business owners can make better decisions with the reports produced by their accounting system. Exhibit B-2 diagrams a computerized accounting system. Start with data inputs in the lower left corner.

Exhibit B-1 The Three Stages of Data Processing

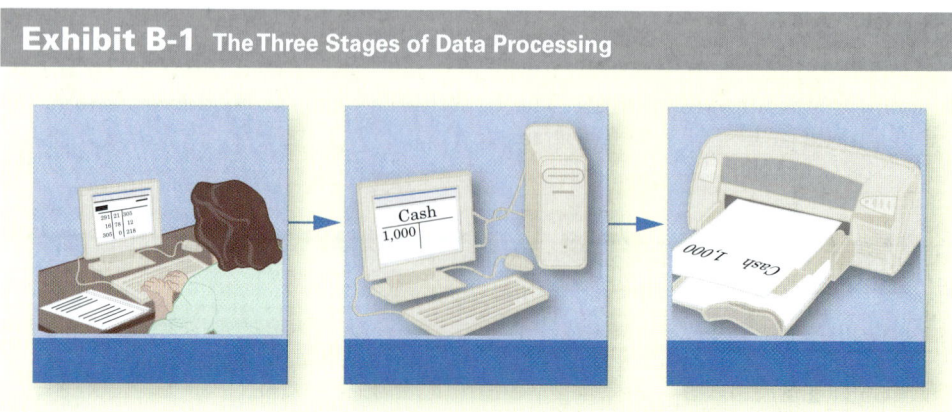

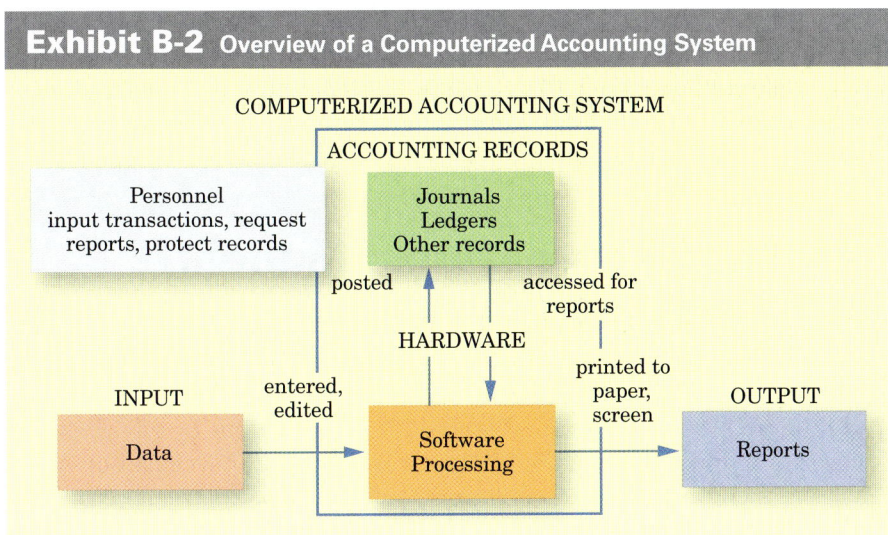

Exhibit B-2 Overview of a Computerized Accounting System

Designing a System: The Chart of Accounts

An accounting system begins with the chart of accounts. In the system of a large company such as Eastman Kodak, account numbers take on added importance. Recall from Chapter 2 that asset accounts generally begin with the digit 1, liabilities with the digit 2, owner's equity accounts with the digit 3, revenues with 4, and expenses with 5. Exhibit B-3 diagrams one structure for computerized accounts. Assets are divided into current assets, fixed assets (property, plant, and equipment), and other assets. Among the current assets, we illustrate only three accounts: Cash in Bank (account no. 111), Accounts Receivable (no. 112), and Prepaid Insurance (no. 115).

The account numbers in Exhibit B-3 get longer and more detailed as you move from top to bottom. For example, Customer A's account number is 1120001: 112 represents Accounts Receivable, and 0001 refers to Customer A.

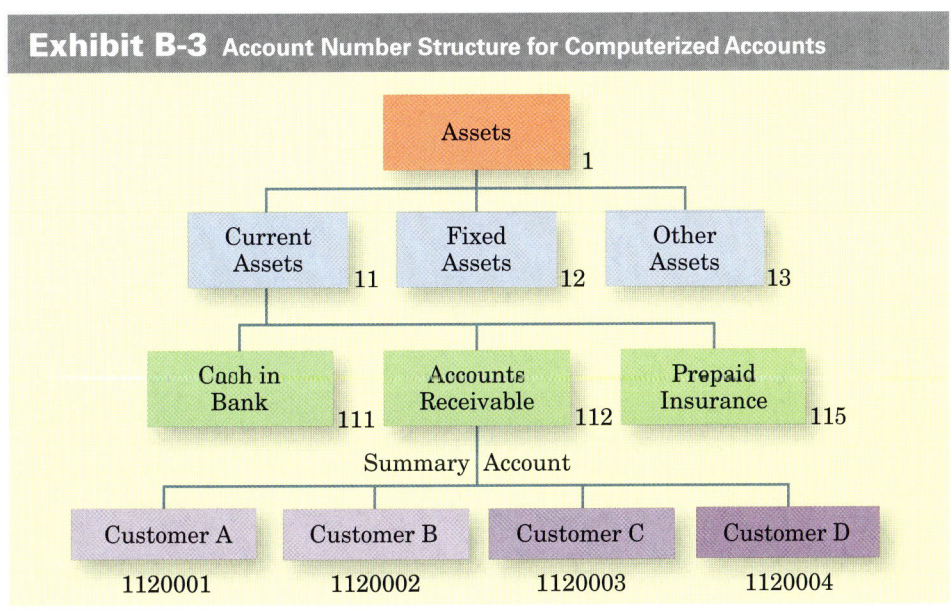

Exhibit B-3 Account Number Structure for Computerized Accounts

Computerized accounting systems rely on account *number ranges* to translate accounts and their balances into financial statements and other reports. For example, accounts numbered 101 through 399 (assets, liabilities, and owner's equity) are sorted to the balance sheet, while accounts numbered 401 through 599 (revenues and expenses) go to the income statement.

Processing Transactions: Manual and Menu-Driven Systems

To enhance efficiency of the accounting process, recording transactions in an actual accounting system typically requires an additional step that we have skipped thus far. A business of any size classifies transactions by type for efficient handling. In a manual system, credit sales, cash receipts, purchases on account, and cash payments are treated as four separate categories. Each has its own **special journal**. For example:

- Credit sales are recorded in a *sales journal*.

- Cash receipts are entered in a *cash receipts journal*.

- Credit purchases of inventory and other assets are recorded in a *purchases journal*.

- Cash payments are entered in a *cash payments journal*.

- Transactions that do not fit any of the special journals, such as adjusting entries, are recorded in the **general journal**, which serves as the "journal of last resort."

Computerized systems are organized by function, or task. Access to functions is arranged in terms of menus. A **menu** lists the options for choosing computer functions. In a *menu-driven* system, you first access the *main menu*. You then choose from one or more submenus until you finally reach the function you want.

Exhibit B-4 illustrates one type of menu structure. The menu bar at the top gives the main menu. The accountant has chosen the General option (short for General Ledger), highlighted by the cursor. This action opens a submenu of four

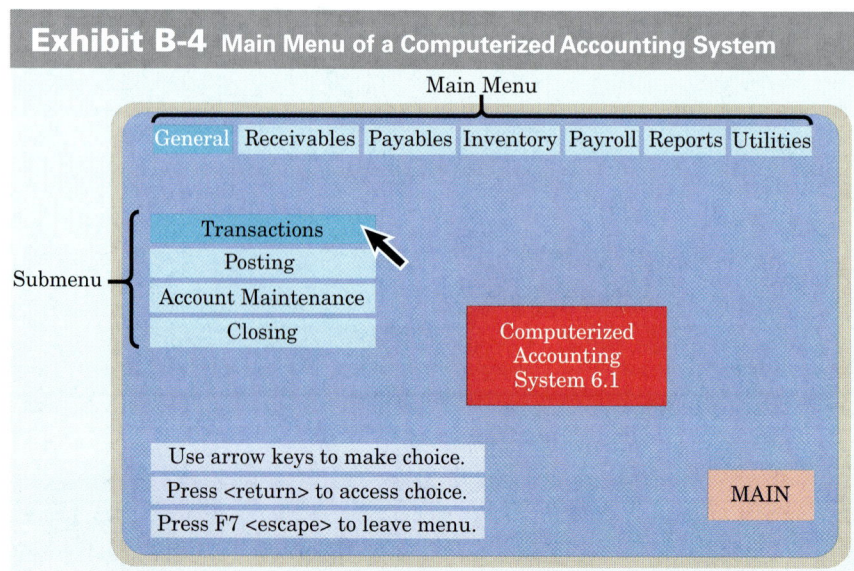

Exhibit B-4 Main Menu of a Computerized Accounting System

items: Transactions, Posting, Account Maintenance, and Closing. The Transactions option is then chosen, as highlighted.

Posting in a computerized system can be performed continuously, referred to as **online processing**, or later for a group of similar transactions, called **batch processing**. In effect, data are "parked" in the computer to await posting. The posting then updates the account balances.

Special Journals

Exhibit B-5 diagrams a typical accounting system and its special journals for a retail business. The remainder of this chapter describes this system.

The journal entries illustrated so far in this book used the general journal. The general journal is used for transactions that do not fit one of the special journals. In a manual system, it is inefficient to record all transactions in the general journal, so we use special journals. A special journal is an accounting journal designed to record a specific type of transaction.

Most transactions fall into one of five categories, so accountants use five different journals. This system reduces the time and cost of journalizing. The five types of transactions, the special journal, and the posting abbreviations follow.

	Transaction	Special Journal	Posting Abbreviation
1.	Sale on account	Sales journal	S
2.	Cash receipt	Cash receipts journal	CR
3.	Purchase on account	Purchases journal	P
4.	Cash payment	Cash payments journal	CP
5.	All others	General journal	J

Adjusting and closing entries are entered in the general journal. Transactions are recorded in *either* the general journal or a special journal, but not in both.

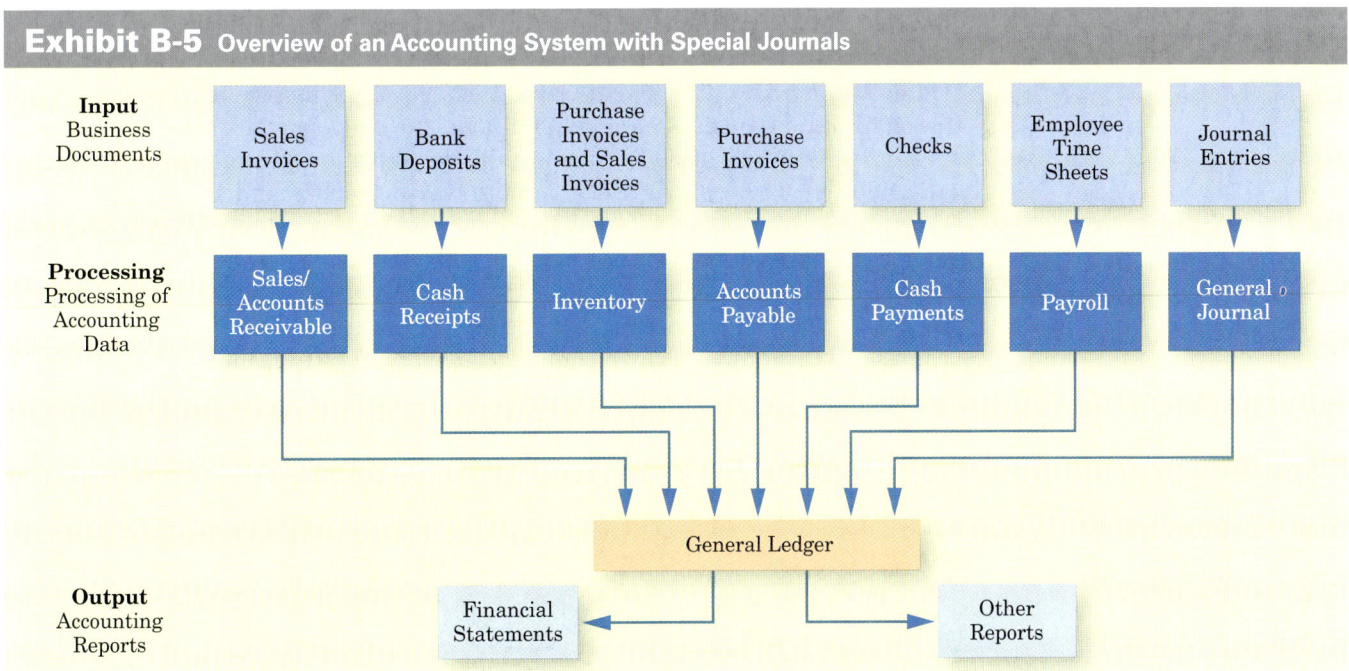

Exhibit B-5 Overview of an Accounting System with Special Journals

You may be wondering why we cover manual accounting systems when many businesses have computerized their accounting information systems. The three main reasons are:

1. Learning a manual system will help you master accounting. Think of the small businessperson who uses QuickBooks for a proprietorship, but knows little beyond which keys to punch. A business owner who knows the accounting can better manage the business and have more confidence that records are accurate.

2. Learning a manual system will equip you to work with both manual and electronic systems. The accounting is the same regardless of the system.

3. Few small businesses have computerized all their accounting. Even companies that use QuickBooks or Peachtree keep some manual accounting records. Also, many small businesses use manual systems, and they follow the principles and procedures that we illustrate in this chapter.

Using the Sales Journal

 Use the sales journal, the cash receipts journal, and the accounts receivable ledger.

Most retailers sell inventory on account. These credit sales are entered in the **sales journal**. Credit sales of assets other than inventory—for example, buildings—occur infrequently and are recorded in the general journal.

Exhibit B-6 illustrates a sales journal (Panel A) and the related posting to the ledgers (Panel B) of Baja Beachwear, the company we introduced in Chapter 5. Each entry in the Accounts Receivable/Sales Revenue column of the sales journal in Exhibit B-6 debits Accounts Receivable and credits Sales Revenue, as the heading indicates. For each transaction, the accountant enters the date, invoice number, customer account, and transaction amount. This streamlined way of recording sales on account saves time. It also tracks the amount receivable from each customer to ensure that the business collects its receivables.

Consider the first transaction in Panel A. On November 2, Baja Beachwear sold goods on account to Maria Galvez for $935. The invoice number is 422. All this information appears on a single line in the sales journal. No explanation is necessary. The transaction's presence in the sales journal means it is a credit sale, debited to Accounts Receivable—Maria Galvez and credited to Sales Revenue.

Recall from Chapter 5 that Baja Beachwear uses a *perpetual* inventory system. Throughout this appendix we illustrate the perpetual system. When recording a sale, Baja Beachwear also records the related cost of goods sold and decrease in inventory. Many computerized accounting systems are programmed to read both the sales amount and the cost of goods sold from the bar code on the package. The far right column of the sales journal holds the cost of goods sold and inventory entry, $505 for the sale to Maria Galvez. If Baja Beachwear used a *periodic* inventory system, it would not record the cost of goods sold or decrease in inventory at the time of sale. The sales journal would need only one column to debit Accounts Receivable and credit Sales Revenue.

Posting from the Sales Journal

Let's see how amounts are posted from the sales journal to Baja's ledgers.

Exhibit B-6 Sales Journal (Panel A) and Posting to the Ledgers (Panel B)

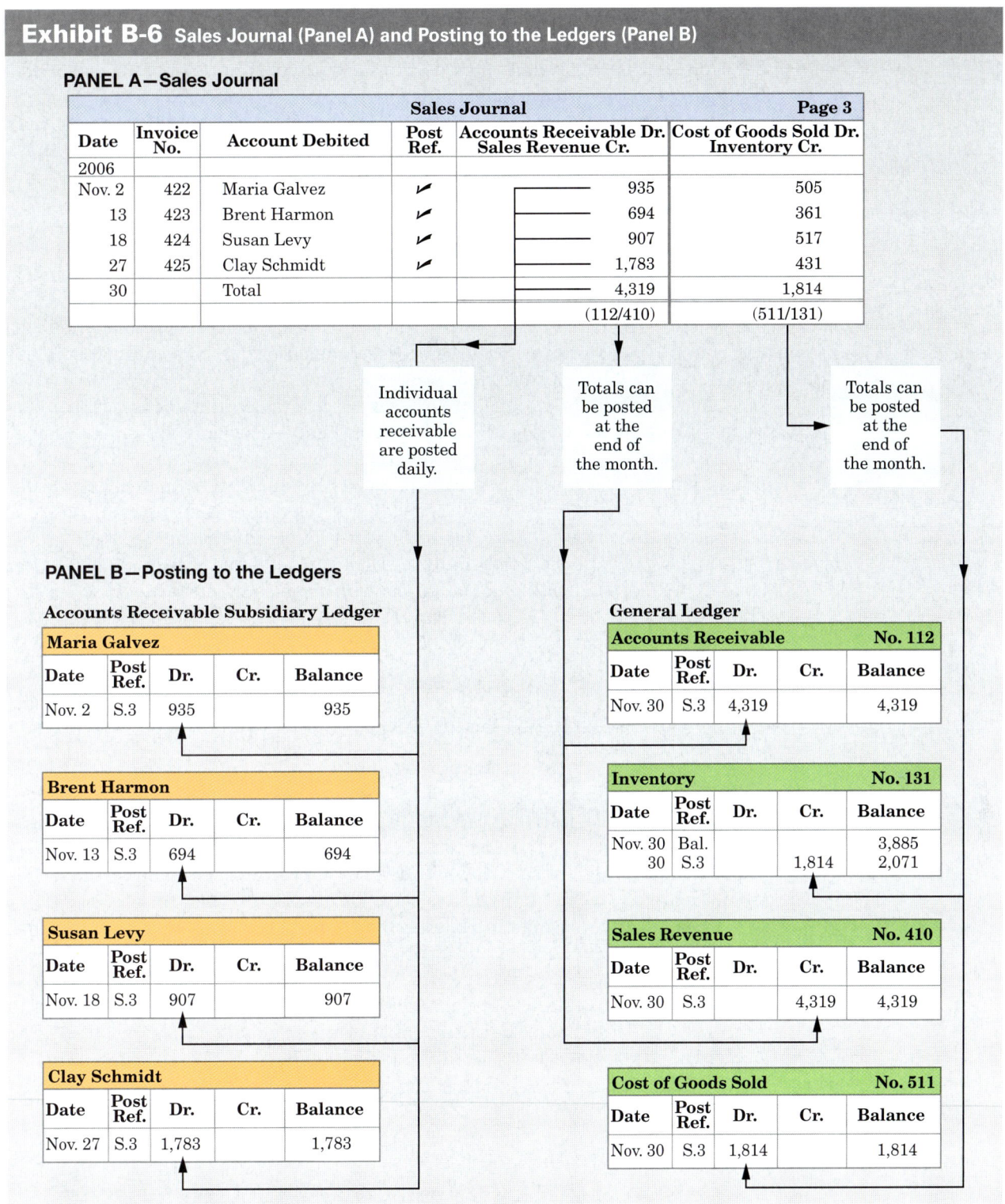

PANEL A—Sales Journal

		Sales Journal			Page 3
Date	Invoice No.	Account Debited	Post Ref.	Accounts Receivable Dr. Sales Revenue Cr.	Cost of Goods Sold Dr. Inventory Cr.
2006					
Nov. 2	422	Maria Galvez	✔	935	505
13	423	Brent Harmon	✔	694	361
18	424	Susan Levy	✔	907	517
27	425	Clay Schmidt	✔	1,783	431
30		Total		4,319	1,814
				(112/410)	(511/131)

Individual accounts receivable are posted daily.

Totals can be posted at the end of the month.

Totals can be posted at the end of the month.

PANEL B—Posting to the Ledgers

Accounts Receivable Subsidiary Ledger

Maria Galvez

Date	Post Ref.	Dr.	Cr.	Balance
Nov. 2	S.3	935		935

Brent Harmon

Date	Post Ref.	Dr.	Cr.	Balance
Nov. 13	S.3	694		694

Susan Levy

Date	Post Ref.	Dr.	Cr.	Balance
Nov. 18	S.3	907		907

Clay Schmidt

Date	Post Ref.	Dr.	Cr.	Balance
Nov. 27	S.3	1,783		1,783

General Ledger

Accounts Receivable   No. 112

Date	Post Ref.	Dr.	Cr.	Balance
Nov. 30	S.3	4,319		4,319

Inventory   No. 131

Date	Post Ref.	Dr.	Cr.	Balance
Nov. 30	Bal.			3,885
30	S.3		1,814	2,071

Sales Revenue   No. 410

Date	Post Ref.	Dr.	Cr.	Balance
Nov. 30	S.3		4,319	4,319

Cost of Goods Sold   No. 511

Date	Post Ref.	Dr.	Cr.	Balance
Nov. 30	S.3	1,814		1,814

POSTING TO THE GENERAL LEDGER

The ledger we have used so far is the **general ledger**, which holds the financial statement accounts. We will soon introduce other ledgers.

Posting from the sales journal to the general ledger can be done only at the end of the month. In Exhibit B-6 (Panel A), November's credit sales total $4,319. When the $4,319 is posted to Accounts Receivable and Sales Revenue, their account numbers are written beneath the total in the sales journal. In Panel B of

Exhibit B-6, you can see that the account number for Accounts Receivable is 112 and the account number for Sales Revenue is 410. Printing these account numbers beneath the credit-sales total in the sales journal shows that the $4,319 has been posted to the two accounts.

The debit to Cost of Goods Sold and the credit to Inventory for the monthly total of $1,814 is also posted at the end of the month. After posting, these accounts' numbers are entered beneath the total to show that Cost of Goods Sold and Inventory have been updated.

POSTING TO THE ACCOUNTS RECEIVABLE SUBSIDIARY LEDGER

The $4,319 debit to Accounts Receivable does not identify the amount that is receivable from each customer. A business may have thousands of customers. For example, the Consumers Digest Company, a Chicago-based firm that publishes the bimonthly magazine *Consumers Digest*, has more than a million customer accounts—one for each subscriber.

To streamline operations, businesses place the accounts of individual customers in a subsidiary ledger called the Accounts Receivable ledger. Remember from Chapter 5 that a subsidiary ledger is an accounting record that keeps track of details; the Accounts Receivable ledger holds the individual accounts that make up the total for Accounts Receivable in the general ledger. The customer accounts in the subsidiary ledger are arranged in alphabetical order.

Amounts in the sales journal are posted to the subsidiary ledger *daily* to keep a current record of the amount receivable from each customer. Daily posting allows the business to answer customer inquiries. Suppose Maria Galvez telephones Baja Beachwear on November 3 to ask how much she owes. The subsidiary ledger readily provides that information, $935 in Exhibit B-6, Panel B.

When each transaction amount is posted to the subsidiary ledger, a check mark is entered in the posting reference column of the sales journal as shown in Exhibit B-6, Panel A.

JOURNAL REFERENCES IN THE LEDGERS

When amounts are posted to the ledgers, the journal page number is printed in the account to show the source of the data. All transaction data in Exhibit B-6 originated on page 3 of the sales journal, so all posting references in the ledger accounts are "S.3". The "S." indicates sales journal.

Trace all the postings in Exhibit B-6. The most effective way to learn an accounting system is to study the flow of data. The arrows indicate the direction of the information. They also show the links between the individual customer accounts in the subsidiary ledger and the Accounts Receivable account. The Accounts Receivable balance in the general ledger should equal the sum of the individual customer balances in the subsidiary ledger, as follows:

General Ledger	
Accounts Receivable debit balance	$4,319

Subsidiary Ledger: Customer Accounts Receivable

Customer	Balance
Maria Galvez	$ 935
Brent Harmon	694
Susan Levy	907
Clay Schmidt	1,783
Total Accounts Receivable	$4,319

As we mentioned in Chapter 7, Accounts Receivable in the general ledger is a control account. A control account's balance equals the sum of the balances of a group of related accounts in a subsidiary ledger.

Using Documents as Journals

Many small businesses streamline their accounting by using business documents as journals. This practice avoids the need for special journals and saves money. For example, Baja Beachwear could keep sales invoices in a loose-leaf binder and let the invoices serve as the sales journal. At the end of the period, the accountant simply totals the sales on account and posts the total as a debit to Accounts Receivable and a credit to Sales Revenue. The accountant can also post directly from the invoices to customer accounts in the accounts receivable ledger.

Using the Cash Receipts Journal

Cash transactions are common in retail businesses. To record a high volume of cash receipts, accountants use the **cash receipts journal**.

Exhibit B-7, Panel A illustrates the cash receipts journal. The related posting to the ledgers is shown in Panel B. The exhibit illustrates November transactions for Baja Beachwear.

Every transaction recorded in this journal is a cash receipt, so this special journal has a column for debits to Cash. The next column is for debits to Sales Discounts. In a typical retail business, the main sources of cash are cash sales and collections on account.

The cash receipts journal has credit columns for Accounts Receivable and Sales Revenue. The journal also has a credit column for Other Accounts, which lists other sources of cash. This Other Accounts column is also used to record the names of customers from whom cash is collected on account.

In Exhibit B-7, the first cash sale occurred on November 6. Observe the debit to Cash and the credit to Sales Revenue, $517. Each sale entry is accompanied by a separate entry that debits Cost of Goods Sold and credits Inventory for the cost of the merchandise sold. The column for this entry is at the far right of the journal.

On November 11, Baja Beachwear borrowed $1,000 from First Bank. Cash is debited, and Note Payable to First Bank is credited. We use the Other Accounts column because the journal has no specific credit column for borrowings; special journals generally only hold specific columns for accounts that are used often. For this transaction, we print the account title, Note Payable to First Bank, in the Other Accounts/Account Title column.

The November 11 and 25 transactions illustrate a key fact. Different companies have different types of transactions, and they adapt special journals to their needs. In this case, the Other Accounts column is the catchall used to record all nonroutine cash receipts.

On November 14, Baja Beachwear collected $900 from Maria Galvez. Back on November 2, Baja Beachwear sold $935 of merchandise to Galvez. The terms of sale allowed a $35 discount for prompt payment, and Galvez paid within the discount period. Baja Beachwear records this cash receipt by debiting Cash and Sales Discounts and by crediting Accounts Receivable for $935. The customer's name appears in the Other Accounts/Account Title column.

In the cash receipts journal, as in all the journals, total debits should equal total credits. For the month, total debits of $6,169 ($6,134 + $35) equal total credits of $6,169 ($1,235 + $3,172 + $1,762). The debit to Cost of Goods Sold and the credit to Inventory are completely separate.

Exhibit B-7 Cash Receipts Journal (Panel A) and Posting to the Ledgers (Panel B)

PANEL A—Cash Receipts Journal

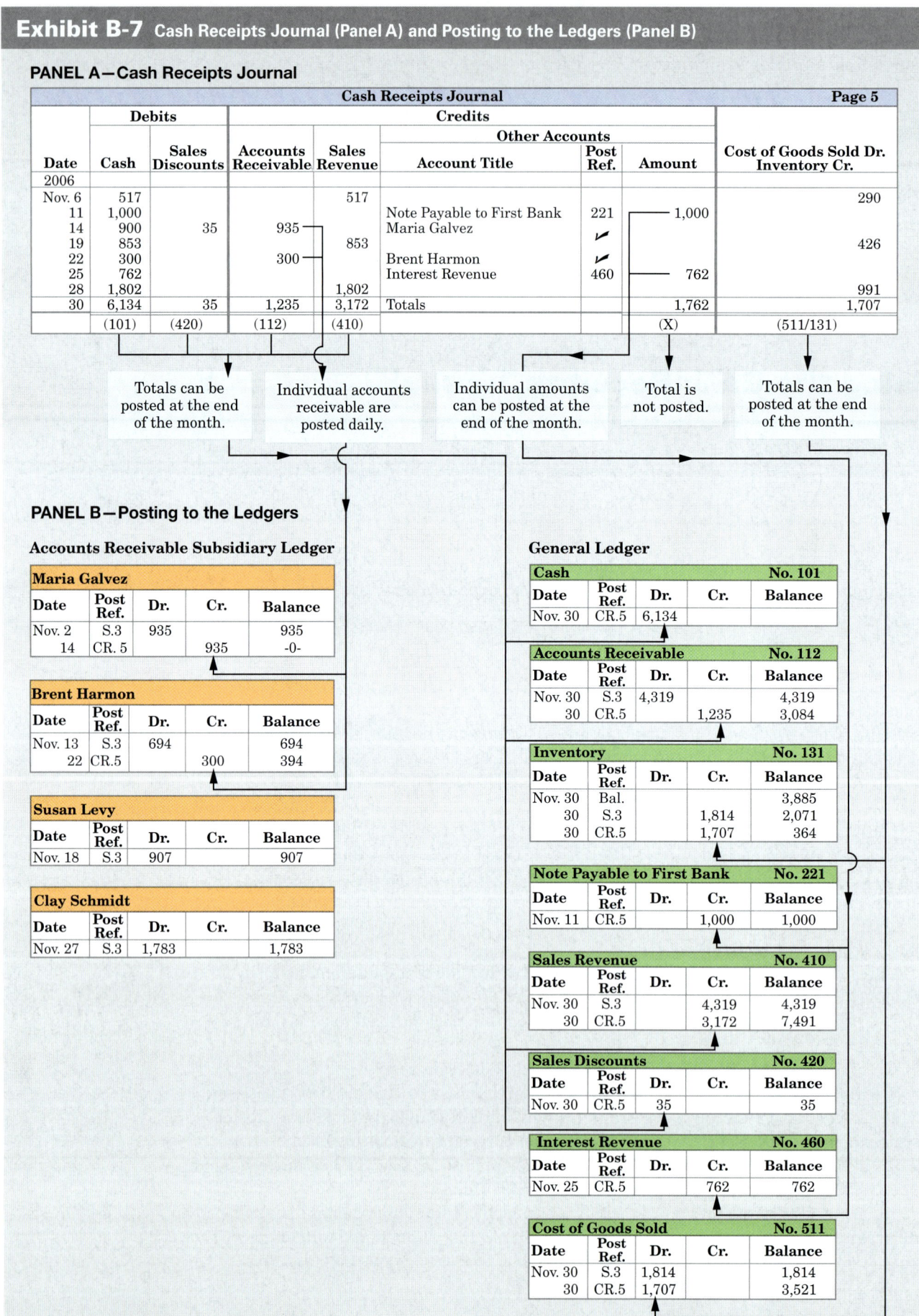

		Debits			Credits				
						Other Accounts			
Date	Cash	Sales Discounts	Accounts Receivable	Sales Revenue	Account Title	Post Ref.	Amount	Cost of Goods Sold Dr. Inventory Cr.	
2006									
Nov. 6	517			517				290	
11	1,000				Note Payable to First Bank	221	1,000		
14	900	35	935		Maria Galvez	✔			
19	853			853				426	
22	300		300		Brent Harmon	✔			
25	762				Interest Revenue	460	762		
28	1,802			1,802				991	
30	6,134	35	1,235	3,172	Totals		1,762	1,707	
	(101)	(420)	(112)	(410)			(X)	(511/131)	

Totals can be posted at the end of the month.

Individual accounts receivable are posted daily.

Individual amounts can be posted at the end of the month.

Total is not posted.

Totals can be posted at the end of the month.

PANEL B—Posting to the Ledgers

Accounts Receivable Subsidiary Ledger

Maria Galvez

Date	Post Ref.	Dr.	Cr.	Balance
Nov. 2	S.3	935		935
14	CR. 5		935	-0-

Brent Harmon

Date	Post Ref.	Dr.	Cr.	Balance
Nov. 13	S.3	694		694
22	CR.5		300	394

Susan Levy

Date	Post Ref.	Dr.	Cr.	Balance
Nov. 18	S.3	907		907

Clay Schmidt

Date	Post Ref.	Dr.	Cr.	Balance
Nov. 27	S.3	1,783		1,783

General Ledger

Cash   No. 101

Date	Post Ref.	Dr.	Cr.	Balance
Nov. 30	CR.5	6,134		

Accounts Receivable   No. 112

Date	Post Ref.	Dr.	Cr.	Balance
Nov. 30	S.3	4,319		4,319
30	CR.5		1,235	3,084

Inventory   No. 131

Date	Post Ref.	Dr.	Cr.	Balance
Nov. 30	Bal.			3,885
30	S.3		1,814	2,071
30	CR.5		1,707	364

Note Payable to First Bank   No. 221

Date	Post Ref.	Dr.	Cr.	Balance
Nov. 11	CR.5		1,000	1,000

Sales Revenue   No. 410

Date	Post Ref.	Dr.	Cr.	Balance
Nov. 30	S.3		4,319	4,319
30	CR.5		3,172	7,491

Sales Discounts   No. 420

Date	Post Ref.	Dr.	Cr.	Balance
Nov. 30	CR.5	35		35

Interest Revenue   No. 460

Date	Post Ref.	Dr.	Cr.	Balance
Nov. 25	CR.5		762	762

Cost of Goods Sold   No. 511

Date	Post Ref.	Dr.	Cr.	Balance
Nov. 30	S.3	1,814		1,814
30	CR.5	1,707		3,521

POSTING TO THE GENERAL LEDGER

Column totals can be posted monthly. To indicate their posting, the account number is printed below the column total in the cash receipts journal. Note the account number for Cash (101) below the column total, and for the other column totals that are posted to the general ledger. Follow the arrows, which track the posted amounts.

The column total for Other Accounts is *not* posted. Instead, these credits are posted individually. In Exhibit B-7, the November 11 transaction reads "Note Payable to First Bank." This account's number (221) in the Post. Ref. column shows that the transaction amount was posted individually. The letter *X* below the column indicates the column total was *not* posted.

POSTING TO THE SUBSIDIARY LEDGER

Amounts from the cash receipts journal are posted to the accounts receivable ledger daily to keep the individual balances up to date. The postings to accounts receivable are credits. Trace the $935 posting to Maria Galvez's account. It reduces her balance to zero. The $300 receipt from Brent Harmon reduces his accounts receivable balance to $394.

After posting, the sum of the individual balances in the accounts receivable ledger equals the balance of Accounts Receivable in the general ledger, as follows:

General Ledger	
Accounts Receivable debit balance	$3,084

Subsidiary Ledger: Customer Accounts Receivable	
Customer	**Balance**
Brent Harmon	$ 394
Susan Levy	907
Clay Schmidt	1,783
Total Accounts Receivable	$3,084

Using the Purchases Journal

A retail business purchases inventory and supplies frequently. Such purchases are usually made on account. The **purchases journal** is designed to account for the purchases of inventory, supplies, and other assets *on account*. It can also be used to record expenses incurred *on account*. Cash purchases are recorded in the cash payments journal.

Exhibit B-8 illustrates Baja Beachwear's purchases journal (Panel A) and posting to the ledgers (Panel B).[1] This purchases journal has special columns for credits to Accounts Payable and debits to Inventory, Supplies, and Other Accounts. A periodic inventory system would replace the Inventory column with a column titled "Purchases." The Other Accounts columns hold purchases of items other than inventory and supplies. Accounts Payable is credited for all transactions recorded in the purchases journal.

 Use the purchases journal, the cash payments journal, and the accounts payable ledger.

---

[1]This journal is the only special journal with the credit column placed to the left and the debit columns to the right. This arrangement of columns focuses on Accounts Payable (which is credited for each entry to this journal).

Exhibit B-8 Purchases Journal (Panel A) and Posting to the Ledgers (Panel B)

PANEL A—Purchases Journal

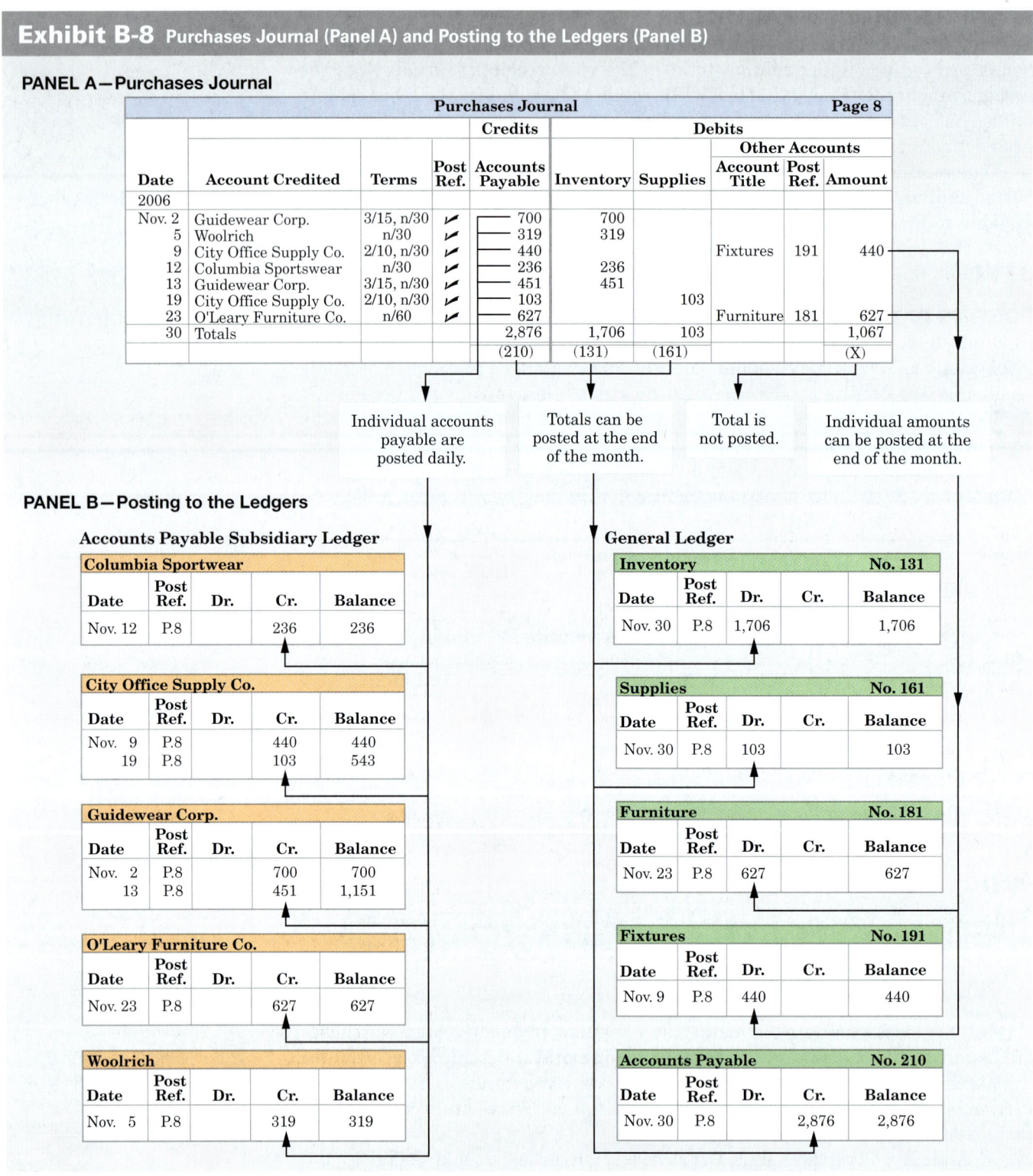

Individual accounts payable are posted daily.

Totals can be posted at the end of the month.

Total is not posted.

Individual amounts can be posted at the end of the month.

On November 2, Baja Beachwear purchased inventory costing $700 from Guidewear Corp. The creditor's name, Guidewear Corp., is entered in the Account Credited column. The purchase terms of 3/15, n/30 are also entered to show the due date and the discount available. Accounts Payable is credited for the transaction amount, and Inventory is debited.

Note the November 9 purchase of fixtures from City Office Supply. The purchases journal holds no column for fixtures, so we use the Other Accounts debit column. Because this purchase was a credit purchase, the accountant prints the creditor name, City Office Supply, in the Account Credited column and Fixtures in the Other Accounts/Account Title column. The total credits in the purchases journal of $2,876 must equal the total debits of $2,876 ($1,706 + $103 + $1,067).

The Accounts Payable Subsidiary Ledger and Posting Process

Just as businesses need to keep track of amounts receivable from each customer, they also need to know the amount owed to each supplier. Posting from the purchases journal to the ledgers allows companies to account for both the total and individual amounts due.

ACCOUNTS PAYABLE SUBSIDIARY LEDGER

To pay debts on time, a company must know how much it owes each creditor. Accounts Payable in the general ledger shows only a single total for the amount owed on account. It does not indicate the amount owed to each creditor. Companies keep an accounts payable ledger that is similar to the accounts receivable ledger.

The accounts payable ledger lists creditors in alphabetical order, along with amounts owed to them. Exhibit B-8, Panel B, shows Baja Beachwear's accounts payable subsidiary ledger, which includes accounts for Guidewear Corp., City Office Supply Co., and others. After all posting has been completed, the total of the individual balances in the subsidiary ledger equals the Accounts Payable balance in the general ledger.

POSTING FROM THE PURCHASES JOURNAL

Posting from the purchases journal is similar to posting from the other special journals. Exhibit B-8, Panel B, illustrates the posting process.

Individual accounts payable in the *accounts payable ledger* are posted daily, and column totals and other amounts to the *general ledger* at the end of the month. In the ledger accounts, "P.8" means purchases journal page 8.

Using the Cash Payments Journal

Businesses make most cash payments by check, and all checks are recorded in the **cash payments journal**, which can also be called the **check register** or the **cash disbursements journal**. This special journal has columns for recording frequent cash payments.

Exhibit B-9, Panel A, shows the cash payments journal, and Panel B gives the postings to the ledgers. The cash payments journal has two debit columns—one for Other Accounts and one for Accounts Payable. It has two credit columns—one for credits to Inventory (for purchases discounts) and one for Cash. This special journal also has columns for the date and for the check number of each cash payment.

Suppose Baja Beachwear made numerous cash purchases of inventory. What additional column would its cash payments journal need? A debit column for Inventory would be added.

All entries in the cash payments journal include a credit to Cash. Payments on account are debits to Accounts Payable. On November 15, Baja Beachwear paid Guidewear on account, with credit terms of 3/15, n/30, for the purchase it made on November 2, shown in Exhibit B-8. Paying within the discount period, Baja Beachwear took the 3% discount and paid $679 ($700 – $21). The discount is credited to Inventory.

The Other Accounts column is used to record debits to accounts for which no special column exists. For example, on November 3, Baja Beachwear paid rent

Exhibit B-9 Cash Payments Journal (Panel A) and Posting to the Ledgers (Panel B)

PANEL A—Cash Payments Journal

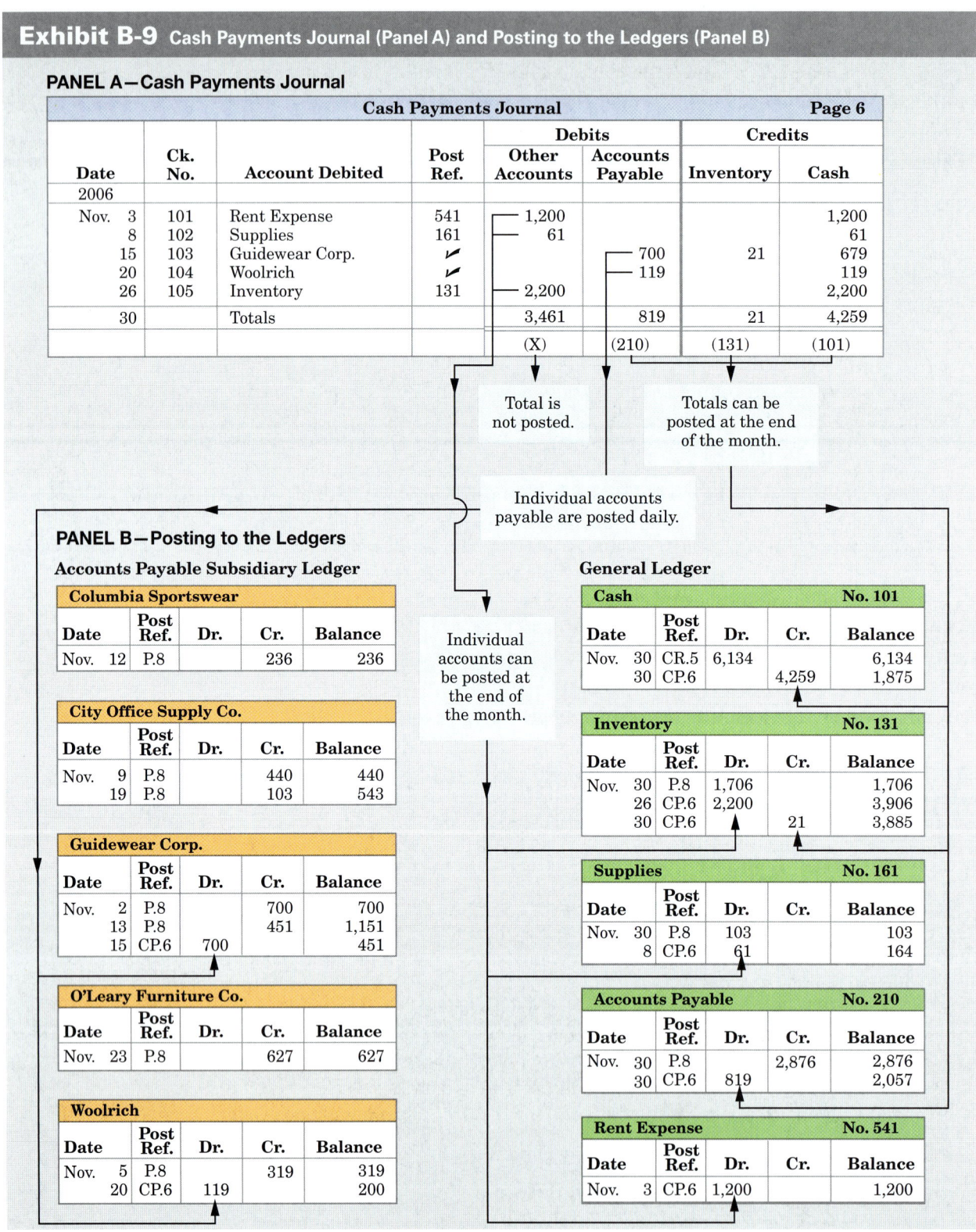

expense of $1,200. As with all other journals, the total debits of $4,280 ($3,461 + $819) should equal the total credits of $4,280 ($21 + $4,259).

POSTING FROM THE CASH PAYMENTS JOURNAL

Posting from the cash payments journal is similar to posting from the cash receipts journal. Individual creditor amounts are posted daily, and column totals and Other Accounts can be posted at the end of the month. Exhibit B-9, Panel B, illustrates the posting process.

Amounts in the Other Accounts column are posted individually, such as Rent Expense—debit $1,200. When each amount in the Other Accounts column is posted to the general ledger, the account number is printed in the Post. Ref. column. The letter *X* below the column signifies that the total is *not* posted.

To review accounts payable, companies list individual creditor balances in the accounts payable ledger. The general ledger and subsidiary totals should agree.

General Ledger	
Accounts Payable credit balance	$2,057

Subsidiary Ledger: Accounts Payable	
Creditor	**Balance**
Columbia Sportswear	$ 236
City Office Supply Co.	543
Guidewear Corp.	451
O'Leary Furniture Co.	627
Woolrich	200
Total Accounts Payable	$2,057

The Role of the General Journal

Special journals save time recording repetitive transactions. But some transactions do not fit a special journal. Examples include depreciation, the expiration of prepaid insurance, and the accrual of salary payable at the end of the period.

 Explain the role of the general journal when special journals are used.

> All accounting systems need a general journal. The adjusting entries and the closing entries are recorded in the general journal, along with other nonroutine transactions.

Many companies record sales returns and allowances and purchase returns and allowances in the general journal. Let's turn now to sales returns and allowances and the related business document, the credit memorandum.

The Credit Memorandum—Recording Sales Returns and Allowances

Customers sometimes return merchandise to the seller. Sellers also grant sales allowances to customers because of product defects or damage during shipment. The effect of sales returns and sales allowances is the same; both decrease net sales and accounts receivable. Recall from Chapter 5 that the document issued by the seller for a sales return or allowance is called a credit memorandum or credit memo, because the company gives the customer credit for the returned merchandise. When a company issues a credit memo, it debits Sales Returns and Allowances and credits Accounts Receivable.

On November 27, Baja Beachwear sold clothing and shoes to Clay Schmidt for $1,783 on account. Later, Schmidt discovered a defect and returned clothing to the store for $500. Baja Beachwear then issued to Schmidt a credit memo like the one in Exhibit B-10.

Exhibit B-10 Credit Memorandum Issued by Baja Beachwear

Baja Beachwear
18 Shoreline Drive
Laguna Beach, California

CREDIT MEMORANDUM #27

To: Clay Schmidt   Date: December 1, 2006
538 Rio Grande, Apt. 236
Austin, TX 78703

Reason for Credit: Defective merchandise returned

Description: Clothing

Amount: $500

To record the sales return and the receipt of the defective clothing and the adjustment to inventory for the $125 cost of the merchandise, Baja Beachwear would make these entries in the general journal:

Journal Entry:

Date	Accounts	Post Ref.	Dr.	Cr.
Dec. 1	Sales Returns and Allowances	430	500	
	Accounts Receivable—Clay Schmidt	112/✓		500
Dec. 1	Inventory	131	125	
	Costs of Goods Sold	511		125
	Record receipt of defective goods from customer, credit memo no. 27.			

Focus on the first entry. Sales Returns and Allowances is debited. Its account number, 430, is written in the posting reference column. The credit entry requires two postings: one to Accounts Receivable in the general ledger, account number 112, and the other to Clay Schmidt in the accounts receivable subsidiary ledger. These credits explain why the document is called a *credit memo*. The account number (112) denotes the posting to Accounts Receivable in the general ledger. The check mark (✓) denotes the posting to Schmidt's account in the subsidiary ledger.

The second entry records Baja Beachwear's receipt of the defective inventory from the customer. Now let's see how Baja Beachwear records the return of the defective clothing to Guidewear.

The Debit Memorandum—Recording Purchase Returns and Allowances

A purchase return occurs when a business returns goods to the seller. The purchaser receives a cash refund or replacement goods. If a business buys items that they are not fully satisfied with, they may keep them and receive a reduction in the amount they owe for those goods.

As we mentioned in Chapter 5, the purchaser may also send a document known as a debit memorandum, or debit memo. This document states that the buyer no longer owes for the goods, or no longer owes the full amount for the goods. The buyer debits Accounts Payable and credits Inventory for the cost of the goods returned to the seller or for the amount of the allowance.

Many businesses record purchase returns in the general journal. Baja Beachwear would record its return of defective clothing to Guidewear as follows:

Journal Entry:

Date	Accounts	Post Ref.	Dr.	Cr.
Dec. 2	Accounts Payable—Guidewear Corp.	210✓	125	
	Inventory	131		125
	Recording inventory returned to supplier, debit memo no. 16.			

Balancing the Ledgers

At the end of the period, after all postings, equality should exist as follows:

1. *General ledger:*

   Total Debits = Total Credits

2. *General ledger and accounts receivable subsidiary ledger:*

Balance of the Accounts Receivable Control Account in the General Ledger	=	Sum of All the Customer Balances in the Accounts Receivable Subsidiary Ledger

3. *General ledger and accounts payable subsidiary ledger:*

Balance of the Accounts Payable Control Account in the General Ledger	=	Sum of All the Creditor Balances in the Accounts Payable Subsidiary Ledger

This process is called *balancing the ledgers*, or *proving the ledgers*. It helps ensure the accuracy of the accounting records.

Blending Computers and Special Journals in an Accounting Information System

Computerizing special journals requires no drastic change in the design of the accounting system. Systems designers can create a special screen for each accounting module. In other words, they can create a screen for each transaction type—credit sales, cash receipts, credit purchases, and cash payments. For example, the special screen for credit sales would ask the computer operator to enter the following information:

- Date

- Invoice number

- Customer name

- Dollar amount of the sale

- Cost of the goods sold

The data input to this screen can generate debits to the accounts receivable ledger and the monthly statements for customers.

Demo Doc

Bookkeeping Ledgers

Learning Objectives   1, 2

Juniper Corp. had the following transactions during November 2008:

Nov.	4	Received $3,300 on a note receivable from Harry Stevenson. This amount includes the $3,000 note receivable plus interest revenue.
	12	Borrowed $8,000 from National Bank by signing a note payable.
	18	Received $1,800 on account from Lisa Henders. Collection occurred after the sales discount period lapsed.
	26	Received $2,400 on account from Peter Wilkins. The full invoice amount was $2,500, but Peter paid within the discount period to gain the $100 discount.
	29	Received $4,000 on a cash sale to a customer (cost of inventory, $2,700).

The general ledger showed the following balances at October 31, 2008:

Account	Account No.	Amount
Cash	10	$1,300
Accounts Receivable	20	6,700
Notes Receivable	30	7,400
Inventory	40	4,000
Notes Payable	50	0
Sales Revenues	60	0
Sales Discounts	70	0
Cost of Goods Sold	80	0
Interest Revenue	90	0

The accounts receivable subsidiary ledger at October 31, 2008, showed:

Lisa Henders	$3,200
Jennifer Collins	1,000
Peter Wilkins	2,500
Total	$6,700

(This total is the same as in the Accounts Receivable general ledger account.)

Requirements

1. Record the transactions in the cash receipts journal. Compute the column totals at November 30, 2008. Show that total debits equal total credits.

2. Post to the general ledger and the accounts receivable ledger. Check that the total of the customer balances in the subsidiary ledger equals the general ledger balance in accounts receivable.

3. The employee at Juniper who opens the mail and physically collects the cash is the same person who updates the cash receipts journal. Does this practice create any problems?

Demo Doc Solutions

② Use the sales journal, the cash receipts journal, and the accounts receivable ledger.

Requirement 1

Record the transactions in the cash receipts journal (page 5). Compute the column totals at November 30, 2008. Show that total debits equal total credits.

Part 1	Part 2	Part 3	Part 4	Part 5	Demo Doc Complete

Remember that the debits and credits in these transactions are *exactly* the same as we have done throughout this book. Only the format of recording the entries changes.

All transactions in the cash receipts journal increase cash and are included in the "Cash" debit column of the journal. Routine transactions in this journal might include cash sales and cash receipts from customers on account. Sales Revenue and Accounts Receivable credit columns are in the journal to fully record these transactions. Whatever other accounts are normally affected when cash is received should be listed in the remaining columns.

Notice that it is not possible to have a column for *every* account. The Other Account column is for accounts that are not used often (and so are not listed separately).

Even though we will actually be recording these transactions in the cash receipts journal, let's first see how they would be recorded in the general journal, omitting explanations.

Nov. 4   **Received $3,300 on a note receivable from Harry Stevenson. This amount includes the $3,000 note receivable plus interest revenue.**

This transaction increases Cash (debit) by $3,300. Notes Receivable decreases (credit) by $3,000. The difference of $3,300 − $3,000 = $300 is an increase to Interest Revenue (credit).

Journal Entry:

Date	Accounts	Post Ref.	Dr.	Cr.
Nov. 4	Cash		3,300	
	Notes Receivable			3,000
	Interest Revenue			300

Nov. 12   **Borrowed $8,000 from National Bank by signing a note payable.**

This transaction increases Cash (debit) and increases Notes Payable (credit) by $8,000.

Journal Entry:

Date	Accounts	Post Ref.	Dr.	Cr.
Nov. 12	Cash		8,000	
	Notes Payable			8,000

Nov. 18   Received $1,800 on account from Lisa Henders. Collection occurred after the sales discount period lapsed.

This transaction increases Cash (debit) and decreases Accounts Receivable (credit) by $1,800. Because the collection happened after the discount period lapsed, sales discounts do not apply.

Journal Entry:

Date	Accounts	Post Ref.	Dr.	Cr.
Nov. 18	Cash		1,800	
	Accounts Receivable—Lisa Henders			1,800

Nov. 26   Received $2,400 on account from Peter Wilkins. The full invoice amount was $2,500, but Peter paid within the discount period to gain the $100 discount.

This transaction increases Cash (debit) by $2,400. However, Accounts Receivable decreases (credit) by $2,500. The difference of $100 is an increase to Sales Discounts (debit).

Journal Entry:

Date	Accounts	Post Ref.	Dr.	Cr.
Nov. 26	Cash		2,400	
	Sales Discounts		100	
	Accounts Receivable—Peter Wilkins			2,500

Nov. 29   Received $4,000 on a cash sale to a customer (cost $2,700).

This transaction increases Cash (debit) and increases Sales Revenue (credit) by $4,000. We also need to record an increase to COGS (debit) and a decrease to Inventory (credit) of $2,700.

Journal Entry:

Date	Accounts	Post Ref.	Dr.	Cr.
Nov. 29	Cash		4,000	
	Sales Revenue			4,000
	Cost of Goods Sold		2,700	
	Inventory			2,700

Part 1	**Part 2**	Part 3	Part 4	Part 5	Demo Doc Complete

Because all of these transactions involved cash receipts (debits to cash), they are all recorded in the cash receipts ledger. Amounts are put in the appropriate column for debits or credits. Posting references are used to help track the transaction through the various ledgers.

We can see that the total debits (cash and sales discounts) are the same as the total credits (all other accounts). All of the transactions recorded in the cash receipts journal had equal debits and credits.

	Cash Receipts Journal							Page 5
	Debits			**Credits**				
					Other Accounts			
		Sales	**Accounts**	**Sales**		**Post**		**Cost of Goods Sold Dr.**
Date	**Cash**	**Discounts**	**Receivable**	**Revenue**	**Account Title**	**Ref.**	**Amount**	**Inventory Cr.**
Nov. 4	3,300				Notes Receivable	30	3,000	
					Interest Revenue	90	300	
12	8,000				Notes Payable	50	8,000	
18	1,800		1,800		Lisa Henders	✔		
26	2,400	100	2,500		Peter Wilkins	✔		
29	4,000			4,000				2,700
30	19,500	100	4,300	4,000	Total		11,300	
	(10)	(70)	(20)	(60)			(X)	

Total Dr. = 19,600   Total Cr. = 19,600

Requirement 2

 Use the sales journal, the cash receipts journal, and the accounts receivable ledger.

Post to the general ledger and the accounts receivable ledger. Check that the total of the customer balances in the subsidiary ledger equals the general ledger balance in accounts receivable.

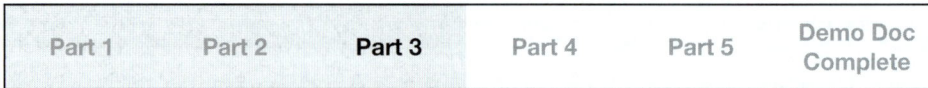

| Part 1 | Part 2 | **Part 3** | Part 4 | Part 5 | Demo Doc Complete |

First, the individual accounts in the accounts receivable ledger are adjusted by posting any accounts receivable transactions.

Some general ledger accounts, such as Accounts Receivable, need to have support for their balances. These accounts are called control accounts. The accounts receivable ledger, which contains each individual customer's name and balance, is called a subsidiary ledger. Whenever accounts receivable is debited or credited in the ledger, the subsidiary ledger for the individual customers affected must be debited or credited as well. *The total of the subsidiary ledger must always equal the control account balance.*

The amounts are then combined to get a total accounts receivable balance.

Accounts Receivable Subsidiary Ledger

Lisa Henders

Date		Post Ref.	Dr.	Cr.	Balance
Oct.	31	✔			3,200
Nov.	18	CR.5		1,800	1,400

Jennifer Collins

Date		Post Ref.	Dr.	Cr.	Balance
Oct.	31	✔			1,000

Peter Wilkins

Date		Post Ref.	Dr.	Cr.	Balance
Oct.	31	✔			2,500
Nov.	26	CR.5		2,500	—

Accounts Receivable Subsidiary Ledger

Customer	Balance
Lisa Henders	$1,400
Jennifer Collins	1,000
Total	$2,400

This total is the same as the total that should appear for the Accounts Receivable account in the general ledger.

Part 1	Part 2	Part 3	**Part 4**	Part 5	Demo Doc Complete

The totals/balances from the cash receipts ledger are now brought to the general ledger. These totals include any amounts in the Other Accounts column that need to be brought forth to specific accounts in the general ledger.

The balance in each account is updated. Notice that the setup for each account is basically a T-account laid out *completely horizontally*!

The balance in each general ledger account is now updated by adding the cash receipts journal transactions to the previous balance. This total becomes the new balance in the general ledger for that account.

For example, the cash account had a balance of $1,300 debit on October 31. The cash receipts journal shows an overall debit of $19,500 to cash. This total is entered in a separate line into the general ledger.

The Cash account is then totaled as the beginning balance of $1,300 debit plus the $19,500 debit of activity for November from the cash receipts journal.

Therefore, the Cash account in the general ledger has a total of $20,800 on November 30.

The other accounts are updated and totaled in the same manner.

General Ledger

Cash				No. 10
Date	Post Ref.	Dr.	Cr.	Balance
Oct. 31	✔			1,300
Nov. 30	CR.5	19,500		20,800

Sales Revenue				No. 60
Date	Post Ref.	Dr.	Cr.	Balance
Nov. 30	CR.5		4,000	4,000

Accounts Receivable				No. 20
Date	Post Ref.	Dr.	Cr.	Balance
Oct. 31	✔			6,700
Nov. 30	CR.5		4,300	2,400

Sales Discounts				No. 70
Date	Post Ref.	Dr.	Cr.	Balance
Nov. 30	CR.5	100		100

Notes Receivable				No. 30
Date	Post Ref.	Dr.	Cr.	Balance
Oct. 31	✔			7,400
Nov. 4	CR.5		3,000	4,400

Cost of Goods Sold				No. 80
Date	Post Ref.	Dr.	Cr.	Balance
Nov. 30	CR.5	2,700		2,700

Inventory				No. 40
Date	Post Ref.	Dr.	Cr.	Balance
Oct. 31	✔			4,000
Nov. 30	CR.5		2,700	1,300

Interest Revenue				No. 90
Date	Post Ref.	Dr.	Cr.	Balance
Nov. 4	CR.5		300	300

Notes Payable				No. 50
Date	Post Ref.	Dr.	Cr.	Balance
Nov. 12	CR.5		8,000	8,000

Notice that the total in the accounts receivable general ledger account ($2,400) is the same as in the subsidiary schedule ($2,400). This comparison is a good check to make sure all of the transactions were posted correctly.

Requirement 3

The employee at Juniper who opens the mail and physically collects the cash is the same person who updates the cash receipts journal. Does this practice create any problems?

| Part 1 | Part 2 | Part 3 | Part 4 | **Part 5** | Demo Doc Complete |

Any employee who collects the cash *and* records the receipt of the cash in the accounting system faces an opportunity for fraud. The employee could steal the cash and delay recording the cash receipt or perhaps never record the cash receipt.

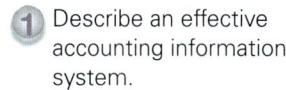

1 Describe an effective accounting information system.

| Part 1 | Part 2 | Part 3 | Part 4 | Part 5 | **Demo Doc Complete** |

Accounting in Action

ACCOUNTING INFORMATION SYSTEMS

Suppose you start a business to do valet parking for large parties. It's not economical to computerize, so you set up a manual accounting system. How do you get started?

Decision	Guidelines

What are the main components of an accounting system?

Journals
- General journal
- Special journals

Ledgers
- General ledger
- Subsidiary ledgers:
  - Accounts receivable
  - Accounts payable

Where do I record
- Sales of inventory on account?
- Cash receipts?
- Purchases on account?
- Cash payments?
- All other transactions?

- Sales journal
- Cash receipts journal
- Purchases journal
- Cash payments journals
- General journal

How does the general ledger relate to the subsidiary ledgers?

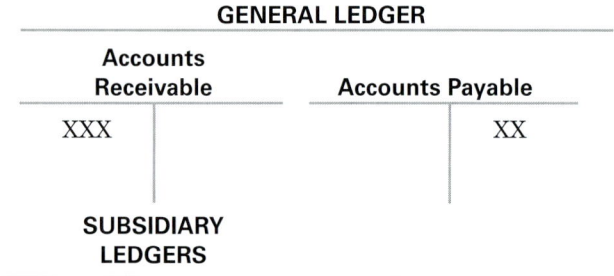

When do I post from the journals to the
- General ledger?
- Subsidiary ledgers?

How do I achieve control over
- Accounts receivable?
- Accounts payable?

- Monthly (or more often, if needed)
- Daily

Balance the ledgers, as follows:

General Ledger		Subsidiary Ledger
Accounts Receivable	=	Sum of Individual *Customer* Accounts Receivable
Accounts Payable	=	Sum of Individual *Creditor* Accounts Payable

Review

Accounting Information Systems

Word Power

Batch processing Computerized processing of similar transactions in a group or batch.

Cash disbursements journal Special journal used to record cash payments by check; also called the *check register* or *cash payments journal*

Cash payments journal Special journal used to record cash payments by check; also called the *check register* or cash disbursements journal.

Cash receipts journal Special journal used to record cash receipts.

Check register Special journal used to record cash payments by check; also called the *cash disbursements journal* or *cash payments journal*.

Database A computerized storehouse of information.

General journal Journal used to record all transactions that do not fit one of the special journals.

General ledger Ledger of accounts that are reported in the financial statements.

Hardware Electronic equipment that includes computers, disk drives, monitors, printers, and the network that connects them.

Menu A list of options for choosing computer functions.

Network The system of electronic linkages that allows different computers to share the same information.

Online processing Computerized processing of related functions, such as the recording and posting of transactions, on a continuous basis.

Purchases journal Special journal used to record all purchases of inventory, supplies, and other assets on account.

Sales journal Special journal used to record credit sales of inventory.

Server The main computer in a network where the program and data are stored.

Software Set of programs or instructions that drive the computer to perform the work desired.

Special journal An accounting journal designed to record one specific type of transaction.

Quick Check

1. John Alden's Rifles purchased inventory costing $6,500 from Pilgrim on account. Where should John Alden's Rifles record this transaction, and what account is credited?

   a. Cash payments journal; credit Cash
   b. Purchases journal; credit Accounts Payable
   c. Sales journal; credit Sales Revenue
   d. General journal; credit Inventory

2. Every transaction recorded in the cash receipts journal includes a

   a. Debit to Cash
   b. Debit to Accounts Receivable
   c. Debit to Sales Discounts
   d. Credit to Cash

3. The purchases journal is used to record all

   a. Purchases of inventory
   b. Purchases on account
   c. Purchases of assets
   d. Payments of purchases on account

4. The individual accounts in the accounts payable subsidiary ledger identify

   a. Customers
   b. Debtors
   c. Amounts to be collected
   d. Creditors

5. Which of the following is *not* a general ledger account?

   a. Sales Discounts
   b. Accounts Receivable
   c. Supplies Expense
   d. Jackson Wholesale Company

Answers are given after Apply Your Knowledge (p. B-34).

Accounting Practice

Short Exercises

SB-1. Use the following abbreviations to indicate the journal in which you would record transactions a through n.

Describing an effective accounting information system.

J = General journal   P = Purchases journal

S = Sales journal   CP = Cash payments journal

CR = Cash receipts journal

Transactions:

_____ **a.** Cash sale of inventory

_____ **b.** Payment of rent

_____ **c.** Depreciation of computer equipment

_____ **d.** Purchases of inventory on account

_____ **e.** Collection of accounts receivable

_____ **f.** Expiration of prepaid insurance

_____ **g.** Sale on account

_____ **h.** Payment on account

_____ **i.** Cash purchase of inventory

_____ **j.** Collection of dividend revenue earned on an investment

_____ **k.** Prepayment of insurance

_____ **l.** Borrowing money on a long-term note payable

_____ **m.** Purchase of equipment on account

_____ **n.** Cost of goods sold along with a credit sale

Exercises

EB-1. Match account numbers from the list that follows to the accounts of Picasso Art Supplies.

Describing an effective accounting information system.

Inventory   Paul Picasso, Withdrawals

Accounts Payable   Sales Revenue

Paul Picasso, Capital   Depreciation Expense

continued.....

Numbers from which to choose:

101	202	312
128	292	415
182	302	527

1 Describing an effective accounting information system.

EB-2. The accounts of Mozart Music Stores show some of the company's adjusted balances before closing:

Total Assets	$?	Long-Term Liabilities	$?
Current Assets......... 34,900		Ronaldo Madrid, Capital............ 6,900	
Plant Assets 50,700		Ronaldo Madrid, Withdrawals... 1,600	
Total Liabilities........ ?		Total Revenues........................... 32,000	
Current Liabilities... 32,900		Total Expenses........................... 16,800	

Compute the missing amounts. You must also compute ending owner's equity.

2 Using the sales journal, cash receipts journal, and accounts receivable ledger.

EB-3. The sales and cash receipts journals of DaVinci.com include the following entries:

			Sales Journal	
Date	Account Debited	Post Ref.	Accounts Receivable Dr. Sales Revenue Cr.	Cost of Goods Sold Dr. Inventory Cr.
June 8	D. Brown	✔	120	60
11	R. Langdon	✔	90	45
11	S. Neveu	✔	20	10
13	L. Teabing	✔	180	90
30	Total		410	205

	Debits			Credits				Cost of Goods Sold Dr.
		Cash Receipts Journal				Other Accounts		
Date	Cash	Sales Discounts	Accounts Receivable	Sales Revenue	Account Title	Post Ref.	Amount	Cost of Goods Sold Dr. Inventory Cr.
June 17					D. Brown	✔		
19					S. Neveu	✔		
25	450			450				225
29					R. Langdon	✔		

Complete the cash receipts journal for those transactions indicated. No sales discounts are given. Also, total the journal and show that total debits equal total credits.

EB-4. The partial cash receipts journal (without columns for Cost of Goods Sold Dr. and Inventory Cr.) of The Louvre Gallery follows.

② Using the sales journal, cash receipts journal, and accounts receivable ledger.

	Debits		Credits				
					Other Accounts		
Date	**Cash**	**Sales Discounts**	**Accounts Receivable**	**Sales Revenue**	**Account Title**	**Post Ref.**	**Amount**
May 2	873	27	900		V. de Milo Corp.	(e)	
9	654		654		M. Rocks, Inc.	(f)	
19	6,740				Notes Receivable	(g)	6,200
					Interest Revenue	(h)	540
30	441	9	450		M. Lisa	(i)	
31	3,534			3,534			
31	12,242	36	2,004	3,534	Totals		6,740
	(a)	(b)	(c)	(d)			(j)

Cash Receipts Journal — Page 7

The Louvre's general ledger includes the following selected accounts, along with their account numbers:

Number	Account	Number	Account
101	Cash	511	Sales Revenue
122	Accounts Receivable	512	Sales Discounts
123	Notes Receivable	513	Sales Returns
139	Land	521	Interest Revenue

Requirements

Indicate whether each posting reference (a) through (j) should be a

- Check mark (✔) for a posting to a customer account in the accounts receivable subsidiary ledger.

- Account number for a posting to an account in the general ledger. If so, give the account number.

- Letter (X) for an amount not posted.

EB-5. The purchases journal of N. Turtle Company follows.

③ Using the purchases journal, cash payments journal, and accounts payable ledger.

	Purchases Journal								Page 7
				Credits	Debits				
							Other Accounts Dr.		
Date	Account Credited	Terms	Post Ref.	Account Payable	Inventory	Supplies	Account Title	Post Ref.	Amount
Oct. 3	Donatello Unlimited	n/30		1,200	1,200				
7	Leonardo Supplies	n/30		265		265			
11	Donatello Unlimited	2/10 n/30		2,114	2,114				
28	Raphael Company	n/30		1,374			Equipment		1,374
31	Totals			4,953	3,314	265			1,374

Requirements

1. Assuming the beginning balances in all accounts is $0, open ledger accounts for Inventory, 128; Supplies, 132; Equipment, 165; and Accounts Payable, 202. Post to these accounts from the purchases journal. Use dates and posting references in the accounts.

2. Assuming the beginning balances in all accounts is $0, open accounts in the accounts payable subsidiary ledger for Donatello Unlimited, 202.01; Leonardo Supplies, 202.05; and Raphael Company, 202.08. Post from the purchases journal. Use dates and posting references in the ledger accounts.

3. Balance the Accounts Payable control account in the general ledger with the total of the balances in the accounts payable subsidiary ledger.

③ Using the purchases journal, cash payments journal, and accounts payable ledger.

EB-6. During August, Brahms Music Supplies had the following transactions:

August 1	Made payment on account to Seranade Associates, $735 less $15 discount for an earlier purchase of inventory.
5	Purchased inventory for cash, $1,540
9	Paid $525 for supplies.
16	Paid $5,687 on account to Sonnet Company; there was no discount.
21	Purchased furniture for cash, $1,340.
26	Made payment on account to Lullaby Company for an earlier purchase of inventory. The amount owed was $5,570. The discount was $110.
30	Made a semiannual interest payment of $1,100 on a long-term note payable. The entire payment was for interest.

Requirements

1. Prepare page 6 of the cash payments journal similar to the one illustrated in this chapter. Omit the check number (Ck. No.) and posting reference (Post Ref.) columns.

2. Record the transactions in the cash payments journal.

3. Total the amount columns of the journal. Determine that total debits equal total credits.

Problems

PB-1. The general ledger of Pickax Electronics includes the following selected accounts, along with their account numbers:

② Using the sales journal, cash receipts journal, and accounts receivable ledger.

④ Explaining the role of the general journal.

Cash	111	Sales Revenue	411
Accounts Receivable	112	Sales Discounts	412
Notes Receivable	115	Sales Returns and Allowances	413
Inventory	131	Interest Revenue	417
Equipment	141	Gain on Sale of Land	418
Land	142	Cost of Goods Sold	511

All credit sales are on the company's standard terms of 2/10, n/30. Sales and cash receipts transactions in September were as follows:

Sept.	4	Sold inventory on credit to J. Quilleran $1,200. Pickax's cost of these goods was $480.
	7	As an accommodation to another company, sold new equipment for its cost of $1,115, receiving cash in this amount.
	7	Cash sales for the week totaled $3,162 (cost, $1,264).
	10	Sold a surround sound system to Duncan, Inc., on account, $4,245 (cost $1,698).
	11	Sold land that cost $34,000 for cash of $53,000. The difference is a gain on sale of land.
	12	Sold goods on account to Weatherby Good, $2,100 (cost $840).
	13	Received cash from J. Quilleran in full settlement of his account receivable from September 4.
	14	Cash sales for the week were $2,795 (cost $1,118).
	17	Sold inventory on credit to Riker and Riker, a partnership, $1,260 (cost $504).
	20	Received inventory sold on September 10 to Duncan, Inc., for $170. The goods we shipped were unsatisfactory. These goods cost Pickax $68.
	20	Sold a stereo to Weatherby Good on account, $5,500 (cost $2,200).
	21	Cash sales for the week were $3,260 (cost $1,304).
	22	Received $1,700 cash from Duncan, Inc., in partial settlement of its account receivable. There was no discount.
	24	Received cash from Riker and Riker for its account receivable from September 17.
	25	Sold goods on account to H. Rice Co., $2,830 (cost $1,132).

continued.....

27 Collected $5,880 on a note receivable, of which $380 was interest.

28 Cash sales for the week totaled $4,160 (cost $1,664).

29 Sold inventory on account to Klingenschoen Corporation, $3,200 (cost $1,280).

29 Received goods sold on September 25 to H. Rice Co. for $950. The goods were damaged in shipment. The salvage value of these goods was $134. Record the inventory at its salvage value.

30 Received $2,375 cash on account from Duncan, Inc. There was no discount.

Requirements

1. Use the appropriate journal to record the preceding transactions in a sales journal (omit the Invoice No. column), a cash receipts journal, and a general journal. Pickax Electronics records sales returns and allowances in the general journal.

2. Total each column of the cash receipts journal. Determine that total debits equal total credits.

3. Show how postings would be made from the journals by writing the account numbers and check marks in the appropriate places in the journals.

3 Using the purchases journal, cash payments journal, and accounts payable ledger.

4 Explaining the role of the general journal.

PB-2. The general ledger of Moose County Something includes the following accounts:

Cash	111	Equipment	189
Inventory	131	Accounts Payable	211
Prepaid Insurance	161	Rent Expense	562
Supplies	171	Utilities Expense	565

Transactions in July that affected purchases and cash payments were as follows:

July 1 Paid monthly rent, debiting Rent Expense for $750.

3 Purchased inventory on credit from Koko Co., $4,000; terms 2/15, n/45.

5 Purchased supplies on credit from Yum Yum Sales, $640; terms 2/10, n/30.

6 Paid gas and water utility bills, $340.

8 Purchased equipment on account from K. Fund Co., $840; terms 2/10, n/30.

9 Returned the equipment to K. Fund Co. It was defective.

10 Paid Koko Co. the amount owed on the purchase of July 3.

11 Purchased inventory on account from K. Fund Co., $850; terms 2/10, n/30.

continued.....

13 Purchased inventory for cash, $1,268.

14 Paid an insurance premium, debiting Prepaid Insurance, $1,930.

16 Paid electricity utility bill, $140.

18 Paid our account payable to Yum Yum Sales, from July 5.

19 Paid account payable to K. Fund Co., from July 11.

20 Purchased supplies on account from J. Goodwinter Supplies, $90; terms net 30.

21 Purchased inventory on credit from Brodie Brothers, $2,750; terms 1/10, n/30.

25 Returned inventory purchased for $450 on July 21, to Brodie Brothers.

30 Paid Brodie Brothers the net amount owed from July 21, less the return on July 25.

Requirements

1. Use the appropriate journal to record the preceding transactions in a purchases journal, a cash payments journal (omit the Check No. column), and a general journal. Moose County Something records purchase returns in the general journal.

2. Total each column of the special journals. Show that total debits equal total credits in each special journal.

3. Show how postings would be made from the journals by writing the account numbers and check marks in the appropriate places in the journals.

For Internet Exercises, Excel in Practice, and additional online activities, go to the Web site www.prenhall.com/pollard.

Quick Check Answers

1. *b* 2. *a* 3. *b* 4. *d* 5. *d*

Appendix C

Partnerships

LEARNING OBJECTIVES

1 Explain the differences between the two basic types of partnerships.

2 Account for the partners' investments in a partnership.

3 Allocate profits and losses to the partners.

4 Account for the admission of a new partner.

5 Account for a partner's withdrawal from the firm.

6 Account for the liquidation of a partnership.

7 Prepare partnership financial statements.

Types of Partnerships

The two basic types of **partnerships** are general and limited.

1 Explain the differences between the two basic types of partnerships.

General Partnerships

A **general partnership** is the basic form of partnership organization. Each partner is an owner of the business with all the privileges and risks of ownership, including **unlimited personal liability**. The profits and losses of the partnership pass through to the partners, who then pay personal income tax on their income.

Limited Partnerships

A **limited partnership** consists of at least two classes of partners.

- At least one *general partner* takes primary responsibility for the business. The general partner also takes the bulk of the risk in the event the partnership goes bankrupt Usually, the general partner is the last owner to receive a share of profits and losses. However, the general partner may earn all excess profits after satisfying the limited partners' demands for income.

- The *limited partners* are so named because their liability for the partnership's debts is limited to their investment in the business. Limited partners usually have first claim to partnership profits and losses, but only up to a specified limit. In exchange for their limited liability, their potential for profits is also limited.

Most of the large accounting firms are organized as **limited liability partnerships (LLPs)**, which means that each partner's personal liability for the business's debts is limited to a certain amount. The LLP must carry a large insurance policy to protect the public in case the partnership is found guilty of malpractice. Medical, legal, and other firms of professionals can also be organized as LLPs.

S Corporations

An **S corporation** is a corporation that is taxed the same as a partnership. This form of business organization derives its name from Subchapter S of the U.S. Internal Revenue Code.

An S corporation offers its owners the benefits of a corporation—no personal liability for business debts—and of a partnership—no double taxation. An ordinary, Subchapter C, corporation is subject to double taxation. First, the corporation pays corporate income tax on its income. Then, when the corporation pays dividends to the stockholders, they pay personal income tax on their dividend income.[1]

An S corporation pays no corporate income tax. Instead, the corporation's income flows directly to the stockholders (the owners), who pay personal income tax on their share of the S corporation's income. The one-time taxation of an S corporation's income is an important advantage over an ordinary corporation. From a tax standpoint, an S corporation operates like a partnership.

---

[1]From time to time, U.S. presidents and Congress members propose eliminating the tax on dividends received by individuals.

To qualify as an S corporation, a company can have no more than 75 stockholders, all of whom must be citizens or residents of the United States. Accounting for an S corporation resembles accounting for a partnership because the allocation of corporate income follows the same procedure used by partnerships.

The Partnership Start-Up

2 Account for the partners' investments in a partnership.

Let's examine the start-up of a partnership. Partners in a new business may invest assets and liabilities. These contributions are entered in the books in the same way that a proprietor's assets and liabilities are recorded—debit the assets and credit the liabilities. Subtraction of liabilities from assets yields the amount of each partner's capital. Often, the partners hire an independent firm to appraise their assets and liabilities at current market value at the time a partnership is formed. This outside evaluation assures an objective accounting of assets, liabilities, and capital.

Assume that Dave Barnes and Joan Hogan form a partnership to sell computer software. The partners write up a **partnership agreement** (also called **articles of partnership**) in which they decide on various terms of their partnership. Barnes and Hogan agree on the following values:

Barnes's Contributions

- Cash, $10,000; inventory, $70,000; and accounts payable, $85,000 (The appraiser believes that the current market values for these items equal Barnes's values.)
- Accounts receivable, $30,000, less allowance for uncollectible accounts of $5,000
- Computer equipment—cost, $800,000; accumulated depreciation, $200,000; current market value, $450,000

Hogan's Contributions

- Cash, $5,000
- Computer software: cost, $18,000; current market value, $100,000

The partnership records the partners' investments at current market value because the partnership is buying the assets and assuming the liabilities at their current market values. The partnership entries are as follows:

Journal Entry:

Date	Accounts	Post Ref.	Dr.	Cr.
June 1	Cash		10,000	
	Accounts Receivable		30,000	
	Inventory		70,000	
	Computer Equipment		450,000	
	Allowance for Uncollectible Accounts			5,000
	Accounts Payable			85,000
	Barnes, Capital ($560,000 − $90,000)			470,000
	Record Barnes's investment in the partnership.			

Journal Entry:

Date	Accounts	Post Ref.	Dr.	Cr.
June 1	Cash		5,000	
	Computer Software		100,000	
	Hogan, Capital			105,000
	Record Hogan's investment in the partnership.			

The initial partnership balance sheet appears in Exhibit C-1. The assets and liabilities are the same for a proprietorship and a partnership.

Exhibit C-1   Partnership Balance Sheet

BARNES AND HOGAN				
Balance Sheet				
June 1, 2008				

Assets			Liabilities	
Cash		$ 15,000	Accounts payable	$ 85,000
Accounts recievable	$30,000			
Less: Allowance for uncollectible				
accounts	(5,000)	25,000	**Capital**	
Inventory		70,000	Barnes, capital	470,000
Computer equipment		450,000	Hogan, capital	105,000
Computer software		100,000		
Total assets		$660,000	Total liabilities and capital	$660,000

Sharing Profits and Losses, and Partner Drawings

Allocating profits and losses among partners is one of the most challenging aspects of managing a partnership. If the partners have not drawn up an agreement or if the agreement does not state how the partners will divide profits and losses, then they share equally. If the agreement specifies a method for dividing profits but not losses, then losses are shared in the same proportion as profits. For example, a partner who gets 75% of the profits likewise absorbs 75% of any losses. Partners may agree to any profit-and-loss-sharing method they desire.

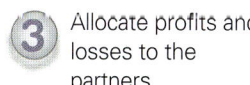

3 Allocate profits and losses to the partners.

Typical arrangements for dividing profits and losses among the partners include the following:

1. Sharing based on a stated fraction for each partner, such as 50/50 or 2/3 and 1/3 or 4:3:3 (which means 40% to Partner A, 30% to Partner B, and 30% to Partner C)

2. Sharing based on each partner's capital contribution

3. Sharing based on each partner's service to the partnership

4. Sharing based on a combination of each partner's stated fraction, capital contribution, and service

The sections that follow illustrate some of these profit-and-loss-sharing plans.

Sharing Based on a Stated Fraction

Partners may state a particular fraction of the total profits and losses each individual partner will share. Suppose the partnership agreement of Lou Cane and Justin Doak allocates 2/3 of the business profits and losses to Cane and 1/3 to Doak. This sharing rule can also be expressed as 2:1. If net income for the year is $90,000 and all revenue and expense accounts have been closed, the Income Summary account has a credit balance of $90,000:

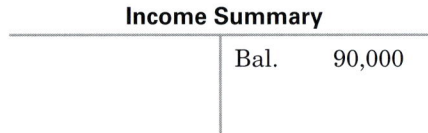

The entry to close the profit to the partners' capital accounts is

Journal Entry:

Date	Accounts	Post Ref.	Dr.	Cr.
Dec. 31	Income Summary		90,000	
	Cane, Capital ($90,000 × 2/3)			60,000
	Doak, Capital ($90,000 × 1/3)			30,000
	Allocate net income to partners.			

Consider the effect of this entry. Does Cane get $60,000 cash and Doak $30,000 cash? No. The increase in the partners' capital accounts cannot be linked to any particular asset, including cash. Instead, the entry indicates that Cane's ownership in *all* the assets of the business increased by $60,000 and Doak's by $30,000.

If the year's operations resulted in a net loss of $66,000, the Income Summary account would have a debit balance of $66,000. In that case, the entry to close the loss to the partners' capital accounts would be

Journal Entry:

Date	Accounts	Post Ref.	Dr.	Cr.
Dec. 31	Cane, Capital ($66,000 × 2/3)		44,000	
	Doak, Capital ($66,000 × 1/3)		22,000	
	Income Summary			66,000
	Allocate net income to partners.			

Sharing Based on Capital Contributions and on Service

One partner may contribute more capital. Another partner may put more work into the business. Even among partners who log equal time, one person's experience may command a greater share of income. To reward the harder-working or the more-valuable person, the profits and losses may be divided based on a combination of contributed capital *and* service to the business. The Chicago-based law firm Baker & McKenzie, for example, has about 500 partners. Baker & McKenzie takes seniority into account in determining partner compensation.

Assume that Rita Ruiz and Nancy Skeen formed a partnership in which Ruiz invested $60,000 and Skeen $40,000, for a total of $100,000. But Skeen devotes more time to the partnership and earns the larger salary. Accordingly, the two partners have agreed to share profits as follows:

1. The first $50,000 of partnership profits is allocated on the basis of the partners' capital contributions.

2. The next $60,000 is allocated on the basis of service, with Ruiz receiving $24,000 and Skeen $36,000.

3. Any remaining amount will be allocated equally.

The partnership's net income for the first year is $125,000, and the partners share this profit as follows:

	Ruiz	Skeen	Total
Total Net Income			$125,000
Sharing of First $50,000 of Net Income,			
Based on Capital Contributions:			
Ruiz ($60,000/$100,000 × $50,000)	$30,000		
Skeen ($40,000/$100,000 × $50,000)		$20,000	
Total			50,000
Net Income Remaining for Allocation			75,000
Sharing of Next $60,000, Based on			
Service:			
Ruiz	24,000		
Skeen		36,000	

continued.....

	Ruiz	Skeen	Total
Total			60,000
Net Income Remaining for Allocation			15,000
Remainder Shared Equally:			
Ruiz ($15,000 × ½)	7,500		
Skeen ($15,000 × ½)		7,500	
Total			15,000
Net Income Remaining for Allocation			$ 0
Net Income Allocated to the Partners	$61,500	$63,500	$125,000

For this allocation, the closing entry is:

Journal Entry:

Date	Accounts	Post Ref.	Dr.	Cr.
Dec. 31	Income Summary		125,000	
	Ruiz, Capital			61,500
	Skeen, Capital			63,500
	Allocate net income to partners.			

Partner Drawings of Cash and Other Assets

Like anyone else, partners need cash for personal expenses. Partnership agreements usually allow partners to withdraw assets from the business. Drawings from a partnership are recorded exactly as for a proprietorship. Assume that both Randy Lohman and Gerald Coble get monthly withdrawals of $3,500. The partnership records the March withdrawals with this entry:

Journal Entry:

Date	Accounts	Post Ref.	Dr.	Cr.
Mar. 31	Lohman, Withdrawals		3,500	
	Coble, Withdrawals		3,500	
	Cash			7,000
	Record monthly withdrawals of cash.			

During the year, each partner gets 12 monthly withdrawals, a total of $42,000 ($3,500 × 12). At the end of the period, the general ledger shows the following balances for the partners' drawing accounts:

Lohman, Withdrawals		Coble, Withdrawals	
Dec. 31 Bal. 42,000		Dec. 31 Bal. 42,000	

The withdrawals accounts are closed at the end of the period, exactly as for a proprietorship: Credit the partner's withdrawals account and debit his or her capital account.

Admission of a Partner

The addition of a new partner or the withdrawal of a partner dissolves the old partnership. We now discuss how partnerships dissolve—and how new partnerships arise.

> **4** Account for the admission of a new partner.

Often, a new partnership is formed to carry on the old partnership's business. In fact, the new firm may retain the dissolved partnership's name. PricewaterhouseCoopers LLP, for example, is an accounting firm that adds new partners and retires old ones each year. Thus, the old partnership may dissolve and a new partnership begins many times during a year. But the business retains its name and continues operating. Other partnerships may dissolve and then re-form under a new name. Let's look at the ways a new member may be admitted into an existing partnership.

Admission by Purchasing a Partner's Interest

A person may become a member of a partnership by gaining the approval of the other partner(s) for entrance into the firm *and* by purchasing a present partner's interest in the business. Let's assume that Roberta Fritz and Benitez Gomez have a partnership that carries these figures:

Cash............................	$ 40,000	Total Liabilities....	$120,000
Other Assets...............	360,000	Fritz, Capital........	110,000
		Gomez, Capital.....	170,000
		Total Liabilities	
Total Assets................	$400,000	and Capital........	$400,000

Suppose Fritz receives an offer from Barry Hart, an outside party, to buy her $110,000 interest in the business for $150,000. Fritz agrees to sell out to Hart, and Gomez approves Hart as a new partner. The firm records the transfer of capital interest in the business with this entry:

Journal Entry:

Date	Accounts	Post Ref.	Dr.	Cr.
Apr. 16	Fritz, Capital		110,000	
	Hart, Capital			110,000
	Transfer Fritz's equity in the business to Hart.			

The debit entry closes Fritz's capital account because she is no longer a partner in the firm. The credit side opens Hart's capital account. The entry amount is Fritz's capital balance, $110,000, and not the $150,000 that Hart paid Fritz to buy into the business. The full $150,000 goes to Fritz. In this example, the partnership receives no cash because the transaction was between Hart and Fritz, not between Hart and the partnership. Suppose Hart pays Fritz less than Fritz's capital balance. The entry on the partnership books is not affected. Fritz's equity is transferred to Hart at book value, $110,000.

The old partnership has dissolved. Gomez and Hart draw up a new partnership agreement with a new profit-and-loss-sharing ratio and continue in business. If Gomez does not accept Hart as a partner, Hart gets no voice in management of the firm. However, under the Uniform Partnership Act, the purchaser shares in the profits and losses of the firm and in its assets at liquidation.

Admission by Investing in the Partnership

A person may be admitted as a partner by investing directly in the partnership rather than by buying an existing partner's interest. The new partner contributes assets—for example, cash or equipment—to the business. Assume that the partnership of Robin Inez and Michael James has the following assets, liabilities, and capital:

Cash............................	$ 20,000	Total Liabilities....	$ 60,000
Other Assets...............	200,000	Inez, Capital..........	70,000
		James, Capital......	90,000
		Total Liabilities	
Total Assets................	$220,000	and Capital.........	$220,000

Laura Kramer offers to invest equipment and land (labeled Other Assets) with a market value of $80,000. Inez and James agree to dissolve the existing partnership and to start up a new business, giving Kramer 1/3 interest [$80,000/($70,000 + $90,000 + $80,000)] in exchange for the assets. Notice that Kramer is buying into the partnership at book value because her 1/3 investment of $80,000 equals 1/3 of the new partnership's total capital of $240,000. The entry to record Kramer's investment is:

After this entry, the partnership books show the following:

Journal Entry:

Date	Accounts	Post Ref.	Dr.	Cr.
July 18	Other Assets		80,000	
	Kramer, Capital			80,000
	Admit L. Kramer as a partner with a one-third interest in the business.			

Cash	$ 20,000	Total Liabilities....	$ 60,000
Other Assets		Inez, Capital	70,000
($200,000 + $80,000) ...	280,000	James, Capital	90,000
		Kramer, Capital ...	80,000
		Total Liabilities	
Total Assets	$300,000	and Capital	$300,000

Kramer's 1/3 interest in the partnership does not necessarily entitle her to 1/3 of the profits. The sharing of profits and losses is a separate element in the partnership agreement.

ADMISSION BY INVESTING IN THE PARTNERSHIP—BONUS TO THE OLD PARTNERS

The more successful a partnership, the higher the payment demanded from a new partner. Partners in a business that is doing quite well might require an incoming person to pay them a bonus. The bonus increases the current partners' capital accounts.

Suppose that Hiro Nagasawa and Ralph Oldham's partnership has earned above-average profits for 10 years. The two partners share profits and losses equally. The partnership balance sheet carries these figures:

Cash	$ 40,000	Total Liabilities	$100,000
Other Assets	210,000	Nagasawa, Capital ...	70,000
		Oldham, Capital	80,000
		Total Liabilities	
Total Assets	$250,000	and Capital	$250,000

The partners agree to admit Glen Pearce to a 1/4 interest with his cash investment of $90,000. Pearce's capital balance on the partnership books is only $60,000, computed as follows:

Partnership Capital before Pearce is Admitted ($70,000 + $80,000)	$150,000
Pearce's Investment in the Partnership	90,000
Partnership Capital after Pearce is Admitted	$240,000
Pearce's Capital in the Partnership ($240,000 × 1/4)	$ 60,000
Bonus to the Old Partners ($90,000 − $60,000)	$ 30,000

In effect, Pearce had to buy into the partnership at a price of $90,000, which was above the book value of his 1/4 interest of $60,000. Pearce's investment of an extra $30,000 creates a *bonus* for the existing partners. The entry to record the receipt of Pearce's investment is:

Journal Entry:

Date	Accounts	Post Ref.	Dr.	Cr.
Mar. 1	Cash		90,000	
	Pearce, Capital			60,000
	Nagasawa, Capital ($30,000 × 1/2)			15,000
	Oldham, Capital ($30,000 × 1/2)			15,000
	Admit G. Pearce as a partner with a one-fourth interest in the business.			

Pearce's capital account is credited for his 1/4 interest in the partnership. The *bonus* is allocated to the partners on the basis of their profit-and-loss ratio.

The new partnership's books then reflect these amounts:

Cash ($40,000 + $90,000)	$130,000	Total Liabilities	$100,000
Other Assets	210,000	Nagasawa, Capital ($70,000 + $15,000)	85,000
		Oldham, Capital ($80,000 + $15,000)	95,000
		Pearce, Capital	60,000
Total Assets	$340,000	Total Liabilities and Capital	$340,000

ADMISSION BY INVESTING IN THE PARTNERSHIP—BONUS TO THE NEW PARTNER

A new partner may be so important that the existing partners offer him or her a partnership share that includes a bonus. A law firm may want a former governor or other official as a partner because of the person's reputation and connections. A restaurant owner may want to go into partnership with a famous sports personality or a movie star.

Suppose Allan Pace and Olivia Franco have a law partnership. The firm's balance sheet amounts appear as follows:

Cash	$140,000	Total Liabilities	$120,000
Other Assets	360,000	Pace, Capital	230,000
		Franco, Capital	150,000
Total Assets	$500,000	Total Liabilities and Capital	$500,000

Pace and Franco admit Martin Schiller, a former attorney general, as a partner with a 1/3 interest in exchange for his cash investment of $100,000. Pace and Franco share profits and losses in the ratio of 2/3 to Pace and 1/3 to Franco. The computation of Schiller's equity in the partnership is:

Partnership Capital before Schiller is Admitted ($230,000 + $150,000)	$380,000
Schiller's Investment in the Partnership	100,000

continued.....

Partnership Capital after Schiller is Admitted $480,000

Schiller's Capital in the Partnership ($480,000 × 1/3) $160,000

Bonus to the New Partner ($160,000 – $100,000).............. $ 60,000

In this case, Schiller bought into the partnership at a price of $100,000, which was below the book value of his interest of $160,000. The bonus of $60,000 went to Schiller from the other partners. The capital accounts of Pace and Franco are debited for the $60,000 difference between the new partner's equity of $160,000 and his investment of $100,000. The existing partners share this decrease in capital as though it were a loss, on the basis of their profit-and-loss ratio. The entry to record Schiller's investment is:

Journal Entry:

Date	Accounts	Post Ref.	Dr.	Cr.
Aug. 24	Cash		100,000	
	Pace, Capital ($60,000 × 2/3)		40,000	
	Franco, Capital ($60,000 × 1/3)		20,000	
	Schiller, Capital			160,000
	Admit M. Schiller as a partner with a one-third interest in the business.			

The new partnership's balance sheet amounts are as follows:

Cash ($140,000 + $100,000)...	$240,000	Total Liabilities	$120,000	
Other Assets............................	360,000	Pace, Capital ($230,000 – $40,000)...	190,000	
		Franco, Capital ($150,000 – $20,000)...	130,000	
		Schiller, Capital	160,000	
Total Assets............................	$600,000	Total Liabilities and Capital	$600,000	

Withdrawal of a Partner

A partner may withdraw from the business for many reasons, including retirement, or a dispute. The resignation of a partner also causes a **dissolution** of the old partnership. The partnership agreement should contain a provision to govern how to settle with a withdrawing partner. In the simplest case, a partner may resign and sell his or her interest to another partner in a personal transaction.

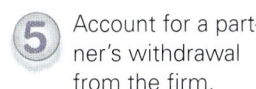 Account for a partner's withdrawal from the firm.

The only entry needed to record this transfer of equity debits the withdrawing partner's capital account and credits the purchaser's capital account. The dollar amount of the entry is the capital balance of the withdrawing partner, regardless of the price paid by the purchaser.

The withdrawing partner may receive his or her share of the business in partnership assets other than cash. Then the question is what value to assign the partnership assets—book value or current market value? The settlement procedure may specify an independent appraisal to determine current market value. If market values have changed, the appraisal will result in revaluing the partnership assets. The partners share in any market-value changes their efforts caused.

Suppose Keith Inman is retiring from the partnership of Gable, Harris, and Inman. Before any asset appraisal, the partnership balance sheet accounts contain the following:

Cash..	$ 69,000	Total Liabilities....	$ 80,000
Inventory...	44,000	Gable, Capital.......	54,000
Land..	55,000	Harris, Capital	43,000
Building $95,000		Inman, Capital	21,000
Less: Accumulated			
Depreciation,			
Building............. (65,000)	30,000	Total Liabilities	
Total Assets	$198,000	and Capital.......	$198,000

An independent appraiser revalues the inventory at $38,000 (down from $44,000) and the land at $101,000 (up from $55,000). The partners share the differences between these assets' market values and their prior book values on the basis of their profit-and-loss ratio.

The partnership agreement has allocated 1/4 of the profits to Susan Gable, 1/2 to Charles Harris, and 1/4 to Keith Inman. (This ratio may be written 1:2:1 for one part to Gable, two parts to Harris, and one part to Inman.) For each share that Gable or Inman has, Harris has two. The entries to record the revaluation of the inventory and land are the following:

Journal Entry:

Date	Accounts	Post Ref.	Dr.	Cr.
July 31	Gable, Capital ($6,000 × 1/4)		1,500	
	Harris, Capital ($6,000 × 1/2)		3,000	
	Inman, Capital ($6,000 × 1/4)		1,500	
	Inventory ($44,000 – $38,000)			6,000
	Revalue the inventory and allocate the loss to the partners.			
31	Land ($101,000 – $55,000)		46,000	
	Gable, Capital ($46,000 × 1/4)			11,500
	Harris, Capital ($46,000 × 1/2)			23,000
	Inman, Capital ($46,000 × 1/4)			11,500
	Revalue the land and allocate the gain to the partners.			

After the revaluations, the partnership balance sheet accounts are as follows:

Cash..	$ 69,000	Total Liabilities	$ 80,000
Inventory	38,000	Gable, Capital ($54,000	
Land	101,000	– $1,500 + $11,500)	64,000
Building $95,000		Harris, Capital ($43,000	
Less: Accumulated		– $3,000 + $23,000)	63,000
Depreciation,			
Building .... (65,000)	30,000	Inman, Capital ($21,000	
		– $1,500 + $11,500)	31,000
		Total Liabilities	
Total Assets	$238,000	and Capital	$238,000

The books now carry the assets at current market value, which becomes the new book value, and the capital accounts are adjusted accordingly. As the balance sheet shows, Inman has a claim to $31,000 in partnership assets. Now we can account for Keith Inman's withdrawal from the business.

Withdrawal at Book Value

If Keith Inman withdraws by receiving cash equal to the book value of his owner's equity, the entry will be:

Journal Entry:

Date	Accounts	Post Ref.	Dr.	Cr.
July 31	Inman, Capital		31,000	
	Cash			31,000
	Record withdrawal of K. Inman from the business.			

This entry records the payment of cash to Inman and the closing of his capital account.

Withdrawal at Less Than Book Value

The withdrawing partner may be so eager to leave the business that he or she is willing to take less than his or her equity. Assume that Keith Inman withdraws from the business and agrees to receive partnership cash of $10,000 and the new partnership's note for $15,000. This $25,000 settlement is $6,000 less than Inman's $31,000 equity in the business. The remaining partners share this $6,000 difference, which is a bonus to them, according to their profit-and-loss ratio.

Because Inman has withdrawn from the partnership, a new agreement—and a new profit-and-loss ratio—must be drawn up. In forming a new partnership, Harris and Gable may decide on any ratio that they see fit. Let's assume they agree that Harris will earn 2/3 of partnership profits and losses and Gable 1/3. The entry to record Inman's withdrawal at less than his book value is:

Journal Entry:

Date	Accounts	Post Ref.	Dr.	Cr.
July 31	Inman, Capital		31,000	
	Cash			10,000
	Note Payable to K. Inman			15,000
	Gable, Capital ($6,000 × 1/3)			2,000
	Harris, Capital ($6,000 × 2/3)			4,000
	Record withdrawal of K. Inman from the business.			

Inman's account is closed, and Harris and Gable may or may not continue the business as a new partnership.

Withdrawal at More Than Book Value

The settlement with a withdrawing partner may allow him or her to take assets of greater value than the book value of that partner's capital. Also, the remaining partners may be so eager for the withdrawing partner to leave that they pay him or her a bonus to withdraw from the business. In either case, the partner's withdrawal causes a decrease in the book equity of the remaining partners. This decrease is allocated to the partners on the basis of their profit-and-loss ratio.

The accounting for this situation follows the pattern illustrated for withdrawal at less than book value—with one exception. The remaining partners' capital accounts are debited because the withdrawing partner receives more than his or her book equity.

Death of a Partner

The death of a partner dissolves a partnership. The partnership accounts are adjusted to measure net income or loss for the fraction of the year up to the date of death. Then they are closed to determine all partners' capital balances on that date. Settlement with the deceased partner's estate is based on the partnership agreement. The estate commonly receives partnership assets equal to the partner's capital balance. The partnership closes the deceased partner's capital account with a debit. This entry credits a payable to the estate.

Suppose Susan Gable (of the partnership at the top of p. C-14) dies, and her capital balance is $64,000. Gable's estate may request cash for her final share of the partnership's assets. Imagine that, at this time, the business has only $39,000 of cash, so it must borrow. Let's assume the partnership borrows $50,000 and then pays Gable's estate. The partnership's journal entries are as follows:

Journal Entry:

Date	Accounts	Post Ref.	Dr.	Cr.
Aug. 1	Cash		50,000	
	Notes Payable			50,000
	Borrow money.			
1	Gable, Capital		64,000	
	Cash			64,000
	Record withdrawal of Gable from the business.			

Alternatively, a remaining partner may purchase the deceased partner's equity. The deceased partner's equity is debited, and the purchaser's equity is credited. The journal entry to record this transaction follows the pattern given on page C-8 for the transfer of Fritz's equity to Hart. The amount of this entry is the ending credit balance in the deceased partner's capital account.

Liquidation of a Partnership

Admission of a new partner or withdrawal or death of an existing partner dissolves the partnership. However, the business may continue operating with no apparent change to outsiders, such as customers and creditors. In contrast, **liquidation** is the process of going out of business by selling an entity's assets and paying its liabilities. The final step in liquidation is the *distribution of the remaining cash to the owners*. Before a business is liquidated, its books should be adjusted and closed. After closing, only asset, liability, and partners' capital accounts remain open.

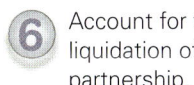 Account for the liquidation of a partnership.

Liquidation includes three steps:

1. Sell the assets. Allocate the gain or loss to the partners' capital accounts on the basis of the profit-and-loss ratio.

2. Pay the partnership liabilities.

3. Disburse the remaining cash to the partners on the basis of their capital balances.

In practice, the liquidation of a business can stretch over weeks or months. Selling every asset and paying every liability takes time. After the partners of Shea & Gould, one of New York's best-known law firms, voted to dissolve their partnership, the firm remained open for an extra year to collect bills and pay off liabilities.

To avoid excessive detail in our illustrations, we include only two asset categories—Cash and Noncash Assets—and a single liability category—Liabilities. Our examples assume that the business sells the noncash assets in a single transaction and then pays the liabilities in another single transaction.

Assume that Jane Akers, Elaine Bloch, and Mark Crane have shared profits and losses in the ratio of 3:1:1. (This ratio is equal to 3/5, 1/5, 1/5, or a 60%, 20%, 20% sharing ratio.) They decide to liquidate their partnership. After the books are adjusted and closed, the general ledger contains the following balances:

Cash............................	$ 10,000	Liabilities	$ 30,000
Noncash Assets	90,000	Akers, Capital	40,000
		Bloch, Capital.......	20,000
		Crane, Capital......	10,000
		Total Liabilities	
Total Assets	$100,000	and Capital........	$100,000

Sale of Noncash Assets at a Gain

Assume that the Akers, Bloch, and Crane partnership sells its noncash assets, shown on the balance sheet as $90,000, for cash of $150,000. The partnership realizes a gain of $60,000, which is allocated to the partners on the basis of their profit-and-loss-sharing ratio. The entry to record this sale and allocation of the gain is:

Journal Entry:

Date	Accounts	Post Ref.	Dr.	Cr.
Oct. 31	Cash		150,000	
	Noncash Assets			90,000
	Akers, Capital ($60,000 × 0.60)			36,000
	Bloch, Capital ($60,000 × 0.20)			12,000
	Crane, Capital ($60,000 × 0.20)			12,000
	Sell noncash assets at a gain.			

The partnership next must pay off its liabilities:

Journal Entry:

Date	Accounts	Post Ref.	Dr.	Cr.
Oct. 31	Liabilities		30,000	
	Cash			30,000
	Pay liabilities.			

In the final liquidation transaction, the remaining cash is disbursed to the partners. *The partners share in the cash according to their capital balances.* (*Gains and losses* on the sale of assets are shared by the partners on the basis of their profit-and-loss-sharing ratio.) The amount of cash left in the partnership is $130,000—the $10,000 beginning balance plus the $150,000 cash sale of assets minus the $30,000 cash payment of liabilities. The partners divide the remaining cash according to their capital balances:

A convenient way to summarize the transactions in a partnership liquidation is given in Exhibit C-2. Remember that, upon liquidation, gains on the sale of assets are divided according to the *profit-and-loss ratio*. The final cash payment to the partners is based on *capital balances*.

Journal Entry:

Date	Accounts	Post Ref.	Dr.	Cr.
Oct. 31	Akers, Capital ($40,000 + $36,000)		76,000	
	Bloch, Capital ($20,000 + $12,000)		32,000	
	Crane, Capital ($10,000 + $12,000)		22,000	
	Cash			130,000
	Pay cash in liquidation.			

After the payment of cash to the partners, the business has no assets, liabilities, or owners' equity. All the balances are zero. According to the accounting equation, partnership assets always *must* equal partnership liabilities plus partnership capital, and they do, even after liquidation.

Sale of Noncash Assets at a Loss

Liquidation of a business often includes the sale of noncash assets at a loss. When a loss occurs, the partners' capital accounts are debited as they share the loss in their profit-and-loss-sharing ratio. Otherwise, the accounting follows the pattern illustrated for the sale of noncash assets at a gain.

Exhibit C-2 Partnership Liquidation—Sale of Assets at a Gain

					Capital		
		Noncash			Akers	Bloch	Crane
	Cash +	Assets =	Liabilities +		(60%) +	(20%) +	(20%)
Balance before sale of assets	$ 10,000	$90,000	$30,000		$40,000	$20,000	$10,000
Sale of assets and sharing of gain	150,000	(90,000)			36,000	12,000	12,000
Balances	160,000	0	30,000		76,000	32,000	22,000
Payment of liabilities	(30,000)		(30,000)				
Balances	130,000	0	0		76,000	32,000	22,000
Payment of cash to partners	(130,000)				(76,000)	(32,000)	(22,000)
Balances	$ 0	$ 0	$ 0		$ 0	$ 0	$ 0

Partnership Financial Statements

Partnership financial statements are much like those of a proprietorship. However, a partnership income statement includes a section showing the division of net income to the partners. For example, the partnership of Lee Gorman and Wayne Harmon might report its statements for the year ended December 31, 2007, as shown in Exhibit C-3. All amounts are assumed.

 Prepare partnership financial statements.

Exhibit C-3 Financial Statements of a Partnership

GORMAN & HARMON CONSULTING
Income Statement
Year Ended December 31, 2007

		(in thousands)
Revenues		$460
Expenses		(270)
Net income		$190
Allocation of net income:		
To Gorman	$114	
To Harmon	76	$190

GORMAN & HARMON CONSULTING
Statement of Owner's Equity
Year Ended December 31, 2007

	(in thousands)	
	Gorman	**Harmon**
Capital, December 31, 2006	$ 50	$ 40
Add: Investments	10	
Net income	114	76
Subtotal	174	116
Less: Withdrawals	(72)	(48)
Capital, December 31, 2007	$102	$ 68

GORMAN & HARMON CONSULTING
Balance Sheet
December 31, 2007

	(in thousands)
Cash and other assets	$170
Owner's equity	
Gorman, capital	$102
Harmon, capital	68
Total capital	$170

Large partnerships may not find it feasible to report the net income of every partner. Instead, the firm may report average earnings per partner, as shown in Exhibit C-4 for a small firm.

Exhibit C-4 Reporting Net Income for an Accounting Partnership

PRICE & YOUNG
Income Statement
Year Ended August 31, 2006

Fees for professional services	$1,500,000
Earnings for the year	$ 600,000
Average earnings per partner (2 partners)	$ 300,000

Demo Doc

Partnerships

Learning Objectives   2–7

The Goode Partnership wants to admit Hanna Storm as a new partner on January 1, 2008. On this date, Goode had the following information:

THE GOODE PARTNERSHIP Balance Sheet January 1, 2008			
Cash	$25,000	Liabilities	$35,000
Other assets	60,000	Janice Wright, capital	15,000
		Ned Frist, capital	35,000
Total assets	$85,000	Total liabilities and capital	$85,000

Janice has a 30% share of the profits, whereas Ned has a 70% share.

Requirements

1. Suppose Janice Wright sold her entire interest to Hanna for $40,000. Journalize the transfer of ownership. What are the Capital balances for each partner after the transfer is made?

2. Ignoring Requirement 1, suppose instead that the Goode Partnership were to admit Hanna as a third partner by selling her a 40% interest for $40,000 cash. Compute Hanna's Capital balance and journalize her investment. What are the Capital balances for each partner after the investment is made?

3. Ignoring Requirement 1, prepare the balance sheet of the Goode Partnership after Hanna is admitted to the partnership.

4. Assume that Hanna was not admitted to the partnership. During 2008, Goode earned $20,000 of net income (in cash). Prepare an updated balance sheet for Goode. How much profit is allocated to each partner (Janice and Ned)? Does the partnership pay income taxes on this profit?

5. Assume the information from Requirement 4. On January 1, 2009, the Goode Partnership was liquidated. All non-cash assets were sold for $90,000, after which all liabilities were paid. How much does each partner receive upon liquidation?

Demo Doc Solutions

Requirement 1

Suppose Janice Wright sold her entire interest to Hanna for $40,000. Journalize the transfer of ownership. What are the Capital balances for each partner after the transfer is made?

Part 1	Part 2	Part 3	Part 4	Part 5	Demo Doc Complete

If Hanna purchases Janice's interest in the partnership, it is an outside transaction of ownership. The only portion recorded in the accounting records of the partnership is the name change on the Capital account. Janice's Capital account decreases (a debit) and Hanna's Capital account increases (a credit) by $15,000.

Journal Entry:

Date	Accounts	Post Ref.	Dr.	Cr.
	Janice Wright, Capital		15,000	
	Hanna Storm, Capital			15,000

The Capital balances are as they were before the transaction, with the exception of the name change:

Before Transaction		After Transaction	
Janice Wright, Capital	$15,000	Hanna Storm, Capital	$15,000
Ned Frist, Capital	35,000	Ned Frist, Capital	35,000
Total Capital	$50,000	Total Capital	$50,000

Once Janice withdraws from the business, the old partnership (between Janice and Ned) is dissolved. A new partnership is formed between Hanna and Ned. The new partnership can even bear the same name as the old one (and will in this example).

Requirement 2

Ignoring Requirement 1, suppose instead that the Goode Partnership were to admit Hanna as a third partner by selling her a 40% interest for $40,000 cash. Compute Hanna's Capital balance and journalize her investment. What are the Capital balances for each partner after the investment is made?

Part 1	**Part 2**	Part 3	Part 4	Part 5	Demo Doc Complete

Hanna purchased a 40% interest in the total partnership's capital. *Regardless* of how much she paid for her share, her capital will be 40% of the *total capital after the purchase.*

2 Account for the partners' investments in a partnership.

4 Account for the admission of a new partner.

5 Account for a partner's withdrawal from the firm.

2 Account for the partners' investments in a partnership.

4 Account for the admission of a new partner.

Partnership Capital before Purchase ($15,000 + $35,000)	$50,000
Hanna's Investment in the Partnership	40,000
Partnership Capital after Purchase	$90,000
Hanna's Capital in the Partnership ($90,000 × .40)	$36,000
Bonus to the Old Partners ($40,000 − $36,000)	$ 4,000

So Hanna's share of the capital after her investment is:

$$40\% \times \$90,000 = \$36,000$$

Because Hanna purchased an interest, the Capital balances of Janice and Ned are adjusted.

Janice's Capital account is now increased for her share of the bonus:

$$\$4,000 \times 30\% = \$1,200$$

Her Capital account is now :

$$\$1,200 + \$15,000 = \$16,200$$

Ned's Capital account is now increased for his share of the bonus:

$$\$4,000 \times 70\% = \$2,800$$

His Capital account is now:

$$\$2,800 + \$35,000 = \$37,800$$

Before Transaction		After Transaction	
Janice Wright, Capital	$15,000	Janice Wright, Capital	$16,200
Ned Frist, Capital	35,000	Ned Frist, Capital	37,800
		Hanna Storm, Capital	36,000
Total Capital	$50,000	Total Capital	$90,000

Because Hanna paid $4,000 more for her share than the Capital amount that is being recorded ($36,000), the difference was split proportionately by the preexisting partners by the preexisting percentages.

For the partnership as a whole, assets increased (a debit) by Hanna's cash investment of $40,000.

Hanna's Capital account increases (a credit) by $36,000, Janice's Capital increases (a credit) by its adjustment of $1,200, and Ned's Capital increases (a credit) by its adjustment of $2,800.

Journal Entry:

Date	Accounts	Post Ref.	Dr.	Cr.
	Cash		40,000	
	Janice Wright, Capital			1,200
	Ned Frist, Capital			2,800
	Hanna Storm, Capital			36,000

Requirement 3

Ignoring Requirement 1, prepare the balance sheet of the Goode Partnership after Hanna is admitted to the partnership.

7 Prepare partnership financial statements.

Part 1	Part 2	**Part 3**	Part 4	Part 5	Demo Doc Complete

The Cash balance increases to:

$$\$25,000 + \$40,000 = \$65,000$$

Hanna Storm, Capital, has a balance of $36,000.
Janice Wright, Capital, increases to:

$$\$15,000 + \$1,200 = \$16,200$$

Ned Frist, Capital, increases to:

$$\$35,000 + \$2,800 = \$37,800$$

Liabilities and other assets do not change.

THE GOODE PARTNERSHIP
Balance Sheet
January 1, 2008

Cash	$ 65,000	Liabilities	$ 35,000
Other assets	60,000	Janice Wright, capital	16,200
		Ned Frist, capital	37,800
		Hanna Storm, capital	36,000
Total assets	$125,000	Total liabilities and capital	$125,000

Requirement 4

Assume that Hanna was not admitted to the partnership. During 2008, Goode earned $20,000 of net income (in cash). Prepare an updated balance sheet for Goode. How much profit is allocated to each partner (Janice and Ned)? Does the partnership pay income taxes on this profit?

3 Allocate profits and losses to the partners.

Part 1	Part 2	Part 3	**Part 4**	Part 5	Demo Doc Complete

Profits are allocated in this partnership based on stated percentages.
Janice receives 30% of the profits, so she is allocated $30\% \times \$20,000 = \$6,000$ of profit.
Ned receives 70% of the profits so he is allocated $70\% \times \$20,000 = \$14,000$ of profit.

After this allocation, Goode has the following balance sheet:

THE GOODE PARTNERSHIP Balance Sheet December 31, 2008			
Cash	$ 45,000	Liabilities	$ 35,000
Other assets	60,000	Janice Wright, capital	21,000
		Ned Frist, capital	49,000
Total assets	$105,000	Total liabilities and capital	$105,000

Cash increases from earning net income of $20,000 and the Capital balances for Janice and Ned increase for their profit allocation.

Adjusted Cash balance:

$$\$25,000 + \$20,000 = \$45,000$$

Adjusted Janice Wright, Capital, balance:

$$\$15,000 + \$6,000 = \$21,000$$

Adjusted Ned Frist, Capital, balance:

$$\$35,000 + \$14,000 = \$49,000$$

Note that *allocation* of profit *does not necessarily mean distribution* of profit. Just as shareholders do not receive all profits a company earns as dividends, partners do not receive all income allocations as cash distributions.

The partnership does *not* pay taxes on this profit. Instead, Janice and Ned are taxed on their individual tax returns for their allocation of profits.

Requirement 5

6 Account for the liquidation of a partnership.

Assume the information from Requirement 4. On January 1, 2009, the Goode Partnership was liquidated. All non-cash assets were sold for $90,000, after which all liabilities were paid. How much does each partner receive upon liquidation?

Part 1	Part 2	Part 3	Part 4	**Part 5**	Demo Doc Complete

The sale of the other assets increases Cash (a debit) by $90,000 and decreases Other Assets (a credit) by $60,000, their book value.

The remaining "gain" of $90,000 – $60,000 = $30,000 is split among Janice and Ned according to their profit-sharing proportions. This "gain" is shown as an increase to Janice's and Ned's Capital accounts.

Janice receives 30% × $30,000 = $9,000 of the "gain."
Ned receives 70% × $30,000 = $21,000 of the "gain."

Journal Entry:

Date	Accounts	Post Ref.	Dr.	Cr.
Jan. 1	Cash		90,000	
	Other Assets			60,000
	Janice Wright, Capital ($30,000 × 30%)			9,000
	Ned Frist, Capital ($30,000 × 70%)			21,000

The liabilities were paid after the non-cash assets were sold. Liabilities decreased (a debit) by $35,000, and Cash decreased (a credit) by $35,000.

Journal Entry:

Date	Accounts	Post Ref.	Dr.	Cr.
Jan. 1	Liabilities		35,000	
	Cash			35,000

After these transactions, Janice's Capital balance totals $21,000 + $9,000 = $30,000 and Ned's Capital balance totals $49,000 + $21,000 = $70,000.

The cash payment received on liquidation is *the amount of the Capital balances*: Janice receives $30,000 cash and Ned receives $70,000 cash on liquidation.

Part 1	Part 2	Part 3	Part 4	Part 5	**Demo Doc Complete**

Accounting in Action

PARTNERSHIPS

Suppose your friend, who is a computer science major, has developed a great new computer game that's already selling well but has no sense for business. So, the two of you form a partnership to take advantage of your respective skills. How do you organize? What decisions must you make? Consider these decision guidelines.

Decision	Guidelines
At what value does the partnership record assets and liabilities?	Current market value on the date of acquisition, because the partnership is buying its assets at their current market value.

How are partnership profits and losses shared among the partners?	• Equally if no profit-and-loss-sharing agreement has been made.
	• As provided in the partnership agreement, which can be based on the partners'
	  a. Stated fractions
	  b. Capital contributions
	  c. Service to the partnership
	  d. Any combination of these factors

What happens when a partner withdraws from the firm?	The old partnership ceases to exist and the remaining partners may or may not form a new partnership
How are new partners admitted to the partnership?	• *Purchase a partner's interest.* The old partnership is dissolved. The remaining partners may admit the new partner to the partnership. If not, the new partner gets no voice in management but shares in the profits and losses. Close the withdrawing partner's Capital account, and open a Capital account for the new partner. Carry over the old partner's Capital balance to the Capital account of the new partner. • *Invest in the partnership.* Buying in at book value creates no bonus to any partner. Buying in at a price above book value creates a bonus to the old partners. Buying in at a price below book value creates a bonus for the new partner.

How is the withdrawal of a partner from the business accounted for?	• First, adjust and close the books up to the date of the partner's withdrawal from the business.
	• Second, appraise the assets and the liabilities at their current market value.
	• Third, account for the partner's withdrawal.
	  a. At book value (no change in remaining partners' Capital balances)
	  b. At less than book value (increase the remaining partners' Capital balances)
	  c. At more than book value (decrease the remaining partners' Capital balances)

Decision

What happens if the partnership goes out of business?

Guidelines

Liquidate the partnership, as follows:

    a. Adjust and close the partnership books up to the date of liquidation.

    b. Sell the partnership's assets. Allocate gain or loss to the partners' Capital accounts based on their profit-and-loss ratio.

    c. Pay the partnership liabilities.

    d. Pay any remaining cash to the partners based on their Capital balances.

Review

Partnerships
Word Power

Articles of partnership The contract between partners that specifies such items as the name, location, and nature of the business; the name, capital investment, and duties of each partner; and the method of sharing profits and losses among the partners; also called *partnership agreement*.

Dissolution Ending of a partnership.

General partnership A form of partnership in which each partner is an owner of the business with all the privileges and risks of ownership.

Limited liability partnership A form of partnership in which each partner's personal liability for the business's debts is limited to a certain amount; also called *LLPs*.

Limited partnership A partnership with at least two classes of partners: a general partner and limited partners.

Liquidation The process of going out of business by selling the entity's assets and paying its liabilities. The final step in liquidation is the distribution of any remaining cash to the owner(s).

LLPs A form of partnership in which each partner's personal liability for the business's debts is limited to a certain amount; also called *limited liability partnership*.

Partnership An association of two or more persons who co-own a business for profit.

Partnership agreement The contract between partners that specifies such items as the name, location, and nature of the business; the name, capital investment, and duties of each partner; and the method of sharing profits and losses among the partners; also called *articles of partnership*.

S corporation A corporation taxed in the same way as a partnership.

Unlimited personal liability When a partnership (or a proprietorship) cannot pay its debts with business assets, the partners (or the proprietor) must use personal assets to meet the debt.

Quick Check

1. How does a partnership get started?

    a. The partners get a charter from the state
    b. The partners reach an agreement and simply begin operations
    c. The partners register with the Better Business Bureau
    d. All of the above

2. Which characteristic identifies a general partnership?

    a. Limited life
    b. No business income tax
    c. Unlimited personal liability
    d. All of the above

3. An S corporation is taxed like a

    a. Corporation
    b. Partnership
    c. Either of the above, depending on the partners' decision
    d. None of the above

4. The partnership of Abbott and Costello splits profits in the ratio of 3/4 to Abbott and 1/4 to Costello. The partnership has a net loss of $600,000. What is Costello's share of the loss?

    a. $150,000
    b. $450,000
    c. $300,000
    d. Cannot be determined from the data given

5. Partner drawings

    a. Decrease partnership liabilities
    b. Increase partnership capital
    c. Decrease partnership capital
    d. Decrease partnership net income

6. Lewis pays $130,000 to Martin to acquire Martin's $95,000 interest in a partnership. The journal entry to record this transaction is

Journal Entry:

Date	Accounts	Post Ref.	Dr.	Cr.
a.	Martin, Capital		130,000	
	Lewis, Capital			130,000
b.	Martin, Capital		95,000	
	Lewis, Capital			95,000
c.	Martin, Capital		30,000	
	Lewis, Capital			30,000
d.	Lewis, Captial		95,000	
	Martin, Capital			95,000

7. Crosby and Hope admit Sinatra to their partnership, with Sinatra paying $80,000 more than the book value of her equity in the new partnership. Crosby and Hope have no formal profit-and-loss-sharing agreement. What effect does admission of Sinatra into the partnership have on the capital balances of Crosby and Hope?

    a. Cannot be determined from the data given
    b. Debit the Crosby and Hope capital accounts for $40,000 each
    c. Credit the Crosby and Hope capital accounts for $80,000 each
    d. Credit the Crosby and Hope capital accounts for $40,000 each

8. Moe retires from the partnership of Curly, Larry, and Moe. The partners share profits and losses in the ratio of 3:3:4. Moe's capital balance is $75,000, and he receives $95,000 in final settlement. What is the effect on the capital accounts of Curly and Larry?

    a. Curly's capital decreases by $10,000
    b. Larry's capital decreases by $10,000
    c. Both a and b
    d. None of the above

9. The book value of the assets of the JFK partnership is $120,000. In liquidation, the partnership sells the assets for $155,000. How should the partnership account for the sale of the assets?

   a. Credit the assets for $120,000
   b. Debit cash for $155,000
   c. Increase the partners' capital accounts
   d. All of the above

10. Partnership financial statements report

   a. Revenues on the income statement
   b. Liabilities on the income statement
   c. Net income on the balance sheet
   d. Expenses on the balance sheet

Answers are given after Apply Your Knowledge (p. 27).

Accounting Practice

Short Exercises

2 Accounting for the partners' investments in a partnership.

SC-1. D. Rowen and R. Martin are forming the partnership Sock It to Me Development to develop a theme park near Virginia Beach, Florida. Rowen contributes cash of $6.5 million and land valued at $12.5 million. When Rowen purchased the land in 2003, its cost was $10 million. The partnership will assume Rowen's $5 million note payable on the land. Martin invests cash of $7.2 million and equipment worth $9.8 million.

    a. Compute the partnership's total assets, total liabilities, and total owners' equity immediately after organizing.

    b. Journalize the partnership's receipt of assets and liabilities from Rowen and from Martin. Record each asset at its current market value.

3 Allocating profits and losses to the partners.

SC-2. Athos, Porthos, and Aramis have capital balances of $40,000, $70,000, and $90,000, respectively. The partners share profits and losses as follows:

    a. The first $60,000 is divided based on the partners' capital balances.

    b. The next $60,000 is based on service, shared equally by Athos and Aramis.

    c. The remainder is divided equally.

Compute each partner's share of the business's $240,000 net income for the year.

7 Preparing partnership financial statements.

SC-3. The partnership of Lewis and Clark had these balances at April 30, 2008:

Cash........................	$28,000	Service Revenue.........	$196,000
Liabilities	56,000	Lewis, Capital	42,000
Clark, Capital.........	14,000	Total Expenses...........	49,000
Other Assets...........	84,000		

Lewis gets 70% of profits and losses, and Clark 30%. Prepare the partnership's income statement for the year ended April 30, 2008.

Exercises

2 Accounting for the partners' investments in a partnership.

EC-1. Honey Water has been operating a party planning service as a proprietorship. She and Olive Oil decide to reorganize the business as a partnership. Water's investment in the partnership consists of cash, $11,200; accounts receivable, $14,800; office furniture, $2,200; a small building, $77,000; accounts payable, $4,600; and a note payable to the bank, $14,000.

To determine Water's equity in the partnership, she and Oil hire an independent appraiser. The appraiser values all the assets and liabilities at their book value except the building, which has a current market value of $99,000. Also, accrued expenses payable equal $1,700.

Requirement

Make the entry on the partnership books to record Water's investment.

EC-2. David Fire and Chip Ice form a partnership, investing $56,000 and $112,000, respectively. Determine their shares of net income or net loss for each of the following situations:

   a. Net loss is $84,000 and the partners have no written partnership agreement.

   b. Net income is $126,000, and the partnership agreement states that the partners share profits and losses on the basis of their capital contributions.

   c. Net income is $138,000. The first $84,000 is shared on the basis of partner capital contributions. The next $42,000 is based on partner service, with Fire receiving 40% and Ice receiving 60%. The remainder is shared equally.

③ Allocating profits and losses to the partners.

EC-3. David Fire withdrew cash of $70,000 for personal use, and Chip Ice withdrew cash of $56,000 during the year. Using the data from situation (c) in Exercise EC-2, journalize the entries to close (a) the income summary account and (b) the partners' withdrawals accounts. Explanations are not required. What was the overall effect on partnership capital?

③ Allocating profits and losses to the partners.

EC-4. Adam Alvin is admitted to a partnership. Prior to his admission, the partnership books show Sean Theodore's capital balance at $80,000 and Kelly Simon's capital balance at $48,000. Compute each partner's equity on the books of the new partnership under the following plans:

   a. Alvin pays $72,000 for Simon's equity. Alvin's payment goes directly to Simon.

   b. Alvin invests $32,000 to acquire a 1/5 interest in the partnership.

   c. Alvin invests $52,000 to acquire a 1/5 interest in the partnership.

④ Accounting for the admission of a new partner.

EC-5. After the books are closed, Ying & Yang's partnership balance sheet reports capital of $80,000 for Ying and $120,000 for Yang. Ying is withdrawing from the firm. The partners agree to write down partnership assets by $75,000. They have shared profits and losses in the ratio of 2/5 to Ying and 3/5 to Yang. The partnership agreement states that a withdrawing partner will receive assets equal to the book value of his owner's equity.

⑤ Accounting for a partner's withdrawal from the firm.

a. How much will Ying receive? Yang will continue to operate the business as a proprietorship.

b. What is Yang's beginning capital on the books of his new proprietorship?

⑥ Accounting for the liquidation of a partnership.

EC-6. Groucho, Harpo, and Chico are liquidating their partnership. Before selling the noncash assets and paying the liabilities, the capital balances are Groucho $34,500; Harpo, $30,000; and Chico, $16,500. The partnership agreement specifies no division of profits and losses.

Requirements

1. After selling the noncash assets and paying the liabilities, the partnership has cash of $81,000. How much cash will each partner receive in final liquidation?

2. After selling the noncash assets and paying the liabilities, the partnership has cash of $67,500. How much cash will each partner receive in final liquidation?

Problems

② Accounting for the partners' investments in a partnership.

③ Allocating profits and losses to the partners.

PC-1. On April 30, F. Astaire and G. Rogers formed a partnership. The partners agree to invest equal amounts of capital. Astaire invests her proprietorship's assets and liabilities (credit balances in parentheses), as follows:

	Astaire's Book Values	Current Market Values
Accounts Receivable	$ 10,800	$ 10,800
Inventory	33,510	36,150
Prepaid Expenses	2,550	2,550
Office Equipment	68,900	41,400
Accumulated Depreciation, Office Equipment	(22,900)	0
Accounts Payable	(28,700)	(28,700)

On April 30, Rogers invests cash in an amount equal to the current market value of Astaire's partnership capital. The partners decide that Astaire will earn two-thirds of partnership profits because she will manage the business. Rogers agrees to accept one-third of the profits. During the remainder of the year, the partnership earns net income of $135,000. Astaire's drawings are $58,500, and Rogers' drawings are $46,500.

Requirements

1. Journalize the partners' initial investments.

2. Journalize the December 31 entries to close the Income Summary account and the partners' withdrawals accounts.

PC-2. The owners of GSR partnership are considering admitting Sue Kurtz as a new partner. On July of the current year, the capital accounts of the three existing partners and their shares of profits and losses are as follows:

④ Accounting for the admission of a new partner.

	Capital	**Profit-and-Loss Share**
Ben Grimm	$ 32,000	20%
Johnny Storm	80,000	25%
Reed Richards	128,000	55%

Requirements

Journalize the admission of Sue Kurtz as a partner on July 31 for each of the following independent situations:

1. Sue Kurtz pays R. Richards $160,000 cash to purchase Richards's interest in the partnership.

2. Sue Kurtz invests $48,000 in the partnership, acquiring a one-sixth interest in the business.

3. Sue Kurtz invests $64,000 in the partnership, acquiring a one-fourth interest in the business.

PC-3. Harry Potter, Sirius Black, and Remus Lupin have formed a partnership. Potter invested $20,000, Black $25,000, and Lupin $35,000. Potter will manage the store; Black will work in the store half-time; and Lupin will not work in the business.

③ Allocating profits and losses to the partners.

Requirements

Compute the partners' shares of profits and losses under each of the following plans:

1. Net loss is $72,000, and the partnership agreement allocates 40% of profits to Potter, 35% to Black, and 25% to Lupin. The agreement does not specify the sharing of losses.

2. Net income for the year ended May 31, 2008, is $252,000. The first $90,000 is allocated on the basis of partner capital contributions, and the next $45,000 is based on service, with Potter receiving $30,000 and Black receiving $15,000. Any remainder is shared equally.

④ Accounting for the
admission of a new
partner.

⑤ Accounting for a part-
ner's withdrawal from
the firm.

PC-4. Mod Party Squad Planners is a partnership owned by three individuals. The partners share profits and losses in the ratio of 36% to Peter Cochrane, 36% to Lincoln Hayes, and 28% to Julie Barnes. At December 31, 2008, the firm has the following balance sheet:

MOD SQUAD PARTY PLANNERS
Balance Sheet
December 31, 2008

Assets			Liabilities	
Cash		$ 18,000	Total liabilities	$112,500
Accounts recievable	$ 33,000			
Less: Allowance for uncollectible				
accounts	(6,000)	27,000	**Capital**	
Building	$465,000		Cochran, capital	124,500
Less: Accumulated			Hayes, capital	75,000
depreciation, building	(105,000)	360,000	Barnes, capital	93,000
Total assets		$405,000	Total liabilities and capital	$405,000

Hayes withdraws from the partnership on December 31, 2008, to establish his own consulting practice.

Requirements

Record Hayes's withdrawal from the partnership under the following plans:

1. In personal transactions, Hayes sells his equity in the partnership to Adam Greer and Billy Waites, who each pay Hayes $60,000 for half his interest. Cochrane and Barnes agree to accept Greer and Waites as partners.

2. The partnership pays Hayes cash of $30,000 and gives him a note payable for the remainder of his book equity in settlement of his partnership interest.

3. Hayes receives cash of $20,000 and a note for $105,000 from the partnership.

PC-5. The partnership of Huey, Dewey, & Louie experienced operating losses for three consecutive years. The partners—who have shared profits and losses in the ratio of Huey, 15%; Dewey, 25%; and Louie, 60%—are liquidating the business. They ask you to analyze the effects of liquidation and present the following partnership balance sheet at December 31, end of the current year:

6 Accounting for the liquidation of a partnership.

HUEY, DEWEY, AND LOUIE
Balance Sheet
December 31, Current Year

Cash	$ 40,500	Liabilities	$196,500
Noncash assets	303,000	Huey, capital	31,500
		Dewey, capital	58,500
		Louis, capital	57,000
Total assets	$343,500	Total liabilities and capital	$343,500

Requirements

1. Prepare a summary of liquidation transactions (as illustrated in Exhibit C-2). The noncash assets are sold for $283,500.

2. Make the journal entries to record the liquidation transactions.

Quick Check Answers

1. *b* 2. *d* 3. *b* 4. *a* 5. *c* 6. *b* 7. *d* 8. *c* 9. *d* 10. *a*

Appendix D

Present and Future Value Tables

This appendix provides present value tables and future value tables (more complete than those in the Chapter 12 appendix and in Chapter 21).

Exhibit D-1 Present Value of $1

Present Value

Periods	1%	2%	3%	4%	5%	6%	7%	8%	9%	10%	12%
1	0.990	0.980	0.971	0.962	0.952	0.943	0.935	0.926	0.917	0.909	0.893
2	0.980	0.961	0.943	0.925	0.907	0.890	0.873	0.857	0.842	0.826	0.797
3	0.971	0.942	0.915	0.889	0.864	0.840	0.816	0.794	0.772	0.751	0.712
4	0.961	0.924	0.888	0.855	0.823	0.792	0.763	0.735	0.708	0.683	0.636
5	0.951	0.906	0.863	0.822	0.784	0.747	0.713	0.681	0.650	0.621	0.567
6	0.942	0.888	0.837	0.790	0.746	0.705	0.666	0.630	0.596	0.564	0.507
7	0.933	0.871	0.813	0.760	0.711	0.665	0.623	0.583	0.547	0.513	0.452
8	0.923	0.853	0.789	0.731	0.677	0.627	0.582	0.540	0.502	0.467	0.404
9	0.914	0.837	0.766	0.703	0.645	0.592	0.544	0.500	0.460	0.424	0.361
10	0.905	0.820	0.744	0.676	0.614	0.558	0.508	0.463	0.422	0.386	0.322
11	0.896	0.804	0.722	0.650	0.585	0.527	0.475	0.429	0.388	0.350	0.287
12	0.887	0.788	0.701	0.625	0.557	0.497	0.444	0.397	0.356	0.319	0.257
13	0.879	0.773	0.681	0.601	0.530	0.469	0.415	0.368	0.326	0.290	0.229
14	0.870	0.758	0.661	0.577	0.505	0.442	0.388	0.340	0.299	0.263	0.205
15	0.861	0.743	0.642	0.555	0.481	0.417	0.362	0.315	0.275	0.239	0.183
16	0.853	0.728	0.623	0.534	0.458	0.394	0.339	0.292	0.252	0.218	0.163
17	0.844	0.714	0.605	0.513	0.436	0.371	0.317	0.270	0.231	0.198	0.146
18	0.836	0.700	0.587	0.494	0.416	0.350	0.296	0.250	0.212	0.180	0.130
19	0.828	0.686	0.570	0.475	0.396	0.331	0.277	0.232	0.194	0.164	0.116
20	0.820	0.673	0.554	0.456	0.377	0.312	0.258	0.215	0.178	0.149	0.104
21	0.811	0.660	0.538	0.439	0.359	0.294	0.242	0.199	0.164	0.135	0.093
22	0.803	0.647	0.522	0.422	0.342	0.278	0.226	0.184	0.150	0.123	0.083
23	0.795	0.634	0.507	0.406	0.326	0.262	0.211	0.170	0.138	0.112	0.074
24	0.788	0.622	0.492	0.390	0.310	0.247	0.197	0.158	0.126	0.102	0.066
25	0.780	0.610	0.478	0.375	0.295	0.233	0.184	0.146	0.116	0.092	0.059
26	0.772	0.598	0.464	0.361	0.281	0.220	0.172	0.135	0.106	0.084	0.053
27	0.764	0.586	0.450	0.347	0.268	0.207	0.161	0.125	0.098	0.076	0.047
28	0.757	0.574	0.437	0.333	0.255	0.196	0.150	0.116	0.090	0.069	0.042
29	0.749	0.563	0.424	0.321	0.243	0.185	0.141	0.107	0.082	0.063	0.037
30	0.742	0.552	0.412	0.308	0.231	0.174	0.131	0.099	0.075	0.057	0.033
40	0.672	0.453	0.307	0.208	0.142	0.097	0.067	0.046	0.032	0.022	0.011
50	0.608	0.372	0.228	0.141	0.087	0.054	0.034	0.021	0.013	0.009	0.003

Exhibit D-1 Present Value of $1 (con't)

Present Value

14%	15%	16%	18%	20%	25%	30%	35%	40%	45%	50%	Periods
0.877	0.870	0.862	0.847	0.833	0.800	0.769	0.741	0.714	0.690	0.667	1
0.769	0.756	0.743	0.718	0.694	0.640	0.592	0.549	0.510	0.476	0.444	2
0.675	0.658	0.641	0.609	0.579	0.512	0.455	0.406	0.364	0.328	0.296	3
0.592	0.572	0.552	0.516	0.482	0.410	0.350	0.301	0.260	0.226	0.198	4
0.519	0.497	0.476	0.437	0.402	0.328	0.269	0.223	0.186	0.156	0.132	5
0.456	0.432	0.410	0.370	0.335	0.262	0.207	0.165	0.133	0.108	0.088	6
0.400	0.376	0.354	0.314	0.279	0.210	0.159	0.122	0.095	0.074	0.059	7
0.351	0.327	0.305	0.266	0.233	0.168	0.123	0.091	0.068	0.051	0.039	8
0.308	0.284	0.263	0.225	0.194	0.134	0.094	0.067	0.048	0.035	0.026	9
0.270	0.247	0.227	0.191	0.162	0.107	0.073	0.050	0.035	0.024	0.017	10
0.237	0.215	0.195	0.162	0.135	0.086	0.056	0.037	0.025	0.017	0.012	11
0.208	0.187	0.168	0.137	0.112	0.069	0.043	0.027	0.018	0.012	0.008	12
0.182	0.163	0.145	0.116	0.093	0.055	0.033	0.020	0.013	0.008	0.005	13
0.160	0.141	0.125	0.099	0.078	0.044	0.025	0.015	0.009	0.006	0.003	14
0.140	0.123	0.108	0.084	0.065	0.035	0.020	0.011	0.006	0.004	0.002	15
0.123	0.107	0.093	0.071	0.054	0.028	0.015	0.008	0.005	0.003	0.002	16
0.108	0.093	0.080	0.060	0.045	0.023	0.012	0.006	0.003	0.002	0.001	17
0.095	0.081	0.069	0.051	0.038	0.018	0.009	0.005	0.002	0.001	0.001	18
0.083	0.070	0.060	0.043	0.031	0.014	0.007	0.003	0.002	0.001		19
0.073	0.061	0.051	0.037	0.026	0.012	0.005	0.002	0.001	0.001		20
0.064	0.053	0.044	0.031	0.022	0.009	0.004	0.002	0.001			21
0.056	0.046	0.038	0.026	0.018	0.007	0.003	0.001	0.001			22
0.049	0.040	0.033	0.022	0.015	0.006	0.002	0.001				23
0.043	0.035	0.028	0.019	0.013	0.005	0.002	0.001				24
0.038	0.030	0.024	0.016	0.010	0.004	0.001	0.001				25
0.033	0.026	0.021	0.014	0.009	0.003	0.001					26
0.029	0.023	0.018	0.011	0.007	0.002	0.001					27
0.026	0.020	0.016	0.010	0.006	0.002	0.001					28
0.022	0.017	0.014	0.008	0.005	0.002						29
0.020	0.015	0.012	0.007	0.004	0.001						30
0.005	0.004	0.003	0.001	0.001							40
0.001	0.001	0.001									50

Exhibit D-2 Present Value of Annuity of $1

| | | | | | | Present Value | | | | | |
Periods	1%	2%	3%	4%	5%	6%	7%	8%	9%	10%	12%
1	0.990	0.980	0.971	0.962	0.952	0.943	0.935	0.926	0.917	0.909	0.893
2	1.970	1.942	1.913	1.886	1.859	1.833	1.808	1.783	1.759	1.736	1.690
3	2.941	2.884	2.829	2.775	2.723	2.673	2.624	2.577	2.531	2.487	2.402
4	3.902	3.808	3.717	3.630	3.546	3.465	3.387	3.312	3.240	3.170	3.037
5	4.853	4.713	4.580	4.452	4.329	4.212	4.100	3.993	3.890	3.791	3.605
6	5.795	5.601	5.417	5.242	5.076	4.917	4.767	4.623	4.486	4.355	4.111
7	6.728	6.472	6.230	6.002	5.786	5.582	5.389	5.206	5.033	4.868	4.564
8	7.652	7.325	7.020	6.733	6.463	6.210	5.971	5.747	5.535	5.335	4.968
9	8.566	8.162	7.786	7.435	7.108	6.802	6.515	6.247	5.995	5.759	5.328
10	9.471	8.983	8.530	8.111	7.722	7.360	7.024	6.710	6.418	6.145	5.650
11	10.368	9.787	9.253	8.760	8.306	7.887	7.499	7.139	6.805	6.495	5.938
12	11.255	10.575	9.954	9.385	8.863	8.384	7.943	7.536	7.161	6.814	6.194
13	12.134	11.348	10.635	9.986	9.394	8.853	8.358	7.904	7.487	7.103	6.424
14	13.004	12.106	11.296	10.563	9.899	9.295	8.745	8.244	7.786	7.367	6.628
15	13.865	12.849	11.938	11.118	10.380	9.712	9.108	8.559	8.061	7.606	6.811
16	14.718	13.578	12.561	11.652	10.838	10.106	9.447	8.851	8.313	7.824	6.974
17	15.562	14.292	13.166	12.166	11.274	10.477	9.763	9.122	8.544	8.022	7.120
18	16.398	14.992	13.754	12.659	11.690	10.828	10.059	9.372	8.756	8.201	7.250
19	17.226	15.678	14.324	13.134	12.085	11.158	10.336	9.604	8.950	8.365	7.366
20	18.046	16.351	14.878	13.590	12.462	11.470	10.594	9.818	9.129	8.514	7.469
21	18.857	17.011	15.415	14.029	12.821	11.764	10.836	10.017	9.292	8.649	7.562
22	19.660	17.658	15.937	14.451	13.163	12.042	11.061	10.201	9.442	8.772	7.645
23	20.456	18.292	16.444	14.857	13.489	12.303	11.272	10.371	9.580	8.883	7.718
24	21.243	18.914	16.936	15.247	13.799	12.550	11.469	10.529	9.707	8.985	7.784
25	22.023	19.523	17.413	15.622	14.094	12.783	11.654	10.675	9.823	9.077	7.843
26	22.795	20.121	17.877	15.983	14.375	13.003	11.826	10.810	9.929	9.161	7.896
27	23.560	20.707	18.327	16.330	14.643	13.211	11.987	10.935	10.027	9.237	7.943
28	24.316	21.281	18.764	16.663	14.898	13.406	12.137	11.051	10.116	9.307	7.984
29	25.066	21.844	19.189	16.984	15.141	13.591	12.278	11.158	10.198	9.370	8.022
30	25.808	22.396	19.600	17.292	15.373	13.765	12.409	11.258	10.274	9.427	8.055
40	32.835	27.355	23.115	19.793	17.159	15.046	13.332	11.925	10.757	9.779	8.244
50	39.196	31.424	25.730	21.482	18.256	15.762	13.801	12.234	10.962	9.915	8.305

Exhibit D-2 Present Value of Annuity of $1 (con't)

Present Value

14%	15%	16%	18%	20%	25%	30%	35%	40%	45%	50%	Periods
0.877	0.870	0.862	0.847	0.833	0.800	0.769	0.741	0.714	0.690	0.667	1
1.647	1.626	1.605	1.566	1.528	1.440	1.361	1.289	1.224	1.165	1.111	2
2.322	2.283	2.246	2.174	2.106	1.952	1.816	1.696	1.589	1.493	1.407	3
2.914	2.855	2.798	2.690	2.589	2.362	2.166	1.997	1.849	1.720	1.605	4
3.433	3.352	3.274	3.127	2.991	2.689	2.436	2.220	2.035	1.876	1.737	5
3.889	3.784	3.685	3.498	3.326	2.951	2.643	2.385	2.168	1.983	1.824	6
4.288	4.160	4.039	3.812	3.605	3.161	2.802	2.508	2.263	2.057	1.883	7
4.639	4.487	4.344	4.078	3.837	3.329	2.925	2.598	2.331	2.109	1.922	8
4.946	4.772	4.607	4.303	4.031	3.463	3.019	2.665	2.379	2.144	1.948	9
5.216	5.019	4.833	4.494	4.192	3.571	3.092	2.715	2.414	2.168	1.965	10
5.553	5.234	5.029	4.656	4.327	3.656	3.147	2.752	2.438	2.185	1.977	11
5.660	5.421	5.197	4.793	4.439	3.725	3.190	2.779	2.456	2.197	1.985	12
5.842	5.583	5.342	4.910	4.533	3.780	3.223	2.799	2.469	2.204	1.990	13
6.002	5.724	5.468	5.008	4.611	3.824	3.249	2.814	2.478	2.210	1.993	14
6.142	5.847	5.575	5.092	4.675	3.859	3.268	2.825	2.484	2.214	1.995	15
6.265	5.954	5.669	5.162	4.730	3.887	3.283	2.834	2.489	2.216	1.997	16
6.373	6.047	5.749	5.222	4.775	3.910	3.295	2.840	2.492	2.218	1.998	17
6.467	6.128	5.818	5.273	4.812	3.928	3.304	2.844	2.494	2.219	1.999	18
6.550	6.198	5.877	5.316	4.844	3.942	3.311	2.848	2.496	2.220	1.999	19
6.623	6.259	5.929	5.353	4.870	3.954	3.316	2.850	2.497	2.221	1.999	20
6.687	6.312	5.973	5.384	4.891	3.963	3.320	2.852	2.498	2.221	2.000	21
6.743	6.359	6.011	5.410	4.909	3.970	3.323	2.853	2.498	2.222	2.000	22
6.792	6.399	6.044	5.432	4.925	3.976	3.325	2.854	2.499	2.222	2.000	23
6.835	6.434	6.073	5.451	4.937	3.981	3.327	2.855	2.499	2.222	2.000	24
6.873	6.464	6.097	5.467	4.948	3.985	3.329	2.856	2.499	2.222	2.000	25
6.906	6.491	6.118	5.480	4.956	3.988	3.330	2.856	2.500	2.222	2.000	26
6.935	6.514	6.136	5.492	4.964	3.990	3.331	2.856	2.500	2.222	2.000	27
6.961	6.534	6.152	5.502	4.970	3.992	3.331	2.857	2.500	2.222	2.000	28
6.983	6.551	6.166	5.510	4.975	3.994	3.332	2.857	2.500	2.222	2.000	29
7.003	6.566	6.177	5.517	4.979	3.995	3.332	2.857	2.500	2.222	2.000	30
7.105	6.642	6.234	5.548	4.997	3.999	3.333	2.857	2.500	2.222	2.000	40
7.133	6.661	6.246	5.554	4.999	4.000	3.333	2.857	2.500	2.222	2.000	50

Exhibit D-3 Future Value of $1

Future Value

Periods	1%	2%	3%	4%	5%	6%	7%	8%	9%	10%	12%	14%	15%
1	1.010	1.020	1.030	1.040	1.050	1.060	1.070	1.080	1.090	1.100	1.120	1.140	1.150
2	1.020	1.040	1.061	1.082	1.103	1.124	1.145	1.166	1.188	1.210	1.254	1.300	1.323
3	1.030	1.061	1.093	1.125	1.158	1.191	1.225	1.260	1.295	1.331	1.405	1.482	1.521
4	1.041	1.082	1.126	1.170	1.216	1.262	1.311	1.360	1.412	1.464	1.574	1.689	1.749
5	1.051	1.104	1.159	1.217	1.276	1.338	1.403	1.469	1.539	1.611	1.762	1.925	2.011
6	1.062	1.126	1.194	1.265	1.340	1.419	1.501	1.587	1.677	1.772	1.974	2.195	2.313
7	1.072	1.149	1.230	1.316	1.407	1.504	1.606	1.714	1.828	1.949	2.211	2.502	2.660
8	1.083	1.172	1.267	1.369	1.477	1.594	1.718	1.851	1.993	2.144	2.476	2.853	3.059
9	1.094	1.195	1.305	1.423	1.551	1.689	1.838	1.999	2.172	2.358	2.773	3.252	3.518
10	1.105	1.219	1.344	1.480	1.629	1.791	1.967	2.159	2.367	2.594	3.106	3.707	4.046
11	1.116	1.243	1.384	1.539	1.710	1.898	2.105	2.332	2.580	2.853	3.479	4.226	4.652
12	1.127	1.268	1.426	1.601	1.796	2.012	2.252	2.518	2.813	3.138	3.896	4.818	5.350
13	1.138	1.294	1.469	1.665	1.886	2.133	2.410	2.720	3.066	3.452	4.363	5.492	6.153
14	1.149	1.319	1.513	1.732	1.980	2.261	2.579	2.937	3.342	3.798	4.887	6.261	7.076
15	1.161	1.346	1.558	1.801	2.079	2.397	2.759	3.172	3.642	4.177	5.474	7.138	8.137
16	1.173	1.373	1.605	1.873	2.183	2.540	2.952	3.426	3.970	4.595	6.130	8.137	9.358
17	1.184	1.400	1.653	1.948	2.292	2.693	3.159	3.700	4.328	5.054	6.866	9.276	10.76
18	1.196	1.428	1.702	2.026	2.407	2.854	3.380	3.996	4.717	5.560	7.690	10.58	12.38
19	1.208	1.457	1.754	2.107	2.527	3.026	3.617	4.316	5.142	6.116	8.613	12.06	14.23
20	1.220	1.486	1.806	2.191	2.653	3.207	3.870	4.661	5.604	6.728	9.646	13.74	16.37
21	1.232	1.516	1.860	2.279	2.786	3.400	4.141	5.034	6.109	7.400	10.80	15.67	18.82
22	1.245	1.546	1.916	2.370	2.925	3.604	4.430	5.437	6.659	8.140	12.10	17.86	21.64
23	1.257	1.577	1.974	2.465	3.072	3.820	4.741	5.871	7.258	8.954	13.55	20.36	24.89
24	1.270	1.608	2.033	2.563	3.225	4.049	5.072	6.341	7.911	9.850	15.18	23.21	28.63
25	1.282	1.641	2.094	2.666	3.386	4.292	5.427	6.848	8.623	10.83	17.00	26.46	32.92
26	1.295	1.673	2.157	2.772	3.556	4.549	5.807	7.396	9.399	11.92	19.04	30.17	37.86
27	1.308	1.707	2.221	2.883	3.733	4.822	6.214	7.988	10.25	13.11	21.32	34.39	43.54
28	1.321	1.741	2.288	2.999	3.920	5.112	6.649	8.627	11.17	14.42	23.88	39.20	50.07
29	1.335	1.776	2.357	3.119	4.116	5.418	7.114	9.317	12.17	15.86	26.75	44.69	57.58
30	1.348	1.811	2.427	3.243	4.322	5.743	7.612	10.06	13.27	17.45	29.96	50.95	66.21
40	1.489	2.208	3.262	4.801	7.040	10.29	14.97	21.72	31.41	45.26	93.05	188.9	267.9
50	1.645	2.692	4.384	7.107	11.47	18.42	29.46	46.90	74.36	117.4	289.0	700.2	1,084

Exhibit D-4 Future Value of Annuity $1

Future Value

Periods	1%	2%	3%	4%	5%	6%	7%	8%	9%	10%	12%	14%	15%
1	1.000	1.000	1.000	1.000	1.000	1.000	1.000	1.000	1.000	1.000	1.000	1.000	1.000
2	2.010	2.020	2.030	2.040	2.050	2.060	2.070	2.080	2.090	2.100	2.120	2.140	2.150
3	3.030	3.060	3.091	3.122	3.153	3.184	3.215	3.246	3.278	3.310	3.374	3.440	3.473
4	4.060	4.122	4.184	4.246	4.310	4.375	4.440	4.506	4.573	4.641	4.779	4.921	4.993
5	5.101	5.204	5.309	5.416	5.526	5.637	5.751	5.867	5.985	6.105	6.353	6.610	6.742
6	6.152	6.308	6.468	6.633	6.802	6.975	7.153	7.336	7.523	7.716	8.115	8.536	8.754
7	7.214	7.434	7.662	7.898	8.142	8.394	8.654	8.923	9.200	9.487	10.09	10.73	11.07
8	8.286	8.583	8.892	9.214	9.549	9.897	10.26	10.64	11.03	11.44	12.30	13.23	13.73
9	9.369	9.755	10.16	10.58	11.03	11.49	11.98	12.49	13.02	13.58	14.78	16.09	16.79
10	10.46	10.95	11.46	12.01	12.58	13.18	13.82	14.49	15.19	15.94	17.55	19.34	20.30
11	11.57	12.17	12.81	13.49	14.21	14.97	15.78	16.65	17.56	18.53	20.65	23.04	24.35
12	12.68	13.41	14.19	15.03	15.92	16.87	17.89	18.98	20.14	21.38	24.13	27.27	29.00
13	13.81	14.68	15.62	16.63	17.71	18.88	20.14	21.50	22.95	24.52	28.03	32.09	34.35
14	14.95	15.97	17.09	18.29	19.60	21.02	22.55	24.21	26.02	27.98	32.39	37.58	40.50
15	16.10	17.29	18.60	20.02	21.58	23.28	25.13	27.15	29.36	31.77	37.28	43.84	47.58
16	17.26	18.64	20.16	21.82	23.66	25.67	27.89	30.32	33.00	35.95	42.75	50.98	55.72
17	18.43	20.01	21.76	23.70	25.84	28.21	30.84	33.75	36.97	40.54	48.88	59.12	65.08
18	19.61	21.41	23.41	25.65	28.13	30.91	34.00	37.45	41.30	45.60	55.75	68.39	75.84
19	20.81	22.84	25.12	27.67	30.54	33.76	37.38	41.45	46.02	51.16	63.44	78.97	88.21
20	22.02	24.30	26.87	29.78	33.07	36.79	41.00	45.76	51.16	57.28	72.05	91.02	102.4
21	23.24	25.78	28.68	31.97	35.72	39.99	44.87	50.42	56.76	64.00	81.70	104.8	118.8
22	24.47	27.30	30.54	34.25	38.51	43.39	49.01	55.46	62.87	71.40	92.50	120.4	137.6
23	25.72	28.85	32.45	36.62	41.43	47.00	53.44	60.89	69.53	79.54	104.6	138.3	159.3
24	26.97	30.42	34.43	39.08	44.50	50.82	58.18	66.76	76.79	88.50	118.2	158.7	184.2
25	28.24	32.03	36.46	41.65	47.73	54.86	63.25	73.11	84.70	98.35	133.3	181.9	212.8
26	29.53	33.67	38.55	44.31	51.11	59.16	68.68	79.95	93.32	109.2	150.3	208.3	245.7
27	30.82	35.34	40.71	47.08	54.67	63.71	74.48	87.35	102.7	121.1	169.4	238.5	283.6
28	32.13	37.05	42.93	49.97	58.40	68.53	80.70	95.34	113.0	134.2	190.7	272.9	327.1
29	33.45	38.79	45.22	52.97	62.32	73.64	87.35	104.0	124.1	148.6	214.6	312.1	377.2
30	34.78	40.57	47.58	56.08	66.44	79.06	94.46	113.3	136.3	164.5	241.3	356.8	434.7
40	48.89	60.40	75.40	95.03	120.8	154.8	199.6	259.1	337.9	442.6	767.1	1,342	1,779
50	64.46	84.58	112.8	152.7	209.3	290.3	406.5	573.8	815.1	1,164	2,400	4,995	7,218

Appendix E

Check Figures

NCF = No Check Figure

Chapter 1

Quick Check

1 b; 2 c; 3 b; 4 d; 5 a; 6 d; 7 c; 8 c; 9 a; 10 d

S1-1	NCF
S1-2	NCF
S1-3	c. Liabilities = $15,000
S1-4	NCF
S1-5	Owner's equity, $3,000
S1-6	Liabilities, $2,300
S1-7	NCF
S1-8	NCF
S1-9	NCF
S1-10	NCF
S1-11	NCF
S1-12	NCF
S1-13	NCF
E1-14	Lundy Plumbing, Owner's Equity, $22,900
E1-15	Increase in owner's equity, $3,000
E1-16	NCF
E1-17	NCF
E1-18	Total assets, $66,500
E1-19	Net income, $1,000
E1-20	Total assets, $25,000
E1-21	2. Net income, $65,200
	3. Withdrawals, $53,100
E1-22	3. Net income, $45,000
P1-23A	2. Net income, $1,140
P1-24A	1. Total assets, $38,320
P1-25A	a. Net income, $37,100
	b. Capital, ending, $71,000
P1-26A	1. Net income, $47,000
P1-27A	Total assets, $47,000
P1-28B	2. Net income, $4,000
P1-29B	1. Total assets, $29,850
P1-30B	a. Net income, $46,000
	b. Capital, ending, $52,000
P1-31B	1. Net income, $64,000
	2. Capital, ending, $174,000
P1-32B	3. Total assets, $88,000
	Know Your Business
	3. Total assets, 2005 = $32,293
	5. Total sales, 2004 = $45,682

Chapter 2

Quick Check

1 c; 2 a; 3 d; 4 c; 5 b; 6 c; 7 c; 8 d; 9 a; 10 a

S2-1	NCF
S2-2	NCF
S2-3	NCF
S2-4	NCF
S2-5	NCF
S2-6	NCF
S2-7	S. Roman, Capital balance, $16,000
S2-8	NCF
S2-9	NCF
S2-10	NCF
S2-11	Trial balance total debits, $74
S2-12	Trial balance total debits, $8,400
E2-13	Trial balance total debits, $3,100
E2-14	NCF
E2-15	NCF
E2-16	NCF
E2-17	NCF
E2-18	NCF
E2-19	Trial balance total, $180,600
E2-20	NCF
E2-21	Trial balance total, $74,700
E2-22	4. Total assets, $59,400
E2-23	5. Trial balance total, $20,400
E2-24	NCF
P2-25A	NCF
P2-26A	5. Trial balance total, $35,500
P2-27A	3. Trial balance total, $33,500
P2-28A	2. Total assets, $168,700
P2-29A	1. Trial balance total, $85,100
	2. Net income, $10,140
P2-30B	NCF
P2-31B	5. Trial balance total, $27,300
P2-32B	3. Trial balance total, $42,000
P2-33B	2. Total assets, $138,700
P2-34B	1. Trial balance total, $200,500
	2. Net income, $6,370
	Know Your Business
	NCF

Chapter 3

Quick Check

1 a; 2 a; 3 b; 4 c; 5 a; 6 c; 7 d; 8 a; 9 d; 10 c

S3-1	NCF
S3-2	NCF
S3-3	Prepaid Rent, $2,400
	Rent Expense, $600
S3-4	Advertising supplies, $1,300
	Advertising supplies expense, $700
S3-5	Book value, computer equipment, $28,750
S3-6	Interest payable, $2,250
	Interest expense, $2,250
S3-7	Subscription revenue, $600
S3-8	NCF
S3-9	Net income, $545
S3-10	Capital, ending, $4,945
S3-11	Service revenue, $1,200
S3-12	Asset, $3,000
E3-13	NCF
E3-14	NCF
E3-15	NCF
E3-16	d. Payments for prepaid advertising, $900
E3-17	NCF
E3-18	Overall, net income is over-stated by $9,300
E3-19	NCF
E3-20	Service revenue balance, $6,900
E3-21	Adjusted trial balance total, $36,500
E3-22	NCF
E3-23	Net income, $7,100
	Total assets, $19,300
E3-24	1. Net income, $87,500
E3-25	1. Capital, ending, $46,000
E3-26	Unearned service revenue balance, $18,000
E3-27	NCF
P3-28A	NCF
P3-29A	NCF
P3-30A	3. Trial balance total, $490,000
P3-31A	1. Net income, $40,900
	Total assets, $41,100
P3-32A	2. Net income, $10,350
P3-33B	NCF
P3-34B	NCF
P3-35B	3. Trial balance total, $55,350
P3-36B	1. Net income, $41,480
	Total assets, $51,480
P3-37B	2. Net income, $7,850
	Know Your Business
	Accumulated depreciation, $5,412
	Accrued liabilities, $1,633

Chapter 4

Quick Check

1 a; 2 a; 3 d; 4 b; 5 b; 6 c; 7 d; 8 b; 9 b; 10 b

S4-1	NCF
S4-2	NCF
S4-3	NCF
S4-4	NCF
S4-5	NCF
S4-6	2. Net income, $500
	3. Capital, change, $200
S4-7	NCF

S4-8	Trial balance total, $8,072 million	**S5-13**	NCF	**S6-2**	NCF	
S4-9	NCF	**E5-14**	NCF	**S6-3**	NCF	
S4-10	NCF	**E5-15**	NCF	**S6-4**	NCF	
E4-11	NCF	**E5-16**	NCF	**S6-5**	NCF	

S4-8 Trial balance total, $8,072 million
S4-9 NCF
S4-10 NCF
E4-11 NCF
E4-12 Adjusted trial balance total, $45
E4-13 Adjusted trial balance total, $49,000
E4-14 NCF
E4-15 Capital, ending, $59,800
E4-16 2. Capital, ending, $72,700
E4-17 Capital, ending, $234,000
E4-18 Net income, $9,300
E4-19 Total assets, $63,700
E4-20 Post-closing trial balance total, $107,505
E4-21 2. Total assets, $18,790
E4-22 Total assets, $124,200
P4-23A Adjusted trial balance total, $126,800
P4-24A Adjusted trial balance total, $299,000
2. Total Assets, $164,000
3. Net income, $17,000
P4-25A NCF
P4-26A Net income, $6,000
Capital, ending, $34,090
Total assets, $46,680
P4-27A Total assets, $81,400
P4-28B Adjusted trial balance total, $193,800
P4-29B Adjusted trial balance total, $314,000
2. Total Assets, $131,000
3. Net income, $90,000
P4-30B NCF
P4-31B Net income, $25,140
Capital, ending, $92,260
Total assets, $105,400
P4-32B Total Assets, $124,600
Know Your Business
2. Inventory, $5,384 million

Chapter 5

Quick Check
1 a; 2 c; 3 a; 4 a; 5 b; 6 d; 7 c; 8 c; 9 c; 10 d
S5-1 NCF
S5-2 Gross profit, $10,044
S5-3 NCF
S5-4 NCF
S5-5 NCF
S5-6 b. Best Buy must pay $225,000
S5-7 NCF
S5-8 NCF
S5-9 b. Gross profit, $29,100
S5-10 NCF
S5-11 Gross profit, 40%
S5-12 Inventory turnover, 3 times

S5-13 NCF
E5-14 NCF
E5-15 NCF
E5-16 NCF
E5-17 NCF
E5-18 NCF
E5-19 a. 2008 Gross profit, $31,000
b. 2009 Net income, $13,000
E5-20 b. Gross profit, $24,000
d. Cost of goods sold, $34,000
h. Net sales revenue, $125,000
E5-21 Net income, $29,830
Total assets, 122,800
E5-22 Net income, $71,000
E5-23 1. Net income, $64,830
2. Inventory turnover, last year, 5.7 times
E5-24 Inventory turnover, 14.1 times
P5-25A NCF
P5-26A 2. September 30 Receivable, S. L. Beauty, $3,800
P5-27A 1. Net income, $47,100
3. Inventory turnover, 2.8 times
P5-28A 1. Net income, $30,000
2. Total assets, $188,000
P5-29A 1. Net income, $27,290
2. Inventory turnover, 2009, 8.5 times
P5-30B NCF
P5-31B 2. Sales discount, $120
P5-32B 1. Net income, $40,680
3. Inventory turnover, 3.38 times
P5-33B 1. Net income, $32,000
2. Total assets, $178,500
P5-34B 1. Net income $50,700
2. Inventory turnover, 2008, 2.83 times
Know Your Business
2. Cost of sales, 2004, $31,445 million
5. Gross margin ratio, 2004, 31.17%

Chapter Appendix 5A

S5A-35 NCF
S5A-36 NCF
E5A-37 2. Capital, ending, $282,430
E5A-38 2. Net income, $32,230
P5A-39 Adjusted trial balance total, $296,880
P5A-40 2. Capital, ending, $71,504

Chapter 6

Quick Check
1 d; 2 b; 3 c; 4 c; 5 a; 6 d; 7 c; 8 b; 9 b; 10 d
S6-1 NCF

S6-2 NCF
S6-3 NCF
S6-4 NCF
S6-5 NCF
S6-6 NCF
S6-7 NCF
S6-8 Adjusted bank balance, $3,200
S6-9 NCF
S6-10 NCF
S6-11 NCF
S6-12 Total current assets, $166,000
E6-13 NCF
E6-14 NCF
E6-15 NCF
E6-16 NCF
E6-17 NCF
E6-18 NCF
E6-19 Adjusted bank balance, $550
E6-20 Adjusted bank balance, $1,200
E6-21 Adjusted bank balance, $1,205
E6-22 Adjusted bank balance, $4,108
E6-23 Adjusted bank balance, $3,175
E6-24 NCF
E6-25 NCF
E6-26 c. Petty cash balance, November 30, $150
P6-27A NCF
P6-28A Adjusted bank balance, $6,900
P6-29A 1. Adjusted bank balance, $12,050
P6-30A NCF
P6-31B NCF
P6-32B Adjusted bank balance, $14,660
P6-33B 1. Adjusted bank balance, $2,000
P6-34B NCF
Know Your Business
5. Cash and cash equivalents, 2005, $2,245 million

Chapter 7

Quick Check
1 d; 2 a; 3 b; 4 a; 5 b; 6 d; 7 c; 8 b; 9 a; 10 c
S7-1 NCF
S7-2 NCF
S7-3 1. Net income, $15,000
S7-4 2. Accounts receivable, net $82,000
S7-5 NCF
S7-6 Uncollectible account expense, $14,000
S7-7 Uncollectible account expense, $2,300
S7-8 Accounts receivable balance, September 30, $4,000
S7-9 NCF
S7-10 Interest, note 4: $1,250

S7-11	NCF
S7-12	NCF
E7-13	Jaxon, quick ratio, 1.33
E7-14	Moore, Day's sales in receivables, 62.50
E7-15	NCF
E7-16	NCF
E7-17	Net accounts receivable, $56,100
E7-18	Net accounts receivable, $58,800
E7-19	2. Net accounts receivable, $289,300
E7-20	Net accounts receivable, $123,400
E7-21	NCF
E7-22	3. Payoff at November 30, 2007, $103,500
E7-23	NCF
E7-24	NCF
E7-25	NCF
E7-26	NCF
E7-27	d. Quick ratio, .86
E7-28	Day's sales in receivables, 2007, 80
E7-29	a. Quick ratio, 1.01 b. Day's sales in receivables, 35
E7-30	Day's sales in receivables, 27
P7-31A	1. Allowance for uncollectible accounts, ending balance, $2,000 2. Accounts receivable, ending balance, $139,000 4. Net accounts receivable, allowance method, $137,000
P7-32A	3. Net accounts receivable, $134,400
P7-33A	1. Note 3, maturity value, $9,075 2. Total interest revenue, $206
P7-34A	NCF
P7-35A	a. Quick ratio, 2005, .74 b. Day's sales in receivables, 2005, 18
P7-36B	1. Allowance for uncollectible accounts, ending balance, $7,000 2. Accounts receivable, ending balance, $100,000 4. Net accounts receivable, allowance method, $93,000
P7-37B	3. Net accounts receivable, $160,100
P7-38B	1. Note 3, maturity value, $15,250 2. Total interest revenue, $785
P7-39B	NCF
P7-40B	a. Quick ratio, 2007, .68 b. Day's sales in receivables, 2005, 20 Know Your Business

	2. Net accounts receivable, 2005, $5,069 million 4. Uncollectible account expense, 2005, $451 million

Chapter 8

Quick Check

1 a; 2 b; 3 d; 4 c; 5 c; 6 c; 7 c; 8 d; 9 b; 10 a

S8-1	NCF
S8-2	NCF
S8-3	Inventory, June 30, $45
S8-4	NCF
S8-5	Inventory, June 30, $39
S8-6	NCF
S8-7	NCF
S8-8	Lower of cost or market total, $23,440
S8-9	NCF
S8-10	Understatement, $50,000
S8-11	NCF
S8-12	Estimated ending inventory, $150,000
S8-13	Estimated ending inventory, $30,000
E8-14	NCF
E8-15	NCF
E8-16	Ending inventory, $240
E8-17	NCF
E8-18	Ending inventory, $220
E8-19	Ending inventory, $235
E8-20	Gross profit, $155,000
E8-21	Ending inventory, LIFO, $102
E8-22	Gross profit, average cost, $4,071
E8-23	Lower of cost or market total, $15,088
E8-24	Gross profit, $72,000
E8-25	b. Gross profit, $75,000
E8-26	Net income, 2009, $44,000
E8-27	Estimated cost of inventory destroyed, $250,000
E8-28	Estimated ending inventory, $49,100
P8-29A	1. Ending inventory, $800
P8-30A	1. Ending inventory, $784 2. Net income, $2,484
P8-31A	1. Ending inventory, $225 2. Cost of goods sold, $1,365 3. Gross profit, $1,315
P8-32A	Inventory, $3,200,000
P8-33A	1. Net income, 2008, $16
P8-34A	1. Estimated ending inventory, $240 2. Gross profit, $2,160
P8-35B	1. Ending inventory, $300
P8-36B	1. Ending inventory, $345 2. Net income, $945
P8-37B	1. Ending inventory, $1,840 2. Cost of goods sold, $4,640 3. Gross profit, $3,270
P8-38B	Inventory, $4,250,000

P8-39B	1. Net income, 2007, $57
P8-40B	1. Estimated ending inventory, $278 2. Gross profit, $2,560 Know Your Business 1. Current assets, 2005, $13,922 million
S8A-41	Gross profit, LIFO, $230
S8A-42	Cost of goods sold, $338
EA8-43	1. Cost of goods available for sale, $4,648 1. Ending inventory, LIFO, $1,280 1. Cost of goods sold, LIFO, $3,368 2. Gross profit, LIFO, $33,092
P8A-44	Cost of goods available for sale, $74,439 3. Ending inventory, LIFO, $17,531 3. Cost of goods sold, LIFO, $56,908
P8A-45	1. Sales revenue, $310,000 2. Cost of goods sold, $195,000

Chapter 9

Quick Check

1 b; 2 a; 3 d; 4 c; 5 a; 6 d; 7 b; 8 a; 9 c; 10 d

S9-1	NCF
S9-2	NCF
S9-3	Cost of land, $60,000
S9-4	2. Overstatement of net income, $600,000
S9-5	1st-year depreciation: 1. b. UOP, $10,000,000; DDB, $18,000,000
S9-6	c. DDB, year 2, $10,800,000
S9-7	$6,000,000
S9-8	Depreciation expense, $10,000
S9-9	Gain on sale, $3,000
S9-10	NCF
S9-11	Goodwill, $500,000
S9-12	Net income, $1,300,000
E9-13	NCF
E9-14	Land $215,000; building $800,000; land improvements, $72,000
E9-15	1. Cost of building, $915,000
E9-16	Cost of bed 1, $2,500
E9-17	NCF
E9-18	NCF
E9-19	2009 Depreciation: SL $6,000; UOP $4,800; DDB $750
E9-20	Revised depreciation, $20,000
E9-21	Loss on sale, $1,500
E9-22	Gain on sale $30,000
E9-23	Units of production, year 4, $10,000
E9-24	NCF

E9-25	Revised amortization, $250,000
E9-26	1. Goodwill, $6,000,000
E9-27	Accumulated depreciation, year 4, $400,000
E9-28	Book value, $6,000,000
E9-29	Book value, $300,000
P9-30A	Building, $990,000
P9-31A	Cost of new motor-carrier, $146,000
	Gain on sale, $406,250
	Cost of land, $100,000
P9-32A	1. Straight line, book value, 2007, $64,000
	Units of production, book value, 2007, $53,000
	Double-declining-balance, book value, 2007, $31,104
P9-33A	1. Goodwill, $2,500,000
P9-34A	2. Net income, $134,000
P9-35B	Apartment building, $1,633,100
P9-36B	Cost of new office equipment, $79,000
	Gain on sale, $84,500
	Cost of assembly equipment, $72,000
P9-37B	1. Straight line, book value, 2012, $23,500
	Units of production, book value, 2012, $22,012
	Double-declining-balance, book value, 2012, $14,200
P9-38B	1. Goodwill, $500,000
P9-39B	2. Net income, $95,000
	Know Your Business
	1. Net property and equipment, 2005, 16,860 million
	3. Total assets, 2005, $32,293 million
	4. Depreciation expense, 2004, $1,232 million

Chapter 10

Quick Check

1 a; 2 c; 3 d; 4 c; 5 b; 6 a; 7 d; 8 a; 9 c; 10 d

S10-1	NCF
S10-2	Interest Expense, $405
S10-3	2. Estimated warranty payable balance, $5,000
S10-4	NCF
S10-5	NCF
S10-6	2. Net pay, $679.39
S10-7	Total expense, $997.51
S10-8	NCF
S10-9	Net pay, $5,588
S10-10	NCF
S10-11	NCF
S10-12	Total current liabilities, $52,612

S10-13	1. Current ratio, 1.18
	2. Working capital, $9,388
E10-14	NCF
E10-15	NCF
E10-16	Unearned subscription revenue balance, $120
E10-17	2. Estimated warranty payable balance, $5,000
E10-18	Net pay, $7,256.72
E10-19	a. Net pay, $464.42
E10-20	Total employee earnings, $88,994; Net pay, $70,114
E10-21	NCF
E10-22	Payroll tax expense, $54,000
E10-23	Interest payable, 2008, $90,000
E10-24	Total current liabilities, $85,000
E10-25	a. Current ratio, 1.76
	b. Working capital, $65,000
P10-26A	NCF
P10-27A	1. Net pay, $68,581
	2. Total expense of employer, $101,476
P10-28A	3. Total liabilities, $200,390
P10-29A	1. Total net pay, $2,264
P10-30A	d. Estimated warranty payable, $9,100
P10-31B	NCF
P10-32B	1. Net pay, $69,263
	2. Total expense of employer, $101,994
P10-33B	3. Total liabilities, $331,440
P10-34B	1. Total net pay, $3,183
P10-35B	d. Estimated warranty payable, $6,000
	Know Your Business
	1. Current liabilities, 2005, $8,220 million
	2. Accounts payable, 2005, $5,779 million
	5. Income tax expense, 2004, $1,146 million

Chapter 11

Quick Check

1 d; 2 d; 3 a; 4 c; 5 c; 6 d; 7 d; 8 d; 9 c; 10 c

S11-1	NCF
S11-2	NCF
S11-3	NCF
S11-4	NCF
S11-5	Paid-in capital in excess of par, $600,000
S11-6	NCF
S11-7	1. Total increase in paid-in capital during 2009, $33,750
	b. Increase in retained earnings during 2009, $250,000
S11-8	NCF

S11-9	NCF
S11-10	3. Preferred gets $6,000; common gets $3,000
S11-11	2. No effect on Transtech's total stockholders' equity
S11-12	NCF
S11-13	1. Shares issued and outstanding, 200,000
S11-14	Treasury stock, $5,000
S11-15	Total stockholders' equity, $736
S11-16	3. Treasury stock purchased during 2009, $10,000
E11-17	NCF
E11-18	NCF
E11-19	2. Total paid-in capital, $59,500
E11-20	2. Total stockholders' equity, $86,000
E11-21	Paid-in capital, $50,000
E11-22	Total paid-in capital, $400,000
E11-23	Dividend declared is $50,000, preferred gets $17,000
E11-24	Preferred gets $40,000
E11-25	2. Total stockholders' equity, $570,000
E11-26	NCF
E11-27	Total stockholders' equity, $800,000
E11-28	d. Increase stockholders' equity by $3,000
E11-29	NCF
E11-30	Total stockholders' equity, $870,000
E11-31	Total stockholders' equity, $400,000
E11-32	Stockholders' equity balance, December 31, 2009, $1,465,000
E11-33	2. Stockholders' equity balance, December 31, 2007, $17,000,000
P11-34A	2. Total stockholders' equity, $266,000
P11-35A	5. Total stockholders' equity, $152,000
P11-36A	3. Preferred gets $11.7
P11-37A	1a. Common gets $155,000 in 2008
P11-38A	Common stock outstanding after split, 20,000
P11-39A	2. Total stockholders' equity, $568,000
P11-40A	1. Par value, $1.80
	2. Price per share, $11.00
P11-41B	2. Total stockholders' equity, $272,0000
P11-42B	5. Total stockholders' equity, $263,000
P11-43B	3. Preferred gets $10,008

P11-44B 1a. Common gets $20,500 in 2008
P11-45B Common stock outstanding after split, 200,000
P11-46B 2. Total stockholders' equity, $414,000
Know Your Business
1. Ending stockholders' equity, 2005, $13,029 million
3. Dividend per share, fiscal 2004, $.31
5. Cash dividends paid, 2004, $272 million

Chapter 12

Quick Check
1 a; 2 c; 3 c; 4 c; 5 b; 6 a; 7 b; 8 a; 9 a; 10 d
S12-1 NCF
S12-2 D. December 31, 2010 principal balance, $196,432
S12-3 NCF
S12-4 NCF
S12-5 b. $102,500
d. $110,375
S12-6 NCF
S12-7 NCF
S12-8 NCF
S12-9 NCF
S12-10 NCF
S12-11 NCF
S12-12 a. Gain on retirement of bonds payable, $11,872
S12-13 a. Carrying value, $1,020,000
b. Gain on retirement of bonds payable, $50,000
S12-14 NCF
S12-15 Total long-term liabilities, $464,000
E12-16 1. D. June 30, 2009 principal balance, $366,730
E12-17 NCF
E12-18 NCF
E12-19 NCF
E12-20 2. Most interest expense, discount price of 95%
E12-21 Loss on retirement of bonds payable, $12,750
E12-22 1. Carrying value of bonds payable, $691,600
2. Gain on retirement of bonds payable, $47,600
E12-23 1. Loss on retirement of bonds payable, $8,000
E12-24 Bonds payable, $270,000
P12-25A 1. D. Period 4 principal balance, $86,966
3. Long-term liabilities, $133,801
P12-26A 3. Interest expense, $49,500
P12-27A 2. Discount

P12-28A 2. Gain on retirement of 10% bonds payable, $13,500
P12-29A Total long-term liabilities, $383,000
P12-30B 1. D. Period 4 principal balance, $141,702
3. Long-term liabilities, $176,092
P12-31B 3. Interest expense, $26,667
P12-32B 2. Discount
P12-33B 2. Loss on retirement of 9% bonds payable, $14,400
P12-34B Total long-term liabilities, $290,000
Know Your Business
1. Long-term debt, 2005, $9,034 million
3. Other non-current liabilities, 2005, $1,037 million

Chapter Appendix 12A

E12A-35 Future value, Plan B $15,870
E12A-36 b. Southern, present value, $226,800
S12B-37 E. Carrying value, March 31, 2009, $546,749
S12B-38 E. Carrying value, May 31, 2008, $217,158
E12B-39 1. E. Carrying value, January 2, 2008, $280,995
P12B-40 2. E. Carrying value, September 30, year 3, $148,095

Chapter 13

Quick Check
1 c; 2 d; 3 c; 4 a; 5 d; 6 c; 7 a; 8 a; 9 d; 10 b
S13-1 NCF
S13-2 NCF
S13-3 NCF
S13-4 Net cash from operating, $48,000
S13-5 Net cash from operating, $40,000
S13-6 Net increase in cash, $39,000
S13-7 Acquisition of plant assets, $100,000
S13-8 1. Payment of long-term notes payable, $2,000
3. Payment of cash dividends, $84,000
S13-9 Net decrease in cash, $10,000
S13-10 Net cash from operating, $50,000
S13-11 Net increase in cash, $54,000
S13-12 2. Payments for inventory, $331,000
E13-13 NCF
E13-14 NCF
E13-15 NCF

E13-16 Net cash for operating, $8,000
E13-17 Net cash from operating, $79,000
E13-18 Net cash from operating, $80,000
E13-19 1. Payment of cash dividends, $34,000
E13-20 NCF
E13-21 NCF
E13-22 Net cash for operating, $8,000
E13-23 NCF
E13-24 Net cash from operating $80,000; investing $(77,000); financing $4,000
E13-25 2. Cash payments for inventory, $89,000
E13-26 b. Cash payments for inventory, $18,516
d. Acquisitions of property and equipment, $1,186
g. Payment of dividends, $143
P13-27A NCF
P13-28A Net cash from operating $87,000; investing $(67,000); financing $43,000
P13-29A Net cash from operating $96,900; investing $(125,700); financing $31,000
P13-30A Net cash from operating $69,100; investing $(37,100); financing $(30,600)
P13-31A Net cash from operating $115,700; investing $(37,000); financing $(70,800)
P13-32A Net cash from operating $69,100; investing $(37,100); financing $(30,600)
P13-33A Net cash from operating $67,800; investing $(10,200); financing $(47,600)
P13-34B NCF
P13-35A Net cash from operating $80,000; investing $(69,000); financing $11,000
P13-36B Net cash from operating $49,000; investing $(179,000); financing $(120,000)
P13-37B Net cash from operating $79,800; investing $(47,600); financing $(29,900)
P13-38B Net cash from operating $(30,000); investing $(40,300); financing $91,700

Know Your Business
2. Cash spent on property and equipment, 2004, $3,068 million
3. Cash required for financing activities, 2004, $2,837 million

Chapter 14

Quick Check

1 d; 2 c; 3 b; 4 d; 5 a; 6 d; 7 c; 8 d; 9 b; 10 d

S14-1 2008 Gross profit increase, 11.8%
S14-2 Cash, 30%
S14-3 NCF
S14-4 NCF
S14-5 3. Inventory turnover, 10 times
S14-6 2. Quick ratio, 1.42
S14-7 1. Profit margin, 25%
3. Rate of return on equity, 1.25 times
S14-8 2. Price/earnings ratio, 11.1
S14-9 Dividend yield, .17
E14-10 Working capital decrease, 2007, $3,000
E14-11 Net income increase, 22.1%
E14-12 Net sales, Year 5, 118%
E14-13 Total liabilities, 54.3%
E14-14 Net income, 2009, 15%
E14-15 a. Current ratio, 2.0
d. Accounts receivable turnover, 8.81 times
E14-16 a. Current ratio, 2008, 2.5
c. Debt ratio, 2008, .42
E14-17 b. Rate of return on total assets, 2008, .144
d. Earnings per share, 2008, $.32
E14-18 Ratios for 2008:
a. Price/earnings ratio, 22
b. Dividend yield, .020
E14-19 EVA, Brandy Pitts Winery, $98,896
E14-20 Total liabilities and stockholders' equity, $26,757
P14-21A 1. Ending total assets, 2010, 130%
2. Rate of return on net sales, 2010, .081
P14-22A 1. Net income, Love Bug, 15%
2. Current assets, Love Bug, 77.4%
P14-23A 1. Current ratio, 1.43
2.c. Current ratio, 1.85
P14-24A 1. a. Current ratio, 2008, 1.91
d. Times-interest earned, 2008, 8.67
g. Price/earnings ratio, 2008, 8.57

P14-25A 1.a. Quick ratio, Build it Right, .86
d. Debt ratio, Build it Right, .40
f. Price/earnings ratio, Build it Right, 4.79
2. EVA, Build it Right, $42,200
P14-26A NCF
P14-27B 1. Ending total stockholders' equity, 2010, 151%
2. Rate of return on common stockholders' equity, 2010, .097
P14-28B 1. Net income, Cue Ball, 6.3%
2. Current assets, Cue Ball, 71.1%
P14-29B 1. Current ratio, 2.11
2.c. Current ratio, 2.88
P14-30B 1. a. Current ratio, 2008, 2.11
d. Times-interest earned, 2008, 2.82
g. Price/earnings ratio, 2008, 7.09
P14-31B 1.a. Quick ratio, Broken Bone Hill, .63
d. Debt ratio, Broken Bone Hill, .74
f. Price/earnings ratio, Broken Bone Hill, 23.4
2. EVA, Build it Right, $(2,200)
P14-31B NCF
Know Your Business
1. Net earnings, 2004, 6.83%
Cash and cash equivalents, 2005, 217.09%
2. EPS, 2004, $3.54
4. Price/earnings ratio, 14.34 times

Chapter 15

Quick Check

1 a; 2 c; 3 d; 4 b; 5 a; 6 c; 7 b; 8 a; 9 d; 10 d

S15-1 NCF
S15-2 NCF
S15-3 NCF
S15-4 Net operating income, $3,000
S15-5 COGS, $46,000
S15-6 a. $3,000
b. $62,000
c. $28,000
d. $200,000
e. $60,000
f. $88,000
g. $27,000
S15-7 NCF
S15-8 DM used, $9,200
S15-9 NCF
S15-10 Total MOH, $12,300

S15-11 COGM, $41,000
S15-12 NCF
S15-13 NCF
E15-14 NCF
E15-15 NCF
E15-16 Net operating income, $7,650
E15-17 Net operating income, $21,000
E15-18 1. Operating income, $15,000
2. $11.21
E15-19 NCF
E15-20 NCF
E15-21 a. $10,000
b. $20,000
c. $4,000
d. $65,000
e. $105,000
f. $80,000
g. $3,000
h. $4,500
i. $4,000
E15-22 COGM, $405,000
E15-23 COGM, $200,000
COGS, $195,000
E15-24 NCF
P15-25A 2. $0.50/foot
P15-26A Operating income, $13,000
P15-27A 1. COGM, $67,000
2. Operating income, $36,200
4. $3.83/unit
P15-28A 1. DM used $55,000; COGM $162,000; Ending FG inventory $68,000; Operating income $100,000
P15-29A 1. COGM, $21.3 M
2. COGS, $21.4 M
3. DM purchases, $2.9 M
P15-30A NCF
P15-31B 2. $33.12/automobile
P15-32B Operating income $35,250
P15-33B 1. COGM, $71,000
2. Operating income, $45,000
4. $54.62/unit
P15-34B DM used $52,000; COGM $150,000; COG available $274,000; Operating income $76,000
P15-35B 1. DM used, $28.2 million
2. COGM, $161.0 M
3. COGS, $158.8 M
P15-36B NCF
Case 1 End. inventory:
1. DM $143,000
2. WIP $239,000;
3. FG $150,000
Case 2 NCF

Chapter 16

Quick Check

1 c; 2 c; 3 b; 4 a; 5 d; 6 d; 7 a; 8 c; 9 d; 10 b

S16-1 NCF

S16-2	NCF
S16-3	Ending Materials Inventory, $42,700
S16-4	Balances: Mat. $25; WIP $50
S16-5	NCF
S16-6	MOH balance, $66,000
S16-7	Total cost, $1,180
S16-8	Indirect materials used, $3,000; COGM $125,000; COGS $110,000
S16-9	3. MOH is $2,000 overallocated
S16-10	3. MOH is $10,000 overallocated
S16-11	NCF
S16-12	2. DL for Client 507, $770
S16-13	2. Indirect cost for Client 507, $280
E16-14	NCF
E16-15	WIP Inv. $6,000; FG Inv. $4,000; COGS $16,000
E16-16	MOH allocated, $18,000
E16-17	NCF
E16-18	1. Ending WIP Inventory, $20,000 4. GP $7,000
E16-19	2. MOH allocated, $80,000 3. MOH underallocated, $3,000
E16-20	2. MOH allocated, $550,000 3. MOH overallocated, $40,000
E16-21	1. MOH underallocated, $10,000 3. Adjusted COGS, $610,000
E16-22	1. b. Indirect cost allocation rate, 60% 2. Total predicted cost, $52,800
E16-23	1. MH used, $10,125 2. MOH underallocated, $25,250
P16-24A	1. c. Nov. COGS, $1,500 Dec. COGS, $3,750 2. Debit FG in Nov., $3,500 Debit FG in Dec., $3,850 4. GP, $500
P16-25A	2. Ending WIP Inv. $274,400 FG Inventory, $116,800 5. GP, $62,000
P16-26A	1. MOH allocated, $600 Total job cost, $2,285
P16-27A	1. PMOH rate, $7.50/MH 3. MOH underallocated, $33,350
P16-28A	2. Ending WIP Inventory, $38,400 FG Inventory, $21,300 4. COGM, $48,850
P16-29A	2. Food Coop, $166,000 3. Mesilla, $10,150

P16-30B	1. c. March COGS, $3,000 April COGS, $2,900 4. GP for Job 5, $900
P16-31B	2. Ending WIP Inventory, $102,400 FG Inventory, $92,400 5. GP for Chalet 23, $42,300
P16-32B	1. MOH allocated, $1,312 Total job cost, $4,352
P16-33B	1. PMOH rate, $25/MH 3. MOH underallocated, $13,000
P16-34B	2. Ending WIP Inventory, $99,600 FG Inventory, $61,000 4. COGM, $61,200
P16-35B	2. Vacationplan.com, $78,000 Port Arthur, $4,800
Case 1	NCF
Case 2	NCF

Chapter 17

Quick Check
1 c; 2 b; 3 d; 4 a; 5 c; 6 a; 7 d; 8 a; 9 b; 10 d

S17-1	NCF
S17-2	NCF
S17-3	$160,000
S17-4	1. 9,600 2. 4,400
S17-5	6,000
S17-6	1. $48,000 2. $0.84/liter
S17-7	2. EU for DM, 200,000; EU for CC, 190,000
S17-8	EU for DM, 40,000 EU for CC, 33,000
S17-9	DM $0.75; CC $0.50
S17-10	1. $37,500 2. $9,000
S17-11	2. 5,000 3. 15,000
S17-12	1. 9,000 2. 15,000 3. 15,000
S17-13	1. 350 2. 230 3. 65 4. 50 5. 150 6. 150 7. 100
E17-14	NCF
E17-15	NCF
E17-16	2. EU of DM 8,000; CC 6,600 3. Ending WIP Inventory, $1,470
E17-17	2. Ending WIP Inventory, $1,470 3. Avg. cost/gal. transferred out, $1.05

E17-18	1. EU of DM, 76,800; CC 74,400 2. DM $2.80; CC $2.00 3. Ending WIP Inventory, $18,240
E17-19	1. EU of DM, 18,200; CC 21,400 5. Ending WIP Inventory, $11,200
E17-20	3. Cost per EU: DM $1.30; CC $0.90
E17-21	2. WIP Inventory balance, $2,929 3. Costs transferred out, $2.20/gal.
E17-22	EU of TI costs: 1. Mixing 90,000; 2. Heating 86,000
E17-23	2. EU of TI, 168,000 6. Ending WIP Inventory, $14,910
P17-24A	2. EU of DM, 100,000; CC 85,840; CC/EU $3.00 3b. Ending WIP Inventory, $116,820
P17-25A	2. EU of DM 4,600; CC 4,600 CC/EU $1.40 3b. Ending WIP Inventory, $260
P17-26A	2. EU of Wood, 3,000; CC, 2,370 3. CC/EU, $1.30 5. Ending WIP Inventory, $1,491
P17-27A	2. EU of TI, $635; CC, 608 TI cost/EU, $40; CC/EU, $94 3. Costs transferred out, $77,500
P17-28A	2. EU of TI, 9,000; CC, 6,000 3. TI cost/EU, $85 3. b. Ending WIP Inventory, $449,000
P17-29B	2. EU of DM, 20,400; CC 19,100 CC/EU $0.30 4. Ending WIP Inventory, $2,210
P17-30B	2. EU of DM, 12,000; CC, $11,700 CC/EU, $26 3b. Ending WIP Inventory, $173,200
P17-31B	2. EU of Green Beans, 15,000; CC, 14,160 3. CC/EU, $2.00 5. Ending WIP Inventory, $4,830
P17-32B	2. EU of TI, $3,600; CC, 2,900 TI cost/EU, $15; CC/EU, $25 3. Costs transferred out, $112,200

P17-33B 2. EU of TI, 35,000; CC 19,800
3. TI cost/EU, $0.14
3b. Ending WIP Inventory, $3,268

Case 3. Operating income, $5,200
5. Selling price per box, $12.74

Chapter Appendix 17A

S17A-34 2. EU of TI, 160,000; CC, 160,600
S17A-35 DM/EU, $0.20; CC/EU, $0.35
S17A-36 Ending WIP Inventory, $15,330
E17A-37 1a. DM, 40%; CC, 25%
2. Mixing Dep't. EU of DM, 75,000; CC, 67,000
Cooking Dep't. EU of DM, 78,900; CC, 76,700
E17A-38 2 EU of TI, 3,600; CC, 3,490
3. b. Ending WIP Inventory, $22,200
P17A-39 2. EU of TI, 28,000; CC, 17,700
3. TI/EU, $0.17; CC/EU, $0.166
3. a. Costs transferred out, $4,208

Chapter 18

Quick Check
1 b; 2 d; 3 a; 4 b; 5 d; 6 a; 7 b; 8 c; 9 a; 10 c
S18-1 NCF
S18-2 NCF
S18-3 1c. Total cost, $33
S18-4 1. $0.40; 2. $2,000
S18-5 6,875 tickets
S18-6 2. $412,500
S18-7 1. 9,167 tickets; $458,350 (or $458,333)
2. 6,111 tickets; $366,660 (or $366,667)
S18-8 BEP, 5,000 tickets; $300,000
S18-9 a. Margin of safety, 125 tickets
b. Margin of safety, $7,500
S18-10 BE sales, $125,000; Units to achieve target, 25,000
S18-11 $13.75
S18-12 1. 3,000;
2. 1,200 individual; 1,800 family
S18-13 NCF
E18-14 NCF
E18-15 NCF
E18-16 1. $1/unit
2. $3,000

E18-17 Op. loss when sales are $250,000, $20,000 BEP, $283,333
E18-18 1. CM ratio, 50%
2. BEP, 100,000 packages; $170,000
E18-19 1. BEP, $12,000
2. Sales required to earn target, $24,500
E18-20 2. Op. loss when sales are $500,000, $240,000
E18-21 3. BEP, 500 students; $50,000
E18-22 1. 625
2. 833
3. 556
4. 500
E18-23 1. Margin of safety, $40,000
E18-24 BEP 200 Std.;
300 Chrome; To earn $6,600: 310 Std.; 465 Chrome
P18-25A NCF
P18-26A North CM ratio, 0.40
East CM per unit, $3.75
South CM ratio, 0.533
P18-27A 1. VC per show, $27,200
2. BEP, 14 shows
3. Target, 144 shows
4. Op. inc., $3,476,800
P18-28A 1. BEP, 82,000 flags
2. Target sales, $1,034,000
3. Op. loss, $93,600
4. BEP, $1,228,032
P18-29A 1. BEP, 40 trades
2. Target sales, $42,000
4. BEP, 35 trades
P18-30A 1. BEP, 8,000 plain; 4,000 custard
2. $52,000
3. $36,774
P18-31B NCF
P18-32B CM ratio: J 0.67; M 0.60
K CM/unit $3.00
P18-33B 1. VC per show, $15,200
2. BEP, 36 shows
3. Target, 94 shows
4. Op. inc., $1,587,200
P18-34B 1. BEP, 160,000 cartons
2. Target sales, $2,104,545
3. Op. inc., $2,001,000
4. BEP, $2,704,800
P18-35B 1. BEP, 24 trades
2. Target sales, $14,400
4. BEP, 30 trades
P18-36B 1. BEP, 12,000 small; 4,000 large
2. $50,000
3. $29,500
Case BEP, 5,000 meals; $225,000
To earn target op. inc. 7,520 meals; $338,400

Chapter Appendix 18A

S18A-37 Op. inc., $75,000
S18A-38 1. Op. inc., $80,000
E18A-39 1. Op. inc.: Absorption $625,000; VC $475,000
3. Increase in op. inc., $75,000
P18A-40 1. Cost/meal: Absorption $4.50; VC $4.00
2. a. Op. inc., $1,900
b. Op. inc., $1,700
P18A-41 1. Cost/game: Absorption $19; VC $15
2. a. Op. inc., $30,000
b. Op. inc., $32,000

Chapter 19

Quick Check
1 d; 2 d; 3 b; 4 b; 5 b; 6 c; 7 d; 8 c; 9 a; 10 c
S19-1 Income variance, $700 F
S19-2 NCF
S19-3 NCF
S19-4 Feb. sales, $60,000
S19-5 June purchases, $1,000
July purchases, $660
S19-6 Feb. cash sales, $48,000
S19-7 Feb. purchases, $36,000
S19-8 Apr. total cash collections, $48,000
S19-9 June total cash payments for purchases, $28,000
S19-10 Ending cash balance, $3,800
S19-11 Must borrow $14,070
S19-12 NCF
E19-13 Op. inc. this year, $200,000
E19-14 Purchases, qtr. ended June 30 $88,500; Sept. 30 $79,500
E19-15 Qtr. 2 NI, $856,960
Qtr. 3 NI, $950,546
E19-16 b. Sept. cash receipts, $106,830
E19-17 Ending cash balance, Jan. $11,500; Feb. $10,600
E19-18 Apr. borrowing, $11,100
May interest expense, $74
E19-19 2. Total assets, $30,280
Owners' equity, $27,980
E19-20 NCF
E19-21 Cell phone total Op. inc., var. $45,000 F
E19-22 a. $105 M
b. $(27) M
c. $ 35 M
d. $113 M
e. $ (7) M
f. $ 10 M
g. $ 70 M
P19-23A $86,000 U
2. Aug. COGS, $120,000
Aug. Op. inc., $37,000
Sept. Op. inc., $40,000

P19-24A 1. Aug. total cash collections, $199,000
Aug. total cash payments for purchases, $124,600
2. Ending cash bal.: Aug. $55,400; Sept. $95,600

P19-25A 2. Ending cash balance, $36,200
3. Total assets, $163,700
Owners' equity, $145,600

P19-26A 1. Op. inc. variance: Phoenix $12,000; Other Ariz. $31,400
Total $44,400

P19-27A NCF

P19-28B 2. May COGS, $15,500
May Op. inc., $17,900
June Op. inc., $11,900

P19-29B 1. May total cash collections, $42,660
May total cash payments for purchases, $18,150
2. Ending cash balance: May $30,610; June $43,460

P19-30B 2. Ending cash balance, $60,000
3. Total assets, $148,900
Owners' equity, $120,600

P19-31B 1. Op. inc. variance: Florida stores $3,900; Other regions $(91,900)
Total $(86,000)

P19-32B NCF

Case 1 NCF

Case 2 1. NI: cotton, $235; linen $225
Total assets: cotton $721; linen $1,511

Chapter Appendix 19A

S19A-33 NCF

S19A-34 Software Dept. $300,000

E19A-35 Marketing cost allocated to Welding, $4,200
Total indirect costs allocated to Priming, $27,400

E19A-36 1. Chrome Op. inc., $75,200

P19A-37 1. Housekeeping expense, $24/room
Total Club expense, $102,720
2. Club cost, $190.22/room
Regular cost, $92.57/room

Chapter 20

Quick Check
1 d; 2 b; 3 a; 4 e; 5 c; 6 c; 7 d; 8 b; 9 a; 10 a

S20-1 NCF

S20-2 NCF

S20-3 Op. inc. @4,000 units, $5,000; @ 6,000 units, $15,000

S20-4 FB Var. for Op. inc., $2,000 F

S20-5 NCF

S20-6 DM Price Var., $770 U
DM Eff. Var., $280 U

S20-7 DL Price Var., $1,750 F
DL Eff. Var., $4,900 U

S20-8 NCF

S20-9 Std. var. OH rate, $7/DLH
Std. fixed OH rate, $3/DLH

S20-10 OH FB Var., $400 U
OH PV Var., $1,200 F

S20-11 Dr. DM Price Var., $770
Dr. DM Eff. Var., $280

S20-12 Cr. DL Price Var., $1,750
Dr. DL Eff. Var., $4,900

S20-13 COGS, $364,000

S20-14 Op. inc., $89,000

E20-15 Op. inc. at 40,000 units, $32,000; 70,000 units, $156,000

E20-16 Total FB Var., $10,000 U;
Static Budget Op. inc., $10,000

E20-17 Sales Revenue FB Var., $21,000F; Static Budget Op. inc., $44,100

E20-18 DM Price Var., $280 U
DM Eff. Var., $200 F
DL Price Var., $375 F
DL Eff. Var., $2,500 U

E20-19 Actual price, $10.50
Eff. Var., $8,000 F
FB Var., $3,200 F

E20-20 DM Price Var., $7,250 F
DM Eff. Var., $5,500 U
DL Price Var., $450 U
DL Eff. Var., $650 F

E20-21 Cr. DM Price Var., $7,250
Dr. DM Eff. Var., $5,500
Dr. DL Price Var., $450
Cr. DL Eff. Var., $650

E20-22 NCF

E20-23 Total OH Var., $2,300 F
OH FB Var., $700 U
OH PV Var., $3,000 F

E20-24 GP, $227,500

P20-25A 1. Op. Inc. FB Var., $175 U;
SV Var., $22,000 F

P20-26A 1. FB Gross profit, $260,068
2. DM Price Var., $1,230 F;
DM Eff. Var., $2,403 U;
DL Price Var., $1,440 U
DL Eff. Var., $1,800 F
OH FB Var., $11,960 U
OH PV Var., $1,200 U

P20-27A 1. DL hrs. worked, 4,350
2. DL Price Var., $2,175 U;
Eff. Var., $1,125 F

P20-28A DM Price Var., $840 F
DM Eff. Var., $135 F
1. DL Price Var., $6,000 U;
DL Eff. Var., $1,428 U
3. OH FB Var., $4,314 U
OH PV Var., $1,134 F

P20-29A 1. DM Price Var., $11,000 U
DM Eff. Var., $1,280 U
DL Price Var., $170 U
DL Eff. Var., $3,360 F
2. OH FB Var., $7,300 U
OH PV Var., $1,920 F
3. GP, $38,530

P20-30B 1. Op. inc. FB Var., $1,000 F;
SV Var., $7,500 F

P20-31B 1. FB Gross profit $4,204,000
2. DM Price Var., $42,840 F;
DM Eff. Var., $58,000 F;
DL Price Var., $24,600 U
DL Eff. Var., $42,000 F
OH FB Var., $28,220 U
OH PV Var., $90,000 F

P20-32B 1. DL hrs. worked, 6,100
2. DL Price Var., $3,050 F;
Eff. Var., $1,000 U
DM Price Var., $3,808 U
DM Eff. Var., $10,880 F

P20-33B 1. DL Price Var., $2,500 U;
DL Eff. Var., $20,680 F
3. OH FB Var., $280 F
OH PV Var., $1,760 U

P20-34B 1. DM Price Var., $13,500 F
DM Eff. Var., $3,300 U
DL Price Var., $1,125 F
DL Eff. Var., $900 U
2. OH FB Var., $6,400 F
OH PV Var., $9,600 F
3. GP, $123,225

Case 1 Total FB Var., $21,550 F
Total SVV, $133,600 U
51. DM Eff. Var., $15 F

Case 2 1. DM Eff Var., $15 F
DL Eff. Var., $96 U

Chapter 21

Quick Check
1 a; 2 b; 3 d; 4 b; 5 c; 6 a; 7 d; 8 c; 9 a; 10 d

S21-1 NCF

S21-2 Expected increase in op. inc., $1,000

S21-3 NCF

S21-4 Drop Accessories & increase op. inc. $15,000

S21-5 CM for equivalent MH:
Deluxe $275; Regular $345

S21-6 Advantage to outsourcing, $23,000

S21-7 NCF

S21-8	Advantage to processing further, $3,000
S21-9	Payback period, 2.5 years
S21-10	Payback period, 5 years
S21-11	ARR, 20%
S21-12	ARR, 10%
S21-13	NPV, $(2,643)
S21-14	NPV, $5,650
E21-15	1. Increase in op. inc., $1,250 2. Decrease in op. inc., $(750)
E21-16	1. Increase in op. inc., $1,000
E21-17	Decrease in op. inc., $30,000
E21-18	Increase in op. inc., $10,000
E21-19	Total CM: Designer $34,500; Mod. $42,000
E21-20	Advantage to buying, $1/unit
E21-21	Cost: Buy and leave idle, $340,000, Buy and use facilities for other product, $310,000
E21-22	Advantage to processing further, $200
E21-23	Payback, 4.8 years
E21-24	ARR Ward, 10%; Vargas, 8.8%
E21-25	NPV: A $(19,855); B $3,616
E21-26	IRR, Project A, between 10% and 12%
P21-27A	1. Increase in op. inc., $2,000
P21-28A	1. Decrease in op. inc., $20,000 2. b. Op. inc., $195,000
P21-29A	2. Spas: CM, $1.95/sq. ft.; Total CM at capacity, $15,600
P21-30A	1. Advantage to making, $38,000 2. Net cost to buy cereal and make cereal bars, $838,000
P21-31A	1. Cost of processing further, $118,750 3. Advantage to process further, $16,250
P21-32A	1. Payback, 7.43 years; ARR, 8.1%; NPV, $(705,500)

P21-33A	1. Payback: a. 5.2 years; b. 4.2 years ARR: a. 8.5%; b. 14.3% NPV: a. $(348,000); b. $77,500
P21-34B	1. Increase in Op. inc., $30,000
P21-35B	1. Decrease in Op. inc., $102,000 2b. Op. (loss), $(50,000)
P21-36B	2. 512 MB CM $1,800/MH; Total CM at capacity, $8,100,000
P21-37B	1. Advantage to making, $3,000 2. Net cost to buy decks and make another product, $31,600
P21-38B	1. Cost of further processing, $51,000 3. Advantage to selling as-is, $21,000
P21-39B	1. Payback, 3.85 years; ARR, 26.8%; NPV, $664,160
P21-40B	1. Payback: a. 5.63 years; b. 9.27 years ARR: a. 15.5%; b. 3.6% NPV: a. $162,500; b. $(230,100)
Case 1	1. Total cost/mailbox $60 2. Total advantage to outsourcing, $12,650 3. Advantage to insourcing extra services, $1,150
Case 2	1. Total earnings if he chooses bottling, $9,439; meat packing, $9,510

Appendix B

SB-1	NCF
EB-1	NCF
EB-2	Total assets, $85,600; Total liabilities, $65,100
EB-3	Total debits to cash, $680
EB-4	NCF
EB-5	3. Total accounts payable, 4,953

EB-6	Total debits to accounts payable, $11,992
PB-1	Sales journal, total accounts receivable debit/sales revenue credit, $20,335; Cash receipts journal, total debits to cash, $79,858
PB-2	Purchases journal, total credits to accounts payable, $9,170; Cash payments journal, total credits to cash, $12,098

Appendix C

SC-1	a. Total owners' equity, $31
SC-2	Net income allocated to Athos, $82,000
SC-3	Net income allocated to Lewis, $102,900
EC-1	NCF
EC-2	Net income allocated to Fire, $50,800
EC-3	Partnership capital increase, $12,000
EC-4	a. Alvin's balance, $48,000 b. Alvin's capital, $32,000 c. Alvin's capital, $36,000
EC-5	Yang's capital, $75,000
EC-6	1. Groucho, $81,000 2. Groucho, $30,000
PC-1	December 31, credit to Astaire, capital, $90,000
PC-2	2. Kurtz' capital, $48,000
PC-3	1. Net loss allocated to Potter, $(28,800) 2. Net income allocated to Potter, $91,500
PC-4	3. December 31, debit to Cochrane, capital, $28,125
PC-5	Payment of cash to Huey, $28,575

Comprehensive Problem (See www.prenhall.com/pollard)

Trial balance totals, $18,400
Adjusted trial balance totals, $18,835
Net income, $2,230

Photo Credits

Chapter 1, Page 2: Courtesy of George D. Lepp, Corbis/Bettmann; Page 3: Courtesy of AP Wide World Photos.

Chapter 2, Page 56: Courtesy of Susan Werner, Getty Images Inc.–Stone Allstock; Page 56: Courtesy of Burke/Triolo Productions/Getty Images, Getty Images, Inc.– Photodisc; Page 57: Courtesy of Spencer Grant, PhotoEdit Inc.

Chapter 3, Page 124: Courtesy of Jim Cummins, Getty Images, Inc.–Taxi; Page 125: Courtesy of Emanuel Dunand, AFP/Getty Images, Inc.

Chapter 4, Page 178: Courtesy of Mark Andersen, Getty Images Inc–Rubberball Royalty Free; Page 178: Courtesy of Getty Images, Inc.–Photodisc; Page 179: Courtesy of Jim Pickerell, The Stock Connection.

Chapter 5, Page 228: Courtesy of Peter Sterling, Getty Images, Inc.–Taxi; Page 229: Courtesy of Ty Allison, Getty Images Inc.

Chapter 6, Page 292: Courtesy of Dorling Kindersley Media Library, Peter Anderson © Dorling Kindersley; Page 293: Courtesy of Dorling Kindersley Media Library, Tony Souter © Dorling Kindersley.

Chapter 7, Page 348: Courtesy of Dorling Kindersley Media Library, Steve Shott © Dorling Kindersley; Page 348: Frank Greenaway © Dorling Kindersley, Courtesy of the Weymouth Sea Life Centre; Page 349: Courtesy of Getty Images Inc–Image Bank.

Chapter 8, Page 404: Courtesy of C Squared Studios, Getty Images, Inc.–Photodisc; Page 404: Courtesy of Dorling Kindersley Media Library, Dave King © Dorling Kindersley; Page 405: Courtesy of Dana White, PhotoEdit Inc.

Chapter 9, Page 468: Courtesy of Getty Images–Stockbyte; Page 468: Courtesy of Dorling Kindersley Media Library, Dave King © Dorling Kindersley, Courtesy of the National Motor Museum, Beaulieu; Page 469: Courtesy of Joe Sohn/Chronosohn, Corbis/Stock Market.

Chapter 10, Page 520: Courtesy of EyeWire Collection, Getty Images–Photodisc; Page 521: Courtesy of Arthur Tilley, Getty Images, Inc.–Taxi

Chapter 11, Page 568: Courtesy of C Squared Studios, Getty Images, Inc.–Photodisc; Page 568: Courtesy of Steve Cole, Getty Images, Inc.–Photodisc; Page 569: Courtesy of Anthony P. Bolante, Corbis/Bettmann.

Chapter 12, Page 624: Courtesy of Altrendo Images, Getty Images, Inc; Page 625: Courtesy of Ron Chapple, Getty Images, Inc.–Taxi

Chapter 13, Page 688: Courtesy of Getty Images, Inc.–Photodisc; Page 689: Courtesy of Peter/Georgina Bowater, Creative Eye/MIRA.com.

Chapter 14, Page 746: Courtesy of Getty Images–Digital Vision; Page 747: Courtesy of Rudi Von Briel, PhotoEdit Inc.

Chapter 15, Page 800: Courtesy of C Squared Studios, Getty Images, Inc.–Photodisc; Page 800: Courtesy of Jim Watt, PacificStock.com; Page 801: Courtesy of Bill Bachmann, Creative Eye/MIRA.com.

Chapter 16, Page 846: Courtesy of David Buffington, Getty Images, Inc.–Photodisc. Page 846: Courtesy of Photos.com; Page 847: Courtesy of Mitch Hrdlicka, Getty Images, Inc.–Photodisc.

Chapter 17, Page 896: Courtesy of Michael Newman, PhotoEdit Inc.; Page 897: Courtesy of Jeff Greenberg, PhotoEdit Inc.

Chapter 18, Page 956: Courtesy of Comstock Production Department, Alamy Images Royalty Free, © Comstock Images/Alamy; Page 957: Courtesy of Jose Carrillo, PhotoEdit Inc.

Chapter 19, Page 1006: Courtesy of Photolibrary.Com; Page 1007: Courtesy of EyeWire Collection, Getty Images–Photodisc.

Chapter 20, Page 1066: Courtesy of Dorling Kindersley Media Library, © Dorling Kindersley; Page 1066: Courtesy of Rachael Epstein, © Rachael Epstein/PhotoEdit Inc.; Page 1067: Courtesy of David Oliver, Getty Images Inc.–Stone Allstock.

Chapter 21, Page 1116: Courtesy of Amos Morgan, Getty Images, Inc.–Photodisc; Page 1117: Courtesy of EyeWire Collection, Getty Images, Inc.–Photodisc.

Glindex

A Combined Glossary/Subject Index

A

Absorption costing. The costing method that assigns both variable and fixed manufacturing costs to products, 1001

and manager incentives, 1003–1004

vs. variable costing, 1001–1003

Accelerated depreciation method. Depreciation method that records more depreciation near the start of an asset's useful life than the straight-line method does, 479–480

Account form. Balance sheet format that lists assets on the left of the report and abilities and owner's equity on the right, just as those accounts appear in the accounting equation, 195–196

Accounting. The information system that measures business activity, processes the results of activities into reports, and communicates the results to decision makers, 6

Accounting cycle. The process of accounting for the transactions of a business for a period of time so that results of these transactions can be reported in financial statements, 180

key decisions in, 203

steps in, 180–182

Accounting equation. The basic tool of accounting that measures the resources of the business and the claims to those resources: Assets = Liabilities + Owner's Equity, 9–10

exercise, 25–30

Accounting period, 127

Accounting principles, 126–127

Accounting rate of return. A measure of profitability computed by dividing the average annual operating income from an asset by the average amount invested in the asset, 1131–1132, 1138

Accounts. The basic summary device of accounting; the detailed record of all the changes in a particular asset, liability, or owner's equity as a result of transactions, 58

after posting to ledger, 77

for assets, 58–59

chart of, 60

for liabilities, 59

for owner's equity, 59–60

Accounts payable. A liability backed by the general reputation and credit standing of the debtor, 13

as current liability, 59, 522–523, 530

Accounts receivable. An asset representing amounts due from customers to whom the business has sold goods or for

whom the business has performed services, 14

account, 58–59

accrual, 137–138

internal control, 355

ledger, 353

liquidity of, 195

notes receivable in exchange for, 366–367

See also Uncollectible accounts

Accounts receivable turnover. Net credit sales divided by average net accounts receivable; measures a company's ability to collect cash from credit customers, 760–761

Accrual basis accounting. Accounting that records revenues when earned and expenses when incurred to produce those revenues; recognizes the impact of transactions as they occur regardless of whether they involve a transfer of cash, 126–127

key decisions, 156

Accruals. Revenues earned or expenses incurred before cash has been exchanged, 128

expenses, 136–137

need for, 129

revenues, 137–138

timing, 138

Accrued expense (liability). An expense that the business has incurred but not yet paid, 59, 526, 530

Accrued liability (expense). An expense that the business has incurred but not yet paid, 59, 526, 530

Accumulated depreciation. A contraasset account that holds the cumulative sum of all depreciation recorded for an asset, 134

Acid-test (quick) ratio. Ratio that reveals how well the entity can pay its current liabilities, 369–370

financial statement analysis, 757–758

Actual cost, 8

Additional Paid-In Capital (Paid-in Capital in Excess of Par). The amount received above par value from issuing stock at a premium, 576, 584, 588

Adjusted trial balance. A list of all the accounts of a business with their adjusted balances, 140–141

preparation of, 153–154

Adjusting entries. Entry made at the end of the accounting period to measure the period's income accurately and bring the related asset and liability accounts to correct balances before the

financial statements are prepared, 127–128

examples of, 139–140, 189

exercises, 144–153

for interest expense on bonds, 640–641

purposes of, 138

recording of, 186

for retailers, 286–287

types of, 128–129

See also Accruals; Deferrals

Administrative errors, inventory shrinkage from, 407, 408

Aging method (balance-sheet approach). Method of estimating uncollectible accounts that focuses on accounts receivable; the accountant calculates the end-of-the-period allowance balance needed according to the aging of the receivable accounts, 359–361, 362

Allocation base. A common denominator that links indirect costs to cost objects. Ideally, the allocation base is the primary cost driver of the indirect method, 856

Allowance for Uncollectible Accounts. A contra asset account that holds the estimated amount of uncollectible accounts receivable, 357–358

Allowance method. The method of accounting for uncollectible accounts that estimates these amounts and uses an allowance account so that the balance sheet shows the amount of accounts receivable expected to be collected in the future, 357–361

American Institute of Certified Public Accountants (AICPA), 23

Amortization. The allocation of the cost of an intangible asset to expense over its useful life, 471

of bond discount, 636–637

of bond premium, 639–640

Amortization expense. Systematic reduction of the intangible asset's carrying value on the books, 488

and cash flow, 696

Amortization schedule. Schedule that tracks the portion of each loan payment allocated to principal and interest, 626–627

Annuity. Multiple investments of an equal periodic amount at fixed intervals over the duration of the investment, 673

future value of, 673–674

present value of, 677–678, 1134

Assets. Economic resources that are expected to be of benefit in the future, 9

accounts, 58–59

Company Index

Chapter 14

Taken from:

Principles of Accounting: Chapters 11-21

by Meg Pollard, Sherry K. Mills and
Walter T. Harrison

LEARNING OBJECTIVES

① Explain the purpose of financial statement analysis.

② Perform a horizontal analysis of comparative financial statements.

③ Perform a vertical analysis of financial statements and prepare common-size financial statements.

④ Compute commonly used financial ratios.

⑤ Measure economic value added.

⑥ Utilize nonfinancial data in analyzing financial statements.

Financial Statement Analysis

Your best friend has a successful career. She has worked very hard to save money, and is now ready to invest. Having recently heard in the news about companies that misrepresented themselves in their financial statements, she is a little nervous about her ability to put her hard-earned money in the right firm. She picked up a tip about a "hot stock" from a friend-of-a-friend, but doesn't know whether that advice can be trusted. Further, she knows that different forms of investment exist; for example, she could buy bonds, common stock, or preferred stock with her savings.

Knowing that you have been studying accounting as the language of business, she turns to you for help. How should she choose the right investment? Would you recommend that she pick large, established companies, or take a chance on new, high-risk entities? What kind of information should she use to make her decision and where is this information available? ●

Look Back

In preceding chapters, you learned how to prepare financial statements including the income statement, the statement of owner's or stockholders' equity, the balance sheet, and the statement of cash flows. You have been introduced to a few ways of evaluating values that appear on these statements, such as the gross profit percentage and current ratio.

Look Ahead

In this chapter, you will learn how to further examine financial statements using several methods of analysis. You will perform both horizontal and vertical analysis of financial statements, and prepare financial statements expressed in common-size format. You will discover how ratios can be used to provide additional insight into financial statement amounts, and measure economic value added.

Some of the most important information about a company's attractiveness as an investment comes from its financial statements. Having prepared financial statements in different formats in previous chapters, you are well aware of the wealth of information available in financial reports. You also understand that the relevance, reliability, and comparability of this information are enhanced by the rules of accounting, Generally Accepted Accounting Principles, as well as the financial statement audit process. You know that, to make an informed decision, you need to be able to analyze those statements, even if the company has been around a long time and is a household name.

With this knowledge, you possess basic information that you can use to help your friend. However, in addition to your understanding of accounting and how it is used to prepare financial statements, various techniques for interpreting these data are also helpful. In this chapter, we examine methods such as horizontal and vertical analysis, common-size financial statements, and ratio analysis, and discover how they can be used to make sound decisions about a business.

Purpose of Financial Statement Analysis

1 Explain the purpose of financial statement analysis.

As we discussed when we introduced the role of accounting in business in Chapter 1, many different parties or stakeholders have an interest in a business's performance. These people range from creditors, such as banks or bondholders, to individual investors, such as you and me, to professional Wall Street analysts. **Financial statement analysis** is the process that these parties utilize when they examine financial statements and other data in order to predict the future of a firm. By determining the financial outlook of a business, stakeholders or users of financial information are able to make informed decisions about it.

Examination of financial statements enables the following comparisons of a company's performance:

- From one year to another

- With a competing company

- Within its industry

Evaluation of a business's financial well-being is based on the two fundamental goals of business entities introduced in Chapter 1, profitability and liquidity, and how well the business is meeting each of these goals. The importance of these goals is underscored by red flags, or warning signs, that may signal financial trouble. If the following conditions are present, the company may be a risky investment and not particularly creditworthy.

- *Earnings problems:* Have income from operations and net income decreased significantly for several years in a row? Has income turned into a loss? Most companies cannot survive many consecutive loss years.

- *Decreased cash flow:* Cash flow validates earnings. Is cash flow from operations consistently lower than net income? Are the sales of plant assets a major source of cash? If so, the company may face a cash shortage.

- *Too much debt:* How does the company's debt ratio compare to that of major competitors and to the industry average? If the debt ratio is much higher than average, the company may be unable to pay its debts.

- *Inability to collect receivables:* Is the average number of days it takes to collect accounts receivables growing faster than for other companies in the industry? Again, a cash shortage may be looming.

- *Buildup of inventories:* Is inventory turnover slowing down? If so, the company may be unable to sell goods, or it may be overstating inventory. Recall from our discussion of accounting for inventory and cost of goods sold in Chapter 8 that one of the easiest ways to overstate net income is to overstate ending inventory.

- *Movement of sales, inventory, and receivables:* Sales, receivables, and inventory generally move together. Increased sales lead to higher receivables and usually require more inventory to meet demand. Strange movements among these items may spell trouble.

A number of financial ratios can help an investor find these red flags. Before we learn how to compute these ratios, however, we will begin our work by using horizontal and vertical analysis and common-size financials. Although a number of techniques are available to analyze financial statement data, know that *all are valuable* because each offers a different perspective, a different insight into the business being examined. In real life, different pieces of information about a business resulting from different forms of analysis may contradict each other; accordingly, financial statement analysis is most effective when all facts are studied in conjunction with one another.

Horizontal Analysis

Many decisions hinge on whether financial statement amounts are increasing or decreasing. Users want to know:

 Perform a horizontal analysis of comparative financial statements.

- Have amounts risen or fallen compared to last year?

- By how much?

Considered alone, the dollar amount of a change is not especially helpful. For example, sales for a company may have increased by $20,000 but without more information, it is difficult to appreciate whether this increase was significant. It is more useful to know that sales increased by 20%. The percentage change in sales over time aids our understanding of the company's performance because it puts the dollar amount of the change in perspective.

The study of percentage changes in comparative statements is called **horizontal analysis**. Computing a percentage change in comparative statements requires two steps:

STEP 1   Compute the dollar amount of the change from the earlier base period to the later period.

STEP 2   Divide the dollar amount of change by the *earlier, base-period* amount; it is against this base that the comparison is being made.

Horizontal analysis is illustrated for Target Corporation[1] as follows (dollar amounts in millions):

			Increase (Decrease)	
	2004	**2003**	**Amount**	**Percentage**
Net Sales	$46,839	$42,025	$4,814	11.5%

Sales increased by 11.5% during 2004, computed as follows:

STEP 1

Compute the dollar amount of change in net sales from 2003 to 2004:

2004		**2003**		**Increase**
$46,839	−	$42,025	=	$4,814

STEP 2

Divide the dollar amount of change by the base-period amount to compute the percentage change for the period:

$$\text{Percentage Change} = \frac{\text{Dollar Amount of Change}}{\text{Base-Year Amount}}$$

$$= \frac{\$4,814}{\$42,025} = 0.115 = 11.5\%$$

Detailed horizontal analyses of Target Corporation are shown in the two right-hand columns of Exhibits 14-1 and 14-2, the financial statements of Target:

Exhibit 14-1 Comparative Income Statement: Horizontal Analysis

TARGET CORP.
Income Statement (Adapted)
Years Ended December 31, 2004 and 2003

			Increase (Decrease)	
(In millions)	2004	2003	Amount	Percentage
Net sales	$46,839	$42,025	$4,814	11.5%
Cost of goods sold	31,445	28,389	3,056	10.8%
Gross profit	15,394	13,636	1,758	12.9%
Operating expenses:				
Selling, general and administrative	9,797	8,657	1,140	13.2%
Other expense, net	2,566	2,376	190	8.0%
Income before income tax	3,031	2,603	428	16.4%
Income tax expense	1,146	984	162	16.5%
Net income	$ 1,885	$ 1,619	$ 266	16.4%

The income statements reveal that net sales increased by 11.5% during 2004. The cost of goods sold grew by 10.8%, and gross profit increased by 12.9%. Net income was up by 16.4%. These results are encouraging.

---

[1]Target Corporation's financial statements have been adapted for use in this chapter.

Exhibit 14-2 Comparative Balance Sheet: Horizontal Analysis

TARGET CORP.
Balance Sheet (Adapted)
December 31, 2004 and 2003

(In millions)	2004	2003	Increase (Decrease) Amount	Increase (Decrease) Percentage
Assets				
Current assets:				
Cash and cash equivalents	$ 2,245	$ 708	$ 1,537	217.1 %
Other current assets	11,677	12,244	(567)	(4.6)%
Total current assets	13,922	12,952	970	7.5 %
Property, plant, and equipment, net	16,860	15,153	1,707	11.3 %
Other assets	1,511	3,311	(1,800)	(54.4)%
Total assets	$32,293	$31,416	$ 877	2.8 %
Liabilities				
Current liabilities:				
Accounts payable	$ 5,779	$ 4,956	$ 823	16.6 %
Other current liabilities	2,441	3,358	(917)	(27.3)%
Total current liabilities	8,220	8,314	(94)	(1.1)%
Long-term liabilities	11,044	11,970	(926)	(7.7)%
Total liabilities	19,264	20,284	(1,020)	(5.0)%
Stockholders' equity				
Common stock	74	76	(2)	(2.6)%
Retained earnings and other equity	12,955	11,056	1,899	17.2 %
Total stockholders' equity	13,029	11,132	1,897	17.0 %
Total liabilities and stockholders' equity	$32,293	$31,416	$ 877	2.8 %

The comparative balance sheet in Exhibit 14-2 shows that some growth occurred for Target during 2004. Assets increased by 2.8%, while liabilities decreased by 5%, and stockholders' equity increased by about 17%.

Trend Percentages

Trend percentages are a form of horizontal analysis because they too are computed by comparing financial statement amounts over time, perhaps the most recent three to five years. Trend percentages indicate the direction a business is taking. They are computed by first selecting a base year and setting its amounts equal to 100%; the earliest year studied is the base year. The amounts for each following year are expressed as a percentage of this base year amount:

$$\text{Trend } \% = \frac{\text{Any Year \$}}{\text{Base Year \$}} = \frac{\$29,740}{\$26,529} = 112\%$$

Target Corporation showed the following net sales for the past six years:

(In millions)	2004	2003	2002	2001	2000	1999
Net Sales	$46,839	$42,025	$37,410	$33,021	$29,740	$26,529
Trend Percentages	177%	158%	141%	125%	112%	100%

For Target, the base year is 1999 and trend percentages for net sales are shown for the five-year period from 2000 to 2004 by dividing each year's amount by the 1999 amount.

Exhibit 14-3 illustrates Target's net sales trend percentages using a graph. Target's net sales increased steadily through 2004. Although the dollar amounts of net sales over this period indicate an increase, trend percentages more clearly present the impact of this increase. You can perform a trend analysis on any item you consider important. We selected net sales because sales drive profits.

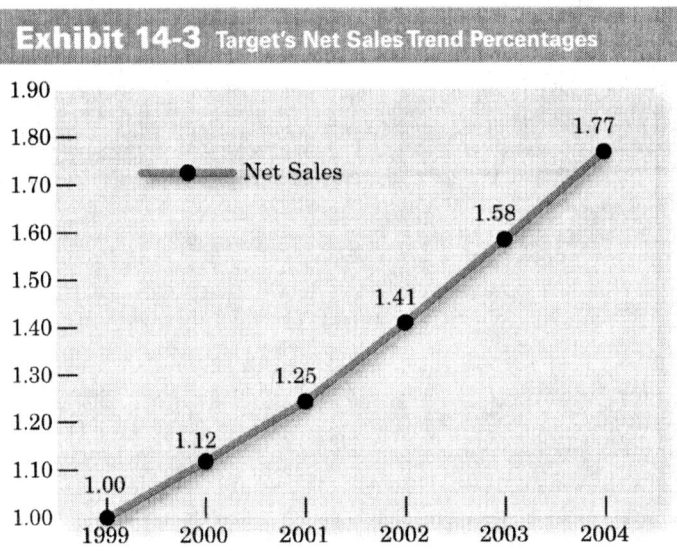

Exhibit 14-3 Target's Net Sales Trend Percentages

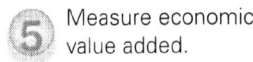

Vertical Analysis

⑤ Measure economic value added.

Horizontal analysis highlights changes over time. In contrast, **vertical analysis** of a financial statement shows the relationship of each item to a common, base amount; every item on the statement is reported as a percentage of that base. For an income statement, net sales is the base. For a balance sheet, total assets is the base. By expressing all financial statement amounts as a percentage of the base, these amounts are presented in proportion to it. Suppose, for instance, that a company's gross profit is 70% of net sales under normal conditions. A drop to 60% may cause the company to suffer a loss. Investors typically view a large decline in gross profit with alarm. Exhibit 14-4 shows the vertical analysis of Target's income statement. For example, check out the vertical analysis computation for cost of goods sold for 2004:

$$\text{Vertical Analysis \%} = \frac{\text{Each Income Statement Item}}{\text{Net Sales}} = \frac{\$31,445}{\$46,839} = 67.1\%$$

This percentage decreased during 2004. Look further. Selling, general, and administrative expenses increased slightly and other expenses decreased.

Exhibit 14-4 Comparative Income Statement: Vertical Analysis				

TARGET CORP.
Income Statement (Adapted)
Years Ended December 31, 2004 and 2003

(In millions)	2004		2003	
	Amount	Percentage	Amount	Percentage
Net sales	$46,839	100.0%	$42,025	100.0%
Cost of goods sold	31,445	67.1%	28,389	67.6%
Gross profit	15,394	32.9%	13,636	32.4%
Operating expenses:				
Selling, general, and administrative	9,797	20.9%	8,657	20.6%
Other expense, net	2,566	5.5%	2,376	5.7%
Income before income tax	3,031	6.5%	2,603	6.2%
Income tax expense	1,146	2.5%	984	2.3%
Net income	$ 1,885	4.0%	$ 1,619	3.8%

Note: Percentage may contain slight rounding error.

Although total expenses increased in 2004, net sales increased at a faster rate, so the percentage for net income increased in 2004.

Exhibit 14-5 shows the vertical analysis of Target's balance sheet, which reveals several things about the company's financial position in 2004:

- Current assets make up 43.1% of total assets, compared to 41.2% in 2003. A high percentage of current assets can be bad because current assets earn a low rate of return.

- Property, plant, and equipment represent 52.2% of total assets. This percentage is high because of the nature of the discount retail business.

- Total liabilities dropped to 59.7%, and stockholders' equity increased to 40.3% of total assets. Overall, Target's creditworthiness improved a bit in 2004.

How Do We Compare One Company with Another?

The percentages in Exhibits 14-4 and 14-5 can be presented as separate statements that report only percentages; in other words, no dollar amounts are shown. Such statements are called **common-size statements**. A common-size statement eases the comparison of different companies, especially of companies of different sizes, because amounts are stated in percentages instead of dollars. **Benchmarking** is this practice of comparing a company with others. Common-size statements help us benchmark a company's performance against the industry average or against another company, maybe an industry leader or key competitor.

BENCHMARKING AGAINST THE INDUSTRY AVERAGE

We study a company to gain insight into past results and future performance. To this point, our analysis has been limited to comparing one company to itself. This

Exhibit 14-5 Comparative Balance Sheet: Vertical Analysis

TARGET CORP.
Balance Sheet (Adapted)
December 31, 2004 and 2003

(In millions)	2004 Amount	2004 Percentage	2003 Amount	2003 Percentage
Assets				
Current assets:				
Cash and cash equivalents	$ 2,245	7.0%	$ 708	2.3%
Other cash assets	11,677	36.2%	12,244	39.0%
Total current assets	13,922	43.1%	12,952	41.2%
Property, plant, and equipment, net	16,860	52.2%	15,153	48.2%
Other assets	1,511	4.7%	3,311	10.5%
Total assets	$32,293	100.0%	$31,416	100.0%
Liabilities				
Current liabilities:				
Accounts payable	$ 5,779	17.9%	$ 4,956	15.8%
Other current liabilities	2,441	7.6%	3,358	10.7%
Total current liabilities	8,220	25.5%	8,314	26.5%
Long-term liabilities	11,044	34.2%	11,970	38.1%
Total liabilities	19,264	59.7%	20,284	64.6%
Stockholders' Equity				
Common stock	74	.2%	76	.2%
Retained earnings and other equity	12,955	40.1%	11,056	35.2%
Total stockholders' equity	13,029	40.3%	11,132	35.4%
Total liabilities and stockholders' equity	$32,293	100.0%	$31,416	100.0%

Note: Percentages may contain slight rounding error.

information is helpful, but it does not consider how other companies performed over the same time period. If a company's net income is increasing as a percentage of sales, for example, is this attributable to good management, a favorable economic environment for the industry, or both?

Exhibit 14-6 compares Target's common-size income statement with the average for the general merchandise discount store industry. The exhibit shows that Target compares somewhat inconsistently with competing companies in its industry. Target's gross profit percentage is higher than the industry average, while the company's percentage of net income is slightly lower.

BENCHMARKING AGAINST A KEY COMPETITOR

You can also use common-size statements to compare two or more companies. Suppose you want to invest in a general merchandise discount company and have narrowed your choices to Target and Wal-Mart. Converting the two companies' income statements to common size enables direct comparison not meaningfully accomplished in dollar amounts; the dollar amounts vary and are not easily comparable because of the difference in the sizes of the firms.

Exhibit 14-7 compares the common-size income statements of Target and Wal-Mart. Notice that the two companies earn similar percentages of net income to sales.

Exhibit 14-6 Common-Size Income Statement Compared with the Industry Average

TARGET CORP.
Common-Size Income Statement for Comparison with Industry Average
Year Ended December 31, 2004

	Target	Industry Average
Net sales	100.0%	100.0%
Cost of goods sold	67.1%	70.2%
Gross profit	32.9%	29.8%
Operating and other expenses	26.4%	22.5%
Income before income tax	6.5%	7.3%
Income tax expense	2.5%	2.8%
Net income	4.0%	4.5%

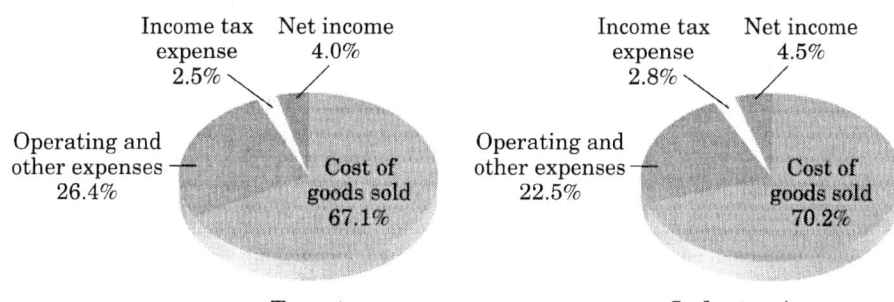

Target   Industry Average

Exhibit 14-7 Common-Size Income Statement Compared with a Key Competitor

TARGET CORP.
Common-Size Income Statement for Comparison with Key Competitor
Year Ended December 31, 2004

	Target	Wal-Mart
Net sales	100.0%	100.0%
Cost of goods sold	67.1%	77.5%
Gross profit	32.9%	22.5%
Operating and other expenses	26.4%	17.8%
Income before income tax	6.5%	4.7%
Income tax expense	2.5%	1.2%
Net income	4.0%	3.5%

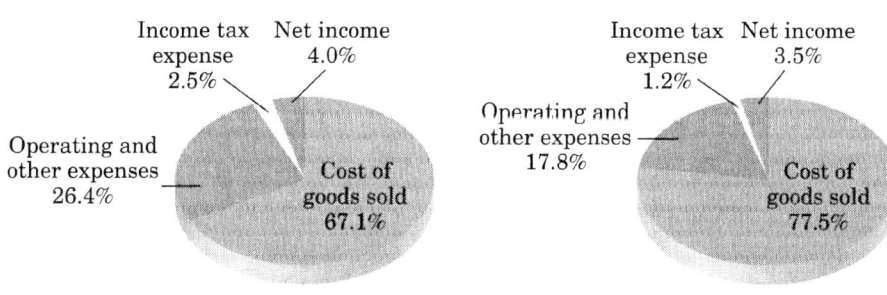

Target   Wal-Mart

Using Ratios to Make Decisions

4 Compute commonly used financial ratios.

Ratios represent comparisons between financial statement amounts. Analyzing ratios is an important part of finding any red flags indicating financial problems so that meaningful conclusions can be reached and informed decisions can be made about a business. Although many different financial ratios can be computed, we will examine some of the ones most commonly used.

Let's employ ratio analysis by looking at the *imagined* financial statements for NoZone, Inc., a company that sells protective clothing. Let's compare it to some assumed industry averages. Exhibit 14-8 gives the comparative income statements for 2007 and 2008 and the comparative balance sheets as of December 31, 2007 and 2008:

Exhibit 14-8 Comparative Financial Statements

NOZONE, INC.
Income Statement
Years Ended December 31, 2008 and 2007

	2008	2007
Net sales	$858,000	$803,000
Cost of goods sold	513,000	509,000
Gross profit	345,000	294,000
Operating expenses:		
Selling expenses	126,000	114,000
General expenses	118,000	123,000
Total operating expenses	244,000	237,000
Income from operations	101,000	57,000
Interest revenue	4,000	—
Interest expense	24,000	14,000
Income before income taxes	81,000	43,000
Income tax expense	33,000	17,000
Net income	$ 48,000	$ 26,000

NOZONE, INC.
Balance Sheet
December 31, 2008 and 2007

	2008	2007
Assets		
Current assets:		
Cash	$ 29,000	$ 32,000
Accounts receivable, net	114,000	85,000
Inventory	113,000	111,000
Prepaid expenses	6,000	8,000
Total current assets	262,000	236,000
Long-term investments	18,000	9,000
Property, plant, and equipment, net	507,000	399,000
Total assets	$787,000	$644,000
Liabilities		
Current liabilities:		
Notes payable	$ 42,000	$ 27,000
Accounts payable	73,000	68,000
Accrued liabilities	27,000	31,000
Total current liabilities	142,000	126,000
Long-term debt	289,000	198,000
Total liabilities	431,000	324,000
Stockholders' equity		
Common stock, no par	186,000	186,000
Retained earnings	170,000	134,000
Total stockholders' equity	356,000	320,000
Total liabilities and stockholders' equity	787,000	644,000

Liquidity Ratios

WORKING CAPITAL

Remember from Chapter 10, that working capital measures the ability to meet short-term obligations with current assets, and is calculated by subtracting current liabilities from current assets.

NoZone's working capital for 2008 and 2007 follow:

	NoZone's Working Capital	
Formula	**2008**	**2007**
Working Capital = Current Assets – Current Liabilities	$262,000 – $142,000 = $120,000	$236,000 – $126,000 = $110,000

NoZone's working capital for 2008 is $120,000, indicating that current assets exceed current liabilities by $120,000. This amount is higher than the $110,000 of working capital that the firm had at the end of 2007.

CURRENT RATIO

Also recall from Chapter 10 that the current ratio is a measure related to working capital, and probably represents the tool most widely used to evaluate liquidity. This ratio is equal to current assets divided by current liabilities. The current ratio measures ability to pay current liabilities with current assets.

The current ratios of NoZone, at December 31, 2008 and 2007, follow, along with the assumed average for the retail clothing industry:

	NoZone's Current Ratio		
Formula	**2008**	**2007**	**Industry Average**
Current Ratio = $\dfrac{\text{Current Assets}}{\text{Current Liabilities}}$	$\dfrac{\$262,000}{\$142,000} = 1.85$	$\dfrac{\$236,000}{\$126,000} = 1.87$	1.50

A high current ratio indicates a strong financial position and that the business has sufficient liquid assets to maintain normal business operations. What is an acceptable current ratio? The answer depends on the industry. The norm for companies in most industries is around 1.50, as reported by the Risk Management Association. NoZone's current ratio of 1.85 in 2008 is strong. In most industries, a current ratio of 2.0 is very strong.

QUICK RATIO

Another measure associated with liquidity is the quick, or acid-test, ratio introduced in Chapter 7. This stricter indicator of bill-paying ability than the current ratio tells whether the entity could pay all its current liabilities if they came due immediately. That is, could the company pass this *acid test*?

To compute the quick ratio, add cash, short-term investments, and net current receivables (accounts and short-term notes receivable, net of allowances) and divide this sum by current liabilities. Inventory and prepaid expenses are two current assets *not* included in the acid test because they are the least-liquid current assets.

NoZone's quick ratios for 2008 and 2007 follow:

	NoZone's Quick Ratio		Industry
Formula	**2008**	**2007**	**Average**
Quick Ratio = $\dfrac{\text{Cash + Short-Term Investments + Net Current Receivables}}{\text{Current Liabilities}}$	$\dfrac{\$29,000 + \$0 + \$114,000}{\$142,000} = 1.01$	$\dfrac{\$32,000 + \$0 + \$85,000}{\$126,000} = 0.93$	0.40

In 2008, NoZone's EPS increased by $2.20 ($4.80 − $2.60) or 85% ($2.20/$2.60). Its stockholders should not expect this big a boost in EPS every year. Most companies strive to increase EPS by 10% to 15% annually, and leading companies generally do so.

Asset Utilization Ratios

INVENTORY TURNOVER

Inventory turnover mentioned first in Chapter 5 measures the number of times a company sells its average level of inventory during a year. A high rate of turnover indicates that a company can sell its inventory fairly easily, but a low rate indicates difficulty in selling merchandise. To compute inventory turnover, we divide cost of goods sold by the average inventory for the period.

NoZone's inventory turnover for 2008 is:

Formula	NoZone's 2008 Inventory Turnover	Industry Average
Inventory Turnover = $\dfrac{\text{Cost of Goods Sold}}{\text{Average Inventory}}$	$\dfrac{\$513,000}{\$112,000} = 4.6$	3.4

Average inventory is figured by averaging the beginning inventory of $111,000 with ending inventory of $113,000.

Inventory turnover varies widely with the nature of the business. For example, most manufacturers of farm machinery have an inventory turnover close to three times a year. In contrast, companies that remove natural gas from the ground hold their inventory for a short period of time and have an average turnover of 30. NoZone's turnover of 4.6 times a year is high for its industry, which has an average turnover of 3.4.

ACCOUNTS RECEIVABLE TURNOVER

Accounts receivable turnover measures the ability to collect cash from credit customers. The higher the ratio, the more successful the business is in collecting cash. However, a receivable turnover that is too high may indicate that a company is not extending credit freely enough to make sales to all potentially good customers. To compute the accounts receivable turnover, we divide net credit sales by average net accounts receivable.

NoZone's accounts receivable turnover ratio for 2008 is computed as follows:

Formula	NoZone's 2008 Accounts Receivable Turnover	Industry Average
Accounts Receivable Turnover = $\dfrac{\text{Net Credit Sales}}{\text{Average Net Accounts Receivable}}$	$\dfrac{\$858,000}{\$99,500} = 8.6$	51.0

Average net accounts receivable is figured by adding the beginning accounts receivable balance of $85,000 and the ending balance of $114,000, then dividing by 2.

NoZone's receivable turnover of 8.6 times per year is much slower than the industry average. Why the difference? NoZone is a hometown store that sells to local people who tend to pay their bills over time. Many larger stores sell their receivables to other companies called **factors**, a practice that keeps receivables low and receivable turnover high. NoZone follows a different strategy.

DAYS' SALES IN RECEIVABLES

Remember from Chapter 7 that the days' sales in receivables ratio also measures the ability to collect receivables. This ratio tells us how many days' sales remain in Accounts Receivable. To compute the ratio, we follow a two-step process:

STEP 1

Divide net sales by 365 days to figure average sales for one day.

STEP 2

Divide this average day's sales amount into average net accounts receivable.

NoZone's ratio for 2008 follows:

	Formula	NoZone's 2008 Days' Sales in Accounts Receivable	Industry Average
1.	One Day's Sales = $\dfrac{\text{Net Sales}}{\text{365 days}}$	$\dfrac{\$858,000}{\text{365 days}} = \$2,351$	
2.	Days' Sales in Average Accounts Receivable = $\dfrac{\text{Average Net Accounts Receivable}}{\text{One Day's Sales}}$	$\dfrac{\$99,500}{\$2,351} = 42 \text{ days}$	7 days

Average accounts receivable is $99,500 [($85,000 + $114,000)/2].

NoZone's ratio tells us that 42 average days' sales remain in accounts receivable and need to be collected. NoZone's days' sales in receivables is much higher than the industry average because, as we mentioned earlier, NoZone collects its own receivables. However, NoZone is able to remain competitive because of its personal relationship with customers. These relationships cause customers to pay promptly and NoZone enjoys good cash flow accordingly.

Debt Utilization Ratios

DEBT RATIO

This relationship between total liabilities and total assets is called the **debt ratio**. This ratio shows the proportion of assets financed with debt and thus allows lenders to evaluate the risk of loaning funds to a business.

- A debt ratio of 1 for a firm indicates that debt has been used to finance all the assets of the firm.

- A debt ratio of 0.50 means that the company has financed half its assets by borrowing; the owners of the business have financed the other half.

- The higher the debt ratio, the higher the strain of paying off loans.

The debt ratios for NoZone at the end of 2008 and 2007 follow:

	Formula	NoZone's Debt Ratio		Industry Average
		2008	**2007**	
Debt Ratio $=$	$\dfrac{\text{Total Liabilities}}{\text{Total Assets}}$	$\dfrac{\$431,000}{\$787,000} = 0.55$	$\dfrac{\$324,000}{\$644,000} = 0.50$	0.64

NoZone's debt ratio of 0.55 is not high in relation to the industry average. Risk Management Association reports that the average debt ratio for most companies ranges from 0.57 to 0.67, with relatively little variation from company to company.

TIMES-INTEREST-EARNED RATIO

The debt ratio says nothing about a company's ability to pay interest. Analysts use the **times-interest-earned ratio** to relate income to interest expense. This ratio is also called the **interest-coverage ratio**. It measures the number of times operating income can cover interest expense and is calculated by dividing income from operations, or operating income, by interest expense. A high interest-coverage ratio indicates ease in paying interest expense, while a low ratio suggests difficulty.

Calculations of NoZone's times-interest-earned ratio follow:

	Formula	NoZone's Times-Interest-Earned Ratio		Industry Average
		2008	**2007**	
Times-Interest-Earned Ratio $=$	$\dfrac{\text{Income from Operations}}{\text{Interest Expense}}$	$\dfrac{\$101,000}{\$24,000} = 4.21$	$\dfrac{\$57,000}{\$14,000} = 4.07$	2.80

The company's times-interest-earned ratio of about 4.00 is significantly better than the average for retailers. The norm for U.S. business, as reported by Risk Management Association, falls in the range of 2.0 to 3.0. Based on its debt ratio and its times-interest-earned ratio, NoZone appears to have little difficulty paying its interest.

Analyzing Stock Investments

In addition to analyzing liquidity, profitability, and asset and debt utilization, investors may want to evaluate stock investments based on the return provided by the investments. Investors purchase stock to earn a return in one of two ways:

1. Receiving a gain from selling the stock at a price above the purchase price paid

2. Receiving dividends

The ratios we examine in this section help analysts assess stock in terms of market price appreciation or dividends.

PRICE/EARNINGS RATIO

The **price/earnings ratio** is the ratio of the market price of a share of common stock to the company's earnings per share. It shows the market price of $1 of earnings. This ratio, abbreviated P/E, appears in the *Wall Street Journal* stock listings for publicly-owned companies. P/E ratios play an important part in decisions to buy, hold, and sell stocks.

Calculations for the P/E ratios of NoZone follow. The market price of its common stock was $60 at the end of 2008 and $35 at the end of 2007. These prices can be obtained from a financial publication, a stockbroker, or the company's Web site.

	Formula	NoZone's Price/Earnings Ratio	
		2008	2007
P/E Ratio =	$\dfrac{\text{Market Price per Share of Common Stock}}{\text{Earnings per Share}}$	$\dfrac{\$60.00}{\$4.80} = 12.5$	$\dfrac{\$35.00}{\$2.60} = 13.5$

NoZone's P/E ratio of 12.5 means that the company's stock is selling at 12.5 times earnings. The decline from the 2007 P/E ratio of 13.5 is not necessarily a cause for alarm because the market price of the stock is not under NoZone's control, although it is an indicator of investor confidence in the stock.

DIVIDEND YIELD

Dividend yield is the ratio of dividends per share to the stock's market price per share. This ratio measures the percentage of a stock's market value that is returned annually as dividends. Preferred stockholders, who invest primarily to receive dividends, pay special attention to dividend yield.

NoZone paid annual cash dividends of $1.20 per share of common stock in 2008 and $1.00 in 2007, and market prices of the company's common stock were $60 in 2008 and $35 in 2007. The firm's dividend yields on common stock follow.

	Formula	Dividend Yield on NoZone's Common Stock	
		2008	2007
Dividend Yield on Common Stock* =	$\dfrac{\text{Dividend per Share of Common Stock}}{\text{Market Price per Share of Common Stock}}$	$\dfrac{\$1.20}{\$60.00} = .020$	$\dfrac{\$1.00}{\$35.00} = .029$

*Dividend yields may also be calculated for preferred stock.

An investor who buys NoZone's common stock for $60 can expect to receive 2% of the investment annually in the form of cash dividends.

Economic Value Added

Coca-Cola, Quaker Oats, and other leading companies use **economic value added (EVA®)** to evaluate performance. EVA measures whether a business's operations have increased its stockholder wealth. The idea behind EVA is that the returns to the company's stockholders as net income and to its creditors as interest expense should exceed the company's **capital charge**. The capital charge is the amount that lenders and stockholders *charge* for the use of their money. A *positive* EVA amount suggests an increase in stockholder wealth, and

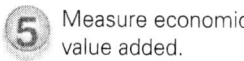
5 Measure economic value added.

the company's stock should remain attractive. A *negative* EVA indicates a decrease in stockholder wealth, resulting in stockholders who will probably be unhappy and sell the stock, causing a decrease in the stock price.

EVA can be computed as follows:

$$\text{EVA} = \text{Net Income} + \text{Interest Expense} - \text{Capital Charge}$$

Capital charge is computed using the formula:

$$\text{Capital Charge} = \left(\frac{\text{Notes}}{\text{Payable}} + \frac{\text{Bonds}}{\text{Payable}} + \frac{\text{Stockholders'}}{\text{Equity}}\right) \times \frac{\text{Cost of}}{\text{Capital}}$$

The **cost of capital** is a weighted average of the returns demanded by the company's stockholders and lenders. The cost of capital varies with the company's level of risk. For example, stockholders and lenders would demand a higher return from a start-up company than from Coca-Cola because the new company is more risky. A new company would thus have a higher cost of capital than Coca-Cola.

To illustrate the use of EVA, let's imagine the following information from CTK Corporation for 2007, assuming that its cost of capital is 10%:

Balance Sheet Information		Income Statement Information		Cost of capital
Notes payable	$180,000	Net income	$350,000	10%
Bonds payable	270,000	Interest expense	2,000	
Stockholder's equity	1,200,000			

You may calculate the capital charge and then compute the EVA, or you may use a formula that computes EVA in one step, as follows:

$$\text{EVA} = \frac{\text{Net}}{\text{Income}} + \frac{\text{Interest}}{\text{Expense}} - \left[\frac{\text{Loans and}}{\text{Notes Payable}} + \frac{\text{Long-Term}}{\text{Debt}} + \frac{\text{Stockholders'}}{\text{Equity}}\right] \times \frac{\text{Cost of}}{\text{Capital}}$$

$$= \$350{,}000 + \$2{,}000 - [(\$180{,}000 + \$270{,}000 + \$1{,}200{,}000) \times 0.10]$$
$$= \$352{,}000 - (\$1{,}650{,}000 \times 0.10)$$
$$= \$352{,}000 - \$165{,}000$$
$$= \$187{,}000$$

By this measure, CTK's operations during 2007 added $187,000 of value to its stockholders' wealth after meeting the company's capital charge. This performance is outstanding.

Analyzing Nonfinancial Data

Utilize nonfinancial data in analyzing financial statements.

Analyzing financial statements requires more than performing horizontal and vertical analysis and computing the standard ratios. The nonquantitative parts of the annual report may hold more important information than the financial statements. For example, the president's letter may describe a turnover of top managers. The management discussion and analysis will reveal management's opinion of the year's results. The auditor's report may indicate a major problem with the company. Let's consider each of these parts of a corporate annual report.

President's Letter to the Stockholders

The president of the company gives his or her view of the year's results and outlines the direction top management is charting for the company. Often, the president will highlight the major decisions made during the year. For example, in its 2005 annual report, the president and CEO of Gap Inc. said, "Gap is focused on re-establishing the brand's iconic positioning. Our product design is true to Gap's heritage and will help us regain our authority in key categories."

Management Discussion and Analysis (MD&A)

Management is accountable for its actions. The MD&A section of the annual report discusses why net income was up or down, how the company invested the stockholders' money, and plans for future spending. Through the MD&A, investors may learn of the company's plan to discontinue a product line or to expand into new markets. These forward-looking data are not permitted in the historical financial statements, which are based on past transactions. Gap's 2005 Management Discussion and Analysis states, "In fiscal 2005, we made continued progress against our strategic priorities and continued to position ourselves for long-term growth. Despite disappointing top line results, we continued to deliver solid earnings, completed our $2 billion share repurchase program, doubled our dividend, and delivered on our growth initiatives."

Auditor Report

Investors are aware of the possibility for management bias in the financial statements. For this reason, the Securities and Exchange Commission, a federal agency mentioned in Chapter 1, requires that all financial statements of public corporations be audited by independent Certified Public Accountants. Investors want to know whether the company followed Generally Accepted Accounting Principles and presented its financial statement amounts fairly. The auditor's report is how stakeholders gain assurance that they can rely on a company's financial statements to make decisions. The Report of Independent Registered Public Accounting Firm in Gap's 2005 annual report says, "In our opinion, such consolidated financial statements referred to above present fairly, in all material respects, the financial position of The Gap, Inc. and subsidiaries as of January 28, 2006, and January 29, 2005, and the results of their operations and their cash flows for each of the three years in the period ended January 28, 2006, in conformity with accounting principles generally accepted in the United States of America."

Demo Doc

Horizontal and Vertical Analysis

Learning Objectives 2–3

Cassidy Inc. (from Chapter 13 Demo Doc) has the following information for 2007 and 2008:

CASSIDY INC. Income Statement Years Ended December 31, 2008 and 2007	2008	2007
Sales revenue	$550,000	$600,000
Cost of goods sold	320,000	350,000
Gross profit	230,000	250,000
Salary expense	165,000	158,000
Depreciation expense	21,000	16,000
Insurance expense	19,000	23,000
Income from operations	25,000	53,000
Gain on sale of furniture	3,000	0
Net income	$ 28,000	$ 53,000

CASSIDY INC.
Balance Sheet
December 31, 2008 and 2007

Assets	2008	2007	Liabilities	2008	2007
Current:			Current:		
Cash	$ 28,000	$ 33,000	Accounts payable	$ 20,000	$23,000
Accounts receivable	26,000	15,000	Salary payable	10,000	8,000
Prepaid insurance	30,000	42,000	Total current liabilities	30,000	31,000
Total current assets	84,000	90,000	Notes payable	40,000	50,000
Furniture, net	90,000	74,500	**Stockholders' Equity**		
			Common stock (no par)	4,000	3,500
			Retained earnings	100,000	80,000
Total assets	$174,000	$164,500	Total liabilities and stockholders' equity	$174,000	$164,500

Requirements

1. Prepare a horizontal analysis of Cassidy's balance sheet and income statement for 2008.

2. Prepare a vertical analysis of Cassidy's balance sheet and income statement for 2008.

Demo Doc Solutions

Requirement 1

Prepare a horizontal analysis of Cassidy's balance sheet and income statement for 2008.

Part 1	Part 2	Demo Doc Complete

② Perform a horizontal analysis of comparative financial statements.

Horizontal analysis goes *across* the rows of each financial statement, looking at *one* account and how it has changed from the prior year.

To prepare a horizontal analysis, we need to calculate the *dollar* amount of change and the *percentage* change for *every* number on the balance sheet and income statement.

Dollar Amount of Change = This Year's Amount (Balance) − Last Year's Amount (Balance)

For example, the dollar amount of change for Accounts Receivable and Sales Revenue would be:

Accounts Receivable = $26,000 − $15,000 = $11,000 Change

Sales Revenue = $550,000 − $600,000 = $(50,000) Change

Notice that the parentheses around the change in Sales Revenue indicates that it decreased, whereas the positive value of the change in the amount of Accounts Receivable indicates that it increased.

Expenses are assumed to be negative numbers on the income statement, in that they are subtracted to calculate net income. However, we use the *absolute value* of the expenses (ignoring the fact that they are already negative numbers) to calculate the dollar amount of change.

So the dollar amount of change of Depreciation Expense and Insurance Expense would be:

Depreciation Expense = $21,000 − $16,000 = $5,000 Change

Insurance Expense = $19,000 − $23,000 = $(4,000) Change

The positive amount of change indicates that Depreciation Expense increased and the negative amount of change indicates that Insurance Expense decreased.

$$\text{Percentage Change} = \frac{\text{Dollar Amount of Change}}{\text{Base-Year Amount}}$$

The base-year amount is last year's amount (balance).

Using this formula, the percentage changes in Accounts Receivable and Sales Revenue would be:

$$\text{Percentage Change in Accounts Receivable} = \frac{\$11,000}{\$15,000}$$

$$= 73.3\% \text{ Change}$$

$$\text{Percentage Change in Sales Revenue} = \frac{\$(50,000)}{\$600,000}$$

$$= (8.3)\% \text{ Change}$$

Notice that the percentage change numbers are positive for Accounts Receivable (which had a dollar amount increase for 2008) and negative for Sales Revenue (which had a dollar amount decrease for 2008).

The percentage change for expenses uses the *absolute value* of expenses. The percentage changes of Depreciation Expense and Insurance Expense would be:

$$\text{Percentage Change in Depreciation Expense} = \frac{\$5,000}{\$16,000}$$

$$= 31.3\% \text{ Change}$$

$$\text{Percentage Change in Insurance Expense} = \frac{\$(4,000)}{\$23,000}$$

$$= (17.4)\% \text{ Change}$$

If an account did not exist in the prior year (such as the Gain on Sale of Furniture in this example), then horizontal analysis is irrelevant and a percentage change cannot be calculated.

Extending these calculations to all of the accounts on the balance sheet and income statement:

CASSIDY INC.
Income Statement
Years Ended December 31, 2008 and 2007

	2008	2007	Increase (Decrease) Amount	Increase (Decrease) Percentage
Sales revenue	$550,000	$600,000	$(50,000)	(8.3)%
Cost of goods sold	320,000	350,000	(30,000)	(8.6)%
Gross profit	230,000	250,000	(20,000)	(8.0)%
Salary expense	165,000	158,000	7,000	4.4 %
Depreciation expense	21,000	16,000	5,000	31.3 %
Insurance expense	19,000	23,000	(4,000)	(17.4)%
Income from operations	25,000	53,000	(28,000)	(52.8)%
Gain on sale of furniture	3,000	0	3,000	—
Net income	$ 28,000	$ 53,000	$(25,000)	(47.2)%

CASSIDY INC.
Balance Sheet
December 31, 2008 and 2007

	2008	2007	Increase (Decrease) Amount	Increase (Decrease) Percentage
Assets				
Current:				
Cash	$ 28,000	$ 33,000	$ (5,000)	(15.2)%
Accounts receivable	26,000	15,000	11,000	73.3 %
Prepaid insurance	30,000	42,000	(12,000)	(28.6)%
Total current assets	84,000	90,000	(6,000)	(6.7)%
Furniture, net	90,000	74,500	15,500	20.8 %
Total assets	$174,000	$164,500	9,500	5.8 %
Liabilities				
Current:				
Accounts payable	$ 20,000	$ 23,000	$ (3,000)	(13)%
Salary payable	10,000	8,000	2,000	25.0 %
Total current liabilities	30,000	31,000	(1,000)	(3.2)%
Notes payable	40,000	50,000	(10,000)	(20.0)%
Total liabilities	70,000	81,000	(11,000)	(13.6)%
Stockholders' Equity				
Common stock (no par)	4,000	3,500	500	14.3 %
Retained earnings	100,000	80,000	20,000	25.0 %
Total stockholders' equity	104,000	83,500	20,500	24.6 %
Total liabilities				
and stockholders' equity	$174,000	$164,500	$ 9,500	5.8 %

Requirement 2

Prepare a vertical analysis of Cassidy's balance sheet and income statement for 2008.

Part 1	**Part 2**	Demo Doc Complete

3 Perform a vertical analysis of financial statements and prepare common-size financial statements.

Vertical analysis compares *every* number on a financial statement to all others in the same year (that is, *down* the columns of the financial statements).

To prepare a vertical analysis, we need to calculate the vertical analysis percentage for each account.

Balance Sheet

On the balance sheet, each number, *whether it be for an asset, a liability, or an equity account,* is calculated as a percentage of *total assets*.

$$\text{Vertical Analysis \% (Balance Sheet)} = \frac{\text{Balance Sheet Account}}{\text{Total Assets}}$$

So in the case of Accounts Receivable:

$$\text{Vertical Analysis \% (2008 Accounts Receivable)} = \frac{\$26,000}{\$174,000}$$

$$= 14.9\%$$

In other words, approximately 15% of all the assets are Accounts Receivable.

Income Statement
On the income statement, each number is calculated as a percentage of net sales revenues.

$$\text{Vertical Analysis \% (Income Statement)} = \frac{\text{Income Statement Account}}{\text{Net Sales Revenue}}$$

So in the case of Gross Profit:

$$\text{Vertical analysis \% (2008 Gross Profit)} = \frac{\$230,000}{\$550,000}$$

$$= 41.8\%$$

This figure means that $0.418 of gross profit resulted from every dollar of sales revenue.

The calculation is the same for expenses. The vertical analysis percentages for Depreciation Expense and Insurance Expense would be:

$$\text{Vertical Analysis \% (2008 Depreciation Expense)} = \frac{\$21,000}{\$550,000}$$

$$= 3.8\%$$

$$\text{Vertical Analysis \% (2008 Insurance Expense)} = \frac{\$19,000}{\$550,000}$$

$$= 3.5\%$$

Extending these calculations to all of the accounts on the balance sheet and income statement gives us the following:

	CASSIDY INC. Income Statement Years Ended December 31, 2008 and 2007			
	2008		**2007**	
	Amount	**Percentage**	**Amount**	**Percentage**
Sales revenue	$550,000	100.0%	$600,000	100.0%
Cost of goods sold	320,000	58.2%	350,000	58.3%
Gross profit	230,000	41.8%	250,000	41.7%
Salary expense	165,000	30.0%	158,000	26.3%
Depreciation expense	21,000	3.8%	16,000	2.7%
Insurance expense	19,000	3.5%	23,000	3.8%
Income from operations	25,000	4.5%	53,000	8.8%
Gain on sale of furniture	3,000	0.5%	0	0.0%
Net income	$ 28,000	5.0%	$53,000	8.8%

Note: Percentage may contain slight rounding error.

	CASSIDY INC. Balance Sheet December 31, 2008 and 2007				
	2008		**2007**		
	Amount	**Percentage**	**Amount**	**Percentage**	
Assets					
Current:					
Cash	$ 28,000	16.1%	$ 33,000	20.1%	
Accounts receivable	26,000	14.9%	15,000	9.1%	
Prepaid insurance	30,000	17.2%	42,000	25.5%	
Total current assets	84,000	48.2%	90,000	54.7%	
Furniture, net	90,000	51.8%	74,500	45.3%	
Total assets	$174,000	100.0%	$164,500	100.0%	
Liabilities					
Current:					
Accounts payable	$ 20,000	11.5%	$ 23,000	14.0%	
Salary payable	10,000	5.7%	8,000	4.8%	
Total current liabilities	30,000	17.2%	31,000	18.8%	
Notes payable	40,000	23.0%	50,000	30.4%	
Total liabilities	70,000	40.2%	81,000	49.2%	
Stockholders' Equity					
Common stock (no par)	4,000	2.3%	3,500	2.2%	
Retained earning	100,000	57.5%	80,000	48.6%	
Total stockholders' equity	104,000	59.8%	83,500	50.8%	
Total liabilities and stockholders' equity	$174,000	100.0%	$164,500	100.0%	

Note: Percentage may contain slight rounding error.

Part 1	Part 2	**Demo Doc Complete**

Accounting in Action

How do stakeholders measure a company's ability to pay bills, sell inventory, collect receivables, and so on? The standard ratios covered throughout this book help people evaluate business performance in order to make decisions.

Ratio	Computation	Information Provided
Measuring ability to pay current liabilities:		
1. Working Capital	Current Assets − Current Liabilities	Measures ability to pay current liabilities with current assets
2. Current Ratio	$\dfrac{\text{Current Assets}}{\text{Current Liabilities}}$	Measures ability to pay current liabilities with current assets
3. Quick Ratio	$\dfrac{\text{Cash} + \text{Short-term Investments} + \text{Net Current Receivables}}{\text{Current Liabilities}}$	Shows ability to pay all current liabilities if they come due immediately
Measuring ability to sell inventory and collect receivables:		
4. Inventory Turnover	$\dfrac{\text{Cost of Goods Sold}}{\text{Average Inventory}}$	Indicates salability of inventory, the number of times a company sells its average inventory during a year
5. Accounts Receivable Turnover	$\dfrac{\text{Net Credit Sales}}{\text{Average Net Accounts Receivable}}$	Measures ability to collect cash from customers
6. Days' Sales in Receivables	$\dfrac{\text{Average Net Accounts Receivable}}{\text{One Day's Sales}}$	Shows how many days' sales remain in Accounts Receivable, how many days it takes to collect the average level of receivables
Measuring ability to pay long-term debt:		
7. Debt Ratio	$\dfrac{\text{Total Liabilities}}{\text{Total Assets}}$	Indicates percentage of assets financed with debt
8. Times-Interest-Earned Ratio	$\dfrac{\text{Income from Operations}}{\text{Interest Expense}}$	Measures the number of times operating income can cover interest expense
Measuring profitability:		
9. Profit Margin	$\dfrac{\text{Net Income}}{\text{Net Sales}}$	Shows the percentage of each sales dollar earned as net income

Ratio	Computation	Information Provided
10. Rate of Return on Total Assets	$$\frac{\text{Net Income} + \text{Interest Expense}}{\text{Average Total Assets}}$$	Measures how profitably a company uses its assets
11. Rate of Return on Common Stockholders' Equity	$$\frac{\text{Net Income} - \text{Preferred Dividends}}{\text{Average Common Stockholders' Equity}}$$	Indicates how much income is earned for each dollar invested by common stockholders
12. Earnings per Share of Common Stock	$$\frac{\text{Net Income} - \text{Preferred Dividends}}{\text{Average Number of Shares of Common Stock Outstanding}}$$	Gives the amount of net income earned for each share of the company's common stock
Analyzing stock as an investment: 13. Price/Earnings Ratio	$$\frac{\text{Market Price per Share of Common Stock}}{\text{Earnings per Share}}$$	Indicates the market price of $1 of earnings
14. Dividend Yield	$$\frac{\text{Dividend per Share of Common (or Preferred) Stock}}{\text{Market Price per Share of Common (or Preferred) Stock}}$$	Shows the percentage of a stock's market value returned as dividends to stockholders each year

Review

Financial Statement Analysis
Word Power

Accounts receivable turnover Net credit sales divided by average net accounts receivable; measures a company's ability to collect cash from credit customers.

Benchmarking Comparing a company with other companies that are leaders or with industry averages.

Capital charge The amount that stockholders and lenders charge a company for the use of their money; calculated as (Notes Payable + Bonds Payable + Stockholders' Equity) × Cost of Capital.

Common-size statement Financial statement in which all amounts are expressed as percentages of a common base amount.

Cost of capital A weighted average of the returns demanded by the company's stockholders and lenders.

Debt ratio Ratio of total liabilities to total assets; shows the proportion of a company's assets that is financed with debt.

Dividend yield Ratio of dividends per share of common stock to the stock's market price per share. Tells the percentage of a stock's market value that the company returns to stockholders annually as dividends.

Earnings per share (EPS) Amount of a company's net income for each share of its outstanding common stock.

Economic value added (EVA®) EVA = Net Income + Interest Expense − Capital Charge; used to evaluate a company's operating performance.

Factors Businesses that buy accounts receivables and collect them.

Financial statement analysis The process of using financial statements and other data to predict the future of a business and make decisions about it.

Horizontal analysis Analysis of percentage changes in items on comparative financial statements.

Interest-coverage ratio Ratio of income from operations to interest expense that measures the number of times operating income can cover interest expense; also called the *times-interest-earned ratio*.

Leverage Earning more income on borrowed money than the related interest expense, thereby increasing the earnings for the owners of the business; also called *trading on the equity*.

Price/earnings ratio Ratio of the market price of a share of common stock to the company's earnings per share that

measures the value that the stock market places on $1 of a company's earnings.

Profit margin Ratio of net income to net sales that indicates a measure of profitability; also called *return on sales* or *rate of return on net sales*.

Rate of return on common stockholders' equity A ratio of net income minus preferred dividends to average common stockholders' equity that measures profitability; also called *return on equity*.

Rate of return on net sales Ratio of net income to net sales that indicates a measure of profitability; also called *profit margin* or *return on sales*.

Rate of return on total assets A ratio of net income plus interest expense to average total assets that measures a company's success in using its assets to earn a return for the groups who finance the business; also called *return on assets*.

Return on assets A ratio of net income plus interest expense to average total assets that measures a company's success in using its assets to earn a return for the groups who finance the business; also called *rate of return on total assets*.

Return on equity A ratio of net income minus preferred dividends to average common stockholders' equity that measures profitability; also called *rate of return on common stockholders' equity*.

Return on sales Ratio of net income to net sales that indicates a measure of profitability; also called *profit margin* or *rate of return on net sales*.

Times-interest-earned ratio Ratio of income from operations to interest expense that measures the number of times that operating income can cover interest expense; also called the *interest-coverage ratio*.

Trading on the equity Earning more income on borrowed money than the related interest expense, thereby increasing the earnings for the owners of the business; also called *leverage*.

Trend percentages A form of horizontal analysis in which percentages are computed by selecting a base year, setting its amounts as 100% and expressing amounts for following years as a percentage of the base year amount.

Vertical analysis Analysis of a financial statement that shows the relationship of each statement item to a specified base, expressing every item on the statement as a percentage of that base.

Quick Check

1. Net income was $245,000 in 2005, $240,000 in 2006, and $276,000 in 2007. The change from 2006 to 2007 is a (an)

    a. Increase of 5%
    b. Increase of 10%
    c. Increase of 15%
    d. Increase of 20%

2. Horizontal analysis of a financial statement shows

    a. The relationship of each statement item to a specified base
    b. Percentage changes in comparative balance sheets
    c. Percentage changes in comparative income statements
    d. Both b and c

3. A statement that reports only percentages is called

    a. A comparative statement
    b. A common-size statement
    c. A condensed statement
    d. A cumulative statement

4. Working capital is

    a. A measure of the ability to meet short-term obligations with current assets
    b. Defined as current assets minus current liabilities
    c. Defined as current assets divided by current liabilities
    d. Both a and b

5. Cash is $15,000, net accounts receivable amount to $6,000, inventory is $10,000, prepaid expenses total $4,000, and current liabilities are $20,000. What is the quick ratio?

    a. 1.05
    b. 1.55
    c. 1.25
    d. 1.75

6. Days' sales in receivables is computed by

    a. Dividing net sales by 365
    b. Dividing average net accounts receivable by sales
    c. Dividing sales by average net accounts receivable
    d. Dividing average net accounts receivable by one day's sales

7. Rubble Company is experiencing a severe cash shortage due to its inability to collect accounts receivable. Which of the following would most likely identify this problem?

    a. Current ratio
    b. Working capital

c. Accounts receivable turnover

d. Return on sales

8. Which of the following statements is true of financial statement analysis?

    a. Horizontal analysis expresses all items on a financial statement as percentages of a common base

    b. Vertical analysis involves comparing amounts from one year's financial statements to another year's statements

    c. Ratio analysis is more important than either horizontal or vertical analysis

    d. None of the above

9. Which statement is most likely to be true?

    a. An increase in inventory turnover indicates that inventory is not selling as quickly as it was

    b. A decrease in inventory turnover indicates that inventory is not selling as quickly as it was

    c. A change in inventory turnover cannot be accurately assessed without considering the change in profit margin

    d. None of the above

10. How are financial ratios used in decision making?

    a. They eliminate uncertainty regarding cash flows

    b. They can be used as a substitute for consulting financial statements

    c. They are only used in evaluating business liquidity

    d. They help to identify reasons for business success and failure

Answers are given after Apply Your Knowledge (p. 799).

Accounting Practice

Short Exercises

Performing a horizontal analysis of comparative financial statements.

S14-1. Britain E. Spears, Inc., had net sales of $250,000 and cost of goods sold of $150,000 in 2006; net sales of $275,000 and cost of goods sold of $165,000 in 2007; and net sales of $300,000 and cost of goods sold of $177,000 in 2008.

1. Find the percentage of increase in net sales from 2006 to 2007 and from 2007 to 2008.

2. Find the percentage of increase in gross profit from 2006 to 2007 and from 2007 to 2008.

Performing a vertical analysis of financial statements and preparing common-size financial statements.

S14-2. The 2008 accounting records of C. A. Guilara Records showed the following: Cash, $15,000; Net Accounts Receivable, $8,000; Inventory, $5,000; Prepaid Expenses, $4,000; Net Plant and Equipment, $18,000.

Construct a vertical analysis of the asset section of Guilara's balance sheet for 2008.

Computing commonly used financial ratios.

Measuring economic value added.

S14-3. Match the following terms to their definitions:

a. Inventory turnover

b. Return on sales

c. Quick ratio

d. Dividend yield

e. Return on assets

f. Accounts receivable turnover

g. Cost of capital

h. Debt ratio

_____ 1. Tells whether a company can pay all its current liabilities if they become due immediately

_____ 2. Measures company's success in using assets to earn income

_____ 3. A weighted average of the returns demanded by the company's stockholders and lenders

_____ 4. Indicates how rapidly inventory is sold

_____ 5. Shows the proportion of a company's assets that is financed with debt

_____ 6. Tells the percentage of a stock's market value that the company returns to stockholders annually as dividends

continued.....

_____ 7. A measure of profitability

_____ 8. Measures a company's ability to collect cash from credit customers

S14-4. Identify each of the following financial ratios as:

4 Computing commonly used financial ratios.

- Profitability ratios (P)
- Asset utilization ratios (A)
- Liquidity ratios (L)
- Debt utilization ratio (D)

_____ a. Inventory turnover

_____ b. Debt ratio

_____ c. Return on equity

_____ d. Days' sales in receivable

_____ e. Quick ratio

_____ f. Return on assets

_____ g. Profit margin

_____ h. Receivables turnover

_____ i. Current ratio

_____ j. Earning per share

_____ k. Times-interest-earned ratio

S14-5. The 2007 and 2008 balance sheets for Alan Jack and Sons showed net accounts receivable of $10,000 and $14,000, respectively, and inventory of $8,000 and $6,000, respectively. Their 2008 income statement showed net sales of $109,500 and cost of goods sold of $70,000. Compute the following ratios for 2008:

4 Computing commonly used financial ratios.

1. Accounts receivable turnover
2. Days' sales in receivables
3. Inventory turnover

S14-6. In addition to the information from S14-5, assume that cash on the 2008 balance sheet was $20,000 and current liabilities totaled $24,000. Compute the following ratios for 2008:

4 Computing commonly used financial ratios.

1. Current ratio
2. Quick ratio

S14-7. The 2008 financial statements for Fay Thill Country Stores show total assets of $490,000, total liabilities of $290,000, net sales of $1,800,000, net income of $450,000, income from operations of $520,000, cost of goods sold of $1,080,000, preferred dividends of $225,000, and interest expense

4 Computing commonly used financial ratios.

continued.....

of $20,000. Total assets and total liabilities for 2007 were $430,000 and $270,000, respectively. Compute the following ratios for 2008:

1. Profit margin
2. Return on assets
3. Return on equity
4. Times-interest-earned
5. Debt ratio

4 Computing commonly used financial ratios.

S14-8. Using the information from S14-7, a market price of $25 per share, and 100,000 shares of common stock outstanding, compute the following for 2008:

1. Earnings per share
2. Price/earnings ratio

4 Computing commonly used financial ratios.

S14-9. In 2007, common stockholders received $2 per share in annual dividends. The market price per share for common stock was $12. Compute the dividend yield for common stock.

Exercises

2 Performing a horizontal analysis of comparative financial statements.

E14-10. What were the dollar and percentage changes in Nat Portman Pawn Shop's working capital during 2006 and 2007? Is this trend favorable or unfavorable?

	2007	2006	2005
Total Current Assets	$410,000	$380,000	$360,000
Total Current Liabilities	250,000	217,000	240,000

2 Performing a horizontal analysis of comparative financial statements.

E14-11. Prepare a horizontal analysis of the following comparative income statement of Charley Theron Taxis, Incorporated. Round percentage changes to the nearest tenth of a percent.

CHARLEY THERON TAXIS, INCORPORATED Income Statement Years Ended December 31, 2009 and 2008		
	2009	**2008**
Revenue	$492,000	$447,600
Expenses:		
Cost of goods sold	242,000	226,000
Selling and general expenses	117,600	111,600
Interest expense	8,000	5,000
Income tax expense	50,400	44,400
Total expenses	418,000	387,000
Net income	$ 74,000	$ 60,600

continued....

Why did net income increase by a higher percent than total revenues increased during 2009?

E14-12. Compute trend percentages for net sales and net income for the following five-year period, using year 1 as the base year:

	Year 5	Year 4	Year 3	Year 2	Year 1
Net Sales	$2,405	$2,185	$2,125	$2,005	$2,045
Net Income	717	714	683	671	685

Which grew faster during the period, net sales or net income?

2 Performing a horizontal analysis of comparative financial statements.

E14-13. B. Younce Boutiques requested that you perform a vertical analysis of its balance sheet to determine the component percentages of its assets, liabilities, and stockholders' equity. Round to the nearest tenth of a percent.

3 Performing a vertical analysis of financial statements and preparing common-size financial statements.

B. YOUNCE BOUTIQUES
Balance Sheet
December 31, 2008

Assets		Liabilities	
Total current assets	$108,000	Total current liabilities	$ 87,000
Long-term investments	52,500	Long-term debt	177,000
Property, plant, and equipment, net	325,500	Total liabilities	264,000
		Stockholders' Equity	
		Total stockholders' equity	222,000
Total assets	$486,000	Total liabilities and stockholders' equity	$486,000

E14-14. Prepare a comparative common-size income statement for Charley Theron Taxis Incorporated, using the 2009 and 2008 data of E14-11 and rounding percentages to the nearest tenth of a percent.

3 Performing a vertical analysis of financial statements and preparing common-size financial statements.

E14-15. The financial statements of Lowe 'N Swak, Inc., include the following items:

4 Computing commonly used financial ratios.

	Current Year	Previous Year
Balance Sheet		
Cash	$ 27,000	$ 33,000
Short-term investments	22,000	28,000
Accounts receivable, net	54,000	72,000
Inventory	65,000	42,000
Prepaid expenses	7,000	9,000
Total current assets	$175,000	$184,000
Total current liabilities	$ 87,500	$ 92,000
Income Statement		
Net credit sales	$554,800	
Cost of goods sold	331,700	

continued.....

Compute the following ratios for the current year: (a) current ratio, (b) quick ratio, (c) inventory turnover, (d) accounts receivable turnover, and (e) days' sales in receivables.

4 Computing commonly used financial ratios.

E14-16. Brandy Pitts Winery requested that you determine whether the company's ability to pay its current liabilities and long-term debts improved or deteriorated during 2008. To answer this question, compute the following ratios for 2008 and 2007: (a) current ratio, (b) quick ratio, (c) debt ratio, and (d) times-interest-earned ratio. Summarize the results of your analysis.

	2008	2007
Cash	$ 32,000	$ 45,000
Short-term investments	35,000	–
Accounts receivable, net	130,000	142,000
Inventory	340,000	360,000
Prepaid expenses	15,000	12,000
Total assets	580,000	560,000
Total current liabilities	220,800	245,600
Long-term liabilities	24,200	29,400
Income from operations	185,000	179,000
Interest expense	42,000	44,000

4 Computing commonly used financial ratios.

E14-17. For 2007 and 2008, compute the four ratios that measure the ability to earn profits for Jenna Niston Fashions, Inc., whose comparative income statement follows:

JENNA NISTON FASHIONS, INC.
Income Statement
Years Ended December 31, 2008 and 2007

	2008	2007
Net sales	$261,000	$237,000
Cost of goods sold	140,000	132,000
Gross profit	121,000	105,000
Selling and general expense	72,000	65,000
Income from operations	49,000	40,000
Interest expense	32,000	15,000
Income before income tax	17,000	25,000
Income tax expense	5,000	8,000
Net income	$ 12,000	$ 17,000

continued....

Additional data:

	2008	2007	2006
Total assets	$320,000	$292,000	$282,000
Common stockholders' equity	148,000	140,000	132,000
Preferred dividends	4,000	4,000	
Shares of common stock outstanding	25,000	25,000	

Did the company's operating performance improve or deteriorate during 2008?

E14-18. Evaluate the common stock of TomCat Incorporated as an investment. Specifically, use the two stock ratios to determine whether the stock increased or decreased in attractiveness during the past year. Assume that TomCat paid the full amount of preferred dividends.

④ Computing commonly used financial ratios.

	2008	2007
Net income	$ 87,000	$ 83,000
Total dividends..	48,000	48,000
Common stockholders' equity at year-end (100,000 shares) ...	780,000	750,000
Preferred stockholders' equity, 6%, $100 par at year-end	300,000	300,000
Market price of common stock at year-end	$15.18	$11.63

E14-19. Using the information in E14-16 and E14-17, compute the 2008 EVA for each company and determine which company would be the better investment according to this measure. Assume the following additional information:

⑤ Measuring economic value added.

(in thousands)	Brandy Pitts Winery	Jenna Niston Fashions
Net income	$100,000	$ 12,000
Loans and notes payable........	14,200	12,000
Long-term debt	10,000	7,000
Stockholders' equity	335,000	301,000
Cost of capital	12%	8%

E14-20. The following data (dollar amounts in millions) are adapted from the financial statements of Semi-More Company:

Total current assets...................	$12,201
Accumulated depreciation..........	1,738
Total liabilities........................	14,755
Preferred stock........................	10
Debt ratio...............................	55.145%
Current ratio...........................	2.1

Requirements

Complete the following condensed balance sheet. Report amounts rounded to the nearest $1 million:

Current assets		$?
Property, plant, and equipment	$?	
Less: Accumulated depreciation	(?)	?
Total assets		$?
Current liabilities...		$?
Long-term liabilities..		?
Stockholders' equity		?
Total liabilities and stockholders' equity		$?

Problems (Group A)

2 Performing a horizontal
analysis of comparative
financial statements.

4 Computing commonly
used financial ratios.

P14-21A. Net sales, net income, and total assets for Gene Blue Clothing Emporium for a four-year period follow:

(in thousands)	2010	2009	2008	2007
Net sales............................	$381	$357	$321	$331
Net income	31	23	16	24
Ending total assets............	193	177	165	148

Requirements

1. Compute trend percentages for each item for 2007 through 2010. Use 2007 as the base year.

2. Compute the rate of return on net sales for 2008 through 2010, rounding to three decimal places. In this industry, rates of 6% are average, rates above 8% are considered good, and rates above 10% are viewed as outstanding.

3. How does Gene Blue's return on net sales compare with the industry?

P14-22A. Love Bug Used Auto Sales asked for your help in comparing the company's profit performance and financial position with the average for the auto sales industry. The proprietor has given you the company's income statement and balance sheet as well as the industry average data for retailers of used autos.

3 Performing a vertical analysis of financial statements and preparing common-size financial statements.

4 Computing commonly used financial ratios.

LOVE BUG USED AUTO SALES
Income Statement Compared with Industry Average
Year Ended December 31, 2009

	Love Bug	Industry Average
Net sales	$521,000	100.0%
Cost of goods sold	331,000	62.1%
Gross profit	190,000	37.9%
Operating expenses	109,000	27.8%
Operating income	81,000	10.1%
Other expenses	3,000	0.4%
Net income	$ 78,000	9.7%

LOVE BUG USED AUTO SALES
Balance Sheet Compared with Industry Average
December 31, 2009

	Love Bug	Industry Average
Current assets	$230,000	70.9%
Plant assets, net	49,000	23.6%
Intangible assets, net	3,000	0.8%
Other assets	15,000	4.7%
Total assets	$297,000	100.0%
Current liabilities	$136,000	48.1%
Long-term liabilities	41,000	16.6%
Stockholders' equity	120,000	35.3%
Total liabilities and stockholders' equity	$297,000	100.0%

Requirements

1. Prepare a two-column, common-size income statement and a two-column common-size balance sheet for Love Bug Used Auto Sales. The first column of each statement should present Love Bug's common-size statement and the second column should show the industry averages.

2. For the profitability analysis, examine Love Bug's (a) ratio of gross profit to net sales, (b) ratio of operating income to net sales, and (c) ratio of net income to net sales. Compare these figures with the industry averages. Is Love Bug's profit performance better or worse than the industry average?

continued.....

3. For the analysis of financial position, examine Love Bug's (a) ratio of current assets to total assets, (b) ratio of stockholders' equity to total assets. Compare these ratios with the industry averages. Is Love Bug's financial position better or worse than the industry average?

P14-23A. Financial statement data of Barb Wired Fencing, Inc., include the following items:

4 Computing commonly used financial ratios.

Cash..	$ 17,000
Short-term investments	22,000
Accounts receivable, net	103,000
Inventory...	119,000
Prepaid expenses	10,000
Total assets...	660,000
Short-term notes payable	45,000
Accounts payable	105,000
Accrued liabilities	40,000
Long-term notes payable	158,000
Other long-term liabilities.........................	33,000
Net income	75,000
Number of common shares outstanding.....	35,000

Requirements

1. Compute Barb Wired Fencing's current ratio, debt ratio, and earnings per share. Assume that the company had no preferred stock outstanding. Format your answer as follows:

Current Ratio	Debt Ratio	Earnings per Share

2. Compute each of the same three ratios after evaluating the effect of each transaction that follows. Consider each transaction separately, and format your answer as follows:

Transaction (letter)	Current Ratio	Debt Ratio	Earnings per Share

a. Purchased merchandise of $38,000 on account, debiting Inventory.

b. Issued 2,000 shares of common stock, receiving cash of $80,000

c. Borrowed $80,000 on a long-term notes payable.

d. Received cash on account, $22,000.

P14-24A. Comparative financial statement data of Lounge Around Furniture Company follow:

④ Computing commonly used financial ratios.

LOUNGE AROUND FURNITURE COMPANY Income Statement Years Ended December 31, 2008 and 2007		
	2008	**2007**
Net sales	$482,000	$457,000
Cost of goods sold	238,000	229,000
Gross profit	244,000	228,000
Operating expenses	140,000	138,000
Income from operations	104,000	90,000
Interest expense	12,000	14,000
Income before income tax	92,000	76,000
Income tax expense	28,000	23,000
Net income	$ 64,000	$ 53,000

LOUNGE AROUND FURNITURE COMPANY Balance Sheet December 31, 2008 and 2007 (Selected 2006 amounts given for computation of ratios)			
	2008	**2007**	**2006**
Current assets:			
Cash	$ 98,000	$ 99,000	
Accounts receivable, net	108,000	112,000	$104,000
Inventory	164,000	154,000	185,000
Prepaid expenses	28,000	20,000	
Total current assets	398,000	385,000	
Property, plant, and equipment, net	191,000	180,000	
Total assets	$589,000	$565,000	
Total current liabilities	$208,000	$228,000	
Long-term liabilities	121,000	117,000	
Total liabilities	329,000	345,000	
Preferred stockholders' equity, 8%, $100 par	100,000	100,000	
Common stockholders' equity, no par	160,000	120,000	100,000
Total liabilities and stockholders' equity	$589,000	$565,000	

Other information:

a. Market price of common stock: $48 at December 31, 2008, and $30.75 at December 31, 2007.

b. Common shares outstanding: 10,000 during 2008 and 9,000 during 2007.

c. All sales were made on credit.

d. The full amount of preferred dividends was paid.

continued.....

Requirements

1. Compute the following ratios for 2008 and 2007:
   a. Current ratio
   b. Inventory turnover
   c. Accounts receivable turnover
   d. Times-interest-earned ratio
   e. Return on common stockholders' equity
   f. Earnings per share of common stock
   g. Price/earnings ratio

2. Decide (a) whether Lounge Around's financial position improved or deteriorated during 2008 and (b) whether the investment attractiveness of its common stock appears to have increased or decreased.

3. How will what you learned in this problem help you evaluate an investment?

P14-25A. Assume you are purchasing an investment and decide to invest in a company in the home remodeling business. You narrow the choice to Build It Right, Inc., or Structurally Sound Corp. You assemble the following selected data:

Selected income statement data for current year:

	Build It Right, Inc.	Structurally Sound Corp.
Net sales (all on credit)	$298,000	$223,000
Cost of goods sold	155,000	125,000
Income from operations	83,000	47,000
Interest expense	13,000	—
Net income	43,000	29,000

Selected balance sheet and market price data at the end of the current year:

	Build It Right, Inc.	Structurally Sound Corp.
Current assets:		
Cash	$ 12,000	$ 13,000
Short-term investments	11,000	12,000
Accounts receivable, net	28,000	25,000
Inventory	60,000	52,000
Prepaid expenses	2,000	1,000
Total current assets	113,000	103,000
Total assets	197,000	159,000
Total current liabilities	59,000	65,000
Total liabilities	79,000	65,000
Preferred stock, 5%, $100 par	20,000	
Common stock, $1.00 par, 6,000 shares		6,000
$2.50 par, 3,000 shares	7,500	
Total stockholders' equity	118,000	94,000
Market price per share of common stock	$ 67	$ 31

continued.....

(Margin notes)
4 Computing commonly used financial ratios.

5 Measuring economic value added.

Selected balance sheet data at the beginning of the current year:

	Build It Right, Inc.	Structurally Sound Corp.
Accounts receivable, net	$ 29,000	$ 24,000
Inventory	53,000	56,000
Total assets	162,000	155,000
Preferred stock, 5%, $100 par	20,000	
Common stock, $1.00 par, 6,000 shares		6,000
$2.50 par, 3,000 shares	7,500	
Total stockholders' equity	76,000	71,000

Your investment strategy is to purchase the stock of the company that has a low price/earnings ratio but appears to be in good shape financially. Assume that you analyzed all other factors and your decision depends in the results of the ratio analysis to be performed.

Requirements

1. Compute the following ratios for both companies for the current year, and decide which company's stock better fits your investment strategy.

   a. Quick ratio

   b. Inventory turnover

   c. Days' sales in average receivables

   d. Debt ratio

   e. Earnings per share of common stock

   f. Price/earnings ratio

2. Compute the EVA for each company, assuming a 10% cost of capital. Does the EVA confirm the opinion you formed as a result of the ratio analysis?

P14-26A. You have been hired as an investment analyst at Cheryl Winch Company. It is your job to recommend investments for your client. The only information you have are the following ratio values for two companies in the video game industry.

4 Computing commonly used financial ratios.

Ratio	Tomb Crater Co.	Resident Upheaval, Inc.
Days' sales in receivables	46	52
Inventory turnover	8	10
Gross profit percentage	67%	59%
Net income as a percent of sales	15%	21%
Times interest earned	16	12
Return on equity	35%	26%
Return on assets	13%	18%

continued.....

Requirements

Write a memo to your client recommending the company you believe to be a more attractive investment. Explain the reasons for your recommendation.

Problems (Group B)

2 Performing a horizontal analysis of comparative financial statements.

4 Computing commonly used financial ratios.

P14-27B. Net sales, net income, and common stockholders' equity for The Royal Flush Plumbing Supplies for a four-year period follow:

(in thousands)	2010	2009	2008	2007
Net sales	$416	$376	$319	$337
Net income...	32	25	13	22
Ending total stockholders' equity.....	355	305	251	235

Requirements

1. Compute trend percentages for each item for 2007 through 2010. Use 2007 as the base year.

2. Compute the rate of return on equity for 2008 through 2010, rounding to three decimal places. In this industry, rates of 10% are average, rates above 12% are considered good, and rates above 15% are viewed as outstanding. Royal Flush had no preferred stock outstanding.

3. How does Royal Flush's return on equity compare with the industry?

3 Performing a vertical analysis of financial statements and preparing common-size financial statements.

4 Computing commonly used financial ratios.

P14-28B. Cue Ball Billiards Emporium asked for your help in comparing the company's profit performance and financial position with the average for the industry. The proprietor gave you the company's income statement and balance sheet and also the industry average data.

CUE BALL BILLIARDS EMPORIUM
Income Statement Compared with Industry Average
Year Ended December 31, 2010

	Cue Ball	Industry Average
Net sales	$861,000	100.0%
Cost of goods sold	572,000	65.4%
Gross profit	289,000	34.6%
Operating expenses	231,000	26.4%
Operating income	58,000	8.2%
Other expenses	4,000	0.5%
Net income	$ 54,000	7.7%

continued.....

CUE BALL BILLIARDS EMPORIUM
Balance Sheet Compared with Industry Average
December 31, 2010

	Cue Ball	Industry Average
Current assets	$403,000	74.2%
Plant assets, net	114,000	20.2%
Intangible assets, net	38,000	0.7%
Other assets	12,000	4.9%
Total assets	$567,000	100.0%
Current liabilities	$221,000	35.8%
Long-term liabilities	130,000	19.0%
Stockholders' equity	216,000	45.2%
Total liabilities and stockholders' equity	$567,000	100.0%

Requirements

1. Prepare a two-column, common-size income statement and a two-column common-size balance sheet for Cue Ball Billiards Emporium. The first column of each statement should present Cue Ball's common-size statement and the second column should show the industry averages.

2. For the profitability analysis, examine Cue Ball's (a) ratio of gross profit to net sales, (b) ratio of operating income to net sales, and (c) ratio of net income to net sales. Compare these figures with the industry averages. Is Cue Ball's profit performance better or worse than the industry average?

3. For the analysis of financial position, examine Cue Ball's (a) ratio of current assets to total assets, (b) ratio of stockholders' equity to total assets. Compare these ratios with the industry averages. Is Cue Ball's financial position better or worse than the industry average?

P14-29B. Financial statement data of Sight Unseen Optical Company include the following items:

4 Computing commonly used financial ratios.

Cash	$ 42,000
Short-term investments	19,000
Accounts receivable, net	92,000
Inventory	247,000
Prepaid expenses	14,000
Total assets	840,000
Short-term notes payable	65,000
Accounts payable	86,000
Accrued liabilities	45,000
Long-term notes payable	131,000
Other long-term liabilities	70,000
Net income	107,000
Number of common shares outstanding	20,000

continued.....

Requirements

1. Compute Sight Unseen Optical's current ratio, debt ratio, and earnings per share. Assume that the company had no preferred stock outstanding. Format your answer as follows:

Current Ratio	Debt Ratio	Earnings per Share

2. Compute each of the same three ratios after evaluating the effect of each transaction that follows. Consider each transaction separately, and format your answer as follows:

Transaction (letter)	Current Ratio	Debt Ratio	Earnings per Share

a. Borrowed $26,000 on a short-term notes payable.

b. Paid off long-term liabilities, $40,000

c. Issued 12,000 shares of common stock, receiving cash of $150,000.

d. Purchased merchandise of $23,000 for cash, debiting Inventory.

④ Computing commonly used financial ratios.

P14-30B. Comparative financial statement data of April Showers Umbrella Company follow:

APRIL SHOWERS UMBRELLA COMPANY
Income Statement
Years Ended December 31, 2009 and 2008

	2009	2008
Net sales	$600,000	$539,000
Cost of goods sold	340,000	255,000
Gross profit	260,000	284,000
Operating expenses	116,000	132,000
Income from operations	144,000	152,000
Interest expense	51,000	37,000
Income before income tax	93,000	115,000
Income tax expense	31,000	48,000
Net income	$ 62,000	$ 67,000

continued....

APRIL SHOWERS UMBRELLA COMPANY Balance Sheet December 31, 2009 and 2008 (Selected 2007 amounts given for computation of ratios)			
	2009	2008	2007
Current assets:			
Cash	$ 33,000	$ 36,000	
Accounts receivable, net	187,000	136,000	$124,000
Inventory	317,000	257,000	166,000
Prepaid expenses	5,000	18,000	
Total current assets	542,000	447,000	
Property, plant, and equipment, net	258,000	248,000	
Total assets	$800,000	$695,000	
Total current liabilities	$257,000	$240,000	
Long-term liabilities	221,000	212,000	
Total liabilities	478,000	452,000	
Preferred stockholders' equity, 4%, $100 par	45,000	45,000	
Common stockholders' equity, no par	277,000	198,000	133,000
Total liabilities and stockholders' equity	$800,000	$695,000	

Other information:

a. Market price of common stock: $30.50 at December 31, 2009, and $40.75 at December 31, 2008.

b. Common shares outstanding: 14,000 during 2009 and 13,000 during 2008.

c. All sales were made on credit.

d. The full amount of preferred dividends was paid.

Requirements

1. Compute the following ratios for 2009 and 2008:

a. Current ratio

b. Inventory turnover

c. Accounts receivable turnover

d. Times-interest-earned ratio

e. Return on common stockolders' equity

f. Earnings per share of common stock

g. Price/earnings ratio

continued.....

2. Decide (a) whether April Showers' financial position improved or deteriorated during 2009 and (b) whether the investment attractiveness of its common stock appears to have increased or decreased.

3. How will what you learned in this problem help you evaluate an investment?

④ Computing commonly used financial ratios.

⑤ Measuring economic value added.

P14-31B. Assume you are purchasing an investment and decide to invest in a company in the medical supply industry. You narrow the choice to Broke Bone Hill, Inc., or Wounded Knee Valley Corp. You assemble the following selected data:

Selected income statement data for current year:

	Broke Bone Hill, Inc.	Wounded Knee Valley Corp.
Net sales (all on credit)	$467,000	$543,000
Cost of goods sold	348,000	409,000
Income from operations	65,000	84,000
Interest expense	7,000	—
Net income	34,000	50,000

Selected balance sheet and market price data at the end of the current year:

	Broke Bone Hill, Inc.	Wounded Knee Valley Corp.
Current assets:		
Cash	$ 31,000	$ 23,000
Short-term investments	12,000	5,000
Accounts receivable, net	148,000	170,000
Inventory	165,000	190,000
Prepaid expenses	14,000	17,000
Total current assets	370,000	405,000
Total assets	844,000	877,000
Total current liabilities	304,000	329,000
Total liabilities	622,000	600,000
Preferred stock, 5%, $100 par	23,000	
Common stock, $1 par, 135,000 shares		135,000
$5 par, 18,000 shares	90,000	
Total stockholders' equity	222,000	277,000
Market price per share of common stock	$ 42.75	$ 8.25

continued....

Selected balance sheet data at the beginning of the current year:

	Broke Bone Hill, Inc.	Wounded Knee Valley Corp.
Accounts receivable, net	$174,000	$128,000
Inventory	177,000	188,000
Total assets	818,000	758,000
Preferred stock, 5%, $100 par	23,000	
Common stock, $1 par, 135,000 shares		135,000
$5 par, 18,000 shares	90,000	
Total stockholders' equity	$194,000	$237,000

Your investment strategy is to purchase the stock of the company that has a low price/earnings ratio but appears to be in good shape financially. Assume that you analyze all other factors and your decision depends on the results of the ratio analysis to be performed.

Requirements

1. Compute the following ratios for both companies for the current year, and decide which company's stock better fits your investment strategy.

   a. Quick ratio

   b. Inventory turnover

   c. Days' sales in average receivables

   d. Debt ratio

   e. Earnings per share of common stock

   f. Price/earnings ratio

2. Compute the EVA for each company, assuming an 8% cost of capital. Does the EVA confirm the opinion you formed as a result of the ratio analysis?

P14-32B. Take the role of an investment analyst at Ronald Grump Company. It is your job to recommend investments for your client. The only information you have are the ratio values for two companies in the body building industry that follow:

4 Computing commonly used financial ratios.

continued.....

Ratio	Pump It Up Co.	Heavy Weight Inc.
Days' sales in receivables	54	42
Inventory turnover	10	7
Gross profit percentage	56%	49%
Net income as a percentage of sales	9.6%	7.8%
Times interest earned	11	18
Return on equity	22.1%	34%
Return on assets	15.6%	12.7%

**for 24/7 practice, visit
www.MyAccountingLab.com**

Requirements

Write a memo to your client recommending the company you believe to be a more attractive investment. Explain the reasons for your recommendation.

Apply Your Knowledge

BE ON GUARD

Case 1. Robin Peterson, the CEO of Teldar Incorporated, was reviewing the financial statements for the first three months of the year. He saw that sales and net income were lower than expected. Because the reported net income and the related earnings per share were below expectations, the price of the stock declined. Robin held a meeting with top management and expressed his concerns over the declining trend in sales and income. He stated that the reduced profitability meant that he needed to formulate a plan to somehow increase the earnings per share. The vice president of marketing suggested that more advertising might help sales increase. Robin stated that spending more money on advertising would not guarantee an increase in sales, then announced that the excess company cash would instead be used to buy back shares of outstanding common stock; this move would help increase the earnings per share because fewer shares would be outstanding. Robin reminded everyone that the yearly financial statements would be analyzed and the current year would be compared to previous years' results. He then stated that the treasury stock would lower the total stockholders' equity, which could then provide a stronger EPS so the current year would not look as bad. Finally, Robin reminded everyone that with fewer shares of stock outstanding, the dividend per share could be increased and that would help make Teldar stock more attractive. The CFO argued that buying back stock merely to increase performance measures such as EPS was manipulative and unethical and financial analysts would easily see what Teldar was trying to do.

Why did the CEO want to repurchase shares of Teldar common stock? Would the repurchase of common stock really have any impact on the financial ratios? Would an investor or financial analyst be able to see that financial performance measures were improved because of the stock repurchase? Are any ethical issues involved? Were the concerns expressed by the CFO valid? Do you have any other thoughts?

Case 2. Crane Corporation was in the process of completing the financial statements for the latest fiscal year. Susan Randal, Crane's CEO, was reviewing the comparative financial statements and expressed some concerns. In comparing the current year income statement against those of the prior years, she noticed that total sales had decreased slightly. Further, the salary expense had increased while the advertising and research and development expenses had decreased. Although the total operating expenses were essentially the same, Susan was concerned that the increased salary expense would be questioned by the investors and financial analysts in light of the decreases in advertising and research and development. She knew that the lower sales would be blamed on reduced advertising and less spending on research and development. As a result, Susan ordered the accountants to issue a condensed income statement that would present all operating expenses as a single amount. Also, during the year Crane Corporation had purchased another company for a price higher than the total fair market value of the purchased business. Crane properly recorded the excess cost as goodwill, but the total amount of goodwill had increased substantially because of this purchase. Susan was concerned that this rather large increase in goodwill would be seen as an unnecessary purchase and investors and analysts would become upset. Thus, Susan ordered that the goodwill be lumped in with the other assets rather than listed separately on the balance sheet where it could easily be seen. The accountants argued that attempting to hide these items from investors and analysts would be unethical. They further argued that GAAP required full disclosure, and that if Susan insisted on providing condensed statements, details would need to be provided in the footnotes anyway. Susan reluctantly agreed to the disclosure, knowing that often footnotes are not read.

Why would Susan want all the operating expenses lumped together? Why would Susan want the goodwill included as other assets? Were the ethical concerns raised by the accountants valid? Are any ethical issues involved in providing condensed information with the details included in the footnotes? Do you have any additional thoughts?

KNOW YOUR BUSINESS

This case focuses on the financial statement analysis of the Target Corporation. Recall from the chapter that stakeholders use numerous ways to analyze and thus better understand the financial position and results of operations of a company. Tools such as vertical and horizontal analyses are available. In addition, financial ratios can be used to gain further insight into areas such as liquidity and profitability. Other measures include earnings per share and ratios that consider the share price of the company. Finally, nonfinancial information provides additional insights into the performance and financial position of the company. We will now apply some of the analytical tools contained in the chapter. Refer to the Target Corporation annual report found in Appendix A.

Requirements

1. Perform a vertical analysis on the income statements (Consolidated Results of Operations). Discuss your results. What benefit do you see in performing this analysis? Perform a horizontal analysis of the balance sheets (Consolidated Statements of Financial Position). Discuss your results. What benefit do you see in performing this analysis?

2. Look at the income statements (Consolidated Results of Operations). Can you find the total Basic EPS for each fiscal year presented? Has the Basic Earnings per Share increased or decreased each year? Why do you think the total Basic EPS has been changing? Can you compute the total Basic EPS figures given by using the net earnings and the common shares outstanding?

3. Determine the liquidity of Target by computing the working capital, current ratio, and quick ratio at January 29, 2004. What do your results mean? Compute the profit margin ratio and the return on equity ratio for the 2004 fiscal year. What do your results mean? Compute the inventory turnover ratio and the debt ratio for the 2004 fiscal year. What do your results mean? What other ratios are available?

4. The market price for a share of Target Corporation common stock was $50.77 on January 31, 2005. Using this price, determine the price/earnings ratio and the dividend yield at January 31, 2005. What do your results mean? Assume that the industry average was 10 times earnings and the dividend yield was 2.3% for the industry. Now what would your results mean?

5. Look at the letter addressed "To Our Shareholders" in the Management Discussion and Analysis section of the annual report. What information was available in this letter? Did you find this letter informative? Was any information contained in this letter not available from the financial statements and footnotes? Read over the rest of the Management Discussion and Analysis section. Did you find the information useful or insightful in better understanding Target? Read the Report of Independent Registered Public Accounting Firm on Consolidated Financial Statements at the end of the financial statement footnotes. Who were the auditors? Did you find their report informative? Look at the footnotes included at the end of the financial statements. How many footnotes were included? Who wrote and included all those footnotes? Are footnote disclosures useful? Read one of the footnotes and comment about any useful or insightful information you read.

For Internet Exercises, Excel in Practice, and additional online activities, go to the Web site www.prenhall.com/pollard.

Quick Check Answers

1. *c* 2. *d* 3. *b* 4. *d* 5. *a* 6. *d* 7. *c* 8. *d* 9. *b* 10. *d*

Chapter 14

Quick Check

1 d; 2 c; 3 b; 4 d; 5 a; 6 d; 7 c; 8 d; 9 b; 10 d

S14-1	2008 Gross profit increase, 11.8%
S14-2	Cash, 30%
S14-3	NCF
S14-4	NCF
S14-5	3. Inventory turnover, 10 times
S14-6	2. Quick ratio, 1.42
S14-7	1. Profit margin, 25% 3. Rate of return on equity, 1.25 times
S14-8	2. Price/earnings ratio, 11.1
S14-9	Dividend yield, .17
E14-10	Working capital decrease, 2007, $3,000
E14-11	Net income increase, 22.1%
E14-12	Net sales, Year 5, 118%
E14-13	Total liabilities, 54.3%
E14-14	Net income, 2009, 15%
E14-15	a. Current ratio, 2.0 d. Accounts receivable turnover, 8.81 times
E14-16	a. Current ratio, 2008, 2.5 c. Debt ratio, 2008, .42
E14-17	b. Rate of return on total assets, 2008, .144 d. Earnings per share, 2008, $.32
E14-18	Ratios for 2008: a. Price/earnings ratio, 22 b. Dividend yield, .020
E14-19	EVA, Brandy Pitts Winery, $98,896
E14-20	Total liabilities and stockholders' equity, $26,757
P14-21A	1. Ending total assets, 2010, 130% 2. Rate of return on net sales, 2010, .081
P14-22A	1. Net income, Love Bug, 15% 2. Current assets, Love Bug, 77.4%
P14-23A	1. Current ratio, 1.43 2.c. Current ratio, 1.85
P14-24A	1. a. Current ratio, 2008, 1.91 d. Times-interest earned, 2008, 8.67 g. Price/earnings ratio, 2008, 8.57
P14-25A	1.a. Quick ratio, Build it Right, .86 d. Debt ratio, Build it Right, .40 f. Price/earnings ratio, Build it Right, 4.79 2. EVA, Build it Right, $42,200
P14-26A	NCF
P14-27B	1. Ending total stockholders' equity, 2010, 151% 2. Rate of return on common stockholders' equity, 2010, .097
P14-28B	1. Net income, Cue Ball, 6.3% 2. Current assets, Cue Ball, 71.1%
P14-29B	1. Current ratio, 2.11 2.c. Current ratio, 2.88
P14-30B	1. a. Current ratio, 2008, 2.11 d. Times-interest earned, 2008, 2.82 g. Price/earnings ratio, 2008, 7.09
P14-31B	1.a. Quick ratio, Broken Bone Hill, .63 d. Debt ratio, Broken Bone Hill, .74 f. Price/earnings ratio, Broken Bone Hill, 23.4 2. EVA, Build it Right, $(2,200)
P14-31B	NCF Know Your Business 1. Net earnings, 2004, 6.83% Cash and cash equivalents, 2005, 217.09% 2. EPS, 2004, $3.54 4. Price/earnings ratio, 14.34 times

Typical Accounts Used

Service Business

Assets

Cash
Short-Term Investments
Accounts Receivable
Allowance for Uncollectible
    Accounts
Notes Receivable, Short-Term
Interest Receivable
Inventory
Supplies
Prepaid Rent
Prepaid Insurance
Notes Receivable, Long-Term
Land
Land Improvements
Buildings
Equipment
Furniture and Fixtures
Accumulated Depreciation,
    Land Improvements
Accumulated Depreciation,
    Buildings
Accumulated Depreciation,
    Equipment
Accumulated Depreciation,
    Furniture and Fixtures
Natural Resources
Accumulated Depletion,
    Natural Resources
Patents
Copyrights

Trademarks and Trade Names
Franchises
Licenses
Patents
Goodwill

Liabilities

Accounts Payable
Notes Payable, Short-Term
Current Portion of Notes
    Payable
Current Portion of Bonds
    Payable
Salary Payable
Wages Payable
Employee Income Tax Payable
FICA Tax Payable
State Unemployment Tax
    Payable
Federal Unemployment Tax
    Payable
Employee Benefits Payable
Interest Payable
Income Tax Payable
Unearned Revenue
Notes Payable, Long-Term
Mortgage Notes Payable
Lease Payable
Bonds Payable
Premium/Discount on Bonds
    Payable

Revenues and Gains

Service Revenue
Interest Revenue
Dividend Revenue
Gain on Sale of Land
    (Buildings, Equipment,
    Furniture, or Fixtures)

Expenses and Losses

Cost of Goods Sold
Salary Expense
Wage Expense
Payroll Tax Expense
Employee Benefits Expense
Rent Expense
Insurance Expense
Supplies Expense
Uncollectible Account
    Expense

Owner's Equity

Owner's Equity accounts vary based on the form of organization.

Depreciation Expense, Land
    Improvements
Depreciation Expense,
    Buildings
Depreciation Expense,
    Equipment
Depreciation Expense,
    Furniture and Fixtures
Depletion Expense,
    Natural Resources
Amortization Expense,
    Intangible Assets
Income Tax Expense
Interest Expense
Miscellaneous Expense
Loss on Sale of Land
    (Buildings, Equipment,
    Furniture or Fixtures)

Merchandising Business

Same as above except for Assets, Liabilities, Revenues, and Expenses

Assets	Liabilities	Revenues	Expenses
Inventory	Sales Tax Payable	Sales Revenue	Cost of Goods Sold
	Estimated Warranty Payable	Sales Returns and Allowances (contra revenue)	Delivery Expense
		Sales Discounts (contra revenue)	Advertising Expense
			Credit/Debit Card Expense

Manufacturing Business

Same as above, except for Assets and Expenses:

Assets	Expenses (Contra Expenses If Credit Balance)
Inventory:	Direct Materials Price Variance
Materials Inventory	Direct Materials Efficiency Variance
Work in Process Inventory	Direct Labor Price Variance
Finished Goods Inventory	Direct Labor Efficiency Variance
	Manufacturing Overhead Flexible Budget Variance
	Manufacturing Overhead Production Volume Variance

Owner's/Stockholders' Equity Accounts

Sole Proprietorship	Partnership	Corporation
Owner, Capital	Partner 1, Capital	Preferred Stock
Owner, Withdrawals	Partner 2, Capital	Paid-in Capital in Excess of Par, Preferred
	Partner N, Capital	Common Stock
	Owner 1, Withdrawals	Paid-in Capital in Excess of Par, Common
	Owner 2, Withdrawals	Paid-in Capital from Treasury Stock
	Owner N, Withdrawals	Retained Earnings
		Treasury Stock